TABLOID
BABY

by
Burt Kearns

CELEBRITY ★ BOOKS

Nashville, Tennessee

Nashville, Tennessee
Copyright © 1999 by Burt Kearns

Published by Celebrity Books
1501 County Hospital Road
Nashville, Tennessee   37218

Printed in the United States of America
ISBN 1-58029-107-4

Library of Congress Cataloging-in-Publication Data:
Kearns, Burt.
Tabloid baby / written by Burt Kearns.
p.   cm.
ISBN 1-58029-107-4 (hardcover)
1. Television broadcasting of news. 2. Murdoch, Rupert, 1931-
-Influence. 3. Sensationalism on television. 4. Kearns, Burt.
I. Title.
PN4784.T4K44   1999
070.1'95--dc21
99-35747
CIP

DEDICATION

For Alison and Sam

C O N T E N T S

INTRODUCTION

It would be the journalistic coup of the century.

This elusive interview subject would be the most prized quarry in a century marked by the likes of Joseph Stalin, Amelia Earhart, Adolph Hitler, Mohandas Gandhi, Jonas Salk, Thomas Edison, Winston Churchill, Frank Sinatra, Albert Einstein, Marilyn Monroe, Joe DiMaggio, Elvis Presley, Betty Friedan, Muhammad Ali, Martin Luther King, and Mother Teresa.

This exclusive interview would take up the entirety of a two-hour special that would become the most-watched single-network news program in television history; a history marked by the likes of the McCarthy hearings, the murder of President John Fitzgerald Kennedy's alleged assassin, Neil Armstrong's walk on the moon, the execution of Israeli athletes at the 1972 Olympics, Watergate, the Iran hostage crisis, and the explosion of the space shuttle Challenger.

This television news interview would be the crowning achievement of a forty-year journalistic career, an historic moment that would be watched by seventy million people on the evening of March 3, 1999.

Barbara Walters allowed herself one final patdown of makeup and began her interview with a young woman who fellated the President of the United States.

Hard to remember a time when television news wasn't a constant barrage of celebrity, scandal and sensation; even harder to recall a time when a President's extramarital assignations would not only be ignored but protected by the press corps; impossible to imagine a time when there was such a distinction between public and private lives that network news executives would decide the involvement of a United States senator in a high-profile rape case was not worthy of coverage.

Yet, not so long ago, white men who rarely ventured far beyond the twin axises of Washington, D.C. and Manhattan, determined what was and was not suitable for dissemination on network newscasts. Long after Vietnam, after *Life* magazine made way for *People*, after Woodward and Bernstein brought down Richard Nixon—years after Woodward found himself lost in the fastlane trail of John Belushi and Bernstein found greater fame for his adulterous liaisons and party life—television news remained rooted in standards of the distant past, haunted by ghosts in Burberry trenchcoats, mythic cigarette-smoking truthtellers of a Golden Age that may have never really existed at all.

In those days not so long ago, there were but three networks and one 24-hour news channel, three powerful news divisions and three anchormen fighting to deliver the same stories in the same grave authoritative manner from newsdesks on high.

What was offered as television news was sacrosanct. There was a line between news and entertainment that would not be crossed. Gossip, celebrity, and stories of the heart would be relegated to newspapers and magazines.

The white men in their white shirts would decide the information America would be fed at suppertime.

Then the landscape shifted. Suddenly, there were no longer a handful of television channels, but dozens. A continuous stream of information, rumor, and innuendo was unleashed through the Internet. A newspaper mogul from Down Under decided to muscle his way in among the Big Three with a television network of his own.

Suddenly, something was happening here and the white men in their white shirts didn't know what it was. They could only watch as millions of Americans became transfixed by stories they'd dismissed, as the figures who were once relegated to supermarket tabloids and gossipy magazines moved to the forefront of the national agenda.

The stories deigned beneath contempt were now being offered up as zesty dessert after the meat, potatoes, and spinach dished out by the network newscasts—and more and more viewers were skipping the meal and heading straight for the sweets.

A new television era was underway. Figures and events of great portentousness soon became easy targets of fun. Stories that seemed to be of little national significance became national obsessions, fodder for books, TV movies, and afternoon slugfests known as talk shows. Terms like "love triangle," "sex video," "murder-for-hire," and, oddly, "vicar" entered the popular lexicon.

This would be the decade of tabloid television.

Fast-forward to April 1999. The story of the "Long Island Lolita," one of tabloid television's most profitable creations, has reached another climactic moment. Mary Jo Buttafuoco, the woman shot in the head by Amy Fisher, is in a courtroom pleading for Fisher's early release from prison. At the very same time, in Los Angeles, the co-president of Paramount Domestic Television is announcing to the *Hard Copy* staff that the show has been cancelled.

Of the half-dozen tabloid television shows that thrived during the past decade, only two remain. On the day Amy Fisher walks free, the story is the stuff of network news, jostling for airtime with the death of child actress and tabloid siren Dana Plato.

"Tabloid news magazines have... withered because certain kinds of tabloid-style stories have migrated to the traditional news organizations, which have so much more time to fill," Lawrie Mifflin writes in the *New York Times*. "There are three all-news cable channels and the broadcast networks produce 13 hours each week of news magazine programs (soon to be 14, with a fourth night of *20/20*)."

David Kamp, writing for *Vanity Fair*, is more to the point. "While tabloid's heyday was relatively shortlived... its influence lives on in every network program... all five *Datelines*, all three *20/20s* and both *60 Minuteses*. Not only have the major news organizations appropriated tabloid techniques, but they've also placed a greater emphasis on tabloid material at the expense of hard news."

At the dawn of the 21st Century, the networks have regained control of the mainstream, yet the course of the mighty river has shifted irrevocably— and many of those driving the network ships were trained in the tabloid television newsrooms.

This book tells the story of the rise and fall of the last television news revolution of the century. It charts the direct line from Robert Chambers to Rob Lowe to Ted Kennedy to William Kennedy Smith to Clarence Thomas to Joey Buttafuoco to William Jefferson Clinton; from Madonna to Roseanne to Amy Fisher to Princess Diana to Jenny Jones to JonBenet to Monica Lewinsky.

In the beginning, there were five of us.
One of us, legend has it, killed a man.
One of us watched a man die.
One sent a man to his death.
Another escaped death by inches.
Then there was me.
We got together.
We had some fun.
We changed the world.
Then we went our separate ways.
This is the story of what we did... and how we did it.
This is the story of the Tabloid Decade.

PROLOGUE:
LOCAL NEWS

I suppose it all began the day NBC killed my friend Pat Doyle. Doyle was the newsroom tipster, working for peanuts and hired as a favor because he'd been sent out to pasture and needed a reason to stay alive, a relic whom news directors kept around the way they'd display an old manual typewriter or candlestick telephone in the office to show off some link to tradition and the past.

Doyle was hovering on the shy edge of sixty when he walked into the WNBC-TV newsroom, but he could have been a hundred—and he looked like he slipped and fell out of the screen at a showing of *The Front Page* at the Thalia. With forty years in newspapers behind him, he'd remained stuck in the most glorious of his New York City glory days, a lost era when there truly was a light on Broadway for every broken heart, when the crack of gunfire was something that made you look up from your paper, and every reporter grabbed his hat on the run out the door in pursuit of a scoop.

Doyle had the look down cold, from the fedora—a straw in the summer—always tilted to a rakish angle, to the charcoal pinstripe suits with braces to keep the pants from falling down and garters to keep the ink off the shirtsleeves. They used words like "natty" and "dapper" to describe the way he dressed, words they stopped using around the time the likes of Doyle supposedly disappeared.

Yet, he walked among us, this living missing link between the halcyon days of tabloids in the forties and the yuppie days of New York City local news in the eighties; a newsman they called "The Inspector" because he looked more like a detective than the cops themselves; a man who called himself the World's Greatest Police Reporter, listed in the *Guinness Book of World Records*, 1985 edition, for covering more than 20,000 murders in his illustrious career at the *New York Daily News*. That career ended when Doyle's brand of news went out of style and he was convinced to take a buyout in the early eighties. He wound up as a tipster on the assignment desk at WNBC's *News 4 New York*.

That's where I met Pat Doyle. I was the producer of the 11 o'clock news, a rebellious, excitable twenty-seven-year-old, raised in the Connecticut suburbs under the conflicting influences of rock 'n' roll and Roman Catholic repression, and measuring my achievements against a yardstick of what John Lennon had accomplished by the time he was my age.

John Lennon and the Beatles, and all the rebellion and possibility they represented, had been an influence on my life ever since they played *The Ed Sullivan Show* that Sunday night in 1964. I was seven years old. I wasn't sure what was happening, but I knew I wanted to be them—not be *like* them, but be the Beatles themselves, and as the years passed learned to accept that growing up meant realizing I never would.

If I couldn't be a rock star, I could be a writer, because I was always better at writing than I was at playing bass guitar, and by the time it was time to make a living, writing and reading every magazine and newspaper I could get my hands on were really all I knew how to do at all, and that led to journalism. The kid who was always writing landed his first real job as a newspaper reporter for a little chain of weeklys in the affluent Fairfield County, Connecticut suburbs, learning the ropes on *The Ridgefield Press* and moving up to editor of its sister paper, *The Wilton Bulletin*. Left to his own devices and without even realizing it, the kid turned the sleepytown broadsheet into a tabloid, with alliterative headlines, sensational crime stories, superficial investigations, and front page features outing the many celebrities who'd moved to the leafy town seeking anonymity.

Then John Lennon was assassinated and I realized my second quarter century was soon to get underway and it was high time to stop marking time. So I quit the newspaper, said "so long" to my suburban girlfriend, and rode the Metro North into the City for good. It was 1981. I was counting on a job at the *Village Voice*. Thank God, I wound up on the assignment desk of Channel Five's *10 O'Clock News*.

That's how things work. It was beyond living a dream of living in New York City; it was to be suddenly in the middle of the fray, starting from scratch on a scrappy news team that had set the standard for gritty, no-frills news coverage. Based on the third floor of the Metromedia building, tucked among the embassies and posh co-ops on the residential Upper East Side, the *10 O'Clock News* had a third of the budget of the network locals, a smaller staff and fewer camera crews, but ran rings around every other newsroom in town. It was a rare inititation on a rare Olympus: thrust into a newsroom of giants, but no stars—a boisterous, edgy, and familial space, charged with sex, excitement, and coke-fueled energy.

The place was run and the agenda set by a pair of legendary and ballsy New York characters, Mark BvS Monsky and John Parsons Peditto, a newspaperman's son and a veteran documentarian and radio news reporter, both of whom considered each night's rundown a personal crusade.

The sparkplug, though, was a hyper little Italian guy from Queens who sometimes lived out of his van. Nick Loiacono was the assignment editor, working on his feet at the hub of a horseshoe desk, listening to police scanners, scanning wire copy, and directing camera crews and reporters all over the city. Nicky called the shots; he knew every street in the five boroughs and could catch the faintest radio call even while shouting at the top of his lungs and literally stuffing a pain-in-the-ass reporter into a trash can.

Nicky interviewed me for the job and said he'd hire me if I learned the city, so I spent two days riding every subway train as far as they'd take me and went to work as his desk assistant. Nicky taught me the streets, he taught me television news, he taught me to never kiss ass, and, over time, he taught me loyalty. Nicky was ten years my senior. He started out as my mentor and became my best friend, and years later, when his predeliction for the dark side killed him, it took a long time for me to accept that it was in the cards.

Two years on and I was writing and producing the broadcast, being paid my entry-level wage and told by the bosses I should feel lucky for the chance, while hoofing it across town to West 57th Street at 10:59 each night to moonlight at CBS network news, writing for its overnight *Nightwatch* and *CBS Morning News* programs.

The CBS bigs liked my style and soon offered me a job writing afternoon updates for Dan Rather. I begged off. There was something about CBS that didn't smell right—something cultish in the way the employees saw themselves upholding some sacred tradition, carrying out some grand mission to spread the CBS orthodoxy.

It wasn't only that the *Nightwatch* writing gig opened up because the previous writer had gone home after work at sunrise and committed suicide. It wasn't because they were paying tribute to the dead man's despair by keeping his name on the screen credits for an extra year. They all just took things so *seriously*.

I'd leave Channel Five after placing a bet on the day and hour Terence Cardinal Cooke would finally kick the bucket, only to arrive at CBS to find the newswriters sniffling and consoling each other over the imminent passing of brave Barney Clark, the artificial heart recipient. Sheesh.

CBS was Palestine and economic indicators and the Beltway and threshers cutting through fields—it was fucking boring, was what it was. I didn't get into television wanting to be Dan Rather. If I had a TV news hero, it was Geraldo Rivera, making trouble and hanging with John Lennon. I dug the rush of local news: fires and cars smashing into storefronts and Black-

Hassidim race wars, shocking murders and building collapses and abandoned babies the entire city wanted to adopt.

I landed a producing job at WNBC's *News 4 New York*, in the building where they made *Saturday Night Live* and David Letterman's show, where my old radio hero Don Imus did his show and a guy named Howard Stern was starting his, and where I'd get to meet Jessica Savitch.

Ah, Jessica Savitch. There was no woman on television with the appeal of the luscious, lisping blonde sex kitten who read the NBC network news. No other newswoman inspired such slack-jawed admiration among male viewers, though she'd been cut back to popping up at 9:59 p.m. to coo her way through fifty-second updates. I never would have guessed she was a coke-sniffing basketcase whose boyfriend, the previous WNBC news director, beat the shit out of her and turned her into a lesbian.

My first day at WNBC was October 24, 1983. It was a Monday. I was awakened by my clock radio blasting Newsradio 88. The headline at the top of the hour was Jessica Savitch.

She was dead.

In the early morning hours in New Hope, Pennsylvania, Savitch, a male friend, and her dog, Chewy, were leaving a restaurant in the rain when their station wagon veered off the driveway and flipped into a canal. Trapped upside-down in the mud as the car filled slowly with water and debris, Savitch and her friend drowned. So did her dog.

The afternoon of the day of Jessica Savitch's death, the *News 4* producers gave me my first writing assignment:

"NBC news correspondent Jessica Savitch was killed early today in an auto accident."

They were giving me the Jessica Savitch obit.

"Are you sure you want me to do this one?"

Yeah.

"Uh, don't you want your top writer doing this?"

No. Just write it.

"Maybe one of the anchors wants to write something personal?"

No one cared about Jessica Savitch. Even though her body was still warm and waterlogged, her posters had already been removed from the frames in the NBC hallways—no great loss, as security was getting tired of removing the drinking straws pranksters kept taping under her nose. I wrote Jessica Savitch's obit that day, wrote it straight and solemn and ended it with, "Last year, she wrote her autobiography. It was called *Anchorwoman*."

Within weeks, I was producer of the eleven o'clock news. New York

City was moving into the greedy yuppie era, and News 4 was picking up where *The 10 O'Clock News* left off, reflecting the most compelling vision of the city: a more prosperous, prettified, and powerful vision from the seventh floor of 30 Rockefeller Plaza.

This was a newsroom of stars, and somewhere into the middle of all this dropped Pat Doyle. The day he showed up, placing his hat on a file cabinet and folding his jacket carefully over a chair by the door near the corner of the assignment desk, it was as if someone had wheeled in a dinosaur skeleton from the Museum of Natural History. The vets who knew him from the *News* rolled their eyes. You could almost hear the "What the fuck?" whisper from the rest of the room.

This was a fossil who had tumbled out of a time warp down at Lindy's on the corner across from Radio City, a perfectly-preserved specimen from a long-gone age of story-chasing. If you looked close enough, past the bushy eyebrows, rosy cheeks, and Irish eagle profile, if you looked beyond his old manual typewriter, you'd notice the threadbare quality, and that made the package all the more genuine. The style and age of the suits, the yellow-brown sweat stains soaked into the frayed white shirts, the imprint of the tenement T-shirt—Doyle could've been one of those guys you passed in Herald Square who darkened his hair with Kiwi shoe polish and lived in an SRO with a hot plate coil on the sink, a bottle of bourbon on the night table, and a billboard blowing smoke rings outside the window.

I never would have guessed Doyle had a wife and five kids and homes in New Jersey and Austin, Texas; never considered how self-created his image was; never counted back to figure that any guy dressed like that should've been too old to walk.

I just thought he was the real thing. I introduced myself.

"How ya doin, kid." Doyle said it out of the side of his mouth, looking around to see if anyone was watching, like he was passing on a secret. He talked that way.

I used one of Doyle's tips on the air. We became pals.

These were heady days to be producing the number one late-night news broadcast in New York City. It was a time of mob hits, a raging drug epidemic, the crystallization of crack, something they were calling "the gay cancer," the subway gunman, Howard Beach, insider trading, municipal corruption, Andrew Crispo, Cardinal O'Connor, and Mayor Koch. It was also when cheaper technology began to allow local newscasts to encroach on the sacred territory of the networks. Now when there was a plane crash in the Midwest or a big story in holy Washington D.C., the lowly locals could send their own reporters and go live. The network newscasts were usually on half-hour tape delay and assembled hours in advance. Who needed John Chancellor when you had Ralph Penza?

Doyle would call his sources, jot down tips for the desk, and, in his spare time, clack away at his manual typewriter, typing out short stories—sometimes for no other reason than to leave them in my mailbox. They were all knocked off in the single take of the newspaperman: one or two pages, sometimes as many as twenty, but most all of them recalling "a time when one could walk the streets, ride the subways and buses, and go into your home or hotel without being on the alert," when "life was gay, carefree, and without worries or tribulations."

It was a time when every crime had resonance, and Doyle liked writing about the ones that resounded the loudest, like the morning a "two-bit bum of the first class" named Albert Victory shot a cop named Albert Townshend outside the El Morocco nightclub.

> In the darkened parking lot next door, two plainclothesmen pressed their guns against the head of Victory while a third searched him for weapons. They had already disarmed him of a .38 calibre revolver he had shot the cop with. He was lying on his back, his blue uniform saturated with blood.
> No one had to tell me I had a good one. Excitement was on the faces and in the voices of the bulls. The booze I had consumed earlier had, as always, given me more balls than when I abstained from it. I got down on my knees and placed Townshend's head on my lap. His handsome face was a white mask. I said a Hail Mary. I could tell he was going. He breathed his last in my arms.

Doyle's moment of television glory came on December 16, 1986. The time was 5:40 p.m. He was at his desk when the call came in.

"Two guys just got knocked off. Forty-sixth and Third."

"In midtown? Who are they?"

"Don't know. I'll call you back."

Doyle filled everyone in and went back to the the phones. Four sources confirmed it. "Three torpedoes" gunned down two men in a limousine outside Sparks Steakhouse. The vics were dead.

News editor Bob Campbell wrote the story and we got it on the air first, exclusive, beating everyone in town.

Doyle had the scoop, but wouldn't sit back until he got the names of the dead. He chewed his cigar. He called the precinct, One Police Plaza, the FBI—nothing. He was thinking of the next move when his line lit up again. It was another of his tipsters, a retired cop he'd known twenty-five years.

"Get ready for it," his pal said. "It's a big one."

"Cut the bullshit and shoot!"

"Big Paul Castellano and Tommy Bilotti. See ya later."

Doyle inhaled deep and exhaled long. The Godfather.

Doyle got that on the air as well, grabbed his coat and hat and rushed to the elevator. He was young again.

Downstairs, he tipped his hat to the boys at the security desk— "Evenin', Inspector" —pushed his way through the Christmas tourists and shoppers under the tree at the Rockefeller Center skating rink, turned right down Fifth Avenue, and, with St. Pat's at his back, walked past Saks and down 46th to the block between Second and Third.

The bodies of Big Paul Castellano and his driver were still warm. Castellano was half in, half out of the passenger side of the car. Tommy Bilotti still had the car keys in his hand. The cops nodded and let Doyle past the yellow tape. The Inspector was on the scene.

The next day, he left eight pages in my mailbox.

> I walked on Paul Castellano's blood. It was just
> after the ventilated bodies of New York's multi-
> millionaire Don and his weight-lifting bodyguard
> were punctured with quarter-ounce slugs pumped
> into them by swearing hit men on a busy street
> with Christmas shoppers in a classic Mob set-up.
> Ninety minutes later and not too tenderly, morgue
> attendants hoisted the sheet-draped stiffs onto
> stretchers and laid them on the floor of the dark-
> colored van. Destination: Bellevue Mortuary...

Not long after, one of the defendants in the Pizza Connection mob drug trial got it in the back while carrying groceries out of Balducci's on Sixth Avenue in the Village. Doyle got the tip; we sent Anna Bond downtown to do a live shot and got the story on *News 4 at Six*—first, as usual.

After the show, I took the F train home. My stop at Sixth Avenue and Eighth Street just happened to be two blocks south of the crime scene, so I walked up into the fresh evening action, past the live trucks and police cars, flipped out my police press pass and strolled on through. The victim had been taken to St. Vincent's with three slugs in his back. He was still breathing. His blood was fresh on the sidewalk.

I stepped up to the blood. I thought of Doyle's great lead...

Doyle couldn't stop laughing when I told him. Wiping his eyes, he loaded some copy paper into his manual and began typing away.

The next day there were more pages in my mailbox. Doyle had written a story about me, rushing from the newsroom to the latest mob hit, shouting,

"I'm going to do the Inspector one better!" and, after threatening a cop who won't let me cross the police line to step on the blood, getting thrown clear across the rooftops of the West Village onto the Christopher Street pier.

All that, when in reality, I never stepped on the blood in the first place. I didn't feel I deserved to put myself on Doyle's level.

My own imagination helped lead to my being sacked as producer of the eleven o'clock news. It was under the reign of news director Jerry Nachman, a former TV street reporter who fancied himself a combination of Hildy Johnson, Edward R. Murrow, and James Bond, but who in reality was a short, round man who had trouble breathing. Nachman played out a 1930's newsboy fantasy on television and later as editor of The *New York Post*. He kept a "Sweetheart get me rewrite" poster on his office wall and played up tough, personalized news with all the frenzy and heart of the old tabloids. You'd think we'd have gotten along. But, as real as it got, WNBC was no Channel Five. It was corporate television, and for all his talk of good old tabloid, Nachman was torn between his romantic dream life and corporate ambition.

He told me to keep the Nielsen numbers rising on the eleven. He urged me to follow my tabloid instincts. "It's your job to walk all the way out to the end of the cliff, and it's my job to pull you back before you fall off," he promised, but when the suits said I went too far, he flicked a finger and sent me into space.

Can't really blame him, though. I could be a loose cannon. I walked the line along that cliff, and the words I put onscreen went beyond the preferred flat newsspeak—like the time a windsurfer set off from the Jersey shore, sailed into the horizon, and was never seen again. It was a sad story. My graphic read, GONE WITH THE WIND. Everyone was offended.

I was producing one Sunday night when an unusual story came over the newswire: a farmer had been killed in India—one single farmer. Reports from India usually had them going by the hundred. This guy was leading a cow into a field to sacrifice for Ramadan when he stopped for a moment and put the rope around his neck. The cow took off running; the Indian man was strangled. My onscreen graphic said "HOLY COW!"

"...Well, it *was* a holy cow. Cows are sacred there. And the idea of the man being sacrificed when he was going to kill the sacred animal—well, you just gotta say 'holy cow,' don't you?"

The bosses didn't buy it, especially after the staff of *Nightline* called to complain en masse.

Soon after Nachman left for an NBC corporate job in Washington, General Electric bought RCA for $6.3 billion and got NBC as part of the bargain. GE's chairman, "Neutron Jack" Welch, took a look at NBC News and saw waste. Television news divisions were no longer regarded as instruments of public service, but as cheap vehicles for pure profit. To ensure more profit, there would have to be a massacre. The intended victim was NABET, the union of 3,000 technicians, producers, writers, and editors in six cities, including the newsroom of *News 4 New York*.

The strike began on June 28, 1987. For the next seventeen weeks, I spent my time on the Cadillac of Unions' picket line in front of Rockefeller Center. I got to yell "scab" a lot, hold up signs, visit the unemployment office, and shave my head. In solidarity, the bartender at my local in the Village stopped charging me for drinks, and he never charged me again.

In the end, the union lost. GE won the right to replace unionized veterans with temporary workers, overtime was phased out, jobs were combined, and, from then on, everyone seemed to be doing piecework, resigned to life as interchangeable cogs making a product for bosses they resented. The bean counters had taken over.

On November third, the night before we returned to work, I got a call from Tina Press, the assistant news director. Tiny, serious, from a family of journalistic educators, and cute as a button, Tina treated me like her wild teenage son. "I wanted you to know, because you're his friend, that we're laying Pat Doyle off this week."

"How can you?" I asked. "You don't even pay him."

"We pay him something," she said.

"Yeah, but hardly anything. This is his life. You can't fire Pat Doyle."

"We have to," she said. Though Doyle was on a stipend of something less than a couple of hundred dollars a week, his was another head to be cut from the count.

John Miller, *News 4*'s police reporter and successor to Doyle's legacy, made a personal appeal to keep him on, but John Lane, the NBC bureaucrat brought in as news director shortly before the strike, wouldn't be moved.

"Now, don't tell him," Tina ordered me.

"Don't worry. I'm not gonna tell him. If you have the heart to let Pat Doyle go, *you* tell him."

News 4 New York was a different place when we returned, the changes camouflaged by an unsettled mix of anger and sheepishness, resentment and relief. Along with the homecoming troops came middle-aged radio employees and network news rejects who, under the new deal, found themselves reassigned to lowly local. They wandered around, stunned, like plane crash survivors.

Then there was Doyle. He walked in, dropped his hat, and rubbed his hands together.

"Welcome back kid! Good to have ya back!"

"Hiya, Pat."

"Why're ya lookin down, Boit?"

"Pat. I'm fucking disgusted with this place. We both oughta quit and I oughta write your book. Your life story."

He motioned me closer, confidential-like. "I'm writin' it," he said. "I've just finished a piece on my pal Henry Ford."

"Great. Put it in my box. I wanna see it."

Then it was back to work, during a week with little time for moping. One of the biggest stories of the decade broke that very day when police entered a brownstone on West 10th Street in Greenwich Village, just a few blocks from my apartment, to find a filthy and horrific scene: a beautiful little girl named Elizabeth "Lisa" Steinberg had been beaten into a coma and her adoptive parents were charged with the abuse.

It seemed no one in the city could fathom what had happened, or why. Joel Steinberg was a middle-class attorney. His lover, Hedda Nussbaum, was an author of children's books. When the couple was brought into the precinct, Hedda looked like she'd been through ten rounds with the heavyweight champ. She too had been beaten to a pulp. Her nose was flattened, ribs and wrist broken, and her leg a gangrenous mess.

It was the type of story that all New York took personally, the type that can't happen here, the type of story that Doyle lived for. We named it "The House of Horror" and gang-covered it.

On Wednesday, a rumor spread through the newsroom that little Lisa had died. It was countered by another that she was brain dead but alive, technically.

"You must know some of the nuns down at St. Vincent's," I told Doyle. "See what you can find."

Doyle got on the phone. "Get it straight," he barked at the source of the rumor. "Get the facts right!"

He was impressed with Bob Campbell's lead to the show that night, a line about the little girl "lying in the twilight of a coma, her life ebbing away."

That evening after the six o'clock show, news director Lane called Doyle into his office. After a few minutes, Doyle came out and gathered his hat and jacket.

"Everything all right, there, Pat?"

"Everything's fine, kid," he assured me, grabbing my arms too hard the way he used to do and clapping me on the back. "I'll see ya tomorra." Doyle went off.

Little Lisa died the next day. The city cried in an outpouring of grief that would culminate in a funeral attended by thousands of strangers.

That morning I was flipping through the newspapers when Jim Unchester called me over to the assignment desk.

"Burt, Pat's been involved in a fatal accident," the assignment editor said.

"Who died?"

"He did, apparently."

Before I could ask if this was a joke, Unch picked up the phone. "It is? He's dead?" He put the phone on hold. "Pat's dead."

It was all pretty straightforward. According to Sgt. Ed Burns at the police public information office, Doyle was on his way to his second-to-last-day of work, driving southbound on the FDR Drive, when his car went out of control and skipped a center divider near 120th Street. The car careened two hundred feet along a service road before crashing into a parked bus on Paladino Avenue.

Doyle was pronounced dead at the scene.

I walked out of the newsroom with Bob Campbell. "At least he died before he found out he was getting laid off," I said. "That would have killed him. Poor old Pat."

Less than an hour later, Nicky called from Channel Five. "I guess you already heard about Doyle," he said. "They laid him off last night."

I thought of Doyle coming out of John Lane's office the night before. "Everything's fine, kid," he said.

John Lane's secretary, Terry, confirmed the worst. She wept as she remembered Doyle's last words to John Lane: "Well, John, I guess Friday is my last day."

Word came that afternoon that the *New York Post* was going to play up the layoff story. The *News 4* executives began playing up their own cover story.

"Pat knew for two weeks he was being let go," Tina said. I looked her in the eye. She knew what she'd told me on Monday.

I left the newsroom again and walked around Rockefeller Center with Bob. He listened and made sure I didn't hurt anyone. "They killed him," was all I could repeat. "Those bastards. They fucking killed Pat Doyle."

I got back and suggested to Terry Baker, another assistant news director, that John Miller do a package—that *somebody* do a package—on Doyle, The World's Greatest Police Reporter.

"No," Baker said. "Nobody knows who he is. Nobody gives a shit."

I looked at the six o'clock rundown. What about the kicker—the final story in the show that leaves you with a smile or a tear? Connie Collins was doing a three-minute package on her grandfather, an anonymous citizen who'd recently passed away of natural causes. Three minutes for "Paw Paw"— and he didn't even live in the tri-state area.

It was decided instead that I should write Pat Doyle's obit. It was hard getting focused through my anger and grief, so I played it straight, the way they like it on TV news. With a little stringer tape of the crash scene, the item ran forty seconds at the most. Two minutes and twenty seconds less than Paw Paw got.

The next day was supposed to be Doyle's last at *News 4*. Instead, it was the day he made all the papers except *The New York Times*. The *Daily News* ran an old photo of Doyle witnessing a handshake between Cardinal Spellman and Bobby Kennedy. The headline read, "Crime was his passion." The story was as bloodless as the *News* had become.

Those guys at the *Post*, though, Rupert Murdoch's Aussie bastards, they got it right:

NEWSPAPER LEGEND
GOES OUT IN STYLE

They ran a three-column photo of Pat Doyle's crumpled car smashed into the bus, cops looking down at the EMS attendants bent over the sheet-covered corpse, and a great Weegee punchline prop—a Hurst "Jaws of Life" resting useless in the foreground.

The article rhapsodized about the glorious, fiery crash, and added that "even in death, Doyle enhanced his legend."

Reporters were barred by the Medical Examiner's guards as the body of Elizabeth Steinberg was brought into the morgue. A moment after the van left, an ambulance brought Doyle in. Doyle had once more bypassed rival reporters to enter the scene of a top police story.

The coroner said Doyle died of multiple external and internal injuries. The cops said he probably had a seizure or heart attack before the crash. John Lane told the *Daily News*, "Pat was very up" about being let go. "It didn't come as any shock," he said. "The sad part is he's gone."

Some in the newsroom speculated that it might have been suicide. I knew better. I knew Doyle and I knew it wasn't an accident and it wasn't his health and it wasn't suicide. NBC and GE took away the man's reason for living. They were warned. They knew what they were doing.

As far as I was concerned, it was murder, and sitting in the newsroom of the flagship station of the NBC television network, I was unable to get out the truth.

---◆---

They laid out Pat Doyle at John Barrett's Funeral Home in Hell's Kitchen. They had him in the charcoal pinstripe suit he favored, with his hair and eyebrows combed back and pancake makeup on his face like he was ready to go on camera. To the left of his head, under the cross hanging over the open lid of the casket, they laid his brown fedora. All that was missing was his cigar, but that was probably in his inside breast pocket.

All the New York journos were there, from Nick Pileggi to John Miller, who arrived with Marty Eisenberg from P.J. Clarke's. "There are two versions of Pat's firing," Miller said. "One is the party line about Pat being laid off three weeks ago." He paused for effect and said the next line out of the side of his mouth. "The other is when I walked into John Lane's office the night before Pat died and Lane said, 'I just told him.'"

Pat Doyle's funeral took place at St. Patrick's Cathedral. The morning was bitter and the sky the color of cigarette smoke. A cold drizzle stung as the hearse pulled up on Fifth Avenue and the police honor guard carried out the flag-covered casket. More cops stood at each street corner, keeping the sidewalk clear as tourists poked around behind them, trying to get a glimpse as the priests exchanged the flag for a vestment and made some blessings over the box before leading everyone to their seats on the right side of the cathedral. The mourners stretched back many rows. Mark Monsky was there. Tina Press was there too, and so was John Lane, the born-again Catholic who'd laid off Doyle the night before his death.

John Miller stood lurking near the wall, like a cop, like Doyle.

"Patrick Doyle. I believe that he was a colorful journalist and reporter." The celebrant, assisted by a Doyle family friend named Father Walsh, had a lush brogue. He seemed to know of Doyle from what he read in the papers. "He reported for the *Daily News* on the crimes of this city. He also succeeded and got great scoops, pretending he was a police inspector. And having got the story, he would share the story with his fellow journalists; a sign of a good journalist."

The priest swung the incenser over the casket. "The smoke is a symbol of our prayers, rising to heaven on behalf of Patrick Doyle."

I thought of Doyle's cigar smoke as I watched the incense fill the great space above the altar.

Jerry Nachman gave the eulogy, and compared Doyle to a bigger-than-life character who stepped off a movie screen. "We're here today because we love Pat and love him because he reminded us of the romance that brought so many of us into his business," he said, slightly choked up by his own written words. "Years ago, there were lots of Pat Doyles carrying press cards. But years ago, there were places like the *Trib* and the *Mirror* and the *Journal-American* and the *World-Telegram & Sun* and the *Eagle* and the *Long Island*

Press and the International News Service.

"But it all began to change. The cops moved into a corporate-looking building and the bosses started calling themselves 'police executives' and went to grad school and took management courses.

"And we in the press, so long run by simple pirates or mere robber barons, became part of conglomerates. And newspeople put on suits and hired agents and fantasized three-picture deals and development situations and options.

"But no matter how many computers invaded how many newsrooms, no matter what mergers and acquisitions changed journalistic parentage, no matter how young or short the cops got, Pat stayed Pat, a loving and beloved anachronism in a world of faded color..."

Back at the newsroom, I wrote the story of the funeral for the five and the six:

> New York was his town.
> And today, New York said "so long" to Patrick Doyle.
> (go to video)
> He was the man they called the world's greatest
> police reporter.
> And it was a police honor guard that escorted him on
> his final visit to St. Patrick's Cathedral.
> Doyle was the last of a breed.
> Forty years at the *Daily News*.
> And a living legend amid the TV journalists, as
> *News4*'s crime specialist.
> Our old boss Jerry Nachman delivered the eulogy.
> He said Pat was a larger-than-life character who
> stepped off a movie screen.
> Nachman recalled the wisecracks, the thumbs in the
> suspenders, the fingers snapping the brim of his fedora.
> Doyle lived by the police blotter.
> He was an entry on the blotter last week.
> He was killed in a car crash, driving to work.
> Pat Doyle was 62.

It was factually correct, but the truth couldn't be found even between the lines. That was it. I'd had it with local news, angered that they didn't have any room for my imagination or excitement over a story, disgusted that the nuclear reactor-building, land-wasting corporation could destroy something so pure as news—that they could kill a man like Pat Doyle.

Fuck them. I was going into show business...

Meanwhile, even as they were shipping Doyle's bones to Austin, Texas, something else was going on about twenty blocks uptown.

Rupert Murdoch had taken over Metromedia, where I'd begun my TV career. *The 10 O'Clock News* was now part of Murdoch's Fox Television empire, and the hard-hitting Upper East Side news broadcast had been turned over to Rupert's newspaper boys from Sydney and spun into a frothy blend of blood and sex and fun. The news director was a guy from the supermarket tabs, a stumpy bloke whom everyone called "The Pig." Steve Dunleavy, the blood and guts street dog of the *New York Post*, learned to be a TV reporter in about three weeks and was starring in a new show called *A Current Affair*. Some distracted genius named Brennan was running the show from the bar across the street.

A Current Affair was using the news to get to bigger things. They didn't merely report the Jessica Savitch story—they re-enacted her death scene; held some production assistant underwater and videotaped her struggling for breath. When Robert Chambers killed Jennifer Levin in Central Park, they dramatized the murder and then got their hands on a tape of the killer at a girls' slumber party twisting off a doll's head. They paid for stories. They were breaking rules. They were turning their backs on the networks and their pretentious notions of TV news, dropping their pants and giving them the mooning they deserved.

These guys weren't pretending to be characters. They were the real thing, like Doyle.

It wasn't long before the phone calls started coming from my old friends from Channel Five. They were working for the Aussies now. They said I'd be perfect for them. C'mon over. Give it another try. It's different, we promise. You've got to meet these guys...

CHAPTER ONE:
KIDNAPPED!

Start by telling the story, then tell it again.

Put all your best material at the beginning. Tease it. Don't make them guess what's coming up. You see, mate, if you give them all the good stuff at the top, they'll stick around to watch it unfold all over again.

When you write the story, focus on one character. Think of it as a saga, or a movie: when you see a movie, let's say it's about a war, they don't cover the whole war, they focus on one soldier or a platoon. You have the star in the middle and the others are the co-stars.

Always remember—and this is most important—tell the story the way you'd tell it to your mates in the pub. Think about it: whenever you get back from a story, you stop in at the pub and the first thing your friends ask is, "What *really* happened?" If what you tell them isn't in the story you just wrote, then you didn't tell it the right way.

That's our job: to tell the story the way we'd tell it to our mates in the pub; to take what's between the lines and make that the story. We tell the story between the lines. Now...

"I'll have a Stoli and tonic."

It's January 24, 1989, and it's the bar of a restaurant called Nickel's, a small well-dressed place on 67th between Second and Third, crowded with East Side professionals stopping in for a quick one or dinner.

A bar will be the one constant wherever the story takes us, the place where ideas are born, friendships bonded, and the future planned; the place where all the dreams will be washed away when everything falls apart.

Most important, this was how it was sealed: standing at this bar, with that wince-making first slug of Stoli to settle the nerves. It was sort of a homecoming, being at Nickel's. Five years earlier, I'd worked up the block at Channel Five's *10 O'Clock News*, and my pals who'd stayed on after Murdoch took over had gotten me back uptown to meet with Fox Television's new vice president of news. Gerald Stone was a Yank who'd found success in Sydney with a Down Under franchise of *60 Minutes* and had been brought back to take over Murdoch's flagship magazine, *A Current Affair*, and its new weekly companion, a cartoony version of *60 Minutes* called *The Reporters*.

Stone wanted to hire me, an experienced TV news producer, to help run and bring some sense of stability to *A Current Affair*, taking over for a couple of producers who'd jumped ship to start up a rival tabloid TV show for the KingWorld syndication outfit. Those producers were a couple of lucky bastards, worker bees who got the show on the air every day and got credit for its brilliance.

The heart and soul, the inspiration, "the, ahem, genius," of *A Current Affair*, Stone said, was an Australian named Peter Brennan.

Brennan was back on board after leaving to launch a live local morning show with the audaciously Australian name of *Good Day New York*, but problem was, he wasn't exactly the office type. He liked to do most of his work across the street, running the show from another pub, a dark and smoky joint called the Racing Club, set up like a bookie at a corner of the bar, with phones sharing space with his drinks and plans jotted down on wet-ringed cocktail napkins.

"What I need is someone like you," Stone said, "to take Brennan's ideas from the pub—" He seemed a little embarrassed. "—and put them into effect in the office."

Stone wanted me to take the job then and there.

"It sounds great," I said. "But I think I should meet Peter Brennan first."

"I don't have a lot of time. You'll like Brennan. Don't worry about that."

"I think we oughta be sure he wants to work with *me*."

So there I was at Nickel's, back amid the well-heeled crowd at the bar with the five cent pieces under the plexiglas, nursing a vodka and tonic and wiping sweat from my hands on this blustery New York City January night.

When Peter Brennan swept in, I tend to remember a halo of snow swirling in the backlit sky before the door closed behind him and he pushed his way through the crowd toward the nearest bartender. He could have been some kind of Irish literary hero with his curly gray-red hair, red nose, flushed cheeks, and literal twinkle in his eyes as he shook hands, waved hellos around the room, wiped the steam off his round glasses, and ordered a Stoli and soda with a twist of lemon.

Brennan wore a long blue overcoat with a red scarf tangled around his necktie. As he slipped out of the coat, Stone appeared from the opposite end of the bar, edging his way through the bodies to make the introductions.

"I'll need an answer soon," Stone reminded me, leaving Brennan and me with our drinks, shoulder to shoulder at the crowded bar.

Brennan took a test sip and settled in with an exhale. "So. Gerald told me a lot about you."

"You too."

"So what do you think of our little show?"

I gave an answer I don't remember, but I'll never forget what Brennan said after asking what shows *A Current Affair* reminded me of and I responded by naming some news or magazine shows.

"The idea with *A Current Affair*, mate," Brennan said, "is that it's like *The Dick Van Dyke Show*."

The Dick Van Dyke Show. I knocked back my Stoli.

"It's something that's different to everyone."

Before he got much further, Brennan was interrupted by one of the video editors from his show, a woman whining a plea to be made chief of operations. Brennan acted like the intrusion was business as usual, muttered something noncommittal, and carried on. "It's all pretty simple what we do, mate. We're like the old tabloid newspapers back in Sydney. We don't do stories about gays, or incest, or child abuse stories, not for any other reason than we're aiming the show at the average American sitting in his average living room. We're not out to educate or push any agenda." He lit a Marlboro Light and continued as if he'd given the speech a thousand times to people who never understood what he was talking about. "We don't do sad stories, not for any other reason than we're guests in people's homes at dinner time. It's all fun."

Brennan soon had several conversations going at the bar, giving me time to look into my Stoli and think about Dick Van Dyke. In time, I'd find Brennan was totally serious. I'd come to understand the importance of a show providing something different for everyone. On this night, though, all I knew was that Peter Brennan thought *A Current Affair* was the fucking *Dick Van Dyke Show*.

I was sold.

"So," Brennan said. "What will it take to get you?" The bartender had already put another Stoli and soda with a twist of lemon in front of him.

"Well..." I caught my breath. "I'm looking for ninety."

"Hmmm. I think we can manage that." He raised his spillingly fresh drink. "Why don't you come over, mate? We'll have some fun."

Shit. My next thought was that I should have asked for a hundred. Everything was up for grabs in those days.

On the afternoon of February twentieth, I rode the Number Two train from 14th Street in the Village to Times Square, walked to the Grand Central shuttle, then took the Six train to 68th and Lex. It was a trip I hadn't taken in the five years since I left Channel Five: three trains and the scope of Manhattan in a half hour.

The 68th Street station, entrance to Hunter College and the elite Upper East Side, was retiled and brightly new. Up on the sidewalk, college kids walked past wealthy wives, the crisp air filled with the sound of construction. The old neighborhood was in transition. Skyscraping sliver apartment buildings were on the rise. The old police precinct on 67th Street was closed. There were no protesters at the Soviet Embassy across the street.

The block between Second and Third had changed most of all. What used to be WNEW was now WNYW, and what was once the gray Metromedia building was now the shiny Fox TV headquarters, the sidewalk level covered with mirrored steel so passersby could turn and look at themselves. They'd also catch the reflection of the Racing Club, the bar on the other side of the street.

That Monday afternoon was spent in a meeting with Brennan and Peter Faiman, a Murdoch intimate on board as a consultant in the *A Current Affair* overhaul.

Faiman cut the quintessential Aussie figure with his hatchet nose and rough-hewn wardrobe, but he wasn't one of Murdoch's gonzo journos. He was a bit of the artiste, a reknowned TV director who a year earlier helped cement the world's image of the archetypal Man from Down Under when he directed a little movie called *'Crocodile' Dundee*.

Peter Faiman spelled out my job description and gave me my first lesson in speaking Australian. I was to be the show's first managing editor— to select, assign, direct, write, and edit stories, and to "liaise" with Brennan and the staff, which, according to Australia's *Macquarie Concise Dictionary*, meant "to maintain contact and act in concert (usu. fol. by *with*.)" When the meeting was through, we were to go "over the road," which meant across the street to the Racing Club bar. There, we would talk, plan and "get pissed."

That meant get drunk.

"Brennan, this coffee stinks. Like a lot of other things around this fucking place. You see last night's ratings? The coffee's better." Maury Povich paced around Peter Brennan's office using his coffee cup as a prop. He was a gray eminence with a hip haircut, a craggy face that seemed covered with a permanent layer of makeup, and a suit that seemed too big for his tall, wiry frame.

It wouldn't matter if he splashed the cup's contents across the room. The place already resembled the rec room of a frat house, with a stained and dusty old couch, one lumpy chair, and several metal folding chairs scattered about. The spatterings of old milk, beer, and God knows what other liquids and secretions were crusted on the small portable refrigerator in the shadow of the inflatable palm tree near Brennan's desk. The TV and tape decks were antique and usually on the blink.

"Yeah, yeah." Brennan leaned over a desk that was scuffed and covered with papers, tapes, and a thin layer of cigarette ash. He sipped his coffee without complaint and flipped through that day's *New York Post*. "Maury, your picture's in the paper."

Maury spun on his heel to see. "Where?"

"Heh heh."

Maury sneered and played with the coffee maker.

I sat on the couch under a large Australian flag tacked to the wall. It was Tuesday, February 21, my first real day on the job, and it began by watching the show's host lope around and continue his crotchety screed without much enthusiasm. It was clear Maury was only acting like a grouch. He was actually athletic, laid back, most cooperative and amused by the successful show built around him.

Brennan would explain that Maury didn't know what the fuck anyone on the show was doing, but that he was the lynchpin to the show's success. A local news anchorman pulled from two decades of obscurity and thrust to stardom by this band of pirates, he provided the bemusement, disapproval and distance from the material that made the show's most unseemly and amateurish moments acceptable.

Besides, his glamorous marriage to up-and-coming superstar Connie Chung—soon to split NBC for a $6 million deal with CBS—actually gave a dash of credibility to the enterprise. Maury *was A Current Affair*.

"I hear you're hot stuff," he said by way of introduction to me. "Get us some ratings."

He walked out with his bad coffee like a tall Groucho Marx, passing the show production team on the way in. Peter Brennan was about to give me lesson one in how a tabloid television show was supposed to be assembled.

"So, whaddawe got today?" He folded the *Post* and got the day's show meeting underway. The show was in the middle of the all-important February sweeps, when ratings are measured and advertising rates determined. It was also the first month of a new competitive tabloid television era, in which *A Current Affair* faced an upstart imitator.

The company behind *Inside Edition* had tried to hire Brennan, tried to lure Maury, tried to buy up the *A Current Affair* brain trust, but wound up with the show's line producers, John Tomlin and Bob Young. They were the ones who took the brilliant material provided by Brennan and the gang, got it edited, timed it out and got it on the air. They were not innovators, and their new product reflected it. *Inside Edition* had debuted as a conservative slug of a show, hosted by the aging, pompous, tippling Brit David Frost, who kicked off the premiere with a windy speech promising that his show would *not* be tabloid or sensational. In fact, he promised it would be a dull, dry half-hour following the same rigid journalistic rules and prejudices as the gasbag news shows that *A Current Affair* was making irrelevant.

Within weeks, Frost would be pushed out, while claiming his ethics forced him to resign. For now, he was riding a phony high road with the second night of his interview with Robert Kennedy's killer Sirhan Sirhan. Despite a promotional push by Tom Brokaw on NBC's *Nightly News*, part one didn't rate, as they say, for shit.

Brennan was more concerned with what the competition had in store for the following night. For Wednesday, *Inside* was promoting an exclusive interview with a man named Mark Christian, lover of the late Rock Hudson. This would rate, as they say in television, with no little irony in this case, up the ass.

"Hudson. Let's do Rock Hudson," Brennan said.

There was silence from his producers.

"*Inside's* running an interview with his lover tomorrow. So I reckon we oughta run an interview with his lover tonight."

"Uh, Pete, *Inside's* got him exclusive," Dennis O'Brien, the latest line producer, pointed out.

"They paid thousands, darling," a female Fleet Street vet added between puffs.

Brennan smiled. He knew that if we ran a Rock Hudson story tonight, viewers who'd tune in *Inside Edition* on Wednesday would figure they'd already seen the same story on *A Current Affair* the night before.

"Exclusive, huh?" He groaned and ran a hand through his tangle of curly hair. "I, uh, seem to remember Mark Christian did an interview on Channel Nine in Sydney right after Hudson died."

Brennan got on the phone and cut a quick deal with some old mates in Sydney. Later that morning, the old footage was fed in and turned into a package with a script that made it seem the interview could have been recent. In fact, if you didn't listen closely, you'd be forgiven for assuming the interview had taken place that very day.

The show was recorded quickly that afternoon, as if it were live, on ancient Channel Five equipment in the old *Wonderama* studio, then fed to stations around the country at four p.m. The Rock Hudson segment was billed as an "exclusive, rare interview" with his lover, Mark Christian.

Inside had probably wasted tens of thousands for their exclusive with the male hustler, and their producer probably wasted weeks preparing his special sweeps piece.

Brennan ripped it off for the price of a satellite feed. It might be considered underhanded, dirty pool, but he did it with a wink and a smile and such charm that there was no way you could fault him for it. This was war, and Brennan was the happiest warrior in television.

When work was done, we all headed over the road to the Racing Club to get pissed again.

Steve Dunleavy was at the Racing Club that evening. Dunleavy, the ageless legend with his silver pompadour, eagle beak profile and rakish charisma, was the paragon of everything that made journalism romantic and dangerous. He was friend to cops and criminals, bums and kings. He knew the words to any show tune you could toss at him. He could do more dialects and accents than Sid Caesar. He was a master raconteur and joketeller, his words a perfectly constructed Shakespeare of the street.

While covering a story, Dunleavy would be moved to tears. He'd tell a story and move himself to tears. Dunleavy, it was said, would fuck anyone, do anything—*fuck anything*—for a story.

I'd first been introduced to Dunleavy a couple of years earlier, shortly after Fox took over Metromedia. It was a *10 O'Clock News* party, in a bar, of course, somewhere on Second Avenue. One of my pals from the WNEW days dragged him through the crowd. Dunleavy extended a bony hand, smiled, began to speak—and his false front tooth fell out of his mouth and plopped into my drink.

Now, here we were at the Racing Club, he the legend and me the celebrated new arrival, colleagues—mates at the horseshoe bar.

"Mate, what're you havin? It's on me. Mohammed, a drink for Mister Kearns here. Put it on my tab!"

Dunleavy deepened his bottomless tab and regaled us with a story of himself and Eddie Burns, the NYPD spokesman who was a great, close friend to all the Aussie journos. He and Eddie had been "drunk as hell" one night, driving up the LIE to their homes in Long Island, when Eddie pulled over to rest. They both fell asleep on the side of the expressway.

Dunleavy took his time with the tale, lining it with laughs along the way. Finally, he was nearing the punchline. "I awake in the car, to a high view of water, and I look over and I see Burnsie doesn't have his hands on the wheel!"

Pregnant pause. Collective intake of oxygen and cigarette smoke from his audience. "Our car was in a backhoe—*being loaded onto a truck!*"

There was much laughter and we all ordered another round. I drank vodka and tonics until 9:30, took a cab back to my apartment in the Village, and passed out.

The next day, I had a chance to get my bearings and a feel for the lay of the land. The *A Current Affair* office was a cramped and smoky maze with pictures of Madonna, James Dean, and Marilyn Monroe on the walls and newspapers stacked on desks. This wasn't a newsroom, it was a free-for-all television refugee camp.

There were the somewhat disoriented local news reporters and producers, some transferred from Fox's *10 O'Clock News*, trying to forget what they'd been taught in the past, tabloid print journalists trying to remember that what goes over in the supermarket and Fleet Street rags must be toned down for television, and a lot of youngsters offered the opportunity to get as far as they wanted—even on-air—if they were talented, attractive, or just plain aggressive enough. The women flirted openly, men spoke suggestively, and sex jokes flew through the room along with the Nerf football lobbed over everyone's heads by reporter Bill McGowan in his constant games of catch with the cameramen hanging around waiting for assignments.

One of the female producers cuddled against Dennis O'Brien and whispered in his ear as he gave a perfunctory glance at her script before sending her into an editing room. I could tell which women didn't get along with him. They were coming on to me.

"We have to have a drink." Karen, a tiny reporter with a Jessica Savitch lisp, was standing a bit too close to my pressed shirt. "You mutht tell me all about yourthelf."

Maureen O'Boyle came up behind her. She was a tall, sassy young gal with a large face and hips that swung when she walked. "You can do that later," she said in a Southern drawl. "Ah'm ready to work. Burt, whatever you want me to do, Ah'm ready to go."

She picked up a pack of Marlboro Lights and lit one theatrically. Folding her arms and gesturing with the cigarette like a drag queen, she threw back her shoulders and thrust her obvious breasts. "Honey, Ah'm ready!"

On Thursday, Wayne Darwen came into view, hunched in one of the tiny, airless edit rooms, trying to cut down an interview with Linda Gray, an aging TV star who'd just quit the show *Dallas*. The actress thought she was pretty hot stuff as she sat in the studio in Los Angeles, being interviewed via satellite by Maury back in New York—pretty hot, that is, until a young female producer in the New York control room spoke into her IFB earpiece: "How do you spell your name?"

Wayne had three tapes displayed on three monitors before him: one showed Linda Gray; one showed Maury; and a third showed both of them, sharing the screen, in boxes. His job was to mix the shots and shorten the interview into one cohesive, three-minute package.

"Any time you wanna jump in, mate, feel free," he said to me. Wayne was another recent arrival at *A Current Affair*, another Aussie pirate transferred from the *New York Post* and new to television. He knew what he wanted, but didn't know the lingo or shortcuts.

"Why don't you cut it there," I suggested, "and cover the middle part with the split screen." To the editor I added, "Can you leave her sound over Maury's picture? That way you can butt the two bites together without a jump cut."

Wayne blew some smoke and sipped from his ever-present half-pint milk carton. "Good, good, do it."

Wayne was a couple of years my senior, a skinny bloke with an alcohol gut and a face bloated red by the hard stuff and scarred by a car crash. He dressed like a member of Spinal Tap, in faded t-shirts, bright red suspenders and torn jeans, bracelets and earrings, topped off by the curly locks of a rock star. His voice was an exorcist growl urged by too many ciggies and nodes on his throat.

Wayne had gotten his first newspaper job at age seventeen when Brennan hired him on the *Sydney Daily Mirror* amid a brawling bite-off-your-ear-and-spit-it-out world in which seven papers competed for stories. When he landed in America, he worked under Dunleavy as an intern at the *Star* before joining the *Post*. Wayne had been through a couple of marriages and was currently shacking in a swank highrise on 57th Street with an elderly widow named Susie while on the side banging the Channel Five news director, a waitress at the Racing Club, and, it seemed, the very editor we were working with.

"Oy'm a wombat, baby," he'd say with a leer. "Eats roots and leaves."

Wayne was a wombat, all right. He was also possessed by a naive brilliance Brennan was just beginning to tap. Completely new to the medium, without any of the prejudices or training to restrict his imagination, Wayne saw television as another sheet of newsprint ready to be filled with anything he wanted to slash across it. The key would be to let that imagination run wild, uncensored, so the raw ideas could be harnessed and turned into a new kind of television.

As the clock ticked closer to deadline, my suggestions in the edit room turned to orders. The job got done. Wayne stamped out his cigarette and exhaled the last of the smoke.

"Thanks, mate," he said as we left the edit room. He was a little shaken by the pressure and took a sip from the milk carton to steady himself. "Good work."

"Get ready for this!"

Maury Povich rushed into Brennan's office. "A horse named *A Current Affair* ran today at Belmont and won twenty-eight dollars on a two-dollar bet!"

"We gotta get the tape," Brennan said.

"We gotta find the horse!"

"We'll run the race at the end of the show." Brennan was excited. He tapped out a cigarette and added the dash of genius. "And after the race is called, we'll add, 'And just leaving the gate, *Inside Edition!*'"

That night, Wayne was raging as we drank over the road at the Racing Club. *Inside Edition* had outbid us, buying up an exclusive interview with the author of a new book alleging that Cary Grant was homosexual. Wayne wanted to trump them with a story alleging that Grant had an affair with Grace Kelly in their later years.

"Only problem is, it ain't true," someone at the bar mumbled.

"I have a problem with ethics!" Wayne growled back. "I don't have any! And there are a lot of people with ethics around here!" Wayne liked to say that "ethics" is a county outside London. He turned to me and blew his cigarette smoke away from the drinks. "Look, mate, I've got this bloke in Hollywood, see?" He lowered his voice, conspiratorial-like. "We pay him a bit and he'll say whatever we want."

"You mean it's *not* true?"

"Bullshit!" he said. "It may not be true, but fuck it! Cause they're both dead! And if it ain't true, nobody'll know!"

"What's the first sign you've got AIDS? A pounding in your ass."

Wayne chuckled at his joke until his laugh turned to a hack and deepened into a smoker's phlegmy seizure. He wore a rugby shirt that read REDFERN ALL-BLACKS.

I took a seat in the petri dish couch and gestured to his chest. "The All-Blacks?"

"It's an all-aborigine team," he explained.

"Are you allowed to wear that in America?"

Wayne shrugged and pulled off the shirt to reveal a Mets 1986 championship T-shirt underneath.

It was the second of March, the last day of sweeps, and everyone was gathered in Peter Brennan's office. Brennan was more rumpled than usual, having slept on the office couch the night before. Young female producers splayed across the floor. Karen was draped on the armrest of Wayne's chair—after refusing the offer of his lap.

"What do we have on Liz?"

"We have the press conference, and we're trying to get a live shot with the medical board."

"Do you want to see any of these?" Supervising producer Judy Sokolow sat near the video deck with tapes of the packages scheduled for that day's show. One of them had been heavily promoted on television, radio and in Maury's phone interviews. Maury was tireless in his work for the show, sitting in his office for hours speaking to radio stations around the country and helping make the show a true grassroots phenomenon.

None of that mattered. The pattern for *A Current Affair* was clear: Scour the papers and wires each morning and find the fresh story people would be talking about that day—be it Roseanne's facelift, Johnny Carson's ex-wife, or Robert Chambers in a jail brawl—and do it differently than anyone else. Get an exclusive interview, buy up some photos, find a new angle to lead the show or tease throughout to attract viewers and keep them hooked.

The most important words were "day of air."

"You can't do this!"

David Miller burst into the room, a barking jangle of nervous tics. If Miller appeared a bug-eyed shouting parody of those reporters on network magazine shows, his segment for that day was satire right down to its title. "Lindbergh Baby Killer" was another story about the kidnapping and murder of Charles Lindbergh's son more than fifty years ago, this one based on a new book promoting the innocence of the executed convicted kidnapper, Bruno Hauptmann.

"You can't kill the Lindbergh baby!"

"We're not," Brennan said. "We're only putting it off a day."

Miller's story was being killed like Hauptmann to make way for breaking news: Elizabeth Taylor's Dr. Feelgood was under investigation for writing her too many prescriptions.

"But—but I promised Bruno Hauptmann's widow the story'd be aired on the 57th anniversary of the kidnapping!" Miller said.

Brennan lit a cigarette and came up with a most rational response. "Why don't we just say *tomorrow* is the anniversary?"

Miller sighed, flapped his arms and walked out.

"Any more stories?"

"A great one in Florida." I waved a tiny clip from *USA Today*'s "Across America" page, the one that each day includes two one-line stories from each state. "Get this. Police in Cocoa Beach get a call that Muammar Khadaffi is eating at a Denny's. Khadaffi!"

"How'd he get into America?" Karen, the reporter on the armrest of Wayne's chair, was piping up.

"Well, wait. Three carloads of deputies show up at this Denny's and they roust this poor schmuck who's eating his eggs or whatever. And it turns out he *does* look like the guy. But of course, he's not Khadaffi."

Maury could do a live two-way with the Libyan madman's doppelganger from the booth in Denny's where he was almost riddled with police bullets.

Brennan chuckled. "That's fuckin great."

Karen looked confused. "Why doesn't he just shave his beard?"

No one volunteered that Khaddafi's well-known face was clean shaven. We were already riffing on how to take the story a step further. Perhaps we could find lookalikes for other hated people.

"Like the Ayatollah," one of us suggested.

Karen chirped in: "Or Khomeini!"

By now, my job was clear: do a little bit of everything and as much as I could take control of. This meant assigning breaking day-of-air stories, writing them with Wayne, producing in the edit room, sorting through hundreds of big city and small town newspapers for stories, editing reporters' and producers' scripts and giving them direction and encouragement in the field.

First, the phones: Bob Martin was on the line. He was a veteran of Channel Five, a veteran of Vietnam, a martial arts expert, and the show's only black reporter, wrapping a story in Houston and heading to Dallas for a segment on an outrageous truckstop. He was looking for one more story.

We found him a psychic in Oklahoma City. Hop, skip and jump. It was amazing. The networks would think twice if they thought at all about sending crews and reporters into small towns for what would be considered small feature stories. Oh, they'd fly Charles Kuralt to meet his crew in their Winnebego for his special segments, but the bulk of their coverage was directed almost entirely to Washington, New York, overseas and the occasional dead movie star or natural disaster in Los Angeles. America, to the networks, was a shot of a thresher cutting through a field or a factory worker pouring molten metal.

At A Current Affair, Danny Meenan and the other former local newsmen on the desk treated the map of America as a blown-up grid of the five boroughs. We'd send reporters and producers on wide story-gathering loops around the country, going to towns and cities the networks wouldn't touch unless a 747 crashed, and in the process elevating small town stories into national issues, and giving blue-collar America a vision of the country they'd never seen on a nightly basis: the one they lived in.

Bob Martin was worried about Oklahoma City. It was cold up there and he didn't bring a coat. I looked at the map. It seemed so close. I traced with a finger the route from Houston to Dallas to Oklahoma City, picturing him running in his shirt sleeves, being chased by guys wearing sheets.

"Okay. I've got a good story."

My reverie was interrupted by David Miller, pitching a story about a prison in Illinois whose inmate newspaper had won a lot of awards. Instinct said it paid to unleash reporters on stories they were passionate about. I told him to go for it.

He went off to call the prison.

"Burt. Dorian on two."

Robin Dorian was on the phone from Tupelo, Mississippi. She too, had reservations about her assignment, but for different reasons. Two men were charged with attempted murder—through voodoo. Both were in jail for poking pins in a doll and sprinkling chicken blood around the room.

"I think the story's dead. No one's talking."

"It's a good one, Robin. You really oughta keep trying."

Robin was a tiny blonde from Florida who joined the show as a segment producer. She was known for making things look pretty in the edit room, and after Brennan made her a reporter, concentrated on making herself look pretty in meticulously-lit standups and reversal shots.

Dorian wanted to be a star, which was fine, but a real pain when I needed her to be a reporter.

"Did you know Rafael Abramovitz is on this story for *The Reporters*?" she said. "We shouldn't bump heads with them."

"It's too good to give up. We're there. We'll get it on first."

She tried another tack. "Then there's the B-factor," she said. "This story is very 'B.'"

"B" meant "black." It wasn't that Dorian was racist—she wasn't. She was merely parroting a term that I'd heard whispered in the office to flag stories the bosses might reject. No wonder *A Current Affair* was getting a rap for avoiding stories about African Americans—its very employees were confused by the new Aussie rules, and interpreting the show in those very terms.

I was only there a month and I got it. Why didn't they? *A Current Affair* avoided the police blotter ghetto crimes that filled local TV newscasts—the drug-related shootings, broken-bottle stabbings and senseless urban violence born of poverty and underclass despair.

Dorian seemed to be using the "B" excuse to avoid the work needed to get the story. I told her to keep trying.

"Forget the prison newspaper story." Miller was back at my desk. "It's dead."

"What happened?"

Miller said a prison official called back to cancel the story. After making arrangements for Miller and a crew to get inside, the official told the murderer-editor and his assistant, the rapist, about his plans to put their paper on national television.

They replied, "*A Current Affair*? No way! That show's too sleazy!"

Pepsi premiered a two-minute commercial that night during *The Cosby Show*. The ad starred Madonna, playing with religious imagery, dancing around with Catholic school girls, and bouncing about with a church choir. Any offensive elements were magnified by Madonna's appearance in the current issue of *Rolling Stone*, shirt open, smoking a joint and grabbing her crotch.

The story was a natural. Madonna was a tabloid TV icon, up there with Liz Taylor, Michael Jackson and Elvis; a star whose every move made news and who was familiar to everyone in the family, from grandma down to the kids, whether they knew her music or not.

The next morning there were already grumbles about the spot's blasphemy. The news shows might run a few seconds of video and report objectively that some viewers found the ad to be distasteful. *A Current Affair's* point of view could be unobscured.

In the worldview of *A Current Affair*, people didn't insult the Church, and sex was naughty—the word unsaid, only spelled out, S-E-X—values needed to be upheld, and all offensive images needed to be shown in as explicit detail as the lawyers would allow.

After a couple of coffees, all my Jesuit pistons were apump. Wayne was pumping, too. "This is an outrage!"

"Insulting Catholics the world over—and during *The Cosby Show!*"

In Brennan's office, I came up with the idea of setting up a TV monitor on the steps of St. Patrick's Cathedral, where we'd screen the Pepsi spot to passersby, tourists, worshippers—even clergy.

Pepsi pulled Madonna's commercial soon after.

Yeah! This was it. *A Current Affair* was a forum for cutting through the bullshit, for doing true enterprise stories that people cared about—all those stories that NBC had rejected, the ones that were laughed away because they weren't clipped out of the *News* or the *Times*, the stories everyone in the newsroom talked about but which wound up filed away in my desk.

At *A Current Affair*, we could send a reporter deep into backwater Arkansas for the story of a bride who won't sleep with her husband because she's in love with Johnny Mathis! We could set an agenda because we were doing stories people were interested in. This was power. *We could tell the truth.*

That night, we celebrated in Nickel's.

"This was the best, mate," I said to Wayne. "They would have laughed that Madonna story out of NBC!" We clinked glasses.

He leaned back on a barstool and pulled his girlfriend the WNYW news director onto his knee. "This guy's all right," he announced, motioning to me with his bottle. "I like him. He hasn't got that 'E' word."

She nodded. "Good. None of that 'E.'"

"Yeah, a lot of people come through here, they're full of that fuckin 'E.'" He sneered the letter with disgust, and I had to smile with pride, thinking to myself, he's right, I'm not a big *egotist* like some of the others.

"Yeah," Wayne said with a treasure chest laugh. "No ethics!"

CHAPTER TWO:
MORLEY: WHAT HAPPENED ?

It was fitting that the *A Current Affair* office wasn't actually in the Fox building at 205 E. 67th Street, but next door, literally sharing space with celebrity, big money, and scandal in the building topped by the posh penthouse home of John Kluge, the mogul who sold Metromedia to Rupert Murdoch. Kluge had built his home atop the existing offices as a love nest for his young bride, a former skin magazine model from England. Upstairs, there was unspeakable luxury; down in the lobby, two security guards at all times, expensive artwork on the walls, and a turntable for Kluge's limousines in the garage.

When Kluge announced plans to raise the building, neighbors called it a violation of zoning regulations; their protest led by the cultured Morley Safer of CBS's *60 Minutes*, whose rear windows and courtyard looked onto the Metromedia and Kluge structures. Kluge agreed to scotch the plans for the penthouse—with one minor caveat. If the city wouldn't let him build, he'd move his Metromedia operations to New Jersey.

The neighbors lost.

Morley Safer watched the penthouse go up, and, in years to come, after Kluge sold his stations, got to have his news business turned upside down, literally in his own backyard.

There was no difficult labor involved in the birth of *A Current Affair*.

It began when Australian newspaper mogul Rupert Murdoch expanded his empire and horizons in 1985, buying 20th Century Fox and the Metromedia TV stations and turning it all into the Fox Broadcasting Corporation.

He wanted to start a TV network to compete with the Big Three, so he hired Barry Diller, the brilliant and ambitious former chief of Paramount Studios. Diller assembled a team of young executives in Los Angeles and aimed for a spot somewhere below the belt of America's lowest common denominator.

When Murdoch looked to create a news magazine show to lead the charge for a Fox News Network, he searched no farther than his own team: the wild and unruly Australian journalists who'd manned outposts around the world for his NewsCorp print empire. He set up his old gang a continent away from the Diller team, in New York City.

To oversee development of this new show, Murdoch plucked his most loyal employee. Ian Rae was a dedicated fifty-year-old soldier who went to work for the *Sydney Daily Mirror* in 1952, first came to the states nine years later as foreign correspondent for Murdoch's Australian papers, and made his mark when he took over *Star* magazine in 1977 and helped reinvent the supermarket tabloid.

The one to conceive the program would be the closest to artistic genius in the Murdoch fold. Peter Brennan was a decade younger than Ian Rae. He also got his start at the *Mirror*, but from the beginning wanted something of his own, and had spent the past twenty years bouncing in and out of the Murdoch orbit trying to find it.

While a star reporter in Sydney, Brennan jumped ship to start up a regional newspaper with his brother, Lorrie. He later sold his interest in the *Sutherland Shire Seer* when he moved to New York as one of Murdoch's foreign correspondents. Brennan rebounded to Sydney for Ian Rae's old job as *Daily Mirror* city editor; he worked for Rae when he returned to the States as national editor of the *Star*.

Through it all, Brennan made stabs at independence. He wrote a quickie book with reporter Steve Dunleavy in 1976, *Those Wild Wild Kennedy Boys*, and copied the structure of a Harold Robbins bestseller to write a tennis novel a couple of years later.

He knocked off his magnum opus in 1980. *Razorback* was the story of a gigantic wild pig on a killing rampage in the Australian Outback. Warner Brothers snatched up the rights and made a movie with Gregory Harrison that had little to do with the book but went on to become a cult classic on video.

From newspapers to books and back again, there was only one way for Brennan to move in the 1980's. Yet, he resisted. "Television," he sneered. "Nobody in the group wanted to get into television in those days. All the guys who left the papers for television were the ones who couldn't hack it as writers or reporters. It was like going into advertising."

Brennan took the leap in 1981 and, like that, changed the television world when he created *Good Morning Australia*. The country's first national morning show was live and dangerous and walked the edge, starring a six-foot-seven youngster named Gordon Elliott.

Then there was Dunleavy. Rupert Murdoch's alter-ego, the man who'd singlehandedly pull the weight of national magazines, metropolitan newspapers—the corporation itself—would of course be the star reporter of Murdoch's new television endeavor. Steve Dunleavy was the Street Dog, Mr. Blood and Guts: the most incomparable, despised, feared, hated, envied, beloved, over-the-top legend in journalism.

Dunleavy began his career in the same year and city as Ian Rae, on the rival *Sydney Sun,* before joining Murdoch's *Mirror* a year later. Son of a newspaper photographer, Dunleavy was born to the trade of Australian "journo," the rough and tumble, do-anything-for-a-story madmen who faded from American newspapers around the time Pat Doyle was checking out hat sizes.

Dunleavy had done it all. He could out-drink, out-talk, out-screw, out-fight, and out-live the Devil himself. He spent years in Hong Kong, on papers with wondrous and romantic names like the *South China Morning Post* and the *Far East American*, ran his own bar, and did song and dance as a sideline, before leaving the Far East under mysterious circumstances, smuggled out of the region with a price on his head courtesy of the local triad.

When he finally hit the New York City streets, Dunleavy realized he'd found his home. This foreigner in the hand-tailored Hong Kong pinstriped suits and physics-defying pompadour was a natural New Yorker, holding court at Costello's bar and bringing his winner-takes-all fervor to every story. As news editor of *Star* magazine, he exhibited a greater handle on the middle- and lower-class American psyche than any graduate of an American journalism school. His column, "This I Believe," was a weekly spewing of hilarious reactionary patriotism, winning him, a foreigner, the American of the Year Award from the John Birch Society.

Dunleavy began the ascent to his peak in the late seventies when he set the city aflame as metro editor of Murdoch's *New York Post*, a yellow paper of fear, excitement, and opinion in hot black and red ink and headlines like HEADLESS BODY IN TOPLESS BAR. Dunleavy turned New York at the cusp of the eighties into 1950's Sydney all over again, with newspaper reporters fighting to the death to get, own, and hype stories to Hell and back in the name of circulation and survival.

Speak of his literary output? Speak of the devil again. With a wife he wrote *The Happy Hooker*, the legendary memoirs of call girl Xaviera Hollander. His novel *The Very First Lady* concerned a woman who murdered her way to become the first female President of the United States. *Elvis: What Happened?* was an explosive paperback that tore the lid off the King of Rock 'n' Roll's secret life of drugs and violence and became a scandal itself when Elvis toppled off his toilet and dropped dead days after the book was published.

Dunleavy received something in the neighborhood of $25,000 for the

Elvis book, a best-seller that made many millions and pushed Murdoch's NewsCorp earnings over the top in 1977. Yet he never asked for more, never sought financial freedom and creative independence like Brennan did. He saw himself as a simple journo, lucky to have a job and security in an organization that would take care of him and his family for life.

Dunleavy would always be the Dog. No matter what heights he'd climb—or to what depths he'd sink, according to his competition—he'd feel the same rush for every story, the same burst of adrenaline and excitement, always driven by the raw, cold fear that he'd be beaten in the chase. Sociopathic in his need to be first, Dunleavy would do anything for a friend—but he'd do anything for a story.

When Murdoch bought Channel Five in New York, he installed Dunleavy among the 10 O'Clock News team. Dunleavy rode with the crews and tailed reporter Steve Powers in a three-week TV crash course. He never saw the great difference in television, never realized as Brennan did that newspapers were hot and ragged and full of alliterative exaggeration that leapt off the page. Television needed to be cool, bland, and inoffensive.

It's a wonder he lasted ten years in the game.

The show would be called *A Current Affair*. To Americans, the double-entendre name was obvious and later taken to further genitalial extremes by copycats like *"Inside" Edition* and *"Hard" Copy*. Actually, the title was stolen from one of Australia's most upstanding and dull news and interview, or, as they call them, "current affair," programs.

The show's distinctive logo came from the man who rounded out the creative team: young Joachim "J.B." Blunck, a rangy graphics whiz who worked the cutting edge as art director and journalist for publications like the *Village Voice*. J.B. came up with the triangular prism through which America would now be viewed and could view itself.

It was a masterwork of simplicity, a three-dimensional icon radiating power and depth—while also reflecting the show's concentration on the "love triangle" stories so popular in the Australian tabloid press. The creation wasn't enough, though. J.B. was insistent. This was television. He had to find a sound.

The show also needed a host. He had to be a Yank, that went without saying, but he had to be unlike any Yank on Yank television.

The team found their man languishing in Murdoch's newly-purchased Washington, D.C. station. Maury Povich was a quirky anchorman who in twenty years in television had been around the horn and back and was currently hosting an afternoon talk show called *Panorama*. He took a ten-week leave of absence from Washington in the midst of its sticky July and expected to be back by October.

Maury arrived in New York in time for J.B. to unveil the audio version of the *A Current Affair* logo. It was a synthesized whoosh that combined the sound of a golf swing and paper cutter and whapped into mind-blowing, resonating *ker-BONG!*

Each show and each throw to commercial break would be announced into every living room with the explosive force of a golf club to the head. They gave the sound a name that day. They called it the KA-CHUNG, in honor of Maury's wife, the esteemed NBC correspondent and anchorwoman, Connie Chung. Every show would have a ka-chung—and soon every story would have a ka-chung as well—an unexpected or ironic twist that would club the viewer over the head.

They had a name, they had a logo, they had a sound. They even had the makings of a team. Now, all they needed was a show and they had about four weeks to find one.

A Current Affair made its debut in New York City at 11:30 p.m. on July 28, 1986, broadcast live, straight up against Ted Koppel and *Nightline*. The first segment was an "exposé"of Benny Ong, whom cops called the Godfather of Chinatown. The second was a piece on a dating service. The reviews ranged from "disappointing" to "rough around the edges."

The most telling comment came from Maury Povich, the fish out of water, hostage of the buccaneers: "We don't have marching orders," he said. "We have a time period. All we have to do is fill it."

Brennan and J.B. had filled *A Current Affair* with a crew of television misfits: David Lee Miller, a hyper and intense local news reporter bounced from his last job in Cleveland; Mary Hughes, a patrician, award-winning journalist and daughter of Time-Life's distinguished John Emmett Hughes; Steve McPartlin, a good-time sportscaster and modern-day Broadway Joe from the Upper East Side's Thank God It's Friday singles scene; and Cora Ann Mihalik, an apple-cheeked wholesome blonde with obsessions for Marilyn Monroe and baking cakes and cookies for the staff.

"*A Current Affair* is tabloid journalism at its best...zippy and knowledgeable...the equivalent of a good afternoon newspaper..."

A surprise rave review in *The New York Times* was enough to move Rupert Murdoch to upgrade the show that September from its late-night perch to the prime spot of 7:30 p.m., replacing the local *PM Magazine*, the light lifestyle show featuring Jill Rappaport and Matt Lauer.

In January 1997, the show began to be broadcast by the Fox affiliate in Boston. Brennan began giving it even more of a national focus, sending reporters into the hinterlands with orders to come back with the goods to fulfill the promotional teases he'd write in advance. *A Current Affair* was developing a real identity. Dunleavy was on board, and Maury Povich had long forgotten about returning to Washington.

It was Brennan's masterstroke to keep Maury away from most of the stories so he'd see them for the first time while on the set recording the show. Maury would have an honest reaction and unscripted moment to express it after each story played.

Be it a comment or simple shake of the head, Maury's uncensored responses would make him a stand-in for the viewer and make the torrid goings-on acceptable in homes across the country. Maury, it was written, had the most expressive eyebrows in the business—and the most valuable.

A Current Affair was also taking advantage of the new satellite truck technology rolling across the television landscape, with "two way" interviews between Maury in New York and story subjects in other parts of the country. At the time, the only other shows doing this on a regular basis were the PBS *McNeil-Lehrer Report* and ABC's *Nightline*. J.B. created an infrastructure of stations, studios, and satellite trucks by climbing on the backs of these respected and staid network news broadcasts, using their affiliates to cover stories PBS and ABC wouldn't touch with rubber gloves. The ones who'd be most offended and threatened by tabloid television would be the ones who'd help get it off the ground.

In June 1987, A Current Affair was rolled out on other Fox stations and syndicated across America. Its national debut was accompanied by a news release which included the following program description:

> Live, nightly, 30-minute news feature magazine that dares to go places others do not and report stories no one else uncovers. Unpredictable and unique in its approach, *A Current Affair* reaches into every corner of the country searching for and finding stories of intense human drama—stories about people and their emotions—the serene and the bizarre, the humorous and the tragic, the proper and improper,

The release dressed up the show with respectability, highlighting past stories like an exclusive interview with fickle surrogate mother Mary Beth Whitehead, the PTL scandal, "an inside look at a Russian community trying to maintain its traditional faith and way of life in an Alaskan village" and the "first televised tour of the home of Ferdinand and Imelda Marcos." What it didn't trumpet were the elements that were making the show so popular: the combination of sex, scandal, celebrity, opinion, straight talk, and innovative story-telling techniques that threw stuffy news convention out the window.

There were, simply, major stories that the networks deemed unworthy of coverage, stories that affected individuals but resonated in households throughout the nation. *A Current Affair* stepped into the void and for a few years had an entire genre of news to itself. Network news watched its ratings slide. Ted Koppel watched his rise when he devoted *Nightline* to sensation subjects like the PTL scandal.

The ability to recognize the undercurrents of America beyond the Beltway and across the Hudson was key to *A Current Affair's* success. The men behind the show were foreigners who had a far better understanding of the national psyche than the network newspeople who spent their careers in windowless newsrooms or trading notes in gang bang press briefings. These men were *writers*, trained in the cadet system of Australian newspapers, cynical veterans of the world's most hardscrabble newspaper wars from Fleet Street to Hong Kong, men who had imagination and balls and little respect for the trenchcoat and hairspray conventions of American television news.

For them, news-telling wasn't the privilege of the elite. They didn't model the cloak of public service and were unapologetic in their quest for ratings. If being first meant paying a subject for exclusivity, so be it—and they didn't obscure the payment under terms like "consultancies"or "travel expenses." If an event took place when cameras weren't there, they recreated it in something called a "re-enactment." They'd used word pictures to bring scenes to life in newspapers and saw no reason not to use television's ability to do the same.

A Current Affair was taking a blank page, a half-hour of television every night, and filling it. It all looked so easy—but there was a catch.

You had to get it.

Tabloid TV was a fragile and volatile mix. Some stories had to be handled with a nudge and a wink. Stories about sex weren't about sex at all. They were "sexy." A story about a brutal murder wasn't about the murder. It wasn't even about crime. It was about the incredible events and emotion that led to the moment a life was taken and the quest for justice that followed. Every story had a twist— a *ka-chung!* You never made fun of the little guy. You never, ever picked on the victim.

There was a fine line that would often be crossed. "Some shows like *Geraldo* will have a hooker with AIDS from Florida," Brennan was quoted in *Newsweek.* "We would never do that. If we could get the hooker's mother to talk about it, mothers all over could empathize with her."

If *A Current Affair* was to work, anyone who walked through the door, from the Americans trained in the finest journalism schools to the second- and third-generation Fleet Street and Lantana, Florida tabloid hacks, from the pretty girls who nuzzled their way in from secretarial or modeling jobs to the kids fresh out of college with bachelor of science degrees in television production—all of them had to unlearn everything they thought they knew if they were going to get the hang of this new thing called Tabloid TV.

They needed to stay close to the source from which all this genius flowed. For in the wrong hands, tabloid TV was a cheap, exploitative cavalcade of blood, bodybags, tits, ass, dirt and scandal.

Ultimately, that's what it would become, as the boilerplate was copied, turned over, and filtered through the inexperience and arrogance of the ones who didn't get it, couldn't get it or thought they knew better.

With the advent of *Inside Edition*, word that Paramount was developing its own copycat show, and a rush to fill all the jobs the competition created, the seeds were planted by the time I arrived at *A Current Affair*. What once was a unique, renegade television show was spreading into a new TV genre and the wrong hands were everywhere.

"'Ave you heard of the Umedic bird?" Brennan sounded serious.

"I don't think so."

"It's got no legs."

"Really?"

"Yeah, every time it lands, it says, 'Ooh, me dick! Ooh, me dick!'"

Brennan threw back his head and let out a lusty guffaw as Wayne and I laughed ourselves silly at the Racing Club bar.

"We'll have another round, darlin." Brennan wiped his eyes and looked to Wayne. "You never heard that one? It goes back to Sydney. Used to be called the Ooh-me-doodle bird."

"Naw, mate." Wayne stepped closer. "Bruce and Sheila, walkin across the Sydney Harbor Bridge. Sheila says, 'Bruce, I'm pregnant. And if you don't marry me now, I'm gonna jump off this bridge and kill meself.' Bruce says, 'Sheila, not only were ya a great fuck, but you're a good sport, too!' AAAAAGGGHHH-HAAAA!"

When the laughing and heaving subsided, I tried out a joke I hadn't told since the eighth grade. I got to the punchline: "'No thanks. If twelve didn't wash the taste out of my mouth, I don't think thirteen will.'"

"AAAAAAAAGGGGHHHAAAAAAA!" It was easy to make these Australians laugh. They liked a dumb joke as much as they liked a good drink.

Yet there was something far more substantial than laughter and smoke in the air in the evenings and nights and sometimes lunchtimes I was spending in the pub over the road from the office. The subtleties that were key to the show and Peter Brennan's genius—of competition and inventiveness, cameraderie and the purity of a good old stupid joke—they were all there waiting to be passed down. The catch was that they couldn't be learned in any place but at Brennan's right elbow at the bar.

So the bar became my classroom, lecture hall, living room, boxing ring, and confessional. This was the place where stories were conjured, written, and deconstructed, where new angles were concocted and war plans hatched, and where all along the barroom cliches proved true, with defenses dropped, voices raised, truths revealed, and the holy liquid alcohol washing over the sins of the day.

Every night, I learned more and more just by sitting at the bar and listening to Brennan. "Think of a movie," he explained. "When they make a movie about a corporation, they don't do it on the entire corporation, they focus on a secretary or an executive. They tell that person's story.

"That's what we do. We tell a story from one person's point of view. We're not reporting news, we're telling stories. Think of it, mate, every time a reporter gets back from a story, he cuts his piece, he goes over the road to the pub, and what do his mates ask him? They ask, 'What really happened? What's the real story?' That's the story we tell."

Night after night, I returned to the bar. I soaked in the sacred cynicism. I matched Brennan vodka for vodka and I took notes on cocktail napkins and stuffed them into the pockets of my suit, deciphering them the next morning, sometimes finding them days later, forgetting I'd written them in the first place.

Mostly though, I listened and I learned.

"I make it simple, mate, I tell them, put everything good up top. Tell the story, then tell it again. That way the audience knows you've got the goods. They'll wait to see it again. We're not here to educate; we're here to entertain. All that matters is the ratings, mate. The ratings. We're used car salesmen.

"And never forget, this ain't brain surgery we're doing here. It's not life and death. *It's only television.*"

Each day, I learned a little more about how tabloid TV differed from television news.

Steve Schwartz, an easygoing veteran producer, relayed a message from the attorney for a woman who was suing the actor William Hurt for child support. It was a great story that exposed the proper WASP heart-throb as an abusive drunk who did things like pee on his girlfriend's couch. Her attorney said he'd let us interview the woman as long as he could confiscate the tape if he didn't like the way the questioning went.

"No way," I said.

Dennis O'Brien, the line producer, looked up. "No way!" he repeated. It was instinct. No journalist, TV or otherwise, ever gives story approval to the subject.

By the time I walked into Brennan's office, he was a step ahead of me, already discussing the offer with Schwartz. "It's not in writing or anything, is it, mate?"

"No," Schwartz said.

"Well, if it's not in writing," Brennan reasoned, "why not?"

Then there was the case of old James Richardson, a black man wrongfully accused of murdering his seven childen. He'd spent twenty years in a Florida prison, some of them on Death Row, until Mark Lane, the Kennedy assassination conspiracy zealot, made the old man's case a cause.

Bob Martin had done the first prison interview with James Richardson the previous summer. The old man was toothless, barely understandable and not telegenic, but Brennan saw the soul in the man's eyes and his innate gentleness despite the years behind bars.

Brennan took Martin's script and wrote in special mention of the way Richardson spoke, a small but deliberate touch that made all the difference in getting viewers to love the man. An audience who might not otherwise care for an aged black baby killer would see reason to at least feel sorry for him—if only because his lack of teeth gave him a gentle lisp. James Richardson became a national cause. *A Current Affair* owned the story.

"A story like this is good for credibility," Brennan explained. "We do something nice and serious and they'll forgive us for the dirty stuff later on."

Inside Edition liked the story as well. Days before the show's premiere, KingWorld fed *Inside's* promotional spots to stations around the country via satellite, advertising that the Richardson story would lead its very first show. Of course, back in the Fox feed room, Brennan was dialing up the satellite coordinates to get an illegal preview of the promos and a jump on the new competition. He couldn't believe what he was seeing. James Richardson was already *A Current Affair's* story, and now *A Current Affair* would have several days notice to play catch-up.

Brennan sent Bob Martin back to Florida to interview Richardson again. *A Current Affair* ran the story the Friday night before *Inside's* Monday debut. *Inside* was stuck running a story that viewers had seen on *A Current Affair* the previous week.

Now, weeks later, at the end of this February sweeps, word came that Ole Man Richardson was going free. Once again, Mark Lane gave us the exclusive. Bob Martin had filed reports from Florida all week, counting down to what would be the fulfilling, joyous, and crowning moment he and James Richardson had waited so long to reach. Together they would walk out of the wretched swamp prison; Martin would return home with Richardson to meet his faithful wife, sit in his living room, and conduct Richardson's first interview as a free man.

This was the kind of story that made the wires and the *New York Times*, and gave *A Current Affair* some respect. It was downright glorious, and *Inside* was slavering to steal it. Despite the ignominy of their debut, they were still following *A Current Affair* as we followed James Richardson. On liberation day, *Inside's* reporter was hopping up and down outside the prison and outside Richardson's house, begging for an interview, a word—a scrap of any kind—to feed back in time for the show.

As deadline approached, the *Inside Edition* reporter could take no more. In the middle of Bob Martin's interview, he burst through the screen door, camera crew in tow, tape rolling. He wheedled, he cried, he tried to get something, anything from Richardson before skittling off to feed it back to New York.

Bob Martin could take his time. He got the interview. He did a stand-up. He walked back to the feed truck with gold.

There was one problem. This week hadn't been up to par, ratings-wise. Every morning, Brennan pored over every story in the papers, trying to scratch out every possible percentage of a rating point he could possibly wring out of the Nielsen boxes. We had hot dog sellers in thong bikinis, we had topless barber shops, we had porn stars gone soft core.

On this day, Morton Downey, Jr., the original king of so-called "trash" talk shows, was in the news. It may have been the day he sneaked into an airport men's room and drew a swastika on his face—backward, because he was looking in a mirror when he did it—and blamed it on skinheads; perhaps it was his country music album—in any case, Brennan knew more people would tune in for Morton Downey, Jr. than would hang in for old James Richardson.

James Richardson would be killed after all.

What? I tried to change Brennan's mind. "But mate, this Richardson story is national!"

"I know."

"This is big news! It's our story! We have it! We've been covering this from the start and now he's finally free! It's not like we can pretend he's getting released tomorrow—"

"Yeah, mate. I understand. He's a nice old guy. But he doesn't rate for shit."

Ratings were everything, and there was more than one way to win a ratings point.

One of the field producers on *The Reporters* was able to help both his show and *A Current Affair* in the ratings wars. It wasn't that he was particularly good in the edit room or known for nailing down great exclusives. No, this producer had a talent that was far more valuable.

He lived next door to a Nielsen family.

The Nielsen Media Research company owns the ratings system by which all shows live or die, relying on approximately 10,000 viewers nationwide to measure the viewing habits of all us millions and thereby determine the millions of dollars in advertising rates for every television market in the country. Some of their "Nielsen families" have "People Meters" attached to their television sets that measure what they watch. A smaller number are on an honor system, writing their viewing choices in "diaries."

Wouldn't you know it, the neighbor of *The Reporters* producer was on the honor system.

Few people needed to know. On the eve of each sweeps, the producer from *The Reporters* was slipped a few hundred dollars to bring his neighbor into the city and fix him up with a great steak dinner and, after dessert, a hooker.

I was learning. I was finding out where the bodies were buried and discovering who was anxious to bury ours.

The chain of command at Fox was deceptively simple. There was me. There was Brennan. There was Gerald Stone and there was Rupert Murdoch. There were no layers of vice presidents or departments or labyrinths to crawl through to get to the top. In those early days, that was how Fox worked—at least on the east side of the country.

There was a dangerous schism in the overall organization. On the West Coast, Hollywood veteran Barry Diller was trying to establish America's fourth television network in Murdoch's name. Most of the new Fox shows were lower-class failures, and to Diller's chagrin, *A Current Affair*, created by Murdoch's alternative government of Aussie boyos in New York, was not only the one moneymaker in the Fox fold, not only Diller's in-house competition, but was basically bankrolling his dream.

It was inevitable that Murdoch's "Australian Mafia" would clash with Diller's "Velvet Mafia."

To the West Coast contingent, the Aussies were unwashed homophobic ruffians with no respect for the way the game was played. Hollywood was a place where untold secrets unfolded in the back of limousines and behind the walls of cloistered mansions, where rubber sheets covered priceless bedspreads and baggies were used for foot covering in thousand-dollar-a-night hotel suites.

The manly men from Down Under had little reverence for the pampered poobahs of screenland and the secrets they held. These blokes were so democratic they sat in the front seat of New York City taxis and pissed on police cars in front of the swankiest pubs. They laughed at the Diller crowd and their fancy-pants airs. To be blunt, the Aussies regarded Barry Diller and many of his young male executives to be gay, and the Aussies referred to gays as "poofters," which, according to the *Macquarie Book of Slang*, is a derogatory term, possibly derived from the French word for "prostitute."

Barry Diller never made a public declaration of his sexuality, but he let it be known that he hated *A Current Affair*, and would not rest until he fucked us in the ass.

For Wayne Darwen and me, who together were writing most of the day-of-air stories filling more and more of the shows, the most immediate threat was in an office across the stairwell and down the hall: the lawyers.

Lawyers were the ones who told us that what we were doing was illegal, that we couldn't use certain pieces of videotape or say things we knew to be true. Lawyers were the ones who censored our perfectly acceptable stories on topless maid services or X-rated film stars. Lawyers were the ones we had to get around to give *A Current Affair* the ratings that kept the lawyers in silk.

"Fuckin' Muriel doesn't fuckin' understand," Wayne fumed at the Racing Club bar. "The stuff we do is extremely unethical and it involves thievery and she can't grasp that!"

The Muriel in question was Muriel Reis, a tiny stick insect of a woman of a certain age, with dyed blonde hair teased high, and outfits sure to combine cleavage-baring tops and supershort miniskirts often constructed of material resembling leather. She looked more like one of Wayne's conquests than vice president and chief attorney for Fox Television.

Muriel had been with WNEW-TV long before it was acquired by Murdoch, and in the past concerned herself with license renewals, contracts, and other yawning legalities. She and the Fox legal team were ill-prepared for the borrowed video, poetic license, opinion, bawdiness, and excess that *A Current Affair* brought to American television—especially now that the show was facing direct competition.

Muriel responded by reaching beyond her role as legal counsel to that of moral censor. She was a bizarre sight in an edit room, this woman dressed like a tart, standing on her tiptoes and leaning over the edit board. Peering over bifocals spattered with facial powder, her nose less than an inch from the monitor, she'd tap the screen with a pencil, and say, "Is that a pubic hair? Stop it right there. Clearly, that's a hair."

"It's a shadow, Muriel. And only when you freeze it."

"No, clearly, that's a pubic hair."

Muriel didn't trust Wayne and she didn't trust me. In the weeks to come, we'd give her more than ample reason to stay on her toes.

"Burt, we've got Sandra. But she wants to see our Charles interview before she'll agree to do our show."

I was working on someone's script while taking the call from the L.A. bureau. Riva's birdlike British trill made the request seem so respectable.

"Who's Charles?"

"Why, Charles Manson." She referred to the mass murderer with such charming nonchalance and familiarity I thought she was talking about the fucking Prince of Wales. Sandra, of course, was Sandra Goode, one of the psycho girl followers still pining for Charles after all these years. "Can we get it for her? And can we change the package to make it more favorable to Charles if it's too negative?"

"Are you serious?"

"But then again, it can't be too negative, can it?" Riva reasoned. "These Manson pieces mostly just have him talking away anyway, don't they?"

That was the logic at *A Current Affair*'s L.A. bureau on the Fox Television Center lot in Hollywood, across town from the Fox Tower and studios in Century City where Barry Diller reigned. The distance from Diller was a healthy one, since our outpost was a dangerously unsupervised mess basically being run from the telephone I was speaking into.

Riva represented a third of the L.A. production staff—or rather, half, since she shared her job with a woman named Lisa, a sweet, fast-talking politician's daughter and former Miss Philippines with a unique knack for getting unattainable stories from Hollywood bigs, Vegas slicks, and underworld lowlife. Lisa was the beautiful frontwoman who'd get an interview, book a crew and shoot it. Riva, who despite the tweetybird voice was a grand billowing bird with even grander and more billowing breasts, was an unsung tabloid talent who'd write the story.

Together, the strange two-headed producer called "Lisariva" brought us exclusives from the slippery, seedy edge of Hollywood Babylon, with tips from people like Alex Adams, the low-key melting sundae of a Hollywood madame who operated from a queen-sized bed in a small house off Doheny Drive, or the skinny kid with the black nail polish who wandered around the Sunset Strip telling people he was Charles Manson's son.

Sharing the L.A. office was a tiny woman with enough personality, will, unchanneled talent—and twice the trouble-making ability—to make up for her half.

Audrey Lavin was our great female hope, a tabloid supervixen who had us wrapped around her little finger and was, potentially, our greatest weapon. Ultimately, she would break all our hearts as our dreams fell down around us.

Audrey was only in her late twenties, yet she and Peter Brennan went back donkey's years, to the days when he was national editor of the *Star* and she was one of his eager young reporters. Born and raised in Beverly Hills, daughter of the cowboy boot king of Hollywood Boulevard, Audrey could never quite forgive herself for betraying her neighbors' secrets as one of the best tabloid journos in town. *Rolling Stone* once featured her as "The Stakeout Queen of Beverly Hills," though Palm Springs was the place she probably set the world record, waiting and hoping outside Liberace's mansion as he lay dying from the wasting effects of his watermelon diet.

Back in the byegone, Audrey and Brennan bonded. Older, perhaps a little wiser, Brennan knew she was a kindred spirit, that like Dunleavy, she'd do anything, and anyone, for a story.

"Hi, Burt. Can I call you Burt? Are you as sexy as you sound?" Audrey's voice was a put-on squeak, curling around the telephone lines and blowing in my ear when we needed to talk about work.

Dennis O'Brien had warned me that Audrey was a dangerous manipulator who couldn't write, knew nothing about television, and would be fired if not for her closeness to Brennan. His warning intrigued me and made me certain Audrey had something very special to offer. After all, the Dennis camp didn't appreciate Cheridah, the Jamaican woman with the wherewithal to get Muammar Khadaffi to come to the phone, or Isabel, the publicist turned associate producer who was able to talk her way into the living room of Mary Jo Kopechne's parents, where she cried with them, in all sincerity, so many years after Chappaquiddick.

Brennan taught me that *A Current Affair* was built on these eccentric people with special talents that could be channeled into stories and angles no one else would have imagined.

"That doesn't matter, Audrey. Tell me what stories you have."

"Oh, you're no fun."

It was clear from our first conversation that Audrey was a sexual flirt and a bit of a user. It was equally clear she had the balls of a bull elephant. I'd use *her*, use her for the show, and just hope she didn't use me more.

A redhead production assistant named Mary Beth stood at my desk with urgent news. She had word that authorities were reopening the investigation into the death of Princess Grace.

"What?"

I grabbed a phone and called the Monaco Police myself, handing the receiver to a Frenchman named Hughes who was working in the office. I gave him the questions and he asked them in French. We did the same at the Paris office of Reuters, Grimaldi Palace, and anywhere else we could think of. No one admitted to knowing of any probe.

A half hour passed. If we got confirmation soon, the story could make that day's show. I questioned Mary Beth once more. "Where did you hear about this Princess Grace story?"

"From my sister."

"Your sister. Is she in the news business?"

"No. She said she heard it somewhere."

At the Racing Club after work, Wayne had an idea.

"This Princess Grace story, mate—"

"It's fucking dead. Forget about it. It was bullshit. She heard it from her sister."

"Yeah." He lit a cigarette and took his time before speaking again. "But it's a rumor now, isn't it?"

He smiled slyly and I got the drift immediately.

"Yeah. On both sides of the Atlantic."

"So look, mate. Why don't we send David Miller to do a standup on the road where Grace died? We have him say *A Current Affair* has learned from sources that they may reopen the probe. Then we do an entire sweeps series on it! Just like we did with Jackie O."

"Yeah, but Wayne, with Jackie O, there was that new book. There were a few facts. This is made up."

"And we made it up!" He clapped his hands. "It'll be fuckin' great! We'll pay Stephanie's ex-boyfriend! He's mad! He'll talk—for money!"

Wayne laughed and called for another drink. He had another brainstorm. "We pay Liz Taylor $80,000 for an exclusive. We'll give the money to AIDS research." He lowered his voice again. "You know, her son Wilding has AIDS."

He didn't. "He does?"

Wayne smiled and gave a knowing nod. "Yeah. And, oh yeah, you know JFK kept a gay lover shacked up here in New York."

"Wait a minute? President Kennedy?"

"John Fitzgerald."

"He wouldn't have time!"

"Oh, no. He did." Wayne paused and sipped his drink. "I have a guy who'll tell us he did. See?"

The life was far more intoxicating than the booze that was now running through my system twenty-four hours a day. Only months earlier, I'd wind down after work with a run around Lower Manhattan or a session at the New York Health & Racquet Club. Now, from the time I awoke to past the time I fell out drunk in bed, I was thinking, living, dreaming tabloid.

Somehow, in short order I'd found my place among the gods. I even had an "image": while everyone dressed casually, I stuck to a suit and tie—

white shirts and dark suits so the sweat wouldn't show. My hair was Tenax-slicked in the Wall Street predator look and my demeanor was businesslike.

With the staff, I was cagey about my past and over-the-top in my enthusiasm and demeanor. With the Aussies, I was able to stand up among the recreational alcoholics because drinking was the one subject I'd learned too well in college. If they were wild, I'd be wilder. If they had crazy ideas, mine would be farther out.

Make no mistake, I had to fight for my place. There was real animosity from Dennis O'Brien, who'd volunteered to become show producer when Tomlin and Young left to start up *Inside Edition*. Dennis was holding on by any means possible, which usually meant countermanding my orders behind my back, but he wasn't a bad guy, just a balding hippie with long, thinning red hair, an earring, and too-tight seventies designer jeans with an iron-on patch on the crotch.

Dennis and I were simply caught in the Murdoch organizational structure. On paper, they gave me power. On paper, they gave Dennis much of the same power. No one was going to tell either one of us who was in charge. It was a matter of seizing control. So I did.

I'd only been at *A Current Affair* two months, and my life had changed completely. At last, there was purpose to all the books I'd read, all the music I'd sought out, all the newspapers and magazines I'd absorbed—all the popular culture I'd been immersed in since I was a boy. I knew that finally my life and career had come together.

Yet, inescapably, my old life—and after only sixty days, it had become old—was coming apart. All of a sudden, my old pals from Channel Five days, the ones who stayed in "straight news," weren't the same. They represented the old way, network believers who outwardly despised what my new mates and I were doing but secretly looked up to us because we didn't give a fuck. They were weak, clutching forks and knives at swish restaurants every Friday night.

I'd arrive at our weekly get-togethers already pissed from however many hours I'd already spent at the Racing Club after the show. Tie askew, face glistening, I'd regale them with stories about the celebs we exposed and the important truths we revealed to America that week.

There was the night I harassed my friend Kiki, who worked at *Saturday Night Live*. "You get me the dirt on the stars, I'll pay you a hundred dollars a tip," I slurred across the table.

"I don't need the money." She tried to change the subject. "I need liposuction, not money."

"You tell me where I can find the guest host this week, I'll pay for your liposuction!"

"Let's talk about something else."

Sitting next to me, my girlfriend cast her eyes downward. I'd met her when we both worked for Nicky on the Channel Five assignment desk. She'd become a producer at CBS News, where conversation like that would not go down well at all. Already, we'd reached an impasse from which neither could retreat.

CHAPTER THREE:
NO MORE FAG JOKES

April 1989 was springtime for *A Current Affair*. Maury and Connie made the cover of *People* magazine.

> "Watch out, America: Connie Chung and Maury Povich are commanding the airwaves... Week in and week out, Povich's audience swells; these days when he tramps the sidewalks of New York, cabbies and hard hats yell out admiringly, "Hey, Maury!"... His nose-thumbing *A Current Affair* may look like a cross between *60 Minutes* and the *National Enquirer*, but it is a syndicated ratings blockbuster now seen by 7.2 million people spread across 146 cities..."

Events flashed by quickly. We were charged by alcohol and adrenaline. Wayne was in an edit room, putting together a piece on Happy Hooker Xaviera Hollander's return to New York City, twenty years older and fifty pounds heavier. Maury interviewed her in the back of a limo on the way in from JFK as she pointed out buildings in which she'd been laid.

"So, I see the old juices haven't run out," he said.

"And the juices haven't dried up, either," Xaviera replied with a laugh. Wayne loved that line. I had the editor remove it.

In the edit room across the hall, we were editing sex scenes from a softcore porn movie and covering the breasts with black bars. A high school principal had been suspended that day for showing the movie in school. We were running it as credits.

Peter Brennan, meanwhile, was distracted again. He had a new show that was getting a late night Sunday spot on Fox. *Live & Dangerous* was everything its title indicated, with big Gordon Elliott roaming the country, knocking on doors, rattling society and shaking up civility.

Gordon Elliott, the big baby bear of an Australian TV personality, had followed the Murdoch mob to East 67th Street in search of a job and wound up as the havoc-wreaking star of *Good Day New York*. Gordon's specialty was the live "doorknock," showing up at people's houses unannounced, with eggs, juice, and camera crew rolling, asking to be invited in for the duration of the breakfast. Gordon had lured Bill Cosby onto the sidewalk by leading a marching band outside his brownstone. When the *Today* show went live from a yacht near the Statue of Liberty, Gordon commandeered a dinghy and used a megaphone to harass and upset the prickly Bryant Gumbel to no end. He was larger than life in every way, from his booming voice to his massive ego to his indisputable Aussie charm that let him get away with anything. Now he'd be getting away with it on a national level.

The premiere was a wedgie for Barry Diller: a secret invasion of his backyard. There's Gordon and two camera crews in formal attire, driving down Sunset Boulevard stuffed into a Caddy convertible with the show's name scrawled across the side in gaffers' tape. There he is in Venice, banging on the door of Dudley Moore's beach house. There's Dudley on the intercom, begging, "Go away!" There's Gordon opening Dudley Moore's mailbox, sorting through his mail; Gordon ringing Dudley's buzzer, demanding he come out. Now there's six-foot-seven Gordon and five-foot-two Dudley doing shtick in the street; Gordon shoving champagne bottles in Dudley's pockets and down his pants.

The show only got more live and more dangerous from there: Gordon trudging along the beach of the Malibu star colony, trailed by two camera crews scampering behind and around, all in tuxes; Gordon walking up to beach houses, surprising Pierce Brosnan on his patio, bullying him and demanding to be let through the gate, unaware that his beloved wife Cassie was dying of cancer inside.

"And look who's there!" Gordon was distracted by the sight of neighbor Larry Hagman in caftan and floppy hat, running off to call the police.

It wasn't only live and dangerous. It was illegal!

The first show did top ratings.

As May sweeps approached, we had a new mission: to democratize Hollywood! To show that the emperors were wearing no clothes! To reveal that these stars we held in such unnaturally high esteem were, indeed, just plain folks.

There was an item in the paper. Jim Belushi had trashed the production office of *Wired*, a movie based on Bob Woodward's book about the drug death of his brother, John. A few years back, young Jim had done the same to the display window at his neighborhood Barnes & Noble in the Village, which was advertising the book with a tasteful tableau of hypodermic needles and bottles of booze.

Belushi was filming a movie in Chinatown. I called on one of our "special talents," Cheridah Walters. Cheridah was loyal and tireless in her dedication to getting what we wanted. When Peter asked her on a whim to get an interview with Fidel Castro, she kept calling until she got a refusal from the man's personal assistant.

Cheridah's most legendary moment came early on. Brennan was passing her desk when he heard her berating someone on the phone.

"I'm sorry. Mr. Brennan is a very busy man! I will not put you through!"

Brennan stopped and smiled at Cheridah's authority.

"That is too bad. What is your business and what is your first name, Mr. Barrydiller?"

Now it was on to Chinatown to bag Belushi.

Cheridah and the camera crew descended on the set and found Jim Belushi in his trailer. When he refused to talk on camera, Cheridah chased him down the street through the movie set.

"Why won't you talk to me? John! John Belushi! Talk to me, John! John!"

Later, I watched the tape over and over again: the way Belushi winced when Cheridah inadvertantly called him by his dead brother's name. That was the downside to special talents. I had to feel sorry for the guy. We never ran the tape.

Then there was poor Fred Gwynne, the great actor who tried for years to shed his image as Herman Munster.

When I was in high school, I went on a class trip to a performance of *Twelfth Night* at the American Shakespeare Theatre in Stratford, Connecticut. It was a schoolkids' matinee, with big yellow buses dumping off loads of teenagers, the kids screaming and shouting, jumping about like monkeys, and running off to the picnic tables near the mouth of the Housatonic River to smoke as many joints and knock back as many cans of Maximus beer as possible before the show began.

The Shakespeare Theatre was the ultimate cultural experience for a suburban kid in the seventies. There was nothing like the sight of old Morris Carnovsky playing Prospero in *The Tempest*, having his soliloquy interrupted by the splat of a spitball in his beard, stopping the performance to roar at the offenders.

Carnovsky's complaint paled, however, compared with the plight of poor Fred Gwynne, a serious actor working so hard to shake the Munster curse by disappearing into theatre roles. On this afternoon, he would be featured as Sir Toby Belch.

Sir Toby makes his entrance at the opening of Act I, Scene III. The lights come up on the modern stage. Fred staggers out, fake belly protruding over his belt, jug in hand, wine bladder strapped across his chest, and hat obscuring his familiar features. He approaches the front of the stage to deliver his first lines, but before he can get a word out, some kid in the mezzanine stands, points and yells:

"IT'S HERMAN MUNSTER!"

As one, the audience erupts: a thousand schoolkids with mouths open wide, contraband snacks flying in the air, screaming, cheering, stomping, and chanting: "Her-man! Her-man! Her-man!"

Poor Fred Gwynne, head lowered, eyes closed, shakes his head in bitter resignation and waits for the tumult to die...

Now it was close to twenty years later and Fred Gwynne had finally broken free as a star on Broadway, character actor in film, writer of children's books, and, on this night, proud artist, opening an exhibition of his paintings in a Greenwich Village gallery with wine, cheese, and a photo op.

I sent Gordon Elliott to cover the triumph of the pop culture hero. I also sent along the actor Al Lewis, who played Grampa Munster in the TV series, and two sexy actresses dressed as Elvira. Gordon walked into the gallery with the aged actor, who at this point in life needed no makeup to look like the centuries-old vampire, with camera lights blazing.

Poor Fred was explaining one of his works when he was distracted by the hubbub. He turned, smiled, and over the course of an instant realized what was lurching toward him. He dropped his cheese. He freaked.

"Not tonight! Not tonight!" he cried, his face contorting unintentionally into Herman Munster's tantrum mask. You'd half expect him to stamp his boot and yell "Darn! Darn! Darn!," causing the gallery to shake and the paintings to rattle off the walls, but it was just a man trying to be recognized for his art, hustling Gordon and Grampa and the busty vampirettes back onto the sidewalk as Howard Stern's Stuttering John trailed behind, shouting questions like, "Was it hard to get the green p-p-p-paint off your face? Were you in competition with G-g-gomez Adams?..."

Some American students on Spring Break on San Padre Island in South Texas wandered south of the border into Mexico and were kidnapped by Satanists. One boy's head was found in a pot on a remote farm. A beautiful young woman was held as the reigning witch.

"This woman, she is evil. Evil does exist—"

I was trying to hear David Lee Miller on the phone from the Mexican jail, but Gordon was running through the newsroom with two camera crews and Tony Randall, who was pointing at people with cigarettes and railing about second-hand smoke...

That April afternoon, I was sprawled on Brennan's couch, coffee in hand, waiting for him to get off the phone and trading jokes with Wayne as the three of us tried to find promotable stories for May sweeps. Four times a year, four weeks each in February, May, July, and November, every show's ratings were measured and those ratings determined the ad rates.

May sweeps was most important. Stories were bought up and saved, outlandish promotions were conceived, the sex quotient was jacked up several notches, and each day would mean another wartime strategy of programming and counter-programming.

James Dean. Marilyn Monroe. Liz Taylor. Elvis. We pulled out all the tabloid standbys. We found tie-ins to run the same nights as the big network shows, concocting segments like the "Secrets of Larry Hagman" and news exclusives like "Roseanne's Love Child."

"What about Cosby?" Peter asked.

No show was bigger than *The Cosby Show*, and no story idea was a bigger challenge. We'd already done every angle of Lisa Bonet we could think of. We'd have to get back to Bill later.

"Rex Reed?"

"I spoke to him." It was Peter's idea for the cranky critic to do a "Ten Worst List." "He said he doesn't know if he can. He said he's going on hiatus." Pregnant pause. "To Greece."

Snickers spread around the room.

Brennan liked my idea of using an Elvis reporter one week. "We do regular pieces, but we have an Elvis impersonator track them. We have him do a standup, maybe even an interview, but we do it totally straight, with no mention of the fact that he's Elvis!"

"I like it," Brennan said. "I don't know what the hell it means, but I like it."

Peter's assistant Penny was at the door. He had an important call. He left the room to take it.

He returned a few minutes later. "Barry Diller killed *Live & Dangerous*."

I looked for signs of despair. There seemed to be none, but after the meeting, Brennan headed straight for the bar.

There was a sorrow inside Peter Brennan I couldn't yet begin to fathom, a hellhound on his tail that I felt I was keeping at bay by staying close to his side as he tried to drink the demon away.

Brennan had kids, he told me: five of them spread across two wives, two coasts, and two continents. He had a girlfriend, a producer for *A Current Affair* who lived in grand style on Central Park West and was a probable heir to one of the greatest American musical legacies of our century.

He also had a stalker. Laurie was an executive for Fox in the next building, a small, attractive blonde with a snappy direct manner and madly intense eyes. Peter had made the mistake of dating her, vacationing with her, giving her a poke or two, and drifting off in his own inimitable way. Laurie didn't want to let go.

When we came to work in the morning, she'd often be sitting at a desk outside his office, just waiting. Earlier this same evening at Nickel's, she was seated at the other end of the bar, stirring her drink and staring at Brennan as he drank in the notion of Barry Diller killing his show.

"Peter."

"Huh, what is it, Laurie?"

"We need to talk. Now."

"Fuck off!"

She did, in a gulp of tears.

"When I hired Wayne, I told him part of his job was dating her," he said, and laughed. "Fa-a-ack."

It was late now, around the time I was ready to pack it in, and, as I'd grown accustomed, around the time Brennan's slow easing into inebriation crystallized into totally focused sobriety.

"Give me something to write on."

"Here." I pulled a cocktail napkin off the stack and leaned back as he collected his thoughts about a new ad campaign for *A Current Affair*. Brennan folded the napkin like a greeting card, took a pen, and wrote on the cover:

EROTIC

REPULSIVE

&

INSPIRED

He opened the napkin and wrote on the inside:

LAUGHABLE

DESPERATE

PITIFUL

ABSURD

"That's the show," he said. "That's the ad. *A Current Affair*. In a nutshell."

I folded the napkin again and put it in my breast pocket. When the ad came out, the words were somewhat different:

Provocative.

Incisive.

Compassionate.

Inspirational.

Successful.

Irresistible.

Unique.

—◆—

The next morning, Greg Snead rattled into the office. Greg was our promo man, a bearded, nervous guy who always seemed to be tapping his foot and was always ready for a laugh. Though Brennan himself jotted off the twenty-second promos for each day's show and had one of the producers edit them, Snead was in charge of the major promotional and print campaigns.

"Sweeps time, gentlemen. Who'd believe so soon? What have we got?"

"Uh, we're sort of working on it, mate." Brennan was trying to draw straight lines with a ruler, finishing a grid for the month of May. Each day of the week had a box we had to fill with a story slug that would be promoted.

"Well, make it good, boys. We're getting daily promotions in *TV Guide*. Quarter-page display ads for each day of sweeps."

"Ripper," Wayne drawled.

"Great," I added, squinting. I was getting used to waking up feeling drunk behind my eyes.

Snead sat on the couch as we improvised the calendar, coming up with story titles and deciding who'd be assigned to come up with stories to live up to promos like:

SOMETHING
ABOUT
MADONNA

"Something about Madonna. Okay." Snead was confused by that one. He let out a hair-trigger laugh that seemed to be a plea for a drink. "What does that mean?"

"It means we don't know what the fuck the story is gonna be, mate," Brennan explained. "But we'll do something about Madonna. If people see it's something about Madonna, they'll tune in."

Snead shrugged and wrote it down. "Something about Madonna, it is!"

"Don't forget our man Cary Grant," Wayne said.

Snead started tapping his foot again. "Cary Grant? What do you have with Cary Grant? Is it the new book? The one that says he was gay?" He giggled.

Wayne growled. That was the book *Inside Edition* nailed down as an exclusive. "Fack that."

"No," I said. "*Inside* has that gay story. We're doing the opposite."

"Yeah," Peter added. "Every housewife in America loves Cary Grant. He'll always be remembered as a ladies' man."

"He was no poofter," Wayne said. "Fuck *Inside*. Fuck the book."

"Our story is about Cary Grant as the ultimate lover! C'mon, he was married to Dyan Cannon!"

"A piece of ass," Wayne mumbled.

"That author's full of shit," I said. "He's getting away with saying anything he wants because Cary Grant's dead and if it's not true, nobody'll know it's not true."

Wayne cocked an eyebrow.

I was caught up. "It's a tribute! Our tribute to Cary Grant, ladies' man! We'll call it—we'll call it: 'Cary Grant: No More Fairy Tales!'"

Everyone laughed at that one. We sent Snead on his way to come up with the sweeps titles.

I found an intriguing story while leafing through the *Weekly World News*. The wacky tabloid wasn't usually a source for stories; we got most of our wild love triangles and murder plots from the hundreds of small town newspapers we subscribed to.

Weekly World News was a tabloid afficionado's joke paper. They'd been printing pictures of Elvis and aliens and stories from remote Andean villages for years. Yet, if this article didn't ring of total veracity, it could be investigated easily enough: the report of a strip club patron who literally dropped dead of a heart attack when a stripper revealed her eighty-eight-inch bust on stage.

Busty Heart was the stripper's name. Like Morgana, she'd made headlines, and was often featured as a funny kicker to local news sportscasts, running out onto professional sports fields and hugging the athletes against her gargantuan, beachballian breasts.

I had Cheridah chase down the story. She not only found that the *Weekly World News* had actually printed something *true*—she found Busty Heart, who was performing that very day, just over the river in a town in New Jersey called Manville.

The strip club was called Frank's Chicken Shack. *Ka-chung!*

Local blue laws did not allow alcohol to be served where nudity was showcased, so the joint served chicken instead. The very image of a woman with breasts bigger than her head performing for a room full of wankers with greasy hands and chicken legs and breasts hanging out of their mouths was, again, enough to warrant a story.

Peter Brennan had reservations about covering it.

"But it's a tragedy!" I argued. "And imagine the sight of all those guys eating chicken!"

He gave in to my enthusiasm on one condition: the story must be played totally deadpan, dead serious.

We sent cleancut family man John Johnston to the Chicken Shack with a crew. He returned a few hours later with a catapult-proportioned brassiere autographed for Maury Povich and one of the most legendary lost stories in the canon of tabloid TV.

Johnston was sublime. Throughout the interview, he kept Busty in a tight shot, her face framed and lit softly as he prodded her ever-so-gently to recount her tragic ordeal.

Busty said she was used to men in the audience joking around, grabbing their throats, clutching their chests, and feigning death when she began her strip act. That evening in Boston, though, when the well-dressed man near the stage not only keeled over but turned blue, she knew this was serious.

There were tears in her eyes as she recounted the paramedics' unsuccessful attempts to revive the man. Yet, trouper that she was, Busty Heart was philosophical, finding the bright side. "Everyone dies," she said. "Some guys die in car crashes. At least when that man died, the last thing he saw—" and with this, she lifted her prodigious, veiny tits into camera view, obscuring her face, "—were these."

The story is still sitting on a shelf somewhere.

With a week to go before May sweeps, we had a visitor in the morning meeting. Elizabeth was a noisy little middle-aged woman from Australia, in town to write an article on the show for a new Sydney newspaper called *The Age*.

As we screened the tapes for the day's show, Elizabeth chirped up with comments, made suggestions—even shot down other people's ideas. Hers was quite different from the fly-on-the-wall approach most reporters would take, but it had the same effect. Elizabeth made such a pest of herself that within a few hours she was part of the scenery. No one was on guard when she was around. We were too busy shooing her away or ignoring her.

The morning was especially busy. Cheridah was on the phone from Texas, negotiating with a woman with 306 personalities. One of the personalities had trouble with the terms of the interview. Cindy Garvey, a perky yet sultry blonde who'd become popular as the former wife of L.A. Dodger Steve, was serving as guest anchor and we needed to find a live guest for her to interview. I was counting on a young actor named Patrick Dempsey who was married to a woman thirty years his senior. We'd been talking to his people for a week and were still waiting for an answer. When someone yelled that Morton Downey, Jr. was a possibility, I remembered seeing a picture in the tabloids showing him with no teeth. "Get me the *National Enquirer*!" I called to my assistant.

Elizabeth popped up in front of me. "That's definitely going in the article!"

An assistant producer walked up. "Dempsey's people just turned us down."

"Fuck!"

"He won't do the show."

"Fuck!"

"By the way, he appeared on *Good Day New York* this morning."

"Fuck!" I exclaimed again. "Fuck! Fuck!" I'd had too much coffee. I descended into a fuck fit, repeating the expletive over and over while Elizabeth jotted each curse in her little Aussie notepad.

I bolted for Wayne's desk in the small room outside Peter's office.

"Fuck!"

"Mate, what is it?"

"Fuck! Dempsey! We're fucked! Fucked!"

"Calm down, mate." Wayne stood and held out his usual half-pint milk carton. "Have some warm milk. It'll calm you down."

"I don't drink milk."

"Mate, believe me." He pushed it toward my lips. "It's an old Australian remedy. Have a sip. It'll calm you right down."

I took the carton and sipped. The taste registered.

"That's not milk!" I spit out the mouthful in a wide spray against the wall. "*This is vodka!*"

Wayne smiled with satisfaction.

I looked to the doorway to see Elizabeth, quiet as a churchmouse, writing it all down.

That night, Steve Dunleavy was at Nickel's bar, planning his funeral. He wanted sixty pallbearers carrying his little body in a thirty-foot coffin.

Brennan was intent, writing something on a cocktail napkin. He pushed it toward me.

"Read those words aloud," he ordered.

"Okay."

I looked down at what he'd written:

WHALE

OIL

BEEF

HOOKED

I tried to work out the connection among the words, to figure which one didn't belong. To—

"Don't think about. Just read it."

"Right. 'Whale oil beef hooked.'"

"Well, I'll be fucked, myself!" Brennan roared.

Dunleavy had tears in his eyes. "Old Da, he taught me three rules in life. Never pick a fight when you think you're going to win, never cheat a friend, and never touch a woman—well, you can touch a woman..."

⋯◆⋯

The true crime sagas and small town scandals were the main course at *A Current Affair*, but it was the celebrity stories that really drove the ratings up. Most stars wouldn't cooperate with us, and that tended to make the stories better. The ones who did cooperate were either washed up or had axes to grind, were on their way in or out of jail, or were so high-flying and above it all—in such a parallel universe—they didn't give a fuck.

No one gave less of a fuck than Sammy Davis, Jr. In what would turn out to be the last year of his life, Sammy was a favorite at *A Current Affair*, a show biz patron saint—a legendary performer whose life was an open book, who did it all, good and shameful, was proud of every moment, and happy to talk about it.

When Sammy wrote his last autobiography, *Why Me?*, Cheridah set out to get an interview. She hounded his publicity people, bothered his publisher, and befriended his wife, Altovise. She did what no one else could. She got us the exclusive.

Maury could have Sammy backstage at London's Royal Albert Hall before his performance with Frank Sinatra and Liza Minnelli. The interview was full of possibilities. Maybe Liza would pass out drunk in front of us. Perhaps the interview would lead to an audience with Mr. Sinatra himself.

The latter chance was what sent Maury and Brennan flying across the ocean on a day's notice. To increase the odds of a Sinatra appearance, Maury brought along a couple of framed, autographed 8x10 glossies of his wife Connie Chung—one for Sammy and a special one for Frank, marked with an appropriately flirtatious message.

Sammy's interview wouldn't be too difficult. His book was chockablock full of stories about orgies, three-way marriages, satanism, blowjobs with Linda Lovelace, *Deep Throat* movie parties with Lucille Ball, sex and drugs and more sex. Sammy could hardly fit it all in. I went through the book and stuck post-it notes in the most outrageous pages. All Maury need do was crack open to any point, read a line or so, and let Sammy take off.

An hour or so before showtime, Sammy sidled up to the bar in one of the spacious dressing rooms. Maury was perched on a barstool across from him, a copy of the book in hand.

The camera rolled. Maury began. Orgies, fucking, sucking, humping, bumping—the Candyman, indeed. He closed the book, his face red, trying in vain to hide a smile as he shook his head in mild reprobation. "Sammy... Sammy... Sammy...."

Sammy clapped his hands, brought his knees chinward and erupted into his trademark cackle. That became the title of the show:

Sammy...

Sammy...

Sammy...

We were at the end of April when Greg Snead showed us the promos he'd assembled for *TV Guide*. Every show in the month of May would have its own display ad. I shuffled through them. Good. Good. "Something About Cosby." Great.

I got to the second Tuesday of the month. Oh, no. I couldn't believe it. He really did it:

CARY GRANT:
NO MORE
FAIRY TALES

Oh well. I supposed it *could* be taken as innocent.

The day before sweeps, John O'Connor in *The New York Times* referred to a Jackie O story we'd done the week before as "vile." O'Connor's target was Cindy Adams, the *New York Post* gossip columnist who was friend to deposed dictators, fallen beauty queens, indicted politicians, and scummy millionaires. Cindy was the smartest and most over-the-top columnist in the country, and we were using her every day in sweeps. Brennan had even come up with a unique idea for showcasing her: sitting her on an actual throne.

Cindy was now enthroned in the middle of the newsroom like her friend Imelda Marcos, draped in a flowered sheet while a makeup woman applied colorful globs from two actual artist's palettes of paint pots. The palettes contained every color in the spectrum, and the makeup woman was swabbing on so much that it was if she were actually painting a picture of Cindy Adams' face on a blank canvas. I handed Cindy her copy for another JFK and Jackie O story Wayne and I wrote. She liked it, though she changed every JFK reference to "JF Superstud" or "President Sex Machine."

I walked by the display into Brennan's office for the morning meeting. Peter Brennan wasn't in, so I knew it was going to be a fight. He refused to say who was in charge in his absence. He liked the power struggle and the dominance of the fittest.

I had a great day-of-air story in my hand. *USA Today* reported that Amy Irving was divorcing Steven Spielberg. Spielberg had shacked up with the shiksa actress Kate Capshaw from his *Indiana Jones* movie, placing wife Amy in line for a divorce settlement of something in the neighborhood of ninety-two million dollars.

Dennis O'Brien had other plans. He'd recently convinced Gerald Stone it would be a good idea to run repeats of old stories, which was easier than coming up with new ones when Brennan wasn't around.

"No, no." He sat behind Peter Brennan's desk, shaking his head. "It's not sweeps yet. We should use one of these great repeat stories."

"That's not how Peter would do it."

Everyone else simply watched. Judy Sokolow cradled the stack of repeats. Marlene the director looked tired of the constant battling. Wayne sipped a coffee, inscrutable behind dark glasses.

"Steven Spielberg is getting divorced!" I exclaimed. "It's a fucking natural."

"We should look at some of these others."

"This isn't a show of repeat stories. It won't cost us anything. We're doing it."

"Burt, you only win because you talk louder than everyone else," Judy observed.

I agreed. I could also back up the talk by writing and cutting the piece myself. It was time to work.

I used clips from Spielberg movies to tell the story, the *Jaws* theme to portray Kate as a shark moving in on Spielberg's marriage, and then calculated how much Amy Irving would be paid for each time she'd slept with Spielberg. It was over-the-top, and looked great because it was wall-to-wall movie clips.

"Crocodile" Peter Faiman, still consulting for the show, loved it. The next day, he asked for a similar piece on Sondra Locke's galimony suit against Clint Eastwood.

Then came word from the West Coast.

Barry Diller wasn't happy. He wasn't happy at all. He was in his office when he got the phone call that ruined his day. It was Steven Spielberg on the line. They told us the conversation went something like this:

"Hello, Steven!"

"Barry. If I live to be ninety, I will never do a movie for Fox."

Spielberg hung up.

In the short term, my little story may have cost the company something like $500 million worldwide.

As we entered May sweeps, New York City was literally shaking with rage over the rape and near murder of a female jogger on the 102nd Street transverse of Central Park. The press said a "wolfpack" of young black kids swarmed and brutalized her in a practice known as "wilding."

In the weeks to come, in the intense arena of our office on East 67th Street, only a short walk from the park where the attack occurred, the same park where Robert Chambers choked the life out of Jennifer Levin during an act of sex, leading to *A Current Affair's* highest ratings to date, Peter Brennan, Wayne Darwen, and I would meld into a wolfpack that would unleash the most notorious act of wilding syndicated television would ever see.

It would only be the beginning.

We were off and running, leading off sweeps with a week of reports from Hollywood. "Hollywood Weeks" always did well for us, beating the leader, *Entertainment Tonight,* regularly in New York and L.A. As the week progressed, the tactic worked again.

The week ended with a phone call from Hollywood to the office of Greg Snead. Barry Diller was on the line.

Snead coughed a few times and cleared his throat. His foot tapped involuntarily as he waited to be put through. The secretary in L.A. told him there was a group in Mr. Diller's office. She connected him. Snead felt his hands go cold as he held the phone to his ear. He heard the wind tunnel sound that told him he was on a speaker phone in a large office.

He spoke first. "So! Hello everybody! How's that weather in L.A.?"

There was only silence in response. Snead said he felt the first droplets of sweat run down his back before Barry Diller's unmistakable Brooklyn bark cut through the silence.

"The... word... fairy... makes... my... BLOOD... BOIL!"

Diller cancelled the entire month of *A Current Affair's* TV Guide ads and demanded to see copies of every promotional item Greg Snead had written in the past two years.

It took more than a couple of drinks for Snead to stop shaking at Nickel's bar that evening. Brennan was there, ignoring Laurie watching him from a table against the mirror behind him, and hearing the troubles of one of the young female producers. She was drunk as all hell—sloppy loud drunk.

Her behavior wasn't unusual. For the most part, except for the elite crew of Aussies and their honorary numbers, of which I'd become one, most of the male staffers avoided the after-hours drinking binges. The next generation of tabloid acolytes was female. They were the ones who followed us to the bar, flirting, grabbing, inviting, trying to drink in our supposed magic while attempting to match us drink for drink. They were ours for the taking, but their feminine faces reddened and shone with sweat; their womanly bodies began to swell with alcohol bloat.

On this night, the producer wept because she'd been dropped by her boyfriend. As a friend pulled her toward the door, she kissed Brennan sloppily. I took her barstool and mentioned the Diller escapade.

Brennan only laughed as he wiped the slobber from his cheek. "Hey, we should have told Diller the real name of the piece: 'Cary Grant: No More Fag Jokes.'"

"Or 'Greg Louganis, the man behind the man!'" someone added.

The distress dissolved into laughter and more vodkas.

CHAPTER FOUR:
ROB LOWE'S BIG DICK

The truth has to be protected with a batallion of lies.
—Winston Churchill

If Barry Diller didn't like *Live & Dangerous* and if he didn't like our tease lines, his horn definitely wouldn't be tooted by my latest weapon in the entertainment coverage wars. We'd begun using Audrey, she of the squeaky voice and coquettish disposition, as our one-woman Hollywood strike force.

This new area of possibility was opened the day Wayne and I wrote a piece on a woman who was suing Eddie Murphy, claiming she was fired from his *Harlem Nights* movie because she wouldn't put out. We figured the best way to get Murphy's side was to send Audrey to his house to knock on the door—or at least to ring the buzzer at the gate of his mansion in Benedict Canyon. Audrey wound up in a running intercom conversation with Murphy's cook. We ran her attempt to get an interview as credits.

Now we were using her all the time, like the segment running on tonight's show: little Audrey in a flowery dress and hat, walking through the mountains of Malibu, dropping in at the front gates of everyone from Mel Gibson to Farrah Fawcett to Cher.

We watched the show unfold in Brennan's office. When Audrey walked up to Johnny Carson's wooded Malibu compound, a guard dropped from the trees.

Some of the other staffers didn't like seeing her onscreen because they didn't like Audrey personally.

I couldn't agree. "I think she has star quality."

"Burtie, you may have something there," said Brennan, his eyes narrowing as he watched her give-and-take with another intercom.

The segment ended. Maury appeared onscreen. He looked deep into the lens. "There's no reason to believe Audrey was on helium."

Someone brought helium balloons into the newsroom after the show and everyone took hits off them. Gordon Elliott sucked in more than anyone and got great laughs, this behemoth with the Audrey voice. He became giddy and said he wanted to play slave to Cindy Adams, waving a palm frond over her as she spoke from her throne.

"Can I do it in blackface?" he asked with enthusiasm. Then he caught himself. "You can't do that in this country, can you?"

That night I had dinner downtown with Bob Campbell, my old pal from NBC. It had been four months since I'd left local news, but I'd aged years in self-confidence and cynicism. Bob was hearing all about it at the Cottonwood Cafe on the far west end of Bleecker Street when we ran into Jeff Madrick waiting for a table. Madrick was News 4's financial reporter, a very intelligent and hip guy who lived in the neighborhood.

A Harvard-educated economics expert and ghostwriter of Ivan Boesky's autobiography, Madrick wasn't your typical local news star, but the stock market boom and insider trading shenanigans of the eighties made him a familiar face, explaining to us all the cowardly crimes of this brave new world.

Madrick was fascinated by my stories of tabloid TV, but for some reason, in his presence I felt I needed to justify my involvement.

"In the end, I figure I can get a great book out of it," I said.

"Hey, why not? I've done that." Madrick was serious. "The important thing is, do it right. Keep meticulous notes. Write down every moment. When you go into a meeting, you've got to come out and list the details—the color of the socks the person wore, who said what, the words, the details. And if you can tape record it—even better."

The wilding continued. We were still looking for a Bill Cosby story to promote for a Thursday night so people would turn to us before tuning in to the Cos at eight. Somehow someone came up with the idea of getting John Simon to review the show.

John Simon was the theatre reviewer for New York magazine, known as America's most curmudgeonly critic. He didn't believe black people should play Shakespearean roles written for white actors. He ridiculed the features of homely Streisandian and Minnellian actresses. Currently, he was in the midst of a scandal in which he was accused of writing a racist and anti-Semitic critique. There was no way he'd come on A Current Affair—but hey, it never hurt to try. I made the call anyway.

"Is this about 'Subject A'?" his assistant asked. She was referring to the scandal.

"No," I said. "We want America's number one critic to review America's number one TV comedy star."

She put Simon on the line. "I'd love to have you come to my house and let me watch the show, depending on the renumeration," he said in an accent vaguely reminiscent of Colonel Klink. He added that he'd do less if we offered only "a pittance."

I got him for two grand.

Lisa Marie Presley was bursting, about to give birth to Elvis Presley's first grandchild. Audrey sent a segment she edited in Los Angeles. It was surprisingly flat, but we were on deadline and the story was promoted.

The only way to spice it up was to have Elvis himself tell the story. This was a job for the Elvis Reporter! Audrey hit the yellow pages in search of an Elvis impersonator to read the script. She found one about fifty miles from L.A. and chauffeured him to the Fox Television Center in Hollywood.

There was a minor problem once she got him into the recording booth for the reading.

The man was illiterate.

"What's that? Right there. I clearly see a nipple."

"Muriel, that's a shadow. I wouldn't let a nipple on the air."

Muriel Reis stood inches from the monitor in the edit room, squinting over those spectacles covered in face powder. "And hold it right there, the tape thing. That bikini clearly shows too much there."

"It's a thong, Muriel."

"I don't care what it is. Look at how much of her—"

The sixty-something attorney leaned forward on her toes, causing her miniskirt to rise even higher up her thigh. She manipulated her eyeglasses for better focus, her nose inches from the butt crack of another thong-wearing hotdog vendor in Broward County, Florida.

Wayne was disgusted. "The pussy police," he muttered.

Muriel ignored him. She was the most paradoxical figure in the office, cutting the sexual content of the show considerably while dressed like a Downtown party girl looking for action. A clattering jumble of clashing Victorian values, Muriel disapproved of the moral tone of the show while she loved, and in fact became girlish and giddy, around Peter Brennan, who set the tone.

"I'll cover it with a black bar, Muriel." Wayne sighed.

"I think you should, because clearly this is a violation—"

"Don't use black bars, mate," I said. "Use *A Current Affair* triangles."

Wayne was excited again. "I'll use hot dogs!"

Bob Campbell called from NBC. "Heya, mate." He got a kick out of that. "Mate, do you remember Ken Bell? He was a writer with network weekend news. He worked with us at *News 4* for a while after the strike."

Ken Bell must have been around fifty; one of the more expensive veteran writers GE was trying to phase out. After the strike, GE offered him a buyout—a one-time lump sum of money to give up his permament union job so he could be replaced by cheaper, daily labor. Bell refused.

After a while, Bob said, Ken Bell simply quit without taking any payoff at all. That week, he'd called another producer at *News 4* and tried to give him some expensive stereo equipment.

"He walked out of his house the other day," Bob said, "the day before he was supposed to enter an alcohol detox program. He told his wife he couldn't do it. He didn't think he could face reality sober. Then he stuck a gun in his mouth and pulled the trigger."

After that, I went to Nickel's and got drunk on four vodkas.

The next day, we ran the segment with John Simon reviewing *The Cosby Show*. He was so dull, not even Elvis would help. So I added a laugh track.

Meantime, a man in Biloxi, Mississippi was ready to give away his mansion to Elvis Presley, should the King show up in person to claim it. I sent Maureen O'Boyle down to Biloxi with another Elvis imitator from L.A. to surprise the guy and see if he'd give up the housekeys.

I was in the Racing Club with Wayne when Maureen called in.

"He backed out. What am I gonna do? This idiot's been hitting on me the entire time we've been down here, and listen, honey, Elvis or not, he's not my type—and now he's backin' out!"

The Elvis imitator had an emergency. He'd bounced a check on a new home he was trying to buy and had to return to California to pay the realtor in person.

"Can't you find another one?"

"At eight o'clock at night in Biloxi, Mississippi? Where am I gonna find—"

"Maureen, think about it. You're around the corner from Graceland. The place must be crawling with them."

The only impersonator we could scrape up by morning was a skinny fella who sort of looked like Elvis from the right angle, but even more like Barney Fife with sideburns.

Now we'd never get the house.

I returned to the bar, where Wayne was in conversation with a tabloid writer named Susan Crimp. He stabbed out his cigarette and raised his Molson's bottle to me.

"He's worse than I am," Wayne said in admiration. "He's the prince of fucking darkness."

———◆———

That weekend, the darkness broke. A local news anchor from Phoenix was appearing nude in *Playboy*. Gilda Radner died. Lisa Marie Presley was experiencing her first contractions of labor and word came that the actor Rob Lowe was about to be indicted for appearing in a sex video with an underage girl.

This was when our triumvirate was bonded, when trust was cemented, when my friendship with Peter Brennan and Wayne Darwen would be guaranteed until death. This was when Gerald Stone realized that the straight-arrow news producer he hired away from NBC was a wilder card than the ones he was trying to control.

Word came the weekend of May twentieth. The video, showing Lowe in the act, was being played in nightclubs in Atlanta—and not some *Hee Haw* line-dancing clubs, either. Atlanta was ground zero for one of the strangest, gothic, gay S&M-flavored nightclub scenes in the country. Pierced body parts, shaved heads, industrial, ambisexual—you name it, Atlanta was years ahead of its time.

Rob Lowe had been in town the year before as one of the pretty Hollywood poster boys at the 1988 Democratic Convention. When he and his Brat Pack buddies weren't trying to act intelligent for the cameras, they were at the nightclubs, out to fuck everything and anything in sight.

Unfortunately, two of the things Lowe wound up with were a lesbian and her fifteen-year-old girlfriend. Lowe brought them to his hotel room and had his video camera rolling as they did him, he did them and they did each other. He passed out. They got up, grabbed his videocassette, and vamoosed.

Lowe made his way back to Hollywood. The tape made its way into the nightclubs the women frequented and ultimately into the hands of the District Attorney. Always willing to endure some painful national publicity, the D.A. decided to go public with the charges.

We had about a week left in sweeps. We had to get the tape. I called Bill McGowan and Andrea Spiegel, the available reporter and producer, and told them to get to Atlanta as soon as possible.

Their mission was three-fold:

>Get the tape.
>Get the tape.
>Get the tape.

I figured we could rely on McGowan and Spiegel to do anything and anyone to get the tape. *A Current Affair* was Spiegel's first job. She was a smart, inquisitive type who worked her way up to producer. She wasn't a flirt and she wasn't a drinker. She even got us Mandy Smith, Bill Wyman's bulimic child bride in London, when I assigned the story out of thin air.

McGowan was also hot. He was in his late twenties but looked older; a chubby guy with bushy eyebrows and a penchant for hiking his pants up a bit too high on his stomach. Like Robin Dorian, he was hired on as a producer but saw and took the opportunity to front pieces himself. He was typical of the successful Yank at *A Current Affair*: he got his job because he had the guts to seize it; the laidback Australians were willing to give anyone the ball if they'd run with it.

McGowan's forte was bitchily funny hatchet jobs; unfortunately for him, he'd begun taking himself a bit seriously since winning a local Emmy for a tearjerking segment about a dead kid and his mother's quest for vengeance. He was imagining himself as some sort of serious crusading journalist when, truth be told, he was among the sleaziest in the office.

That's not meant as an insult. That's why Brennan liked him.

The previous year, McGowan had shot a story in New England that required videotape from the local CBS affiliate. Someone from the office called in the request only to be told that the holier-than-thou news director would have nothing to do with *A Current Affair*.

McGowan hitched up his pants, walked into the station and flashed his old CBS ID card. He walked out with the tape.

After the hijacked video aired, the honcho at the CBS affiliate went ballistic and the shit hit the fan. The Fox lawyers decided there was no choice. McGowan had to be interrogated and then fired. Brennan intervened. He blew smoke. He sent McGowan on the road, indefinitely.

McGowan roamed the backroads of America for weeks, chasing stories far from the major markets, safely out of the line of fire until the fire was put out, the heat died down and a new crisis overshadowed his scandal. Peter Brennan saved Bill McGowan's career. There was no way McGowan would let us down.

Spiegel was on the phone by Saturday afternoon. One of the local stations in Atlanta was airing exclusive excerpts of the Rob Lowe video on its newscasts. The tape, leaked by the D.A.'s office, was a record of Lowe's weekend at the convention. One scene followed another: Lowe at the convention; shaking hands with Tom Hayden; playing around with the Atlanta Braves; in his hotel room; playing patty cake with the lesbian and the minor; coming around into frame himself, smiling for the camera.

"What about the fucking?" I demanded. "I thought this was a fucking sex tape!"

"They only showed a still from the bed scene," she said. "But the tapes's out there. Bill's out now meeting a guy from one of the discos."

"Find it."

For the time being, we had to get the tape that was airing on the local news. Lucky for us, the station was a Fox affiliate. Unlucky for us, the news director was a prick who despised *A Current Affair* and refused to give us a dub.

We didn't have time to fuck around. I told Spiegel to have the camera crew set up in her hotel room, record the segment off the six o'clock news, and get it on a plane to us in New York, pronto.

"Oh yeah," she added. "*Inside's* here."

Inside Edition had sent a producer-reporter named Craig Rivera to get their piece of the story. Craig was Geraldo's little brother, a strapping, handsome version of the American tabloid godfather, a nice young man who seemed to change designer suits as often as his cameramen changed tapes.

If he got this one for *Inside Edition*, it would do volumes for their reputation as a show that could get as down and dirty as the best. We had to beat Geraldo's little brother.

Peter, Wayne and I sat in the Racing Club all day Saturday, figuring out how to get our hands on the actual sex video. I called the assignment desk at the Atlanta station and tried to bribe a lowly assistant to steal it for us. When that didn't work, I made plans to fly to Atlanta that night to pay off or pose as a janitor.

There was no need. Spiegel came through. She'd recorded the newscast and the tape would arrive in New York Sunday morning. McGowan, she said, was hot on the trail.

The next morning, we were back in the office with a tape editor on overtime to help put something together for a promo. The elevator doors opened. A courier walked in with the package. We crammed into the edit room and watched it unspool. The tape showed Lowe, all right, but no sex. There was another slight problem: graphics all over the lower third of the screen, trumpeting "EXCLUSIVE" and the name of the local station.

I had the editor wheel in the Abakus, an attachment that allows the editing machines to do all kinds of tricks; in this case, blow up the picture, thereby eliminating the chyrons. The editor made us a new, clean dub.

Meanwhile, McGowan found the nightclub deejay who was playing the actual sex video. He was going to sell it to us.

Craig Rivera was on the same trail, so McGowan called his hotel room, and using a funny voice, told him to sit tight and wait for the tape to be delivered. He did.

On Monday morning, Rob Lowe's scandal and *A Current Affair's* name were splashed all over papers across the country. Photographers from AP, UPI, the *News*, the *Post* and *Newsday* had come to the *A Current Affair* office

Sunday to shoot stills for the Monday editions, so the show's name accompanied every still photo of the tape we ripped off from Atlanta. More straggling photographers, victims of less-experienced weekend assignment editors who didn't know the Rob Lowe sex tape was news, lined up for more shots.

Peter, Wayne, and I squeezed past them into another edit room. We had another very special package. We had the sex tape. The editor dimmed the lights, rewound to the beginning and hit 'play.'

The sex tape was worth the trouble. We extracted enough clips for an updated promo and made plans for another round of still photographers. Then we stepped out into the newsroom.

Everyone was looking at us.

They all wanted to see the tape.

Peter Brennan directed that a screening machine be wheeled to the center of the office for the New York premiere of the Rob Lowe Sex Video. By the time the tape was ready to roll, it seemed the entire staff of Fox and every resident of East 67th Street was assembled in anticipation. Even Morley Safer was probably leaning out his back window trying to get a peek.

I popped in the tape. The screen showed hash; color bars; then the action began. It was a grainy, poor quality dub that had been copied so many times all the figures seemed colored in with pastel chalk. A fixed camera recorded the scene. A woman lay on a king size bed, smoking a cigarette nonchalantly. Her legs were spread wide. A naked male climbed onto the bed, then onto the woman, and the show got underway.

As the couple got it on, a second naked male figure walked past the camera and knelt on the bed next to them. Even in the shadowy, poorly-lit and poor-quality video, the aroused figure was unmistakeably the B-movie pretty boy Brat Packer Rob Lowe. Or, to be more accurate, the figure was unmistakably a huge cock with the unmistakable Rob Lowe attached. The man was hung like a Modigliani.

"Rob Lowe, that bastard," a young male producer muttered. "Not only is he handsome, but he has a big dick, too."

Everyone else sat stone silent, eyes glued to the screen. I'd never seen a room full of people so sexually excited by what they were watching on television. Rob Lowe knelt by his buddy and began wanking. "Is it hot in here, or is it me?" he asked.

The heat had definitely spread through the female spectators in the office. I half-expected brassieres to be slipped out of and tossed toward the screen at any moment. Lowe's buddy climbed off. Rob climbed on and started screwing. The bed was creaking. He kept going. The woman was moaning. He continued. Women in the room were reaching for cigarettes and coffees. The men were looking at their watches. He was like the fucking

Energizer Rabbit! Every male in the room felt like a lesser man, while every woman—well, every woman probably wished the room wasn't full of so many lesser men.

Wayne and I pulled the tape back into the edit room and got to work on the package. Muriel Reis was in and out of the edit room in her little miniskirt watching what we were constructing—and oh, what a sight it was.

What we were doing belonged on some X-rated cable access channel. After setting up the story of Lowe, the convention and the tape, we let it roll. Rob's comments about the heat, the squeaking of the bedsprings and the obvious in and out thrusting of his tight little movie star ass. We showed everything except his member, and that probably bounced out of the area of tiny blurry squares we used to cover the private parts.

Muriel watched. She consulted. She came back and peered over the rims of her smudgy spectacles. She took them off and chewed on the stems. She told us to cut. She demanded we digitalize large sections of the screen. We got the old Abakus back in and began placing those squiggly foggy boxes over more potentially offending parts. The deadline ticked toward four. We just about had it.

Then, around three thirty, Muriel snapped.

Be it from arousal, frustration, excitement, or pure legal overload, Muriel could take no more. She demanded we black out the entire screen except for the subjects' heads.

"What?"

Wayne and I were apoplectic. *Inside* and *E.T.* had copies of the tape by now. They were going to show it! We had to be in the forefront!

Muriel called in Gerald Stone. Gerald was a quiet man and he need not raise his voice when he looked at what we were ready to put on the air. He'd never seen anything like it before, either. There was little room for compromise. In the end, we were able to show some full screen shots of the hotel room setting, but as soon as Big Rob was unleashed and the banging got underway, we went with the black masqueing.

Even so, it turned out that *A Current Affair* went far beyond the boundaries of what anyone else dared. *Inside Edition* limped in with a couple of stills. For all we knew, Craig Rivera was still waiting in his hotel room for the man with the funny voice.

Like the Robert Chambers story, the Rob Lowe tape was a milestone for the show and tabloid television. Sex, celebrity, politics, crime, morality, and America's obsession with home video cameras were all rolled into one.

Barry Diller could hissy fit all he wanted. The networks could harrumph and complain that this wasn't news, but there was no denying this was a legitimate story. Rob Lowe faced jail for canoodling with a minor on video.

We ruled.

I spoke to Speigel and McGowan on the phone. "Congratulations! You guys did it," I said. "Now go out and find the girl!"

After the show was fed out that afternoon, we all sat in Peter's office. Wayne and Peter and Judy Sokolow and Marlene and Dennis and I were laughing it up, patting ourselves on the back, sipping a beer or two from the refrigerator and telling war stories, when Gerald Stone came to the door.

He coughed to get our attention.

I noticed right away he wasn't smiling.

"You've been accused of stealing a tape."

Everyone got quiet very quickly. I looked to Brennan. He was looking straight at Stone. Wayne was looking anywhere but. I felt my face redden.

Stone stood stiffly and read from a note in his hands. "The news director from the Fox affiliate in Atlanta called. He said he saw his station's chyrons on the tape we used."

"That's impossible," Brennan said.

"There were no chyrons," I added.

"Apparently," Stone continued to read, "the tape was recorded off air and blown up to eliminate the chyrons. But they weren't blown up enough."

Stone explained that news director Mark Hoffman played the show in "superscan"—an edit room screen that shows more of the picture than appears on television sets at home—and saw quite clearly the tops of his chyrons.

Damn! Fucked by an editor!

"That's bullshit," Brennan said. "Everything we used we bought."

"Where's the tape?" Stone asked.

Brennan looked to me.

"Uh, it's out there somewhere. I'll get it."

"Bring it to my office." Stone turned on his heel and was gone.

The room remained silent.

"I'll take care of it," I said.

I slipped out of the office and moseyed to my desk. The tapes were in the bottom drawer: the sex tape McGowan bought in Atlanta and the tape I had Spiegel record off the hotel TV. I took the tapes and found an editor I could trust. We went into her edit room and shut the door.

"I need you to do something really quick and then forget you ever did it."

"Yeah, fine, no problem."

In a matter of minutes, we'd taken the purloined material and copied it onto the end of the sex video. Now all the material was on one tape. I brought it into Gerald Stone's office and suggested that the person we bought it from had added the TV material as a bonus. The tape had been played in all the nightclubs, you know.

Stone didn't seem to buy it.

"Let's take a walk," Brennan suggested.

We stood at the doorway and scanned the newsroom. Everyone seemed to be going about their business. Brennan lit a cigarette and smiled at his employees as he walked, looked twice at a newspaper headline that interested him, and continued out the back door into the stairwell.

"So, the tape is taken care of?" He spoke softly and not directly to me, more to the air.

"Yeah. I copied it."

"Where's the problem tape?"

"It's locked in my desk. I'll take care of it."

We wandered down the hallway, into the *10 O'Clock News* studio, up the metal stairs through their control room and back into the hall.

"The next thing is to get McGowan and Spiegel on the phone. Tell them what's going on. Tell them what the story is and make it clear they only need to stick to the story."

They were to stay in Atlanta, and if Gerald Stone or anyone else called to ask about the tapes, they should say they bought the tape from the source at the nightclub. They only scanned through the tape and didn't know anything about the TV material at the end.

They weren't to mention anything about recording the news off the hotel television set.

We walked through the accounting department, Brennan talking distractedly and me taking it all in, back into the Kluge building and across the offices of the beeper company on the floor above our newsroom.

If Speigel and McGowan continued working in Atlanta and stuck to the story, we'd be all right. Brennan returned to his office. I found a secluded telephone and got Spiegel in her hotel. She was nervous but cool about the situation. She understood.

McGowan, the one Brennan not only created but saved, expressed a different reaction. He started screaming.

"You guys, you guys, I'm sick of you guys going over the edge and dropping it in my lap!"

"It's not in your lap, Bill," I said as quietly and evenly as possible. "We just have this situation and this is how *Peter* says we should handle it."

"I'm not taking the fall for this! I'm not gonna be left in the cold because of you guys! I'm not going down alone, I'll tell you that!"

"Bill, nobody's going down. We're in this together. Just stick with the story."

Man, I was high on the excitement that night, sitting in the back of a taxicab bouncing over the potholes of Second Avenue on the way home from Nickel's. We got the story of the season at the tail end of sweeps and our ratings were bound to skyrocket. We'd taken television to a delirious and dangerous edge, and if that weren't enough, we were walking that cliff ourselves. We could be fired over this.

I patted the bag in my lap, feeling the hard plastic Beta cassette tape inside, the tape I'd copied over to hand to Gerald Stone. That was when I felt something else in the bag: my microcassette recorder. I thought of Jeff Madrick's advice: "Keep meticulous notes. If you can tape record it, it's even better. When you go into a meeting, come out and list the details, the color of the socks the person wore, the words, the details."

As the cab turned onto Broadway for the rattling crash through Times Square and down Seventh Avenue, there in the backseat I related the story of what happened since the weekend. I remembered the quotes, the details, the color of the socks—though I don't think Rob was wearing any.

The cabbie let me out at the corner of Eleventh Street, where I clicked open the safety guard of the problem videocassette and unspooled yards of shiny brown metallic tape from its innards before tearing the tape and stomping the plastic cassette shell to pieces. I stuffed the mess into a trash can across the street from my apartment. I'd destroyed the evidence.

Rob Lowe was a ratings bonanza. Celebrating at the Racing Club the following night, Peter Brennan and I stood with Muriel Reis, who was still recovering from the hours she'd spent watching the young movie star in a three-way fuckfest.

"We were screwed," I said to Muriel over the Barry Manilow song blasting on the jukebox. "Whoever sold us that tape, recorded part of a TV newscast at the end of it."

"It's that bastard news director," Brennan said. "He's jealous of the show because it runs before his five o'clock news and doubles their ratings."

Muriel looked deep into Brennan's eyes. "I still can't get over how quickly you manage to get all this on the air."

I gave Brennan a soft kick to the shin. We looked Muriel in the eye and lied some more. I pictured the two of us, Peter and I, standing at the bar with shovels, digging a deeper and deeper hole until we couldn't reach our drinks.

As the week progressed, more fires flared and were put out. Peter rehired the Atlanta crew who'd recorded the newscast in the hotel room and we sent them to Texas on another story with another producer. Spiegel phoned and said Gerald Stone asked her a couple of questions about the tape. She said she stuck with the story.

McGowan didn't say anything.

The conspiracy widened when we got a bill from the Atlanta crew that actually itemized "recording Rob Lowe video from newscast off hotel TV set." A few dabs of white-out took care of that one, and the Rob Lowe caper promised to dissolve into memory as just another distraction in the homestretch of a highly-charged sweeps—if only Gerald Stone would let it be.

Brennan and I continued our long walks throughout the week, building lies upon lies until they turned into the truth. When he told me to meet him in the fifth floor men's room, I felt I was in the middle of a Watergate-level conspiracy, one that was only as strong as its weakest link.

I stood at the urinal to use it as Brennan washed his hands, talking in a low voice into the mirror.

"Gerald keeps asking questions," he said. "He's fucking stupid."

"So what do we do?"

"I'm going to give him a little time." Brennan pulled a paper towel from the dispenser and walked along the row of toilet stalls, kicking the doors open as he spoke. "Then I'm going to explain that we're keeping him in the dark for his own fucking good."

"Deniability." Flush.

It made me feel special, like I was being tested in an initiation rite and entering something legendary, much bigger than myself. I knew I'd never give up the truth, and in that determination realized I'd have to be ready to lose my job if this house of cards collapsed.

There was no question I'd lay down my reputation in the name of friendship and the team. Brennan and Wayne showed me there truly was honor among thieves. I'd show them I could be trusted.

Besides, there was a greater purpose to this small incident of pilfery. If we didn't steal the tape, no one in America would have seen the rest of the Rob Lowe video. The entire story could have been suppressed. We were only lying so we could tell the truth.

Gerald Stone got the message. Brennan had to ask if he really wanted to know the dirty details of how we pushed his ratings so high. Stone accepted the luxury of deniability.

By the end of the week, the situation was defused. The internal investigation was closed. For the first time in a week, I drank at the Racing Club without a care.

We were the fucking champions of the world! I sat at the bar surrounded by female producers talking about how hot the Rob Lowe tape was, how long he lasted, how wild—one of them pressed in against me and used the jukebox music as an excuse to speak right into my ear. Fingers touched. There was an invitation to see the balcony of her new apartment a few blocks away...

I had to take a rain check. I had to get home. I accepted a farewell brush of lips against my cheek and leaned over to grab my shoulderbag from the back of the barstool.

It was gone. Someone had stolen it.

Mohammed, the owner of the place, said there'd been a series of ripoffs recently, mostly women's handbags, but overcoats as well. I ordered another vodka; one for the road. They'd gotten my notes, some story lists. Ha. They got my microcassette recorder, the one I'd spilled my guts into every night the past week; an expensive little Olympus that contained a cheap little cassette that just happened to contain the entire story of the theft and the coverup, naming names and places and—

After all we'd been through to get away with this, I'd handed over the evidence myself. I had to laugh.

"What's so funny?"

I settled back against the bar and took that first throat-burning sip of the fresh Stoli and tonic. "Ah, nothing. What were you telling me about your balcony?"

The microcassette never surfaced, while the Rob Lowe story continued over the next couple of months. We'd find that the infamous sex video wasn't shot in Atlanta after all, and presented no illegality. It was shot in a hotel room in France, with a woman who was not underage, and just happened to be on the tape Lowe used to record his Atlanta escapade. As it would turn out, the material we lifted from the local station was the only Atlanta footage America was allowed to see.

No one ever discovered the identity of the woman in the most famous sex video of all time.

A Current Affair, meanwhile, focused on that strange nightclub scene where Lowe found his video partners. When we learned they congregated by day around a hair salon outside Atlanta, I sent Audrey to go in undercover and have her hair done while her crew got surreptitious "bag camera" shots of the place and its denizens.

Audrey got caught. The owners of the salon sued for invasion of privacy.

The prick news director at the Atlanta station sued us, too.

In the end, it would all come down on me.

I had a lot to learn in this new tabloid world.

CHAPTER FIVE:
HOT STEAMY SEX

*You learned the two greatest things in life. Never rat
on your friends and always keep your mouth shut.*
—Robert De Niro in *Goodfellas*

May sweeps were too successful for our own good. We'd pulled out so many stops with sex and stunts that June had to be a time of pulling back. All the station managers in the Bible Belt who were blindsided by the Rob Lowe tape and other sexy video we crammed in for the sake of extra ratings points had to, for now, believe their eyes had fooled them. Sex, for the time being, was out.

Inside Edition hadn't fared so well. In the months to come, they'd hover on the brink of cancellation, saved only by the determination and brilliant positioning of the King Brothers. Their host David Frost was long gone, replaced by a self-important doofus from network news named Bill O'Reilly, who opened each show with heartfelt thanks to the viewer for tuning in.

A Current Affair was the champion, but there was no sitting back. We were about to face the birth of yet another imitator, this one from a most unlikely mother, with an unlikelier pair of midwives.

Paramount Television, provider of the Hollywood shill *Entertainment Tonight*, was launching its version of *A Current Affair*. The show's working title was the obvious *Tabloid*, but word had filtered back that Paramount was raising the sexual stakes of show titles by calling it *Hard Copy*. We all agreed the name would be fitting, because it would be hard to make the show work and it was bound to be a copy of *A Current Affair*.

The real surprise was the production team Paramount hired to start it up. Mark BvS Monsky and John Parsons practically invented smart, tough local TV news when they ran Channel Five's *10 O'Clock News* in the days before Murdoch bought Metromedia. They were my first bosses in television news, a couple of New York City characters who owned the city in the seventies, but whose visions were thrown for a loop by the Australian invasion. Parsons in particular had reason to want payback: Ian Rae replaced him as Channel Five's news director—then fucked him out of the company. One way or another, this was going to be war.

On the morning of June twentieth, Gerald Stone was waiting when I stepped out of the elevator. He invited me into Peter Brennan's office, closed the door, and gave Peter and me the news. Rafael Abramovitz, who'd left *A Current Affair* for a starring role on *The Reporters*, had quit the new show after a fight over a story.

Instead of letting Raf out of his contract, Gerald was transferring him back to *A Current Affair*.

This was not good news.

Rafael Abramovitz was quite a piece of work, with quite a history to explain why. He was a Lithuanian Jew who, as a child, escaped the Holocaust in the arms of his mother as she outraced the crunch of Nazi jackboots in the march across Europe. Swept by the broom of history into a displaced persons' camp in Linz, Austria, they eventually found refuge and a home in Sweden, before finding a new life in America.

His family settled in Baltimore, and Rafael grew into a screaming red liberal whose first job in journalism was as a reporter for a black newspaper. He moved into television as a producer of the NBC *White Paper* documentaries, worked with John Parsons on the idealistic PBS show, *The 51st State*, and was most proud of winning the prestigious DuPont Award in 1984 for *Whispering Hope*, a documentary on Alzheimer's disease.

Rafael spoke a dozen languages. He was grounded in the classics. He had a law degree, and for a time, put journalism on hold to work as a defense attorney. He handled mostly death penalty cases and saved the lives of indigent defendants, only to see his practice "go down the toilet" amidst a million dollar police brutality case he won but was unable to collect.

Rafael had first come to *A Current Affair* as a middle-aged producer. He virtually invented the use of re-enactments, beginning with the notorious "Preppie Murder" in which Robert Chambers killed teenage Jennifer Levin and pleaded a defense of "rough sex."

In May 1988, after Chambers copped a plea and got five to fifteen years in prison, Raf scored his biggest hit when he came up with that tape of Chambers joking and twisting off the head of a doll at a girls' slumber party. *A Current Affair* spread the story over several nights and got its highest ratings ever.

Yet, even though he parlayed the Chambers stories into a regular on-air role, Raf could not rest with victory. He was dogged by rumors the Chambers tape was actually Steve Dunleavy's scoop.

Rafael had a distinct presence on and off camera. He wore a beard, a small ponytail, and leaned on an elaborately-carved walking stick. Though he'd never lived west of Maryland, he dressed like a cowboy, from the four-beaver Resistol hat to the Levi jeans and lizard boots.

He read his tracks in a rabbinical drone, which, combined with his *Midnight Cowboy* look and gimmick of opening each segment at his word processor, helped create a persona that was so anti-television it was almost cinematic, as instantaneously recognizable as Clint Eastwood's Man with No Name.

Yet, Rafael Abramovitz, with all his talent and breadth of experience, with his beautiful schoolteacher wife, two model-gorgeous daughters and pampered life with them on Manhattan's vibrant Upper West Side, was consumed with a rage that made him all but unapproachable. He'd worked hard at his reputation as a temperamental, macho braggart who strutted around with his walking stick boasting of the day he gave *A Current Affair* its highest ratings.

As far as I was concerned, this Rafael Abramovitz was a blowhard.

We were back at Nickel's the following night to toast Maury Povich's latest success. Maury could keep up with the best of them, and tonight he was doing his best. "A guy with balls like you have, you must be reveling in the freedom of a place like this." He had his arm draped over my shoulder.

"No kidding."

"I know. I worked at the NBC O and O's."

Maury was a long way from his days anchoring the news at NBC Owned and Operated stations. That day, after much negotiation and a report that *Inside Edition* had offered him four million dollars for two years, he announced he'd signed for another two years as host of *A Current Affair*. He was Fox's first three million dollar man.

There was a news conference and staff meeting on the fourth floor. "Call him Maury Moneybags," Gerald Stone said as Maury beamed.

"I didn't think I'd be on the air at age fifty," Maury said. "I'm somewhat surprised by all the interest shown in me."

The assembled reporters wanted to know what else Maury got out of the deal; whether, like Dan Rather, he'd demanded editorial control.

"For what reason?" Maury was genuinely baffled. He said he was always part of the process.

"Looking for editorial control," Gerald interjected stiffly. "That's the type of thing that brought the networks into a morass."

"Maury, are you getting paid too much?"

"Hey, I know guys who are hitting .186 who make a million."

"The President only makes two hundred thousand."

Brennan cut in. "The President has editorial control."

When the questions were through and the jealous low-paid TV writers made way for their photographers, Maureen O'Boyle and a producer named Laura came forward in "Maury Povich Fan Club" T-shirts and posed for pictures, each kissing one of Maury's cheeks.

As the photographers packed up, Gerald announced to the staff that Rafael Abramovitz was joining us "in a special capacity."

"That means asshole," Brennan chimed in, to uncomfortable laughter.

The bad feeling spread through the office, with word that Raf would be taking on a management role as "creative producer."

Back in Peter Brennan's office, I told Wayne and Maury that I wasn't about to take any shit from the old nut in his cowboy boots, jeans and hoodoo cane. They counseled me to be cool and let Raf do his thing. A moment later, Raf sauntered in. "Welcome back," I said, still hot. "And when are you hitting the road?"

He looked me over and nodded with a trace of a smile. It would be the start of a beautiful friendship.

On the last Friday in June, Raf and Dunleavy sat in Brennan's office trading execution stories. Dunleavy's silver pompadour looked as if it were piled in a hairnet. Any sleep he'd gotten the night before was snatched sitting up at a desk in the back of the newsroom. Only his snores told the custodian he was alive. Now, taking time from *The Reporters* to recall witnessing electrocutions and hangings, he seemed energized and excited.

Raf stared off with ghosts in his eyes. He remembered being on the road in the early days of *A Current Affair*, when he wound up in a town called Belzona, Mississippi. On the front page of the local paper was a story about an execution that very night at the infamous Parchman Prison.

Raf drove to the prison on a whim. He walked into the makeshift press room at the exact time a prison official was holding a lottery to determine who'd get to witness the killing.

"They always want a reporter to be a witness. Everybody was putting their press cards into a box. I threw mine in. I never won anything before." He paused dramatically. "But I won this.

"They took us into a room with whitewashed walls and a curtain. Everybody sat in these folding chairs. I stood up in the back, with my foot up on this ledge to get a better view. The only thing I worried about was that I was gonna have to take a leak." Raf spoke slowly, as if he were unfolding a story on the show. "They pulled back the curtain so we could see the gas chamber. A black man was strapped in with seatbelts. His name was Edward Johnson. He'd killed a marshal."

"Good for him, then," Dunleavy muttered.

"When the execution began, they asked him if he had anything to say. He mouthed the words 'I love you.' Then the execution began. There was a wisp of smoke, like from a cigarette." Raf illustrated with his fingers, the thread of smoke dancing slowly before us. We could tell Raf was reliving the death. "Every time I thought it was over, he'd take another breath."

There was silence for a moment. Then Dunleavy spoke.

"Who says seatbelts save lives?"

Raf had yet to hit the road, but he was good at talking about the roadwork he wanted to do, like starring in a series of reports based on the Tony Curtis film, *The Great Race.*

"We should connect it with a cause," Peter said. "Connect Maury to some childhood disease."

"We connect it to the environment," Raf said. "I can raft up the Mississippi."

"*Against the Current Affair* we'll call it," I said.

Peter Brennan was preoccupied. He wasn't happy. He went off to the Beach Cafe, a few blocks north on Second Avenue, to spend some time with Dunleavy.

Fortified from the evening that ended only hours before, Dunleavy and Brennan didn't need long to get their vodka levels back into gear and to be leaning against each other at the handsome bar, drunk as two rats.

"Don't let that Gerald Stone get to you, mate. What does he know about anything?" Dunleavy demanded. "The man's thick as two short planks. He's run *The Reporters* into the ground and now he's doing the same to *A Current Affair.*"

"No, no, he's right," Brennan said. "It's my fault. I went off, I left the show alone and it lost its way."

"Aw, that's a bunch of bollocks and you know it."

"No. I came back for February sweeps and I had to reach low to beat *Inside.* We didn't have a fuckin' choice. But these new kids, these new reporters, they think that's all there is. They don't get it."

"You can't blame yourself for those morons."

Brennan brooded and picked at the beginnings of a patch of psoriasis on the back of his left hand. He'd been successful as hell two sweeps in a row, fighting off the threat from *Inside Edition,* but Gerald Stone was appalled that he did it with the exuberant mix of celebrity, saga, and sex that was the core of the show's very being.

"Ratings are all it's about," Brennan repeated.

"Fuckin' right they are," Dunleavy agreed.

They both knew Stone's reputation as a great TV mind in Australia had been greatly exaggerated by distance and rumor. He was just a Yank who had to go all the way to Sydney to make his name with a by-the-numbers imitation of *60 Minutes*. Now he was killing *The Reporters* with his big-issue international stories, setting up a bureau in Cali, Colombia for reports on the cocaine wars—spending millions, for nothing.

Stone had similar plans for *A Current Affair*. There was only one way to save the show. By the time Brennan finished his vodka, he knew he had to start at the bottom, with the troops.

"How can these people be so fucking stupid? They don't get it. After all the work we did, I have to teach them all over again."

"Aw, mate," Dunleavy said. "Take a few days, head up to that Tarrytown Hilton where you brought the kids. Play some tennis—"

"That's it!" Brennan lurched from the bar toward the payphone.

Dunleavy looked to the barman. "Was it something I said?"

The following afternoon, Peter Brennan was in the Racing Club with Rafael, trying desperately to shake loose his memory.

"So I've called a fucking all-day staff meeting and I don't remember why I called it."

"You did what?"

"Aw, I was getting pissed with Dunleavy and yelling about Gerald Stone and I come in this morning and Penny's got everything set. We're taping the show in advance, chartering buses, renting out the damn Tarrytown Hilton. It was my fucking order and I just don't remember why!"

Raf started laughing and couldn't stop.

"At least I'll get a weekend of tennis out of it."

Raf slapped his cowboy hat against his knee. "I can't believe you did this." He tasted his Johnny Walker Black to calm himself. "Wonderful. Just wonderful."

"I'm here, I suppose, to speak about what *A Current Affair* is, why it is, and where it's going." Peter Brennan swayed at the podium and scratched his head, as if to dislodge the thoughts from his foggy brain. "It's still a good show, probably as good as it was a year ago, but it's not good enough...a show with this kind of mix..."

He sighed and pulled a pack of Marlboro Lights from his shirt pocket. It was two days after Independence Day and the *A Current Affair* retreat was underway at the Hilton Tarrytown Inn, about forty-five minutes outside the city. The show's entire staff was invited, and now, in the spacious banquet room, they were waiting for their leader to tell them why.

"...this kind of mix is gonna kill it." Brennan lit the cigarette. "I'm rambling," he said, "'cause I'm trying to think of why we're here."

Their laughter gave him a moment to take a thoughtful drag and focus somewhere beyond the sea of expectant faces. It was a typical Brennan performance, the absent-minded demeanor only a cover for the rage that led him here. The genius behind television's most successful innovation in years was under pressure to compromise, and I was hoping it wasn't going to happen.

"*A Current Affair*," he said, "has always been the product of people sitting around thinking the most average thoughts possible. But I think we have to look at the show as a person—someone who comes around at 7:30 every night and knocks on your door. You have to make a decision, since he's knocking around five times a week, whether you want to let him in.

"Now, Gerald thinks *A Current Affair* let itself down, with the perception that we'll do anything to get a rating—"

I caught a glimpse of Rafael, sitting alone near the front of the room. He looked toward the ceiling when he heard the name that led him to quit his starring vehicle, *The Reporters*.

Brennan merely raised an eyebrow. "We have to get back to that guy who comes around at 7:30. Because if you tell a story, and you remember you're in someone's living room, and you're a guest, if you tell the story the right way, if you're witty, if you're not offensive, you should be able to tell any story to your mother or your grandmother or the Queen of England. It all depends on how you tell it.

"Now you get back from a story, what happens? You talk to people. You go to a bar, and your friends say, 'What were they really like? What really happened? If you give an answer that wasn't in the story, if the viewer or your mother can ask what the people in your story are really like, you've told the typical television version of the story. *A Current Affair* tries to do the story between the lines, and turn it into lines."

Brennan would speak for more than an hour, explaining every aspect of the genre to his workers and to Gerald Stone. No one moved. There was no doubt. This was Brennan's call to arms.

"*A Current Affair* stories are nothing more than stories about people, emotional stories," he said. "It's a straight theft from what worked in the past, long before there was *A Current Affair*. Think of them as sagas, mini-movies—when Hollywood did movies, there was one star. They made a movie about World War II, they focused on one soldier, or a platoon. Take that Naked Civil Servant, about the homosexual Quentin Crisp or whatever, who dressed like a woman in straight-laced Britain—there's no more ultimate *A Current Affair* story."

Brennan fired up another cigarette. He was fired up, as well. "This show has the freedom to do anything we like! We can do a live show, take Maury to the moon! Yeah, right now we have too many murders, too many tits and ass stories. We'd be fools not to do certain things the audience is expecting, but we can't become imitators of ourselves. We must continue to nudge the show toward new areas, turn it into a different person than it was."

He paused and realized everyone was waiting to hear what those areas would be. "We don't realize our power. We have to think we're important enough to ring up and demand to talk to Cher or the Chief Justice of the Supreme Court. We're handcuffed by the holiday weekend now, but the abortion decision seems to be the most emotional issue in the land, and to not do the *A Current Affair* story means we're locked into formula. They ought to be asking, 'What would *A Current Affair* do on this?'" He dropped a spent butt and stabbed it with his tennis shoe. "There's no reason *A Current Affair* shouldn't be the number one show."

I looked over at Raf and saw he was smiling like I was. Peter Brennan was pushing for his vision to evolve without compromise. That was something I'd never expected from the television business. I knew then and there, I'd follow this man anywhere.

"Now, if anyone has any questions..."

A production assistant named Todd stood, looking as if he finally understood, but for one minor point. "Why would we do a transvestite story when we don't do stories on gays or blacks?"

When we returned to East 67th Street, Brennan began to reassert control of the show he created. He was named Gerald Stone's co-executive producer, and set the stage to expand the *A Current Affair* agenda to include the great news stories of the day.

The first opportunity came on July 19th, when a United Airlines jet with 296 people on board crashed in Sioux City, Iowa. Miraculously, 184 people survived the fiery disaster, and in an even greater miracle, someone recorded the crash with a home video camera, proving it all the more unbelievable that anyone walked away from a jet that tumbled end over end in a ball of flames.

We dispatched a team of reporters to the crash site. Maury Povich went along to anchor the show from the scene. The idea was to tell the story our way, not doing news reports but getting the story between the lines: the personal tales of heroism and tragedy from survivors, rescuers, and loved ones.

Ragtag as it may have been, our coverage provided the prototype for what the networks would send back from Oklahoma City six years later. As Brennan had envisioned, it was a matter of focusing on that one person. Mike Watkiss sent back a story on a group of tourists who lived through the crash. Amid all the soundbites and B-roll were a few quick quotes from a Norwegian exchange student who emerged unscathed. She was a modern-day Noxema girl, blonde and tan and robustily busty, who'd turned eighteen that very day.

Back in New York, Wayne and I tore the piece apart, rewrote it and centered the story on her. Some habits die hard.

Maury took some days off. Maureen O'Boyle filled in. She was good for the job, sitting at the anchor desk all serious and anchorlike, as if one of the *A Current Affair* kids was filling in while Dad was away on business. It was evident she wasn't up for the role as permanent host. Maureen didn't have the presence needed for a show like this. When she sat on the set, she left her bawdy, brassy personality and swinging behind, well, behind.

On this day she was doing a two-way interview with a man in Vancouver who bought John Lennon's psychedelic Rolls Royce and found some movie reels under the seat. I was at my desk in the newsroom, watching the interview on a monitor while on the phone to Andrea Spiegel in the control room, who, in turn, spoke to Maureen through her IFB earpiece. I was supplying the interview questions.

"What's on the reels?" I suggested.

Andrea repeated. "What's on the reels?"

There was a beat. Then Maureen onscreen: "What's on the reels?"

"Did you contact Yoko Ono?"

"Did you contact Yoko Ono?"

"Did you contact Yoko Ono?"

I cracked up. It was funny—until I noticed. Maureen was just sitting there, silent, like Charlie McCarthy without Edgar Bergen. If I didn't ask a question, she didn't ask a question.

We kept the ratings on an even keel that summer. Gerald Stone was very happy we were able to do so without the usual "tits & ass"—the industry's standard term for sexy items—the show relied on traditionally to keep viewers hooked in.

Things were not boding so well for Wayne and me. After months of obfuscations, diversions and outright lies to get tapes and stories on the air, we'd finally driven Muriel to distraction. She didn't believe a word we said and had spread word throughout the company that we were on thin ice.

The low point arrived when Riva came up with a spectacular scoop in Los Angeles. A cameraman who'd done work for Michael Jackson came forward with close to an hour of video footage he'd shot for the star a few years earlier at the family compound in Encino. The tapes showed Jackson making fun of his sister Latoya, kissing his animals, talking low-down jive with the family factotum, and camping it up with songs from *Peter Pan*.

There was also a scene that on the surface was so disturbing that back in 1989 we were all certain it had to be innocent. In a curtained room, Jackson practiced moonwalking steps with the tiny actor Emmanuel Lewis, until the pop star swept the miniature child in his arms and waltzed him around like Fred with Ginger.

The cameraman said Michael had given him ownership of the tapes and his blessing to do with them what he pleased. It was almost too perfect, but Wayne and I weren't about to argue. We flew him and his wife to New York, put them up at a fancy hotel, and got the tapes for a song. Muriel said all we needed was a signed statement verifying ownership, so I had Cheridah rush over in the early morning hours to wake the cameraman and have him sign on the dotted line before he was totally cognizant.

Wayne and I went to work. This would be our greatest triumph yet. We called in the photographers, wrote press releases, and set about writing and producing a special half hour. The promos went out for "Michael Jackson's Home Movies."

We finished editing the special over the weekend. On the morning it was to air, there were articles in all the newspapers and more press at our door.

By afternoon, Muriel the attorney was developing a case of cold feet. She called the cameraman into her office and questioned him again. She grilled me, and after I left her office, she told Peter Brennan, "I don't believe a word he says." I wasn't sure why. Peter said it had something to do with the Rob Lowe lawsuits.

Shortly before 3:00 p.m., an hour before the show was to be sent by satellite around the country, Michael Jackson's attorneys called, claiming that Jackson owned the tapes and would consider filing a lawsuit if we aired them.

They rattled the sabre. Muriel went weak at the knees. She advised Gerald Stone not to run the tapes. Gerald Stone's knees buckled, too. Michael Jackson's home movies would not be shown. Gerald was visibly upset; one might say, panicked. "What will we do? What will we do?"

"Don't worry. We'll take care of it." Defeated, shoulders slumped, Wayne and I walked back to the edit rooms, pulled two old stories off the shelf, knocked out a quick story about Jackson's people stopping us from airing the tape, and got the show on air.

We got more publicity from the censored show, but Wayne and I knew something was up. The wonder boys were too successful for their own good. Gerald didn't like the show's direction, and we were taking the fall to appease the station managers, advertisers, and Barry Diller.

At the end of July, a young production assistant named Matt Singerman came up with the story of the summer.

He found it in one of the hundreds of small-town papers we relied on: a photograph of two kids, a girl who looked to be thirteen years old and a boy, about ten. They were lying on a mattress in what appeared to be a van, bound and gagged, with electrical tape over their mouths, terror in their eyes.

The caption said a woman found the photo in the parking lot of a convenience store in Port St. Lucie, Florida. No one knew who the children were or under what circumstances the photo was taken. No one had picked up the story nationally.

We did. We led with the story the next day. We showed and analyzed the mystery photo. We interviewed the woman who found it. We spoke to the FBI. There were no answers, but it was captivating, frightening, and potentially heartbreaking stuff; it showed that *A Current Affair* cared and could handle the big ones.

This was a story that should have brought our team together, but it would be the one Dennis O'Brien chose to use in a desperate and obvious strike for control of the office. It was a big mistake.

The story aired on a Friday. I awoke Monday morning to the sound of my alarm, clock radio, television and phone ringing with the six a.m. conference call. Dennis was reporting matter-of-factly that he'd been in the office all weekend working the mystery photo story with Andrea Spiegel and Catherine, a producer he fancied.

Two sets of parents had called after the airing of Friday's show, he said, claiming the kids in the photo were theirs. Both couples were from New Mexico. Each called us independently. The boy, named Michael, disappeared in April 1988. The girl, who would have been twenty, vanished five months later. Her name was Tara. The children were still missing.

I sat up in bed. Nobody told me. Why hadn't anyone told me? The adrenaline surged through every inch of my body. I was awake in less than thirty seconds and already standing.

"Which reporters are on the story?"

"No reporters. I sent Catherine to New Mexico yesterday."

"What? You only sent one producer?"

"Uh, yes. Catherine."

Within the hour, I was charging from the office elevator, asking questions and barking orders. What reporters do we have anywhere near New Mexico? Get them to both families now. What are the cops saying? Are there any other leads?

Dennis had more surprises. He'd booked a live shot with the girl's parents, but decided to leave out the parents of the boy.

I repaired the damage, ordering Catherine to gather all the parents in one place and moving reporters to the area. The next day, we tailed the FBI as they followed up tips and made raids on houses in different parts of the country. The assignment desk moved reporters and crews around the United States like they were back chasing NYPD radio calls around Lower

Manhattan.

Through it all, Dennis continued to countermand my directives behind my back. The cumulative effect took me to the edge. I'd been polite, even respectful to the guy. That evening we almost came to blows.

For the first time, Brennan intervened. He brought me to Nickel's.

"That's it, mate," I told him as I gulped a Stoli and tonic to settle down. "I've had it with this backbiting. This is bullshit. The man is a fucking amateur. You've got two people running that office and nobody knows who's in charge. You've got to choose."

Brennan stirred his drink. "It's yours."

"If you want to go with him, it's cool, I just need to know. Cause it can't go on like this. He's moving crews. The man has no clue. That's my job—"

"It's yours. You own it."

I stopped, mid-rant. "What?"

"You own the show. It's yours." Brennan sipped. "Be diplomatic. You've got it, mate. You're born to this. I don't know where you get it from, but you're a cross between Wayne Darwen and—and I don't know, whatever highbrow whatever, I don't know. But the show is yours."

"Oh."

"You've just got to do something about your absolute wild card mentality, mate. And be diplomatic."

The next morning, I awoke sick as a dog from all the vodkas. Our story was in *The New York Times*, with a two-column picture and many mentions of the show. Tara and Mike though, were never found, and as far as I know, no one ever confirmed it was them in that mysterious photo.

Maury Povich's *A Current Affair* third anniversary party took place in New York harbor aboard a cruise boat called the Carrousel.

Among the revelers was Audrey Lavin, who'd flown in from Los Angeles with the rest of the crew. It was the second time I'd met her, a small yet sturdy woman with big eyes and a bobbed nose. The first time was back at the Tarrytown seminar. It wasn't more than an hour after we were introduced that she suggested we get a room for an hour or so. I didn't take her seriously.

This time, as the boat chugged off from Queens toward the lights of Lower Manhattan, she'd turned her flirtation game into a seduction competition, and I found myself in the odd position of being the quarry of two adventuresome females, a producer from the East and one from the West.

Maury was giving a speech when I felt the first pinch on my ass. It was Audrey. There was dancing and an invitation from her competitor. I headed for the bar and found faithful Cheridah, who watched my and Brennan's sides against the ones who'd take advantage.

"Watch that Audrey, she's playing games with you, she's bad news," she said in her rapid-fire, proper Jamaican accent. "Here, Stoli and tonic."

"Thank you, Cheridah."

The night got later, I had more Stoli and tonics, and the party got wilder and flowed to a stateroom downstairs. Audrey was winning the game.

Somehow we wound up in the "head," which was actually a fully-equipped bathroom, complete with a stall shower, and somehow Audrey and I wound up in the shower, with the water running and the party raging on above us. I was management, at an office party, in a shower. I kept my head out of the flow as steam filled the tiny cubicle and seeped through the louvered door into the stateroom.

There was a commotion outside—a rattling of the door handle and a banging on the door. Someone was trying to get in. I turned off the water and squeezed my eyes shut. What the fuck was I doing?

The captain was at the door. We toweled off and went back upstairs where the party was in full wild swing with a sweaty drunken crowd dancing at the open air stern. With my hair slicked back to begin with and my tie in place, there was little to give away what went on.

Audrey appeared a bit soggier, with a victorious smile as she signaled to her competition. When the boat docked and we staggered off to various taxicabs back to the city, Audrey invited me back to her hotel. I said I didn't think it was a good idea, and carried on drinking with Brennan and Wayne at Dorrian's Red Hand on the East Side.

The next morning, Maury was genuinely perplexed. The boat owners charged him for a tankload of shower water and he didn't know why.

"Who the fuck took a shower?"

There were only smiles and whispers. Only two would know for sure, and one of us was already winging back to Los Angeles. When I returned to my desk from a meeting in Brennan's office, Gordon Elliott was sitting at a typewriter near my desk like a schoolkid trying in vain to suppress his laughter.

On my desk was a showercap. It was from Audrey's hotel.

Under questioning, I denied all. If anyone asked what we were doing locked in the bathroom, I told them we were doing drugs. We lit a joint, I said, and turned on the shower to kill the smell.

It was preferable to anyone thinking anything else.

CHAPTER SIX:
LESBIANS, CRIPPLES & CLOWNS

The next day I had a message from Jerry Lewis. I'd written him a letter, asking permission to shoot behind the scenes at his *Muscular Dystrophy Telethon*. Jerry had called me back.

Jerry Lewis was my show business hero. His telethons were, to me, the ultimate in reality television, edge-of-your-seat psychodramas from an alternate show business universe where time stopped in the sixties and only Frank Sinatra was a bigger star than Jerry himself.

I had dozens of VHS tapes at home filled with complete 21-hour telethons from years of Labor Day weekends. Two years earlier, when my friend Kiki worked as an assistant director for the telethon from Caesars Palace in Las Vegas, I volunteered as a production assistant just so I could stay awake the entire time and hang with Jerry and Sammy and the gang.

One of the producers had assigned my first task the moment I arrived in the production trailer: fix the show rundowns that were distributed to all studio personnel. Someone had typed "Muscular Dystrophy Telethon" at the top of the sheets. Jerry had passed through the office, noticed the misprint and demanded it be corrected on every page. It was my job to white out the words "Muscular Dystrophy" and type in "Jerry Lewis." This wasn't the *Muscular Dystrophy Telethon*, it was the *Jerry Lewis Telethon*. I was in fucking heaven.

That Labor Day weekend, I'd witnessed many moments of reality drama: Sammy Davis, Jr., days away from a hip-replacement operation, hobbling on two canes and tossing them aside to rock the house at four a.m. with "Birth of the Blues"; a uniformed chauffeur unfolding two wheelchairs from a Mercedes limousine, then opening the rear door so two of Bobby Berosini's orangutans could hop on; Berosini in the wings before his spot, slapping and yanking one squealing orangutan's face, to form its mouth to say "mama" onstage.

As the telethon reached its climactic moments, I waited backstage as Jerry wept his way through "You'll Never Walk Alone." I had to see for myself if my man was for real or whether he'd drop the emotional facade once he stepped out of camera range.

Jerry thanked the audience, walked offstage into the arms of his wife, and wept some more.

My idea to follow Jerry Lewis through this latest telethon was a long shot, but it would be great television. I dialed his home number.

"Hello." The voice was as unmistakable as Rob Lowe's member.

"Mr. Lewis."

"Mr. Kearns."

Jerry liked my idea but had a few things to clear up. "Now in your letter, you mentioned the possibility of converting the cynics."

"Yeah, well, you know—"

He paused, then exploded. "*I FUCK THEM!* After forty years, I have to prove I'm sincere? Fuck them!" He changed personalities like the Nutty Professor, then switched back again. "Now," he said, calmly. "What do you need from me?"

I explained that we wanted to follow him around with a crew. "Fly-on-the-wall stuff."

"What convinced me is that you have a copy of *Jerry Lewis Just Sings*," he said, naming a classic lost album he cut in the fifites. "I can't find a copy of *Jerry Lewis Just Sings*."

I told him I had four and would bring him one.

"The only thing I ask is I want fifteen minutes of airtime, not the usual three-minute story like some of these other shows have done to me."

"Well, I can't say—hey, why not! Whatever you want, I'll work it out!"

"You will have total access, total cooperation from my crew."

Jerry Lewis was true to his word. He told me to make sure our camera crew was in place when he arrived at the telethon arena, then made a most dramatic entrance, rolling up slowly in his long Cadillac coupe with swinging jazz blasting from the car stereo. He stepped from the car wearing a football jersey, athletic shorts and high white socks, gave a casual hello and sauntered into the production offices leading an army of flunkies and producers. This was right out of *The Bellboy*.

Jerry Lewis was a prince to us over the next four days. He loved the attention. He threw a tantrum when his freezer wasn't stocked with Dove Bars. He bullied. He clowned. He was a supplicant to Sinatra in a two-way from Atlantic City. He cursed and made lewd comments about the world-famous Rangerette marching team from Kilgore, Texas.

"Look at that one. She has a box like a Samsonite briefcase," he commented for our cameras as one teen after another slammed to the floor in painful splits.

Backstage between appearances, Jerry slurped chicken soup in his trailer, whined when one of the crippled kids wanted to come in and meet him, and even accidentally on purpose let the door swing open as he eased his chronic back pain by sucking on an oxygen mask.

We returned each night to the Flamingo Hilton on the Strip, where we'd had an editing system installed in one of the rooms, and edited the show as we went along. Robin Warner was the editor, a fan whose devotion to Jerry Lewis far outstripped mine; she adored Jerry and didn't want us to include any intimate scenes that might embarrass him. I explained that in a way, we *had* to; no matter how much we loved Jerry, we weren't responsible to him. but to the viewers. It was our job to show what really happened.

Besides, Jerry may have *seemed* unguarded in front of the cameras, but he was a professional. He knew when the cameras were there, and much of the time he played to them. I focused on the *most intimate* scenes, bleeped the curses, and showed it all, pulling together an entire verite half-hour show, with no reporter or narration, to run as a special edition of *A Current Affair* the day after the telethon.

If we were *48 Hours* or any other network magazine, if we were PBS, we would have won awards. We were *A Current Affair*. We had to settle for ratings, and they were good.

We also had to settle for the expected response from Barry Diller. Days after the broadcast, he forwarded us a letter:

> Dear Mr. Diller:
>
> I am writing in reference to the rude language used on a recent *Current Affair* program...
>
> I heartily agree with the producer's decision to bleep out profane language uttered by Mr. Lewis, yet I am as disheartened by the the the fact that the producer felt compelled to leave in Lewis' derogatory and defaming remarks about God...

Jerry had uttered a "goddamn." I'd broken a cardinal rule of tabloid television, and television in general, by letting someone say the name of the Lord our God in vain. You can get away with a "shit" or even a "fuck" in the right circumstances, but throw in one "Jesus Christ" and you've alienated a quarter of the country. Jesus Christ, how could I have been so stupid? Goddamn it.

Jerry was appearing onstage in Atlantic City a few weeks later. Wayne and Robin and I drove to the dismal boardwalk and a seventeen-hundred seat showroom in a hotel called Trop World to see him perform the exact same act he'd recorded for an eight-year-old tape I'd bought at a Times Square video store. He told dumb jokes, did his old typewriter routine, tossed some canes in the air and sang some standards.

After the show, we went to the stage door to let our pal know we were in the house.

His manager Joey Stabile emerged, clearly upset. "No, you can't see Jerry!" He was waving his arms. "Go away! He's so angry!"

They hated the show we did. It was worse than defaming God; we'd defamed Jerry.

I realized with sadness we were merely paying the price for doing our job, but Wayne was outraged because Robin looked so sad.

"Write that ungrateful bastard a letter, mate," he said. "Tell him if he didn't like what we aired, too fuckin' bad! We've got lots more where that came from, and it rated so well that Brennan's making us use it—*unless* Jerry does something else for us."

Wayne was right. What an ungrateful bastard. I thought of all the footage we didn't have room for—like Jerry's mini-fit over his dear friend Sammy Davis, Jr., who'd co-hosted the telethon from New York. As the minutes ticked toward the grand finale, word came that Sammy was refusing to perform an extra, unscheduled number.

Sammy's wife Altovise was backstage with us in Vegas. She whispered to Jerry that Sammy wasn't feeling well, something about his throat hurting. That wasn't good enough. Jerry freaked. "What the fuck do you mean he's not going on?"

Wayne and I began the letter the same way we promoted the Sammy Davis interview:

Jerry...Jerry...Jerry...

Two days later, Jerry Lewis was on the phone again.

"Burt, I'm sorry. I never knew you were in Atlantic City. Tell Robin I am so sorry. I loved the show. I thought it was the best thing anyone's done in a long time. These people who work for me, they're *FUCKED.* They think they're protecting me. I apologize. For them."

"They had problems with the show?"

"Ah, the MDA didn't like it because you didn't show any kids—"

"The story was about you."

"You're telling me? They didn't like the language. So what? You did a great job."

"Well, it rated so well, our boss does want us to run more—"

"I'll do anything for you. Look, I'm going to Europe. Call me in three weeks when I get back."

"Hey, I found another copy of *Jerry Lewis Just Sings* in Soho."

"See? See what I mean? With a fan like you, who needs these people around me?"

Jerry never did anything with us again.

It was something we had to do. *A Current Affair* was about showing the story between the lines and turning it *into* lines.

"What would they ask in the pub, mate?" Brennan's words echoed. "What really happened?"

Sometimes it's a matter of having to kill your heroes, sometimes simply learning from your mistakes. I'd never forgive myself for the one time I let my sympathy for an interview subject get in the way of the true story.

It was shortly before I joined *A Current Affair*. The country singer with the lower-case name, k.d. lang, was just beginning to make waves when I saw her open for Lyle Lovett at the Ritz in Manhattan. She hit the stage in a crewcut and glittering Nudie suit, changed into a cartoony cowgirl dress with sawed-off cowboy boots, and wailed a spine-chilling version of Roy Orbison's "Crying" that marked her as one of the best pop singers *ever*.

She was also gay as all hell, but no one was mentioning the obvious.

When Legs McNeil suggested I write something for his section in *Spin* magazine, k.d. lang became my first subject. I arranged to interview her on the phone from work at WNBC, then meet her later in the day when she appeared on *Live at Five* and *Letterman*.

On the phone, k.d. lang was serious, pretentio-arty and rock star bored. I was going to wake her up. I saved the microcassette, from July 7, 1988:

> Me: When I saw you at the Ritz, I guess the other thing is, your image on the stage...It's like, people, you know, 'Is she a boy? Is she a girl? Is she Wayne Newton?' It seemed to be evenmore than just androgyny. It seemed like a heavy political statement you were making.

She laughed, then burst out with an excited giggle.

> kd: Yeah.
> Me: Right?
> Me: So is it as innocent as, like, you want the guys to like you and you want the girls to like you, so you want to be androgynous?
> kd: No. It's just that I grew up as a tomboy and I prefer my hair being short and I love Nudie suits.
> Me: Uh huh.

kd: You know. *(laughs more defensively)* I don't—yeah, sure. The boys can be attracted to me. The girls can be attracted to me.
Your mother can be attracted to me, your uncle—sure. It doesn't really matter to me. I mean, you know—

I was hungry, circling. I was going in for the kill. I lied.

Me: You're like a real heroine to a lot of gay friends I have.

She knew I was lying. She was ready, too.

kd: Yeah.
Me: And at the Ritz, when I was there, there were a lot of people who were dressed like you.

k.d. lang knew where this was headed.

kd: Uh hum.
Me: People I know that work in card shops were dressed like cowboys—
kd: Uh hum.
Me: —that I didn't even know had cowboy boots. Are you like the first, like, gay country singer? Are you going to want to come out like that?

I'd blurted it out. I waited to hear the phone slam down.

kd: Well...

Now the laugh was truly defensive.

kd: I don't even, I don't even know if I think I'm gay. I mean it doesn't—

She didn't think she was gay.

Me: I'm just talking about image, you know.
kd: Well, I would, I would assume that I'm one of the first androgynous country singers. I think Porter Wagoner was kind of androgynous.
Me: Uh huh. Yeah. Same kind of suits.
kd: Yeah, and you know, really pouffy hair, which is the same as

me having, you know, a sort of a flattop. Yeah, I think my imagescan be taken that way or, or you know, eccentric. I'm sure a lot of people look at me as a gay image, but uh, really it's just—as I said before—it's just, as I said before, just how I feel comfortable on stage and my natural reaction to life.

I had my lead. There were a few more questions.

Me: Anything you want to say to *Spin* magazine? To their readers?
kd: No. Just don't print a lot about the gay stuff, because I can't deal with it right now with country. I'm having a hard enough time getting played as it is.
Me: Well, there goes my lead.
kd: (*nicely*) Yeah.

A little later, she begged me again not to go with the gay angle.

kd: Be kind to me. Don't say anything controversial.
Me: Well, it's *Spin* magazine. Give me one thing controversial to say—about meat eaters or something.
kd: No. I don't want to be controversial at all. Not today. I feel a little vulnerable today, so be good to me.

I told her not to worry, and she didn't have to. I wrote a piece they titled "Country Cowpie," about her being an androgynous *Green Acres* cartoon who's more like Eb the farmhand than Lisa Douglas and made references to gym teachers and Anne Murray, but didn't use the best quotes I had because I felt some kind of responsibility to this person who was pushing a record.

From the moment I saw the article in print, I regretted the lapse. I was using her. She was using me. I knew I should have been responsible to the *story*. If k.d. lang is the lesbian queen of country and asks not to have it mentioned, she's savvy enough to think it will be.

A year or so later, a writer named Michelangelo Signorile started "outing" gay stars and k.d. lang came out on her own. Who knows? I may have helped her career by not jumping the gun. Maybe history would have been changed if that early article was headlined:

k.d. lang: "DON'T CALL ME GAY!"

I vowed never to hold back again. Too bad poor Jerry paid the price.

On September 18th, 1989, a couple of weeks after the telethon special, *Hard Copy* premiered with a thud.

It wasn't supposed to be that way. Monsky and Parsons had big plans for their tabloid debut. They wouldn't copy *A Current Affair* after all. They were going to throw the tabloid TV rules out the window and reinvent the form as a hard-hitting, investigative, MTV version of *60 Minutes*, launching with a big New York news-style sting that would announce the dawning of a new era.

Instead, they showed they'd ignored some vital tabloid rules. *Hard Copy* planned to set up and embarrass one of America's most-loved stars.

A young musician was claiming he had an affair with Dolly Parton when he was a thirteen-year-old traveling with her show. He had pictures of Dolly with her arm around him and he had his mother to back up his claims.

It wasn't enough that the *Hard Copy* boys would stick Dolly with charges she really couldn't refute, but they went a step beyond the bounds of propriety and the law. They set up a sting; arranged to meet Parton's manager at the Le Dome Restaurant on the Sunset Strip and with hidden cameras, videotaped the gentleman handing over an envelope of money in return for the incriminating photos.

Now, celebrities have to deal with this blackmail all the time. Bad guys have to accept being stung; but Dolly Parton, the woman represented by one of Hollywood's most powerful men, the Velvet Mafia's underboss, Sandy Gallin, close friend to Barry Diller himself? Stung by Paramount Pictures?

Hard Copy was almost cancelled before it went on the air. The story was killed from on high—way, way on high.

Monsky and Parsons scrambled for a replacement story. They got a producer to drag a couple of teenagers to the Atlantic City boardwalk and sent them into a casino with another hidden camera rolling. They were going to show how easy it was for underage kids to gamble.

It didn't actually pan out as planned. Casino security pounced on the kids immediately. The producer ran away, leaving the kids high and dry. The casino went to the police and the D.A. filed charges against the producer and the show.

We at *A Current Affair*, in our new role covering the important stories of the day, did several on the *Hard Copy* scandal.

Ultimately, Monsky and Parsons learned the important tabloid rule of choosing one's targets carefully. They were forced to lead off the *Hard Copy* era with stories like the one focusing on struggling actors in Hollywood. I watched the piece back in New York and recognized the actor they profiled. He was John Parson's son.

It was almost too easy a target: out of all the worthy actors in Hollywood, etc. I got the item in the papers. *Hard Copy* began with a red face and a whimper.

Monsky and Parsons were in over their heads. They were great New York City newsmen, they were journalists, they were documentarians, but this tabloid TV thing required something far beyond these credentials. The important threads of tabloid TV—the senses of humor, perspective, and the absurd—only seemed easy to imitate. The bottom line was, Tabloid TV wasn't news. And it wasn't as simple as mixing sex, violence, celebrity, and Elvis.

Hard Copy had the added disadvantage of being the first tabloid TV show to be based in Hollywood, three hours behind the New York-based shows and saddled with Paramount's entertainment mentality. Frank Kelly, the man in charge of syndication, had several ideas about what made good television, including a thirty-eight-week production schedule—with thirteen weeks of enforced repeat shows—and a perky and innocuous male-female anchor team. Monsky and Parsons' production team included an ambitious blond lieutenant named Linda Bell, who was straight out of bubbleheaded L.A. local news and Charmin-soft hour magazine shows, and a staff of local news producers, *Entertainment Tonight* rejects, and members of their own hard news inner circle.

As the season progressed, *Hard Copy*'s onscreen body count would rise while the ratings would fall. Monsky and Parsons' show began to resemble a bloody, hard-boiled local news broadcast. Their innovative herky-jerk MTV-style camerawork often resembled Letterman's monkey-cam. The show would fall apart and so would the Monsky-Parsons team.

We were back on the news bus in October when a major earthquake hit San Francisco. David Miller, Robin Dorian, and several producers scattered through the city looking for individual stories while we in New York decided how to narrow down such a widescale catastrophe to *A Current Affair* proportions.

Brennan found the answer in a section of double-decker highway in Oakland that collapsed onto itself and traffic, crushing dozens of cars and trapping drivers in a concrete coffin. The road was supposed to be earth-quake-proof.

While our team in San Francisco scrambled to get the goods at the scene, we in New York went all-out to recreate the moment in our edit room. Jerry Burke took a crew onto the George Washington Bridge to shoot footage from a moving car: the speedometer, the passing girders, the clock, the radio, and the wheels. Then they shook the camera to simulate a quake.

By combining that with actual news footage, we were creating a scenario of the moments leading up to the disaster. Wayne and I wrote the story as we usually did, taking turns at the word processor: he giving it a run-through, me polishing and adding, getting up and letting him take over; tag team tabloid that pushed the story closer to perfection and farther over the top. It was a combination of strict facts and undeniably true embellishment that only heightened the reality.

"Did you find out about the radio stations?" I had story coordinator Mike Larkin call up various San Francisco stations to find what songs were playing at the time of the quake.

The kid held the phone to his chest. "The quake knocked most of the stations off the air. But the one FM station that stayed on was playing 'Hotel California.'"

"Are you serious?" Wayne and I exchanged high-fives.

"That's what they told me. But I'm calling back to confirm it—"

Wayne and I spoke in unison. "Hang up."

We both had learned. Many a good story could be ruined by making one phone call too many.

Brennan gave the script a few finishing touches. It was an awesome countdown to death as compelling as any earthquake movie. Wayne and I went into the edit room with Mike "Mikey" Squadron, one of the show's more straight-arrow producers and the son of Rupert Murdoch's attorney, Howard Squadron. He was appalled that we were taking a tragedy—a real-life event—and turning it into over-the-top drama on the very day it happened. It went against everything he was taught. Mike sat in the corner of the edit room shaking his head and wringing his hands.

He stood. "I'm sorry. I can't be a party to this. I can't have anything to do with this."

He left the edit room.

Within weeks, Mikey had himself transferred to Fox News.

Before we knew it, November was upon us, and so was another sweeps period. *Hard Copy* was already hard up. They'd made open inquiries about buying the list of our sweeps stories and even hired away one of our lowly L.A. assistant producers for big money, in hopes he'd bring along our story list.

It didn't matter. *Hard Copy* didn't know how to do it. We simply pushed along and pulled out all the regular stops. James Dean stories always rated big when we ran them on Wednesday nights in sweeps, so Wayne got Juliet Mills' young husband Maxwell Caulfield to host our "James Dean Playhouse" of never-seen Dean footage.

Wayne also dug up unseen footage of Marilyn Monroe's unfinished final film, *Something's Got to Give*, but before we could air it, Barry Diller's people took it out of our hands and turned it into a Fox special. They even took full credit for the discovery.

We filled each day with great promotable taglines. There was a story on the long and lasting love of Dean and Jeannie Martin. Our Madonna story focused on her new public friendship with the comedienne Sandra Bernhard. We called the Martin story "Hollywood's Greatest Love Story";

Madonna and Bernhard were "Hollywood's Oddest Couple." On the day the promos ran, the titles were accidentally switched.

We decided the captions fit anyway.

There wasn't a hiccup from Barry Diller.

Of course, there was Elvis. Early on in my tenure at *A Current Affair*, I'd returned from a visit to Nashville and Jimmy Velvet's Elvis museum with a huge velveteen wall hanging of the King and posted it on the wall in the middle of the office. "The Elvis Shrine" became a repository for *Weekly World News* headlines and tacky King-related memorabilia that producers brought back from places from all over the country. The watchful eye of Elvis served notice of who we were, the world we covered and who we represented.

A Current Affair's original star reporter, Steve Dunleavy, had written the ultimate Elvis book, the shocking *Elvis: What Happened?* and we continued to stay on top and ahead of the Elvis curve. It helped give the show a place in American pop culture, as reflected at the time by a cartoon in the short-lived SMART magazine. Under the heading, "Crisis on *A Current Affair*," and a sketch of an Elvis lookalike wearing a sheriff's badge was the caption:

> When live coverage from Tiananmen Square was
> interrupted, Elvis impersonator Roy Saposhnik
> was summoned to discuss his brand of law & order.

If Elvis was really dead, we brought him back to life that November. Peter Brennan had a pal in London who was a tabloid newspaper editor and part-time Elvis impersonator. He'd cut a cassette called *Songs Elvis Would Have Sung*—accent on the *would have*—twelve songs you'd figure Elvis recorded, if they hadn't been written after he allegedly died; songs like "Feelings" and "Lady."

Brennan decided to bring the concept to America. We found the best singing Elvis impersonator in the country and put him in a Manhattan studio with a group of fine studio musicians, recording songs like Bruce Springsteen's "I'm on Fire," the Rolling Stone's current hit, "Mixed Emotions," and "Crazy Little Thing Called Love" by Queen—all done Elvis-style, with rockabilly guitar and Sweet Inspiration-style back-up singers.

One of our producers made MTV-quality videos of the songs, funny two-and-a-half minute bits we'd tease through the show and run at the end. It made for great publicity—and promised great spinoffs.

The first of the videos aired on a Monday. By the time we showed the second, the threats of lawsuits started coming in. We didn't have rights to the songs. We didn't have synch rights to put pictures to the songs or the rights to let Elvis sing them. We were forced to scrap the final two or three videos—but we allowed the impersonator to use them in his stage shows. Apparently, they're still a big hit around Ohio.

We had similar trouble when Prince cut a song with Kim Basinger. Someone got hold of the audiotape, exclusively, and at the last minute, I put together "the video they would have made" by using a split screen, combining footage of Basinger writhing in *9 1/2 Weeks* with a clip of Prince simulating sex in one of his music videos.

They were lining up to sue us over that one.

CHAPTER SEVEN:
ACHTUNG, BABY!

Thursday, November 9, 1989, was a pretty rough day. I went home without hitting the bar, ordered some Japanese food from Obento Delight around the corner and was settling in to watch some television when the phone rang. It was about eight o'clock. It was Wayne.

"Get down to the Fortune Garden, mate. They're tearin' down the Berlin Wall! Communism's over and the place is going fackin' nuts."

The Fortune Garden up on Third Avenue was our latest bar of choice. The Racing Club was too crowded with hangers-on. A lot of us were suspicious that Mohammed the owner was inflating our bar tabs, and that Czechoslovakian waitress Wayne had been seeing was accusing him of being the father of her unborn child or something.

There was more room at the Fortune Garden.

I scarfed my Japanese takeaway in the cab on the way back uptown and arrived at the old Chinese restaurant to find most of the office staff there. Brennan was at a corner, on the phone. Gail the bartender was in her tightly-packed miniskirt, working doubletime filling drink orders.

We were sending a team of reporters and producers to East Germany, where everyday people were literally knocking down the Berlin Wall.

Brennan had already dispatched Ian Rae to the dais of a bigwig black tie event at the Pierre Hotel to beg Rupert Murdoch for permission to use his private jet. Rupert said he needed it to fly to his uncle's funeral but gave the okay to charter a similar aircraft for a hundred thousand dollars.

Peter must have felt guilt over pushing Dennis O'Brien aside. As I settled in at the bar, he asked Dennis if he wanted to go to Berlin. Dennis had no passport. Peter turned to me.

"I'm there."

David Lee Miller was already off getting packed. Gordon Elliott was ready to go. He wanted to hire a bulldozer and crash the Wall! Somebody was making calls to find one. Producer Nancy Gershwin had returned that very day from Berlin, where she'd interviewed Hitler's secretary for sweeps.

She could speak German and her bags were ready. We had Dick and Theresa Fisher for the crew, Maury as host—there was one other person we were still trying to locate.

We needed a German. Peter's daughter Yasmin was combing the bars in Germantown on the Upper East Side to find someone who'd fled East Germany whom we could bring back for a reunion with the loved ones left behind.

One by one, the powder blue Skyline towncars pulled up at Teterboro Airport in New Jersey to dislodge personnel and gear. There was Miller and Gordon and Maury and Nancy and Dick and Theresa—and our German. In typical *A Current Affair* fashion, Yasmin found Luther at an *Irish* pub called Ryan's Daughter. He was already a few sheets to the wind when she'd cajoled him into coming along for the ride of his life. In fact, he was so half-hearted about the prospect that Brennan had someone sit on him physically at the Fortune Garden while Yasmin went to the Bronx to pick up his passport.

If Benny Hill were to portray a Deutschlander, Luther would be him. He was a befuddled man, about fifty, with a messy head of sandy gray hair and a sweater and windbreaker over a big gut. Luther said he was in the construction business, though he did a few other things on the side. He came to America around the time the Wall was being constructed, leaving behind a brother named Helmut with whom he'd kept in some contact. Helmut would meet us at the Wall for the touching reunion.

I watched Luther as we waited for the jet. His eyes roved nervously. His face was covered in a film of sweat. As the pilot came out to tell us the jet was ready, Luther sighed and his shoulders slumped. He acted as if he were a war criminal, shackled and about to embark on an inevitable journey to face justice in his homeland.

Luther did not seem psyched to see his brother.

Another small plane later, we were in Berlin. It was early evening. We commandeered the first five taxicabs in line outside the terminal and headed to the Brandenburg Gate, the center of activity at the wall.

I was in the backseat with Maury. Police cars led motorcades of small, sputtery plastic sedans spewing puffs of smoke and making lawnmower noises.

"Those are the Trabis," the taxi driver said in decent English. "Trabants. The cars they drive in the East. Pieces of shit. People drive in from East Germany since the Wall opened and they can't find their way back."

We passed a fruit stand. It was cleaned out.

"Bananas," the driver said. "They cannot get bananas in the east. The East Germans took them all."

We were soon at the wide boulevard leading to the Brandenburg Gate, the magnificent centerpiece of what once was Berlin's major thoroughfare, now rising above and behind the cement and cinderblock Wall that was a slash through the soul of the western world. The Germans on the west had attacked the wall in recent years with their piss and layers of spray-painted graffiti. Now they'd risen up with hammers and picks and punched holes through various sections, creating their own checkpoints to let in cars from the East.

Even from half a mile away, it was a moving sight. Just as crowds gathered at the Dakota when John Lennon was murdered, ordinary Germans were drawn to the gate. It was the focal point for the celebration, the image the world would see.

We had to park blocks away on the esplanade and run through the crowds toward the action. There were young hippies and old folks, families of stunned parents and laughing children, moving closer to the cheering and din at the wall blocking the avenue.

When we approached the surreal scene, we could have been rushing to catch the opening act at a rock concert. Atop the graffitied Wall was another wall of young people in a moving, chanting mob. They sat, they stood, they danced. If they had tried something like this a few days before, they'd have been riddled with bullets, but tonight everyone was laughing and cheering and celebrating.

Behind them rose the statue of four horses and the Goddess of Peace, lit shadowy by the blinding television lights focused on the scene. The American networks had turned this section of the Wall into a giant television studio, and the stars of the show were not the young people who together brought down an economic and social system because of a collective love of rock 'n' roll and Levi jeans— no, the kids on the Wall would be reduced to an out-of-focus blur, an incomprehensible "natural sound up" between the lines of bland reporter script.

The stars of this show were, indisputably, the anchormen.

Two of the American networks, ABC and NBC, had big scaffolding platforms in place so their anchormen could stand in dramatic framing as they pontificated about the end of the Cold War era.

CBS did them one better.

Dan Rather was in the bucket of a cherrypicker. His hair was sprayed into an immovable helmet. His Burberry trenchcoat was set off by a jaunty, bright red scarf, seemingly stapled to his shoulder as he was sent winging and dipping and soaring over the crowd like some Holy Avenging Angel of news. If only they had let him carry the Bible he toted around the CBS newsroom. Gordon and I looked at Brother Dan. Gordon seethed.

A cherrypicker! That was Gordon's shtick! One morning on *Good Day New York*, Gordon used a cherrypicker to rise up the side of an apartment building in the Bronx to see who'd let him in a window for breakfast. When a grizzled old man pushed up his window, Gordon nattered away as usual and stuck his wireless microphone into the man's face. To Gordon's horror, the man held an electronic voice box to a wound at his throat. He was a victim of throat cancer! Gordon was ready to move up to the next floor, but before he could, the man began to speak. It turned out he hadn't spoken for months since the cancer operation, was in fact ashamed to speak— that is until Gordon showed up at his window. The man began to speak and wouldn't stop. He spoke to all New York. He spoke to all the tri-state area. His relatives saw him on the television, called other family members and cried. People who never knew the man cried as well, while Gordon and the old man with the voice box laughed and laughed.

Now Dan Rather was on Gordon's cherrypicker! We looked around to see who we could pay off for a moment at the controls, to send Dan on the ride of his life, but there was no time. We had a show to feed and we had only about an hour to collect the material because the only satellite time we could get was three p.m. New York time.

We hooked up with two camera crews from London and were ready to roll. We knew that Checkpoint Charlie was somewhere to the right. If we followed the Wall, eventually we'd run into it. David Miller took off on foot to stake our claim there. When Yves returned with a pickax he rented from a firehouse, Gordon grabbed the ax and ran, his overcoat flapping behind him, toward Dan Rather.

I feared it was the end for Dan, but the six-foot-seven-inch giant hurtled past the cherrypicker and bulled his way through the crowd to the Wall. Those on top took his hands, those below pushed his big beefy ass and Gordon was there, centerstage, towering above the others. Our cameras rolled with everyone else's. He pushed the crowd back, raised that pickax like John Henry standing up to a steam locomotive and—CLANK!—there was a shower of concrete and sparks and the crowd went berserk.

Gordon soaked in the applause, then found the smallest kid he could see and handed him the ax. The kid swung the ax, and as it was over his head, a hundred cameras flashed. The picture made magazine covers around the world.

Gordon hopped down. Maury did some quick segments. David Miller came back huffing and puffing with the goods. We had enough for a half hour show, all of it ready to be fed back in order.

The truck they'd booked for us from New York was the size of a Winnebego, run by two Germans whose command of English was left a deliberate mystery. One was a typically professional techie. His partner had greasy black hair, wore a leather coat and spectacles. He clenched a cigarette in his teeth and sneered as the Amerikaners boarded his bunker on wheels only a few hundred yards and across the Wall from where his hero died with Eva Braun.

The truck was impressive. It had two rooms, a couch, monitors, and a refrigerator. It was useless. CNN, with a pup tent and portable 12-inch dishes from Radio Shack, was bouncing signals off satellites to points all over the world. We couldn't even get the tapes to play back.

"What's going on?" I demanded.

The German in the coat pretended he couldn't understand us. Too bad he couldn't hide his nicotine grin.

The techie twirled some dials. "Is this PAL tape?"

"What's PAL tape?"

Adolph laughed.

"We use NTSC," Dick Fisher said. NTSC is the videotape standard in the States. In Europe, they use a system called PAL, which meant our tapes couldn't be played back on their machines.

"This truck only deals with PAL tape," the techie said.

"Yeah, well, we'll get it transferred. How long will it take?" There was no answer. The minutes were ticking away. I grabbed their phone to get in touch with New York. We needed PAL cameras and we needed to transfer this tape. The leatherman laughed and mumbled something.

"What's the trouble?" I asked.

"You will never leave Berlin," he said flatly.

"What are you talking about?"

"Heh heh heh."

I hung up. "What?"

"Thees ees a microwave truck, not a satellite truck, you fools."

I got in his face. "What are you telling me?"

"Your tape will never leave Berleen."

We were fucked. We missed the feed. Gordon carried me backward down the steps of the truck as I dragged the German, prying my fingers off his sauerbraten-stained leather lapels. My head bucked back and forth, attempting a version of the Glasgow kiss Dunleavy taught me a few weeks earlier at the Fortune Garden.

Gordon and I rushed through the journalistic encampment, opening our wallets and pulling out hundred dollar bills, trying to find someone who'd let us borrow some feed time, just enough to get some tape back for Friday night's show.

Meanwhile, someone in the New York office made a deal for us. ABC would let us feed some tape, and feed Maury live. Though we'd missed the early feed of the show, we'd be able to go live in New York and any other market that would take us.

⋯⋯◆⋯⋯

7:29 p.m., New York time, a minute away from 1:30 in the morning in Berlin: Tom Brokaw is standing on a crate, the Wall behind him, ready to do his standup. He turns to wink at his compadre Peter Jennings as the countdown to his standup begins—only to see Maury Povich standing in Jennings' spot.

Brokaw's jaw drops.

Back in New York, the screens in the control room are hash as *A Current Affair* is about to be sent out live, off the cuff to stations across the country. There are color bars. There is sound. There is Marlene, standing and conducting and praying, trying not to knock her headset off as she closes her eyes and hears the "three-two-one..." She looks up and through the hash there comes an image: Maury in his gray trenchcoat and turtle neck, live from Berlin and feeding tape as he spoke.

They cheer.

We were the only non-network show to go live from the Wall that first night. *A Current Affair* had edged into network news turf in the most brash manner. We weren't only covering the big stories, we were covering the biggest story of all. We had arrived.

Gordon gave me a boost to the top of the Wall. It must have been about six feet wide, a rush job with cheap eastern cinderblocks covered in slabs of muddy concrete. Where the kids had used the pickax I could see down into the Wall, and wouldn't you know it, most of it was hollow; I could see straight through the blocks into the ground. Not much of a wall at all, but it was packed with people, all of us moving against our wills as if caught in a roiling tide at Jones Beach, riding a collective surfboard that could wipe out at any time.

On the Western side, the crowds sang and cheered. To the East, there was only darkness, and in the shadows a scary formation of gun-toting soldiers.

Looking back, it seems so easy, but that night no one knew what would happen next. All those kids on the Wall were reveling in the exhilaration that comes only in knowing that at any moment the bullets could start flying and your life would be over like that. Just five months earlier, a youthful, triumphal protest turned to a massacre of hundreds—maybe thousands—at Tiananmen Square.

You never knew if the phone call would come from the Kremlin that they'd seen enough of this shit on CNN.

West Berlin was cold, a clinical and sixties-modern city, yet beautiful in its way, with the steel and glass buildings set against the deep green forest within and around it. We got a tour trying to find a hotel in the middle of the night, since our reservations went the way of the satellite truck. We somehow found rooms at the Hotel Berlin and scrounged up some beer and cheese before passing out.

The next day, Yves and I leased the biggest BMW towncar we could find, equipped with a car phone and large enough to fit six with room to spare. The sun began setting around four p.m. so we had a lot to get done in the daylight hours.

It was time to do our thing. The networks would be reporting the cold clinical facts. They'd run old footage of the Wall being built and people being killed trying to cross No Man's Land. They'd keep everything unemotional and aboveboard. *A Current Affair* was going to wallow in the great human stink of it all.

While David Miller was off on a shopping spree with a young East German couple, Gordon borrowed the BMW. He was hosting a radio talk show for the ABC network at the time, so he had Yves drive him around East Berlin while he went live from the car phone. Use of car phones was illegal in the East, so Gordon lay flat out on the back floor. Later, Gordon would interview prostitutes on the Reeperbahn to find how their new East Berliner clientele measured up.

Maury and I filed reports from East Berlin for the Fox stations' newscasts before recording segments for Monday's show. We got more material at the Wall and used hotel knives and whatever we could to hack off layers of graffiti paint, cheap cement, and pebbles from the Wall to bring home as souvenirs. We carried off large chunks from the base.

On Sunday, Maury and I drove with Luther, Yves, and one of the British camera crews past Checkpoint Charlie back into East Berlin. Our passports would allow us into the city for a few hours. We had to be out by curfew.

The plan was to interview some ordinary East Germans and then meet up with Luther's brother at the Alexanderplatz, the city's modern plaza centered on a tall tower with an onionbulb observation deck. We hauled everyone to the top while Luther called his brother to set up the reunion. It was to be the highlight of Monday's show.

"Hey, I can see Hitler's bunker from here!" I was so enthralled by this view beyond the Iron Curtain that I almost didn't notice the young man next to me. He was Fisher Stevens, the nerdy American actor who at the time happened to be living with Michelle Pfeiffer. Sorry, but for *A Current Affair*, the fall of the Berlin Wall and the end of communism was big—but an exclusive with Michelle Pfeiffer was bigger.

I told Maury to keep an eye on the actor as I ran the perimeter of the observation deck, checking out all the women. Michelle Pfeiffer was nowhere to be found. I introduced myself to Stevens and asked if he'd talk to Maury about his experiences.

"And it would be great if we could talk to your girlfriend."

No such luck. She was in Moscow, he said, shooting *Russia House* with Sean Connery. Stevens was making a stopover on the way home when the Wall came down.

Downstairs, Maury did a quick interview with Stevens and his pal anyway. Then we caught up with Luther, who seemed to be lost, scampering back toward Checkpoint Charlie. Yves and I blocked his path with the BMW and made him get in. We picked up Maury and strategized.

"So Luther, when's your fucking brother showing up?" Maury growled from the front passenger seat. "It's fucking cold, I wanna get this over with."

Luther sat in the back with me. "It is not possible. My brother, he will not come to East Berlin."

"But Luther. You promised."

"No. He will not do it."

"We didn't fly you all the way to East Berlin so you could go shopping," I said. "We promoted this piece. We have to do it."

"No."

"Then we'll go to him. What town does he live in?"

Luther named it. "It is far away. It is in the forbidden zone. No. It is impossible."

Impossible. Saying that word to me was like Lou Costello saying "Niagara Falls" to that psycho in the jail cell. Step by step. Inch by inch. Slowly I turned.

"Impossible? It's not impossible. If he won't come here, we'll go to him. We're driving there. We'll surprise him."

Luther was in a panic. "You cannot! We will be arrested. We are not authorized to leave the city. They will put us in jail."

"You have a German passport. They won't do anything to you."

"No. It is impossible. I will not."

"God-*damn* it!" I punched the roof of the car and punched it again. "Fuck! Whatever torture the East Germans can think up isn't half as bad as what'll happen to me if I don't deliver the story we promised. Do you understand?"

"He is crazy," Luther observed. "Maury, talk to him."

Maury looked straight ahead and tried almost successfully to suppress a grin. "I don't know, Luther. He's the boss."

"We promoted this fucking reunion!"

"I'm not going."

"Fuck you're not going!" I punched the ceiling again.

"You cannot force me."

"Watch me! You're my hostage. I'm forcing you. I'm taking you hostage!"

"Maury. Please—"

Maury shrugged and a laugh escaped.

I was in a frenzy. "And if the police stop us, you can say you were taken hostage by a crazy American!"

Yves piped up. "Uh, I'm with you, but I'm not authorized to drive. I could lose my license."

"I'll drive then. You're my hostage, too. The crew is my hostage. We're getting this fucking story!"

We dropped Maury off near a break in the Wall. He'd get a cab back to the hotel and do the rest of the news spots with Nancy Gershwin. We were off to hit the Autobahn, a motley crew of me, Yves and in the back seat, Luther surrounded by the British camera crew, Philip and Bob, two easygoing blokes who were ready for anything.

The BMW was made for the straight flat highway, cutting through the fields and forests on the way to Luther's brother's house. The sun went down over the Black Forest and the chill set in. Everyone was silent as we moved farther and farther from the safety of Berlin.

We stopped twice; once so we could all have a leak on the side of the highway, and again for petrol at the one service station on the Autobahn. We knew we were approaching the rest area when we hit the traffic jam, stretching over a hill and around a bend as far as the eye could see. All the little Trabis were lined up for the one island of gas pumps working that East German Sunday evening.

Yves said I should simply roll past them. In our tanksize BMW, not even the police would have the balls to pull us over. He was right. Emergency flashers ablink, I drove alongside the long queue to the gas pumps. When the manager saw us approaching, he opened an island especially for us.

The service station featured a big fluorescent store with sparsely-stocked shelves of items that were generally too expensive for the average East Germans who might stop in. One of the hundred Deutschmark bills in my wallet equalled a month's pay for most of them, Yves said.

"What does your brother need?" I asked Luther. "Chocolates? Nylons? Bananas?"

"There are no bananas," said Luther, glumly. We were no more than twenty kilometers from his brother's town. "Give me some money, please. I will buy him something special."

I pulled out a wad and Luther waddled off down the aisle with it.

Yves and I stocked up in a supermarket sweep of goods. If Luther's brother wasn't happy to see him, he'd at least be satisfied by all the goodies.

I dropped my armful on the checkout counter and looked around for Luther.

"You seen our boy?" I asked Yves.

"I have not seen him since you gave him the Deutschmarks."

"Shit." I thrust some bills at Yves— "Pay for this" —and burst onto the pavement. The crew was leaning against the BMW, chewing pork rinds and sharing a spliff.

"You seen Luther?"

Philip the cameraman shrugged. "Thought he was with you."

He and his partner burst into giggles.

I fucking lost Luther! I checked the men's room, looked across the highway. What if he got run over? Then, far down that line of flickering Trabant headlights, a jiggling shadow caught my eye.

I ran toward it. "Luther!"

Luther was working his way down the queue, holding up his crumpled bills, offering them to any driver who'd take him back to Berlin. He got panicky as he saw me approaching.

"Please! Please!" he pleaded in German. "Take me to Berlin!"

He backed up toward the highway, but stopped stepping into traffic and denting one of the slow Trabants crawling up the Autobahn. I took him by the elbow back to the BMW. Luther muttered to himself and whimpered. "No, no."

We were so close. I couldn't figure why this guy didn't want to see his brother.

I was hoping to be back in Berlin by seven p.m., but with the traffic, wrong directions, and the hubbub at the rest area, it was well past that time already. There was no way we were going to make it back to Checkpoint Charlie before the curfew.

We pulled off the Autobahn around 8:30. The town actually existed. It was Dr. Frankenstein time here; big mossy stone buildings side by side with Third Reich factories. The strong smell of noxious chemicals hung in the air, strong enough to taste and make us wary of breathing in the mist.

"So Luther, now where?"

Luther was broken. He'd given in. "It's here somewhere. A sugar factory. My brother lives in a house behind the gate. But I don't know how to get there, I swear."

We drove around until we came to a housing development. A young husband was unloading his wife and child from a car in front of their tract house. Maybe they'd spent their day lost in West Berlin, buying bananas. I instructed Yves on what to say. "Tell him if he brings us to the factory, we'll give him one hundred Deutschmarks."

"No. Fifty will be fine!"

"Yves! This is no time to get cheap. We're lost in the middle of fucking Uberland! They could call off democracy any minute here! Offer him a hundred!"

Yves made a deal. The man's eyes widened. A giant BMW, filled with smelly foreigners who wanted to get to the sugar factory. Who knows what really went on at the sugar factory? But fifty Deutschmarks? A hundred? He yelled something to the wife and he was off, leading the way.

The anonymous East German led us over hill and dale, across fields, through forests and around green lakes. "I bet the place is around the fucking corner, and he's trying to give us our money's worth. *We're running out of time.*"

Twenty minutes later, the Trabant slowed as it climbed a small one-lane road leading to a gate. Behind the gate was a big stone building that must have been the sugar factory. A stone house was alongside. A lone light blazed above the factory entrance.

"They're not home. Let's go," Luther said.

"C'mon, Luther. It's showtime." I turned to the crew. "You all set? Batteries, tapes?"

"You got it, guv."

"Yves, you take the goodies. Let's hit it."

Like a tabloid A-Team, we hit the house. I stood next to Luther at the oversize wooden door and placed his hand physically on the knocker.

He knocked twice, weakly. "No one is home, I tell you."

"Goddamn it." I took the clapper and banged away. "Hello! Hello!"

A light went on upstairs. There were noises.

"Hello! Hello! Helmut!" I yelled. Luther's brother was probably getting his gun. "Get this, guys."

The sun gun atop the camera went on as the door creaked open. Helmut was in his bathrobe. He shielded his eyes as he looked out into the glare. Then Luther stepped forward.

Helmut uttered a German curse and slammed the door.

"See, I told you!" Luther turned to run.

"What the—" I started banging again. "Yves, do something."

When the door opened abruptly, young Yves began his best bullshit rap, inveigling, begging, crying. Helmut let us in.

We stood in the kitchen, camera rolling, as we handed Luther the gifts and Luther, on camera, handed them to Helmut and his wife. Helmut's wife was weeping with consternation, and she trembled as she opened some of the booze we brought. I poured doubles for the brothers. Helmut calmed down a bit after the gift presentation. I stood to the side of the camera and threw them lines to say.

"Thank Maury Povich for reuniting you."

"What is Maury Povich?" Helmut asked.

"Please, just thank him and we'll go," Luther said.

"God bless you, Maury Povich."

I gestured for them to hug. They did, gingerly.

In the end we got a good fifteen minutes of reunion, lots of B-roll in the house—we got the story and it more than satisfied the promo. This was history.

On the way out, Philip stopped to shoot some exteriors of the big Bavarian house with all the lights on.

The young husband was waiting in his car by the gate. Yves gave him the high sign and he sped off, leading us back to the Autobahn. He pulled over when he got us in sight of the highway. Yves and I got out of the car and loaded him down with all the sundries we had left over.

I handed him a pack of nylons and a bottle of booze. "Tell him to give this to his beautiful wife," I instructed Yves. Then there was the chocolate—boxes of it. "And this is for his handsome son." Yves translated. "And this—" I pulled out 150 Deutschmarks and handed it to the driver before Yves could stop me. "This is for him. Tell him he must never tell anyone where it came from. And he must never—ever—tell anyone that he saw us here. Ever."

Yves gave him the instructions, gravely, and the man nodded back. He took my hand and spoke. "He says thank you on behalf of his family," Yves said.

"No," I said. "Tell him we give *him* thanks on behalf of the people of *A Current Affair*."

We were off, leaving this poor flabbergasted East German sitting on the side of the road in his Trabant with a year's worth of chocolate, a few nights' worth of booze, stockings that were bound to get him laid with the fraulein—and a month and a half's salary—all because he happened to step out of his car in the middle of former communist nowhere on a Sunday night.

That was the glory of *A Current Affair*.

Luther fessed up on the road back to Berlin. His brother hated him.

"We could see that, Luther."

"Ever since Las Vegas."

"What?"

Yes, these two brothers, separated by that great Berlin Wall, had not seen each other in over eight months, not since they met for a vacation in a hotel-casino on the great Las Vegas Strip. It seems Luther was into more than one business about which Helmut did not approve.

"Everything moved so quickly when that girl pulled me out of Ryan's Daughter. By the time I was sober enough to realize, I was in a jet with you crazy nuts."

We'd deal with that later. The lights of East Berlin had enveloped us. I switched places with Yves as we narrowed down on Checkpoint Charlie, hours after it had closed for the night. We could be spending the night in detention—which would mean we'd miss another feed.

"Give me all your passports," Yves ordered as he rolled toward the gate. Luther whimpered.

"Should we hide the grass?" Philip asked.

"Shhh!" Yves was smiling toward the approaching German guards. He stuck his head out the window and spoke quickly, with many hand gestures.

The guard leaned over and squinted as he looked us over. The camera crew, hippy dippy and trying not to laugh, Luther, visibly sweating, and me, with the tapes inside my coat.

The guard exchanged more words with Yves before walking into the administrative building with our passports.

"What did he say?"

"He wanted to know why we're here past curfew. He said it's very bad."

"Should we bribe him?"

"No, we have to wait."

Luther moaned.

I looked at the black and white striped gate that kept us from freedom, the spikes in the road, the gate to the West, the armed guards pacing around us. It was only about thirty yards to freedom. I could run around the gate and not look back, just keep running across the bridge, run right along the Wall and into the city. As long as I didn't look back, they wouldn't shoot me. Not now. Not this weekend.

My hand was on the door handle. "Yves, I'm going."

"You can't go." He snapped the master door lock.

"Open it, man."

Yves refused. "Now you are *my* hostage."

"You can't run, mate," soundman Bob said. "Are you fuckin' crackers?"

"We've got to make the feed. We only have an hour. Unlock the fucking door."

Yves unlocked it. The border guard was returning to the car with our passports. "If he says we can't get in, I'm running for it."

The guard leaned into the car and said a few harsh words to Yves. Yves lowered his head and acted contrite. God, this kid was good. What was he saying? I looked around. The coast was as clear as it was going to get.

The border guard handed back the passports and signaled for the other soldier to raise the gate.

Our feed point was another truck at the Brandenburg Gate. The crowds were gone now, but the networks and news organizations remained. Gordon, David Miller, and Dick and Theresa were in the truck feeding their raw material. Everything had gone well, beyond expectation, but I was holding the gold.

"Maury told me. You hijacked the crew to East Germany?" Gordon laughed.

"Wait til you see it. I got tears, the brothers hugging, they thank Maury, it's fucking great."

I handed the tape to Theresa and she popped it in. There were the color bars. There was some roadside B-roll, shots of the East, the exterior of the house and factory.

"Here it comes. Watch this."

The shot was out of focus, but eventually Luther and Helmut came into view. They hugged. Luther said a few words. The brothers raised their glasses in a toast. They spoke to the camera. There was an exterior of the house with the lights on.

"Great mate, all thirty seconds of it," Gordon laughed. "Really worth the trip."

He was exaggerating, but not by much. My eyes widened. "No, wait. There was more. I have like fifteen minutes. They do teases and everything. The wife cries. Theresa, roll it back."

There was no more. Sure enough, most of the reunion was missing.

"Great stuff, Dirty Burtie!" Gordon let loose a lusty laugh.

I bolted out of the truck and found Philip. "Mate, did you shoot the reunion on another tape?"

"No, only one tape, dad."

"But it goes from the B-roll to about thirty seconds of the reunion to the exterior again. It's not there."

"Aw, it's the bleedin' camera, dad. I meant to get that looked at. It does 'at sometimes, dig? Rewinds on itself."

"Oh." I walked into the truck in a daze. "His camera rewinds on itself once in a while."

Gordon laughed. "And you went all that way!" He teased. "HAHAHAHA!"

"NO!" I reared back to punch the wall, but Gordon grabbed my fist and again lifted me out of the truck and planted me in the middle of the boulevard.

"Take a deep breath, mate."

Instead, I found the nearest garbage can and went berserk, pummeling and kicking it while Gordon laughed and applauded.

Luther wandered over. "What is he doing?"

I stopped and walked toward Luther. "We're going back. We're going back!"

Luther scampered away in terror. Gordon took off after him.

Theresa handed me the phone. It was Brennan in New York. "Mate, it's fine, it's enough, don't worry, we've got a couple of minutes. It's great."

"But the good stuff isn't there."

"No one knows what you don't have. What you got is great. Everyone here agrees."

The crew got away unscathed. Yves drove Gordon, David Miller, and a very nervous Luther back to the hotel. I stayed on the car phone, talking to a producer in New York, asking about the real reaction to the reunion and whether I should go back to reshoot it.

"We got what he wanted. What does this crazy man expect?" Luther mumbled. "I cannot go back. I will have a heart attack and drop dead if I do that again."

Everyone got out of the car at the hotel, leaving me in the back seat with the phone. Maury was waiting upstairs with the drinks. When I hung up, I learned another secret of BMWs. They lock from the outside. I was stuck in the car for a half hour before Yves came down to get me.

Monday's show rated its ass off (though Raf with his usual team spirit attributed the ratings to the earlier promotion of a David Miller love triangle murder story that ran all weekend). After lobbying Brennan unsuccessfully to let us roll on into Amsterdam to shoot sex stories, we organized a final party with the crew.

There were a dozen of us at one of the hipper brasseries. Americans, Germans, Brits, and anyone else who happened by, all of us jetlagged and wired, trading war stories and drinking up all the beer and vodka they could throw our way.

The strong among us carried on to a stark Schprockets-like nightclub tucked away in one of the damp back alleys. Once Yves got us inside, we saw why the place was such an attraction. Every woman was Nico, their slim bodies swathed in velvet and their eyes smudged with black shadow. The Krautrock thumped on the speakers and variations of Jagermeister rattled on the tables.

Gordon and I walked into the men's room and stopped in our tracks. Lines of cocaine were spread out on the urinals and sinks and strangers were sharing their stashes. They beckoned us over.

Communism had fallen.

There was one last mission. In the early morning as dawn broke gray and cold over the city, Yves drove the BMW through the empty streets of West Berlin toward the Brandenburg Gate. He skidded off the road and fishtailed to a rest on the dark dirt footpath along the Wall. The forces-that-be had indeed seen enough of the frenzied displays atop it. Soldiers were again posted sentry on the Wall above us.

The soldiers regarded me curiously as I staggered toward them, a bottle of Lowenbrau in my hand. "Mate. I want to buy your hat. Your hat, mate. I'm from America and I want to buy your hat."

The soldier didn't respond. I had Yves try it in German, and with a few apologies added, he did.

The soldier shook his head grimly.

"Mate, a hundred Deutschmarks for your hat. Let the breeze blow it off your head. No one will be the wiser."

No response.

I stood tall and saluted, catching my balance as I roared this time: "In the name of Peter Brennan, *A Current Affair,* and the people of the great United States of America, I hereby ask you for your hat in the name of peace. And as a gesture of goodwill, I will give you two hundred Deutschmarks!"

"No—" Yves was staggered by the amount.

Another soldier meandered to his colleague and whispered something under his breath. They both shook their heads.

This went on for a few more exchanges, me getting louder and more insistent.

"C'mon, man, it's a month's pay. You can buy a new fucking hat. It's for my boss! C'mon! This is history!"

Finally, the soldier spoke. "Go away."

"Aaaagh!" I heaved the Lowenbrau bottle. "I piss on your Wall! I piss on this symbol of hatred and division! One world! Someday you will see!" The guard remained imperturbable, even when I whipped out my dick and pissed on his Wall.

TO: ALL ACA STAFF
FROM: PETER BRENNAN
    Without getting too schmaltzy, there's no episode of my time in media that's given more pride than the effort and effect of the Berlin Wall experience, both at this end and in Berlin. Next to war itself, it was the most important story of our time in my opinion, and *A Current Affair* was involved and delivered to the most demanding expectations. Monday night's show was as good as we've ever done and by far better than anything produced by a network or other TV organization in this country.
    Thanks.

CHAPTER EIGHT:
KINGS OF COMEDY

Oh, it's lonesome away from your kindred and all,
by the campfire at night where the wild dingoes call.
But there's nothing so lonesome, morbid or drear
than to stand in the bar of a pub with no beer.
— "Pub With No Beer," Australia's national anthem

We were drunk; drunk with glory, drunk with power, drunk with the very excitement of being around ourselves. After Berlin, the Fortune Garden became our permanent center of business. We'd trudge up there sometime around five, walk into the traditional, classy restaurant, take a right at the murky lobster tank, and sweep into the large bar-lounge that opened into the kitchen. There was a piano no one played and a karaoke machine no one sang along to. The regulars were few: affluent alcoholics seeking refuge for a few hours on the way home from the office. Among them was a hangdog newsbreak anchor from the NBC network who lived in the neighborhood. Each night he'd sag over his scotch in silence, watching us wrestle and hoot and talk too loud, never joining in, never shaking his head in disapproval.

Behind the bar most nights was Gail, a ripe young dead ringer for Demi Moore who poured her babyfat body into tight, short skirts and liked to shimmy herself up on the ice chest near the telephone, drinking Shirley Temples between orders and giving the male patrons a look at more of her legs than anyone but her loved ones had a right to see.

We'd position ourselves near the center of the bar. The room was ours and it would begin to fill early. We'd line up the vodkas and spread the cigarette packs across the bar. Occasionally, unwary females from the office would settle in next to us and defile the holy drinking space with pupu platters of gelatinous dumplings and dried-out spareribs. The hardened female proteges would match us for the first several rounds and entice us to the seats wedged in against the wall for slurry ear talk and come-ons.

Then there was Raf. Whether he arrived alone or in a group, Rafael would take a seat near the corner of the bar, six or ten barstools from the crowd, cowboy hat tipped over his eyes as he nursed a glass of Johnny Walker Black and muttered monotonal words of depth to Gail, who sipped her Shirley Temple through a straw and giggled in agreement.

We'd stay at the Fortune Garden well toward midnight. The crowd would thin to a few diehards. Brennan would drink himself to a point of ultimate clarity, dispensing wisdom, advice, instructions, and charm.

There were a half dozen of us left a week or so after Berlin. Wayne smoked, held a beer, and growled at his news director girlfriend until she was reduced to a silent wiping of tears from her eyes. Dunleavy sparred with one of the producers from *The Reporters*.

"There's gonna be three hits in this fight, mate," he warned. "I'm gonna hit you. You're gonna hit the ground, and the ambulance is gonna hit eighty."

"I'll fight ya," Wayne offered.

"Not unless you want a shirtful of broken ribs," Dunleavy taunted.

Brennan excused himself to use the men's room. He backed off the stool, caught his balance on the second step, stuck the cigarette back in his mouth and walked out the door.

Dunleavy was back to his boxing lesson. "Look at him. He ducks and weaves like Clive Churchill!"

The hour was late. The talk was getting more vague. I finished my last vodka and tonic of the night and was ready to head home when there was a clamor at the door.

"No! No! You put back! You no take robster! No take!"

"Aah!" In one hand topping a wet sleeve, Brennan held a flexing live lobster away from the grasp of the small Chinese owner. In the other hand he held his cigarette. "I'm buying it," he said. "I am liberating this lobster!"

He tossed the crustacean onto the bar and the creature made a sad crawl for freedom. "How much?"

"No. No riberate," the old man insisted. "You no buy. People eat robstah here. I have to charge furr price. Twenty seven dorrah!"

"Twenty seven dorrah then. Put it on my tab." Brennan looked fondly at the lobster in front of him and picked at the thick red rubber band holding its big claw closed. "I'm saving your life, mate."

"I take care." The owner brought the lobster into the kitchen.

"My good deed for the day, mate," Brennan said. "Every night I walk past that lobster tank and every night I see those poor creatures awaiting death. If I can save just one—"

"Here you robstah." The old man had wrapped the live lobster in brown paper. It moved like a mummy, struggling to free itself.

"Have fun, mate," I said. "I gotta go."

"Here." Brennan handed me the damp package. "Take this."

"What am I gonna do with it?"

"I want you to set it free."

"Where? In the sewer?"

"In the river. You're going down to the Village. Have the cabbie drive you to the piers."

"I'll get raped at the piers."

"Have the driver wait. Walk to the river and set the lobster free."

"It'll be poisoned in the river."

Brennan stood. He'd regained the clarity. "Listen to me. This is your job." He looked me in the eye. "Tonight, I want you to set this lobster free. Go."

I sat in the back of the cab, rushing through the sparse traffic in the middle of Times Square, stroking my little bundle. At Madison Square Garden, I whispered, "It's your lucky day, guy."

I left the cab at the triangular corner of Waverly and Charles. It was late. I'd bring the lobster to the riverside in the morning. In the kitchen I unwrapped the parcel in the sink. The lobster's movements were slower and more pained.

"Hey lobster, wake up." I ran some water over its back, but the refreshing chill had no effect. When I returned from the bedroom, there was no change in its condition.

So I filled a pot with water, lit the stove, and boiled the fucker.

In December, Gerald Stone had another idea to throw into the *A Current Affair* mix: consumer stories. He'd entered into a deal with a freelance investigative reporter out of Florida.

Steve Wilson seemed to have turned up on every local news and syndicated show in the country at one time or another. He was a solid, entertaining reporter with an instantly recognizable style; a portly, disheveled pitbull who got on a story and didn't give up. Be it governmental rip-off or consumer scam, Wilson would get the goods and go for that age-old local news trick, the unexpected on-camera confrontation. "Sir, why are you stealing from these people?"

At worst, the alleged offender would invite Steve and his crew in for a coffee and a sit-down interview. At best, he'd run away or attack the cameraman and Steve in a torrent of obscenities.

Wilson was so good because he was so untelegenic. Years before Michael Moore cashed in with his fat boy outsider routine in *Roger & Me*, Steve Wilson played the archetypical tubbo who everyone picked on in school, now all grown up and getting revenge.

He was still getting compliments at the time for pursuing a story about

CBS News for a short-lived syndicated afternoon show. His target was Dan Rather, and for days, Wilson would lie in wait like a big game hunter, poised to ambush Gunga Dan when he arrived at the CBS studios on West 57th Street. When Dan came into the clear, Wilson would follow him down the sidewalk and hector him with questions the tightly-wound Rather would not answer.

One afternoon, it happened one time too many. When Rather got to the revolving door of CBS, he snapped. He grabbed Wilson's microphone, went chin to chin with the fat man and said the two words no network TV anchor ever wants his public to hear him utter, not even in rage: "*Fuck you.*"

The soundbite, translated as "bleep you," turned up on every local newscast in the country—except, of course, on CBS affiliates.

It was great television. The only question was whether this type of local news activism had any place in the saucy, racy, though current events-conscious mix of *A Current Affair*. Wilson's reports seemed better suited to a show like *Inside Edition*, which had taken on former *20/20* executive producer Av Westin as a consultant.

Gerald Stone was to be humored, though. So Peter and I went over Wilson's list of suggested stories, found a few that had some promise of humor and emotion, and sent him off to do his thing.

All good things come to an end. Wilson's ended with a story he chased down without telling us. I guess he wanted to surprise us. Wilson had a tip that *Cops*, Fox's new reality show which followed law enforcement officers through White Trash and Black Ghetto America, was staging some stories. A cameraman had given him a piece of tape that allegedly showed the producers or cops planting or moving heroin paraphernalia at the scene of a drug bust because it made the segment work better.

With evidence in hand, Steve Wilson and crew burst in on the *Cops* production offices. "I'm Steve Wilson from *A Current Affair!*" he announced. "I'd like to speak to the producers of *Cops!*"

The *Cops* people told him to wait in the lobby and got on the phone to Gerald Stone's office in New York. "What the fuck is going on here?" they inquired.

So now we were sitting in Gerald Stone's office with Steve Wilson on the speaker phone. Gerald leaned foward and asked Wilson if it was true that he raided the office of *Cops*.

"Why, yes. I had the goods. They planted evidence for their show."

"That remains to be seen," Gerald said. "But did you realize that *Cops* is a Fox show?"

"Yes. What does that matter?"

"Did you realize that *A Current Affair* is a Fox show?"

"Yes, so?"

"Did you ever think that you were exposing a show on our network?"

"Yes, but they did wrong."

"But they're a Fox program."

"I know. I heard you. What's the point?"

Gerald leaned back, exasperated. Even in the land Down Under, he'd not been subject to this kind of logic. How could he argue?

"Uh, Steve—" I spoke to the speaker phone. "I think the problem is, they're us. It's like *A Current Affair* doing an expose on *The Reporters* show down the hall. It's like us exposing... ourselves."

"I don't understand the problem."

Gerald's face relaxed into inscrutable calm. He'd reached a state of Zen breakdown.

We had Wilson unclench his jaws and drop the *Cops* story. He faded into the wide television waters, to resurface again and again, bobbing up on everything from national news magazines to local newscasts.

Gerald would soon be returning to calmer waters, as well.

Going into December, Bruce Springsteen laid off the E Street Band and there was an explanation of why Sammy Davis, Jr. didn't want to sing that extra number at the end of the *Muscular Dystrophy*—I mean *Jerry Lewis*—*Telethon*. He had throat cancer.

Sammy's sixty-fourth birthday was on December eighth. We ended the show with a tribute. Maury mentioned Sammy's throat trouble and wished him the best. Dissolve to video of Sammy performing. Roll credits.

I happened to wander into the edit room where a young producer was editing the credit roll. There on the screen was great footage of Sammy, singing and dancing onstage—at age four.

The only trouble was the song he was singing: "I'll Be Glad When You're Dead, You Rascal You."

I had the producer select an alternative.

I encountered 1990 on the island of Mustique in the Caribbean West Indies. Robin Dorian had told me it was the place to be on New Year's Eve because Mick Jagger and David Bowie always performed at a party in a tiny harbor bar called Basil's.

I booked a boat and captain on the last day of 1989, sailed over from Bequia and, as promised, pulled up in front of Basil's, an open-air bar and restaurant built on a dock over the tiny harbor, serving up huge lobsters and giant drinks.

I was walking from the bar with another Hurricane drink that afternoon when I bumped into a little barefoot man surrounded by children. It was Mick Jagger.

Back at our table, I put the 35mm still camera to my eye, and pretended to photograph my girlfriend while actually snapping off half a roll of the craggy little rock star.

That night, curtains of rain whipped down and gale force winds battered the postage stamp island. Basil's New Year's party carried on regardless, water dripping through the thatched roof and washing up on the dock floor as the reggae music throbbed on. Jagger's daughter Jade hosted the bash, and all the locals, of which they thought we were some, were invited. We drank champagne and shots of warm liquids and when the clock struck twelve stood in the drenching torrent to welcome in the nineties.

Mick Jagger remained behind the walls of his Japanese-style estate, but around one a.m., I got a picture of David Bowie sweeping in, his orange hair slicked back wet. He was wearing a sarong.

A few weeks later, Howard Stern appeared on Joan Rivers' talk show and got Angie Bowie to admit she once caught her ex-husband David and Mick Jagger in bed together.

We ran a story on that evening's show, mentioned the official denials, and pulled out my Mustique photos. "Coincidentally," we wrote, "one of A Current Affair's producers caught Jagger and Bowie on New Year's Eve, in the same tiny bar in Mustique, the postage stamp island of the rich and famous." It sounded as if we'd been on the story for weeks. "Mick was dressed for the beach. David was dressed...more formally." That's where we revealed Bowie wearing his dress.

Later that winter, Wayne and I went to Las Vegas to shoot a series of specials for February sweeps. It was the beginning of the end of the old Vegas era, and we caught it on the way out. We shot a mix of emotional A Current Affair stories, like the one about the black owner of an escort service who received a transplanted heart from the body of white actor Jon-Erik Hexum. A newspaper columnist was rallying against the man because he didn't change his ways once he got a second chance at life. We also did stunts, getting Maury onstage at the Hilton with Wayne Newton and convincing Maureen O'Boyle to perform as a showgirl at the Aladdin.

The story that most impressed Wayne, though, was a feature I put together on the Hilton's Elvis Presley Suite. The place where Elvis stayed was believed to be haunted by his ghost, ever since the jacuzzi bubbled on mysteriously while Englebert was sleeping there.

After we picked up some file tape from the Las Vegas News Bureau, I saw why the story might be true. There was footage of Elvis outside the hotel while it was being built. Wearing a hardhat and colorful scarf, he looked over blueprints with the construction workers and architects. "If Elvis *were* to haunt a hotel, the Hilton would be the place," I wrote. "It's a little known fact that Elvis helped design the hotel..."

Wayne howled at the line, holding it as proof I could never tell the truth. I argued that it was true. "Look at the picture..."

Back in New York, there were rumors Dennis O'Brien would be shunted off to *The Reporters*, which was sinking fast. Gerald Stone was no longer in charge of *A Current Affair*. Soon he'd be on a slow boat back to Sydney, where he'd find success again with the franchise version of *60 Minutes*. The damage he left behind in the states would never be repaired.

We were now at the mercy of Ian Rae, vice president of news, and now Brennan's co-executive producer. Ian was an unpolished, rough and tumble capo in the Murdoch Mafia; the apotheosis of the Murdoch loyalist-lifer; a man of simple talent who would be guaranteed a job for life because he'd gladly lay down that life for his Boss.

Ian's nickname was "the Pig," whether because of his pride, integrity and guts or his disconcerting—and one would think singularly Outbackian—habit of simultaneously picking at his butt crack and nose was never made clear. In any case, the Pig title was affectionate and used by most everyone. Ian himself was proud of the appellation. It made him feel like one of the boys he could never really be, because Ian lacked the derring-do and reckless merriment of his crew. He would always be management, and though Aussies like Brennan were joined to Ian Rae like family, it didn't mean they liked working for him. Brennan, especially, didn't like it at the *Star* and he didn't like Ian taking credit for inventing *A Current Affair*.

By March 1990, Peter, Wayne, Raf and I had *A Current Affair* working like a well-oiled gun. Raf led the way in perfecting a new kind of re-enactment based on Peter's vision of the "mini-movie," not only telling stories and building up to ironic twists, but shooting and editing them like actual films.

The show was evolving, after all, and no part was evolving in a more strange way than the day-of-air stories. They were often more commentary on the news and personalities than simple recaps of the latest tabloid headlines of the day. Be it from Hollywood or Washington, there was little we took seriously.

There was nowhere else this particular direction could take us but straight into comedy.

One of the most important ingredients in the success of *A Current Affair* was a sense of humor, a sense of fun. The loss of this humor along the way was a major factor in the decline of the genre. At the dawn of the nineties though, everything was a laugh, nothing was serious, and no story brought out the yuks in grander proportions than the adulterous doings of

Donald Trump.

Trump had been the butt of *A Current Affair* humor in the past. When Soviet president Gorbachev was in town, Gordon Elliott found a lookalike, drew a purple stain on his forehead and squired him around town in a limousine. When Trump heard that Gorby was on the sidewalk outside his Trump Tower, he actually took the golden elevator down and walked out to the sidewalk with his aides for an official greeting.

He was exposed as the self-important asshole he was.

Now, Trump was apparently dumping his wife Ivana for a patootie named Marla Maples. Marla was a Southern belle doing whatever she could to claw her way to the top in the entertainment business. This was made clear by the number of videotapes sent our way—Marla bouncing braless in a proposed aerobics video, Marla in various beauty contests, Marla cozying up to an older, grabby, smoochy contest judge—we couldn't write checks fast enough to buy up all of the video people tried to sell us.

A couple of years earlier, *A Current Affair* had gotten great publicity staging a phony telethon for Peter Holm, who was suing Joan Collins for alimony. They'd even gotten Holm on the show, thinking he was really going to get the money toted on the mock "Peter Meter."

Raf had that in mind when he took his re-enactment and mini-movie innovations to the next step by staging the first "pre-enactment," an entire show dedicated to the inevitable Trump divorce trial. He shot mock testimony in an old courtroom in Queens and when he had it all edited, Wayne and I got pissed out of our brains at the Fortune Garden, rolled back to the office at one in the morning, and wrote a script to wrap around the segments. We cracked ourselves up to the point of urination with teases like "the breast is yet to come."

The show aired on a Friday night. The following week's *Newsweek* said it was funnier than *Saturday Night Live*.

We weren't just top tabloid journos now. We believed we were comedy writers. Brennan even got the Fox station to put up the money for us to do a comedy pilot.

We'd call it *FUNY*, as in "funny"—as in "Fuck You New York."

The show would be performed in the style of a local newscast, with taped comedy bits interpersed with mock news items and interviews. Gordon would play the sportscaster. Robin Dorian wanted to portray the gossip columnist. We'd get a tall beautiful blonde to play the weather girl.

One night that week, after hours trying out jokes on Gail in the Fortune Garden bar, Peter, Wayne, and I set off in search of our anchorman.

We piled into a cab, Wayne and I in back, Peter up front with the driver. "Mate, we need to go to a comedy club."

"What comedy club is?" the driver replied. "Address club comedy you want."

Wayne and I cracked up again. "We gotta put this guy in the show!" Wayne wheezed.

"The Comic Strip," I told the driver.

"Who strip?"

I gave Wayne a whack. "Second Avenue in the eighties somewhere. Head up to the nineties and work your way down."

We stumbled into the Comic Strip flashing press and business cards in time for the late set. A comedian named Don McHenry was on the stage. He was a smart aleck in a working class Dennis Miller mode, with a good outer boroughs accent. We hired him on the spot. A star was born.

The taping and creating of *FUNY* would have to be done around *A Current Affair* when various technicians were available. That meant taping would begin at midnight Wednesday. On Tuesday after work, I went to the Friars Club and got five old Borscht Belt comics to sit around a table. There was Cindy's ancient husband Joey Adams with Henny Youngman, Gene Bayliss, Mickey Friedman, and Ed Melvin. The idea was for me to throw out a famous name, like Dan Quayle, Ed Koch, or new Mayor Dinkins, and one or more of them would respond with an instant joke, the cameraman moving around to catch the zingers as they flew.

I began with Dan Quayle.

"Who's Dan Quayle?"

"Dan Quayle? He's not funny," said Friedman.

"Do we get paid for this? I want to get paid," Melvin said.

Joey Adams popped up. "A lawyer joke. Lawyers are funny."

Bayliss poked Youngman. He jumped awake with a start. "Take my wife, please." He said it automatically.

"Man goes into a lawyer's office..."

We finished the writing and gathered in the news studio sometime after midnight. The director was Paul Nichols, a young man with long blond hair and a serious manner who directed *Good Day New York*. He and his staff were out of sight in a control room a floor above. We had enough script for an hour-long show with a few taped pieces. I managed to get a minute or so of useable material out of the old comics and there were some slapstick bits done by some of McHenry's comedy pals, including a cab ride with the doubletalking hipster comic, Professor Irwin Corey.

Wayne produced a taped segment on a fictional reporter named Justin Time who always arrived at the scene of a story moments after everyone else left. Without anyone to interview or anything to shoot, he was forced to re-enact what happened. In this case, he pretended to be old Harry Helmsley, falling down a flight of stairs and breaking a leg. It was in the best of taste:

a young comedian imitating the addled geriatric Alzheimer's victim, moaning and groaning in pain.

Most of the jokes followed the *Saturday Night Live* news format, with McHenry reading funny captions for news photos of the week, one-liners like "Back home in New York, fears of Japanese takeover fanned again...at the gland opening of Klazy Eddie's in Lockafeller Center," enlivened with recitations of actual corrections from *The New York Times*.

Cheridah was to read a commentary in her proper accent called "Why is it So?" She rehearsed it and was funny enough, but as soon as the camera light went on, she froze. She didn't foul up, she didn't stumble. She froze. I'd only heard of something like that happening. We were so shocked that after a dozen tries, we cancelled the bit instead of playing it for laughs.

It got worse from there. Another of my contributions was the weather report, indeed performed by a statuesque, leggy beauty in a spandex miniskirt, standing with a pointer at a map of the United States.

"Temperature's been normal in most parts," she said. "But down here—" she pointed to Florida on the map, "—You see there's a slight chill moving up the leg."

As she moved the pointer from the Keys toward Daytona, the camera was supposed to shift and move up her legs before getting back to a wide shot of the map.

"It's climbing up past the panhandle...and around the bottom of the country." She turned. Her pointer slid toward Texas, and with side-splitting hilarity, the camera was to zoom in on her hips!

"But that's turning to a warm front across the entire lower third, lingering around the farmbelt—" you guessed it, "—moving ever so slowly across the midsection and over the plains, while there's more warmth sliding down the Gulf Coast."

She licked her lips. "Should get mighty steamy down there.

"In the north, Jack Frost should come calling by morning! Snow is lingering over the mountains; skiing is especially good in the Rockies and Grand Tetons."

Fuck Noel Coward. To hell with Steve Martin and Monty Python. Move over, Benny Hill! At the point the actress talked about mountains, the directions called for the camera to push in on her heaving breasts! This was comedy!

The routine was supposed to wind up with "humidity rising but *going down* overnight, with relief by morning, followed by showers"—but a shout from the control room ended everything.

"Stop. Hold it. No, no, no!" The director didn't think it was funny. The woman behind the camera was outraged. She simply moved the camera up and down from the weathergirl's foot to head.

After a break and an explanation to the director that this was supposed to be bawdy, over-the-top comedy, Gordon Elliott got to the anchor desk to perform his bit as sportcaster Adrian L. Adrian.

"Ah yes, the continuing story of man's inhumanity to man," he said, reading from the TelePrompTer a script he wrote himself. "The flesh, the flash, and the fumble. Cold locker walls and men with balls. It's irresistible viewing to any red-blooded American. And tonight is no exception, the mighty muscled few who play the field with force.

"I will always be there to offer my support—size twelve—but I draw the string at unprovoked contact. Without so much as a phone call or an appointment, the thuggish throwing of knuckle against buckle. Children, avert your eyes as we look back in anger at some of the season's more unpleasant peasants and how they take sport one step too far."

Of course, Gordon read the entire script in the lisping, effeminate voice of the stereotypical Australian "poof." It didn't go over well with the director. Nichols was gay and proud. His angry voice boomed through the studio that the segment didn't work.

Then he walked out of the control room.

Everything stopped until Gordon agreed to read it "straight."

Needless to say, *FUNY* never saw the light of day. With crew expenses and an overtime shoot lasting from midnight til dawn, the cost neared $50,000, but the pilot was never seen by anyone in the organization—not even the executive in Los Angeles who authorized it.

Brennan took one look at the pilot and had the master tapes destroyed.

There was other funny business that month at *A Current Affair*. Word was out that *Hard Copy* found someone to provide them with our list of planned sweeps stories.

There are few things more frustrating to an innovative tabloid journalist than coming up with a story out of thin air, developing it, turning it into a totally rateable idea—and then seeing it first turn up on another show or in one of the tabloid newspapers.

Our stories were the very essence of what made the show a hit. We had the imagination that the other shows couldn't provide, and the theft of ideas was costing Fox money.

It was obvious the culprit was stealing the stories by hacking into our computer system, so Fox set a trap. With J.B. Blunck leading the team, they let the LAPD and Treasury Department in on the plan, then laid the bait in the system and waited for the hacker to bite.

It was a false story in the *A Current Affair* computer system that would be too good to pass up. It said that Ron Reagan, Jr. had a gay lover named

Tyrone living in a suburb of Los Angeles. The information included a fake contact number and address.

The hacker hacked in. *Bingo*. A federal trace on the Fox computer phone line led straight to an apartment in Studio City. Within minutes, police, federal agents, and Fox cameramen knocked down the culprit's door and found him still logged in at his computer, with incriminating floppy discs and a gun to boot.

Turns out he was a freelancer who'd worked in the L.A. office around the time I arrived at *A Current Affair*. Stuart Goldman was an eccentric who'd played bluegrass music in the seventies and presented himself as an investigative reporter. After his freelance gig was finished, he apparently kept Riva's access code to our system and used it to break in.

Goldman claimed he was gathering evidence for a big expose on the inner workings of tabloid television, which was a reasonable enough defense but was, in a word, bullshit.

Still, we couldn't help but feel sorry for the guy. In the years to come, Stuart Goldman would go through Hell because of his little alleged scheme. I ignored several subpeonas to testify against him as he was dragged through court after court. He went broke. His wife left him. Eventually, he agreed to a plea bargain.

Things worked out in the end, though. Years later, Goldman finally wrote a story about tabloid television and the torment it caused him. He sold his story to *Spy* magazine and a Hollywood production company bought the movie rights.

The sting engineered by *A Current Affair* was a success but, as might be expected, it was not well-received by one particular member of the Fox organization. Barry Diller's team had been trying to work out a television special deal with Nancy Reagan and her family.

In light of those dealings, Mrs. Reagan's representatives demanded to know why Mr. Diller's people would plant a libelous story on an unprotected computer system, alleging that her son, the controversial Ronnie Jr., was gay.

Negotiations ended.

Shortly afterwards Ron Reagan Jr. wound up with his own talk show on Fox. He also got a role on Fox's failed newsmagazine, *Front Page*. No one ever knew if the Goldman scandal was the reason the company wasted so much money on him.

That same month, *The Reporters* was put on hiatus. It was a polite term for cancellation. Gerald Stone's unfamiliarity with the American viewing public had driven the final nails into the coffin. When the show began, it was a comic book superhero series; a cartoon version of a news magazine show, but at least it was a caring, gritty cartoon that warranted attention.

Under the Stone regime, tabloid legend Steve Dunleavy spent his days chasing down Colombian drug dealers in far-away Cali. Olivia Newton-John hosted ponderous tours of the Amazonian rain forest. There were bland profiles of yuppie faves like the Neville Brothers. A new breed of young, j-school ethical, and television-illiterate reporters and commentators was on board. The blood was let until there was no life left.

With *The Reporters* cancelled, there were forty employees out of work—and some of them had contracts. Stone's last act in regard to *A Current Affair* was to force layoffs among the staff so we could absorb some of *The Reporters* employees.

It was a case of good news and bad news.

The bad news was that we'd have to lay off about fourteen people.

The good news?

We were getting Steve Dunleavy.

CHAPTER NINE:
DEAD HEAT ON A MAURY-GO-ROUND
(or SAMMY'S GLASS EYE)

Peter Brennan never wanted to fire anyone, couldn't stand to see someone out of work, and would never force someone to go out on a story if he or she didn't want to. Some saw it as weakness. I mistook it for the same until the night Rafael told me the story at the Fortune Garden.

It was the *Sydney Daily Mirror*, in the midst of another tabloid war. City editor Brennan assigned one of his reporters to a story in the Hinterlands. It was a massacre, front page news; competition was fierce, they had to be there first.

The reporter demurred. He'd have to take a helicopter to get the story and he was afraid to fly in helicopters. Brennan had no time for such illogical fear. He ordered the man to cover the story or clean out his desk.

The reporter went out on the story.

The helicopter crashed, killing all on board.

No matter how many vodkas, Brennan could never get the picture of the widow and kids out of his head.

Yet, when Black Friday came, Brennan showed the steel behind his accommodating and often nonconfrontational demeanor. He was Australian, and when the chips were down, he could be one of the toughest motherfuckers you'd hope to meet. He brought each employee into his office and told them they'd have to go. It was something he hated to do, he made sure in advance they'd receive generous severance, but he did it.

On the fourth of April, he even hosted a party for the fourteen people who were let go. The party took place in a private dining room upstairs at the Sign of the Dove restaurant, a posh eatery a couple of blocks south from the office on Third Avenue, one of the places we'd go if we needed to drink away from the crowd.

It was a sad and strange evening, not unlike being trapped in one of those Irish plays where all the dead people get out of their coffins and walk around begging for another chance at life while regretting the moment that led to their deaths.

It had finally come to pass. For one brief, shining moment, the complete Wild Bunch was in place at *A Current Affair*: Brennan, the soulful genius; Steve Dunleavy, the legendary street dog; Rafael Abramovitz, the masterful philosopher; Wayne Darwen, the trigger-happy kid; and me, the wild card, second-generation Prince of Darkness.

On the bench, we even had Wayne's pal from the *New York Post*, a long tall Scotsman named Dickie McWilliams who, like Wayne not long before, was learning television on the job.

Wayne and I welcomed Dickie into our special club without hazing. We invited him to join us when we rode Amtrak to Washington D.C. for a concert by George Jones, Merle Haggard, and Conway Twitty, an unholy trinity of country western music, all on the same bill.

Twitty and Hag were enough of an attraction, but the man I wanted to see was George Jones, the tragic, hard-drinking legend who Frank Sinatra himself described as the "second-best singer in America." Sitting amid the crowd of rednecks in the Virginia arena, I began to hear something new in his ballads of cheating lovers, revenge, lifetimes of regret, and devotion beyond the grave. They were short stories in two-and-a-half minutes time, with surprise punchline twists whose literary and literate ironies were often lost on those who couldn't hear past the steel guitars and fiddles.

There was the man going to the funeral of a friend who'd held a torch for thirty years: "First time I'd seen him smile in years." The DJ whose wife would entertain her lover while he worked the midnight shift—until the night of their first wedding anniversary, when the DJ taped his show as a surprise. "The radio was playing as he walked in on her and her lover. He heard himself saying the last words that they ever heard."

That was when it hit me. I realized America's connection to *A Current Affair* and the reason our show connected to all the people in this crowd. Our stories were like George Jones' songs. Not only were we giving importance and weight to events that effected ordinary people in out-of-the-way towns, we were making them universal. It wasn't only the old *Collier's* magazine or O. Henry we invoked when we provided justice and morals and surprise endings. The epics on *A Current Affair* were, in a nutshell, re-enactments of the songs that had this audience teary-eyed.

That night, George Jones dethroned Elvis Presley as avatar of our work. George Jones was king.

Despite our religious conversion, we rode back into Washington after the show and visited every strip club in the capital. It was in a small showroom on the second floor of a building downtown, while we sat around an elpee-size table crowded with drinks, that a woman danced onto the stage and into Wayne's heart. She didn't look like the others, with their skinny legs, boys' asses and big fake tits. This one was fuller, fleshier; ghostly pale with platinum hair and a face that bore an eerie resemblance to Marilyn Monroe.

She was moving languidly in and out of the smoky spotlight beam when the first of us noticed what else set her apart. She was scarred. There was a fine line running down the center of her pale chest, along the inner curve of her left breast, a thin pink scar no wider than a thread, but almost glowing in contrast to the translucence of her skin.

After the show, she sat at our table wearing a Japanese kimono, impressed by the business cards of these bigtime producers from New York City. In a whispery voice, catching her breath between sentences, she told us her story. She called herself Stephanie Hart, though "Hart" wasn't her real name. She chose the name because her heart had overtaken her life. It was failing, becoming weaker with every beat; after many surgeries, she was in Washington to be near an experimental hospital program that might possibly save her life.

A tear rolled down Wayne's cheek.

It was long after midnight when the three of us crowded around a payphone near the door. Wayne had awakened Brennan and was pleading with his bleary-eyed boss back in New York. "Mate, please, you've got to let us bring her back with us. It's the ultimate story."

"Peter." I took the receiver and controlled my voice to sound as sober as possible. "He's serious. He's not doing this because he wants to fuck her. This Stephanie is a great story."

"Aye!" Dickie piped in.

"Oy've got a heart-on for it!" Wayne stage-whispered.

I shushed him. He was going to blow it. "You've got to approve it," I told Peter. "I'm serious."

Wayne grabbed the phone. "Mate, listen to me. We take her back to New York, right? We make her up, we dress her up at the finest shops on the Upper East Side. And we introduce her to New York high society—we get her invited to parties, we throw a big coming out for her. Mate, no one will know she's a fucking stripper!"

Back at the table, Stephanie Hart pulled her kimono tighter and looked toward Wayne expectantly.

"Mate, it's her last wish. We can save her life. Or when she comes home from the ball, she could go to sleep and never wake up. Can't you see? Either way, it's fucking great! No, listen, it gets better, I've got the title. You ready for this? 'My Bare Lady!'"

Wayne paused, triumphant. "Peter—wait! Hello? Hello?" He held the phone away from his ear and looked at me in shock. "I don't believe it, mate. He told me to fuck off and hung up."

Back at work, Rafael actually hit the road, but he was living up to his reputation for not always following through. He'd spend a week on a story, come back with as many as twenty tapes and often not know what to do with them. Either he'd hand off a script so the segment could be cut by another producer or he'd leave the tapes under his desk.

Raf was restless. For him, the process ended when he was done gathering material and doing the interviews. Raf was a talker—a good adviser and coach. When he did finish a story, it was often multi-layered and thoughtful, some of the best material we aired.

Dunleavy was another story altogether. He'd drink with Brennan til closing time at the local bars, then sneak into the back room bar at the Silver Star diner on Second Avenue and drink til dawn. He'd sleep an hour at his desk, stick his head under the sink faucet and come up ready to do a live shot for *Good Day New York*.

Dunleavy was voracious and greedy in his quest for airtime and stories. Every morning, he'd come up with fifteen ideas out of the papers. Oprah's show is being bought by the Japanese? Why not run part of her show, dubbed with voices from a samurai movie?

He sent me into the edit room. I walked in with the tapes and looked around at the Amerasian baby pictures on the wall. The editor was married to a Japanese man. She found Dunleavy's concept very distasteful. I got the work done, catching glimpses of Dunleavy in the hallway pointing and laughing.

Around the time of Dunleavy's return, explosive charges were leveled in *Life* magazine by Albert Goldman, author of another famed autobiography of Elvis Presley. Goldman was now claiming the King committed suicide—because of Steve Dunleavy!

It all went back to Dunleavy's *Elvis: What Happened?*, the most famous Elvis Presley book of them all. In the as-told-to, three of Presley's former bodyguards revealed his abuse of drugs and women and his obsession with death. The book was released in 1977. Fifteen days after publication, Elvis Presley was dead.

Goldman's new theory was that the book had Elvis "terrified that his audience would see him for the first time, stripped naked, with all the kinkiness they'd never suspected."

I had Raf report the story and interview Dunleavy on the set. The two of them sat at a small table. Raf brought up the charges and Dunleavy grew more visibly upset. His lip curled in a sneer that, combined with his pompadour, made him absolutely Elvis-like. He grabbed the *Life* magazine from Raf.

"This is absolute garbage!" he thundered, slamming the magazine down to the floor. "Garbage!"

Then silence, broken by Marlene the director's voice over the studio intercom. "Uh, Steve, can you do that one more time? We want to make sure the camera gets the magazine on the floor."

Dunleavy shrugged, his face passive and friendly. "Was it good, though?"

Take two. "This is absolute garbage! *Garbage!*"

Steve and I rushed down the stairwell from the studio to the edit room where we were finishing up the Elvis package. At the landing he stopped and held my arms. "This book, this accusation that I killed him, that he committed suicide, mate—" His eyes lit up. His lips spread into a gleeful smile and he giggled. "It's true, you know. I think it's true! I think I really killed Elvis!"

The Wild Bunch was riding high, and more than ever we were outlaws. It wasn't long before Dunleavy, freed from the restraints of the oh-so-proper *Reporters*, was back to his old tricks, running two steps ahead of the press pack and a soft-shoe shuffle ahead of the law.

Through his many contacts on Long Island, he'd snagged an interview with Robert Golub, a 23-year-old man convicted of murdering the thirteen-year-old girl who lived next door.

The story was all over the New York tabloids, a sordid and grisly tale of a girl who was missing for days, only to turn up dead and mutilated in a neighbor's cluttered basement. The investigation and subsequent trial had turned the neighborhood into a war zone, and young Golub was regarded as the spawn of Satan.

Now Steve was in trouble and the show under scrutiny by the New York State Crime Victims' Board because he'd paid five thousand dollars to get the exclusive. Under New York's "Son of Sam" law, it was illegal for convicts to profit from their crimes.

Officially, *A Current Affair* insisted that neither Dunleavy nor the show "paid any money whatsoever to Robert Golub, or his defense fund or his attorney." That was true. Dunleavy paid the five grand to Golub's father.

The bottom line was, so what? "Paying for interviews is standard procedure for entertainment shows," one "industry insider" told the *Post*. "Paying someone else who is not a criminal happens all the time. It's a competitive marketplace and the exclusive interviews help the ratings."

Those words may have startled the naive student of journalism, but paying for stories was indeed a standard practice at *A Current Affair* and all the tabloid and reality shows to follow. This new genre was profit-motivated entertainment and it was a matter of expediency and urgency to get the stories and ratings exclusively.

Even so, though there were no apologies for paying for stories, the standard line was that we didn't pay for them: we paid for material like photographs or documents, or people's time if they had to miss work to appear on the show. We drew a moral line at never paying a killer or rapist or convicted felon, but if the story was good enough, we'd find a way to funnel the money to his family or attorney.

As the genre became more successful, story subjects became more savvy, hiring lawyers and agents and demanding money before saying a word. We were cashing in on their lives and they knew they deserved a cut—the same as if they sold book or movie rights. Every show did it. The only secret was that the networks did it too, and they did it long before tabloid TV existed.

That *Post* article on Dunleavy and Golub made sure to mention historic instances of network payments for exclusive interviews, such as CBS paying $15,000 to Watergate felon G. Gordon Liddy and another $100,000 to his pal H.R. Haldemann for an interview with Mike Wallace. The networks brought up their guidelines allowing themselves only to "pick up the tab for transportation and hotel arrangements," but didn't bring up the practice of hiring story subjects as "consultants."

In the Golub case, the "E word" aside, Dunleavy had apparently stepped on the wrong side of the fence in brushing up against the Son of Sam law. It wouldn't be the last time Son of Sam would almost prove to be his undoing.

While Dunleavy prepared to bring in great ratings for his killer interview, Wayne and I returned to Los Angeles to tape a second Hollywood week. The year before, we'd attacked Hollywood with great fanfare, featuring Cindy Adams and Cindy Garvey on outdoor sets and grand stunts. Now, everything had to be much more low-key.

Maury, Wayne, and I hit Los Angeles like guerrilla commandos, recording a week's worth of standups and reports on the run. We didn't want Barry Diller to know we were in town.

Maury was beaming. He had a three million dollar contract. He had a book deal. After years of struggle in the middle reaches of local television, he had made it in a big way.

"The last time I was in this town, at the end of the seventies, I was a fucking joke," he said, piloting the luxury rental car from the Four Seasons Hotel to lunch at Geoffrey's in Malibu. "They ran this big billboard campaign, 'Who is Maury Povich?' They made it like a puzzle, and every week they'd reveal another piece of it, revealing me.

"Well, the big graffiti in town was 'Who's Maury Povich? Who gives a shit?'"

Now, Maury was a star. As he walked through the hotel lobby, people stopped him for autographs and handshakes. When we did standups on the roadside, cars pulled over and people shouted his name.

Working with Maury that past year and a half, I realized that no one deserved it more. In a business full of pompous assholes and nasty pieces of work, Maury was truly a nice guy. For once in this fucking world, a nice guy finished first.

Good for him.

On our last night in L.A., Maury took us to Spago's, the glitzy California pizza joint overlooking the Sunset Strip. They gave us the best table in the house and when we sat down, the entire restaurant sneaking glimpses our way, we found a big bottle of expensive Dom Perignon waiting for us.

Maury read the attached card and chuckled. "'From your friends at Paramount.'"

We thought it was cool. Champagne from one of the big studios. If Barry Diller didn't appreciate us, at least someone did. Wayne and I ordered a couple of vodkas. The significance of the bubbly eluded us.

The bubbles dissolved and the meaning of the champagne became clear in the middle of May when Maury Povich announced he was quitting *A Current Affair*. He'd signed a deal with Paramount to host his own talk show, beginning in the fall of 1991.

"I was looking for something new to do with new people," Maury told the *New York Post*. "It's a fresh challenge."

In five years, Maury had gone from a $90,000 a year talk show host in Washington D.C. to a three-million-dollar man and national star at *A Current Affair*. Never had an anchorman been so perfectly suited to a show. Maury was our journeyman everyman, and the show's entire style, savoir faire, and distance from its more salacious stories was attributed totally to him.

His departure was potentially devastating. The person chosen to replace him could define or destroy the genre.

Peter Brennan saw a great opportunity amid the crisis. He suggested that Fox involve Maury in launching a nationwide search for a new host.

"Imagine the publicity, mate," he told Ian Rae. "Who can replace Maury? We'll make it a national obsession. We'll get Maury involved and have him help choose his successor. We'll have a big ceremony, on air, so he can pass the baton. Send him off on his new career with a pat on the back and a bon voyage!"

"Fuck him!" Ian Rae groused. "That facking Povich. We don't need him. He'd be nothing without us. We made him, that ungrateful bastard."

Plans were underway to get Maury off the air as soon as possible.

The day Maury made his announcement, Frank Sinatra began a long stand at Radio City. The engagement had been sold out for weeks, but on opening night, a few of us walked up to the cancellation window and walked away with ninth-row seats. It was like a New York City World Series. Any Sinatra performance could be his last.

Frank opened with "Come Fly with Me," looking every bit of his off-key seventy-four years, but with each song to follow gained momentum, strength and cool. It was an ultimate performance by the lion in winter; his bracing emotionalism and craft offset by his pedestrian taste and tough-guy boorishness.

After a poignant "Soliloquy," Sinatra swaggered to the lip of the stage to introduce his son, Frank Jr., who was leading the orchestra. "Somebody had to get him a job," he muttered. There was an audible gasp from the crowd.

Sammy died the next morning.

Sinatra cancelled the rest of his engagement. We scrapped the show we'd scheduled and, by mixing Sammy's Albert Hall interview, performance clips, and a bit of heartfelt narration, turned A Current Affair into an instant half-hour tribute.

The show was a fine example of the way A Current Affair elements could fit into place. In any other context, our Sammy Davis, Jr. special would be considered a damning expose. Part three, for instance, led off with Sammy talking about his dabbling in Satanism, his many orgies, drug use, sex addiction and open marriage, ending with him saying something about never thinking he'd live so long.

Then there was a slow dissolve from Sammy's face to a shot of him onstage, singing "What Kind of Fool Am I?" for a full forty-five seconds—an eternity in TV, taking in the entire final verse and fanfare at the end—and when you thought it was over, Sammy was back with one more line about how he'd finally learned to appreciate being alive and was at last happy with what he saw when he looked in the mirror.

There was a real slow dissolve from the interview back to Sammy on stage, a bowler derby cocked on his head, singing the end of "Mr. Bojangles:" "Please come back and dance...man, that cat could dance..." and Sammy did a little dance, came to a stop, looked down, raised an arm over his head, bent a knee, tipped the hat—and froze in a spotlight that faded to black and applause.

As the show was fed out, many staff members gathered around the monitor in the newsroom, watching in tears. The show was drink and drug and suck and fuck and a minute of pathos and—*bingo!* You walked away with a good feeling.

The ability and luxury of throwing out a show and dedicating an entire half-hour to the story we felt was most important that day—that was freedom and that was power. That was the magic of television.

No one was doing anything like it on television at the time. No one is doing it now.

"I'll get the shot of the decade," I promised. "I'll get you Sinatra crying over the box. I will, mate. I'll get Sinatra at the wake, crying over his little buddy in the box."

That night at the Fortune Garden, I convinced Peter Brennan to let me go to Sammy's funeral. Cheridah had kept in touch with Sammy's widow Altovise since setting up the Albert Hall interview, and Altovise invited her to the funeral at Forest Lawn Cemetery in Los Angeles.

There was trouble with the Sammy shoot even before we left Kennedy Airport. Storms delayed all flights for hours. Waiting in the terminal bar, downing vodka tonics in frustration, I couldn't erase the vision of Sinatra leaning over the casket at that very moment, weeping inconsolably, his tears plopping off the made-up face of his dead little friend. We missed the wake. We'd have to settle for the funeral and graveside service.

The producer in the L.A. office was supposed to set me up with a tiny hidden camera, but when Harley arrived at my hotel in Century City the next morning, he handed me a family-sized VHS recorder. It was about the size of your average boom box; nothing I could slip up my sleeve or stick in my pocket and shoot surreptitiously. When I took that thing out, it would be like hauling out a rocket launcher. People would scatter.

A vow, however, is a vow. I wedged the camera in a shoulderbag and Harley drove us to join the mourners at Forest Lawn. We arrived to find that the local Fox station was broadcasting the funeral live, with an open feed going out across the country. Nobody told us. This would be like getting exclusive home movies at the Super Bowl.

Cheridah and I mingled outside while people back in the New York office watched us among the celebrities on the feed. I was the only mourner carrying a huge black shoulderbag. We walked through a gauntlet of flashing still cameras—the paparazzi shot us in case we turned out to be someone famous—and took seats in the sixth row. Little Richard was a few seats down the row. Casey Kasem, a subhost on Jerry's telethon, sat behind us. We shared some small talk. Sammy was on stage up front, doing his last show from inside the box.

As mourners entered from the back of the hall, a door opened near the front at the side of the stage. Silhouetted for a moment against the bright sunlight behind them, Frank and Barbara Sinatra were escorted in and given seats front and center—Sinatra, just five short rows ahead of us, his silver Caesar hairpiece taunting like a bullseye. I had to get a shot.

Slowly, ever so slowly, I took out the bazooka-size camera and placed it on my knee. Not good enough. I couldn't raise it high enough to get a shot. If only I had a small camera, I could have held my bag up near my face and taped without anyone noticing.

A professional still photographer was shooting from the side aisle. I decided to give it a try. Very nonchalant, I got up and stood near him and hoisted the huge camera to my shoulder.

A hand clamped down on my other shoulder.

"What do you think you're doing?"

"Uh, um, I'm just getting—"

"Who are you?" The man wore a black Italian suit and talked in an angry stage whisper.

"I'm a friend of the family. I'm sorry. Sammy, you know—"

"I'm the Davis family attorney—"

"I'm sorry. I just wanted to remember him, my mother—"

"You put that camera away, and if I see it—"

I sat down. Little Richard leaned over and brushed his forefingers in a "naughty naughty" sign. "You got caugh-ghtt," he mouthed, giggling.

The show went on. The family attorney stood at the side of our row, staring at me. I apologized again, pretended to pray until he walked away and watched Sinatra jealously throughout the rest of the service. The game was in my sights and there was nothing I could do about it.

People talked. Gregory Hines wept. They played a Sammy song on tinny loudspeakers. Then it was over. The Rev. Jesse Jackson stood at the pulpit, did a few rhymes and told everyone to wait to follow the Sammy box out the back.

Amid the shuffling, Sinatra and Barbara were helped to their feet and led out that door near the stage. I hoisted the heavy black bag, waved goodbye to Little Richard and bolted from my seat, burst through the door on the feet end of the casket and blinked in the bright wash of sunshine. Scrambling up a grassy hill, I pulled the unwieldy camera out of the bag and searched for Sinatra. There he was, uphill from me, to the left, about twenty feet away, the silver hairpiece glittering in the sun. He was moving slowly and reflectively toward a limousine.

Crawling uphill, aiming, target locked in, I shouted, "Frank!"

Sinatra turned, in slow motion, in my direction.

Our eyes met and I was falling, swarmed by Forest Lawn security personnel. Shooting, waving, yelling, "Wait, wait! Do you know who I am? Mr. Sinatra!" Sinatra regarded the rumble, his face impassive, and he took his time being helped into the limo.

The driver shot out the way JFK's driver should have back in Dealey Plaza. Hands blocked my camera lens and held my shoulders down as I watched Sinatra's sleek black limousine circle over the hill, around and out, past all the ground-level markers of the graves of the dead bodies of all the people who romanced to his songs.

Sinatra gone, the security men in their polyester sports jackets shrugged and walked off, leaving me on my knees on the grassy knoll.

I met Cheridah in front of the chapel. Next stop was the burial, and then Sammy's house in Beverly Hills, where his new widow Altovise had invited some of the mourners.

Limo after limo dropped off B-grade celeb after B-grade celeb at the gate on Summit Drive. There was Liza Minnelli; Mary Hart and her husband stood on line for food; I was introduced to Rita Moreno or Chita Rivera— one or the other, I don't recall. Sinatra was probably on his way back to Palm Springs. Altovise remained locked behind a bedroom door, accepting visitors. We were starting on the Stoli and tonics by the pool when I noticed someone watching me from behind a tree. It was the Davis family attorney.

He followed me as I walked around the house and sat in Sammy's piano room, listening in on celebrity conversations. He head the good taste not to confront me, but still kept me in his sights.

Eventually, I had enough, and ducked into a bathroom to get away. Locking the door and sighing with relief, I turned around to realize that I'd landed in a goldmine. After checking to make sure the door was secure, I opened the medicine chest and began rummaging through the shelves, looking for glass eyes.

CHAPTER TEN:
SPARE PRICKS AT THE WEDDING

How did we wind up in the middle of Kansas? The last week of June, 1990, Wayne and Dickie and I were in a rented car, barreling through the flat farmlands under threatening skies in search of a ball of string.

"It's my favorite line in my favorite movie," Wayne had said one night at the Fortune Garden. "*National Lampoon's Vacation*. When Chevy Chase says, 'If we turned left we could have seen the World's Second Largest Ball of Twine!'"

"I know the ball of twine," I said. "It's in a book at home."

"It's real?" Wayne didn't believe it.

"Nae," said Dickie. "You've got to be kidding."

"I'm serious," I said. "It's in Kansas or somewhere. I can look it up."

"He knows all this shit, mate," Wayne said. "His mind is like a fucking steel trap of information."

Somehow, I convinced them to take a long weekend, fly to Kansas City, and drive the rest of the way to the middle of nowhere, to Cawker City, Kansas, to visit the World's Second Largest Ball of Twine. On the way, we'd tasted beef fries—breaded bull's testicles—at a small-town diner, visited a man-made obsession and backyard mausoleum called the Garden of Eden, and stood at a stone marker in the middle of a cornfield that marked the exact geographic center of the conterminous United States.

We also captured everything on home video cameras we'd brought along for the ride.

It was near sunset when we found our way down Route 24 heading into Cawker City, a one-ball town with its name on a water tower and the twine nestled under a gazebo on Main Street.

We checked into the local motel, which was actually a collection of mobile homes—we got a good one, with washer and drier, for twelve dollars a night—and that evening, went to the local tavern, which was a residential house with the windows painted black.

Wayne had an unnatural fear of rape by the rural gentry and refused to leave the car in a neighborhood so far from Manhattan, so Dickie and I walked up to the Winchester Bar without him.

The door opened to a house that was gutted into one big room with a bar in the middle and a pool table where the living room should be. The mood was lively and the music rollicking when we walked in, though the conversation and clack of pool balls ceased and the bartender lowered the jukebox and placed his palms on the bar as we approached.

He and the rest of them were looking us over and staring us down.

"Hi. Can I get a beer?" I asked.

The bartender took his time answering. "Are you a member?"

"A member of what?"

"A member of the club."

"No, I don't think so."

"Then you ain't getting a beer."

"Hey, your loss, pal. Thanks." I turned and headed for the door. Dickie kept his back to the door as he watched mine.

"Hey." It was the bartender.

I turned.

"You all from ABC?"

"No." I looked at Dickie, confused. "We're from Fox."

Now it was everyone else's turn to be confused.

"Where are you guys from?"

"New York City."

An audible murmur spread through the bar. Dickie kept a hand on the doorknob.

"New York? What the hell are you doing in Cawker City?"

"Why else?" I replied. "We're here to see the Ball of Twine!"

A moment of silence was followed by a whooping cheer from everyone.

"Well, come on in and let me buy you a beer!"

The bartender cranked up the music, pool balls popped into pockets, and I grabbed a frosty Budweiser as Cawker City locals patted my back and laughed heartily.

Dickie gave a whistle and Wayne hurried inside.

That night, in the midweek cold in the middle of America, no more than twenty miles from the geographic center of the conterminous United States, we'd found another unassuming bar that we turned into the center of our television universe.

"What's this stuff about ABC?" I asked the barkeep. "Has ABC News been here?"

"No, ABC, the Alcohol Bureau of Control. We're a private bottle club. They're always sending people in to check on us to see if we're selling to the public. Pains in my butt."

We drank into the night. Billy the bartender reminisced a good twenty years back to his high school days, when he and his pals rolled the Ball of Twine into the center of Main Street and set it afire. We had to keep that one under our hats, he said, since the perpetrators were still at large.

Wayne beat everyone in the place at pool, but I kept the locals from getting angry by losing every hand of liar's poker at the bar. Billy told us about his day job as a realtor and offered to sell us a house for five thousand dollars.

Word spread quickly that the guys from *A Current Affair* were in town. At the diner the next morning, the waitress revealed herself to be the town historian— "the twine historian," Wayne said— and lugged out her scrapbooks of news clippings and photos tracing the history of the ball from a few pieces of string in the pocket of a farmer named Frank Stoeber to the pride of Cawker City. Each year, she said, the entire town threw a big party and everyone brought their own pieces of baling twine to add to the ball. They called the event the Twine-A-Thon.

We paid up and walked the several blocks up Main Street to visit the Ball of Twine in daylight. Behind us, we noticed a small but growing parade of townfolk. Shopkeepers flipped the "gone fishin" and "Back in an hour" signs on their doors and joined the throng until it seemed all of Cawker City was with us as we stood and videotaped the impressive, ten foot high orb.

In a matter of moments, the sound of backfiring and rattling machinery filled the air. An aged pickup truck was pulling up. A grizzled little man in overalls and baseball cap got out of the cab and ambled up to us. He was Frank Stoeber's cousin, the official caretaker of the ball.

Old Man Stoeber pulled a piece of paper out of his bib and began to read. "The ball is fourteen thousand, nine hundred and ninety six pounds. It uses approximately three million, two hundred and ninety nine thousand, one hundred and twenty feet of twine. Way we arrived at that is there's so many feet per pound. I check on it every day."

"You're doing a fine job," Wayne said.

"Well, you see the top ain't cropped any more. Roof's down too close. It's my idea to get the twine there in the air, keep it round." He held up his wooden t-bar and spool of twine. "Two pounds on each spool. We know the ball's two pounds heavier."

Then, without further ado, the old man tied the end of the twine on his spool to a spot on the ball and began walking around it. The spool squeaked like a coopful of chickens as new twine flowed neatly around. We watched in amazement and applauded at this latest step in world recorddom.

Then he let us try.

The bartender's house was an unpainted two-story on the edge of a small town a few miles away. It was a bargain for five thousand dollars, even if we decided to tear it down and sell off the wood and pipes. Wayne wanted to buy the place on the spot. He thought it could be a perfect retreat if any of us found ourselves out of work or in need of a getaway.

Dickie and I begged off. There were railroad tracks across the street, and in the next field, beyond the grain elevators, something that looked suspiciously like a missile silo.

When we got back to New York, we put together a special segment that ran on the Fourth of July. It was *National Lampoon's Vacation* meets *The Three Stooges*. No one had seen anything like it before. The Ball of Twine segment would prove to be a defining journey and actually lead to the next step in the evolution of reality television, one Wayne and I would take in a poignant reunion five years later.

Life remained unchanged for decades in little Cawker City, but we returned from Kansas to find our little world was about to undergo traumatic transition that dwarfed the imminent departure of Maury. It came in the shape of a tiny, hundred-pound woman named Anthea Disney.

Anthea, Ian announced, was joining the *A Current Affair* staff on the orders of the Boss himself.

There was a history of Murdoch sticking his favorite print or Australian TV lieutenants into the mix of *A Current Affair* or local news as a way of learning the television ropes before being transferred to another corner of the operation. We were always generous with our attentions, in the way we helped Dunleavy and Wayne along and gave Dickie a year's worth of television education in a matter of months.

Anthea's situation was different. Something was up. With Dickie on board the management team as our new assistant, Raf helping out, and Dennis wandering around, one thing we didn't need was another manager. There was a visible unease among us higher-ups that this editor of women's magazines would be dropped into the roiling stewpot of success and change the flavor.

Something was up, all right, and that would turn out to be the jig, for us.

Dunleavy filled us in at the Fortune Garden. Anthea was in her early forties; British, small, sharp, and ambitious. "Not a bad looker, but she's tough, mate. She's like a mate."

Anthea started as a reporter on Fleet Street and was viewed as aggressive and as good as the best of them. Over the years, editing newspapers and magazines, she'd become one of Murdoch's favorites. The fact that she didn't know anything about television was a small matter. She knew Rupert. She knew how to accomplish what he directed. She was his protegée. She was a threat.

As Dunleavy charged on, Brennan sat quietly, almost distracted.

"So, mate," I asked Brennan. "What's her title going to be?" Raf and I had gotten into the habit of calling everyone "mate." We figured it sounded better than "pal" and agreed to make the term universal.

"What's a title, mate?" Brennan said. "It doesn't matter." He was uncomfortable, shrugging off the question. He had reason to be. The title she would get would be mine.

When Anthea arrived, Dunleavy was proven right. She was a sharp woman in her early forties, and though she'd never worked in television, it was clear she didn't have to. Her brown eyes showed she had a mandate and was carrying the authority. Anthea wasn't looking to us for direction or help. She was looking at us, studying and judging.

That week there was a nice press release announcing that Anthea Disney was joining *A Current Affair* as its first managing editor. Something was up, all right. I'd been a very well-publicized managing editor for the past year and a half.

"Print princess Anthea Disney has been appointed to the new position of managing editor at *A Current Affair*, a decision that has upset some staffers at the show," the *New York Post* reported.

> The dissenters are believed to be irked by the
> fact that their new boss has no television experience,
> but Disney, one-time editor-in-chief of *Self* magazine
> and a former editor at the Sunday *Daily News*,
> remains confident.
> "A print background is not a stigma here," said
> Disney. "A good story is a good story."
> ...While Disney acknowledges that fixing the
> troubled program is her mandate, she says she
> needs time to assess the program's weaknesses. "I'm
> still learning where the ladies room is," she said...

I knew it was over the day Maureen O'Boyle stopped bringing me cappuccinos. Every morning, she'd arrive at the show meeting with two steaming cups, and in front of everyone else in the room, hand one to me. It was thanks for helping write her scripts. It was a show of her closeness to the circle of power.

Within a week of Anthea's arrival, the cappuccinos were cut off.

The floor was moving under us and it was all we could do to hold on. Ian Rae stepped aside as executive producer and Brennan took back the title again. The senior producer spot had yet to be filled.

I expected to get the title. Dennis O'Brien was lobbying hard for it. Brennan had to choose again. He chose Dennis, explaining to me that in doing so, Dennis would effectively be "kicked upstairs" and kept away from show content altogether. He'd no longer be pushing for repeat stories or trying to maneuver behind my back. He'd also act as a buffer between me, who was calling the shots in Brennan's absence, and Ian Rae, Muriel, and other executives.

Brennan still felt he owed Dennis O'Brien for taking over the show in the months before I arrived, but there was more to it. After the Michael Jackson and Rob Lowe scandals, I was "too hot." All the things we'd done had been great for the show, but bad for me politically.

Brennan, with his charming style, cunning skills, and sharp intellect, was a Teflon leader. Any illegal deeds and schemes he'd masterminded, all the sex he injected into the show, all the disappearances and hangovers, all of it slid off because of his charisma and genius. Everyone loved him. Muriel, who despised the show, gushed in his presence. Male executives respected him.

Then there was me: the new Prince of Darkness; the Lyin' King; Mr. Love Him or Hate Him. I was the Hitman. If Peter was rubber, I was glue. Anything they threw bounced off him and stuck to me.

I accepted the role, gladly. I'd chosen a persona to take my place among the gods, and just as Brennan felt he owed O'Brien, I knew that I owed Brennan. My salary continued to climb with every success.

Most important, I'd decided to pledge total loyalty to my newfound mates. One for all and all for one. If worst came to worst, I would gladly take the fall.

Wayne Darwen and I were named show producers, now paired officially as a team, writing and running the show on a daily basis. The old formula, in which I'd add humor, a dash of insight, and TV cool into Wayne's perfect hot tabloid prose, was now incorporated.

We were no Tomlin and Young, though. More and more, we found ourselves running ideas past Anthea Disney. At first it was out of politeness, to explain what we were doing in this new medium called television. Soon, it was just plain instinct. Just as nothing needed to be spelled out when I wrested control from O'Brien, nothing had to be spoken here. Anthea was suddenly in charge of taste control. She was out to make stories nicer, friendlier, more polite and magazine-like; more palatable to Barry Diller and his bunch.

None of us was too happy about it; especially not Peter Brennan. By the end of that second week, he'd circled the wagons. Wayne, Dennis, and I were in his office. The door was closed.

"I have to leave town for a few days," he said. "I'm going to L.A. and we need to make sure things work smoothly while I'm gone. Dennis, I want you to move into this office. Set up shop in here, if you know what I mean. I want to make sure no one moves into my desk while I'm away."

We all got the picture. He didn't want Anthea to set up camp and take control in his absence. This was also a way to deal with the latest "Dennis problem," for although Dennis had gotten his big promotion to senior producer, he refused to leave his old desk in the main office and take on the new responsibilities. He realized too late he was being pushed out and was holding on by his fingernails, leaving solid Steve Schwartz, who was supposed to be taking over as line producer, with nowhere in the office to sit.

This was Brennan's way of confronting the problem without confronting the problem. It worked. Dennis was anxious to play boss. The pictures of his daughter and hippy-dippy knick-knacks were transferred from his desk into Brennan's office. Schwartz slid into Dennis' old desk and set up his own family pictures as fast as he could.

Once Dennis settled in behind Brennan's desk, he didn't leave the entire time Peter was gone, except to go to the bathroom. When Anthea walked into the office, he treated her as an underling. He played hardball and she wasn't sure why.

Wayne convinced me, meanwhile, to play softball.

"You can't fight it, mate," Wayne counseled. "I've seen this happen before. These things happen in waves, and if this is what Rupert wants, there's nothing we can do. We're cool. We'll be taken care of. Just let it play out."

So I did.

By July, everything at *A Current Affair* was totally out of whack. Maury, whose trademark was to criticize stories after they aired, was now interrupting his intros and distancing himself before he saw the segments. So afraid was he of offending any of his new colleagues in Hollywood or respectable television, he'd apologize going in— "I don't have any idea what this story is about, but I'll tell you I don't like it and I didn't have anything to do with it."

Ian, fearful of offending the Boss after all the money thrown at Maury, began a series of on-air auditions for the anchor post. At Brennan's insistence, Dunleavy got the first week, followed by Jim Ryan from *Good Day New York*, and Jack Cafferty, who'd recently been lured from WNBC with his own local late night news show.

On July 18th, Peter Brennan returned from his trip with two words: "I quit."

The announcement was low-key. He told Ian, word spread around the office, a funereal air descended on the place, and Brennan stopped in to confirm the news and shake a few hands before disappearing over the road into one of the bars.

Brennan, too, was going with Paramount. He took a job as executive producer of *Hard Copy*. He was replacing Mark BvS Monsky. He was moving to California.

There was an impromptu party for him the following night, over the road at the Racing Club. Everyone got gloriously, depressingly drunk. In the middle of the festivities, Brennan sidled over and told me we needed to talk.

That time came around three a.m. It was a work night. The place had thinned out to about me and him and the bartender. We stood at the back end of the bar, near the payphone, facing the street and the Fox News building across it.

"So, mate, I'm going to *Hard Copy*. I want you to come along."

"Great. Thanks. I'm there."

"Like that?"

"Like that."

"Uh, don't you have personal details to work out? Don't you live with your girlfriend?"

"Don't worry about that. I'll do it. Let's do it."

"Good. Great." Brennan shrugged and ordered another vodka and soda. He was surprised at how easy it was.

"Who else are you bringing over?" I asked.

"Rafael, so far."

"Great."

"It should be," he said. "I'm going over for more than *Hard Copy*. They've got other avenues, other opportunities. Once we get *Hard Copy* straightened out, we'll be able to move onto other things, other shows."

"Mate, I want to work with you. The one thing I'm afraid of doing is boring, ordinary television. We can go out there and do great things. I'm there."

Back in the office, Anthea was named interim executive producer and finally wangled the executive producer's office from Dennis, who was walking around in a sort of daze because he thought he'd get the job. After all, he already had the office.

Anthea asked me to stay after the morning meeting to discuss the show. "You've got obvious talents," she said. "You're a great writer and producer. But I've been watching you and talking to people in the office, and I've got to say you've got terrible people skills. People think you shut them out, you have favorites. You're probably the worst people person I've ever seen.

You're not much of a manager at all."

I was a little taken aback. "Yeah, well, with the speed of things here, I've been more of a worker than manager—"

Anthea was already onto the next victim. "And Dennis. I don't like him. Do you? The way he acts with some of these female producers, I find it very disturbing. He really gives me the creeps. He's like some kind of New Age cult leader."

Within weeks, she fired him.

I met with Peter Brennan at the Conservatory Bar of the Mayflower Hotel, in the shadow of the Paramount building clear across Central Park from the *A Current Affair* haunts. Raf was signed, sealed, and gone. Now the legal department would concentrate on my contract.

Brennan told me how much money Paramount would pay me, the perks I could negotiate, and about the latest addition to our team: John Parsons.

The first season of *Hard Copy* had not gone well for the Monsky-Parsons alliance. As the months progressed, Mark BvS Monsky had less of a hand in the work, and eventually, they say, disappeared from the scene altogether.

Parsons took up the slack, and almost single-handedly managed to keep the show on the air. As a reward, Paramount was giving him another year on his contract.

Brennan and Raf already had a sit down with Parsons. He told them he knew we could all work together, he and Brennan and Raf and me: the Four Musketeers.

I laughed and hoisted a light beer. "Let's do it," I said.

"What would it take to keep you?" Anthea faced me from across the low table in her new office. "What do you want? What can we give you?"

"Nothing," I said. "It's not about money. It's about working with Peter, and you know, a chance to move to California. So I'm thinking."

Actually, I was stalling. I was definitely leaving *A Current Affair*; only I couldn't announce it until I'd signed with Paramount. It had taken their legal department a full week to call me about the contract, and as their young attorney justified her job by going through the motions of negotiating, Anthea was left holding the bag.

"I understand fully," Anthea said. "But I'd appreciate it if you'd let me know soon." She was antsy, understandably; she couldn't get on with her sweeps planning as long as I was hanging around ready to jump to the competition.

The other shoe dropped on Friday when Wayne told me to meet him at the Fortune Garden. He'd eased off on his drinking that summer, and without a vodka in front of him, he was nervous enough. This latest news had him shaking.

"Mate, Anthea told me to tell you. She said to tell you to take the *Hard Copy* job because she might have to fire you."

"Fire me? Why?"

"She said you may have perjured yourself in the Rob Lowe suit."

"How could I have perjured myself when I didn't swear to anything?" Those bastards.

"That's what she said, mate. Oh yeah, she also said she thinks you don't like her."

"C'mon."

"I'm worried. It's Muriel's hit list. Everyone who Barry Diller doesn't like. I think I'm next."

Those bastards were scapegoating me. A couple of months earlier, Muriel and a Fox attorney from Washington deposed a group of us about the lawsuit filed by the hair salon Audrey infiltrated while covering the Rob Lowe story.

I told what happened, the whole truth and nothing but the truth. Muriel and her colleague, however, kept reverting back to the Rob Lowe video and the lawsuit threatened by the prick news director at our Atlanta affiliate. As the stenographer typed away on the machine between her legs, Muriel asked how we got the tape and who did what, all the while trying to trip me up.

Again, I told the truth, the whole truth, and nothing but the truth Peter and I had agreed upon a year earlier.

I didn't know I was being double-crossed. Audrey didn't want to take the blame for the salon incident, so she simply put it all on her cameraman and me, then called me and confessed merrily to what she had done. That was Audrey. She had a perverse streak and enjoyed causing any trouble she could. She'd say I'd think it was cute.

Then someone else cracked under questioning about the purloined video. Someone ratted me out. The ghost of Rob Lowe was hovering.

There was a joint on the Upper West Side called the Raccoon Lodge, a theme bar in name only, with a pool table, long bar, and decent jukebox. We had a get-together that final summer, a cross section of *A Current Affair* staffers raising more toasts to a time and camaraderie we'd never know again. Everyone knew I was gone. She knew I was long gone, and I knew I wouldn't be seeing her much anymore. She was someone who'd spent many nights at our side at the many bars we'd closed in many nights of drinking. She'd racked up as many wild myths and stories as the best of us. It was inevitable it would happen before we left. Close drinking at the bar led to close dancing by the jukebox and now we were in a taxi driving down Broadway. We couldn't go to my place and she didn't want me coming to hers.

We wound up back at the *A Current Affair* office. The actors and actresses who worked nights transcribing our tapes looked up from under headphones and smiled as we walked into one of the back offices and shut the door.

The papers on the finance officer's desk wound up on the floor, but this wouldn't do. We wandered through the Fox building, on the same tour Peter and I had taken long before when we were on the edge of enforced retirement because of the Rob Lowe scandal.

On the fifth floor, there was a locker room with a shower and a sink and a window to the courtyard. Many mornings, Dunleavy would be dragged in here by his female producers, stripped naked, and held under the stinging cold shower to jolt him awake to work again.

We bolted the door, dropped to the cold tile floor and made our way past the sink to the open windowsill, illuminated by the August moon. Months of anticipation and electricity had given way to this. I was leaving, and I suppose she was saying goodbye.

The details will fade into the Jaegermeister mist of past glories, a place none of us will ever be again, and the knowledge that if Morley Safer put down his book of art history and peered out a back window into his courtyard that night, he would have seen, framed in a fifth floor window of the Fox building, a vision that would have made him forgive all the changes Rupert Murdoch brought to his life and world.

Wayne and I pulled off one last triumph.

On August eighth, the United States was ready to respond to Saddam Hussein's aggression. War with Iraq was another news event throwing a cold splash of reality into the tabloid world we'd created. *A Current Affair* needed to weigh in with a story. It wouldn't bring us ratings, but would again show we had the ability to give our spin to any event. We had to take this war and personalize it, boil it down to the story of one person.

That person was ten-year-old Penelope Nabokov, a little girl from northern California. She was one of dozens of passengers aboard a commercial airliner that was rerouted from Kuwait and detained in Baghdad by Saddam Hussein's forces.

The story was simple to cast. Penelope was an innocent American abroad. Saddam Hussein was the Bully of Baghdad.

We had tape of Penelope, tape of the jetliner, tape of Saddam—enough to do a story, but we needed something to dress it up and take it over the top into *A Current Affair* land.

Baghdad...Arabian nights...flying carpets...Wayne and I took a step we figured would be a step too far, but at least would serve as a proper sendoff on my trip to Hollywood.

"When I was a kid, I remember watching movies like *Ali Baba & the Forty Thieves*," we had Maury say. "And it was every kid's dream to be carried off to a magic land called Baghdad, full of genies and flying carpets..."

It was so shameless and over-the-top, I was embarrassed even writing it. This made the earthquake piece look like McNeil-Lehrer. We'd dug up an old movie starring Sabu, *A Thousand and One Arabian Nights* or something, with bad special effects of rugs flying past minarets, green genies appearing in puffs of smoke, and little Sabu up against a giant genie's foot or sitting in his hand. Using that video, we weaved fantastical storybook tales around the serious news story of Penelope and the new Bully of Baghdad. For a finale, we taped little kids saying "We love you, Penelope." It was sappy and more than maudlin, and Maury read it expertly, as if he was actually moved and took it seriously.

That night, we celebrated the fourth anniversary of *A Current Affair* on dry land, at a decadent preppie restaurant at 32nd and Broadway called the Grolier Club. There was a gag reel that McGowan put together, with gags ranging, as did McGowan's work, from amusing to mean. Some people danced. Everyone drank.

This would be Maury's final party. He was pretty much in his cups when he made his way through the well-wishers, clasped my shoulder and mentioned the Baghdad piece. I tensed. What a way to go—with the anchor slugging me for embarrassing him.

"You really challenged me," he said. He shook his head. His eyes misted. "You challenged me."

He thanked me and said it was a great job.

As Maury steadied himself and moved on, I burst out in a laugh and looked around for Wayne, only to turn to Ed Harris, the show's chief engineer. Ed was our technical whiz. He kept everything running and pulled off many a miracle.

"That Baghdad piece," he said.

Now it was coming. I braced for a shove or a drink splash. I deserved it.

"I just had to mention how well-written the Baghdad piece was," he said. "You guys do it every day. But this one was special. I just had to mention it. It was a great job."

You never know what's going to touch people.

The next day, one of my friends over at CBS network news called. She'd seen the piece we ran on Penelope and the Bully of Baghdad, and she too was impressed. She said CBS had a reporter in Penelope's neighborhood in California, and found out that no one liked the little girl. It seemed Penelope herself was regarded as a bully, feared by all the other kids. Penelope was a brat.

"Of course, we couldn't report the truth," she said.

A few days later, the deal was done. There was a farewell party for me at the Fortune Garden. Anthea gave me a kiss and a bottle of champagne. She was, undeniably, a class act. Unfortunately, she was now free to set out trying to make *A Current Affair* a class act, as well. The seeds of destruction that Gerald Stone nurtured and Barry Diller fertilized would be sprinkled by her watering can.

The headline in the next day's weekly *Variety* told it all:

FOX SEEKING TO CLEAN UP AFFAIR
**Honcho says tv mag will change,
but won't get kinder or gentler**

A Current Affair, the show that brought a brash tabloid style to the tv magazine genre and hit syndication gold, will attempt to go upmarket.

Affair's new topper, Anthea Disney, is telling associates that she's been given the directive from 20th Century Fox corporate chiefs Rupert Murdoch and Barry Diller to make the show "more *New York* magazine and less *New York Post*."

Although Diller declined to talk about the developments at *A Current Affair*, it's been an open secret at Fox that Diller is no fan of the show.

The layoff of a dozen people in New York, as well as two *Affair* producers in Hollywood, was said by show staffers to reflect Diller's feeling that the show was "too tabloid." And it was Diller, according to several sources, who issued the directive that nobody tainted by *Affair* would be hired to work on the company's new syndicated property *Personalities*.

The article went on to lay out the facts: *A Current Affair* cost $350,000 a week to produce. It was generating twenty-five million dollars a year in profits, earnings that paled compared to more "benign" shows. *A Current Affair* was scaring off advertisers and getting on the blacklists of right-wing censorship zealots like the Rev. Donald Wildmon and Terry Rakolta, and of course, few in the industry had the courage to tell them to piss up a rope.

Anthea's plan would go beyond mending fences with Barry Diller, whose wet kiss of a show called *Personalities* was soon to fail. She told *Variety* she'd woo back the advertisers personally, even seek their input about show content, without going too far in "sanitizing" the show.

"The stories on *A Current Affair* will always be about people who toy with the Commandments and the Seven Deadly Sins," she said. "You can have a lot of fun with stories of crime and passion. But you shouldn't have to feel like you have to wash your hands after you watch it."

Anthea and Ian Rae were keeping mum on Maury's replacement, and downplaying the impact of his departure.

"When Maury came here, nobody knew him from a bar of soap," Ian blustered to *Variety*. "We promoted the hell out of Maury. The show drove Maury. Maury didn't drive the show."

The experts were skeptical. "If they don't get the right anchor, the show could crash and burn," said Michael Linder, the former executive producer of *America's Most Wanted*. "A lot of the show's appeal, after all, is Maury Povich—the guy with the best eyebrows in show business. You need somebody like Maury who can take you through this delightfully sleazy world and bring you back alive."

It was urgent that *A Current Affair* find a host, a standard-bearer to lead the fight against the formidable new competition from us at *Hard Copy*.

For the time being, Anthea and Ian decided to stick with Maury's fill-in, young Maureen O'Boyle.

CHAPTER ELEVEN:
HOLLYWOOD BABBLE ON

*A world seen at dawn through a hangover, a world of
cheap double entendre and stale smoke and drinks in
which the ice has melted: a true comedy of despair.*
—Joan Didion on the films of Billy Wilder

Hollywood; just like I pictured it. There I was, rounding the corner in
the red LaBaron convertible Paramount provided for me, turning left onto
Melrose, past the famed El Adobe Mexican restaurant and left again after the
historic Nickodell's restaurant and bar. I rolled through the fabled
Paramount gates and stopped at the guard shack barrier. Looming ahead of
me were the cavernous soundstages, the famous blue sky backdrop against
which they filmed movie dogfights, and the unlimited Cinemascope dreams
Hollywood promised to make a reality.

The kindly old security guard leaned over my car with a clipboard in
his hands, just the way he would in the movies.

"Morning."

I peered over the top of my shades and gave him my name. "I'm
starting at *Hard Copy* today."

"Kearns. Kearns." He searched for the name. "That's with a K?"

"Yeah."

"Nope. Sorry. Hold on a minute."

The line of cars grew behind me. Too bad, suckers. In a second, I'll be
cruising through—

"Mr. Kearns, I can't let you in."

"Excuse me?"

"You're not authorized to park on the lot. You'll have to go back around
to Gower and park in the structure across the street."

"Across the street."

"That's right. You can turn around right here. And have a nice day."

⟞⟐⟝

It was a movie lot, the same lot F. Scott Fitzgerald wrote about in his Pat Hobby stories, the same lot where Cagney and Coppola and Billy Wilder worked. There were big soundstages painted tan, tall office buildings, and small cottages where producers set up shop. VIPs and runners alike tooled about in golf carts down narrow streets and paths where Jerry Lewis and Eddie Murphy once wreaked havoc in theirs.

Near the far southeast end of the lot was the original Paramount gate, half the size of the one I tried to drive through. It was the gate Gloria Swanson's limousine rolled through in the movie *Sunset Boulevard*. It remained open for walk-ins. Just outside the gate were apartments where Rudolph Valentino had to live at the height of his fame; it wasn't safe for him to venture much farther. Valentino remained only a few hundred yards away, filed away in a mausoleum in the Hollywood Memorial Park off Santa Monica Boulevard.

Eddie Murphy's production company shared a low-rise near the main gate with notorious producers Don Simpson and Jerry Bruckheimer. Their personalized golf carts were plugged into big batteries near their steps.

Out in back were the outdoor sets: warehouse and office fronts and old New York City streets with a subway stop I'd see in an old Jimmy Cagney movie that very week. With the latest *Star Trek* series in full swing, Klingons walked the streets in full regalia. There was always a movie in production, the stars housed in trailers outside the soundstages.

The *Hard Copy* offices were tucked away in the northwest corner, across a Paramount street from the huge offices of *Entertainment Tonight* and next to the soundstage where they filmed *Cheers*. To the north was Arsenio Hall's soundstage, slapped against a wall of the Hollywood Jewish Cemetery.

Mark BvS Monksy designed the *Hard Copy* operation in a style that defined his Hollywood dream. It was built into a bisected soundstage. One half was turned into the main newsroom, with desk cubicles, filing cabinets, and flakes of asbestos drifting through the makeshift chicken wire reinforcement on the high hangar ceiling. On the other side of the prefab wall was the studio where *Hard Copy* was taped each day. You had to walk up a perilous metal staircase to reach the executive area, four offices around a reception area with a window looking down into the studio, far from the general staff.

Raf and I shared a roomy office with windows facing out on the Billy Wilder Building. All the buildings on the lot were named after past stars. Jerry Lewis had a building. You had to enter Lucille Ball to get from the parking structure to *Hard Copy*.

Raf, the immigrant from Eastern Europe, was especially taken by the fact that he was so close to a symbol of Wilder's greatness. He began reading Neal Gabler's book, *An Empire of Their Own*, about the Jews who created

Hollywood and was soon spouting trivia about the tailors and agents who came west with a dream of their own.

I did my first lunch that first day. Lunch was a very important occasion in Hollywood; a time when projects were pitched, connections were made, and deals went down. No one, it seemed, ate dinner.

We got a table in Paramount's main commissary, an actual restaurant in the middle of the lot with actual Oscar statuettes in a display case outside.

Gathered around Peter Brennan and Raf were a few other members of the team Peter inherited when he took over *Hard Copy*. There was Parsons, in his Hawaiian shirt and white pants, assignment editor Tom Colbert, a police buff with red hair and loud clothes of unnatural fibre, and Linda Bell, a puffy, somewhat hysterical bleached blonde who insisted on telling me everyone's story on the way over.

"I know who to watch out for," she said, talking a mile a minute between cackles. "I'll tell you the good people and the bad ones..."

There was Richard Dreyfuss at the next table—a tiny man in white pants, open grey shirt, and sneakers getting up to plant a kiss on the cheek of Carol Kane, who until then was talking dreamily into the microcassette recorder a male journalist held in front of her as they picked at their Oriental chicken salads. Oh man, we were in Hollywood, all right, but what did this have to do with tabloid television?

Once the initial thrill wore off, it was clear to see that all would not be smooth sailing at *Hard Copy*. When Brennan accepted the job, he got an entire production staff—and there wasn't a writer among them. They could report, they could package; some could even piece together alliterative sentences and lay in music and sound effects. Not a one of them was trained in how to tell a story, to find the heart and the character to lead us through it.

We were going on the air in two weeks. The staff would have to be worked with and around.

Later that week, we got in some drunk driving training with strong margaritas and weak Mexican food at the popular and cheesy hangout El Coyote on Beverly Boulevard, and then a drive to Mark Monsky's birthday party at his home in Brentwood.

Monsky had retreated to a secluded compound in a tightly-packed residential neighborhood. There was a pool and jacuzzi out back, completely hidden from neighboring eyes by foliage and palm trees. Monsky walked around with a slightly demented grin. His t-shirt showed a mushroom cloud over Iraq and the slogan, "That's All, Folks."

Everyone ate and drank and the *Hard Copy* veterans whispered and snickered about the skinny-dipping parties the season before. When it was time to leave, Linda Bell insisted I drive her home in my leased convertible.

She played my cassette tapes and asked me questions about Parsons and Monsky and my girlfriend back in New York. I didn't give up too much, curious about the motives of this frantic woman who talked constantly, burst frequently into a high-pitched gargling giggle, and kept urging me to drive faster and faster. She leaned close and acted palsy-walsy like a porculent Doris Day, but when I pulled up at her apartment—an executive housing block on the edge of CBS Television City—she jumped out of the car quickly and left without ceremony or embarrassment.

I knew then something was up with Linda Bell. It took only days to find out how far up it actually was, how Brennan was making a disastrous and potentially fatal decision to keep this woman in place as supervising producer.

Linda Bell claimed to be my age, though she appeared older and more weary. A product of the Midwest, she gathered most of her experience in Los Angeles local news, a market that at the time was the exact opposite of my TV news roots. New York was focused, intense, and without frills; Los Angeles was, and remains, all big hair, frothy happy talk, sunshiney kissy-poo coverage, and smiley-face clones spread thinly across an unmanageable territory that encompassed a vast and heterogenous "Southland."

Linda Bell was a producer for the CBS affiliate before moving on to *This Evening* and *Hour Magazine*, the ultralite syndicated lifestyle shows that *A Current Affair* made obsolete a few years before. She claimed credit for keeping *Hard Copy* on the air that troubled first season, and believed she deserved to be executive producer in the second.

Peter Brennan had the job for the moment, and the arrival of Rafael and me put two physical barriers between her and the top slot. So while Brennan, Raf, and I struggled with scripts, tried to teach old dogs new tricks, and managed against all odds to turn the show into a tabloid TV force to be reckoned with, Linda Bell worked equally hard pushing her own agenda behind the scenes.

This wasn't the TV dream I was working to fulfill. This wasn't why I came to Hollywood. At a time when we should have taken tabloid television to new heights, when all the innovations we'd managed to lay down at *A Current Affair* were about to be elevated to a new level, we found ourselves embroiled in Vatican-style politics that forced us two steps back for every one forward, and which ultimately would destroy both our hopes and the genre.

Peter Brennan refused to use word processors or computers. His one concession to modernity was that his typewriter was electric. He sat over it, his cigarette ash falling onto the keys, looking for a symbol.

A Current Affair had its triangle and ka-chung. *Hard Copy* needed something of its own. A square, a circle, something with balls—the ball. The typing ball on his IBM Selectric.

He pulled the letter- and number-covered silver sphere out of the typewriter and envisioned it spinning toward the camera and crashing in with letters: *H* BANG! BANG! *A* BANG! BANG! Until it spelled out *HARD COPY*. Each segment would be introduced with and go out on the brain-crunching slam of the ball.

BANG! BANG!

Next, Brennan had to deal with problems that to him were more serious than Linda Bell—beginning with the anchor team.

Alan Frio and Terry Murphy were hairdos off the *Entertainment Tonight* assembly line, whom syndication boss Frank Kelly selected before he even hired a team to start up the show. Off the set, Frio was unassuming and even meek—very much the way he was on air. Terry Murphy was a horse of a different color, a woman who managed to camouflage a colorful and wholly American past.

Terry was three when her parents divorced and she went off to live with her father. When her father remarried, young Terry found herself in a home full of half brothers and sisters, living apart from the rest of the family, *in the attic*. As little girls will do, she turned to food for comfort, grew fat, and got the nickname "Sergeant Garcia," after the portly sidekick to Zorro.

Terry was twelve years old and 165 pounds when her father died. She moved in with her mother, a supportive woman who encouraged the girl and even entered her in the Junior Miss Pageant. By the time she was sixteen, Terry had grown three inches, lost many pounds, and was modeling. She later married and divorced her high school sweetheart, and in the 1970's, began the hopscotch journey through local TV news markets: Cincinnati, Detroit, Chicago, and ultimately Los Angeles, where she was a popular reporter and anchorwoman for the ABC affiliate.

She met her future second husband at a female impersonator club. David was an Israeli jeans magnate. Terry realized she was pregnant three months into their marriage. During her pregnancy, she returned to her childhood eating obsession. By her fifth month, she'd gained fifty pounds; by the time she delivered their first child, she was up to 217 pounds, bigger, she recalled, than the biggest maternity clothes they made.

"I loved talking baths," she told *Complete Woman*, a fat ladies' magazine, "but I had to put a minimal amount of water in the tub, because once I got in, the water rose, and if I filled it normally, it overflowed. David would cry when he saw me like that. He told me, 'I would love you if you were a tank.' I wish he hadn't said that because that's just what I became."

It took Terry Murphy six months to lose the weight, but she did, and fared far better with the birth of her second child. A few months later, Frank Kelly offered her the *Hard Copy* job.

By then, Terry Murphy was hovering around forty; like Maury Povich, she'd been through life's mill and back. She knew what it was like to be a lonely kid, a woman with weight problems. She was a journeywoman anchorwoman, in a position to put all of those hard-earned miles to good use.

Instead, she played the diva, breezing into the makeup room early in the morning, where Linda Bell would sit with her for hours as the heavy pancake was applied, then read her lines on the set and get the hell out. She was hard-boiled, hard-looking, and hard to get to do anything, balking whenever asked to do a special assignment and even refusing to screen packages before adding her voice to them. "I'm a professional," she'd sniff. "I don't need to see what I'm reading about."

On air, however, she couldn't have been more different, affecting the persona of the eager young bimbo: brainless, submissive to her male counterpart, resembling nothing so much as a happy, panting golden retriever or one of those head-bobbing dolls you put in the back window of your car.

Peter Brennan wanted Marlene Phillips, *A Current Affair*'s whipsmart director, to come with us to complete the new *Hard Copy* team, but when she decided to remain in New York, Brennan settled on Paul Nichols, the attractive young director of *Good Day New York*—the one who manned our *FUNY* fiasco.

In New York, Paul Nichols was a serious TV artist with a professional demeanor. In the California sun, he came out of his shell, untying his luxuriant blond hair, letting it flow past his shoulders and celebrating in the freedom of liberation.

As show director, Nichols would be a crucial part of the new team, but because he wasn't one of the "journo mates," Linda Bell saw him to be a weak link in Brennan's invading army. In no time at all, Linda and Paul were close friends, sharing an office and paying frequent and much-discussed visits to the female impersonator club on La Cienega Boulevard owned by the family of the male secretary to Charlotte Koppe, Paramount's vice president of programming, the intermediary between *Hard Copy* and the Paramount brass. She had all the bases covered.

"Hiya! How are ya? You look great today! California's sure agreeing with you!" Linda Bell was in my office. She took a wide berth on the couch and didn't wait for me to answer how I was or how California was agreeing with me. "Lookie, I've been talking to Peter about how you and I can best divide our work. Now, you know more than I do about scripts and Peter's style and all, so I suggested I work in the control room, getting the show out every day." She kept a big wide smile on her face, but her eyes were cold.

"Uh, sure, that sounds fine. Whatever Peter says."

"Great!" She was standing. "Have a nice day!"

It sounded innocent enough. Boy, did I have a lot to learn.

Hard Copy was assembled and fed to its stations via satellite each day at noon. At *A Current Affair*, this was a technical task that took about an hour in a cramped control room peopled by few others than the director, assistant director, and line producer.

Linda Bell turned the process into the heart of the operation and the command center for her *Hard Copy* alternative government.

She began by establishing a chain of command, seizing for herself the producer's role from the woman hired for the position. Robin, a sharp and cynical redhead, accepted her role as Linda Bell's assistant. Cheri Brownlee, a haggard woman at least a few years Linda Bell's senior, had been appointed coordinating producer. Cheri had transferred to the show after years running around as a field producer for *Entertainment Tonight*. Now she was to make sure all tape segments were completed and delivered to Linda Bell in the control room. Cheri became Linda Bell's field commander, taking a tiny desk in the office Linda Bell shared with Paul Nichols.

Linda Bell's most uncomfortable alliance was with a big-bellied, mustachioed Irishman named Mike O'Gara. O'Gara was the "executive in charge of production," a member of Paramount's permanent government assigned to the show to handle payroll, the hiring of crews, and other budgetary items. O'Gara ran a government of his own, including the finance, travel and technical departments.

Linda Bell and Parsons had scrapped publically with O'Gara the first season. She let it be known she despised him, but in the interest of the greater goal, joined forces with him.

With its four rows of desks and room for thirty people, their control room headquarters resembled the star deck of the Starship Enterprise in the *Star Trek* movie being shot at the opposite end of the lot. Each morning, Bell's crew and acolytes and O'Gara's lieutenants would gather and plan. A job that took an hour at most was stretched to six hours a day in a scene combining a slumber party with NASA's mission control.

This drawn-out process was key to Linda Bell's positioning with Paramount brass. Each morning, we'd work on day-of-air stories or mandate fixes to segments edited during the night. Cheri Brownlee often made the repairs herself, and by working as close to feedtime as possible, helped create a false sense that *Hard Copy* might not be recorded in time to make its satellite deadline.

Once the show was recorded, those in the control room would cheer as an entry-level production assistant ran the tape to the satellite transmission point in imitation of the opening scene of the movie *Broadcast News*—whose poster Linda Bell kept in her office along with a framed photo of herself sitting with Charles Manson in his prison cell.

When the feed began, Linda Bell would call the Paramount executives to report that she'd managed to make the feed—often despite delays caused by Brennan, Kearns, and the editorial side.

In late September, Rafael and I sat with Peter Brennan at the pool of his rented mansion in Coldwater Canyon.

Raf got right to the point. "Mate, you've got to do something about that Linda Bell. There's too much at stake here."

Brennan got up and picked out a flower that had dropped onto the water. "These pools are hard to maintain."

"We have a very difficult job to do, and this woman is working against you."

Raf had already ingratiated himself to the *Hard Copy* staff when he tracked a piece written by an emotionally fragile producer. Standing in the recording booth as he scanned the script for the first time, Raf asked if he could fix some grammatical errors and change a few instances of alliteration so the words would trip more comfortably off his tongue—and not make him sound like an idiot.

"You should read it as written," the producer replied.

"Yes," explained the young man with the featherbedding job of timing the tracks. "See, there are puns written in."

"Oh, these are puns. Thank you for explaining to me what a pun is." Raf's slow burn was heating quickly. "I don't know if you people know who I am, but I know when something's not written in English. But who cares? Who am I? I don't know what a *pun* is."

With headset on, Raf continued his low-key tirade in the tracking booth, not realizing that the tape editor was recording him and that the female producer had been reduced to uncontrollable tears.

Venting what to him was simply frustration over another insult and act of incompetence, Raf didn't realize that the tape would be copied and saved by Linda Bell, the same woman who'd cuddled the blubbering producer and wiped the mascaraed tears from her face.

"Mate, there's nothing I can do," Brennan said, studying some tiny imperfection in the tiling of the pool. "She's under contract."

"You're the boss there. She's undermining you, mate. You ought to send her to the New York office or someplace. It's bad enough Parsons is telling his people that what you're doing is sleazy. This woman is starting her own separate government."

"Raf's right, mate. She's bad and there's no reason we should have to work around this."

"Look at that," Brennan said. "Is this filter working or what?"

Brennan began to pick at the rough skin on his hand. He wasn't responding for reasons he wasn't yet letting on. He'd realized only recently that he didn't have the power he expected; Peter Brennan, executive producer, was considered hired "talent." Real power rested in the hands of Paramount's permanent bureaucracy, and its president of syndication, Frank Kelly.

Brennan also knew what Raf wasn't ready to admit. It was a different game in Hollywood, and you had to play by the rules. The game was to get ahead and accumulate power. The rules, well, the rules were to do anything you needed to do to get ahead and accumulate that power—as long as you kept a smile on your face and reminded everyone to have a nice day.

Raf and I hung around Brennan's dark-tiled swimming pool for a while longer before heading off for a drive. We were living in the next canyon over from Brennan's place, in a small cottage two and a half miles behind the Beverly Hills Hotel.

The inevitable had taken place. I'd cut the last cord tying me to my old New York life when my girlfriend decided she wouldn't move to Los Angeles with me. In the past year and a half, the clashing sensibilities of CBS and the newly liberating tabloid ethic (or lack of it) led to new strains in our relationship. She'd been living her own life, spending much of it on the road, chasing the major news stories of the day. At *A Current Affair*, I began leading a separate life as well.

Everything had gotten out of hand. It was a relief to let it go.

As a final gesture, I helped her set up the season premiere of the CBS reality show, *48 Hours*. She was responsible for coming up with several stories centering on the issue of murder in America.

"It's easy," I said. "Follow one of those spec crews, the cameramen who go out at night in New York City and shoot the dead bodies. Spend forty-eight hours in the worst emergency room in America.

"And hang out with that guy Ice Cube—the rapper from the group NWA? He's gone solo. His music's like a documentary on murder in America. He's like a spokesman."

She took my advice. *48 Hours: Murder U.S.A.* aired on September 13, 1990. Walter Goodman wrote in *The New York Times*: "What's going on here? Does this first show of the season signal a descent into the snap-crackle-pop journalism of *Hard Copy*?"

Audrey was still working in *A Current Affair*'s L.A. office, but without

Brennan's protection and with Anthea Disney's Diller-friendly mandate, she knew her days were numbered. She laid low, and in her spare time, drove me around Los Angeles

She'd even helped me find the house on Benedict Canyon Drive, up the road from the legendary pink hotel. "The compound," as it came to be known, was a country cottage with two bedrooms, an outdoor jacuzzi, lemon trees, and a high wooden fence to keep everything private.

Raf took the second bedroom. He was in a curious position. When he accepted Peter's offer to come along to *Hard Copy* as its senior correspondent, he neglected to tell his wife of twenty-five years that the job was in California. He couldn't admit to himself that he'd made the move.

In Raf's mind, he was only camping, so he equipped himself with a sleeping bag, a mess kit, and his books, and set up his room like an indoor campsite. In the closet was a collection of blue denim shirts and jeans, cowboy hats, boots, and socks. He didn't bring underwear. Raf liked to let everyone know he didn't wear any.

At the office, Raf was in the process of taking stories shot by *Hard Copy* producers and shaping them into compelling sagas—but with a difference. Brennan decided that Raf wouldn't bring along his gimmick of opening each segment with his laptop and map.

"Mates, you're making a big mistake. People know me. You wouldn't believe how many people come up to me in airports." Raf made typing gestures with his fingers.

"I agree with Peter, mate," I said. "It's like we've stolen a segment and gimmick from *A Current Affair*. We're taking the show to a new level, we can do the same with you."

Raf shook his head. "You fucking guys..."

One thing you had to admit about Raf, no matter how depressing he might be to be around, he was dead-on right when it came to nailing people and their motives. In that respect, he had true wisdom, and the first time Linda Bell stole a look in his eyes, she knew it, too. She didn't like Raf's style or manners. She didn't think he looked like a reporter—he certainly didn't dress like one. More to the point, she didn't like the fact that Raf was suspicious of her motives.

The following Monday, Raf was walking down the steel stairwell from our office to the studio when he passed Linda Bell on her way up.

"Hiya, Raf!" she enthused, as if she were his best friend.

"How—"

Raf held up a hand. "Wait. Don't ask me how my weekend was, because I know you don't care. Don't tell me I look great because I know you think I look awful. Don't ask me how I'm feeling because I know you won't wait for an answer and want me to feel bad. Don't tell me you liked my story, because I already know you didn't like my story. Don't tell me to have a nice day, because I know you want me to have a bad day. As a matter of fact—" He took his first breath. It was impressive. "Don't ever speak to me at all."

Raf continued on his way. Linda Bell froze for a moment. Her face reddened. Her eyes narrowed even further. Raf was dead meat.

For me, it was a constant yet polite bumping of heads until a Friday morning a couple of weeks later. Peter wanted to shake up the show; do something different, test the control room staff's ability to bring in a "live" show, and stretch the boundaries of the *Hard Copy* format.

It was simple. We'd let Gordon Elliott do his thing.

Gordon was working for us part-time. He'd been sailing some rough waters since his career took an unexpected sidetrip over the summer when he heard about open auditions for a cable channel game show. Would-be hosts dressed in their best suits lined the block outside the building on Manhattan's East Side when Gordon rolled up in a car direct from the beach, wearing baggy shorts, a Hawaiian shirt, and sand and suntan lotion still on his bare treetrunk legs.

Gordon took a number. When it was his turn, he waltzed onto the set, grabbed a wireless mike, ignored the prepared script, and did his audition off the cuff. He insulted the contestants, wreaked havoc on the set, and had the crew in stitches—the very thing that had made him such a phenomenon on morning television.

In offices throughout the building, where a feed of the auditions had run in the background like a leaking toilet since morning, executives perked up, ended phone calls, shushed their visitors, and scrambled for remotes to turn up the sound.

Suddenly, Gordon was a game show host, a new career that was only complicated when the legendary Mark Goodson, creator of *To Tell the Truth*, tried to hire Gordon away for a new version of the old chestnut. Gordon's agent said, "Go for it."

The cable channel sued. While Gordon's game show career was on hold, he'd be barging in on homes again.

On this day at *Hard Copy*, he'd go live from Zsa Zsa Gabor's home in Bel Air. Zsa Zsa had "adopted" a homeless woman she met while serving jailtime for slugging a Beverly Hills cop. She'd give Gordon a tour of the mansion, show how she lived with her new roomie, and even play a pickup game of basketball in the driveway. It promised to be different, wacky TV, and we'd have a couple of hours to whittle down whatever Gordon got into a good sixteen minutes of television, which was all it took to fill the show.

Brennan gave me editorial control and left the lot for the morning.

Linda Bell, meanwhile, was sulking. She didn't like the idea of running a single story. She didn't like the concept. She didn't like having me in the control room—or hearing me explain what Peter expected from her, the show, and the control room staff.

As we got the signal from the microwave truck and Gordon got down to business, the crowd in the control room laughed and applauded while Linda Bell paced. She snarled. She picked up the hotline to the office of Charlotte Koppe. She didn't like it. This may have been Peter Brennan's idea of *Hard Copy*, but it wasn't hers.

So she went over his head. Right in front of me, she got on the phone to Koppe and got her to override Peter's orders. When she hung up, she began shouting orders to the control room staff. The Zsa Zsa piece would be shortened. We'd knock it back to one section and add packages to the show. Business would go on as usual.

On Monday morning, I met Linda Bell alone in the darkened studio.

"That was wrong what you did," I told her. "You know it was wrong. Peter Brennan is our boss, you knew what he wanted and you did the opposite. You've got to realize, you're not going to save this show and make it a success. And the Paramount executives aren't going to save this show. Peter Brennan is—and as long as you have your own agenda and go over his head, you're dangerous to the show."

Her eyes went cold. She stormed off. Now I was dead meat.

Later that afternoon, Charlotte Koppe came into my office and said Linda Bell told her I didn't want her or any other Paramount executives "interfering" with their own show.

It was an impressive tactic. From then on, the war was in the open.

Linda Bell was married to her former news director, a balding, nebbishy chap who was out of work for at least part of that season. He'd drive his wife to work every morning and hang around the office. After my confrontation, he'd drop his wife off at the steps to the *Hard Copy* entrance and wait in their car until I came along. He'd just sit there, staring me down as I made my way into the office.

Every morning, I'd walk by and give him a hello, a smile, or a nod. He'd just squint back, trying to look mean. The intimidation tactic continued on and off for the next three years.

Brennan was having trouble on another front that would have a crucial effect on the ratings. Frank Kelly told him to stay away from the show's promotions. Paramount had an outside contractor handling the daily advertising for both *Entertainment Tonight* and *Hard Copy*: an old chum of Kelly's named Robert Faulk.

With his uniform of shorts, sandals, and granny glasses, the tall, pudgy Faulk might, on first meeting, be mistaken for an accomplished director or adult magazine czar, as he surrounded himself with blond women of various temperaments who basked in his wisdom. Yet Faulk was a tyro in this business of tabloid.

Brennan, on the other hand, invented tabloid TV promotions when he invented tabloid television in 1986. Nothing was so important as bringing viewers into the tent, and no one was better at writing those twenty- and thirty-second teasers than Peter Brennan.

A Current Affair didn't even have a promotions department until *Inside Edition* came on the scene, and even then, Brennan would write the promos for the young ad person who'd edit the spot to Brennan's directions.

Faulk wasn't interested in Brennan's expertise. He was dismissive in our presence, and most disconcertingly, burst into tears on more than one occasion when Brennan confronted him. His promotions for *Hard Copy* were more suited to a children's cartoon show. Striking reality footage was run through special effects machines, stop-framed, played with, labeled "*HOT! HOT! HOT!*", and any sense of reality was bled out.

Brennan fought for weeks over control of the promos. Eventually a deal was struck, by which Brennan would collaborate each day with one of Faulk's women. The first candidate, with all of a year of television experience under her insubstantial belt, would lecture Brennan on how to write. "The stupid bitch," as she came to be known, was replaced by a taller and more amenable blonde whose cluelessness was a blessing. She was happy to take what Brennan wrote and edit it to his specifications.

While *A Current Affair* relied on a seat-of-the-pants, unfinished quality that made the show real and immediate, Paramount demanded a slick product in the mold of *Entertainment Tonight*. It wasn't bad enough that just as *ET* had two perky anchors, so would *Hard Copy*. To make the show a "Hollywood" version of reality TV, the suits deemed that the anchors would be shot against a blue screen, with videotape of a working newsroom in Detroit projected behind them. The anchors looked like two people sitting against a projection, while our actual working newsroom was only several yards away, under asbestos skies on the other side of the prefab wall.

The bigger challenge would be keeping up with stories in a city like L.A., where news didn't matter and where the plugged-in, Manhattan-based competition had a three-hour headstart.

We got around the time problem by dividing up the day. The content of each show would be decided the previous afternoon. Each morning we'd have a six a.m. conference call with the New York office and decide whether to throw out one of the stories for something new. We'd have until noon to whack something together.

This split approach worked well, yet would soon develop into a dangerous pattern: wake up with a hangover before dawn, review the stories, write a day-of-air lead, record the show at noon, go to lunch, drink til four, come back and work til six or so, drink til midnight, up with a hangover at six a.m.—but we're getting ahead of ourselves.

For now, in these first months of *Hard Copy's* second season, we managed to re-establish the show, make people forget the embarrassing bad writing, two-minute copy stories, blood, body bags, and general ineptitude of the first season. We pulled out all the stops to get noticed in a big way. We went after serial killers. We tracked down the voluptuous Barbi Twins. We even had Gordon ambush Maury Povich on East 67th Street. It wasn't too difficult because we'd arranged the meeting with Maury the day before.

Most important, we took the idea that Brennan came up with in Tarrytown and gave it a Hollywood twist. *Hard Copy* would be the home of the reality mini-movie. We'd spend big money on high-quality dramatizations, sometimes spooling out the drama over several nights in the style of a TV miniseries.

Our first attempt came from a one-column item I pulled out of a newspaper from a town near San Diego. A middle-aged divorcee walked into the home of her ex-husband and his new wife and shot them dead in their marital bed. Betty Broderick was facing murder charges, cut and dried, yet the most cursory background check revealed a story that would win her the sympathy of every housewife in America.

Betty and Dan Broderick married when they were kids in college. She worked to put him through medical school. She bore him several children. She made the mistake of getting older. Dan left her for his beautiful young secretary.

There were many warning signs before Betty's ultimate explosion. She broke into Dan's house and set his clothing on fire. She vandalized the newlyweds' house. She gained weight. She broke down.

We recreated the story on film—which was unheard of in the quick-shooting video world of tabloid TV—and wrote the story as a three-act tragedy. We called it *A Woman Scorned.*

We followed Betty Broderick through her trial, conviction, and troubles in prison. Eventually, Meredith Baxter starred in the television movie. They called it *A Woman Scorned.*

CHAPTER TWELVE:
GOD'S FUCKUPS

Hard Copy was a new show. We brought in new producers. We phased out old producers. I spent most of my time at my desk, writing stories, rewriting producers' stories, and coming to the conclusion that the art of tabloid television could not be taught. Either you got it or you didn't.

The best of the *Hard Copy* veterans was Doug Bruckner, an eccentric refugee from L.A. local news who spoke in an over-enunciated tabloid voice of doom, but was actually a mild-mannered gentleman who worked in miniature, crafting intricate pieces he wrote section by section. Bruckner had a unique style and was free to do as he pleased.

The reporters and producers John Parsons had brought on from his New York days were at a loss when it came to the competitive and ethical challenges tabloid television required. When they were on the road, they turned to Parsons for guidance, and he couldn't help. The Brennan way represented the antithesis of the standards he upheld so proudly.

One by one, we had to let them go, including the reporter I sent to Thunder Bay, Canada, where fugitive murder suspect and former *Playboy* bunny Bambi Bembenek had been arrested after escaping from prison. He called to say the story was wrapped and that he and David Lee Miller, his competitor from *A Current Affair*, were chartering a plane back to the States—together.

"Are you out of your fucking mind?" I roared. "You go to that pilot and you pay him extra. You tell him to fly David Lee Miller to fucking Nome, Alaska. And then you get yourself another flight back—alone."

He chuckled. "Your *Front Page* spirit is all well and good—"

"No, it's not. This is fucking war and you better believe David Miller isn't going to be doing you any favors. He'd kick open the door and fucking throw you out of the plane sure as you're there. This isn't local news where everyone helps each other and makes sure they get the same story. Every exclusive, every rating point means the difference between success and cancellation."

That reporter, incidentally, was the same one my old boss Nick Loiacono the assignment editor had stuffed physically into a trash can back in the Channel Five days. It wasn't long before he was back working for local news.

Parsons' disappointment at his first season failure and the double embarrassment of being replaced by the very Australian contingent who pushed out his *10 O'Clock News* team in New York could be understood. So could his eventual decision that he couldn't have anything to do with our overhaul of the show he invented.

He kept his office while he floated off, back to New York and into development deals and other projects.

Of all Parsons' hires from the first season at *Hard Copy*, the least likely to succeed was the bureau chief he'd installed in New York. Eames Hamilton Yates was a large, red-faced rambling ranch of a man; the big, fat, thirty-something black sheep of several first-class families and traditions.

His father Ted was a legendary and respected NBC News producer who was killed in action while covering Israel's Six Day War. His mother went on to marry CBS correspondent Mike Wallace, the grand old black-haired man of *60 Minutes*. Eames' new stepbrother was Chris Wallace, correspondent, anchorman, and smirking heir to the Wallace legacy.

Eames's brother was a noted documentarian and journalist for the *Christian Science Monitor*. Eames was married to the lovely blue-blood daughter of Senator Claiborne Pell of Rhode Island. They had a lovely towheaded son.

Eames Yates was a fuckup. He was in and out of jobs, in and out of rehab, in and out of whoever'd let him do the old in and out; a heavy drinking, heavy eating, heavy smoking, heavy duty heavy boy.

Thanks to his lineage, Eames was dropped into television at the top of the slide. On his own, he'd slid down, around and around until he landed on his big fat ass at *Hard Copy*.

Yet one conversation with Eames and it was evident. He had the spark. His hard knocks on easy street had given him a depth his colleagues and more successful siblings didn't have. He knew what it was like to fall down and pick himself up. His privileged upbringing and exposure to rarified air gave him the perspective of a true outsider to the rest of America.

Eames had a glint of brilliance and he wanted so much to succeed. Succeed he would—and then some. Eames would pack up all his personal baggage and venture throughout this great land, mixing with real, forgotten Americans in places ranging from reservations to family farms to the most exclusive drawing rooms of Palm Beach and Upper East Side society.

Eames would become our secret weapon. Whenever we hit a brick wall on a story, whenever the subjects refused to cooperate no matter how much money was waved in their faces, when we needed someone to go out there and bring 'em back alive, we sent Eames.

When we weren't out recasting *A Current Affair* in our own westward-looking image, Peter, Raf, and I tried to recreate the pub scene of New York. It was near impossible. People didn't drink in L.A. the way they did in New York.

We tried out an Irish bar on Fairfax called Bergin's. It was dark, with paper shamrocks on the walls and ceilings, and a short, stout bartender in white shirt and apron whose attention we couldn't get when we arrived because he was chatting with a customer about the films of Claude Chabrol. The next day, as we walked in with a blast of late afternoon sunlight, he announced, "Uh oh, here come the drinkers."

We found refuge at a place called the Formosa, a ramshackle Cantonese joint on Santa Monica Boulevard that had hip cache among young actors and old drunks. We fit somewhere in between.

The place was built around an old trolley car, and every inch of wall seemed to be covered with another framed 8x10 of an old Hollywood star, with each name displayed in punched-out red tape.

The Formosa was next door to the old Warner Brothers lot; long a favorite hangout of celebritites. Ava Gardner had a favorite red leatherette booth under the fishtank. Bogart and Bacall ate there; Howard Hughes, who'd set up shop a few blocks east, once borrowed a twenty from owner Lem Quon to settle a bar bet.

Marilyn Monroe drank there. Elvis once paid with a check Lem thought of keeping as a souvenir but cashed for the sure thing instead. Old Lem kept Elvis' beer bottles and a collection of Elvis figurines and decanters in a display case. He was past eighty by now. He kept himself on display, every night from five to eleven, slumped at Ava Gardner's banquette under the fish.

Lindy, the ancient barman, had been there since the beginning and claimed he'd written a memoir called *Forty Years Behind Bars*.

The Formosa was a landmark, so it was no surprise that in those early months, it was in danger of being torn down. Warners owned the land and building, and wanted to replace it with a parking structure.

Our official office-away-from-the-office was hidden within the Bel Age Hotel just off the Sunset Strip, our home-away-from-home when we lived in New York. The Diaghilev Bar was a dark den whose only window looked in on the city's best Russian restaurant, patronized by vacationers, celebrities, and an assortment of interesting people who drank and smoked.

The bartender was Nabi Hussein, just plain Nabi to thousands from around the world, a trim and exact man from Bangla Desh, trained in the art of superior bar service. The restaurant maitre d', Dmitri Dmitrov, was a product of the finest European hotel schools. Dmitri didn't walk. He glided. No one was better at the restaurant arts, but when the restaurant closed and his tie came off, Dmitri revealed himself to be one of the toughest characters in L.A., an expert in boxing to boot.

The sophisticated European room was our refuge, where we could plan, dream, and watch celebrities in their most candid moments; watching with discretion, another vodka and tonic always on deck.

After a decade in New York, I'd regained my driving skills on the perilously policed boulevards and dangerously veering canyon drives. It wasn't a question of not driving drunk. It was a matter of knowing how to drive after several drinks—or a dozen. It was a matter of survival.

Audrey called from the road a few weeks after we had settled into the house on Benedict Canyon. It was about one a.m. L.A. time, which meant it was three hours later wherever she was.

"Hi," said the squeaky little voice. "Anthea says I'm not allowed to talk to you, but I need someone to talk to. I'm in Palm Beach doing a story for Anthea, and I know I'm going to get fired any day now."

"You're in Palm Springs, too?"

"What do you mean?"

I was fucking with her. Even roused from sleep, I knew instinctually to screw with the heads of the competition. "You guys are on the Sinatra death watch. I figured they'd send you."

"Not Palm Springs. I'm in Palm Beach. Florida. There's a death watch?" Audrey had made her reputation as a death watch soldier.

"Oh, Palm Beach, right." I stretched and pretended I was struggling for consciousness. "No, never mind. How's work?"

"Anthea hates me."

"Yeah."

"I think my days are numbered."

"Yeah."

"Uh...I heard about the death watch. I think we have Watkiss there."

A week later, Audrey was fired by *A Current Affair*. Peter hired her on *Hard Copy*.

A week after that, I was thumbing through the file of clips sent from the New York office and there was a one-liner from one of the gossip columns about the false rumor that sent Wall Street on a downward blip: the rumor that Frank Sinatra was dead.

I called Audrey right away. It turned out she'd called Dunleavy about the supposed death watch, who called his pal Eddie Burns at police headquarters, who made a call to one of his contacts on Wall Street who knew all the rumors, who made a couple of inquiries, which led to a rumor that spread to the floor and was picked up by the papers.

All from a bedroom in Benedict Canyon in the middle of the night.

There was a bump in the ratings for our first November sweeps. The new depth of the sagas, the wit around the edges of the celebrity pieces, the use of film on extensive re-enactments all gave *Hard Copy* the beginnings of a new identity. For once, a show named after the typewritten version of a newspaper reporter's article was able to tell a story. We had a long way to go, but slowly, painfully, we were on the way.

It was *A Current Affair*, however, that gave us the greatest gift and potential for grabbing the couple of ratings points we'd need to catch up. Days before the beginning of sweeps, they announced the permanent replacement for their legendary host, Maury Povich.

It was Maureen O'Boyle.

"This is the most exciting day of my life," Maureen gushed, understandably, to the newspapers.

The announcement represented the surrender of *A Current Affair* to Fox's West Coast contingent, and was apparently based on money considerations and the advice of dreaded consultants. A look at the numbers showed that ratings hadn't dropped considerably since Maury was taken off the air in the summer. What those numbers didn't show was that most people thought Maury was still the anchor—a perception that would remain for years.

Maureen's ascension was the first major decision of Anthea Disney's reign, and seemed to be the crowning touch on her plans to convert the show from the *New York Post* to *New York* magazine. Behind the scenes, it was also a measure of her control and comfort. Big, tall, and brassy Maureen had not only become the alter ego for the diminutive executive producer, she had also become Anthea's confidante, best friend, and, for a time, roommate.

Amid the fast life as a print-turned-television executive running *A Current Affair*, so did Anthea's personal life become a soap opera. She and her husband reached an impasse in their marriage and Anthea left their home outside the city and moved, briefly, into Maureen's West Side apartment.

Rumors spread quickly in the compressed and bitter atmosphere of *A Current Affair*. Unfair and untrue though the rumors may have been, Anthea and Maureen became the targets of a whispering campaign that labeled them lesbian lovers.

It all reached a head the day the two of them got into a shouting match in Anthea's newly-redecorated office. It was a boisterous, unhinged disagreement that could only happen between close friends. Maureen had the last word before turning on her heel and slamming the door behind her. Anthea rose from her desk, trembling with anger. She pushed back her chair and charged after her anchorwoman, grabbing the doorknob and turning it, ready to throw back the door and end the argument in Maureen's office at the other end of the newsroom.

She never emerged. She couldn't open the door. The force of Maureen's slam had broken and jammed the doorlock. Anthea was trapped in her office in the middle of the workday.

A locksmith had to be called in to free her. In the newsroom, staffers walked about as if they didn't notice what was going on, but the clattering of their computer terminal keyboards spoke differently as the nasty gossip web spread and the phone calls went out far beyond *A Current Affair*, all the way to the office of *Hard Copy* across the lane from the Billy Wilder Building.

Editors of the *New York Post's Page Six* had gotten wind of the lesbian rumors weeks earlier, and the very juicy story of the spat was enough to prompt publication as the lead item of the gossip column. This simply would not do. Anthea and Ian Rae forced Steve Dunleavy to telephone *Post* editor Jerry Nachman and beg him not to run the story. The story never ran.

Our plans for tabloid domination were put on hold late in November when true human tragedy struck our small team. Peter Brennan's ex-wife died unexpectedly in New York City, a terrible event and all the more heartbreaking because she had custody of Peter's two youngest children, his adolescent sons.

The boys would be moving in with Peter and his fiancee, Nancy Gershwin.

Peter and Nancy were married during the first week of 1991. The intimate, formal gathering, captured by a photographer, video crew, film team, and a lensman taking nineteenth-century style daguerreotypes, began with touching candlelit reverence and descended into tabloid mayhem by evening's end.

After the vows, Gordon Elliott, the one guest attired in white dinner jacket, spun himself into the role of master of ceremonies, prompting each of the groom's tuxedoed pals to relate stories of his benevolence and amity.

The more eloquent Gordon waxed, the more it became all too much for a small, gray-haired man sitting with his wife at a table near the wall. "Aw, what a bunch of bullshit!"

Gordon, speaking toward the bubbles of a lofted glass of champagne, was snapped out of his reverie.

The offender was one Neal Travis, creator of *New York Post's Page Six* column, an old newspaper mate of Brennan who was currently living in Los Angeles, editing *California* magazine.

"Ah, Neal, I see you're enjoying the spirits and handling them as well as usual," Gordon said with a dismissive chuckle. "As I was saying, the gentle nature of Peter Brennan—"

"Bullshit! Peter Brennan is not some kind and gentle poof! Peter Brennan is a hardass, cynical son of a bitch, and that's what makes him such a great journalist!"

Travis' elegant wife Tolley placed a hand softly on his trembling arm. "Now Travis," she intoned. "You're getting untidy."

"Thank you, Neal," Gordon replied, totally shaken and stirred. "Back to your drink."

"Bullshit!" Travis was halfway to his feet. "Peter Brennan is a son of a bitch! He's a bastard! He's not like you say! He's tough!"

The groom leaned over in absolute hilarious collapse. The father of the bride began to cry.

I turned to Rafael, who was laughing as well. "Who is this guy? He's fucking great!"

Later that night, the party carried on to the Bel Age. There were about ten of us, sitting on the couches against the back wall, watching the actor Raul Julia and a female companion at the bar.

"J.B." Blunck, one of the *A Current Affair* originators, now developing new Fox shows, recalled Julia had been a guest on *Good Day New York*. He called over a waitress. "We'd like to buy a drink for Mr. Julia."

Rafael groaned.

"Uh, J.B., we try to stay low-key here," I explained. "We never bother the celebs."

"Oh, bullshit." He looked to the waitress. "Please buy a round for Mr. Julia and his friend. Tell him it's from Fox Television."

After the drink, Raul Julia and the woman stopped at our table. "My companion and I wish to thank you," the actor said with a theatrical flourish, "for your generous gift of libation—"

"No." Raf interrupted him. "We wish to thank *you*, sir. For all the pleasure you have given us."

Raul Julia smiled and bowed.

"The pleasure you have given us with your work on stage and film, especially in the movie, the kissing—the one about the bug—the bug that...that kissed the woman, the kiss of, what was it called, the spiderman kissing—"

Julia's smile froze as Raf struggled for the name of the film. *Kiss of the Spiderwoman* was in all our heads as we all leaned toward him, trying in vain to send it to Raf telepathically.

"The one about the spider and the woman, you know, the one with the transvestite in the..."

"Mate, stop staring."

Two weeks into 1991, Raf and I were back at the Bel Age. Raf leaned against the bar, cowboy hat dipped low over his eyes, sipping his Johnny Walker Black and staring at two men sitting on the couch.

The actor Michael Douglas was drinking heavily. Every five minutes or so, he and his pal would run out the door to the men's room and return a couple of minutes later, all the more animated.

"I don't believe this," Raf muttered, watching as Douglas rubbed his nose and drank more.

A beautiful blond who looked like a pro walked in and sat between Douglas and his friend. After another drink, the trio left.

After a time, Douglas would enter a rehab clinic, reportedly for treatment of drug and sex addiction.

Our plans for *Hard Copy* had hit another snag that week as the United States launched Operation Desert Shield against Saddam Hussein. The show's content would reflect the fact that American men and women were being shipped off to kill and be killed.

The war began officially at midnight. We put together a special show focusing on what people were doing at that exact moment, sending a producer to a homeless shelter, another to an all-night convenience store, and Raf on a train from Los Angeles to Phoenix.

The show was pre-empted by network news in most markets. All I wanted was for the war to end, if only to get our time slots back.

"Well, I need four walls around me to hold my life, to keep me from going astray. And a honky-tonk angel to hold me tight, to keep me from slipping away..." Raf and I drove down Santa Monica Boulevard, singing along with George Jones on the tape deck.

"Guess who wrote this, mate?" I asked.

"George Jones. I don't know."

"James Taylor. That's good trivia to remember."

"See, you teach me." Raf tilted his hat. "Who's James Taylor?"

Raf was in a better mood. Saddam Hussein hadn't put up much of a fight and Desert Shield turned to Desert Storm turned to Desert Hanging Around much quicker than anyone had expected.

We were back in business. Raf had more reason to gloat because, back at home, he'd saved my life that very weekend.

Los Angeles was turning out to be a stranger place than I'd expected. An aspiring rock 'n' roll star I'd been dating hadn't taken kindly to my attempt at phasing out our short-lived romance. She took it even less calmly when I responded to her incessant phone calls by telling her to fuck off.

That Sunday morning, while I slept off another long night, Raf awoke to the sounds of someone coming in the front door. He climbed out of his sleeping bag, into his robe and stepped out to the hallway to see the young woman with one hand on the doorknob to my bedroom and another holding a knife.

"You don't want to go in there."

"Why not?"

"Because if you go in, only one of you is going to come out alive."

"I only want to talk to him." She turned the knob. Raf lifted her physically and carried her through the living room.

When he deposited her on the front lawn by the gate, he pried the knife from her hand. A dude on a motorcycle idled in the driveway.

"Are you out of your fucking mind?" Raf asked.

"I want to give him back his things, talk to him."

"I do stories about this every day. Go home. He's not worth it."

After some more discussion, she did leave.

When Raf told me very matter-of-factly about what happened, my emotions were mixed. I was shocked by how close I came to being gutted, impressed by the depth of the woman's feelings, and proud that like Peter Brennan, I finally had a stalker of my own.

"You guys are out of control," Raf reminded me after we handed the car to the valets and settled in at the Bel Age bar. Nabi hovered a few feet away, elbow on the cash register and eye on our drinks, ready to replace them as soon as we were down to the final sip. "This L.A. is a very, very bad place."

"It is an honor when you think about it," I said, still charged by the stalking incident. "I can't imagine feeling like that about someone."

Raf shook his head. "You know, that's something I don't understand about you. Peter, Dunleavy, those guys I can understand. But you're not like them. You're an American. You worked for network news. You should know better."

"No, *you* came from the networks, mate. I worked local. There's a difference."

"You're out of control, mate, all of you. This whole place is spinning

162

out of control. You, Peter. You drink like fucking fish. You drive through these canyons like unguided missiles. You're gonna get killed or arrested."

I responded with misplaced pride. "We're all alcoholics."

"No. *They're* alcoholics. You're worse. You're an alcohol abuser." Raf sighed. "I'm really tired of this, mate. I'm too fucking old."

"Weren't you the one who said we're the heirs to guys like Shakespeare and Testicleese?"

Raf couldn't help but laugh. "No, I said we were the heirs to Homer...and *Soph*ocles." He held up his diminishing glass of Johnny Walker Black. Nabi reached for the bottle. "See, that's what I like about you. You're smart. But you don't act smart." Suddenly, more whiskey was poured. "Nabi, please. You're gonna make me broke."

"No, no, Mr. Raf. This is on me."

Raf accepted, graciously. "Look," he said, leading with his tumbler. "What I said was there's nothing wrong with tabloid stories. They're as classic as they come. *Oedipus Rex*. Incest, homicide, suicide, patricide—"

"I thought there were *two* sides to every story."

"Good one." Raf was easy to make laugh, too. "And no one ever calls Shakespeare sleazy or Aescylus or Euripedes or Sophocles sleazy. Now, Testicleese..."

Raf was questioning the kid about his t-shirt. The production assistant was one of several *Hard Copy* employees wearing a shirt declaring in red ink: "I survived *Hard Copy*'s Serial Killer Week."

"Why are you wearing that shirt?"

"I don't know, we thought it was funny."

"Don't you think it hurts the show and morale to mock the programming? Don't you realize we're trying to get attention for the show? Who told you to wear that?"

We were in the middle of February sweeps, gaining more attention through a series of stories on serial killers. We had the first interview with the nurse who survived the Richard Speck murders twenty five years earlier; Doug Bruckner faced down Charles Manson, who sooner or later would face another parole board; and Diane Dimond had a two-part story on Jeffrey MacDonald, the Green Beret doctor serving life times three for killing his wife and two daughters. Dimond was a local news reporter and former National Public Radio reporter for whom Gerald Stone had paid big money to bring to *A Current Affair* and who we brought over to *Hard Copy* when her fat contract wasn't renewed. She confronted MacDonald with love letters from a female radio host with whom he'd reportedly shared sexual intimacy behind prison walls.

We even had a B-movie director film a mini horror movie on Ed Gein, the old coot who inspired *The Texas Chainsaw Massacre*.

The strategy gained us attention and ratings the show had never seen. That was why Raf was especially attuned to the workings of Linda Bell's alternative government. He was convinced they were involved in the t-shirt rebellion. He knew an attack was imminent.

The attack came two weeks after sweeps ended. It was a hit: planned, planted and directed at the Paramount executives who scanned the front page of the *Los Angeles Times Calendar* section each morning. The hitman was TV critic Howard Rosenberg. The article was entitled "Enquiring Minds Love *Hard Copy*."

Suddenly, *Hard Copy* was stuck with the title of "the most repulsive show on television," "the closest TV equivalent of those spurious scandal sheets, the *National Enquirer* and the *Star*," "by far the foulest of the syndicated tabloid shows," "junk, not journalism," and "deeper in the gutter than *A Current Affair*."

"In its fifteen months of life," Rosenberg wrote, "*Hard Copy* has done to the airwaves what that recent oil spill did to the waters and marine life of the Persian Gulf."

The article was already xeroxed and posted around the office early that morning when I stormed into Brennan's office.

"Do you believe this shit?" I was ready to take on the columnist on each story segment he'd lacerated.

I'd argue that every few years Charles Manson should be carted out and the horror of his crimes retold, especially when heavy metal bands make him a hero to alienated kids; that it's worth mentioning when a convicted killer like Jeffrey MacDonald has fans among the supposed intelligentsia seeking his release—that stories about the Menendez brothers were news.

"Stories like these feed the fright and paranoia of those Americans who take programs like *Hard Copy* seriously," Rosenberg concluded.

I'd answer him in the *L.A. Times Feedback* column. Hell, he knew we needed flashy promotions and teases. He knew the shows we were up against. He knew we were only getting them into the tent—

"*Burtie, stop!*" Brennan brought me back to earth. "It's a hit."

"What?"

"Fuck it," he said, tossing the paper onto the couch in his office. "It's a hit, mate. Hit as in hitman. There's nothing we can do. They've put a hit on us."

Brennan knew. Whether Rosenberg was accurate or not didn't matter. He was only the hitman. There were far more powerful enemies in this company town. I had to get used to it, this new game we had to play in Hollywood.

CHAPTER THIRTEEN:
WILLIE SMITH'S WILD WILLIE

The history of tabloid television was shaped by the response of those in command to the stories that presented themselves to be exploited. There was a reason *A Current Affair* once used the tagline "Guts TV"—not necessarily because of any bravery on the part of its producers, but because of the gut instinct that allowed them to recognize important and rateable stories—days, even weeks before the competition.

One such story was presented on a silver platter on the Monday after Easter Sunday, 1991. It was midmorning in Los Angeles. Peter Brennan was locked in his office in a meeting with the Paramount execs. Rafael Abramovitz was on the road. I was in my office rewriting someone's script when the phone rang.

"Hello, Burt, Vincent Eckersley here." It was a thick Scottish burr belonging to a tabloid newspaper stringer in Florida. Vincent was among the best. He called in often with stories and tips.

"How are you, mate?"

"Burt, look, I've got to talk quickly. We've got a big one here in Palm Beach. There's been a rape at the Kennedy mansion here."

"Really?"

"And apparently the senator's involved."

"The senator?" Something in my chest began to pound.

"That's right."

"The senator? As in Ted?"

"That's right. Burt, I've got to run. I'll be here. You can page me." He left his number and ran off to chase the story.

The phone was suddenly wet and cold in my hand. Oh man, this was the kind of story we lived for. The Kennedys in trouble again.

I ran to Brennan's door. Penny, his assistant, looked up. "You better not bother him. He's in with the suits."

I looked around the office. I heard Paul Nichols and Linda Bell laughing behind their closed office door. I realized I was truly stranded, stuck in fucking L.A. with no one with whom to share this purely visceral feeling of excitement; no Wayne or Dickie or Dunleavy to dance a jig with; no one who would understand.

I ran back to my desk and got the New York office on the phone. Diane Dimond answered. She was teamed in New York with another *A Current Affair* alum, Jerry Burke. They were among the few Yanks to make it as all-out, rabid tabloid journalists. She could appreciate the Kennedy story. Dimond booked herself on the next flight to Palm Beach and was rolling to the airport by the time I strolled into Brennan's office with the news.

The story would be a watershed in American political and sexual mythology. Generations of condoned womanizing by America's royal family had finally led to this: a young woman, claiming she was raped at the famed Kennedy mansion in Palm Beach, Florida in the early hours of Easter morning after a late-night drinking binge with Teddy, his son, and his nephew, William Kennedy Smith.

Willie, as he was known, son of Steve Smith, the late "fixer" of Kennedy scandals, was accused in the biggest family disgrace since Chappaquiddick. This would be the first defining news story of our tenure at *Hard Copy*, and we were sure to come up against massive competition from *A Current Affair*. After all, Brennan and Dunleavy had written *Those Wild, Wild Kennedy Boys* back in the seventies—and it wouldn't get much wilder than this.

We stationed a live truck outside the Kennedy mansion and led the next day's show from Palm Beach. Dimond had Michele Cassone, a young woman who claimed to have gone to the mansion with the victim the morning in question. Cassone accused Senator Ted of chasing her around in a nightshirt while his nephew was having his way with the victim out on the beach.

Back in L.A., we had Mike O'Gara don a nightshirt and stand in his stocking feet while a cameraman did a pan from from his toes up to his belly. As Michele Cassone described her alleged encounter, we threw in the shot in a frightening, almost subliminal, recreation of Ted's lower regions.

The cops weren't talking and that made the story even better. Dimond dug up everything possible and we ran stories every day that week. It wasn't difficult for her to get exclusives, though. For some reason, there was no competition.

It was no surprise that *Inside Edition* stayed away from the story. Supported in sales deals by other King Brothers blockbusters, *Inside* was intent on establishing itself as the most boring, unwatched successful show in syndication. This season, they'd even invoked something they called the "Clean Air Act," promising to cover only the most newsworthy stories, like wheat futures in Russia and defective airplane parts.

We had to feel sorry for Bob Young, known as the Poison Dwarf of tabloid TV, explaining straight-faced to *Variety* why the William Kennedy Smith story was less important than an item about faulty school bus blinkers. "We decided a long time ago we weren't going the tabloid route," he said, "so it wasn't a big story for us."

The networks ignored the story completely. CBS and ABC didn't even run a mention. When taken to task, the producer of ABC's *World News Tonight* said, incredibly, "It wasn't even a tough call. No government official had been charged with anything."

NBC eventually weighed in with a report on the media. Reporter Keith Morrison sniffed at the fuss, declaring, "Reporters stick like greasy glue to whatever doorstep might reveal the next salacious quote"—as if that wasn't a reporter's job to begin with. He probably got a fruit basket that week from his NBC colleague, the Terminator's wife—and Willie's cousin—Maria Shriver.

After years of looking the other way while Teddy stumbled and groped his way around Washington, going as far as to allegedly have relations with a woman under a table during lunch in a popular restaurant—though he apparently won points with the press corp by making use of a private dining room—all these network newsmen in the Brooks Brothers shirts and loosened ties who spent time taking "L's" and "R's" out of Tom Brokaw's scripts actually ran through a list of world events and decided that a story in which Senator Ted Kennedy was embroiled in a rape case wasn't even worth fifteen seconds. The arrogance of the networks was mind-boggling— at least until you considered the Kennedy influence and infiltration.

The JFK assassination was a defining moment for me. I was seven, home sick from school watching television when the first bulletin hit NBC, sat through the weekend vigil with my family and neighbors, and watched the murder of Lee Harvey Oswald on live television.

By the time I was on the Channel Five assignment desk, the Kennedy name had other significance: a reason for checking out every murder and drug item that came over the police wire. It was standard practice to ignore the everyday crime in rougher neighborhoods like Bed-Stuy and Harlem— until RFK's son David was arrested buying smack at a hotel in Harlem. Ever since, every death or bust in a bad place made me remember the words of Nicky the assignment editor: "Check it out. It could be a Kennedy."

In those days at Channel Five, Monsky and Parsons' Kennedy love was amusing. When Monsky hired Jackie O's nephew Tony Radziwill as his personal assistant, it was a matter of status. He had an almost-Kennedy working for him.

A few years later, a couple of lowly production assistants were put out of work so Parsons could hire Kara Kennedy when her dad Teddy was making a run at the presidential nomination.

The Kennedy connection was far more insidious at the networks, long before John-John and *George*. ABC honcho Roone Arledge caused a major scandal, when, at the behest of his close friend Ethel Kennedy, he spiked a *20/20* story on the RFK-Marilyn Monroe affair. Geraldo Rivera quit the show amid the fuss. Maria Shriver went from a failed morning show at CBS to more than one failed evening show at NBC, and Dan Rather, in his autobiography, admitted to giving more weight to JFK conspircy theories when he got an exclusive viewing of the Zapruder film and reported that Kennedy's head was knocked forward by an assassin's bullet—when the head was shown clearly to have jerked backward in an explosion of bones and brain.

A Current Affair and Rupert Murdoch were certainly no Kennedy lovers. When Murdoch bought up Metromedia, Ted Kennedy sneaked through a law stopping him from owning TV stations in the same cities in which he was saving newspapers. It was a dirty trick and not one Rupert would forgive easily. Ted was a fat, liberal target, and any excuse to poke him would be taken advantage of.

Yet, *A Current Affair* didn't touch the Willie Smith story, either. All that week, Diane Dimond had it to herself. We poured money into special feeds and live trucks, going $200,000 a week over budget just to establish a beachhead. The ratings climbed. It was a case of "he said, she said," a story everyone was talking about over water coolers all over the country. *The New York Times* was playing it up bigtime, with prominent space and team coverage.

On television, the story was ours.

Linda Bell didn't like it one bit. I was at her spot on the deck of her Starship Enterprise, feeding Dimond the latest information. Peter Brennan and I had invaded her control room, running the show by the seat of our pants. There should be more of a "mix" of stories, she suggested. Terry Murphy had nothing to do.

By midweek, Linda Bell freaked. When I was out of the room, she ordered Dimond to redo a standup in the rain because her hair was out of place. When Dimond said it wasn't that important, Linda Bell screamed to remind her who was boss. Dimond responded with a curt "fuck you."

"Who is this bitch?" Dimond asked me on the phone. "I'm working my ass off in the rain with the cops kicking me off the property and she's screaming at me to redo standups because my hair isn't perfect? Where are her priorities?"

For days, she refused to speak to or take directions from Linda Bell.

Linda Bell, no fool, responded by flooding Dimond with flowers.

Back in New York, Wayne Darwen toiled as Anthea Disney's senior producer. He knew William Kennedy Smith was a major story—but he knew *A Current Affair* wasn't his show anymore. Anthea insisted that the rape allegations against William Kennedy Smith were not worth reporting, not on a show that was trying to prove to Barry Diller and unnamed advertisers that it was more *New York* magazine than *New York Post*.

The complaining phone calls came to us from *A Current Affair* staffers. Everyone said it was proof that Anthea had no gut. She was smart, she was sharp, she could parrot Peter Brennan's words about the Ten Commandments and Seven Deadly Sins. She could look like a tiny Tina Brown and study Faye Dunaway in *Network*, but in her zeal to make *A Current Affair* respectable she was squeezing out its reason for existence.

By the end of the second week, the New York tabloids were going all-out in their coverage. *The New York Times* was making the story a daily cause. As the scandal spiraled into Washington, even the networks were forced grudgingly to acknowledge its existence.

Ultimately, so was *A Current Affair*. Almost two weeks after we hit Palm Beach, Anthea Disney dispatched Bill McGowan. He did a standup on a pier, and a wrap-up package mixing file footage with recent news coverage. The story was such a low priority that McGowan and his producer checked into the airport Marriott Hotel, forty minutes from the action, so they could collect more "Marriott points" to trade in for future discounts.

All this was too much for Wayne. The day after he finally got the story on the air, he walked into the *A Current Affair* office and threw what the Australians call a "pink fit." Telephones and newspapers went flying in his wake as he stormed out.

When he returned, he announced he was taking a job as senior producer for a new tabloid show to be produced by the Tribune Company. The show was to be called *Now It Can Be Told*. Its star would be Geraldo Rivera.

On April fifth, *A Current Affair* was forced to bring in the big guns—the only big gun it had, Steve Dunleavy—to Palm Beach. He was in the Midwest, interviewing a porn star, and was embarrassed to take the assignment so late in the game. "No, it's McGowan's," he insisted. "I can't take Billy's story, no."

Dunleavy had no choice. He was ordered to do it. The order came from Rupert Murdoch himself.

The following week, I watched *A Current Affair* to see Dunleavy try to play catch up. He was a pathetic sight, jogging shirtless down Main Street in Palm Beach, making a point in his flowery prose about shirtless jogging being illegal yet rape being acceptable in this jet-setting town.

Dunleavy kept running. In the end, he ran away with the story. Diane

Dimond, experienced and hungry as she was, found herself running in second place. *Hard Copy* was at a further disadvantage because the Paramount suits decided we were spending too much time on the Kennedy story. They wanted to lighten things up, add a little variety.. We were forced to turn our attention elsewhere while Dunleavy attacked the story like the proud street dog he was.

He set up camp at the Brazilian Court Hotel, where RFK's son David had been found dead of a drug overdose. He drank and danced at Bar One, where the alleged victim met the Kennedys. He bought up everyone in sight, cops and socialites and witnesses, including $40,000 for Anne Mercer, the woman who fetched the alleged victim from the Kennedy estate—making her testimony worthless at the trial. He duped the police spokesman into reading the arrest report describing the incident, then shot a graphic, brutal re-enactment of what the victim claimed happened.

Dunleavy ran dozens of stories and reclaimed the story personally. It was a grand return to form.

It was also another step in his downfall.

With no one to guide him, Dunleavy was allowed to run wild, and, eventually, go overboard. In April, he interviewed that young woman Michele Cassone, the one who claimed that Senator Ted chased her in his gown the night of the alleged attack. Michele was a typically pathetic Palm Beach wannabe, a baker's daughter with a drinking problem.

Dunleavy lured young Michele to be interviewed at Fox studios in New York, got her drunk at "21," then sat her under the lights in front of two cameras. After setting her up with some softball questions, he flattered the plain woman by bringing up rumors she was planning to pose for a girlie magazine.

"I would never pose nude," she said, pleased to be considered yet putting on mock airs of horror, as a society gal would be expected to do.

Oh no? "Well what of this?" Dunleavy whipped out a snapshot one of Michele's more chivalrous former beaus had sold to *A Current Affair*, showing Michele smiling and posing with his penis in her mouth.

The interviewee responded as any alcohol-impaired woman might be expected. Her eyes grew wide. She gasped. "Where did you get—" She made a grab for the picture, and when Steve held it just out of reach, just as the boyfriend may have tantalized her with his member before snapping the incriminating photo, she slugged Dunleavy, pounced on him, bit his hand, pulled his hair, and body-slammed him out the door.

Dunleavy was in pain, yet he couldn't keep the smile off his face. *A Current Affair* ran it all. The show even broadcast the blowjob snapshot, but apparently in a nod to Anthea's intent to make the show more like *New York* magazine, covered the gentleman's penis with an *A Current Affair* triangle. It was good television. It was also crass, over the top, grimy fingers newsprint ugly. The *A Current Affair* staff cheered their 12.6 rating in New York City, not appreciating that viewers watched the way they'd watch an auto accident. *A Current Affair* had made a victim out of a drunken woman. They were no better than Willie Smith.

Scandal and sex and celebrity were but a few of the ingredients that made up the new mix at *Hard Copy*.

Animal stories and tabloid TV go back to the genre's roots in Australian and British tabloid newsapers. Every issue with a seamy story about the sordid affair between a vicar and choirmistress and a page three picture of a big-jugged lass would also contain an inspiring or heartbreaking story about a little furry creature. The idea was that a nice animal story would make the reader more likely to forgive the nasty material in the rest of the paper.

The same held true in television. Animal stories attracted calls and letters. They made up for other sins you put on the screen.

Our most memorable animal story at *A Current Affair* was about an old dog named Smoke in a town somewhere down south. One day, Smoke ran down the railroad tracks, smack into the path of an oncoming train. When Smoke's distraught owner went out to see if there was anything left of his old hound, he found an ear, a leg, another leg, the tail, a scrap of fur—that was about it.

That would have been the end of the story, except that a week or so later, Smoke picked himself up from wherever he was carried several miles up the track and came hobbling home, minus that ear, tail, fur and those two legs. It was inspirational, all right. Brennan wanted to run it just so he could write in the promo: "It was the day the train kept a rollin...ON TOP OF OLD SMOKIE."

We covered our first major animal story within our first weeks at *Hard Copy*, joining an ASPCA raid on a group of dognappers who stole household pets off the streets and sold them off to be killed in research labs. Joining the strike on the so-called "puppy mill" was a group of activists called Last Chance for Animals.

This animal Entebbee raid turned into a crusade when we learned that the fifty liberated dogs were being held as evidence by the Bakersfield District Attorney's office. Brennan's idea of starting an adoption campaign led to plenty of phone calls, and got everyone else pissed off, including Terry Murphy, who was forced to do a report from the D.A.'s kennel, on her knees, surrounded by dogs. That wasn't her style. (About a year later, Murphy made news when her neighbor's Akita ripped a hole in her face. Everyone was worried she'd have to get painful rabies shots—the dog, that is.)

Peter Brennan found another gold nugget in that first raid: the leader of the animal group, a charismatic actor-activist named Chris DeRose. DeRose was in his early forties, a rugged, handsome guy who'd bounced around Hollywood for years. He'd starred in B-movies and an old Aaron Spelling TV series called *The San Pedro Beach Bums*, but he was best known in the industry for his activism on behalf of helpless beasts. He was a combination Clint Eastwood, Rambo, and Gandhi—a down-to-earth guy and a true believer.

When interviewed at the scene of the kennel raid, DeRose came off like the ultimate tough guy. "What kind of garbage bags could do this to helpless animals?" he growled. "They make me wanna puke." Male viewers saw a thinking man's Stallone. Women in the office creamed over the guy.

We took advantage of DeRose's natural empathy and compassion and hired him to front other animal and human interest stories around the country. The great idea almost forced us to tear a page out of the tabloid handbook, crumple it up and toss it out, abandoning animal stories for good.

On paper, it was one of the best: a captivating justice story about a puppy mill in the mountains of Nevada. A man and woman were arrested by the FBI for allowing dozens of stolen pets to freeze to death. There was tragedy. There was justice.

DeRose was paired up on the story with a young producer named Scott. Scott was typical of the *Hard Copy* producers left over from the first season. As a kid, he was one of *The Bad News Bears*—he actually starred in the movie, playing a little leaguer coached by Walter Matthau. In adulthood, Scott and another former Bear would team up and use those credentials to pick up women in bars. This being L.A., it *worked*, and this being L.A., those were just about his only journalistic credentials.

At that point, we were working with what we had.

Scott and DeRose went off to Nevada and drove with a camera crew up a treacherous, snowy mountain road to the crime scene, where the illegal compound—a house trailer, some utility vehicles, and animal cages—had been cordoned off by the federal agents.

DeRose then confronted the female suspect in an on-camera jailhouse interview.

"I didn't mean to hurt those animals," she said.

"You're lying to me." DeRose leaned forward and jabbed his finger at the plexiglas separating them. "You've been lying this whole interview," he hissed.

"No, I haven't. I did my best for those dogs."

"Find yourself another business. And tell your partner to find another business. Because if not, I'm gonna find him. I'll find him—*if I have to follow him all the way to hell.*"

Chris DeRose may have been overly dramatic, but he meant every word. The man was effective because he was totally sincere.

When they returned, I went through the usual drill. I had Scott sit in my office and tell me what video he'd shot, and as he waited, I wrote the piece for him. DeRose read the script and Scott went into an edit room to put the parts together to have the story ready for the next morning's pre-show meeting.

When I walked in at 7 a.m., Peter Brennan's office was unusually crowded. For some reason, all of Linda Bell's minions were sitting in, crowded around her and Jeff, the lawyer assigned to the show. All avoided my eyes as I took a seat near Brennan's desk. They usually avoided my eyes anyway, so I didn't notice anything was up.

As usual, everyone watched the piece without comment. Unlike the raucous discussions back in New York, people rarely expressed opinions in these meetings. In Hollywood, most people are afraid to express an opinion that might contradict that of their boss. When the segment was over, the only one to speak up was Jeff the lawyer.

"I don't like it," he said. "It's very one-sided."

"Mate," said Brennan, "of course he's one-sided. That's the idea. That's DeRose's style."

"He's an activist," I added.

Jeff glared at me. "He's not an activist, he's a nutcase!"

Excuse me?

There was an uncomfortable moment of silence as everyone let the lawyer's intemperate outburst sink in. Linda Bell put her head down, shuffled some papers, and pretended to be reading something.

Jeff was beside himself. "What about—what about the cars he trashed at the kennel?"

Excuse me?

"What about the crowbars and the trailer and—"

Brennan stopped him. "What are you talking about?"

"The tape. Everyone's seen the tape."

Linda Bell and Cheri Brownlee looked at me with little pursed-lipped smiles. Their faces said "Gotcha."

"What the fuck are you talking about?"

Jeff held up a Beta cassette. It was raw, unedited tape from the shoot. One of them put the tape in Brennan's player and everyone sat silently as the scene unspooled.

There was Chris DeRose, on that Nevada mountain, looking heroic, intense, and angry as he swaggered through the crime scene. His breath was visible in angry bursts of steam. He spoke off the cuff about how enraged he was by the people who let the animals die. This didn't make the piece. It must be an outtake.

DeRose whacked something on a tree for emphasis. It was a crowbar. He walked on, raised the crowbar, and whacked it against the trailer's aluminum side. Then he whacked again, this time smashing out a trailer window.

DeRose stomped toward the camera and the cameraman backed away. It appeared that DeRose was out of control. He approached a gleaming new Jeep Cherokee left behind when the feds raided the place. He reared back with the crowbar, ready to send it cracking down on the windshield.

Where the fuck was Scott?

"Stop! Stop!" Scott's voice piped up from somewhere off camera. Thank God. Someone had common sense. There was a camera cut.

The next shot was from a different point of view. The cameraman was now *inside* the Jeep. We heard Scott's voice.

"Okay, go ahead."

CRUNCH! The crowbar came crashing down, sending spiderweb cracks across the safety glass windshield. This could be a first. Scott had been directing the destruction.

"That's a take!" Scott chirped.

This was worse than the Rodney King tape. This was a federal crime scene he was destroying. What was even more seriuos, and glaringly obvious, was that people had known about the tape and assumed that Brennan and I ordered or approved of the rampage. We'd been set up for a fall.

Brennan's reaction was instantaneous and direct. "Destroy the tapes," he ordered, in front of everyone.

I took the tape out of the machine and brought it to my office.

As the day progressed, Brennan found out that much of the office had known about the tapes the previous afternoon. Linda Bell showed it to the attorney. Of course, she wasn't going to let me in on it. Her mistake was not telling Peter Brennan.

The trap led to a glimpse of Brennan's hidden tough side. He called Linda Bell and Cheri Brownlee into his office. He told them that if he found out any of his subordinates knew about that tape for an entire day and tried to set him up, they'd be fired.

That night, we brought Scott along to the Formosa. Brennan, Raf and I sat with him in a booth under the Elvis decanters, poking at greasy eggrolls and slurping uncarbonated Stoli and tonics.

Brennan told Scott not to worry; it was in Paramount's best interest to keep the tape issue quiet, so he should just lie low and we'd protect him. If the feds even noticed the destroyed trailer and Jeep, they'd have no proof of who did it. "Remember, though. This is a federal offense. They could make a federal case out of it." Once again, our jobs were on the line.

Scott was pale. Brennan went off to use the phone. Rafael sat there, disgust curling up his nose and drawing back his lip into a sneer like young Elvis on the Jim Beam decanter in the display case above us. He swirled his Johnny Walker Black in the cloudy Formosa glass. "I hope you realize what Peter's doing," he said without looking up. "He's going way out on a limb for you and I don't know why. Anyone else would have cut you loose."

"I know. I'm stupid," Scott whined. "I thought it was what you guys wanted."

"You better be ready to do the right thing," Raf said. "There comes a time, like every good Roman soldier, you have to know when to fall on your sword. And sacrifice yourself."

The bad news bear gulped. "I know."

Later that night, I snapped open the cassettes, yanked out yards of tape and tossed it all in the garbage can outside my kitchen door.

The heat died down. The battles continued. Scott lasted another year or so until we had to let him go. As we said our goodbyes, I counseled him that the best thing he could do was to work in a real newsroom for a year. Go out and get some experience, some seasoning. He didn't. He just turned up on some other show.

CHAPTER FOURTEEN:
FAKE TITS & REAL BLOOD

April fifteenth was "tax day." Rafael Abramovitz stood at the Formosa bar, bemoaning his unappreciated status as a tax accountant and introducing me as an FBI agent who was handing him over to the witness protection program after he testified against his Mob employers.

We were well into our drinking night, bullshitting a couple of women sitting next to us, when what appeared to be a homeless man staggered in and flopped onto a barstool. He wore a filthy overcoat too heavy for the weather and a floppy hat pulled over his greasy hair. I recognized him immediately and kicked Raf.

"Look." I was always giving him free pop culture lessons. "Keanu Reeves."

"Who's that?"

"Big actor. You know, the guy from the *Bill & Ted* movie."

Raf stared as the young actor took his drink to a table behind us and dropped his head in his arms. "No way." He returned to his boisterous monologue, and only believed the young bum may have been a Hollywood star when a beautiful blond sat with him and got Reeves to lift his head.

Raf and I were leaving by then. He waved his cowboy hat and bid everyone a loud adieu. As we walked past his table, Keanu Reeves looked up and spoke. "A couple of dicks!"

I stopped and glared. The woman smiled apologetically. Raf took my arm and stopped me from walking back to ask the actor to repeat his fighting words.

"He thinks we're detectives," Raf said with a proud smile.

Raf and I had become fast friends in a slow town, spending much of our time driving my orange Kharmann Ghia or his '67 Mustang up and down the long boulevards of Los Angeles, looking for action, of any kind, anywhere. We were convinced that somewhere in L.A. was a shadow city where men like us and beautiful women filled bars, laughing and toasting and indulging in intellectual conversation.

Instead, we drank at dives like the Formosa and sipped tequila next to poodle-haired men at heavy metal clubs like the Rainbow, consorted with off-duty strippers and tried to urge a smile from the female bartenders.

Raf was working out his deception about moving to Los Angeles, getting back to visit his wife every five or six weeks, and copping a free plane ride by complaining to Brennan that his teeth needed fixing and that his dentist on the Upper West Side was the only one who could do the work.

Living in "the compound," the only friction occurred when he couldn't pay his share of the rent, because his wife held the family purse strings and since he hadn't exactly told her he *moved*, couldn't exactly write five hundred dollar checks every month.

He paid indirectly once. During one of Raf's dental trips, a female companion of mine accidentally let the bathtub overflow and flooded the bathroom. I didn't realize the water had seeped under the wall into his room.

Raf got back to L.A. a couple of weeks later, slipped naked into his sleeping bag, and jumped out with a high-pitched scream, running into the hall swinging his cowboy hat at his ass and the floor and shutting the door behind him.

Seems Raf's carpet and sleeping bag had been soaked, gone moldy and become home to a family of lizards that tried to squirm up his brown-eye when he crawled in for some shut-eye. Raf hopped around the house yelling about Legionnaire's disease and reptiles and when I stopped pissing myself laughing, I poured him a shot of Johnny Walker Black.

When we weren't working or drinking or laughing, Raf and I were writing. We were in Hollywood, so naturally, we wrote screenplays together. Among the first was one about a band of tabloid television reporters who'd made their show too successful for their own good and were being phased out by a new, politically-correct regime that wanted to make the show less *New York Post* and more *New York* magazine when the story of the decade broke out: a U.S. Senator, implicated in the rape of a stripper at his nephew's bachelor party.

It was a wild comedy, starring a character named Phil, who was based on me, and another named Alex, who was something like Raf.

We called it *The Fortune Garden*.

Yeah, it was Sunday night and we were drinking at the Rainbow again. The Rainbow Grill was, and is, a legendary rock 'n' roll hangout on the western edge of the Sunset Strip, sharing a driveway, parking lot, and clientele with the Roxy music club and its private upstairs boite, On the Rox, where John Belushi had his last supper and in more recent years Heidi Fleiss and her friend Victoria Sellers held court and took orders from celebrities.

Back in the fifties, the Rainbow was the site of the Villa Nova, the restaurant where Vincente Minnelli proposed to Judy Garland and Marilyn Monroe met Joe DiMaggio on a blind date. In the seventies, the Rainbow was the place where heavy metal gods Led Zeppelin would rest, surrounded by a never-ending menu of groupies who'd wank the Sunset glam scene through the eighties. These days it was usually jam-packed with heavy metal kids and occasional stars like Slash of Guns n Roses and Jason Bonham, son of Led Zeppelin's dead drummer. The Who's John Entwistle was a semi-regular, as were chubby porn star-director Ron Jeremy and his ever-changing bevy of "actresses."

The Rainbow was dark and comfortable, with checked tablecloths and a specialty in pizza and drinks. Memorabilia like Entwistle's bass and a Stray Cats drum cover adorned out-of-reach parts of the walls. Upstairs, in a third-floor loft above the rest rooms, was a hidden bar and dance floor, but the most singular attraction was the exclusive dining room open only on the most crowded nights. It was in the kitchen: tables and booths and even a bar set up in the space not taken up by the dishwashers, fryolators, and pizza ovens. The party at the Rainbow went on into the early hours under the fluorescent lights.

The place rested on Sundays, the nights Raf and I often stopped in on the way home to the canyon. We didn't exactly fit in at the tiny bar, Raf in his Resistol hat and demim jacket, me in my sports jacket, he sipping his Johnny Walker Black and me trading off between Bud Lights and tequilas.

On this night, the bartender was a slim, attractive woman in her mid-thirties with tight black jeans, a tighter white ass, and a permanent frown that all the bad one-liners in the bar wouldn't erase.

Lemmy Kilmister, mythical leader of the legendary metal band Motorhead, sidled over to give her a kiss. Lemmy was royalty; the bartender offered a rare smile and a cheek, even though Lemmy's face was plastered with boils that prompted British music writers to dub him "The Carbuncular One."

"Raf, it's Lemmy," I pointed out.

"Who the fuck is Lemmy?" Raf was from a different world. He was amazed at my pop culture references.

On the other side of Raf sat two women from a place somewhere between the worlds of stripping and rock 'n' roll. One wore lingerie as a blouse. The other wore leather straps wrapped around her torso until all strategic parts were covered. They were shapely, sturdy girls with a look of the farmland, tainted milkmaids with teased hair and cornfed, tanned skin.

We got to talking. Candy and Renee were sisters. Renee gave me her number. I promised to call.

Later that week, I convinced Raf to accompany me to meet the sisters at another rock 'n' roll haunt in Hollywood. Boardner's was a grungy tavern on a sidestreet off Hollywood Boulevard. It was steeped in Hollywood history. W.C. Fields once drank there; a time since, Raf was convinced, the glasses had not been properly washed.

We were squashed into a booth in back. Rock 'n' roll music played. Across the aisle, a TV scriptwriting conference carried on. A thirtysomething preppie whose Boola Boola demeanor shouted Ivy League lorded over several pitchers of beer and three young men—two white and one black—who could have passed as underclassmen, but were in fact his writing staff. The leatherbound script on the table near his beer glass showed they all worked for a black sitcom.

Raf sat on the aisle, leaning back as far as possible from the two sisters across from us. Both could have been dressed up for a transvestite parade, and traded knowing winks with many of the male rockers trolling the aisles in leather jackets and torn jeans.

I leaned over my beer, talking nonstop, a veritable James Woods of let's-get-it-on anticipation.

"Candy saw you on television this week," Renee said to Raf.

That got his attention. He couldn't resist a smile. "Yes. I spend most of my time hanging around bars. But I try to do some good."

"We thought you might have been bullshitting—"

"You know how dudes are," said Candy.

"Especially at the Rainbow," Renee completed. "Anyway, we thought maybe you could help us."

"You being on television and all," Candy said. She brought her arms close to her chest, forcing her artificial breasts to squeeze out further. "And Kurt—"

"Burt," I corrected.

"Burt said you were a lawyer and stuff."

"Once a lawyer always a lawyer," said Raf.

"See, we have a problem with our mother."

"She has a drinking problem."

"Don't we all."

Renee continued. "She's got this new boyfriend."

"He's an Indian," Candy added.

"He's a motherfucker. He beats her. And our brother—"

"He's in the army, he's stationed in Germany, he's coming home soon, and he knows about what's going on."

"He's coming home soon," Renee added. "And we're afraid that he's going to kill the Indian."

"We thought maybe you could help us," Candy said. "You being on TV and all."

"On *Hard Copy*," said Renee. "Help us before our brother gets back and kills the Indian."

Raf swirled his Johnny Walker Black and tipped back his hat before smiling again and sipping from the cloudy glass. "I can understand. I've heard this kind of story many times before. You'd like me to have a word with your brother—"

"We could do that," I butted in. "Easy."

"—Or perhaps find out about a shelter for your mother."

The two women shifted uncomfortably and traded looks.

"Not exactly," said Renee.

"Not exactly," her sister echoed.

"We were hoping maybe, with your connections—"

"Working for *Hard Copy* and all—"

"That you could help us find a hitman, to kill the Indian before our brother does."

There was a pause in the time it took for the impact of their words to sink in, and for Raf's eyes to widen.

"I don't believe this," he said, standing and sliding out of the booth. "I'm a lawyer. I can't be hearing something like this—"

"Uh, I don't think so." I was thinking on my feet and trying to somehow recoup the evening and those big fake breasts. "Maybe we should talk—"

The sisters heard nothing more. Raf had me by the collar and was dragging me down the aisle past the comedy writers, pushing me past the bar and back onto the sidewalk.

"What are you doing?" I sputtered into the night air.

"Those fucking women asked me to kill somebody!"

"They didn't really. They only asked you to help *find* someone to kill somebody."

"What the fuck's the matter with you?"

"We could of talked 'em out of it."

"Talked them out of it? You're over the edge, man. What's wrong with this fucking town?"

In Los Angeles, far from our families and any concept of reality, Raf was our moral compass with bad teeth. He was the only one who could stand at a bar with Peter Brennan, jab a finger in his chest, and give him advice. Brennan often said Raf was constantly telling him things were wrong without coming up with solutions, but when Raf spoke, Brennan listened. Raf was older, and beneath the prickly exterior, had a real heart.

Raf was also a prime target of what had become referred to openly as

Hard Copy's "alternative government." His days were numbered —though he'd have to wait in line before getting the knife.

Gordon Elliott would be first.

Gordon Elliott was one of the sharpest minds and quickest studies in show business. He had a brilliant and wicked wit, and every little bon mot he threw toward the camera was caught by the viewing audience. Back in Sydney, many of his fellow Australians thought he was a tall poppy too smart for his own facking good and meant to be cut down. Americans, though, saw him as a big cuddly koala and success was inevitable.

Yet by the spring of 1991, Gordon's life and career were in ruins. His decision to jump from a cable TV game show to Mark Goodson's *To Tell the Truth* had ended in disaster. A high court ruled that Gordon be held liable for leaving the cable outfit in the lurch. He was enjoined from hosting another game show for five years, he was bankrupted—and his marriage was ending, to boot.

The defining moment of his crisis came at the end of April. It was about two a.m. on a Sunday in Los Angeles and Saturday night was still going strong. The four of us were in Gordon's rental car, he and Audrey and Peter Brennan and I, all of us well-oiled, having spent the night at various Mexican and El Salvadoran bars on the east end of Sunset, drinking tequilas and heavy Central American cervezas, looking for action among the celebrating-wildly-for-no-reason Third World crowd, while getting farther and farther from the action at each stop.

Bars close early in L.A. The prepared and the alcoholic always have bottles to go home to. I had more than a few at the compound. Raf was off on assignment, so we could stay up the rest of the night drinking whatever we could find. Gordon was behind the wheel. Peter and Audrey were in back. I was in the death seat, pointing the way home up Benedict Canyon Drive while pulling a homemade cassette from my pocket to stick in the tape deck.

I knew Gordon would love it. He, too, was a Sinatra man, and I was carrying the next level in appreciation: *Jerry Lewis Just Sings*, that rare album from the fifties, a copy of the recording Jerry himself couldn't find until I presented it to him, on which Jerry straight-faced belts out standards with a big orchestra arranged by Buddy Bregman.

"Listen to this," I enthused, and popped in the tape of Jerry wailing "I've Got the World on a String." It echoed out the sunroof through the canyon. *"What a world, what a life...I'm in lo-o-o-o-o-o-o-ve!"*

We were as far as Lexington when Gordon announced, "Turn this shit off!" He popped the cassette out.

"Are you crazy?" I punched it back in.

Without warning, Gordon grabbed my head and thrust it toward his crotch. The car veered. Audrey yelped. Peter laughed.

I popped up and without thought responded by punching Gordon in the cheek. Whoops. The car slowed to about five miles an hour, and in a single motion, Gordon reached over, flicked open the passenger door and pushed me out into the street.

I ducked and rolled and came up wobbly on a new pair of cowboy boots I'd purchased that week. He threw me out of a moving car! Getting my bearings, all I could think was, *Cool!*

The car stopped and started up the road, the brakelights flashing on and off while Audrey's squeals and Peter's laughter bounced into the night. I ran, leapt, scrambled onto the car's trunk and splayed myself across the roof, holding on as the car continued up Benedict Canyon, maintaining some kind of balance as I reached into the sunroof, grabbed Gordon by his hair and punched wildly.

Whap! Whap! My fist connected across his big face again and again. Gordon roared like an injured lion and hit the brakes.

Whoaaa! I went flying again, this time off the roof and down the hood, rolling again away from the wheels and opening my eyes once I landed on my back in the middle of the road.

We were at the corner of Tower Road. Take a right and head up the hill and Bruce Springsteen lived just a couple of blocks away on a compound with *two* houses, one for him and one for the wife and kids. We didn't know it then, but had we turned on Tower and kept winding up the hill, we'd find Madame Heidi's house in full swing.

It was in eyesight from where I lay, in the road, blinking at the stars and getting my bearings when suddenly there was a bellowing six-foot-seven Australian charging at me, blinded with drunken rage, screaming he's going to kill me.

I was up, all cylinders of Cuervo stoked, running up the road like a man on stilts. I couldn't run in the fucking boots.

"Wait! Wait!" I yelled, laughing, "No fair!"

Gordon stopped, panting, accepting the called time-out while I pulled off the boots.

"Now!"

I got about three steps before Gordon caught up and swatted me with a beefy paw like a bear brushing away a small dog. Like a battered dog, I skittered across the road onto my back.

"AAAAAARRRGGGHHHH!" Gordon bellowed into the night.

"I give, I give!"

"Yeah! And take yer bloody poofter boots!" He was talking about my new Spanish-heeled Tony Llamas, pointy black with hearts wingtipped on the toes, blue and pink and red tooling on the sides. Yeah, they were a little pooftery, but you couldn't really tell unless you rolled up my pants—

BOINK! Gordon fired the first boot past my sprawled, heaving, too-drunk-to-roll body. The boot bounced off the tar and crashed into the bushes.

"Aarrgh!"

BOINK! The second one bounced, as well—*BOOF!*

For a moment, everything went silver as the boot heel caught me square in the face and ricocheted into the street. Then, as if someone pulled a stopper, I felt my mouth fill swiftly with syrupy fluid. My cheeks puffed trying to hold in the stuff. It was warm.

It was blood.

Gordon lumbered in for the kill. I made my way to one knee, moved a hand from my face and held it up to stop him. "Wait!" I pointed to my mouth with my free hand and then opened wide. Blood gushed forth down my chin and splashed all over my denim shirt.

In the streetlight or moonlight, Gordon froze and his mouth opened as well. "Oh my God, mate!" The fight was over. "Are you all right?"

"I don't know."

It didn't hurt. I was so fucking drunk I could have been shot and not felt it. I was drunk enough to start a brawl with a six-foot-seven Australian. I wasn't going to feel this.

"Mate."

"I'm bleeding."

"Stay still. Let me see." Gordon put an arm around me, and in an act of selflessness, brotherly love and foolhardiness for which I will always be in his debt, held open my blood-spouting mouth and stuck his meaty fingers inside, feeling around gently to see if he'd knocked loose any teeth. He hadn't, but I was a fucking mess.

Gordon helped me into the car. Audrey screamed. Peter laughed. "Mate, we've got to get to a hospital," Gordon said, skidding the car around and rushing back toward Sunset. "And fast."

Audrey directed him.

"Fuck him, mate, I've seen worse football injuries," Peter scoffed, chuckling. He lit a cigarette. "Let's get to the house and put a little vodka on it."

It seemed that when the boot hit my cheek, it came in contact with a tooth and punctured the skin at the smile line. There was a straight-through hole ripped into my cheek, and a tiny blood vessel poking out, venting blood. I slumped in the passenger seat and soon realized that by manipulating my facial expressions, I could direct the flow of blood to spurt forth like a horror movie special effect.

"Mate, mate..." I got quiet, holding my face. Gordon and Audrey, wide-eyed. "*Dawn of the Dead!*"

I opened my mouth and blood shot everywhere. The front of the rental car looked like a fucking abattoir. "Mate, I'm getting cold, I'm getting cold..." I bullshitted. "Ma? Ma?"

"Hang on, mate, we'll get you there."

"Not Cedars Sinai! Please! Not where Sammy died!'

"No worries, mate!"

Audrey leaned over the seat, pointing the way. "Take a right, down Beverly!"

Peter chortled in back.

It was a private hospital on the corner of Beverly Drive and Pico. Gordon and Audrey helped me into a fluorescent waiting room. The receptionist was a black gentlemen behind a glass window, reading something. He looked up. His eyes widened. He stood. Audrey looked at him. Then she turned and got her first good look at me. She gagged, and with a hand over her mouth, ran into the ladies' room to vomit.

"Excuse me everyone," I announced. "I'm okay. I know it looks bad, but I have NOT been shot. It was just a little horseplay."

The man behind the glass opened the door and held out a plastic bag for me to drop in my bloodied shirt, then pointed me toward an examining table, where on the other side of the curtain, a middle-aged man moaned in pain. He couldn't urinate.

"Well, it was a bit of horseplay that got out of hand," I explained when a doctor arrived.

"Did you have anything to drink?"

"Yeah. A few beers."

"How many?"

"Uh, nine?"

"He's had nine beers!" The doctor gave a nurse an urgent look and she scurried about, returning to shoot me with something. "Did you have anything else to drink?"

"A few shots of tequila."

"How many?"

"Uh...nine?"

"*He's had nine tequilas!*" The nurses ran around some more. "No wonder he's bleeding so much. His blood is thinned."

They shot me with something else and got me ready for stitches. The doctor was disgusted. I should have been ashamed of myself, pissed as a rat, next to a man with real problems. He couldn't urinate.

The doctor went off and returned with some satisfaction. The plastic surgeon was refusing to come to the hospital in the middle of the night because of doubt whether my insurance would cover his cosmetic services.

"Now, if you insist he come, we can make some arrangement—"

"No, don't bother."

"There could be a scar."

"That's all right," I said. "Go for it. A scar will give me some character."

The scar was character-making, all right. When the bandaid came off later in the week, I got the same compliment from everyone:

"Cute dimple."

The episode was an embarrassing low point for all involved. I'd carry the physical reminder; Gordon wouldn't drink again for a couple of years and, for a moment, it seemed he might not work again, either.

Some days after the incident, Paramount boss Frank Kelly summoned Gordon to lunch, told the big guy he was the greatest, and offered him a full-time, exclusive contract.

Gordon thanked him, but said he'd prefer to stay freelance, traveling cross country on Mark Goodson's private jet, doing the occasional early-morning doorknock for *Good Day New York*, and waiting for his talent pay off in a big way.

"Are you turning me down?" Kelly asked.

"Why, yes."

The little man underwent an amazing transformation into the leprechaun from those horror movies. He screamed and yelled and even uttered that deathless Hollywood phrase: *"You'll never work in this town again!"*

At the very least, Gordon was no longer working with us at *Hard Copy*.

By Spring 1991, *Hard Copy* had staked its ground. Our crime stories were dramatic and moral, our celebrity stories were tweaking and not fawning, our T&A was naughty, and Howard Rosenberg thought us enough of a force to be knocked down a few pegs.

"We don't do blood and guts crime stories," I told *USA Today*, "we do justice stories. We don't do sex stories, we do sexy." It was an important distinction.

Our on-air staff was small but forceful. We kept the anchors to as minimal a role as possible, and relied on the over-the-top styles of our "correspondents" and "characters" like Audrey and Chris DeRose, who was no longer laying low after the puppy mill incident.

Then there was Eames.

Eames Hamilton Yates was that rare hybrid of creation and creator, and was probably the most successful of my TV "characters" because his true personality was the furthest from his television persona.

Eames was an excellent writer and producer and he got into the role he played. He may have been an educated New Yorker who moved in the most exclusive circles of high society, but to the *Hard Copy* viewer, he was the lovable, slightly lost buffoon whose bosses forced him to venture into strange towns to uncover the seamiest sex and crime scandals that no one wanted to talk about.

Eames didn't sound like a reporter. He didn't have a trained "TV voice." He squeaked and cracked like an ordinary Joe whose job was on the line with every story. He was always getting punched out or thrown out. He was always apologizing. Eames never meant to insult or hurt anyone, he was just doing his job.

The audience was always on his side.

I made sure Eames always wore his best Brooks Brothers suit and jaunty tie. Rather than have him speak to the camera in the traditional standup form, I came up with the "thought track"—we'd show Eames driving or sitting on a fence and hear his thoughts as he looked around, always somewhat nervous in his surroundings, yet resigned to the fact that he had to get the story or lose his job.

There was one more touch. Each segment would feature a shot of Eames taking a breather in the local diner, ordering up the local special and the biggest glass of milk they sold.

Eames crossed this great land to the tune of his own happy theme song, a blazing fiddle western swing tune from a Mel Tillis and the Stateliners album called *Big Balls in Cow Town*, because no one had bigger balls than Eames, trudging into hollers and hamlets, covering stories and scandals that were emblazoned across the front pages of the tiniest weekly newspapers, but which the networks would never think of investigating and the other tabloid shows had no idea existed.

There was the real-life *Scarlet Letter*: a woman whom the local newspaper falsely accused of having AIDS. Eames accompanied her down Main Street with her head held high. There was a murder in a nudist colony: "Where did he hide the weapon?" There was the octogenarian judge accused of molesting his secretary of thirty years. When Eames confronted the jurist, the geezer decked him!

It was a combination of dogged reporting, compelling storytelling, and sly self-parody. Mike Wallace would be proud—and he was. He'd congratulate Eames for taking on stories that were too far out or too sticky for *60 Minutes*; including the mysterious death of Wallace's former *60 Minutes* colleague, Harry Reasoner, who took a fatal header down a flight of stairs. "It is perhaps the biggest story *60 Minutes* has ever missed...," Eames wrote.

Eames' most poignant story was one he got Peter Brennan to approve—after I spiked it.

"You've gone over my head," I told Eames menacingly. "You've taken a valuable chit and wasted it. I hope it's worth it."

The story of a murder on the edge of the Florida Everglades would be a classic. The copy we eventually wrote together was ripe with personal attachment, description, and the small details so many other producers overlooked in their rush to get the facts.

"Ooh, life was simple then," Eames began, as we saw photos of him as a student at the University of Wyoming, working on his agriculture class project: grooming a pig. "And with a middle name like 'Ham,' my fate was pretty much sealed. All I had to do was keep my prize pig Freckles bathed and powdered and looking good for the judges at the college agricultural fair. Gosh, I miss Freckles. Boy, was she fun to be around."

Hit Eames' theme song as Eames drives into another town, wiping something from his eye that may be a tear. "And that's why I had to do this story. This one cut through the fat. And it's what brought me to the town of Fort Pierce, Florida.... a senseless killing that devastated a young girl."

Dissolve to Eames and an adorable twelve-year-old farmgirl named Christie, standing in a dirt pen.

"I can't stop thinking about him," she says.

"Do you know who might have done this?"

"No." She squeezes her eyes shut but is unable to keep from weeping. Eames hugs her close to his beefy chest and strokes her hair. Tears splash into the dirt.

It would be up to Eames to find who killed Sparkle, the girl's prized show pig.

Three weeks later, the killer would be revealed as a local man, age twenty-five. He admitted he'd stolen and slaughtered Sparkles because he needed a main course for a New Year's Day barbecue.

We were left with a final image of the state fairground. Sad little Christie is in the show ring where she'd walked Sparkle to victory in years past. This time, she walks alone.

"Christie's dream of parading Sparkle at the fair never happened," Eames said. "She took one last walk around center ring, alone, saddened that she and Sparkle could have had it all...but for the appetite of one man."

Eames' story yielded one more unforgettable image. It was during his trademark stop at the diner: the waitress places his order on the counter; Eames looks down at his plate and grimaces. We reveal his meal: a plate of scrambled eggs—with four strips of bacon.

CHAPTER FIFTEEN:
RAF GETS KILLED

By May sweeps, in the aftermath of Gordon Elliott's rejection of Frank Kelly, Peter Brennan began to feel heat about Rafael.

Kelly let it be known he didn't like Raf's on-air appearance, Brennan told me. Kelly had also been given a list by someone within our organization showing that Raf was credited as director on fewer stories than reporters like Doug Bruckner or Diane Dimond.

"That's deceptive," I said. "Raf spends a lot of time rewriting other director's scripts. He puts his face and voice on them, but he doesn't get the credit."

Nor did he get the Directors Guild residuals; those often went to the producer-director who screwed up the story in the first place.

We could tell. Another hit was in the air.

Brennan seemed resigned to the inevitable. "Let's just have him put on a tie, mate, and let's see how it works."

While Raf was on the road with instructions to wear a jacket and tie and to shoot more traditional standups, Brennan and I stopped off after work at a place across Santa Monica Boulevard from the Formosa, on a corner where transvestites and rent boys sold themselves openly (and where Eddie Murphy would make his most notorious pickup).

Ports was a former sports pub turned into a pretentious art bar, named not for any nautical considerations but because the first "S" had fallen off the old "sports" sign above the door.

We sipped our Stolis and discussed plans for the rest of sweeps. Brennan was distant, looking off, talking about visiting his hometown Sydney during the upcoming summer hiatus.

"I'm thinking of hiring John Tomlin," he blurted as casually as possible. "I need a senior producer, someone to place between Linda Bell and my job."

I took a thoughtful sip in response.

"It can't be you, mate. I can't make you senior producer. In your position, with Linda Bell, you'd never be the one who brings management together."

"That's cool. The more the merrier, mate. Is Tomlin available?"

"He may be. Can you think of anyone else?"

"What about Dickie?"

"McWilliams?"

"Yeah, he's about running *Current* now that Wayne's gone. He's still learning TV, but he could be good on the management side."

"Yeah. We need to find someone, though. I can't get rid of that bitch. She's tied in with Frank Kelly."

The drink helped ease the path of depression that rolled through my body. It wasn't that I wanted to be senior producer; it was knowing that if Peter Brennan had wanted me for the job, I'd let him down. With his avoidance of confrontation and refusal to acknowledge the constant attacks against his vision by Linda Bell and her gang, I'd made myself his defender, always watching to be sure they followed his instructions, working overtime to maintain the integrity of the show. I was Peter's shield, and there were no brownie points in Hollywood for loyalty.

Now I was sure I'd blown it. All I wanted was to make great television, to take the combined genius of Peter and Raf and myself and bring this tabloid television thing to a new level. All it took was one shrieking politician to throw a spanner into the works and ruin everything.

Again, I could only tell myself that I didn't come to Hollywood to deal with this bullshit. I ordered another Stoli and tonic.

Around four in the afternoon at the end of May, I was in my office, writing someone's script when Brennan stuck his head in.

"Mate, you got a few minutes?"

"Of course."

I hit *save* and *enter* on the word processor and met Brennan out near the Billy Wilder Building. It was another beautiful L.A. afternoon with the deep blue sky, green palm trees, and tan Paramount buildings adding up to any New York boy's California dream.

Brennan lit a cigarette and walked toward Melrose. He was pale and a bit shaky.

"So, what's up?" I asked. Something was definitely up.

"It's Raf."

"Raf?"

"Frank Kelly doesn't want to renew his contract."

Just like that. I could feel Linda Bell watching us from her office window.

"So what did you say?"

"What could I say? There's nothing I could do. Kelly thinks he's not on the air enough. And when he is on the air, Kelly doesn't like him. There's nothing I can do."

It was a pivotal moment. Brennan realized how little power he had and the compromises he'd have to make.

"Where's Raf?"

"I had Penny page him. He'll meet us."

We didn't say much more as we walked out the main gate onto Melrose and down the sidewalk to Nickodell's, the ancient Hollywood haunt built into the front wall of the Paramount lot. With its noirish neon sign and colorful past, Nickodell's was a classic, irreplaceable part of Hollywood history. Naturally, it was on borrowed time, soon to be torn down for the expansion of the Paramount parking lot.

We skipped the entrance to the restaurant that sold dishes like Shrimp Looie, corned beef, and chops, and headed for the discreet side door that opened into one of the darkest bars in America—so dark you couldn't see the drink in front of you.

There were two old-time Italian bartenders, silent horse racing on the television high on the rear wall, and above the leatherette booths, Hollywood prop paintings of naked women, one of whom looked suspiciously like the early Cher.

We took the nearest bar seats. Brennan ordered first.

"Mate, I'll have a double Stoli with just a touch of soda water and a slice of lemon."

"I'll have a Stoli and tonic."

We sat and said little. Every once in a while, a blinding slice of daylight would sear into the bar when someone opened the door. In that instant, the light would spread across the faces at the bar and in the booths. Everyone looked like extras from *Adam-12*.

We were sipping off the last of our second round when the door opened and Raf walked in. He wore a new white shirt from the Banana Republic store and a black knit tie he probably found in an airport gift shop somewhere in the Midwest. He looked like a civil rights lawyer again.

"A little early for Stolis, gentlemen, wouldn't you say?" He had his usual smirk and raised a hand for the bartender. "Johnny Walker Black, straight up," he said, then turned to Brennan. "So, mate."

"So. Frank Kelly doesn't want to renew your contract."

Raf remained stoic. "So I'm out of here."

"He said you're welcome to stay on." Brennan took another slug. "As a producer. He doesn't like you on the air."

"Fuck." Raf could have reacted theatrically, bolting back the Johnny

Walker Black, but didn't. "So that's that."

"I guess so," Brennan said. He was trying to keep up a "that's show biz" front. "There wasn't anything I could do."

"I'll get a flight back to New York. Will they pay for that?"

"Yeah, yeah."

"So that's that. Fuck!"

Raf drank the Black. He left the bar and that was that.

Raf was enraged and embittered and very let down that he wasn't protected. It wasn't that he hadn't been warned. I'd urged him to get as many pieces on the air as possible, that the hit was on, but he wouldn't hear of it. He told me to take care of his Mustang, threw his copies of *The Iliad* and *The Meaning of Shakespeare Volumes I & II* into a knapsack, and boarded a plane for New York.

The next morning, I took my time getting dressed, pulling on a black shirt, blue Levis, and black cowboy boots. I didn't smile that day or the next, and for the next year, wore jeans and cowboy boots every day so everyone in the office would be reminded of Rafael's sacrifice.

Julia Roberts and young actor Keifer Sutherland were to be married in an old-fashioned Hollywood wedding on the Fox lot in June, but Julia called it off three days before the extravaganza.

We had to find out why.

The most obvious reason was Julia herself, whose personal problems were rumored from the set of Spielberg's *Hook*—a movie the great director made for Barry Diller's company, after all—but then came the photos and video from various paparazzi. Keifer had a secret squeeze, a young stripper from the Crazy Girls club he met at a pool hall in Hollywood.

Amanda Rice, also known as "Raven," was a single mother. We had photos of her and Sutherland riding roller coasters with her child, and paid her thousands of dollars to allow us to elevate her to Julia Roberts status by portraying her as Keifer's "real-life *Pretty Woman*."

I was surprised when she came to the office. Amanda was barely five feet tall, freckled, with dyed jet-black hair, in very bad humor and obviously in pain. She sat on the couch in my office and kept her arms folded across her massive chest.

That morning, she'd used the money to get herself a breast implant operation.

In early June, I flew to New York City for a pair of major tabloid events. Maury Povich was throwing a party for his just-published book. He was in the highest of spirits and deserved to be. He was king in a room packed with past and present employees of *A Current Affair*. Anthea Disney was among them. She worked her way through the crowd to plant a kiss on my cheek.

"Hi," I said. "I hear your door got stuck." She smiled thinly and walked away. My arrogance was showing. I'd already been in Los Angeles too long.

That weekend, Peter rented out the Central Park Zoo for a black tie celebration of his marriage six months earlier to former *A Current Affair* producer Nancy Gershwin. The couple sent out video invitations to the affair, and as a sign of their puckishness, the very first invite was messengered to Barry Diller's office. Within an hour, Mr. Diller's secretary called to express his regrets.

Everyone else in television seemed to be at the outdoor bash. There was even a miraculous appearance by David Lee Miller, who days earlier broke his shoulder in four places in a bicycle accident in the same park. He arrived in a wheelchair, pushed about by a porn actress dressed as a cleavage-baring nurse.

Linda Bell was there. She was particulary festive, and, stationed near the canapes and hors d'ouerves as Peter and his bride listened to Gordon Elliott repeat his celebratory benediction of their nuptials, told more than one person that with Rafael gone, the score at *Hard Copy* was "one down, one to go."

On the last day of the season, a minor earthquake struck Los Angeles. It caused the studio lights to swing and knocked books off shelves. We got the show in the can, and then Eames Yates and I drove off in his rental car toward Tijuana and Baja, California.

We parked the car in the international lot on the United States side of the border and walked down the Avenue de Revolucion to a place called Senor Frog's, where we began to plaster ourselves with cheap tequila and beer.

It was a crash decompression. We visited all the strip bars we could find, paying off every bouncer in every joint to watch our backs as we made fools of ourselves, handing out dollar bills and *Hard Copy* business cards to the dancers.

Well after midnight, Eames stumbled back to the United States to retrieve his car so we could drive farther south to Rosarito Beach, where we rented a full condo with an ocean view and set ourselves up like two decadent bachelors in paradise.

The trip lasted less than forty-eight hours. On Sunday, Eames drove back to Tijuana and the border inspection station. He told me the inspector asked if he had anything to declare.

"No," Eames said.

The official pointed to the damp heap on the backseat floor of the car.

"What about that?"

Eames grabbed the heap, which was me, by the hair. The inspector got a good look at my face and let him drive through.

A few miles up the road, I climbed into the front, exhausted and tequila-dazed, and fell back to sleep as Eames drove up the Route Five freeway back to Los Angeles. Eventually, a gentle tap to my forehead prodded me awake. I opened my eyes to see we were surrounded by an Edenic greenery. It took a couple of seconds more to realize I was twisted around in the passenger seat of the car.

The car engine was running. Eames was slumped over the wheel, snoring loudly. He'd fallen asleep at the wheel and driven off the freeway and into the bushes. Had the car veered in the other direction, we would have crossed three lanes of traffic and crashed over the cliff into the Pacific Ocean.

I gave Eames a good shake. He awoke, and without a word put the car in reverse, backed out of the trees and continued on to L.A.

Eames had to fly back east that afternoon to attend a black tie party that evening at a mansion in Newport, Rhode Island. He called me the next day to say he'd made the party, but not without an embarrassing incident at the Providence Airport. He got off the plane in his seersucker suit, still dazed from tequila and the additional spirits he'd imbibed on the flight. As he looked for the limousine driver holding up the placard bearing his name, Eames noticed other people looking at him with expressions of horror. A nun crossed herself. A mother quickly used both hands to cover her child's eyes. It was only later when he reached into his pants pocket to tip the skycap that Eames realized what was wrong: his fly was open and he was fully exposed.

It was a sticky July night, back on 67th Street, over the road from the old office at the old Racing Club, now called Tommy McGrath's Bar, with Dickie McWilliams at my side and Peter Brennan on the other end of the phone in Los Angeles. Brennan and I had made a great attempt to hire Dickie away from *A Current Affair*, and that day Brennan had gotten the Paramount attorneys to cut the red tape and give Dickie a clearcut contract that he could sign immediately.

Dickie was a cautious man. "I don't know what to do, mate," he told Brennan over the phone. "Fox says that if I don't sign a contract, they'll fire me."

"Well, I wouldn't want to work for people like that," Brennan said. "I don't know what the problem is, Dickie."

Dickie knew, but he wasn't letting on. He didn't tell us that Wayne was trying just as hard to get him to work at his side on the new show *Now It*

Can Be Told. Dickie was using both our offers as a wedge to get more money out of *A Current Affair*.

For a few days, we were at a loss. We needed someone to stand between Peter Brennan and Linda Bell.

Brennan and I were back in L.A., sitting at the Boogie Woogie Bar by the pool at the Mondrian Hotel, when it hit me. "What about that guy who was at your wedding? You know, that Peter O'Toole guy. The one who made the scene."

"Neal?"

That was him: Neal Travis, the man slumped over his drink who was driven mad by Gordon's hypocritical ravings. Neal Travis was a Kiwi, from the far outback land of New Zealand. He, too, worked early on for the *Sydney Morning Herald* and came to New York City as one of Murdoch's foreign correspondents in the swinging sixties.

Neal was a trendsetter, the best-read of the Murdoch Mafia and originator of the most innovative gossip column in years when in 1977 he invented the *New York Post's Page Six*.

Page Six provided exciting new targets of gossip and innuendo, putting the bright light on the lives of New York's new stars in the fields of politics, business, media and nightlife.

Neal became a star himself when he wrote a bestselling book called *Manhattan*. The jacket copy said it all:

A NOVEL AS JUICY AND TEMPTING AS
THE BIG APPLE ITSELF!
They make sweet love on Bill Blass sheets
and make big deals at "21." They dance at
Regine's, drink at Elaine's and score at Studio 54.

The copy was also a good way to describe Neal's life. In 1979, he moved up a step in class to revamp *New York* magazine's *Intelligencer* column. Two years later, before they'd have to wrap Neal in a Bill Blass sheet and carry him out feet first, he and his wife Tolley bid the nightlife farewell, pulled up stakes, and moved to Bermuda, where he sat in the sun and wrote more bestselling novels through the eighties.

"So what's Neal doing?" I asked Peter.

"I don't know. We'll find out." He rolled the idea over in his head for a moment. "Neal. Yeah. We'll find out."

When we called Neal, he was still editor of *California* magazine. The timing was in our favor. The magazine was going under. He joined up with us.

CHAPTER SIXTEEN:
GERALDO FINDS HIS HITLER

*Q: What elements of your previous career in news do you feel
have prepared you for hosting* Hard Copy?
*MURPHY: My natural curiosity as a newsperson spills over into
my work on* Hard Copy. *I'm naturally curious about news events
and how people are affected by the world, and as a result,
I'm always suggesting stories to our producers.
NOLAN: Theatre history and psychology helped prepare me
for* Hard Copy.

—From "A conversation with Terry Murphy and Barry Nolan,
Co-Anchors of *Hard Copy,*" 3rd Season Press Kit.

It was snowing in Los Angelesin September.

We were starting our second season at *Hard Copy*. I was walking
through Paramount's back lot with a cup of coffee in my hand, crossing a
street in the middle of the old New York set when I noticed the first flake.
It drifted from somewhere behind me and landed on the sleeve of my black
shirt.

There was no doubt. It was a snowflake. It was a miracle.

I looked up to see the sky above me filled with tiny white crystals.
Beyond, the sky was the same blue it always was, yet it was snowing in the
middle of September in the middle of Los Angeles.

It wasn't a miracle. It was a special effect for a movie they were
shooting around the corner.

By the start of our second season, Alan Frio had been released from his
contract. He flew back to Sacramento to a local news job, claiming he quit
because the show was too tabloid. The last straw, he fumed, was when
Paramount forced him to wear glasses so he'd look more intelligent.

Brennan replaced him with Barry Nolan, a boyish, diminutive, yet

Kennedy-esque man with prematurely gray hair who'd been a correspondent out of the New York office since the beginning. He never quite grasped the new *Hard Copy* style—yet, suddenly, Brennan plucked him from obscurity and made him the frontman.

Brennan knew he had a malleable dummy he could turn into a winner, for, like the phony doctor in the old commercials, Barry Nolan wasn't really a newsman, he just played one on TV. He was an actor whose resume trumpeted leads in an Off-off Broadway production of *The Misanthrope*, an Off-Broadway production of *The Passion of Dracula*, and recurring roles in soap operas like *The Doctors* and *One Life To Live*. Like many actors whose solid looks allow them to play professionals in TV commercials, Nolan found he could get a regular paycheck by taking a detour into quasi-journalistic lifestyle magazine shows, those bastard hybrids of info and tainment that filled the access time slots before the days of *A Current Affair*. He hosted Boston's *Evening Magazine* in the eighties, taking time off to play Jean "Edith Bunker" Stapleton's son in a TV drama.

Brennan wasn't impressed with Nolan's journalistic abilities. He found the guy to be a ponderous bore, as are many actors who feel they're entrusted with social responsibility when they take a role reading TelePrompTer copy.

No, Brennan knew that Barry Nolan at least sounded smart when he read the copy we wrote for him. With that gray hair, he even looked like an anchorman—though he needed to sit on a couple of phone books to be at eye level with his co-host Terry Murphy.

The new season meant a new battle plan for Linda Bell. Unable to get the senior producer job without Brennan's okay, she signed a new contract that allowed her to carry the title of senior supervising producer, though there was no lower supervising producer for her to supervise.

Neal Travis was Associate to the Executive Producer. There would be no senior producer.

Our 1991-92 season began with a new presence that would make our transition to life in the sun a bit more bearable. Howard Stern's syndicated radio show had come to Los Angeles in July.

By that time, more people in the country had heard of Stern than actually heard him on the radio; because the FCC was targeting him, the syndication of his show was being slowed. Every time we ran a Howard Stern story, we had to explain who he was, and explain it from the tabloid point of view: as a six-foot-five, hook-nosed toilet mouth, cutting a swath of aural mayhem toward your town. We couldn't say Stern was a great new Lenny Bruce or the Jesus of cool, liberating us all with his honesty, plain talk, and common sense. We had to remember the position *we* held in viewer's minds. Tabloid represented average, often hypocritical American values, which was why the genre flourished despite howls of disgust from the critics who often didn't share the common morality. As long as we appeared as shocked as the viewers at what we delivered, they wouldn't blame the messenger.

One reason *Hard Copy* almost sank completely in its first season was the flaunting of a hipper-than-thou image of pointy-headed liberals from El Lay. They tried to educate viewers on what to think, and they did, literally, look down on the masses as being in need of education.

Peter Brennan always reminded us to remember who made up our demographics, and to never forget they were a lot smarter than we were. People didn't want to see blood and bodybags at the dinner table, and they certainly didn't want to be told that they should loosen up, baby. When we ran a story about S-E-X, we'd tsk-tsk our way through the raunchiest stuff we could get away with. When we ran a story on nudity on European television, we'd show as much of it as we could, all the while saying, "Can you believe what they're showing on TV in Europe? *We'd* never show that!"

You could not ignore the tabloid rules. It all went back to that seminar in Tarrytown when Peter laid it all out. The show is a person who's knocking at the door at dinnertime. You want to be invited into a home and invited back the next night. You can tell any story there is, and you can tell it to the Queen of England, if you tell it the right way. Peter Brennan was a genius when it came to telling stories the right way.

Peter Brennan recognized a disturbing thread in the tales of Howard Stern's domination of out-of-town radio markets: he was a big bully. The Big Bad Mouth of Radio would attack mercilessly, and ultimately destroy the top deejay in each city his show would invade. Most of his competitors weren't national figures. They were sad voices without faces in mill towns, local celebrities who'd appear at openings of bowling alleys. Howard would attack them before a national audience, treating these little men with big voices as if they were Rush Limbaugh.

First stop was Philadelphia and a pathetic morning deejay named John De Bella. Stern not only humiliated De Bella and predicted his wife would leave him when he was toppled from the number one perch, but when Mrs. De Bella did leave, Stern brought her onto his show and sent her on a date with one of his moronic followers.

The woman was on a binge. Eventually, she would commit suicide.

The attacks seemed crueler the more lowly the victim. The top deejay in Rochester, New York called himself Brother Wease: a sad, fat Vietnam vet who did a lot of charity work. Like most radio personalities, he wasn't especially hip—the guy named himself after a *weasel*, remember—and he wasn't especially witty. He simply played records that people in Rochester liked to hear.

In the weeks after Stern's show was picked up by a rival station in Rochester, Wease became Stern's national whipping boy. Listeners called Stern's show to tell about Wease's ex-wife and their retarded daughter living in Philadelphia. Stern claimed Wease dumped them in pursuit of fame. People across America shared in the shame of this local zero.

I sent a producer to Rochester to interview Brother Wease. When he was asked about his little girl, Brother Wease started to cry.

We had an ulterior motive for running stories about Howard Stern again and again. Each time, Stern would tape our segment to play on his show the morning after it ran. He'd dissect the story, stop and start the tape, replay it, complain, laugh at its extremity—and give us ultimate publicity for a good half hour.

I tried as often as possible to find Howard Stern stories to run on Friday nights. That way, as we promoted the story through the week, Howard could criticize the story before it ran. It was free publicity among the hippest morning audience in the country. Stern fans would tune in when they got home from work or set their VCRs in advance to get worked up over what we said or to see their man on the tube. Viewers in parts of the country where Stern's show wasn't yet broadcast would get to shake their heads or whet their appetites. They'd be sure to be intrigued.

This was before his first book, and there was no doubt *Hard Copy* stories helped increase Stern's popularity. Sitting in Los Angeles, having put together another hilarious Stern package, reading faxed threats from his attorneys and hearing him venting spleen on the radio, we couldn't understand why he didn't get the joke—and Howard Stern truly didn't get it.

His producers didn't call us after segments ran to thank us for the publicity, and they didn't allow us to use snippets from his show when he had a particularly newsworthy interview. If we used a clip from Stern's radio show, his lawyers would demand we pay ten grand. Paramount would pay.

Off-mike, Stern never admitted seeing the tongue-in-cheek humor in the stories I wrote. In fact, in his second book, *Miss America*, Stern printed part of my script about the De Bella affair. The humor was there on the page. He claimed he didn't get it.

In that sense, Stern showed himself to have much in common with the great men of television comedy he so envies.

Shortly before Christmas 1989, a group of us from *A Current Affair* had a table at the Odeon Restaurant in Lower Manhattan. David Letterman and his entourage were a few tables away.

Letterman didn't know who we were, but we knew he was peeved with our show for airing an interview with a deranged woman who kept breaking into his house, claiming to be his wife. "Mrs. Letterman" did part of the interview standing on her head. She was, to borrow an Australianism, mad as a gumtree full of galahs.

Letterman's people had asked us not to run the interview. We countered that it might finally lead to the help and incarceration the poor woman needed so badly—not mentioning the increased ratings we needed and accepted so gladly.

As the salty french-fried shoestring potatoes mixed with the potato-based vodkas in the din of the bistro night, Peter Brennan had the idea of sending Dave a humorous peace offering. He called over the waiter and asked for a cheap bottle of wine.

"I'm sorry sir, we do not serve cheap wine."

"Mate, not any cheap wine. I'm talking about the *cheapest—cooking wine!* Something with a screw top!"

The man shrugged and brought over a bottle. I took out a business card and scrawled a message on the back, referring to the catchphrase "Bite Me," which Dave had been repeating on his show:

> *To Dave:*
> *Bite Us.*
> *Drink This.*

Letterman seemed confused when the bottle arrived, but accepted it without comment. We all sat back, napkins to our lips, suppressing titters of anticipation, holding our collective breath, waiting for Letterman to screw up his face, read the card, see the *A Current Affair* logo on the reverse side, slap his forehead and guffaw, waving us to his table for toasts and pats on the back.

Letterman removed the cigar from his mouth and the card from the tray. He read the card, dropped it, and resumed his conversation. He didn't even crack a smile.

That's comedy.

When Stern came to L.A. to do his first talk show on the E! channel, we'd see him at the Bel Age bar, hulkier than we expected, fat and hairy in ill-fitting clothes, scrunched in a corner with his people like a heavy metal Tiny Tim. We didn't bother saying hello.

Yet Stern on the air in Los Angeles was a new morning. We were connected again, able to wake up to an inkling of what the rest of the world outside the L.A. smog zone was talking about.

We didn't feel so bad for Brother Wease, knowing that Stern would aim his barbs at those maudlin clowns Mark & Brian, whose cloying kissypoo radio show I'd listened to in the car just to get worked up. We had no way of knowing that Stern's assault on Los Angeles would lead to a confrontation that put one of our own in true physical peril.

Wayne Darwen, meanwhile, was doing very well for himself at *Now It Can Be Told*. Thanks in no small part to the success Peter and I were having at *Hard Copy*, he'd managed to get himself one of the most lucrative contracts of any of us. Despite reservations about the tabloid bunch, the buzz within the television industry was that like it or not, this cadre from *A Current Affair* knew how to make money-making television.

When the Tribune Company offered Wayne $175,000 a year to come on board as senior producer of Geraldo Rivera's new show, he laughed at the not insubstantial offer. The bluff worked. Tribune raised their offer by $100,000 a year, and offered him two years, pay or play.

Wayne had been through some changes in the past year, struggling to stay fit and sober. Deprived of his alcohol, he developed a new intensity while dropping an astonishing thirty pounds of bloat. Most important, he found a new woman in his life. Norah was a tall, wholesome Canadian girl who'd turned herself into a doyenne of the New York nightclub scene. She'd soon become Wayne's third wife, but for now was showing him a side of life he'd never imagined.

With his first new paychecks and Norah's help, Wayne binged in a way he had never done before; not on alcohol, but clothing. The man who wore beer- and puke-stained All-Blacks rugby jerseys was now swathed in $900 designer shirts. His motorcycle jackets and jeans were traded in for $1,500 Tierry Mugler suits, $2,000 Claude Montana getups with epaulets and zippers on the sleeves; his Reeboks kicked off in favor of soft leather Versaces.

The self-described "gutter rat journo" had his first taste of the highlife. He and Norah moved into a luxury apartment 40 floors above the East River. They searched for the perfect Connecticut estate in their new black Mercedes towncar.

In Geraldo, Wayne had found a new soulmate, a man who actually talked in the hyperbole Wayne had been writing for twenty years. "He was Mr. Fucking Tabloid, he was P.T. Barnum," Wayne enthused later. "We were two peas in a pod. Tribune thought they found a zookeeper for Geraldo. They wanted a harness; instead they had a nutcase who drove him to obscene lengths."

For his part, Geraldo recalled that when Wayne walked into his office, with his long hair, fringed jacket and silver-toed cowboy boots, "the nutmeter went off, the needle went way into the red." As they talked, Geraldo realized what had walked into his life. He echoed Zero Mostel's famous line from Mel Brooks' *The Producers*: "That's our Hitler!"

Now It Can Be Told could have been a Mel Brooks production. Tribune's dream was to make it the first totally respectable tabloid television show; one that combined high-minded investigative reporting with high-rating trash. It was a lofty goal, and from the start, things were a bit off kilter.

In forming an on-air team, Geraldo cast his reporters the way he'd cast a movie. He didn't go after the best TV journalists—he hired individuals who looked like tough young reporters in the Geraldo mode. There was the zoned-out Krista Bradford, hired by the original *A Current Affair* because of her fuck-me looks and most recently the girlfriend of J. Geils' keyboard player and shopping her own rock 'n' roll demo tape; Alexander Johnson, a smashingly handsome black man fired from *Hard Copy* because of an inability to get a handle on any story; there was even a young Robert Redford lookalike discovered when he was a guest on a segment of Geraldo's afternoon talk show titled "The Problems of Handsome Men."

Behind the scenes, the chemistry looked just as good on paper but was equally toxic when exposed to air. Wayne found he was only part of Tribune's high-minded, high-rating formula. He was paired with a second senior producer to balance out his tabloid excesses.

Pete Simmons was a gray, tired journeyman in his fifties who'd seen too many bars and too many warzones. The crusty old veteran of *20/20* was to provide "the meat."

Wayne was "the heat."

Indeed, when *Now It Can Be Told* made its debut in September 1991, many had wrung their hands in fear that Geraldo Rivera would bring tabloid television to a new low level of sleaze, yet it proved to be rather mild and more a macho version of *20/20* than a clone of *A Current Affair*.

Its premiere show was supposed to feature an excoriating interview with former President Gerald Ford, who was using his declining years as a corporate shill and golf partner for hire. When he got Ford on a two-way interview, however, Geraldo spent most of the time gushing about the man's greatness.

The second week of the show highlighted an intense investigation into the explosion of the space shuttle Challenger. The story was produced, in a coincidence of no little irony, by the wife of the NBC *Dateline* producer who used incendiary devices to blow up a truck in the historic, deceptive "demonstration" of its faulty gas tank.

The story had its tabloid elements, with accusations of astronauts dying slow and excruciating deaths and bodies trundled off in Hefty bags, but for all its sensation, could have been an *Inside Edition* report on defective bus parts.

Wayne knew the show needed more heat. He knew it couldn't survive on syndicated imitations of network probes, and he had a surefire hit in his pocket. A producer named Maury Terry had access to letters from David

Berkowitz, the notorious Son of Sam killer who held New York City in a grip of terror in 1977. The letters mentioned Charles Manson, Jeffrey Dahmer, and Satan; they provided the first insight into the twisted mind of the madman.

The Tribune executives were against it. Geraldo's image was sullied enough. They didn't need him to start wallowing in the tabloid mire so early in the game.

Pete Simmons sniffed and turned his nose. "Spare me. Please."

Wayne fought. He appealed to Geraldo's survival instincts and convinced the mustachioed host to back him on an ultimate ratings grabber. They sent Alexander Johnson to bring back the goods. Johnson returned with a four-minute news package.

Wayne found himself in the same quandary we were in three thousand miles away. These guys just didn't get it. He took the story and the huge stack of letters from Johnson, locked himself in an office with Maury Terry, and came out with three complete shows. The heat was on.

The shows rated, as they say in the tabloid business, up the ass. Even Pete Simmons was forced to bow before Wayne's instinctual genius. Yet their partnership was not to find its common ground. The constant see-sawing of bland news and exciting tabloid may have seemed as brilliant as hiring actors who looked like reporters. In reality, the clashing sensibilities would lead ultimately to an explosive showdown.

The only question was whether the heat would beat the meat.

October brought the Clarence Thomas Supreme Court confirmation hearings and the ensuing pubic-hair-on-the-Coke-can sexual harassment charges from Professor Anita Hill. We at *Hard Copy* were fascinated by the sexual war being waged on Capitol Hill and, with Senate committee chairman Ted Kennedy rendered ineffective by the Palm Beach sex scandal, could only send an "I told you so" to the know-it-all network newsbosses who thought the incident beneath consideration.

We were even more fascinated by Professor Hill's description of Judge Thomas's taste in pornographic films, including his affection for a long-gone star named Long Dong Silver, a sad genetic freak at the other end of the penis scale from Howard Stern. His hung limply below his knees.

Somehow, someone in the *Hard Copy* organization found a copy of one of the only Long Dong Silver movies in existence, one of those wacky skin flicks from the seventies that included a singalong bluegrass number about the wonders of Mr. Silver's long dong. We all agreed that *Hard Copy* would be the first and only show in America to reveal Mr. Silver.

I handed the tape over to one of the day-of-air producers and instructed her to masque the offensive portion, which covered the area from

Mr. Silver's waist to a point slightly below his knees.

"Should I cover the whole bottom two thirds of the screen?" she asked. "Do you want a black bar or do you want it digitized?"

I was already distracted by another story. "Just put a black box over the head of it," I said jokingly, and went back to work.

It was a half hour before feed time when I happened into the control room. Mike O'Gara was red in the face. The assistant director wasn't sure about this one, but he was going along if that was what the producer wanted.

"I don't think we should do this," O'Gara said again.

"Burt said to do it," the loyal producer repeated. "That's what we have to do."

They were covering the X-rated Long Dong Silver video by merely placing a black box over the head of his penis, leaving fourteen or so inches of his long dong exposed.

I took the nearest seat and lowered my head. Methodically, I pounded it into the desk. They were going to let it go on the air. We were a half hour away from losing a lot more than our jobs.

It wasn't all sexual politics and war. October 1991 also brought storybook romance, with Elizabeth Taylor marrying a construction worker she'd met kicking drugs at the Betty Ford Clinic. The wedding would take place on Michael Jackson's Neverland Ranch. The press couldn't get anywhere near it, yet we dispatched Audrey Lavin to the press encampment outside Jackson's sprawling ranch.

It was around 11:30 a.m. the Friday before the Neverland nuptuals when Brennan stepped into my office. "Dunleavy's in town. We're going to meet him."

Great. I grabbed my jacket and away we went.

Dunleavy was into his first Heineken at the bar of the Columbia Bar & Grill when Penny dropped us off shortly before noon. He said he was in town to cover another story.

"They don't have you on the wedding?"

"Nah, mate, fuck it. It's on Saturday, all the networks'll be there, it'll be old news by Monday. Otherwise I'd be on it like a rat up a drainpipe."

Dunleavy looked a little green around the gills. He'd been on a nonstop cavalcade this past year, racing after every breaking news story the assignment desk came up with. There was no one to tell him to slow down, no one to temper his hot-blooded tabloid style.

"Well, here's to Liz," Neal said.

"One more facelift and she'll have a goatee," Dunleavy said. "One more facelift and she'll have a fucking tracheotomy!" he added, one-upping himself. He got an extra kick when I reached for a cocktail napkin and borrowed a pen from Neal to write it down.

We stood at the bar, hoisted some beers, and told old stories while watching the lunch crowd and seeing which celebs were jockeyed to which tables. We saw the lunch crowd go. It was an hour or so later when we were ready for our fifth round.

"I'm sorry, guys," the bartender said. "I can't serve you any more."

"Excuse me? Are we causing a disturbance here?" Dunleavy was incredulous.

"No sir, you're all fine. But we have a four drink limit."

"Mates," he said, amused. "They're giving us the Spanish archer."

"The what?"

"The El-*bow*," Dunleavy said, amused at his joke.

Brennan wasn't amused at all. "Mate, none of us is driving here."

"Maybe we'd get busted for drunk walking."

"This is outrageous," Neal said, truly offended. "Surely we can have one more."

"I'm sorry, guys. It's the rule."

Brennan's eyes narrowed. "I wish to see the manager."

The manager came out from the back, a clean-cut young guy in white shirt and tie. "Guys, sorry, we do have a limit—"

Brennan cocked a finger. "Sir, I have been in bars from Sydney to New York, Hong Kong to London, and I have never been at a place where there is a four drink limit—"

The manager rolled his eyes. He'd heard it all before. "Look, that's just the way—"

"No. Let me finish! This is your rule?"

"It's my rule."

"Well, let me say that never has any tavern manager exhibited as much care about me and my safety! I produce a television show and I will use it to nominate you man of the year!"

Hoorah! We all backed him up.

"Yeah, yeah." The manager knew Brennan was, as they say in Sydney and London, taking the piss; he'd say he was being goofed on. He backed off toward the kitchen. "Okay, I get it. Thanks, guys."

"No! No! I'm serious! You're the first one to care about us! I'm putting you on television as man of the year!"

The day was still young and we were adrift in the wincing sunlight of a bad part of Sunset Boulevard. We were without vehicular transportation and had no intention of returning to work. The only question was where we would find a drink.

We walked up the road to the depressing Old Spaghetti Factory, but the place was closed. "Try the Columbia Bar & Grill," the custodian suggested.

We wound up at an outdoor cafe near Gower, drinking warm bottles of beer next to a table of Fly Girls from Fox's *In Living Color*.

Neal's wife showed up around five and gave us a lift into West Hollywood, dropping Peter, Dunleavy, and me at the Bel Age before continuing on to their place on Roscomere in Bel Air. We drank for hours under the watchful eye of Nabi and took a breather by walking up the Strip to Nicky Blair's, the sleazy Italian place filled with B-movie actresses, would-be producers, middle-aged TV stars, and Iranian wheeler-dealers with cell phones and beepers.

The bar was packed. We'd found a cantilevered B-girl to whom we could gesture with our Stoli and tonics when Dunleavy disappeared for a few minutes and returned a bit shakily, his pompadour floating a bit less high than it did at noon.

It wasn't surprising, even for Dunleavy. Despite the obstacles, we were well into our tenth hour of drinking.

"Mate," he whispered to Brennan. "I think I've had a bit too much. I just vomited. I've gotta get back to me hotel."

"You sure you're all right?"

"Ah, nothing a cuppa tea, a Beaks, and a good lie down won't cure, Burtie, my boy." The poor guy; we all hugged goodbye and Peter and I got back to the B-movie actress. Brennan and I carried on, back to the Bel Age, into the wee hours of Saturday morning...

On Monday, the wedding of Elizabeth Taylor and Larry Fortensky was still big news after all, the local and network news organizations having given the story shorter shrift than public interest might indicate it deserved.

Audrey came back with enough to build a good package around, including helicopter footage we bought from one of the paparazzi.

"I saw Steve there," she said. "Saturday morning, he was all over the place."

What? We watched *A Current Affair* that evening, and sure enough, the show opened with a special report on the marriage of Larry and Liz, and sure enough, there was the man leading the coverage: Steve Dunleavy, hanging out of a helicopter, shouting over the whirring blades as he pointed to the ceremony below him. Had they given him a parachute, he would have dropped in.

Dunleavy later admitted he was never ill at all on Friday night. He'd been sent, or sent himself, on a complicated mission: to meet up with us, the *Hard Copy* brass, convince us that the Elizabeth Taylor story was not worth losing sleep over, then incapacitate us with alcohol while he sneaked off to the telephone every once in a while to make sure *A Current Affair's* preparations were underway.

When Dunleavy left us at Nicky Blair's Friday night, he was taken by taxicab to a strategy meeting at the Beverly Hills Hotel before making the trip to the ranch near Santa Barbara.

His words echoed: "Do anything for a friend. But do anything *to* a friend to get a story. All's fair in love, war, and reporting."

We went into November sweeps with real momentum. Figures showed that our fourteen months at *Hard Copy* were paying off. For the week ending October sixth, ratings were up 37% compared to the same week two years before, from a lowly 4.1 to a 5.6. Something else was growing, as well. In a Paramount ad touting the ratings jump, a picture of the anchors showed Barry Nolan as a good four inches taller than Terry Murphy.

On the seventh of November, word came that Magic Johnson had called a news conference to announce he was quitting the NBA because he was infected with the AIDS virus.

We crowded into Peter's office and explained to him that Magic Johnson was one of the biggest stars in America.

"Is he gay?"

I recalled that about two weeks earlier, *Parade* magazine ran an item about Magic on its Personality Parade page, the gossip column that gives opinionated answers to phony letters. The question: "I know there are gay players in the NFL, but is it true there are two gay stars in the NBA?" The answer: "You must be talking about Magic Johnson and Isaiah Thomas, who kiss on the court whenever they compete. No, they're both married and are just good friends..."

That was the undercurrent of the story, but it wasn't something we could harp on so early in the game. This was a tragedy. When Barry Nolan came up from the studio after taping the show, we decided to send him to the press conference with two cameras, one to focus on Magic and one on him. We gave Barry the questions, and he got to ask one of them:

"What do you have to say to the kids?"

Amid the reverential and sport-oriented questions at the news conference, that simple query got a lot of attention around the world, and the second-camera image of our anchor, peeping up through the crowd asking it, was a memorable one for the show.

Asking questions and creating one's own agenda at press conferences seems simple enough, but it was another innovation we pioneered back at *A Current Affair.* Unbelievably, many of these events where journalists stand with notepads and microphones are not always forums for pointed questioning. Most of the time, the person setting up the press conference sets the agenda and everyone follows along, waiting for the same quote.

It really hit me back in May 1989, when the media had the chance to capture the physical and metaphorical equivalent of *Moby Dick*. The great, elusive and reclusive Marlon Brando made himself available after his son Christian was arrested for shooting his sister's lover to death at Brando's home—in the same compound where Jack Nicholson lived and where Audrey once spent a memorable evening.

It was an incredible Hollywood story, containing a turbulent family saga, mental illness, sex, B-grade hangers-on, whispers of incest, death, and standing at a bank of microphones outside the courthouse in Santa Monica, Marlon Brando himself.

Brando was clearly a broken man as he lisped his immortal words about "the methenger of mithery" visiting his house. Standing in the feed room at *A Current Affair*, I foresaw numerous opportunities for a half-hour special once the reporters began peppering him with questions. No one bit. When Brando finished speaking, most of the press corps was shown to be kneeling at his feet. They thanked him and let him waddle off with attorney Robert Shapiro.

I couldn't believe I was watching Moby Dick submerge without a single harpoon hurled toward his exposed flank. I got Mike Watkiss on the phone. Watkiss was a cocky bantam of a reporter with an overdeveloped upper body and a pompadour rivaling Dunleavy's. He used to be a local news reporter in his hometown of Salt Lake City and was perfect for *A Current Affair*: he acted a character who personified the new Wild West; he'd recently been made L.A. bureau chief.

I told Watkiss to show up at the courthouse the following day, and if God granted us another shot at Brando, to position himself in the front of the others and start firing away.

I faxed him the questions:

"Christian, do you think you can survive in jail?"

"Mr. Brando, do you love your son?"

"Christian, are you ashamed you hurt your father just as he's making a comeback?"

"Christian, why did you do it?"

"Mr. Brando, how is Cheyenne?"

When Brando surfaced, Watkiss was standing three feet away. He got every question in, and some good answers in return. It was relevatory and it worked.

It was a slightly different tack with Michael Jackson around that same time. He was making a rare appearance to announce a shoe endorsement deal at the same time his sister LaToya was making lots of noise, appearing naked in magazines and making abuse allegations against their father.

Of course, the pack of press that morning obeyed a warning by veteran public relations man Lee Solters that Mr. Jackson would not entertain any questions and should be accorded the utmost respect.

While they listened like sheep as Jackson whispered a couple of lines about the children of the world, Audrey waited in the parking lot between the stage door and Jackson's limousine. The star hotfooted it outside and ran smack into little Audrey's microphone.

"Michael, what about LaToya? Do you have any comment on what your sister is saying?"

Jackson looked at her and the camera, stunned. "I love her," he whispered before he was trundled into the limo and raced away. The camera rolled. Audrey turned and was accosted by old Lee Solters. We ran everything, and chyroned Michael's words as we played them over and over:

"*I love her.*"

We were doing more than taking the piss out of Hollywood pretension. We were asking questions people wanted answers to. Unfortunately, we were doing so in concurrence with the rise in power of the Hollywood publicist, women like Pat Kingsley who began exercising an iron grip on the images of their often troubled charges, trading print interviews for magazine covers, television chats for promises that certain subjects would not be broached.

Everyone was playing along—except *A Current Affair*, and later, *Hard Copy*. It wasn't a matter of ambushing people or making up stories. We were treating celebrities like real people, and that wasn't how the game was supposed to be played.

Howard Stern took it to the next level with his Stuttering John, the interviewer who asked embarrassing—but often relevant—questions. The fallout was double-edged. Now, whenever you send someone out to ask an "impolite" yet legitimate question at a news conference—like, "Hey Magic, are you gay?"—they cluck and call you a Stuttering John; not the interview subjects, the other reporters.

Yet, when a Diane Sawyer or an Oprah makes a deal for an "interview of the century" and, because of pre-conditions, doesn't ask the questions everyone wants to hear or lets a sleazy answer get off without a followup question, they're held to task.

Thank tabloid for that.

CHAPTER SEVENTEEN:
A FATAL SUPPOSITORY

November 1991 brought surprise and unsettling change to *A Current Affair*. A year after she named Maureen O'Boyle permanent host, Anthea Disney was out, pulled by Rupert Murdoch to take over as editor of *TV Guide*.

As a sign that the show had been taken over by the West Coast contingent, the new executive producer was selected by Lucie Salhany, who'd followed Barry Diller from Paramount to take over 20th Century Fox Television.

The new executive producer didn't come from within the Fox or News Corp ranks. He wasn't a veteran of any of *A Current Affair*'s tabloid competitors. He was selected after Salhany's office interviewed job applicants off the proverbial street.

Nobody ever heard of John Terenzio—nobody in tabloid at least.

John Terenzio was an NBC network vet, producer of what may have been the most soporific news show in network television history, Garrick Utley's *Weekend News*. More recently, Terenzio was working out of Miami, attempting to start TV shows of his own.

Once again, Fox let it be known that Terenzio was brought on board to continue the *A Current Affair* "cleanup." To Terenzio, "cleaning up" meant making the show harder-edged, rougher—more newsy, including gritty urban crime stories, tales of child abuse, and investigative pieces.

It was as if a virus had been downloaded into the computer that was tabloid television. For the first time, an American network newsman was put in charge of one of the shows. He would bring in more "serious journalist" types and spread the constipated network news mentality around the free-wheeling arena. The clock would tick toward the virus exploding, taking tabloid television with it.

Yet, perhaps because Terenzio realized he was out of his depth in the tabloid field, he hedged his bets by appointing Steve Dunleavy managing editor. In time, Terenzio would attach himself to the grand old man of tabloid and try to learn the business by osmosis, drinking himself into dullness every night at Tommy McGrath's on glass after glass of white wine with ice.

Dunleavy would run unfettered, racking up more air time than any other reporter in tabloid television during the Terenzio era; but, though it appeared he was calling the shots, right down to the hiring of notorious *Star* bureau chief Barry Levine at the height of the "clean-up," there was a higher power approving all decisions.

John Terenzio was embarrassed to admit it, but everything he put on the air—every script, package, and rundown—had to first be approved by Lucie Salhany on the West Coast.

"Lilting laughter rippled across the castle of Camelot last night, where happiness had so often been put on hold!"

On December twelfth, as Steve Dunleavy read his purple poetry into a microphone in a room at the Brazilian Court Hotel, anyone could be forgiven for thinking tabloid television was reaching a new peak. The day before, the William Kennedy Smith trial had ended in acquittal; a trial in which Dunleavy had become as important a figure as the defendant himself.

He'd filed more than forty reports since he took that first shirtless jog through Palm Beach, chasing lead after lead and buying up scoop after scoop. When it was revealed in court that *A Current Affair* paid $40,000 for an interview with Anne Mercer, the woman who gave the alleged victim a ride home from the Kennedy mansion, the prosecution's star witness was discredited and it was Willie Smith who was on his way home.

"I have to thank Steve Dunleavy for what he did with Anne Mercer," Smith's attorney Roy Black told a press conference.

"Does that change your mind about *A Current Affair*?" someone asked.

Black sneered and shook his head. "They'd pay the lawn man if they thought he'd say something nasty about Will and his family."

The following weekend, Dunleavy was the subject of a major feature in *The New York Times*. "Every famous trial has its chronicler," David Margolick wrote. "The Scopes trial had H.L. Mencken, the Eichmann trial Hannah Arendt. And the just concluded rape trial of William Kennedy Smith had Steve Dunleavy.

"If this is a media circus, Mr. Dunleavy is the ringmaster and he knows how to make the most of it."

Dunleavy and the *A Current Affair* team may have missed the irony of the comparison to Mencken, the anti-Semitic editor from Baltimore, but there was no doubt he was on a roll.

A week later, the *Times* ran another picture of Dunleavy in a story on the booming success of tabloid television.

> In the November sweep-month ratings, all three programs increased their ratings substantially. *A Current Affair*, which still commands a sizeable lead over its rivals, had an 8.8 rating, up from 8.2 a year ago. *Inside Edition* had a 6.8 rating, up from a 5.6 *Hard Copy* had a 6 rating, well up from the 4.6 it had in November of 1990. (Each rating point currently represents 921,000 homes).

Interviews with various programming honchos pointed to a more newsy direction for all the tabloid shows. A Fox executive claimed *A Current Affair* was moving in a more "sensitive" direction, because "the attitudes of the viewers have become more conservative."

Crinkly *20/20* vet Av Westin, consulting over at *Inside Edition*, crowed that his "Clean Air Act" was working well. He pointed to the investigative, consumer, and crime segments, a mix that was very similar to his old ABC network show.

It would soon become clear that everyone was fooling themselves. Tabloid television was about to get dirtier than ever. A story would soon come along that was so sordid and out of control, it would seem like manna to a famished people. In the end, it would fertilize the seeds of destruction for the show that started it all.

With Neal Travis on board at *Hard Copy*, we had an added level of sophistication we'd always hoped for. Neal came up with stories from different angles and places; he chose fine wines at lunch. Most unexpectedly, this international traveler and I came up with one of tabloid's most bizarre concepts yet: the imaginary reporter.

November sweeps had brought us some sex stories that were so out there, there was no way we could run them and not have the slime rub off on us. Yet, we knew we should be able to tell any story, even to the Queen of England...

Thus, the Old Timer was born.

The Old Timer was a character from the hills, an old hayseed who'd seen everything in this century from the vantage point of the creaky rocking chair on his front porch, learned about the birds and the bees by watching the hogs and cows, and couldn't quite cotton to the newfangled ideas these city folks had.

The intro to each "Old Timer" story would go something like this: "This story was so weird, we sent an old timer to cover it."

Richard Halpern, a young actor who did voices for Rick Dees' radio show, provided the voice of the Old Timer. We discovered Richard when he played Pee Wee Herman in one of our comic re-enactments. He also supplied Richard Burton's beyond the grave narration for a story about Liz Taylor. Now he was a cross between Titus Moody, Walter Brennan, and Granny Clampett.

"'Gosh durn it!" Richard rehearsed. "These people are naked as a turnip on a skillet!'"

"Not naked— *nekkid!*"

"Yeah, yeah! 'I ain't seen nothing like this since me and Junior got us some moontans down at the swimmin' hole.'"

Neal lit his pipe and laughed his ass off. "Not since I was plowing the back forty!"

We traded off countryisms, made stuff up. We howled.

Afternoons, we set up shop at the finer restaurants in West Hollywood; long, leisurely lunches during which bottles of wine would flow and we'd chart our course to success.

Hard Copy had become bright, colorful, loud, and innovative. While the other shows were doing the only thing their new bosses were schooled in—straight news—we were venturing farther out on the creative limb, taking that mini-movie idea to a new extreme.

It was a three-part miniseries on the death of Marilyn Monroe; three entire shows aired on three consecutive nights of February 1992 sweeps, shot on film, on location, with a stunning Marilyn lookalike and a recreation of her death scene in the actual house and bedroom in which she died.

Peter Brennan got the idea when an ad in *Variety* revealed that Marilyn's death house on Fifth Helena Drive in Brentwood was available for rent. Timing proved to be on our side when, midway through the preparation, we received galleys of a new book claiming the star didn't commit suicide at all, but was killed by Mafia hitmen with an overdosing drug suppository.

The dramatic scenes were shot by a quiet *Hard Copy* director named Joe Tobin. To chase down the interviews, to provide—to borrow a term—the "meat" around which the series would be based, we used freelance producer Peter Herdrich. Herdrich was a news intellectual and one of my pal David Peterkin's instructors in his days at Columbia University's School of Journalism. For years, Herdrich was a journalistic snob with anachronistic long thin hair falling to his shoulders, but he'd traded in his tenets when he got the chance to make some real money as a producer for *The Reporters*.

Herdrich cut his hair, began wearing suits and, with his highbrow journalistic zeal, helped grease the show's slide into oblivion.

Herdrich found the freelance life to be a good living after *The Reporters*. We used him on several stories, and because he'd come back with handsome-looking interviews, Brennan decided Herdrich would be our "classy," journalistic producer.

When we flew Herdrich out from New York for the Marilyn project, he was full of enthusiasm and awe after a recent vacation to Turkey, where he'd used his Hi-8 video camera to shoot deteriorating works of art. It took a bit of doing to get him focused on the suppository jammed into Marilyn's shapely ass.

Brennan was willing to blow the budget on this one. Tobin came through like a young Spielberg, shooting dozens of reels of filmstock—and even making use of a crane—to shoot TV-movie-quality re-enactment scenes. Herdrich traveled as far as Ireland to round up interviews. When he returned, he handed us a version of the show script that made *The McNeil-Lehrer Report* look like the *Weekly World News*. "The actress Marilyn Monroe, according to a new book, may have died by possible complications from a suppository administered by alleged Mafia hitmen, though there is no concrete evidence to back up the theory. Her alleged affair with President John Fitzgerald Kennedy, though never proven..."

Zzzzzzz...

Brennan and I rewrote the script from top to bottom on his IBM Selectric.

We wrote it as a drama. The thesis was that Marilyn was killed by the Mob. There was no other reason to devote three days to the story. Anyone who thought otherwise—anyone who doubted thirty years down the line whether Marilyn fucked JFK—they should be shooting Hi-8 footage of fucking Turkish art objects.

We wrote it good.

The Marilyn Monroe miniseries drew the highest numbers in *Hard Copy* history.

Lisa stopped by Peter Brennan's office. Peter had hired her and her partner in the LisaRiva team after they were swept out of *A Current Affair*'s L.A. bureau in Anthea Disney's clean-up campaign. At *Hard Copy*, they continued to use any means necessary to bring us exclusive interviews with denizens of the Hollywood underworld. One of those creatures was Alex Adams— Madame Alex to her friends.

Alex was an overflowing, balding woman in a stained housedress who was the unlikely yet well-known Hollywood Madame to the Stars. We'd done many a story with her girls, testifying about everything from white slavery in the Orient to the secrets of the Hollywood casting couch.

"Hi guys." Lisa had news. "Thought you'd want to know. Everybody's talking about a new Hollywood madame. Her name's Heidi."

"Great name."

"Yeah. Alex is really upset that she's stealing her business. She supposedly runs a house that used to be owned by Michael Douglas."

"Wow."

Peter and I walked out by Penny's desk to tell Neal the story.

"Heidi," Neal said. "What a great name."

Big Mike O'Gara happened to be walking past at that very moment, and when he heard Neal repeat the name, his ears perked up.

"Whoa!" he said. "You talking about *Madame* Heidi?"

"Yeah."

"We don't do stories on Heidi. Whoa. No way."

Hmmm.

In March 1992, Maureen O'Boyle achieved the ultimate distinction for a rising television personality. Maury Povich had done it three years earlier, but only in conjunction with his equally famous wife, Connie Chung. Maureen did it alone.

She made the cover of *People* magazine.

Yet, this silver cloud was lined in black. Maury and Connie's cover headline advertised a story about their accomplishments:

> CONNIE CHUNG &
> MAURY POVICH
> A VERY
> CURRENT
> AFFAIR
> The new $6 million
> woman of CBS News
> goes home at night
> to the brash king
> of tabloid TV—and
> they're crazy about
> each other. Here's
> one power couple
> who won't let work
> kill a fine romance

Maureen's cover trumpeted something far more tragic:

"THIS IS
MAUREEN
O'BOYLE. I'VE
JUST BEEN RAPED..."
It was six
years ago
when she
placed the
terrified
call to 911. Now the A CURRENT
AFFAIR host talks for the first
time about her ordeal at the
hands of a brutal intruder—and
her painful recovery.

Maureen made the cover in a roundabout way. She got a call that one of the seamier tabloid papers had gotten wind of the story from her local news days and planned to publish it in a most sensational manner. The matter was turned over to *A Current Affair*'s public relations man, Jeff Erdel, for damage control.

Jeff came through famously, giving Maureen's exclusive story to *People*, which gave it a more sympathetic and Oprah-like tone.

When the magazine hit the office of *Hard Copy*, a young producer who'd worked with Maureen shook his head and offered the sympathy only one from the tabloid world could muster.

"Poor Maureen," he said. "She finally gets her picture on the cover of *People* and she can't hang it in her office."

Brennan walked into my office. "I got an interesting call from Lurch." "Lurch" was Cliff Lachman, second-in-command to Frank Kelly; a tall, lumbering man who resembled his nickname. "He said, 'Um, I hear you're following up on a story on, um, Madame Heidi.' I said, 'No Cliff, we're not doing any story on any Madame Heidi.' 'Well, um, I hear you are, and you should know, Paramount will not do any stories on Madame Heidi.' I said, 'What are you talking about, Cliff?' He said, 'No, Paramount will do no Madame Heidi stories. That comes directly from Robert Evans and that's that.'"

Robert Evans was the former Paramount chief whose career was destroyed by drugs and his involvement in *The Cotton Club* murder case. After years on the outs, he'd returned to Paramount as a producer the previous summer. We'd see him being driven around on the back of golf carts, a bronzed lizard with extravagant sunglasses and neckerchief, balanced on a cane.

"I told him, 'Cliff, we're not doing any stories on Madame Heidi.' He said, 'Well, you better not. That comes straight from Robert Evans.'"

"Is he stupid?"

"Uh...yeah! Let's go to lunch."

"Over there's where they make *Cheers*. And *Entertainment Tonight's* offices are there. It's huge, like a network compared to *Hard Copy*. Over there's where people get their hair cut."

We had visitors on the lot. Brennan, Neal and I were walking them back from the commissary: Peter Faiman and the wife of one of his producer friends in London.

Alison Holloway was the statuesque anchorwoman for the evening news on Murdoch's new Sky TV venture. She was a star in England, having been in the TV news business since she was fourteen, with a show for schoolkids. Her hair was cut like Princess Di's, but her face was far more classic, with high cheekbones, an upturned nose, and green eyes permanently narrowed in a smile.

The two Peters and Neal walked behind while I gave Alison the tour. She nodded thoughtfully and spoke in the clipped, Queen's English accent of a BBC broadcaster as I pointed out the sights.

Alison was beautiful; in her late twenties, tall, lithe, athletic, and built for speed. She said she'd be glad to do some work for us back in England.

Neal and I worked out a deal as soon as we got back to the office. Alison would be our London correspondent.

Wayne Darwen's showdown with Pete Simmons took place in Geraldo Rivera's office at *Now it Can Be Told*. The room was crowded and the atmosphere was tense. There was crisis and fear in the air, and Geraldo's penis was in the thick of it.

Wayne paced and looked at the faces of the others. There was fellow senior producer Simmons, Geraldo's lieutenant Marty Berman, a couple of very nervous Tribune executives, Geraldo's agent from William Morris, and Geraldo himself.

On Geraldo's desk was the morning's edition of the *New York Post*. On the front page of the paper was a headline that had Geraldo's boxer's hands shaking as he held it up for the room to see:

GERALDO
DATE-RAPED
ME
—says
Bette Midler

The item came from an episode recounted in Midler's new autobiography. *Entertainment Tonight* had already done a story on the allegation. They had a producer and camera crew at the door downstairs. Other vultures were beginning to circle. Geraldo didn't know what to do.

Wayne could take it no longer. He snatched the paper. "We oughta address it on tonight's show, mates."

Pete Simmons shook his head vigorously. "We can't," he told Geraldo. "You cannot use this show as your personal forum."

Wayne had enough. "Pete," he said. "You are out of your fucking mind. You're telling me we have the host of our show in a story on the front page of the fucking papers, and *ET* doubles it's ratings on false charges of date rape against Geraldo and we're not supposed to do anything about it?"

"We must have dignity," Simmons said. "We have to be above it."

"Above it? You're out of your fucking mind! *You* are the reason our show is getting its ass kicked! ET *is doubling its fucking ratings on our back!*"

Wayne was thundering now. "We will do a whole show on this. Can't you see? This story has been sent by God to save this show!"

The blood drained almost audibly from the faces of the Tribune Company executives. Their worst nightmare was playing out before their eyes. They looked to Geraldo.

Their star drew in a breath. "You're fucking right," he said. "We're gonna do it!"

"But, but you can't. You can't do it!" Simmons was appalled.

"We will not let Bette Midler make up lies—not while *ET* is cashing in and calling him a fucking rapist!" Wayne countered.

"She's a fucking liar!" Geraldo thundered. The fear was gone. The scrappy pugilist had put on the gloves. "Now, everyone out of the office. We've got a show to do!"

Wayne charged out to start writing the show of his lifetime. Marty Berman and the man from William Morris followed. The Tribune execs hemmed and hawed and made their way to the elevator. Pete Simmons remained behind. He shut the door after the last man left the office.

Fifteen minutes later, Simmons returned to the newsroom. Witnesses recall he was white as a ghost, choking back tears.

"Mate, what is it?" Wayne asked.

"I just quit."

Simmons cleaned off his desk and walked to the elevator.

The showdown had taken place. The meat was dead meat. The heat was hotter than ever. Wayne corralled the forces and assembled a broadcast whose only precursor was Howard Beale's "I'm mad as hell" speech in the movie *Network*.

Around midday, shortly before the show was to be taped, the call came from the president of Tribune Entertainment.

"If I even hear the words 'Bette Midler' on this show, in any context, there will be no more *Now It Can Be Told* as of today."

The message was clear. They put together an alternate show.

Pete Simmons was already on the street. The journeyman TV journalist who was only doing what had been drilled into him all these years had resigned over nothing.

Peter Brennan liked Herdrich's work on the Marilyn story. He thought the guy was a good, solid journalist who could bring us raw material we could shape into something approximating tabloid. The wooing process began.

We took Herdrich to lunch and offered him a job, on his terms, anytime.

"I'm really flattered," he said. "I like you guys and I appreciate all you've done for me. But I really do prefer to remain freelance."

We accepted him at his word. I'd known Herdrich for years, since the early days at Channel Five when he'd show up at restaurants with Peterkin. We considered him part of the team. He'd been in on more than one May sweeps planning meeting over lunch and wine in the back garden of the Hollywood Canteen.

We had big, expensive plans for May, and Herdrich would be part of them. As a perk, we offered to send him to Carnaval in Rio to shoot some sexy stories we could hold for sweeps.

"That's great," Herdrich said. "But I have to ask one thing." He wanted us to pay to first fly him home to New York City so he could take care of some important business.

"No problem," Brennan replied.

Herdrich promised that if he ever did want a permament job, he'd let us know.

At the end of April, I was back in New York, standing with Herdrich in a men's room downstairs at the Odeon Restaurant.

"So, mate," I said, drying my hands. "Rio must have been a blast."

"Oh, yeah." Herdrich was fresh from his trip to Brazil. He'd returned with a dry piece on a neighborhood samba band and a segment on a hangover cure. The wild, racy side of Carnaval did not appeal to his higher instincts. He stepped to the urinal and began to empty his bladder. "So. I suppose this is as good a time as any to tell you," he said, midstream. "I've signed to take a job at *A Current Affair*."

I stood silent for a moment, staring at the mirror and the reflection of Herdrich's back. "You've already signed?"

"Yeah. It's a done deal."

There was time for a controlling breath. "Wow, tell me, Herdrich, which one of us is holding his dick in his hand?"

Upstairs was a table of mutual friends, including David Peterkin and a few others from the rival *A Current Affair*. It turned out everyone at the table had known all along. I kept things light until I could make a graceful exit. That was when Herdrich asked coquettishly if I'd allow him to give the news to Peter Brennan.

"Hey, no problem, mate. It's the least you can do."

I went straight for a payphone and woke up Brennan in L.A.

"You're not gonna believe this one, mate. Remember when you sent Herdrich to Rio? Remember how he asked us to fly him home to New York first so he could tie up some important personal business? Well, the motherfucker went there to sign a fucking contract with fucking *A Current Affair*."

"You're kidding me."

"I'm not. The bastard signed with *A Current Affair*."

Brennan sighed in disgust. "Oh, well. What can we do? Just tell him that all we ask is that he be honorable and discreet and keep confidential the contents of the sweeps meetings we invited him to."

I relayed the message to Herdrich the next day.

"Uhh...too late," he mumbled.

The Ivy League dilettante had sold us out, divulging the contents of our sweeps list to *A Current Affair*, stories we'd already spent money to shoot—and that was only the tip of his devious iceberg. It turned out he'd sold himself to *A Current Affair* on the premise he'd produced the high-rating Marilyn Monroe series himself.

Terenzio wanted Herdrich because he liked the re-enactments; Herdrich shot only the interviews.

Herdrich betrayed us because he didn't understand the rules. Like the other carpetbaggers moving in on tabloid turf, he thought this was how the game was played—that you were supposed to be underhanded to your friends. Like the others, Herdrich missed an essential point, the very core of what made this genre so special: *Do anything for a story. But a friend is a friend.*

We'd teach Herdrich a lesson. We'd teach them all a lesson in a way they'd never expect. In that May sweeps period, a story was about to break that would define tabloid television yet again. It was a story with all the elements, one that no tabloid show could pass up, but one that needed to be handled with great care.

What *Hard Copy* would do with a piece of that story would stun *A Current Affair* like a blow to the head. They'd have dizzy spells from that day until the plug was pulled on the granddaddy of tabloid television.

Raf was back in Los Angeles. Denied his role as an on-air talent, he returned to *Hard Copy* with the somewhat lofty status of freelance specials producer, free to stage sophisticated re-enactments and stories on expensive, movie-quality film.

Since we did so well with the miniseries about Marilyn Monroe's suppository and her affairs with the Kennedys, Raf had the idea of leading off May sweeps with a three-part retelling of brother Teddy's weekend at Chappaquiddick in July, 1969. A 23-year-old Kennedy scandal may have seemed less than captivating, but in wake of the Willie Smith trial, Uncle Ted's peccadillos were of renewed interest.

Raf even had something almost newsworthy. All these years after Ted drove his car off a canal bridge, leaving pretty Mary Jo Kopechne to claw unsuccessfully for life in the back seat, no one made much hay of the 764-page transcript of testimony from the inquest that took place in January 1970. Some of the material was pretty embarrassing, even damning, to Ted.

Raf gathered a group of actors in a courtroom in downtown L.A., dressed them in colorful swingin' sixties costumes and had them act it all out. He shot a re-enactment of the beachhouse party Ted and his married male cohorts threw for the young female campaign workers known as the "boiler room girls," and he capped it off with the scene of an actual car overturned in a canal.

Three shows of Ted were to begin on April 28th. Thanks to a new promotional approach Brennan came up with—running short ads for the special weeks in advance—Wayne over at *Now It Can Be Told* "scooped" us by more than a week. He and Geraldo assembled a hasty mock trial of Senator Ted, using actual residents of Chappaquiddick as the jurors. The jury voted that the senator should have been indicted for "criminal responsibility" in the death of Mary Jo Kopechne. Then they voted ten to two to re-elect him to the Senate.

Peter Brennan and I watched Raf's first Chappaquiddick show the afternoon it was set to air. The problems were evident immediately. Raf didn't shoot enough re-enactment. Over and over, he ran the same scene of his actors dancing and drinking to "Spinning Wheel" and then he'd go back to that overturned car.

Maybe that was why the report took on a dream-like quality, the story told in reverse, with pieces fitting together as if the special was a Nicolas Roeg film.

"Mate, we've got to set up Chappaquiddick," Peter said. "This assumes people know what it is. It happened about twenty-five years ago."

"You can do that in the intro," Raf said.

"Then we'd have a two-minute intro. It's got to be on tape."

"You guys take care of that."

I shook my head. Brennan scribbled on his desk blotter. "Here. We make segment two run first, then go to segment one and we need to open it up explaining what Chappaquiddick is."

Raf looked as if he'd lost final cut of *Citizen Kane*. "I don't care. You guys do what you want," he said, and walked out.

There he went again. In the end, the Chappaquiddick shows wouldn't rate very highly. Nor would a three-part special on Elvis Presley, highlighting great moments from his career, including a little-known summit with the Beatles at his home in Bel Air, and concluding with a disgusting recreation of the last fifteen minutes in the King's life, complete with a big fat Elvis impersonator drooling and dying on a bathroom floor.

We were going to call that one "Naked Elvis," until Brennan toned it down to "I, Elvis," which was totally lost on our audience, and I must admit, on me. Dunleavy beat us to the punch with a couple of pre-planned Elvis Presley stories the week before, because the Elvis series was on the story list brought over by Herdrich.

By the time I'd written a half-hour dramatizing the murder of Paul Castellano and the fall of John Gotti, with narration culled entirely from court testimony of Sammy "the Bull-turned Rat" Gravano and done in the style of *Goodfellas*, it was too late. Brennan saw that full-show dramatizations weren't working.

We were over the hill in Studio City the following evening; Raf and I eating pizza and watching television along with everyone else in the middling Italian restaurant on Ventura Boulevard owned by Vanna White's husband. The expressions of nausea on the faces of the all-white clientele could not be blamed on the food. On the screen, a white man was being dragged out of a semi-truck by a group of young black men. The LIVE chyron hung in the corner of the picture as Reginald Denny was bashed about the head with a cinderblock and fire extinguisher.

Our acquaintance, Johnny Roastbeef, a star of *Goodfellas*, supped with a group of actors from *Who's the Boss*. He patted his lips with a napkin and shook his head. "This is very fucking bad," he said. "This would never happen in New Yawk."

Hours earlier in another valley, a jury of ten whites, one Latino and an Asian acquitted five police officers in the videotaped beating of motorist Rodney King. All around Los Angeles, African-American citizens and their sympathizers were responding to the verdict.

"It's a fucking riot, mate," I said to Raf. "Should we drive down into it?"

"No," Raf said. "We're not working, so we stay away. You don't be a tourist on something like this. Remember that."

We left the restaurant and stopped at a nearby sporting goods store to pick up some socks. The manager rushed from the back and met us at the door. "I hope you're not looking for guns, cause we're all sold out!"

"Mate, you should see this! Shopping centers are on fire. People are running around with guns, looting." Raf was phoning from a car taking him to the airport the next morning, an inadvertant tourist to the riots as he headed back to New York. "It's amazing."

Robert Faulk was crying. He was on the couch in Peter Brennan's office to discuss promotions, but as he watched the continuous live television coverage, it all became too much. He removed his granny glasses and pressed the bridge of his nose. "Boo hoo hoo," he said.

Onscreen, local news helicopters followed mobs of Angelenos moving from one shopping center to another, smashing through display windows and taking what was inside. With each helicopter news report that police weren't stopping the thievery, more people switched off their TVs and joined in. Faulk watched and sniffled.

"*They're coming!*"

I wished Rafael luck and looked toward the door with everyone else. "Who's they?" Brennan and I said together.

"The, the looters! They're two blocks away!" It was Joe Tobin, in a literal sweat. The quiet producer was supposed to begin editing a sweeps piece but was more likely to hit the road at any moment. "We gotta get out of here! We could be in danger!"

"Joe," I suggested calmly, "you'll be in an edit room in the basement of a building in the middle of the guarded Paramount lot. I don't think anything's gonna happen."

"Can you guarantee my safety?"

Neal puffed his pipe and stifled a laugh.

There was panic. A few blocks away, bands of festive neighbors stepped over shattered storefront glass on Western Avenue and wandered off with couches and the like.

Chief Darryl Gates and his criticized police force had proven their point by letting the riots get out of control. By afternoon, Paramount had been shut down and Tobin was sent to a safe edit house in the Valley as the city prepared for a dusk-to-dawn curfew.

Brennan and I drove west along heavy Melrose Avenue traffic and into a scene out of a bad apocalypse movie. Merchants hammered plywood over storefront windows in haste. Women sobbed inside locked BMWs. Cars sped from service station pumps with the nozzles left hanging from their tanks. When a lone black driver attempted to wedge into traffic, everyone stopped to let him through.

We left our cars with the Bel Age valets and walked to the back of the restaurant with the window beneath which the Los Angeles basin was laid out like a game board. With our feet up on the windowsill, we watched as portions of the city burned below us. To the east, past Dodger Stadium and south toward Compton, entire blocks raged unchecked, the smoke rising black with hints of orange flame. The outbreaks spread like forest fires, where embers drift for hundreds of yards on the winds before settling at random and exploding another distant patch of dry wood. As the arsons neared the Beverly Center and the West L.A. aristocracy, they'd be extinguished quickly, the black smoke turning papal white, as if the lawmen had drawn an imaginary fire line at Pico Boulevard.

Visible through the restaurant windows was a billboard on the corner of Sunset and Larrabee, advertising a radio station with a painting of Marvin Gaye and the question, "What's Going On?" Sly Stone's answer raged before us. There was a riot goin' on. Brennan and I drank soberly, brushing the ashes from our Stolis and tonic, fiddling while our new home burned.

CHAPTER EIGHTEEN:
FUCKING WITH THEIR HEADS
(or STEALING SATELLITES)

On May 10th, 1992, a single gunshot rang out in a quiet neighborhood in Massapequa, Long Island. When police got the call, they assumed it was an incident at the home of John Gotti, Jr. The actual address was just around the corner. A woman was lying on the front steps of her house with blood pouring from her head. The shooter was long gone. The shot would be heard around the world, whether the world wanted to hear it or not.

The victim, as it turned out, was a thirty-seven-year-old housewife named Mary Jo Buttafuoco. Soon, the shooter would be identified as seventeen-year-old Amy Fisher. Amy would admit to the shooting, claiming she was having an affair with Mary Jo's husband Joey, and that she was driven to the act after Joey tried to break it off.

It was everyone's idea of the ultimate suburban nightmare, and as Mary Jo Buttafuoco lay in a coma, the messengers of this particular misery rolled into position. This was the ultimate tabloid story.

Yet, it had its drawbacks, for the crime took place in a suburbia that would be considered distasteful to much of America, a suburbia of harsh New York accents, blunt characters in gold chains and muscle shirts, and teenage girls with purple hair.

As days passed and sleazy allegations flew about all parties, there was a miracle, as, incredibly, the victim rose from the dead. Mary Jo Buttafuoco came home from the hospital, and soon she was on her front steps again, facing the media and adding a new, unexpected layer to the story.

"My Joey would nevah have an affair," she insisted against all evidence. "People forget who's the victim heah. That little bitch shot me in the head!" The bullet remained lodged in Mary Jo's skull, behind her ear. Her mouth drooped pathetically, stroke-like, where a nerve had been severed.

All through May sweeps, the tabloid shows competed with the networks, locals, and afternoon talk shows for ownership of the story. *Hard Copy* was at a bit of a disadvantage. Diane Dimond and Jerry Burke of the

New York bureau, so excited to be in the midst of a big story in the compressed locale of Palm Beach, were adrift when sent out to sprawling Long Island to come up with scoops. *A Current Affair* had Dunleavy, with his connections within the Nassau County court system, and a team of New York City journalists.

In the final days of May, *A Current Affair* wrote a check to purchase what was, at that point, mind-boggling proof of the ultimate twist to the story. Some guy in Long Island had called a prostitute to his home and videotaped the encounter. It was a year later that he realized the importance and value of his sordid video. He called *A Current Affair*.

Despite his quest for a more sensitive broadcast, Terenzio went for it: a fourteen minute and thirty-six second, grainy, dirty, sleazy, X-rated video of a fat slob in boxer shorts rutting with a child. Yet the child charged a hundred and eighty-five dollars an hour and she was Amy Fisher, the Long Island Lolita herself.

When Dunleavy called us on a Sunday with the news that he had the ultimate tape in the Lolita story, Brennan was crestfallen. Once *A Current Affair* went with the video, they'd own the story forever. Every year or so comes a story that redefines tabloid television. From Robert Chambers to William Kennedy Smith to Michael Jackson to O.J. Simpson, these stories change the course of television history. The Amy Fisher story was the most recent and there was nothing we could do about it.

Nabi's bar was closed Sunday nights, so we sat at the Bel Age Brasserie that Sunday night, power drinking Stolis—Peter's with sodas with a twist of lemon, mine with tonic and wedge of lime. We were approaching double figures when I noticed the glint in Brennan's eye. He had the answer. He knew what he was going to do, but he didn't say anything.

We arrived at work early Monday morning. I'd awakened with that great quasi-hangover feeling where your head feels like it's underwater and it isn't until an hour or so after you've been walking around that you realize you're still drunk from the night before. It adds great purpose to the day.

The Lolita Tapes were all over the front pages of the New York tabloids. The networks, which tut-tutted about tabloid irresponsibility, were eager to run the story on their local affiliates, even though the identity of the girl in the tape was not confirmed by any means other than that she looked a whole lot like Amy.

We were beaten on this one.

Or were we? Brennan brought me into the office and shut the door. "We're leading with the Amy Fisher story."

"I knew you were up to something. How can we do it?"

The answer was obvious. The New York papers and Associated Press had run still photos from the video. We had the New York office shoot every photo available, and told them to have the shooter move the camera a bit to give the pictures the sensation of motion.

Then we went further: we had one of the producers re-enact the sex tape. We had to do it quickly. We had a couple sit on a bed and pretend to negotiate and consummate a sex act. We made it blurry and badly-lit and played the tape through a monitor behind Barry Nolan as he did a standup.

We did it all that Monday morning and wrote a nice juicy package describing everything on the sex video. We never lied. We never said we had the sex video, but the casual viewer could be forgiven for assuming *A Current Affair* didn't have much of an exclusive after all.

As we got the package underway, Brennan stayed on the phone with the Paramount lawyers and higher-ups. He argued, cajoled, demanded over and over that we had to get our hands on the tape. He didn't make much of the fact that the only way to get the tape would be to point our satellite dish at the correct satellite at the time *A Current Affair* fed out its show to the affiliates *and steal it.*

Every day, the syndicated tabloids and strips like *Entertainment Tonight* record their shows and feed them via satellite to stations around the country. The feeds are taken in and aired live or recorded for broadcast later in the day.

Though the practice was technically illegal, the tabloid shows dialed up the satellite coordinates and brought in rival show and promo feeds as a matter of course—to see what the other guys were promoting for the next day and get an edge on the competition.

It was one thing to spend money playing peekaboo for a little lead time in a game of catch-up; quite another to steal footage off the satellite and then air it. That would be a violation of federal law. Nothing even similar had ever been done since, well, not since the Rob Lowe video scandal, and that video was taken off a television set and shown after it aired locally.

This was out-and-out air piracy, and it had never been attempted.

Not until now.

Brennan had it planned. He began by calling Paramount Television's top lawyer, Tom Fortuin. Fortuin was an archetypal Hollywood attorney; tough, gay, intimidating, and scary. With his cool Teutonic demeanor, he looked like he could have run the concentration camp in *Schindler's List* and even his most preppie wool suit had the sheen of leather.

Tom Fortuin was also probably the best TV attorney I've worked with. As much as he may have detested *Hard Copy*, he never let that get in the way of his responsibility to the show. He was no Victorian avenger like Muriel Reis. Fortuin was a dispassionate professional who knew which side he was playing for. He backed us when we were right—and if we were wrong, he'd make it right. We could trust him.

Brennan hammered the argument that we had the right, under fair use laws, to air a portion of *A Current Affair's* video. Portions of the Amy Fisher tape had already been given out to the morning shows in New York City. It was on the front pages of the papers. It was big news. We could surely use ten seconds under the same fair use laws that allowed us to take a clip from *The Tonight Show* if something newsworthy took place.

Fortuin said, "Go for it."

We scrambled. We took in the *A Current Affair* feed and selected maybe ten seconds of the Amy Fisher sex video—okay, fifteen seconds at the most. We put a bit of it in the open of the show. We stuck a little in the package. We slowed the video down and stretched it out. That, combined with the re-enacted footage, the stills, and anything else we may have throw in, made our show look pretty damn impressive.

We had it together in time for the second feed at one p.m. Most of the stations around the country took this feed, and we had a production assistant call every one of them to let them know it was coming. WCBS-TV in New York was one of them. *Hard Copy* aired in New York at 7 p.m., a half hour before *A Current Affair* ran on Fox.

We did it. We watched the feed go out. We went to lunch.

Meanwhile, back in New York, John Terenzio, Herdrich, Dunleavy, and the boys at *A Current Affair* were feeling darn good about themselves. They'd even stayed around the office late to watch their triumph as it aired at 7:30 p.m. Ha ha! they snickered. We are the champions of this tabloid form. We've won!

As a laugh, they tuned in *Hard Copy* a half-hour before their exclusive to see what measly scraps we'd try to throw against them.

They say that if we had only listened, had Peter, Neal, Raf, and I put down our glasses of Silverado wine at the Mustache Cafe on Melrose Avenue at 4:01 p.m. that afternoon, we may have heard the anguished screams emanating from the fourth floor office on East 67th Street. They say the boys at *A Current Affair*, this generation of desk assistants, associate producers, and newspaper hacks promoted to leadership roles through attrition, went fucking ballistic.

Dickie McWilliams, they say, was crying. Danny Meenan was punching the walls. Peter Herdrich, who jumped to *A Current Affair* with our sweeps list, went red in the face. And John Terenzio was running back and forth like a naked customer looking for his pants in a whorehouse fire.

"I'll get them! They'll pay! They won't get away with this! I'll sue! I'll get them! They broke the law!"

Dunleavy was alone among them. He watched the *Hard Copy* piece unspool, smiled a thin crooked grin, and nodded. "They really did it. Gotta hand it to em. Gotta hand it to em," he said to deaf ears. "Mates, mates, it's only television, it's only business... touché, they got us..."

Terenzio was having none of it. He fired off a memo to the *A Current Affair* staff, promising that Twentieth TV was "instituting a lawsuit calling for a permanent injunction on the use of material...seeking statutory damages...We will pursue all legal avenues available to us..."

Peter Brennan and I stepped carefully on Tuesday. My office was beseiged by phone calls from former mates at *A Current Affair* saying we went too far this time. We figured everything would cool down once the guys got back to their senses, but it was not to be.

We came to work Wednesday morning to a very bad omen. We saw the lead story of *Variety*, and it was us:

HARD COPY COPS
AFFAIR SEX TAPE

Current says Par show stole signal

Twentieth TV's *A Current Affair* has accused Paramount's rival tabloid *Hard Copy* of intercepting the *Current Affair* station satellite feed Monday and stealing nearly two minutes of exclusive footage for its own broadcast.

Hard Copy removed the ACA logo from the feed, the program's officials charge, and scooped *Affair* with the allegedly pilfered video in New York, a virtually unheard-of practice in the television industry...

Terenzio was spluttering in the *Hollywood Reporter*: "If we allow this to go down the pike, then what will happen next? The industry would be in anarchy..."

It was sad. On that day, tabloid television officially ended. The ones we trained, who owed their six-figure salaries and inflated senses of selves to Peter Brennan, were now puffing up their chests behind Terenzio and calling for Brennan's head—for his job. Our old mates, who'd played hide the salami with lots of stories and video, were all caught up in this new hypocrisy. They forgot Brennan's most important lesson: It's only television.

Maybe we did go too far. For from that day on, from June 1st, 1992, *A Current Affair* would never recover. Everything its staff believed was sacred no longer had meaning. When a satellite feed could be pirated in direct violation of the law, what mattered?

None of them saw its lineage; that the caper was a direct descendant of the finest tabloid scams in history. They forgot the legend upon which their very heritage was based, the story of the teenage Steve Dunleavy, working for the *Sydney Daily Mirror*, slashing the tires of a rival in order to beat him to a crime scene. That rival was his father.

They forgot the second part of Dunleavy's story, about how later, father and son were rivals again in the chase after the Kings Grove Slasher. Dunleavy was hiding in an outhouse, hoping to catch the man himself, when he heard a deadbolt fall over the door outside. He remained locked in as the criminal was arrested only yards away.

"The man who locked me in? My father," Dunleavy would recall as he wiped a tear. "I said, 'Do you realize I could have got fired over this?' He said, 'Remember the day you let down my tires?'"

None of this mattered. Terenzio was grandstanding for Lucie Salhany and her assistant Gregg Meidel, a blond beachboy who would do literal jumps and splits while leading surreal pep talks for the *A Current Affair* staff.

Terenzio wore artsy ties emblazoned with headlines from the *New York Post* and he drank his white wines and ice while listening to Dunleavy plot the course of coverage, but he was the final break in the chain that kept *A Current Affair* anchored.

Nobody had a sense of humor.

There was no room for pirates any more.

A few weeks later, I flew into New York and called Dickie to meet me at the Whisky Bar at the Paramount Hotel. I knew he wasn't doing well at *A Current Affair*. Herdrich had taken his senior producer role and he was left with little to do. I didn't hold it against him that he used us as a bargaining chip when we tried to hire him away the previous summer, and felt bad that things weren't working out for him at Fox.

After all, it was only business. We were mates. We'd sit at the Whisky Bar and reminisce about the Ball of Twine or something.

When I arrived, the place was crowded with Armani suits, male and female, shoulder to shoulder from the bar to the window. Dickie was at the bar and he wasn't alone. He was with Herdrich.

They were both so disappointed. They spent the evening grilling me about the satellite piracy. They wanted to know how I thought we'd ever get away with it. They, like Muriel Reis and everyone else, took it for granted that I was behind the theft, that only Burt would be wild enough to steal from a satellite feed. The Prince of Darkness dragged Brennan too far over the line this time—and they'd all be happy if we learned our lessons by being fired.

In a way, they were right. For a couple of days after we pirated the footage, with the story the lead of *Variety* and prominent on the front of the *Hollywood Reporter* and Terenzio offering self-righteous, self-serving quotes to all the papers about the sanctity of his checkbook scoops, it looked grim. For forty-eight hours, at least one person on the *Hard Copy* staff walked on eggshells of anticipation, knowing that at any moment Brennan and I could be gone and replaced by a deserving new regime.

Sorry, but truth be told, I had little to do with it. There was no way either Brennan or I could be disciplined over this matter because we had approval from the top. The Paramount executives approved it. Tom Fortuin said it was okay.

Looking back, one can't help wonder why Tom Fortuin, this smart, by-the-book attorney, would allow us to do something so crazy; why he'd allow us to break criminal laws and FCC statutes; why this tough-as-nails Paramount lawyer agreed with the words of Tom Cruise in *Risky Business*: "Sometimes, you've just gotta say 'What the fuck?'"

We'll never know.

A year later, Tom Fortuin was dead from complications of AIDS.

CHAPTER NINETEEN:
THE RESURRECTION OF RAFAEL

INT. BAR - DAY OR NIGHT
Phil and Alex drink, heavily.

                    ALEX
    Your what?

                    PHIL
    My autobiography. Right now I'm
    living "The L.A. Years." I'm
    gathering material.

                    ALEX
    You go through life living your
    autobiography? Are you INSANE?

                    PHIL
    How else do people have anything
    to write about? They go out of
    their way to get into interesting
    situations.

                    —from My Future Ex-Wife,
                    another Kearns & Abramovitz
                    screenplay

The Fall 1992 season began with *Inside Edition* leading the tabloid pack for the first time. Its "Clean Air Act," promising a sleaze-free broadcast, couldn't have done much for viewership, but its good-faith placement in sales packages that included *Oprah* and *Wheel of Fortune* got the show good lead-ins and time slots in the best markets. *A Current Affair*, under Terenzio, was slipping.

After the summer recess, we at *Hard Copy* worked to restore the ratings destroyed by months of enforced rerun shows and resumed our long lunches and evening drinking sessions. We'd also expanded our pub turf from the Bel Age to a bunker-like structure over the road from Paramount. Small's was a jam-packed nightspot for the late-night leather jacket crowd. We had the windowless concrete box to ourselves as we started on the vodkas around five.

Rafael was back with us, officially a freelance producer, but working just about full-time. He was restless again, anxious to reassert himself in TV journalism. As Amy Fisher neared her date in court, he worked all sides of the fences, trying to get a scoop to rival *A Current Affair*'s sex video.

It was only a matter of weeks before he'd come through with the wildest and most controversial story in the history of tabloid television, one that threw a curveball into the faces of so-called "serious" journalists and left his tabloid compadres scratching their heads in amazement.

The subject, the victim, the star, was Amy. After a summer of wild tabloid headlines and revelations that got sleazier by the day, her attorney Eric Naiburg was finally making a plea bargain in the case. Amy would admit shooting Mary Jo. She would express contrition and she would blame Mary Jo's husband Joey for leading her astray. She would go to prison.

The debate among feminist columnists, news hands, afternoon talk show hosts and parents around the country was over Amy Fisher's character; whether she was an impressionable schoolgirl driven to violence by a devious older lover, or a bad-seed wild child who deserved to be in a cell with door locked and key thrown away.

Judging by the tips we were receiving, nothing was so simple. Amy may have been a love-bitten teen, but she also had at least one other adult lover.

Paul Makely was a bodybuilder with a couple of drug arrests in his background. With Amy on her way to jail, he was more than happy to sell her out for money. He couldn't think of enough ways.

Raf could. He came up with a scheme that would serve up Amy to *Hard Copy* on a silver platter.

It only cost us about $10,000 to get Makely's cooperation and assistance. Peter Brennan knew that Raf's plan would be too much for the Paramount legal department to handle, so, without telling them about the monetary layout or the plans to follow, he flew to New York. Sick with the flu, he holed up at his wife's apartment on Central Park West, surfacing only to go on a long drinking binge with Rafael that worked its way to the Upper East Side and continued through the weekend.

The deal went down on a Thursday night. Raf wound up holding a videotape that he'd proclaim to be "an x-ray of Amy Fisher's soul."

The last time Raf took an x-ray was when he came up with the very story that put *A Current Affair* on the map. It was May, 1988; he got his hands on the videotape of Robert Chambers pretending to strangle himself at a party before decapitating a doll and saying, "Oops, I killed it."

It always burned Raf that he had to share credit with Dunleavy on his claim to fame and in the TV movie based on the Preppie Murder case. He'd insinuated that Brennan forced him to cut Dunleavy in, out of loyalty to his old mate, but in reality it was Dunleavy's tip that sent Raf on the trail.

This time, Rafael had the story all to himself, and in having it, beat any of Dunleavy's scoops in this case or any other.

It was a surveillance tape, recording a meeting between Paul Makely and Amy Fisher in the reception area of the bodybuilding gym Makely owned, hours before Amy was to walk into court to be sentenced for her crime.

The tape was, by any account, spectacular.

As the camera rolled, Makely asked the questions and Amy gave the answers. She told Makely she wanted to marry him so they could have sex on conjugal visits in prison. She insisted she deserved a Ferrari for her troubles. She made a move for Makely's crotch in an effort to have sex with him on the counter.

This mysterious tape served to tarnish Amy's promoted image as an innocent driven to distraction. Peter Brennan knew this had the potential to be the biggest hit in the history of tabloid television. He released the first publicity about the tape on Friday. The New York tabloids went into a frenzy.

On Saturday, Amy Fisher's attorney Eric Naiburg retaliated, announcing that news of the videotape had spurred the teenage girl to gulp a handful of pills in an attempt to commit suicide.

Brennan could tell it was transparent bullshit, that Naiburg was merely stealing the headlines that the surveillance tape won. He also knew that Paramount, still new to reality television, would likely go weak at the knees and not allow the surveillance tape to run. He had to steal back the headlines.

Brennan and Rafael spent the day investigating the alleged Friday night suicide attempt. They found out what phone calls were made to whom in the hours following the crisis, that an ambulance had not been called to the house until five hours later, that Naiburg had alerted a newspaper photographer to meet them at the emergency room—that it was all a publicity ploy.

Months later, Naiburg would be even more creative when he would sell Amy Fisher to *Inside Edition*, and get around the Son of Sam law by having KingWorld cloak the hundreds of thousands of dollars it paid Amy as an "investment" in a production company that was supposedly developing a TV movie about the Fisher family.

For now, Peter Brennan had to tell the world that Amy Fisher's suicide attempt was a fraud, and come up with a headline to replace Naiburg's.

It being a weekend, all the Paramount attorneys were off frolicking in Palm Springs or were otherwise unavailable. Nobody knew Brennan was calling his own press conference at a hotel on Central Park to announce new evidence in the Amy Fisher case.

The evidence was something Raf had hoped to hold back—an audiotape Makely had sold him. Incredibly, as if there weren't enough Amy Fisher tapes floating around, Amy herself had tape-recorded a "letter" to Makely from her jail cell after her arrest, accusing her father of unspecified abuse, and her mother of doing nothing to stop it.

As the press conference got underway, Peter Brennan could only hope the tape would show that *Hard Copy* was not the victimizer in this case. His more immediate problem, though, was talking. He'd been up for nights on end, his flu had led to laryngitis, and he could barely croak out an introduction of Rafael Abramovitz.

The wary and grumpy weekend press corps leaned forward to make out Brennan's strangled words. They looked askance at *Hard Copy*'s lonesome warrior, Eames Hamilton Yates, standing watch in suit and Wayfarer sunglasses like a Fruit of Islam bodyguard. Then Rafael stepped to the microphones and everything really went haywire.

Rafael was on edge, defensive and angry as usual as the audiotape was played, and then the reporters demanded to know how he got his hands on this tape and the one from Makely's gym.

"If I comment on how things are done, then I can never do investigative work again," Raf told his colleagues.

"Who are you?"

"What do you mean, who am I?" Raf became more indignant. "I have won the DuPont Award, I have—"

"How do you spell your name?"

"Spell my name? Fuck you!"

"Fuck you!" the genial weekend A.P. reporter screamed back.

The press conference descended into shouting.

Peter Brennan could only stand by, helplessly. He had no voice.

All the reporters at the gathering went away with the phony suicide timeline and soundbites from the audiotape. The young reporter representing the local CBS station—the station that aired *Hard Copy*, determined on his own to report the story but not play the tape. The young man was criticized when the tape led every other newscast in New York. He was in more hot water when the tape appeared the next day on the CBS network morning show.

He was fired after he was quoted as saying he decided not to air the audiotape because "CBS doesn't do that sort of thing."

CBS did do that sort of thing, and more.

The audiotape did little to quell the media uproar over Raf's surveillance video. In the days to follow, the "serious" media went berserk. When *Newsday* ran a doctored quote of Brennan saying, "Rafael Abramovitz is an investigative journalist following in the finest tradition of Edward R. Murrow," Don Hewitt from *60 Minutes* got in the act to set the record straight about *Hard Copy*'s, and his, roles in journalistic history. "I knew Edward R. Murrow," he quipped, "and Rafael Abramovitz is no Edward R. Murrow."

New York magazine's Edwin Diamond dedicated an entire column to the tape. In a fight among tabloid shows for the title of "most repulsive show on television," he wrote, *Hard Copy* had "all but retired the sleazeball cup.

"Is this really the true face of news, a psychiatric ward where everyone points video cameras at everyone else and all news sources are for sale?"

Raf, meanwhile, couldn't understand why he was being pilloried by those whose respect he knew he had earned. Here was a man, dumped unceremoniously from a show, who came back to provide its highest ratings with its biggest and most controversial exclusive, yet, like Rodney Dangerfield, he couldn't get no respect.

His fellow journalists may have envied Raf's perseverence and, secretly, his outlandish exclusive, yet they couldn't help but cringe at the notion that Raf may have *engineered* the set-up—that he was taking an advocacy position that no journalist could reconcile with his or her code of ethics.

Criticism even came from Raf's old friend, John Parsons, who upon leaving *Hard Copy* had hitched a ride for the final miles of *Now It Can Be Told*. Though Parsons bragged of his Sicilian roots and respect for the code of omerta, he went public with his comments. "I think what he did is outrageous," Parsons said. "Just fuckin outrageous. He totally set her up. Rafael and I began in *The Fifty-First State*, when we were chasing the real criminals and now he's in bedrooms for a buck. Everything's for a buck. I told him he made me feel tawdry, made me want to get out of the business."

We saw Parsons's words as nothing less than a betrayal. I called the New York gossip columns and spread the word that Parsons was angling for the executive producership of *Hard Copy*.

Yet, Rafael himself was responsible for some of the uproar over his actions in this story. While the gym tape made Amy Fisher seem like a cunning vixen, the desperate release of the audiocassette made her appear an abused child all over again. Raf's willingness to present both sides of the girl showed that his only agenda was pursuit of the truth, but it didn't do much to help his reputation.

It was almost as if he was defeating himself.

Never mind all that. How did Raf get that video?

Through it all, some have bandied about the amount of money we may have paid for the gymnasium videotape, but no one knew exactly how *Hard Copy* "obtained" the footage—whether Paul Makely had come up with an enterprising money-making scheme himself and simply popped the tape from his gym's security camera or if Rafael was hiding in a closet or behind the wall.

As it happened, Rafael had taken destiny into his own hands. He worked hard and showed tremendous self-restraint on a night when everything could have gone so wrong.

Makely, going over his laundry list of ways to make money off his teenage lover, told Raf that Amy often ventured out to meet him for sex. Despite the ring of national media, police, and spectators around her home and attorney's office twenty-four hours a day, this eighteen-year-old on two million dollars bail was scooting all over town in her hot little car doing whatever she wanted.

Makely insisted he knew for sure Amy would meet him at his gym that very Thursday night, even though she was to be sentenced the very next morning.

About an hour before the planned rendezvous, Raf and a cameraman ran into the gym and set up three small, concealed cameras on a high shelf facing Makely's counter. Then they went outside into the parking lot and waited in the crew's van.

They waited. Raf sat thinking of all that had gone down in his career, praying that the cameras would work and hoping Amy Fisher would show up. The camera crew talked about how hungry they were and what they were going to eat when they got their dinner break. Raf called Peter on a cell phone.

Brennan was back at the apartment, feeling the full effect of the week's partying and that goddamn flu.

"We're waiting," Raf said. "There's nothing we can do but wait."

"Well, whatever happens, mate."

Suddenly Raf's voice raised in pitch. "I'll call you back."

A car was pulling up in front of the gym. The engine was cut and the lights flicked off.

Amy Fisher stepped out of the car. Raf couldn't believe his eyes. It was Amy Fisher.

"Oh man, that's her! That's her!" The cameraman scrambled for his gear. His soundman put the cans over his ears. "Let's bang her now! Let's do it!"

Raf told them to shut up and sit tight. He tapped out Brennan's number again.

"The eagle has landed," he said to Brennan.

"Really?" Peter never believed he'd pull it off. It was too outrageous.

Raf spoke deliberately and softly. "The question is, do we wait outside and ambush her when she comes out? Or do we hope the cameras work?"

"I can't guarantee anything, man," the cameraman said.

"Shhhh—" Raf held out a hand to quiet him.

Peter lit a cigarette and spoke in equally measured tones. "I think you should go by your instinct."

Raf hung up. "We wait."

About a half hour later, Amy Fisher walked out of the gym and got into her car. Raf felt a twinge as the quarry got away. He didn't know if he'd blown the chance to get some kind of exclusive footage on the eve of the sentencing. Most important was to get in there and get the tape before Makely did anything funny.

He and the cameraman charged the place. They burst through the door, grabbed the cameras off the shelf and got the hell out before Makely's head had a chance to spin.

They got back to the *Hard Copy* office and played back the tapes. The first camera had malfunctioned. It didn't work at all. The tape from the second camera showed only shadows. That camera malfunctioned, as well.

Resigned to defeat, Raf played the tape from camera number three.

That one remaining camera got the goods.

It was Raf's idea to set up three cameras—not two, not one, but three. That's one reason Rafael Abramovitz is regarded by many as a genius.

CHAPTER TWENTY:
HOWARD RULES & ELTON SUES

Months before Raf's exclusive, Jerry Burke and I met two women at Boardner's and brought them back to my place. At the time, I was living with Nicky Loiacono, my old assignment desk mentor and friend from the Channel Five days, in a big old house at the end of a long narrow road off Benedict Canyon Drive, not far from the compound where Raf and I spent the first season. Brennan had hired Nicky on the *Hard Copy* assignment desk after he was fired from Fox because of problems with drugs and alcohol.

Nicky was cleaned up and getting back on his feet professionally, but was on his back sound asleep upstairs when Jerry and I arrived with the women. Jerry's was more eager than mine. The two of them went into the kitchen and knocked pans and silverware into the sink to make assroom on the counter. Mine and I were on the couch for a half hour listening to Phil Spector's greatest hits and drinking tequila, with me trying in vain to show her the voodoo shrine in my bedroom before she got fed up and decided she wanted to go home.

I insisted I drive her. We threw down the top of the Kharmann Ghia and blasted off down the hill, toward the treacherous twisting canyon drive that led over Mullholland and ultimately to her place in the Valley.

I didn't get far before realizing the extent of my drunkenness. The road swerved in front of me. If I closed one eye, I couldn't see the yellow line at all. With both eyes open it was pick and choose which way to point. Approaching a curve a couple of hundred yards past Eddie Murphy's estate, I pointed wrong. The car bounced off the road, smashed off a rock and was projected into the air.

We were sailing—*BOOM!* The Ghia landed back on the road on the other end of the curve.

"Jesus. Are you all right?"

"You asshole, you almost killed us!"

Sheesh. I got out to inspect the damage. The right front tire was torn to shreds. The wheel was smashed to shit.

I drove the car at a crawl up the hill, for miles down Beverly Glen to Ventura Boulevard, where we finally found a service station to get the tire changed. Sobriety began poking its fingers around the back of my eyes as the pump jockey pried the mangled wheel from the axle.

That was a cliff, with nothing but sky above and Deep Canyon Drive below. What if the car had sailed in a different direction? The top was down. What if she were ejected from the vehicle?

I looked at the woman sitting on the curb at the gas pump island, forlorn and fed up in her black leather jacket and dyed red-black hair. What if I'd killed her?

By the time I got home, Jerry had gone off with his newfound friend. I wiped off the kitchen counter, sat down at the dining room table and cracked open another beer. Nicky padded downstairs, and though he'd been awakened from a dead sleep, cracked open a beer himself.

"You guys were really fucking loud," he said, not complaining. "You were playing that Ronettes music."

"It's not an aphrodisiac, believe me." I told him what happened.

"Wow," he said. "You could have killed her."

I looked at Nicky, who'd been going through an even wilder time left to his own devices. I realized that if I'd crawled away from a dead body in the wreckage, there was only one choice.

"You know, man. You were the only sober one. I was thinking, I'd have to come back and get you to say you were driving."

Nicky shrugged. "Yeah. I woulda did that."

"I know."

I stood in the bathroom and looked at what was staring back in the mirror. All this drinking was taking its toll. Not even the California tan could hide the puffiness of my face or the extra twenty pounds of alcohol bloat I was carrying. Back when I was two months into tabloid, I was walking around New York City like I was John-John Kennedy. Now, two years in Los Angeles and all of a sudden I was Teddy.

As we moved into our third season at *Hard Copy*, I carried one important reminder from that fateful brush with death and loss of my driver's license. The woman in my car that evening told me she'd met Stuttering John at a record company party back in New York. Howard Stern's interviewer, the butt of many jokes because of his severe speech impediment, never stuttered once in their conversation, she insisted. His stuttering was an act.

That anecdote was in my head when I assigned Audrey another Howard Stern story. This one would focus on the people surrounding him, including the interviewer who only pretended to stutter.

It was a hard-hitting, tongue-in-cheek expose that actually chronicled

Stern's continued success, including his new Number One status in Los Angeles. When tiny Audrey waited outside Stern's studio in Manhattan to get some comment before his show, Stern hid his face and ran into the building, providing a provocative visual tease to promote the story. Stern himself mentioned the ambush on his radio show before the segment ran.

The morning after the segment aired, Audrey woke me up about five a.m., excited and upset, saying Stern had awakened her with an on-air phone call. He ambushed *her*, she said.

I listened to Audrey's phone call segment when the show was replayed three hours later in Los Angeles. I heard Stern ask Audrey if she'd agree to be on the air. She gave her approval. She said hello to Robin. She gave back a few "Oh, Howards." She sounded awake.

What happened next took everything over the line. Stern was holding ammunition. He asked if it was true she'd slept with Jack Nicholson for a story or that she'd had sex with her cameramen. He solicited acquaintances to call in with more embarrassing stories about her—and like all of us, Audrey had more than her share.

By the time Audrey got to work, she was claiming a stream of threatening phone calls at home and to her extension at *Hard Copy*. I listened to some of them on her office voicemail.

"*Stern rules!*"

"*You suck! Stern number one!*"

"*Stern is God!*"

"Audrey. From what you told me, I think this is very dangerous. We should consider filing an injunction immediately, and possibly a defamation suit—" It was Audrey's new fiancé, an L.A. attorney, calling from his car phone. "I'm very worried about this..."

"*Howard Stern rules!*"

"*Bababooey! Fuck you!*"

"*How could you dis Howard, bitch? Stern is King of All Media!*"

"*Stern rules! You suck!*"

Next thing you know...

> LOS ANGELES (AP) A producer for the TV tabloid
> show *Hard Copy* said she got hundreds of death
> threats from fans of shock jock Howard Stern after
> one of her stories portrayed Stern as a bully. Audrey
> Lavin said she received nearly 250 threats on her
> answering machine after the Oct. 2 segment on Stern,
> whose allegedly offensive broadcasts led to a record
> $105,000 fine last week against a Los Angeles station.

"It was quite horrible for me," Audrey told the Associated Press. "These people are such lunatics. These are nasty, mean yahoos from hell that he incites."

An L.A. police detective said there wasn't much the cops could do unless they caught one of the callers in the act.

We were running on automatic pilot, if not totally on empty by now. With Neal as our navigator, we steered our way between lunch spots, our boat powered by bottles of Silverado Chardonnay and the winds of our long conversations. After lunch, we'd knock off the show and plan for the future.

In two years under the unforgiving Los Angeles sun and unyielding aggravation from Linda Bell and her gang, expectation had given way to resignation, politeness to arrogance, and celebration to routine elbow-bending in the shadowy haunts of a town in which only losers gathered at bars. Old Lindy the Formosa bartender complained of gut pains one night and woke up dead the next morning. They gave him a twenty-one drink salute at the dirty old bar and old Jimmy stepped in to fill his slow-moving shoes. Jimmy was a gray-haired Irish sprite with a little ponytail who'd cut his teeth behind the mahogany at P.J. Clarke's and was always quick with a joke out of the side of his mouth.

He was also alive enough to recognize us when we came in, knew Raf from television and knew to pour me a Stoli in "a bucket," a wide double tumbler he set down next to the petite vessels of the street alcoholics alongside us.

Backed by more than two thousand signatures on "Save the Formosa" petitions, Old Lem the owner worked out a deal with Warner Brothers to save his joint; they'd lift and move his restaurant a few hundred feet down the road and still have room for their garage.

At the Bel Age, miracles multiplied as the magician Nabi replaced our most proper Stoli and tonics before we'd downed the last gulps of the ones before. The phone was ours for the using to place calls as far away as Sydney. Nicky had turned the joint into his local watering hole in the past year. He'd chow down on the complimentary appetizers and talk boxing with his new pal Sean Penn, who was living at the Bel Age almost full time.

One Friday night, the rock star Slash staggered in with an entourage of roadies and pals. I bought him a double Jack Daniels and thanked him for his contribution to rock 'n' roll. He let slip this was his last night of freedom. He was to be married in the morning.

Brennan shook his hand and offered some congratulations and advice, having been down the aisle at least three times himself. The two of them, the Guns n' Roses guitarist in his leather pants and the old journo in his denim shirt and jeans, wound up at a table by the wall, Slash crying on Brennan's shoulder as the night grew fuzzier.

It wound up in the jacuzzi on the Bel Age roof; me and a woman I'd met at the bar, joined by Slash and two women I'd never been introduced to at all. The security guard who was poking me with the antennae of his walkie talkie and asking to see my room key was kind enough not to throw me off the roof when I answered his request by climbing out with nothing on, dripping water, and demanding "Do you know who the *fuck* I am?"

I awoke alone the next afternoon in a Bel Age suite with someone else's breakfast on the room service cart and my silk and only shirt soaking wet and balled up in a corner. Sean Penn gave me an amused look at the checkout desk and again outside when I realized I'd left my car back at the Paramount lot because I was too pissed the previous afternoon to drive it back to West Hollywood.

There was no way around it. We were spending too many afternoons and nights in too many empty, smelly bars, squinting at the brightness outside through the slats in the window, praying God make that fucking sun go down, making sure to keep to the right of the double yellow lines, veering wildly through the canyons, lurching from Genghis Cohen's to the Mondrian to Dominick's to Barney's Beanery to the Sunset Hyatt, knowing you're in real trouble when you find yourself drinking at a comedy club, those pits of hopelessness and aggression where the minimum is two drinks but the joke's on them because you can walk in five minutes before closing time and they'll insist you order to cover the minimum, so you make it a pair of doubles and an Irish coffee and you harass the comedian and wind up being bum-rushed out the door to the alley and drive home with one eye shut to halve the double vision...

Optimism had given way to despair. We knew all too well it wasn't the same when you stop at only six drinks; it wasn't the same to leave the bar before the night flips over into the next morning or before the slurring, arguments, and raised voices have a chance to melt into the point of clarity. Without that, it was amateur hour, just drinking and nothing more. Nothing gets done.

New York was where I'd rather stay. My bi-monthly jaunts through the concrete canyons of my glory days were comforting homecomings, like landings on Earth after weeks aboard a lonely space shuttle. The elation of arriving back there helped regain my equilibrium and offset the unsettled feeling of homelessness in a place where I'd come into my own.

Yet the deeper I fell into the isolation of Los Angeles, the more often the New York City trips turned into binges of dark release: three-to-seven-day, no-sleep-til-you're-poured-on-the-plane Nighttown adventures that would put Stephen Dedalus to shame.

I'd planned on a trip back the third week of October with Joe Hamill, a Parsons holdover who became the solid rock of the *Hard Copy* assignment desk. In the old days, he'd worked on the Channel Five assignment desk under Nicky. Now he and Nicky worked side by side, for me.

Joe's family connections were as impressive as his credentials. He was the kid brother of the writer Pete Hamill. Another brother, Brian, was Woody Allen's stills photographer. At the height of the Mia Farrow-Soon Yi scandal, Brian helped us arrange an "ambush" interview with Allen while he directed a movie on location in Manhattan. Raf and a camera crew were instructed by Allen's people to wait on a sidewalk so they could "confront" the director when he left his production trailer at a specified time.

This time, Joe had gotten wind of a Bob Dylan tribute concert at Madison Square Garden; we bought tickets and flew out on October 16th to attend the four-hour show, broadcast live on TV around the world. There was a procession of rock stars lined up to sing Dylan songs, from Eric Clapton to George Harrison, Neil Young to Zimmy himself, but the one who'd been getting the most attention—the one I was waiting for—was bald little Sinead O'Connor.

Sinead had hogged more than a few headlines in recent weeks, since she refused to perform a concert in New Jersey because the arena opened events with the National Anthem. Frank Sinatra was incited to comment that he wanted to give her a punch in the nose.

Then she went and tore up a photo of the Pope on *Saturday Night Live*. Joe Pesci hosted the show the following week and provoked great applause by saying he'd like to give her a slap.

With all these brave paisan heroes ready to swat the shaved Irish waif, the New York crowd was bound to be raucous. When Kris Kristofferson walked onstage and began his introduction of "a woman of great courage," I knew who he was talking about. As a goof, I stood up and booed. People around me joined in. When Sinead came out with her shiny head and little lime spacesuit, the booing intensified. Someone down on the floor unfurled an American flag. I felt like the guy who turns on his blender at the exact moment a great blackout occurs and thinks he's the cause. Holy shit, what did I do? I stood again, applauding this time, but it was too late. Sinead soaked in the booing, screamed a few lines from a Bob Marley song and ran off the stage in tears.

Wow.

After the show, we headed downtown and met Jimmy Sheehan at the St. Mark's Bar and Grill in the East Village.

"There's an Irish bar right down the street," Jimmy said. He was a connoisseur of taverns. "The Cafe Sine. I've seen Sinead O'Connor sweeping the floor there."

"Yeah, right."

Maureen, the St. Mark's bartender, noticed the concert program on the bar. "How was the Dylan show?"

"It was great. Sinead O'Connor got booed off the stage."

Maureen sneered. "Good for them. You don't rip up the Pope's picture, not in New York. That little squirt, she tried to come in here the other night, I wouldn't serve her."

"No."

"Hey, Billy!" She called to the Irish kid working as bouncer at the door. "That Sinead O'Connor. Didn't I throw her out the other night?"

"Aye! And Maureen, she just tried to come in a minute ago. I told her to piss off!"

"She's probably down at the Sine, the little bitch."

Joe and I locked eyes. "Watch the drinks," I told Jim, and we were out of there.

The Cafe Sine was a storefront in the middle of the block. It had some wooden tables and chairs, New-Agey Celtic music on the sound system, and, standing at a small bar in the back, still wearing her little green Martian suit and talking glumly to another woman, Sinead O'Connor.

Joe and I walked up to the bar. I ordered a beer and did a mock double-take. "Sinead O'Connor."

She was a knobby little thing, regarding me with suspicious, dismissive doe eyes.

"Miss O'Connor. We've just returned from the Bob Dylan show. And let me apologize on behalf of the people of New York. Those weren't Bob Dylan fans. Those were yahoos, and I personally am ashamed."

"Ye left yer change on the bar." There were nicks and cuts amid the faint black stubble of her shaved head.

"Miss O'Connor." I extended my hand and she shook it, limply. "My name's Burt Kearns. This is Joe Hamill—" I turned to Joe. His mouth was actually hanging open. "He's an Irishman, too. We want you to know that your stand against the patriarchal Papacy and your support of women's rights is so brave. Joe Pesci doesn't have fans. Frank Sinatra doesn't have fans. Dan Quayle doesn't have fans. But you, Miss O'Connor—" I searched for words. "You are a saint. God bless you."

She regarded me as though I were taking the piss. "Thank you."

"Good luck," I said, putting down my beer and heading toward the door. "Oh, yes." I turned on my heel and pulled out the business card I'd stuck in my shirt pocket. "I work for a show called *Hard Copy*. We'd be proud to have you on to talk about what happened. I'll give you all the airtime you want on Monday if you'll come on and give your side."

She took the card and nodded. Joe and I hit the sidewalk.

"Christ Jesus, I thought I heard it all until that," Joe said. "I never heard such a line of bullshit in my friggin life."

I hurried back to the St. Mark's. "Joe, we got a story here."

We rushed past the bouncer. "Didn't I tell ya?" he said.

"You sure did, mate." I got to my bar stool, stood up on the lower rung and called for attention. "Excuse me. Everyone. Yo."

Maureen lowered the volume on the jukebox from behind the bar.

"I'm a television producer. I will pay five hundred dollars to anyone who can find me a home video camera to borrow."

There was silence.

"All right. You're a tough crowd. One *thousand* dollars!"

"He's not kidding," Maureen said. "He's *Hard Copy!*"

Suddenly there was a scramble for the house phones. Drug dealers were being pushed away from the payphones on the corner outside.

"I've got a Polaroid!" one man said.

"Video, we need video!" I turned to Jimmy, who worked as a cameraman for the spec crews that roamed the city at night. "Jim. You're gonna shoot. We'll walk into the Cafe Sine. Just roll and keep a steady shot on her face. If there's a scuffle, go wide. But no matter what anybody says or does, just keep rolling."

No one was coming up with a camera. I stood at the payphone and called all the local news assignment desks I had numbers for in my wallet, but it was well after one a.m. It was too late.

Someone came back with word that Sinead O'Connor had taken a taxi into the night.

We went back to our drinks. It was just another night in the City.

Deborah came into our lives in Los Angeles in early October. She was a tall, vibrant beauty with thick rusty hair who swept into my office like a fury, to my amazement and much to the amusement of Neal. Deborah was a producer from New York City, in Los Angeles looking for work in reality television. Her entree was a phone call from Jonathan Klein, an old acquaintance from CBS Network News.

Jon Klein was one of the producers of CBS *Nightwatch* for which I'd moonlighted more than a decade earlier. At the time, he was a hyper-intense, hyper-intelligent youngster a couple of years my junior but miles ahead in television savvy.

As good as I may have been, I was a beginner in network newswriting. Jon Klein took time with me; helped me learn the CBS system, in which the writers fit their stories to match shot lists of footage pre-cut by producers in another part of the building (0-10 seconds, African village; 11-13 starving child; 13-19 body covered in sheet), and how to do it quickly. Jon Klein remained at CBS; he was big time now, with his own production wing under the CBS News banner.

He'd called me that week, saying he knew a woman who was looking for producing work. She was an Olympic skier who'd done some sports documentaries, specials and segments for MTV and CBS.

"She's really good, and I think what she does is right up your alley," he said. "Will you talk to her?"

"Of course. Why not?"

Now here she was in my office, all hair and legs and enthusiasm, making Neal smile more and more as she bent over my office playback machine, popping tapes in and out, showing us clips of skiers doing loop-de-loops and flips to screechy punk rock music.

"You must, you must give me a try, you have to," she instructed, and Neal and I, just back from lunch, still blinking off the Silverado, he transfixed by those big legs in the black stockings that led underneath that pleated schoolgirl skirt, agreed.

"Yes, we must!"

We operated off instinct and good feeling. Deborah appealed to our animal instinct and it gave us a good feeling to watch and hear her. Sweeps was on the way and we needed to farm out special segments to some good producers.

"You come recommended by Jonathan Klein, and that's good enough for me," I said.

"We'll give you a shot," Neal seconded. "What do we have?"

We had an easy one: a feature on Elton John. The pop star had recently moved to Atlanta to be with his most recent boyfriend, the manager of a Baskin-Robbins ice cream store. He'd been involved in AIDS charity work and marches down there. "Elton's New Life" would be the title of a promotable segment that answered the musical question, "Why would an international pop celebrity move to fucking Atlanta?"

Deborah returned to New York with the assignment. She'd do some research and set off sometime the next week.

That weekend I was back in New York, ensconced at the hip Royalton Hotel on West 44th Street. Wayne's wife Norah had made a call and fixed me up with a big corner room. We promised to hook up during my stay, but when I called their apartment Saturday afternoon, Norah sounded perplexed. Wayne wasn't home. She thought he was with me.

I didn't pay it much mind, figuring he'd call eventually. He did, about a half hour later.

"Mate. We're in the room downstairs. Come on down."

What?

"Yeah, we've got a room below you." He gave me the number. "Come on down, we got a little surprise."

I figured Norah had gotten a deal through her PR connections. I took the elevator down a flight and knocked on the door. Wayne answered with the sly grin of the devil.

"Enter, mate." The shades were drawn and the room was lit softly by a lamp near the bed. There was a tray with a bottle of champagne on the bed, and sitting next to the champage was Deborah.

Deborah?

I did a triple take. "Uh, what the fuck's going on here?"

This was the same woman I'd met three days earlier in Los Angeles. She was supposedly going off to Atlanta to do a story for *Hard Copy*, yet here she was, on Saturday, in a hotel room in the hotel where I was staying, with Wayne.

"This is some kind of sting, right?" I looked around for a hidden camera or microphone.

Wayne poured me a glass of champagne and tried to put me at ease. "Mate, relax. Me and Deborah here just sorta fell in love."

The story as he told it seemed simple enough. Wayne was visiting his friend Susan Crimp in *Hard Copy*'s New York office the previous afternoon. Deborah stopped in as she was setting up the Elton John story, the three of them went downstairs to the Conservatory Bar for a drink, and before you knew it, sparks, as they say, flew.

I was more than a little stunned. I drank more of the champagne and told Wayne about Deborah's assignment.

Wayne became animated. "I know why Elton John's in fackin Atlanta, mate. He's probably got AIDS! The Centers for Disease Control is there. It's gotta be." His tabloid pistons were pumping. He turned to Deborah. "What you do, darlin, you call his people and say, 'Give us an interview with Elton and we'll do a nice piece. If you don't, we'll run a story saying he has AIDS!'"

"Wayne, calm down." I rolled my eyes to Deborah so she'd know he wasn't serious. "We can't do that at *Hard Copy*, mate. The boyfriend angle is hot enough; it's all between the lines. It's a new world. We're doing a nice piece here."

I left them in their shadowy room and didn't see Wayne again until I checked out of the hotel on Sunday morning. He was at the lobby bar, working on another bottle of champagne with Deborah.

As I walked out, Norah walked in, giving her new husband a not pleasant surprise.

"Uh, Norah...here, darlin, have some champagne," he said.

She accepted, and tossed the drink in his face.

By the time Monday rolled around, I was back on the Paramount lot with another crisis to worry about. Deborah checked in with me regularly over the next few days as she shot in Atlanta. I gave her approval to hire a helicopter to shoot some aerials of the city. She told me some people at the gay nightclubs told her they were convinced she'd be charging that Elton John had AIDS.

"Did you tell anyone that?"

"No, of course not," she insisted.

"Why would they think it, then?"

"Someone probably put two and two together and got five."

It was strike two: my second chance to pull her from the story; but I didn't.

At the end of the week, Deborah came to L.A. to write and edit. Around the time she was finding herself a desk at which to work, Nicky ran from the assignment desk up to my office, waving a piece of AP wire copy and forcing me to get off the phone to read it.

> (Atlanta) — Singer Elton John is suing the producers of the TV program *Hard Copy* for slander, alleging that a reporter claimed off the air that John had moved to Atlanta to be near an 'AIDS' treatment center. The suit was filed yesterday in Fulton County Superior Court in Georgia. It seeks at least 35 (M) million dollars in damages.
>
> John's attorneys claim the reporter spied on their client and threatened to run a negative story about him if he didn't grant her an interview...

Holy shit. This was real trouble. I showed the story to Brennan and Neal and told them what happened in New York with Wayne and what Deborah had said on the phone from Atlanta. It was all my fault. I'd fucked up big time.

"Who is this woman?" Peter asked.

"She worked for CBS. She was recommended by this guy Jon Klein, who's a big shot there."

"She had nice legs," Neal said.

"What CBS show did she work for?"

"I don't know. Something about skiing. She had tape. Fuck me!"

When Deborah came upstairs, she read the wire copy and played dumb. She denied everything, conceding only that she did use the helicopter to get some shots into Elton's apartment window.

We next got the lawyers in and took the quickest fix action possible, scrapping part of that day's show and replacing it with a tossed-off celebratory segment on Elton John.

I rushed into my office with Deborah so I could write the segment based on what she'd shot. It would be the same story we'd planned—though no one would believe we were doing it for any other reason than that we were being sued for thirty-five million dollars.

I was on automatic writing mode, my fingers typing bullshit before my mind could formulate the thoughts. "You have footage of the nightclubs? We'll put in the nightclubs."

"And the antique dealer."

"'This is where Elton John buys antiques, one of the finest places in the country. But most of his money is going into—You got footage on Ryan White?"

"Tons."

"'Going into the fight against AIDS. Elton's friendship with brave Ryan White...'"

As I typed away on my word processor, Deborah got up off her chair and began rubbing my shoulders. I stiffened.

"Are we in trouble?" she cooed.

Guilty!

That sealed it. She'd done it. She did what Wayne suggested. I stopped typing and told her I didn't like people touching me in the office. "Why don't you go downstairs and cue up some of those bites? I'll get this tracked and meet you in the edit bay."

As soon as she left, I got Wayne on the phone. "What the fuck did you tell her, mate?"

He had a good laugh. "I just told her that's how we do things, mate. I told her, 'Look, these guys tell you they want you to do a nice piece. But they're the dirtiest bastards around. You want to impress these guys, you got to be down and dirty. Do anything. Take it from me, darlin. I know what these guys want. You tell Elton John's people that if they don't give you an interview...'"

He was still laughing when I hung up.

The next day, Elton John's people said our reasons for running the glowing piece were obvious and transparent. Eventually, though, the lawsuit drifted away and was forgotten.

Wayne got his. Back in New York, he tried to give Deborah the Spanish archer, the "El Bow," and she started stalking him.

Neal and I never saw or heard from Deborah again.

No sooner had Deborah gone than Howard Stern was in our backyard, literally blocks away. As he'd promised, the King of All Media came to Hollywood to celebrate, gloat and preside over a mock funeral for the dethroned Number One deejays Mark and Brian. On the 24th of October, he starred in a rally at the Palace Theatre on Hollywood Boulevard. Despite, and because of her recent publicized problems, we sent Audrey to ask questions at the press conference that would be broadcast on his radio show. Stern was ready for her. He shouted down her questions and mocked her voice while his supporter Melrose Larry Green screamed in her ear through a megaphone. Audrey was jostled. She was shaken up.

During the commercial breaks, Stern and his crew were polite and apologetic, posing for pictures and schmoozing before turning on the vitriol when they were back on the air.

Audrey was in an odd situation. Her fiance had actually convinced her to file a real lawsuit against Howard Stern. It was as if we were in some strange parallel universe where a celebrity can be sued by the tabloid queen of the Beverly Hills stakeout, the ambush princess, the most feared little person in Hollywood.

It got very embarrassing for *Hard Copy*, as tabloid journalism was becoming more concerned with the public doings and private lives of celebrities and bound to clash with them more often. Brennan and I had to call Audrey into the office, shut the door, and tell her that enough was enough. She had to drop the suit.

Benny Hill was six months in the ground when I assigned Alison Holloway a November sweeps story about his death and subsequent desecration of his grave because of rumors he was buried with his money.

Alison had proved herself a classy secret weapon since our first meeting with Peter Faiman: an innovative producer and natural adlibber who buried Terry Murphy with her charm and wit when they shared a two-way. Thanks to Britain's royal family, Alison was getting a lot of airtime, reporting revelations along the lines of Princess Diana throwing up or throwing herself down stairs, Charles wishing he was a tampon, and Fergie getting her toes sucked.

Alison agreed to take on the Hill story, though she and her fellow Brits were gobsmacked by our love for things Benny Hillish. Benny was old hat in the U.K., sacked by Thames Television three years earlier because of pressure from feminist groups. The Brits didn't understand how Benny Hill lived on in reruns here in the States, how he was regarded as an innovative god of television comedy—especially by our group of innovative gods of tabloid TV.

Alison went all out. She knew we wanted comedy, tits, ass, and tears.

She provided all that and more when she interviewed Benny's director, who'd written a book about his long friendship with Benny and his discovery of the star's body.

"He had this fabulous head of hair, lucky devil," the director said, recalling the moment when police let him touch the swollen head of the friend who'd lain dead in his apartment for two days. "It was always sticking up and he was forever wetting it down. I tried to smooth it." He smiled as tears fell down his face. He had to choke the last words. "It wouldn't stay."

What an actor! As we screened the piece in Brennan's office, I knew we had a winner. There was sex. There was comedy. There was the director saying he knew for a fact his pal Benny wasn't gay. There were the facts about Benny's strange life, his final hours, the robbing of his grave. Then came the topper.

In the middle of the segment was a piece of production derring-do that showed how little we all knew about the art of television. It was a shot inserted in the middle of an interview Alison conducted with the director in the garden of Benny Hill's favorite pub. While the man spoke outside, the camera cut away to a shot inside the pub, of a framed picture of Benny Hill on a table. The camera pulled back to reveal a window through which the interview went on. The director was mid-sentence. His lips were perfectly in synch.

Then it cut back to the camera outside. It was amazing. I was certain this was a one-camera shoot. Alison confirmed it. It was no big deal, she said. She'd simply repositioned the camera indoors and had the director repeat what he'd said earlier.

It was a casual yet brilliant production twist. I played it over and over for my producers, showing them how television could be done with a little imagination.

Benny Hill's director was impressed, as well. When the interview was over, Alison said he leaned forward and asked, "Would you fancy a fuck?"

"As a matter of fact, yes, I would," she replied. "But not with you."

Tabloid Adolescent: Ten years old at the Statue of Liberty. Superhero t-shirt, Bob Dylan hat, and brand new transistor radio tuned to the WABC All Americans. Already gone.
                                        —photo credit Frank Gambalesta

Doyle tries not to be first to phone next-of-kin with bad news. "I get a priest to tell them. Then I move in."

Pat Doyle, the world's greatest police reporter.

Nicky and me.

"And then I plucked him from obscurity..." Connie Chung and Peter Brennan.

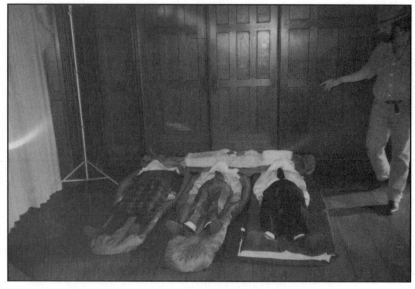

"Who's been sleeping in my bag?"
Rafael directs a re-enactment of a famous murder.

There goes the neighborhood. Steve Dunleavy visits the
Amityville Horror house.

*The Booze Brothers. Burt Kearns and Wayne Darwen, 10 a.m.,
Washington D.C., 1990.*

*Over the road. The Phoenix Park pub, formerly Tommy McGrath's,
formerly the Racing Club.*

"Who's the joker who put the superglue in my Mai tai?"

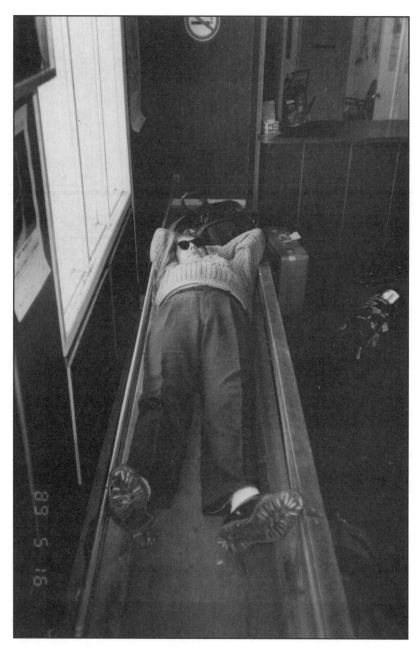

The bag no one would claim. Gordon Elliott on an airport conveyer belt,
Alaska, 1989.

Maureen O'Boyle kisses a moose.

"Of course I'm not making it up. Why would I lie?" The Prince of Darkness in his den. New York City, 1989. (Spot the Elvis photo)

Mrs. Letterman's Top Ten Reasons To Take Your Lithium. Number two: Margaret Ray did most of the interview standing on her head. And the number one reason to take your lithium: Ten years later, she ended it all by sitting in front of a speeding train.

"Dan, Tom, Peter—eat your hearts out!" Maury Povich at the Brandenburg Gate, East Berlin, on Friday, November 10, 1989, the weekend the wall came down.

Get this man to a telethon. Even if he wasn't in the book, I'd still use this picture.

Raf drives, Ken Fuhr shoots. Picture taker hangs off driver's side.

The Censored Showgirl Shoot. Maureen O'Boyle had all the tapes and photos destroyed—almost. The future anchorwoman surrounded by Kearns and Darwen, surrounded by Bill Cassera and Ken Fuhr, tabloid's greatest camera crew.

The Prince of Darkness at the grave of the King. Little did he know that Elvis was standing there watching (see the guy with the cane).

Rebel without a Coors: It's 1989, Hollywood Week at A Current Affair, and outside the Griffith observatory, Wayne Darwen interviews the ghost of his idol.

Eat your heart out, Elton John. Peter Brennan,the father of tabloid television, Melrose Avenue, 1991.

Pardners. Abramovitz and Kearns at the compound in the old days of the typewriter (spot the Elvis picture).

"I know I'm forgetting something." Eames Yates on the job.

Tabloid Wedding: Peter Brennan marries Nancy Gershwin, Coldwater Canyon, 1991. From left: LisaRiva (with original A Current Affair *reporter Mary Hughes behind them), ACA co-founder J.B. Blunck, Audrey Lavin, Gordon Elliott, the groom and bride (with producer Whitney Trilling behind them), Jerry Burke, Wayne Darwen, Burt Kearns, Rafael Abramovitz and Dennis O'Brien. Oh yeah, eight years later, Brennan would marry the woman on the far left.*

Now she knows how Pee Wee felt. Diane Dimond, busted for exposing...Michael Jackson?

A frowner, a downer, and a clowner. Three Stooges, back from the Ball of Twine.

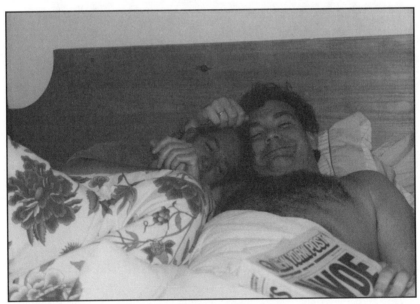

"What was in that drink? I don't have a hangover, but my ass is killing me!" Me and Gordon Elliot in his Tribeca loft. Don't ask.

Raf cruises the Vegas Strip, looking for a place to park his hat.

Hard Copy *scoundrels Burt Kearns and Eames Yates arrive at Tommy McGrath's bar (circa 1993) in attempt to destablize the competition at* A Current Affair. *Kearns looks on in horror as Eames tries to coax producer (and Dunleavy wrangler) Shannah Goldner to the dark side.*

Spot the psycho. Wayne Darwen with the Rev. Ronnie Dickerman, David Berkowitz and Maury Terry. Yes, that David Berkowitz.

Spot the psycho. Inside Edition's *John Tomlin, Geraldo Rivera, A Current Affair's John Terenzio and Wayne Darwen. Yes, that Geraldo Rivera.*

*Who cut the check? Steve Dunleavy interviews the Buttafuocos while attorney
Dominic Barbara passes answers...and gas.*

*"Oh, Ian, stop, you're just too funny!" ACA executive producer Bill Ridley and
his boss Ian Rae at Tommy McGrath's*

"You think that's funny? You should see your hat." A Current Affair *executive producer Bill Ridley, with reporters David Lee Miller and Bill McGowan. At Tommy McGrath's bar.*

Gotcha! Robert Kardashian moseys away with his pal O.J. Simpson's garment bag.

Alison takes one for the team at the O.J. trial. "One of the cameramen hit me with the back of the camera. He said to me, 'Get out the way,' and I wasn't going to get out the way and this is the result."

Jeff Greenfield's Maalox moment. "This is not the way to do journalism. And I feel very sorry for you if you have any hope for a career in it."

"Hi Jeff! Are you hiring?" Hi-8 Joe, aka Video Joe,
aka Joe Guidry, the next generation.

Hello! Goodbye! The censored photo from
Allison's 1994 Hello! Magazine *shoot.*

Staging area for the Stonewall Parade? No. Rafael Abramovitz on the Detour *shoot. He's got a truckin' convoy!*

"Are you sure Clint Eastwood started this way?" Rafael and Peter Brennan in the desert, on the Detour *shoot.*

The Prince of the City. Steve Dunleavy looking cool.

"Hmmmm...maybe I should start a courtroom show. Naah."

"Here now the news..." Alison Holloway and Steve Dunleavy do a Fred & Ginger for Dancing In the Dark, *the great lost newsmagazine.*

Tabloid wedding. Little White Chapel, Las Vegas, April 13, 1996.

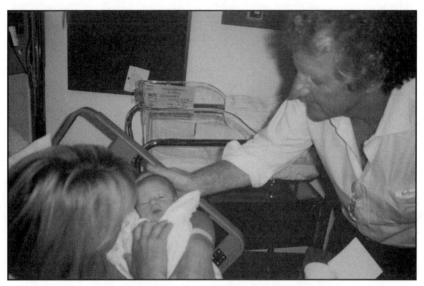

Peter Brennan meets Sam Peter Holloway Kearns.

Tabloid cliché: Tabloid Daddy and Tabloid Baby, crossing Abbey Road.

CHAPTER TWENTY-ONE:
SUICIDES, MURDERS & SLOPPY
EXECUTIONS

"Hey, guess who I'm in bed with right now?"

It was eight a.m. on a Thursday. *A Current Affair*'s executive producer John Terenzio was calling into the office, speaking to a production assistant.

"Who, John?"

"Dunleavy! And he slept right next to me! We were so wasted last night, we just crashed!"

"That's great, John."

"Look, I'm coming in now. You've got to get me breakfast. Get me an egg sandwich with a piece of meat on it."

The continuing saga of Amy Fisher, Joey Buttafuoco, and his wife Mary Jo may have been great for tabloid ratings, but it was ruining tabloid television. There was no one to feel sorry for. Yet, the story was impossible to ignore and everyone from the networks to the afternoon talk shows to Hollywood movie producers to book publishers were fighting for pieces of it.

At *A Current Affair*, that meant buying up every offering, no matter how insignificant. Ever since we at *Hard Copy* stole the sex tape from their satellite feed, the staff fought back with quantity. After all, we couldn't steal everything.

John Terenzio, meanwhile, was giving *A Current Affair* a dark, newsy, and decidedly ugly tone, while keeping up the charade that he was "cleaning up" the show. As he approached his first anniversary as executive producer, he played the part of avenging crusader to the hilt while Max Robins of *Variety* stood back and took notes.

> The screen is filled with hard bodies gyrating on a dance floor to a pulsating rhythm track. A woman's moans soar over the bass. It's sweeps month, and this is a promo for *A Current Affair*.
>
> "No, too much with the moans; that's our history, not our future," says exec producer John

Terenzio in the show's edit room. The promo, for a special report on "Loving American Style," will get a less tawdry soundtrack before it sees air.

"We're at this transitional moment," Terenzio told Max. "We're trying to be more pro-active—that's what will set us out from the pack...If we do a small-town murder, it's not just what happened, it's how the daughter of the victim carried the investigation on after the cops had given up."

Dunleavy threw in his two cents with a straight face. "It's surprising how often when we're chasing a story these days, we find *60 Minutes* and *20/20*'s footprints," he said.

Among the show's pro-active innovations was handing out Hi-8 video cameras to citizen vigilante groups and encouraging viewers to become junior journalists, photographing hookers and johns and litterbugs with their home video cameras.

The culmination of this crusade to bring a new, ratfink American news mentality to tabloid television appeared in Associated Press wire stories in newspapers around the world, with no small irony on the same day *Variety* published its admiring profile of Terenzio.

It was a pro-active tape the news hounds couldn't pass up. A man was caught banging a woman who was not his wife in a pickup truck, parked on a lover's lane outside a town called Fremont, Ohio.

A man named Randy Powers owned a house on the street. He called the police, claiming his kids could see what was going on through the open door of the pickup, and when the cops said they'd need more evidence than his word, he got out his home video camera and shot the couple in the act. The woman was spread out on the front seat; the man stood outside, leaning in with his pants around his ankles, poor schmuck.

They were charged with public indecency, this man and the woman who was not his wife. The man went to court, was fined a hundred and fifty dollars, charged an extra thirty-three in court costs, and sent home to try to make things right with his wife and kids.

That would have been the end of the unfortunate episode had not *A Current Affair* gotten wind of it. They heard there was video involved—pro-active video! Terenzio shelled out $2,500 to buy the exclusive rights. He sent a reporter to town to knock on the man's door and harass him some more.

We knew about the story at *Hard Copy*. We didn't think twice about passing it up. It was dirty to begin with, and whether or not the man was convicted, you had to feel sorry for him. This wasn't a Sheriff Corky, a public official who cheerfully admitted renting a video camera to shoot some hanky-panky with his wife, only to leave the tape in the camera and have the whole town have a gander. This wasn't the creep who secretly shot private video of his girlfriend, then left copies of the tape on her neighbors's doorsteps. This wasn't Rob Lowe with an underage girl. This wasn't a seventeen-year-old Lolita who put a bullet into the head of a housewife.

Garry Offenburg of Fremont, Ohio was an average working stiff making his way through life and getting a little on the side. He probably couldn't afford a motel so he drove to the place where everyone in town went to park and he wound up getting scoped out by someone who ratted to the cops. The common decency at the heart of tabloid TV says you don't treat this guy like a criminal. In many ways, he was a victim.

With the new *A Current Affair*, the victimization went national.

They ran the story and the video, with little smudges to cover the offending anatomical sections, at least twice.

On November 18th, Gary Offenburg, age forty-nine, walked down into his basement, took out a pump-action shotgun, and blew a hole through his chest.

"It was eating at him so much that he couldn't take it anymore," his widow said. "I'm angry about *A Current Affair*."

Terenzio sent Maureen O'Boyle out to face the press while he put on his show for *Variety*. She insisted her program wasn't responsible for the suicide. "I think it's terrible his life took such a deadly turn," she said.

They knew though, that there were two headlines on November 23rd, 1992. The one in *Variety* read:
AFFAIR TO REMEMBER?
AFFAIR TRIES TO KEEP CURRENT

That same day, there was a headline in the *New York Post*:
Affair blamed for suicide

For us at *Hard Copy*, November was a time for executions: firings as a matter of survival. We had too many producers who weren't pulling their weight and we needed to circle the wagons.

There were too many games being played behind the scenes. By allowing the "alternative government" to take on a life of its own, Brennan found himself with a staff divided. Anticipating that he might not be around after the third season, many were choosing sides and aligning themselves with the ones in line to succeed him.

Then there was Audrey.

Audrey was my first "creation." Her persona had been so effective back at *A Current Affair* that when we wanted to interview Jack Nicholson, we had Audrey send him a "video letter" in which she did her best Lolita pleading into the camera and stuck the cassette in his mailbox. She wound up with an invite to Nicholson's house high above Los Angeles on Mulholland Drive.

She and Jack ate from his refrigerator—all the food was in containers marked "Jack's dinner" or "lunch" with the appropriate days of the week listed—and shared a skinnydip in his pool.

Anything else that happened was subject to debate. Audrey had several versions. Nicholson liked her, but because it was well-known he didn't do television interviews—especially not with a show like *A Current Affair*—he compromised. He told Audrey where she and a camera crew could follow his car the next day, get some exclusive footage, and have a story without him saying a word.

Audrey's segments were often hilarious. I saw her potential to be the best Hollywood reporter in television, but she couldn't do it by herself—or she wouldn't. In this season of *Hard Copy*, she began demanding "nice" stories and general assignments and made things very difficult. Confident that her friendship with me and Brennan would prevent her ever being fired, she'd throw her weight around, missing deadlines, and often force me to knock off her scripts just so the pieces would make air.

When Audrey didn't like an assignment, she'd make a display in front of the rest of the staff. "I'll just go sit on Burt's lap and blow in his ear and he'll change his mind," she'd lie.

She'd burst in on the middle of a staff meeting refusing to cover an event like the Oscars. "You're just making me do it because you have a small penis!" she'd shout.

Audrey was unprepared in the edit room. Many of her segments weren't airable. When I criticized or expressed disappointment over a specific story, she'd go to Linda Bell or Cheri Brownlee, who'd tell her how good it was. Soon, she was seeking their approval without realizing it. Soon, Linda Bell was playing her like a jukebox.

I'd put up with Audrey for four years. Whenever she double-crossed me, she'd made it seem cute. Whenever she took advantage of me, she'd made it seem special. Now, though, it was out of hand—and dangerous.

I called Audrey into my office and told her I had a choice: I could either be the managing editor of *Hard Copy* or I could be her friend. She was taking advantage of our friendship and I couldn't operate as a manager of the program as long as she did.

"We can't be friends anymore, Audrey. From now on, you're an employee just like anyone else. I'm not going to punish you, but you're not going to get any more special treatment. You've got to write your own scripts and meet your own deadlines.

"I'm sorry, but you're on your own."

Necessity, meanwhile, gave birth to another innovation when Peter Brennan lost control of the promotions again. He needed to find promotable tape that Robert Faulk's bimbos couldn't fuck up—video that spoke for itself.

It began with video of a drunk driving suspect, a rich kid hauled in by police, kicking and screaming things like, "Do you know who my father is?" and "You guys have no *idea* the trouble you're in," and left to cool his jets in a holding cell, under a sign that read: "Warning: This room is under video surveillance." The kid sat slumped, muttering to himself about fascist pigs and the like, all of it caught on tape, when, all of a sudden, he sat upright— and punched himself in the face!

Whap! He did it again, and proceeded to beat the shit out of himself better than the cops did Rodney King. It was truly funny. Funnier still, he used his injuries to claim police brutality. When the case got to court, the cops played the tape.

The package we put together rated so well, we began running similar surveillance tapes every night: police stings and chases, casino cheats, and convenience store holdups, including one in which two female store clerks beaned a robber with a wine bottle. We ran the scene several times, once with comical slapstick sounds, then again with eerie music to show what a dangerous step they'd taken. We asked the woman who bopped the crook with the wine bottle whether she sought out a bottle of cheap stuff intentionally. She said she had.

It was an *America's Funniest Home Videos* of crime and sex. Peter named the series "Caught on Tape," and sent a private eye-turned-producer named Danno Hanks on a sweep across the Southwest to collect more tapes from police departments.

Neal and I took special care with a segment from Wilton, Connecticut, the wealthy suburb where I used to be newspaper editor. Police stuck a camera in a warehouse to catch a worker suspected of dealing drugs. They taped for days as the young man traded glasine bags and packages for cash, but before the cops moved in, there was one more visitor: a typical suburban housewife who must have been in the wrong place.

The camera revealed she was indeed a customer, though one who didn't pay in cash, but barter—dropping to her knees and favoring the young Latino with vigorous oral sex.

Neal and I sat around the word processor and conjured up the spirit of John Cheever: "Her husband had probably taken the commuter train in his grey-flannel suit to earn the money to pay for the station wagon and country club fees. Perhaps, before she picked up the kids from school..."

We didn't show the woman at work, not even with a digitized grid concealing her mouth action. We didn't give her name or even mention the town. We didn't knock on her door.

The "Caught on Tape" segments were immediate ratings grabbers. As allowed under his contract, Peter put together a proposal and offered

Paramount a show called *Sting: Caught on Tape*. Paramount didn't do anything with it.

Danno the private eye did. He and a producer we'd just hired made copies of the segments and sold them to Dick Clark Productions for a special called *Caught in the Act*. Paramount sued Dick Clark for a million dollars and fired the private eye and the new producer. The "Caught on Tape" segments continued irregularly on *Hard Copy*. In late 1995, Frank Kelly and Paramount stole Brennan's idea for a show called *Caught on Tape*. Around the time Brennan's lawyer sent them a letter, they renamed the show *Real TV*.

We all headed back to New York for the Christmas holidays. I was supposed to meet up with Dickie McWilliams, but he was laying very low at *A Current Affair*. Things had become very strange since Terenzio, despite Dunleavy's pleadings, told Dickie he was fired. Surprisingly, Dickie didn't leave. He had a talk with Ian Rae, who told him to hang tight until he could be fixed up with a gig at Fox News. Dickie continued to show up for work every day, with nothing to do.

After the Terenzio crew leaked a mean item to the gossip columns, characterizing Dickie as a "ghost" who refused to go away even though he no longer had a job, Ian and Dunleavy hid Dickie at a desk in the promotions department, two floors above the *A Current Affair* offices.

With the dawn of 1993, Rafael Abramovitz was on a roll. His image was still high after his Amy Fisher scoop, and he was the subject of a major profile in *GQ*. When Dunleavy was written up in the magazine three years earlier, the title was "The King of Sleaze" and the article depicted him as a duplicitous scumbag who faked a crying shot on camera a la William Hurt's character in *Broadcast News*. That article depicted him wrongly—or at least without the proper empathy.

The piece on Raf was written by the great pop journalist Gerri Hirshey, and though it was called "Sleazy Does It," was generally sympatico, portraying Raf, spot-on accurately, as a man who believed he was doing his best to find justice in an unfair world, and could not understand why he was hated for it.

> Rafael Abramovitz would like you to know that he's a nice guy, really. Fifty-two-year-old father of two grown daughters. Kinda rough around the edges (beard, cowboy boots, jeans). Prone to finishing his sentences with the impatient scatchat: "Baddaboo, Baddabee." Gave up his ponytail but not his commitment to justice. "I'm just trying to

document things I've heard," Abramovitz says, a
trifle sadly...

Raf and I had returned to Los Angeles with a fresh resolve to take tabloid
television to a new level in 1993, even though I'd had my difficulties working
with Rafael, or getting him to work at all on our screenwriting projects.

Brennan theorized that Raf never wanted to offer up his best for fear
that his best would be rejected—as it was with the Chappaquiddick series.
I'd concluded that Raf was simply afraid of success, but I was giving him
another chance to put it on the line with his idea for a show called *Freelance*.

Raf envisioned it as a one hour weekly magazine that would break the
mold in reality storytelling by giving not only the stories people are talking
about, but involving the viewer with the people who report them.

"Think of *L.A. Law* or *Lou Grant* unfolding in a reality TV operation,"
we wrote. "Behind the scenes of every story, there is a movie going on..."

The "stars" of *Freelance* would be the real on-camera journalists and
select members of the support staff—in a word, us.

We put together a quick "sell tape," shooting fake "behind the scenes"
segments based on the Amy Fisher surveillance story. In *Hard Copy*'s New
York office, we shot office strategy sessions; at his hotel in Universal City,
we shot Raf in a van, pretending to wait while the Amy Fisher sting was
going down, Peter learning by phone that "the eagle has landed," and the
two of them in the bathroom before their disastrous press conference.

When edited together with actual news footage, it seemed as if we'd
actually shot everything while covering the Amy Fisher story.

Raf's agent, a young go-getter at ICM named Ari Emanuel, set us up
with a series of meetings to push *Freelance*.

In the big building on the edge of Beverly Hills at 9200 Sunset
Boulevard, we had an audience with Bernie Brillstein, the man who managed
the original *Saturday Night Live* stars and went on to produce some of their
most successful movies and TV shows. Brillstein was a legend, and not only
as "The Man Who Killed Belushi" for supplying him with money his last
week on earth.

Ushered past the picture of "Client of the Month" Garry Shandling and
posters for movies like *The Blues Brothers, Ghostbusters,* and *Wayne's World*
in the reception room, we met Brillstein, a big bear with white hair and a
goatee, settled behind a big desk in a big corner office with big views
straight out to the big ocean. At either corner of the desk, a round fishbowl
containing a live fish faced us and our obligatory black coffees.

"I know you, I know your work," Brillstein said to Raf, and settling back, he looked at me and wagged a finger. "And you, you look exactly like John Hughes."

I wracked my brain to think who John Hughes was. John Cusack, Andrew McCarthy—was he a Brat Packer?

"A young John Hughes. It's amazing."

I thought some more. Then I realized who he was talking about. John Hughes, the guy who produced *Home Alone*. A fat guy with owly glasses. Great.

"I like tabloid TV and this reality TV," Brillstein went on. "I have a good friend, he's fucked a lot of women, he told me the best he ever had, the one he was proudest of doing, guess who it was?"

"You got me."

"Fawn Hall." He was talking about Rob Lowe.

"Yeah. Fawn Hall. With the tooth," I said.

"I've always admired her for using her underwear to transport secret documents," Raf said.

Brillstein was male bonding. I could picture him with Belushi, rhapsodizing about how he'd like to give that skinny Larraine Newman a shot in the ass. "I'll tell you, in all these Amy Fisher movies, you know who I'd love to fuck?" His assistant, whom we'd not noticed—I was looking at the fishies—nodded as if he'd heard it all before. "I'd love to fuck that Drew Barrymore. Oooh."

"*E.T.*, yeah," I said, thinking, well, it took three years but we were in. This was Hollywood; a powerful fat man with a commanding view of the city, fantasizing about fucking a seventeen-year-old.

Yet Brillstein listened carefully to the pitch, interrupting every few sentences for clarifications. He was amused when Raf's rap was interrupted by a page from Joey Buttafuoco. Even I thought it was a bullshit attempt to make an impression until Raf asked for a phone to call him back. While Raf spoke with Joey on one line, Brillstein called the agent Ari on another. "I love these guys," he said with enthusiasm. "We're gonna do something together."

When they hung up, he spoke again. "I like your ideas. Just get them down on paper. We can make lots of money, lots of money on a one-hour reality show. Come back with the specifics on paper and we'll go to a network with it."

It was as simple as that. Bernie Brillstein was good to go.

It was even simpler. Raf let it slide. Our Brillstein meeting led to naught, and I never got to that second meeting to find out if old Bern got to fuck Drew Barrymore.

John Terenzio was fired from *A Current Affair* in March. We were in

New York that very week, Raf and I, and we wound up with our New York bureau host Eames Yates in the modern Asia Restaurant across Third Avenue from the recently closed Fortune Garden. Asia's bar was a small area near the door, looking out on the restaurant with its fish tank wall and well-heeled customers.

That early evening, at a table about ten feet away, the managers of *A Current Affair* said goodbyes to their executive producer. With Herdrich on his right and a changeable cast of well-wishers in the other chairs, Terenzio knocked back his white wines with ice until the table was cluttered with the detritus of cork and bottles.

Rafael could never forgive Herdrich for what he'd done to us at *Hard Copy*. He saw Terenzio as another destroyer of a medium and genre that in its alternate moral universe was rivaled only by some forms of children's programming in its purity. He stood at the end of the bar, cowboy hat cocked over his brow, Johnny Walker Black in his hand, staring at the play acted out at the table.

Eames flirted and acted for the group of women bundled up around the bar. They were the new generation of *A Current Affair*, chattering away but getting quieter when they noticed Maureen O'Boyle outside on the sidewalk, laughing with several black women. The women did not follow her inside. Maureen was leaving her "posse" on Third Avenue.

Maureen had always swung her hips and occasionally affected a "black attitude." Now, as undisputed star of the show, she surrounded herself with a group of females who catered to her and conversed in mock "homegirl" patois. Maureen was conflicted. With those friends, she acted like an octoroon version of Sue Simmons; to her detriment, the blowsy, wowsy good time gal never reared her head on the air.

Nor was she to be found when Maureen left her "girlfriends" on the sidewalk and entered the bar. Maureen had taken on airs.

Heidi stood to give Maureen her barstool. Heidi was a freckled redhead in her early thirties who was hired as a secretary and flattered her way to the exalted post of Maureen's personal writer. Her only drawback was that she couldn't write—at least not for tabloid television. To Heidi, the pathetic was "bizarre," the tragic "shocking," the fashionable "hot," the evil, "heinous."

Heidi spent most of her working day with her legs up on her desk, doing crossword puzzles. Yet she gave Maureen comfort. With Anthea gone, Heidi had become the anchorwoman's confidante. She was there in the morning to hear Maureen's stories of the night before. In the evenings, she was there to share a drink and offer praise for that day's performance.

Maureen gave a distant and affected greeting to us at the bar, thumbing a nose at Raf and betraying none of the familiarity we had only a couple of years before.

"You look good, Maureen," I said.

"Oh, please. You Californians are so full of shee-yut."

I went back to my Stoli and tonic and watched her sashay to the Terenzio table. She snuck up behind the broken man, wrapped her arms around him and nuzzled his ear. Terenzio moaned and returned the buss.

"What are you guys doing here anyway?" It was Heidi, talking too loud.

"We are watching the beginning of the end," Raf said, biblically. "The people who are killing a dream."

"Oh, you guys are so full of shit."

"No we're not," I said.

"It's just a TV show," Heidi replied.

"It's a life."

"It's not. It's work. Nine to five and go home. I knock off a few lead-ins, it's simple. We're only doing simple trash TV."

"That's what's killing it, you people who think you're doing trash," Raf said.

"You'll learn," I added. "You'll learn when you realize how hard it is. Men gave their lives to create what you're destroying. Dunleavy is killing himself for you guys. We've all given up relationships, marriages, our livers."

"Come off it. It's only a job."

"It's not a job. It's a fucking life. And it has to be."

"It is not. You guys are just assholes."

"No. We're not."

Standing behind Raf, Eames was getting into it. Don Hewitt's daughter Lisa was among the women from *A Current Affair* gathered with Heidi, laughing contemptuously. Don Hewitt ran *60 Minutes*. He was the boss and friend to Eames' stepfather, Mike Wallace.

"We are gods of tabloid." The vodka was beginning to speak on my behalf. "I'm a god of tabloid and you're a mere peon who should be honored to drink with us."

"You think you're God?"

"I didn't say I'm God." I was riffing on a line from a Bill Murray movie, the one about Groundhog Day, but these new purveyors of popular culture didn't get the reference. "I said I'm a god."

That line got around the city the next day. Burt said he and Raf and Eames were God. What a bunch of assholes.

That same next day, Asia installed a Chinese screen at the end of the bar so the barflies couldn't stare at people at the tables.

Back in Los Angeles, Peter Brennan was at a restaurant on Melrose

Avenue with his agent Barry and Paramount's Frank Kelly. Kelly was making Brennan an offer.

Only months earlier, the two men has clashed over the licensing of the *Hard Copy* name and its material to an Australian company run by Brennan's mate and sometime partner, Peter Sutton. Sutton's weekly show of revoiced *Hard Copy* packages had been on the air for months when Frank Kelly got wind it was hosted out of Los Angeles by Gordon Elliott, the man who rejected him and was never to work in this town again.

"You tell your friend Sutton," Kelly threatened over the phone, "that if he keeps using Gordon Elliott to host that show, the deal's off. He'll lose the license to the Paramount material and he'll never know this is the reason."

I was in Brennan's office to hear him respond, "You know, Frank, we'd better meet off the lot. "

Brennan hung up, wrote a memo documenting the tirade and faxed it off to Gordon before driving off to meet Kelly at the Columbia Bar & Grill.

In the end, Sutton kept the license to the Paramount material, and Gordon continued to host the Australian show out of Los Angeles.

Even so, Frank Kelly was now offering Brennan a new contract to sign on for another season as *Hard Copy's* executive producer.

Peter Brennan turned him down.

The Madame Heidi secret went public in a big way when Heidi Fleiss was arrested in April, 1993. It was a small story in the papers at first, but soon became wide open for anyone to cover.

Private eye Danno Hanks got into the act while calling upon all his skills to make ends meet after his expulsion from *Hard Copy* over the *Caught on Tape* special. One of Heidi's confidantes offered him a quick $5,000 if he'd tap the Madame's phone, and for this real-life Jim Rockford, a job like that was easy.

As he recalled after the statue of limitations expired, Danno went to a spot about a quarter-mile from Heidi's funhouse, a house which records showed was bought by Heidi and her father, a pediatrician, from the actor Michael Douglas. There, amid the scrubby woodland of Benedict Canyon, he cut into her phone line and installed a simple tape recorder.

Each day, Danno would return to the spot, replace the latest tape, and deliver it to his client. One day, he popped a tape into his car stereo, and immediately made a detour home to make a high-speed dub.

For days afterword, Danno kept making dubs of the tapes. He wound up with hours of Heidi's phone calls, evidence she was still in business, and many famous voices and names. There was the son of the studio boss who took Heidi's girls to Europe. There was the big-time record producer who'd fallen in love with one of the girls he'd paid for. There was the movie producer with an affectation for coprophiliac strolls in Baggie booties. There was the handsome young movie hunk with the AZT in his medicine cabinet.

By transcribing the tapes over hundreds of pages, Danno had found a way to make some much-needed cash, as well as make Hollywood history by generating story after story for newspapers, magazines, and television. The Heidi transcripts became required reading all over town.

Hard Copy paid for a look, and Brennan read the pages carefully. He wanted to know why some Paramount executives were afraid of Madame Heidi. He expected repercussions from his refusal to sign another contract, and he wanted ammunition in case things got ugly.

In his mansion high above all others in Benedict Canyon, at the end of a road that twisted and turned along a mountainside behind the Sharon Tate death house across the canyon from Heidi's lair, Rupert Murdoch took back control of *A Current Affair*. The Hollywood contingent had done enough damage. The mogul was turning to those closest to his heart and gut.

He appointed Ken Chandler, editor of his newspaper, *The Boston Herald*, as executive producer. Chandler was another television virgin, but he was refined and schooled in the tabloid tradition.

Best news to all of us was that our mate Dickie McWilliams was allowed to return and move his belongings back down to the fourth floor office of *A Current Affair*. Wee Dickie, a cautious man to begin with, returned not as an exiled king but as one who'd been held hostage in a windowless room. He'd pledged his troth to Terenzio and Herdrich, and their rejection was devastating.

Events moved quicker than Murdoch expected. In a matter of days, he had the opportunity to buy back his beloved *New York Post*. He seized the opportunity and transferred Ken Chandler downtown to become its editor.

Ian Rae was once again installed as *A Current Affair's* executive producer. "He's had more comebacks than Billy Martin," Dunleavy cracked, but it was only partially true. Ian, tied up with many important Fox News projects, put the future of *A Current Affair* into the hands of those left behind.

It was an odd assortment of newspaper professionals with little inclination for the subtleties of television. Besides the gun-shy Dickie and former *Star* bureau chief Barry Levine, there were others, all British and to the tabloid newspaper born.

Wendy Henry was a sweet woman with a trilling voice, birdlike legs, and a massive chest whose cleavage was left open to public inspection at all times. She was Murdoch's first female newspaper editor, running London's *News of the World* until she was fired for running a front page photo of Wee Prince Willie taking a wee wee in a public park. Rehired by Murdoch after a stint at the scurrilous *Globe* tabloid in Florida, she had little propensity for television, and spent much of her days scanning faxed copies of the most scandalous tabloid rags from London.

For a time there was Bill Ridley, a charming Briton with a devilish wit who'd been editor at the profitable *Star*. Ridley was a lonely man, still mourning the passing of his beloved wife who'd died of cancer two years before. In her memory, he had published a touching book of photographs and remembrances. Life for him was not the same since her passing.

Ultimately, it all came down to Dunleavy. His competitive instincts and natural affinity for the downtrodden had made him the hero of the *A Current Affair* office. Ever since William Kennedy Smith, Dunleavy grabbed as many stories and as much airtime as possible, while doing himself and his career no favors. Rather than appearing as the debonair elder statesman he was showing the sweat, appearing tired, worn-out, out-of-step, and old.

His personal producers, misfits protected under his wing, concerned themselves with keeping Dunleavy awake and filled with enough booze to keep moving, for his success was theirs.

CHAPTER TWENTY-TWO:
SON OF SAM & THE LOBSTER BOY

It's better to regret something you have done
than to regret something you haven't done.
— The Butthole Surfers

In the Spring of 1993, Wayne Darwen bargained his way out of that expensive contract with the Tribune company. Ever since the cancellation of *Now It Can Be Told* months earlier, he'd been sitting in an office in his fancy threads, coming up with specials ideas with John Parsons, who was laying the groundwork for his own future as a successful independent producer.

Now, with his lump settlement, Wayne was a solo producer. All he needed was the right project with which to make a splash.

"Wayne?" The call came from Maury Terry, a large, garrulous Irishman who'd worked as a producer for *Now It Can Be Told* and whose nervous eyes betrayed the terror he saw lurking around every corner. Somewhere between Mark Lane and Oliver Stone was Maury Terry, conspiracy buff of conspiracy buffs. In the early eighties, he'd written a book called *The Ultimate Evil*, a best-seller in newsrooms that painted the Son of Sam terror spree as a massive conspiracy of middle-class Westchester Satanists and the convicted killer, David Berkowitz, as just another Oswald: a patsy.

The book danced on the fringe of speculation but had some credibility. Terry was obsessive in his research and tied every rumor, tip, and whisper into a somewhat believable package.

It was just the sort of bullshit Wayne loved. Terry's work meant headlines, it meant ratings and, most important, meant there was meaning in the tabloid world. All this random violence and illicit sexuality and malfeasance were somehow connected to some greater plan, after all.

"Wayne," Terry repeated. "I think we can get Sam."

Those were the words Wayne needed to hear. Maury Terry had a connection, a traveling jailhouse preacher with the melodious name of the

Reverend Donnie Dickerman, who could get them a meeting with David Berkowitz himself. It would be up to Wayne to convince the killer to sit down for an interview.

Within days, Wayne was sitting with Terry and Rev. Dickerman in a reception room at the Sullivan Correctional Facility in upstate New York. When David Berkowitz walked in, Wayne was taken aback by his appearance. At forty-two, only a year older than Wayne, the infamous killer was a dead ringer for the actor Richard Dreyfuss: a soft-spoken, seemingly intelligent man in horn-rimmed glasses.

Wayne was already writing the special in his head. He'd build up Berkowitz as the Bogey Man, then reveal him sixteen years later. He made his pitch. Berkowitz nodded and said he'd think about it. To Wayne's amazement, a few days later, he agreed.

Wayne returned to the prison with Maury Terry and a three-man camera crew. Terry, the Son of Sam expert, asked the questions—unloading as much as the killer himself after sixteen years of pent-up obsession about the killings. Berkowitz told it all, from his adoption as a child to his involvement with Satanic cults to his role in the killings. Berkowitz was thoughtful. He was apologetic. Most astounding, the story he unreeled fit exactly into the conspiracy theory laid out years before in Terry's book. Berkowitz had insisted, upon his arrest and guilty plea, that he'd acted alone. Now he was saying he belonged to a cult. He spoke of ritual sacrifices. He intimated police may have been involved in the conspiracy. He admitted to pulling the trigger in some, but not all, of the shootings.

Wayne and Terry came away with six hours of interviews. When they were finished, they returned to the prison week after week, bringing the notorious killer small gifts like candy, food, socks, and t-shirts. He didn't want anything more.

"There's rumors and magazine reports I paid him $200,000," Wayne told me. "I'll tell you mate, he did not get one fucking penny. He wanted to send a message. He had become a born-again Christian. He wanted kids to be alerted to the dangers of Satanism, to testify to his Christianity.

"Mate, he did the interview to show nobody was beyond redemption."

Berkowitz had his doubts, however. When the interview was over, Wayne got up to get some sodas from the machine down the prison hall. Maury Terry told him that while he was gone, Rev. Dickerman pressed Berkowitz's hand and told him he did well.

"You know, David, I think society will see you differently," Terry said. "I think we'll be able to integrate you back in."

"Yeah," Berkowitz replied, focusing on the producer in the hall. "But what are we going to do about Wayne?"

On the long drives back to the city, Wayne and Terry would discuss the dichotomy between this gentle Bible-toter and the killer who ranked among the worst of the century. Wayne was conflicted. Not only did he believe Berkowitz, he liked him.

All this forced Wayne to confront his own crimes: the drinking, the philandering, the infidelities, the lying, the cheating, the chiseling, the exaggerations—he'd been through two and a half marriages so far and realized he hadn't learned a thing.

When he got home, he stood at his bathroom mirror and studied the image staring back at him. Under the coiffed curls and neatly trimmed beard he could make out the scars caused by past recklessness. He looked at the trappings of success, the Claude Montana designer suit with the zippers on the collars and the fringe on the epaulets—

Wait a minute. He had a TV special to sell.

Back in Los Angeles, the war had begun. Brennan got word that he'd be blackballed in retaliation for leaving *Hard Copy*.

Already, the rumors were getting back to New York. *Poor Brennan. He never shows up for work. Too bad about his drinking...* Brennan knew this was only the beginning. He was worried he was going to be set up.

He got Danno on the phone. He had some freelance work for the private eye. First, Brennan needed his office and home swept for listening devices. After the bug check, he had a little investigating for him to do. Remember our girl Heidi?

One thing was true: Brennan wasn't showing up for work in the morning. That was my job. No matter how late we were up the night before or what mischief we were into, I was there every morning in time for the seven-thirty meeting.

Every morning, I'd come into the office, face the cold hard stares of Linda Bell and her assistant Cheri, sit behind Brennan's desk, watch the tapes that were going into that day's show, and give instructions on how to tweak them.

On too many mornings, I'd leave the meeting with the last-minute changes for the show taken care of, tell my secretary I couldn't be disturbed, walk into my office, lock the door, take off my shirt, hang it neatly on the wall, vomit into the large blue wastebasket, and fall back to sleep on the couch, rousing in time for lunch and another cold bottle of Silverado.

As we neared the end of our final season at Paramount, Eames Hamilton Yates had reached the mountaintop.

For three years, he'd been the loyal soldier, traveling wherever we sent him, asking whatever questions he was instructed, bringing back the goods without fail. A national fast food chain was talking with his agent about having Eames star in a television commercial touting the All-American wholesomeness of their burgers.

Yet Eames was despised by *Hard Copy*'s alternative government. This unlikely correspondent was one of Parsons's recruits who went over to the other side. He would not be forgiven.

It mattered little to Eames. In the past three years, he'd attained a sense of personal achievement that had always eluded him before among the giants and strivers in his family. At last, he stood tall, as their equal.

Eames had achieved a level of tabloid satori equalled only, in their very different ways, by Dunleavy and Abramovitz. His segments, crafted, collaborative efforts between him and me, were on a plane higher than anything else on the show.

Linda Bell was not on a level to understand them.

Eames' final segment aired the last week of our third season, before the show went into reruns for the summer. It was his crowning moment, a commentary on American tabloid culture, on celebrity and on the dysfunctional modern family.

It was the story of Grady Stiles, Lobster Boy.

The story opened outside Tampa, Florida, in a place, Eames said, "where fire-eating midgets, giants, fat people, bearded ladies, Siamese twins and monkey-faced girls make their livings...the carnival sideshow, the freak show...a tough place to make a living, but when you're different, it's the only place to go."

This was the world of Grady Stiles, born into a family cursed by generations of a limb deformity that could only be named "lobsteritis." With his stunted forty-inch body and hands in the shape of eight-inch claws, Stiles made the best of his affliction as star of his own traveling freak show. He married, and in an extreme example of man's reproductive urge, sired two children who were also stricken with the deformity and also joined the show.

Grady Stiles endured the taunts and stares of paying curiosity seekers for nearly half a century, but his ordeal did not lead him to the serenity of his predecessor, the Elephant Man. Quite the opposite, Eames explained: "Grady Stiles was a monster, fueled by gallons of whiskey and rage...rage and anger he vented on his loved ones. Though confined to a wheelchair most of the time, his kids say Lobster Boy was a violent drunk. He'd knock them down with his wheelchair and head-butt them and their mom."

The family responded by hiring a hitman, who shot the 55-year-old Lobster Boy in the back of the head while he sat in his living room in Gibsonton, Florida.

The story took its time unfolding. It turned out Grady Stiles was on probation at the time of his murder, convicted in 1978 of shooting his daughter's boyfriend to death. His family claimed they hired a hitman only because Grady threatened to kill them next. The entire Stiles family claimed to have suffered from battered wife and battered child syndrome—the first time such a defense was used in a contract-killing case.

Eames traveled to Florida to speak with Lobster Boy's carnival coworkers. He went to the Tampa Jail to interview Grady Stiles' stepson, who was not afflicted, but allegedly contracted the $1,500 hitman. At the last minute, his attorney cancelled, but in an odd gesture allowed Eames to shoot video of the accused as he stood behind glass, pacing in a holding room.

"It was the ultimate irony," Eames deadpanned, "for Harry Glenn was simply put on display, just like his stepdad was in the freak show."

Eames' last words in the segment were: "Which way to Palm Beach?"

When the case went to trial and Grady Stiles' family was convicted of his killing, the story received national attention in such august periodicals as *The New York Times*. On the morning of June 21, 1993, however, when Eames' segment was screened in Los Angeles, this compelling social exposé was met with stunned silence, hands placed over mouths, gasps, and physical revulsion by Linda Bell and her cadre. They'd never seen anything like it before, and would never see its like again.

Imagine if we'd left in the trademark diner scene, where Eames contemplated the tragedy over a tall glass of ice cold milk...and a plate of steamed lobster.

Two days later, Peter Brennan was front page news in *Variety*:

Copy exec
producer
may ankle

Peter Brennan, the exec producer of Paramount's tabloid strip *Hard Copy*, reportedly is having difficulty reaching an agreement to remain with the show after his three-year deal expires on July 23.

...A Par source said the syndicator wants to keep *Copy* "pretty much as it is," while Brennan is seeking to move the syndie tabloid genre into a new direction. "It's no longer good enough to do the reality magazines of six or seven years ago," Brennan told the paper. "My objective is to elevate these shows to

a much more solid and deeper level than they are
now at. We need to search for a moral if there is
one..."

Wayne Darwen wasted no time compiling a twenty-minute sell tape comprised of the greatest moments from his six hours of Son of Sam interviews. By summer, he was ready to start pitching it as a television special.

He'd sunk $30,000 of his own money into this project and was desperate to make all that back and then some. Still, out of a sense of loyalty, he first offered it to his old mates at Fox.

"I have to go to the Pig," he told Maury Terry. "Mate, I'd worked at Fox so long I have to tell them first. Ian was my editor at the *Star*, I've known him twenty years—no matter what I think of him, he gave me the ability to even do this. They're hurting over there at *Current*, babe. This is a good one for them."

Ian Rae viewed the pitch tape in his office on East 67th Street, then hopped up and down with excitement. "Mate, this is stupendous!" he said as Wayne leaned back and gloated. "I don't fackin believe this."

"So, let's make a deal. A special, a series, a bit of both—"

Ian began to sputter. "Mate, this is big money. I need to run this by the others. Please, just give me time to talk to Faiman."

With *A Current Affair's* ratings in a nosedive, Fox's proven TV guru Peter Faiman was called east once again to oversee and perhaps revamp the show completely. It would be his decision.

Wayne met Faiman a week later at the Rihga Royal Hotel in midtown Manhattan. After Faiman and his colleague Tarquin Gotch screened the pitch tape, Wayne again sat back in the comfortable chair with a Cheshire grin spread across his face.

Faiman considered the offer. "Mate, it's a bit of an old story, isn't it?"

Wayne wasn't expecting that one. He leaned forward. "Umm, mate, I agree it happened a long time ago, but I'd figure the fact that he's never talked about it, and now he's talking sixteen years later, not pleading innocent but saying other people did it with him, other people pulled the trigger, that there were Satanists in Westchester and police knew about it and let it go in order to calm a panicked city, and that subsequently all the people he named all fucking died in car wrecks or were shot or died in other ways like the Kennedy conspiracy, I'd say maybe we have something here."

He took his first breath since the words "Umm, mate."

Faiman looked to his associate.

"Mate, maybe you weren't here in New York at the time," Wayne added, "but this guy, he's notorious."

"We'll need some time," Faiman said.

Wayne left the Rihga Royal and waited. He waited for several weeks without a word from anyone at Fox. That twenty-minute sell tape was burning a hole in his pocket.

Wayne's next stop was KingWorld and Bob Young, his old mate from the *Post* who was now working at the bland *Inside Edition* and developing bland new shows with his partner John Tomlin.

As did Ian Rae, Tomlin and Young hopped excitedly. The difference was, they followed up their enthusiastic display with an immediate monetary offer.

Wayne worked out a deal for a sum well into six figures, "and none of it went to Berkowitz," he was quick to remind anyone who asked.

It was the last day of June. I drove my new midnight blue Porsche Targa up to Paramount's main entrance and held the thick blue parking pass against the electronic sensor that would activate the rising gate in the driveway.

The pass had no effect. The gate didn't rise. The same kindly guard who wouldn't let me through on my first day at work three years earlier told me my parking pass had been deactivated.

As he opened the gate manually and waved me through, I smiled. Paramount's effort to keep me out on this day would give me an out permanently.

I was in a tough spot. More than a week after we'd taped our last *Hard Copy* episode of the season, Peter Brennan was gone from the show, but I remained, stuck midway in a second two-year contract Paramount's legal department insisted I sign, to overlap Brennan's and provide "a sense of continuity" if he left the show. There was a real chance that I'd be tied to *Hard Copy* for another year, if only to stop me from going with Brennan to the competition.

I needed an out. With this parking thing, I'd found one.

It all began a few months earlier, when I'd parked my car in the Paramount "tank," the parking lot they filled with water for movie scenes like the parting of the Red Sea in *The Ten Commandments*.

When Paramount re-shot the watery ending to Harrison Ford's *Patriot Games* in the tank, the security department towed my car to another part of the lot, and stuck *Hard Copy* with a bill for $69.50. Now, it seemed Mike O'Gara, Paramount's man at *Hard Copy*, had the security department revoke my parking privilege until I paid the towing bill.

No fucking way.

Those of us who worked with Peter Brennan had gotten used to harassment from Paramount security in the months since he made it known

271

he was leaving the show. We had trouble getting through the gate, our car trunks and backseats were often searched, and guards hassled us about leaving the lot with our personal computers.

It all fit into my escape plan. As I left the office after a second day of deactivation, I handed my assistant a memo to fax to the fifteen names listed before handing it to O'Gara.

Among the recipients were Frank Kelly, producer Robert Evans, new studio chief Sherry Lansing, Paramount owner Stanley Jaffe, my agent, attorney, Rafael Abramovitz, Peter Brennan and Dan Ayckroyd.

The inclusion of Ayckroyd was obvious to anyone at Paramount. The former star of *Saturday Night Live* was on the lot filming the movie *The Coneheads*. A few weeks earlier, after Security wouldn't let one of his assistants past the main gate, Ayckroyd had gone on a rampage, hijacking a Paramount golf cart and, in full Conehead regalia, trashing the Melrose guard shack. He destroyed phones and computers and, most egregiously, opened the gate and let in all cars that happened to be queued.

Of course, being Dan Ayckroyd, he got away with it.

My memo to O'Gara contained the standard shock and outrage, my surprise that "after the effort and time I've spent helping this show earn millions of dollars," no one reached into the petty cash drawer to pay for the tow and, most impressive, a personal note to O'Gara that would be read by all:

> Mike, you and I have had no quarrel...Even
> Linda Bell would say that I have put my heart and
> soul into *Hard Copy*...I don't play politics. I make
> television shows.
>
> And now, as word spreads that you are about to
> become the new co-executive producer here, I
> would hope you would not allow anyone in the
> office to play politics with me.
> ...I expect to work after hiatus...

It was up there with the Lobster Boy script, a mindfuck masterwork with more levels than *Finnegans Wake*, the culmination of my three years of graduate work at the school of *Hard Copy*. I'd learned some bitter lessons about the television business. Hard work and dedication didn't matter. It was all a fucking game.

This memo poked at all their boils. I could imagine the CEO's questions, Robert Evans worrying about a hidden Heidi connection, Dan Ayckroyd's vindication, Sherry Lansing wondering why Evans and Ayckroyd were cc'd, and the ones closest to the action being blown into their own paranoid camps.

They wanted to keep me? They could have me, bigtime.

Within two days, I received the letter I was hoping for:

> Dear Burt:
>
> This is to advise you that Paramount has elected not to exercise its option to employ you for the Option Period...
>
> Paramount does not require you to return to work for the balance of the current employment period, but you will continue to be paid.
>
> Paramount is appreciative of the significant contribution you have made to *Hard Copy* during your tenure and we wish you the best in the future.

I was free.

CHAPTER TWENTY-THREE:
THE MUGGING

Raf and I were in his Mustang, driving east on Beverly Boulevard, past the El Coyote Mexican restaurant and Big & Tall coffee shop. We were headed to a Chevron station on the corner of LaBrea to meet Peter Brennan.

In past months, Paramount and Frank Kelly had played hardball over Brennan's departure from *Hard Copy*. Brennan's contract expired on July 23, but the Paramount lawyers found a clause that wouldn't allow him to work anywhere else until September.

Brennan, who was holding his own ammunition compiled by Danno the private eye, was correct in predicting things would get uglier. He'd gotten a call that day from *A Current Affair*'s Los Angeles bureau. Mike Watkiss called to say someone was selling an audiotape in which Heidi Fleiss talked about Brennan.

"There he is." I pointed to the tail of Peter's Jag in the alleyway behind the filling station. Peter was leaning against the front of the car. He tossed his cigarette when he saw us roll up. Raf parked ahead of him and we got out.

"So." Raf was in his role as consiglierre.

"So. Watkiss calls me and says he saved my ass. Says he bought the tape to get it off the market."

"So why's he calling you about it?"

"That's what I mean. He says he's doing me a favor and he wants me to go over to Fox personally to pick it up."

"Playing power games. Why doesn't he just bring it to you, the little prick?"

"Yeah, well." Brennan tapped out another Marlboro Light. "Who knows what Kelly's up to?"

"So do you know what's on the tape?"

"Something about Heidi saying she knew me. That I hired two of her girls. It's bullshit."

"Is it true?"

"I spoke to two of the girls. About the Paramount connection—"

"Hey. Legally and socially, there's nothing wrong with you calling a prostitute—"

"I didn't call a prostitute. I was building a case. I had Danno out—"

"All that matters is what your wife thinks."

"Nah. I just hope we're only being paranoid. Because I'm just pissed off about what might happen next."

Brennan was angry. All our Hollywood dreams had come to this, a *Goodfellas*-style meeting behind a gas station on the corner of Beverly and LaBrea. Yet, leaning against Brennan's car, watching him pick at the scabs on his hand, I had the feeling we were in the middle of something historic, as if to say, "Wow, we're even involved in the Madame Heidi story. Cool."

Brennan got hold of the tape from Watkiss the next day. It was far less incendiary than he'd indicated. In fact, Watkiss told him it was a set-up from someone we knew all too well. Stuart Goldman, whose life had been ruined since he was arrested for hacking into the *A Current Affair* computer system four years earlier, was continuing his "investigation" of tabloid journalism.

Goldman was said to be one of many people in Hollywood who were calling Heidi, prompting her to mention specific names, and taping the calls. In Goldman's case, the names were those of tabloid TV bigs he blamed for his problems. Somehow, the tapes wound up on the market.

"You know Peter Brennan?"

"I know Peter Brennan. That motherfucker bought two of my girls and tried to get them to rat me out to Alex." Heidi had the mouth of a stevedore.

Peter had more pressing matters to worry about. Two nights later we met up with *Hard Copy* producer Theresa Coffino at the Pearl, a dark loungy bar on LaBrea just down the block from our back alley summit.

"Hey," she said in her fetching Bronx accent. "I heard you guys were meeting behind a gas station. What was that all about?"

Peter realized he was being followed. It was time to get out of Dodge.

The Son of Sam killer was babbling as soon as they brought him into the visiting room. "Wayne, Maury, what's going on? A man, a man was here. You won't believe what he said. How did he get in? You promised no one would bother me!"

It took a few minutes before Wayne Darwen got the story out of David Berkowitz. A visitor had arrived in maximum security earlier that day. He said his name was John Lester, that he represented *A Current Affair*, and was offering Berkowitz one last chance to have his story told by Steve Dunleavy, the man who spread it across New York City in blood red headlines sixteen years earlier. The show would make a substantial charitable donation in return.

Berkowitz panicked and had the man removed by guards.

"Johnny fucking Lester?" Wayne Darwen was dumbstruck. Everyone knew Johnny Lester, a Runyonesque character to whom Dunleavy had thrown a few odd jobs in the past. It was bad enough that Wayne had first offered the story to Fox; never mind that Dunleavy was fucking over his mate.

Johnny Lester was a paroled double-murderer, and it appeared that Dunleavy got him to break *into* prison.

As the summer progressed, Linda Bell's wish was on its way to coming true. She was named co-executive producer of *Hard Copy*, part of a team that included Frank Kelly's subordinate Cliff "Lurch" Lachman, her former rival Mike O'Gara, and a player to be named later. In a move that was not unexpected, she cleaned house of the turncoat Eames Yates and every male employee brought in by Brennan. The women were kept on, though Audrey was once again working on borrowed time.

Hard Copy was left in a perilous state. With no one left who was capable of writing and conceiving long-form stories, the consensus among the new brain trust was that the show would concentrate on shorter, news-style stories about show business, taking on the role of a sort of dirty companion to *Entertainment Tonight*.

Within a week of this decision, a story fell in their laps which made it seem brilliant.

On August 17th, 1993, the day Michael Jackson left the country to begin a concert tour promoting his *Dangerous* album, police in Los Angeles began investigating a thirteen-year-old boy's allegations that the superstar molested him during a four-month romance.

The monumental show business scandal urged *Hard Copy* out of its rerun schedule. A former tabloid writer on the assignment desk bought up an illegally-leaked copy of the Department of Child Services abuse report and handed it to Diane Dimond, who was given credit for tracking down the report herself.

The show's ratings skyrocketed. It was another defining story for tabloid television.

Breaking news like the Jackson story had become a nettlesome quandary on the fourth floor of 215 East 67th Street. There simply wasn't room in the show. Sitting surly and exhausted around a big table in a conference room, the newspaper-journalists-turned-TV-producers discussed stories culled from that week's papers, discussed them again, set them aside for later discussion and turned to the big bulletin board behind them, where rows of file cards represented the upcoming *A Current Affair* schedule.

On each card was another story slug, three or four a show, slotted as early as a month in advance, for the convenience of the fifteen-person promotion department and at the order of Ian Rae.

The meetings went long into the night. Stories breaking each day had to be put aside because the week's shows were already "filled," with space enough only for short, one- and two-minute "exclusives" bought from paparazzi or culled from the sleazy British tabloids.

The ratings at *A Current Affair* had plunged during the summer, but the team was very protective of its work. A defensive, bunker mentality had spread through the expanded staff that overflowed into the office upstairs where producer Dickie McWilliams had waited out his exile.

On August 28th, Elizabeth Taylor jetted off to meet a troubled Michael Jackson in Singapore. Mike Watkiss used his own money to buy tickets on the same flight for him and a crew, got footage of Taylor on the plane and snagged an exclusive interview on landing.

It was a spectacular get, but the team back in New York alloted only a few minutes for the story. They'd already promoted some story about a murder in the heartland.

Peter Faiman, taking control as consultant, realized the show had become rigid and inflexible with another serious misstep each day. The show needed a new look and vision to bring it into the Nineties. He turned to the past. Peter Brennan was soon to be sprung from his *Hard Copy* contract and was amenable to returning to his old show as a consultant.

Brennan brought me on board so we could produce a half-hour special bringing everything in the Michael Jackson story up to date and into long-form context, the first step in getting *A Current Affair* back in the game.

We worked in Los Angeles with Dunleavy at our side, writing quick intros to get Maureen O'Boyle on and off the air as quickly as possible. Dunleavy would track the script we wrote, without alliteration or his usual, breathless over-the-top delivery.

> Michael Jackson was everything we wanted him to be.
> The ultimate entertainer. The ultimate humanitarian.
> At once a grown-up whose music pulsated with
> sensuality...
> Yet the eternal kid...whose greatest joy was having
> other kids visit the home he calls Neverland Ranch....
> But now...suddenly...darkness threatens to envelope
> the light.

There is real fear tonight...that true or false... these
terrible accusations will force Michael Jackson to
close the curtain of seclusion he only recently opened
to the world...fear that the catastrophic publicity of
the past two weeks will result in the destruction of a
billion dollar empire...and the ruin of a man.
Tonight... a special report:
Michael Jackson, The Curtain Closes.

We fed the segments back to New York and waited for the phone calls
of praise. The *A Current Affair* team wasted few words. They hated it. Dickie
led the critics, saying the sober Dunleavy sounded drunk. The script was
too dry. There was no alliteration.

Brennan couldn't believe what he was hearing. The founder had
returned to save his show, and the ones who were driving it into the ground
were telling him he didn't know what he was doing. He walked out to get
an early afternoon drink, leaving Dunleavy to add words and sensational
adjectives to the so-carefully worded script.

"We think the combination of Linda Bell and Linda Ellman will create
one of the most dynamic teams heading any news program on the air today
and we are pleased to make these appointments from within our family."

When Linda Bell read the statement from Frank Kelly, she most likely
hid her conflicting emotions behind a tight smile. It was September seventh,
and word was out on the *PR Newswire*: the naming of her co-executive
producer on *Hard Copy*.

Linda Ellman was another stranger to tabloid, a network producer
who'd spent a decade at NBC News before joining *Entertainment Tonight* as
supervising producer earlier that year. She was also, coincidentally, a close
friend of John Terenzio, having loaned him her New York apartment when
he took over *A Current Affair*.

Linda Bell moved quickly to stake her ground before Linda Ellman was
named her equal. She would be in charge of day-to-day operation of the
show. Linda Ellman would handle the more indistinct "big picture," or as
the memo stated, "strategic planning and long-range projects."

People were already calling them "The Two Lindas." Linda Bell could
swallow a momentary feeling of hysteria. She knew it was only a matter of
time before there would be but one.

On Sunday, September 19th, I was packing up and moving out of my
third home in Benedict Canyon. Built into the side of a rustic hill and
reached by climbing ninety-six perilous steps, the place was more of a

houseboat than a house, with two floors, two big rooms, and a mysterious 12x12-inch square cut into the wall of the laundry room.

The landlord explained that a previous tenant named George Lucas made the hole to turn the laundry into a film projection room almost twenty-five years earlier. This was the house where Lucas wrote the script for his first feature, *THX 1138*.

I found the legacy inspiring, and had recently completed my latest screenplay at the kitchen table. It was to be a collaboration with Raf, but when I couldn't get him to do any writing, I wrote it myself: another story about the tabloid TV gang, this time stranded in Los Angeles. While the first script had the glorious name of *The Fortune Garden*, this one reflected the current zeitgiest: *Fucking the Dead*.

In the morning, I'd be returning to New York. After three seasons at *Hard Copy*, three houses in Benedict Canyon, hundreds of scripts, thousands of stories, gallons of vodka, any number of women, and too many close calls, I had no choice. Three years in Los Angeles and I'd squandered more than half a million dollars on bar tabs, hot cars, restaurant checks, airline tickets, hotels, women, friends, and God knows what else.

Peter Brennan had a deal with ABC to produce a pilot for an afternoon talk show in Manhattan. I would be senior producer.

I had no choice. I was dead broke.

When I arrived at Kennedy Airport, the story was on the cover of weekly *Variety* and all hell was breaking loose in tabloidland:

Son of Sam sparks
tag-team tab tiff

Anyone who doubts that the tabloid magazine shows are spinning out of control should talk to David Berkowitz. But Berkwowitz, the infamous serial killer who called himself Son of Sam, isn't talking to just anybody— and that's what started the latest tabloid donnybrook...

When word filtered back to *Current Affair* star correspondent Steve Dunleavy that his competition had scored the Berkowitz material, "he went ballistic," according to a Fox source...

According to (Maury) Terry, Dunleavy hatched a

plan to get his own Son of Sam interview with the
help of John Lester, an ex-con who told Dunleavy
he could get to Berkowitz in prison...

Now that the story was out in the open, no one would admit to first
tipping the trade paper, not Wayne and certainly not Bob Young, who
wanted to keep the Son of Sam interview a secret so he could spring it on
the world in November.

Strangely, all fingers pointed to Herdrich, who since John Terenzio's
departure had kept a low profile at *A Current Affair*. Office buzz said his
ethical hackles were raised by Dunleavy's stunt. He was innocent, though.
All journalistic differences aside, Herdrich loved Dunleavy as much as any
young journo who'd spent time with him. Herdrich ignored the gossip.
Within weeks, he'd be gone, taking a job with John Terenzio in Los
Angeles— but not before the Son of Sam episode took another sinister twist.

Wayne Darwen's descent into an alcoholic tailspin was only heightened
by Dunleavy's betrayal. Writing the Son of Sam special at Maury Terry's Fire
Island retreat, he went through several bottles of vodka a day, and at one
point attempted suicide by walking into the ocean. The surf spit him back.

Dunleavy, meanwhile, was back at Tom McGrath's bar, working on his
tenth Heineken. As far as he was concerned, there was no fault involved;
this was business and survival was on the line. If it weren't for him, David
Berkowitz would be a nobody. While he was off shooting people and writing
letters to Jimmy Breslin, Dunleavy was the one writing the great stories that
struck fear in the hearts of New Yorkers and the rest of America. That
fucking Darwen, while Dunleavy was making history, he was a fucking cub
reporter at the *Star*. Dunleavy had been his boss.

Dunleavy thought back to the night in 1977 when Stacy Moskowitz
and Robert Violante were shot. Those poor kids, doing what teenagers do
on a lovers lane in Brooklyn, unaware of anything beyond where their hands
explored when the Son of Sam madman got into the police crouch and
began blasting away.

When the call came, Dunleavy felt the rush in every pore. It never
paled in intensity; it was always the same combination of adrenaline,
excitement, and raw fear. Every story was the King's Grove Slasher all over
again. He'd either be number one or locked in the outhouse while
everything happened around him.

His cop source said the nearest emergency room to the shooting scene
was Coney Island Hospital, and that's where every journo, TV crew, and
police buff was rushing. Dunleavy, the foreigner, knew the vics would be

diverted to Kings County, the hospital that best handled shots to the head. He walked in alone, straight into Stacy's parents.

Poor fools, they thought he worked for the hospital. Dunleavy spent the night with them and the Violantes. A bullet had carried one of young Robert's eyes out of his skull. Poor Stacy was in a coma from which she'd never awaken. Dunleavy cried honest tears with the parents, drank with them, shielded them from the rabid pack of reporters that showed up late and out of breath at the automatic doors to emergency.

It was Dunleavy who had the exclusive of exclusives on page one the next morning:

> For 13 1/2 hours, a *Post* reporter stood at the
> side of four courageous people in a painful and
> often stirring vigil—praying, talking about God and
> swearing at an unknown madman who has
> launched a guerrilla war against the young and
> beautiful of this city...

Fuck! He did it for the Boss. The night they arrested Berkowitz, that fat fuck Breslin was lolling about out in the Hamptons! Steve had the story to himself. No one would forget the front page showing the killer curled up on a bunk in his cell; the legendary headline:

SAM SLEEPS

Now, because Ian Rae was too slow, because Faiman didn't see the story, *Inside* would get the grand prize: *SAM SPEAKS!*

"So Steve, uh, what's the score?" Johnny Lester couldn't hide his agitation. His eyes had more movements than a Swiss watch.

Boy, had this spun out of control. After *Variety* ran the story about Johnny sneaking into prison, breaking his parole, came word that the state might send him back upstate to finish his sentence. Relief came in a phone call from a public official. The woman said she could take care of things— for the small fee of $1,500.

That should have posed no problem, except it was Friday night, Dunleavy's bank card was tapped out from flying all over the country on stories *A Current Affair's* new finance department wouldn't reimburse him for because he didn't keep receipts, and anyone who could loan him money was home or in the fucking Hamptons, probably with Breslin.

Dunleavy couldn't hit up Tommy McGrath. His credit line with Tommy was drier than a dead dingo's donger. He'd managed to scrape up six hundred dollars. Somehow he needed nine hundred more, and he needed it by the next morning.

The door to McGrath's opened and Ian Rae walked in. Dunleavy gave a nudge and Johnny Lester made himself scarce.

"'Ello, mate."

"How are ya, mate. What're you havin?"

"Nothin for me. I'm stepping out with my lady love." Ian was moony lately over his new girlfriend. "Just want you to know, don't take it too hard, mate. There's other stories. We'll get the bastards back. That fackin' rat bastard Darwen."

"Yeah, onward and upward." He thought for a moment about asking Ian for the money. No way. It was Ian who got him into this. "You gotta stop Wayne Darwen at any cost," were his words. "Get in there and try and stop it; try and match it." Big talk. If Ian heard where it'd led, he'd drop a darkie, cack a Richard the Third, pass an Edgar Britt right there in the bar. Dunleavy shuddered at the thought, wished Ian well, and went back to his Heineken.

Johnny came back out when the coast was clear. There was resolve in his darting eyes. "So whatta we need? Nine hundred?"

"Somehow."

"I know where to get it. Don't worry."

"Mate, no." Dunleavy reached out and grabbed Johnny by the arm. "Don't do anything...silly."

"Don't worry. I know this guy. Uptown. I'll get the cash."

Four hours later, Dunleavy was still at the bar dreaming about David Berkowitz when Johnny Lester walked in and plunked nine hundred dollars on the bar in front of him. Dunleavy opened his eyes. It was a miracle.

"Johnny! Brilliant! I shouldn't ask, but where did you get it?"

Johnny smiled. "It was nothin. I mugged a guy."

CHAPTER TWENTY-FOUR:
SEEMS LIKE OLD CRIMES

"I'm telling you, mate. You'd like him. He's a mate, I swear."

"Wayne. Stop. Listen to me. He's not a mate."

"But he is, you have to meet him. He's a good guy."

"Wayne! In this century, in our society, there are like four people who cannot be mates. They're banned from consideration of ever entering matehood, ever. Four names, mate. There's Hitler and there's Manson and there's Nixon and there's David Berkowitz! David Berkowitz cannot be a mate! He's one of the worst fucking criminals of the century!"

Wayne shrugged. "Ah, you never met him. I'm tellin ya, he's a mate."

We were all back in New York, back in the bar drinking and talking nonsense like we'd never left.

Neal Travis had returned to the *New York Post*. The man who revolutionized the gossip industry with *Page Six* now had page seven all to himself for a new column called *Neal Travis' New York*.

Rafael was back at *A Current Affair*, having pulled out of *Hard Copy* and finding security the moment word leaked that Peter Brennan was leaving.

Brennan was back dividing his time between the ABC pilot and his sweeps consultancy at *A Current Affair*. My ABC paychecks meant I'd now worked for all four networks, but the money was hardly enough to cover my Manhattan living expenses. I needed to moonlight at *A Current Affair*, too. The only obstacle was Ian Rae, who was telling people he didn't want me in the Fox building.

Dunleavy set things straight. He arranged a meeting in the heart of the Fox building, in Ian Rae's office. I told Ian I'd changed. Ian said he'd changed, too, and had no problem with me coming over. He sounded as if he were under orders from Faiman.

It seemed like easy money, rewriting some scripts, assigning some stories, and picking up an extra couple of grand a week. I forgot. There's no such thing as easy money. It seems Brennan had again spread himself too thin and made promises he couldn't keep. Faiman expected him to be at *A

Current Affair full-time through November. We worked out a compromise. Brennan would be in charge of strategic planning and long-range projects. I'd be in charge of day-to-day operations of the show, in the office every day.

I was back running *A Current Affair*.

It was like that scene in *It's A Wonderful Life*, where Clarence the Angel shows George Bailey what Bedford Falls would be like had he never lived to influence it.

The *A Current Affair* office looked the same as when we'd left in the summer of 1990, but at the same time, somehow, it was very different.

Maybe it was the air, literally oppressive, thick with the stink of a million cigarettes, bodies too close together, and defeat. Constant smoke had left trails of thick black soot at the ceiling near the air conditioning vents. Stacks of yellowed newspapers gathered dust on tabletops. Spent coffee cups and paper stuck together in corners. Cobwebs and dust collected on the velveteen "Elvis Shrine" against the back wall.

Then there were the gnats, a most strange phenomenon for a New York City newsroom. The miniscule insects hovered over trash cans and certain desks. Reporters noticed them bouncing off the screens of their word processors as they wrote their short stories; producers swatted them absently while working the phones.

The gnats were a byproduct of a recent attempt to boost morale among the staff. Some of the female producers decided, and no one put up much of a fight in disagreement, that it would be a good idea to allow employees to bring their pets to work. One of Dunleavy's chain-smoking assistants brought in her dog and a turtle. Someone else had a lizard.

Maureen O'Boyle's writer Heidi topped them all by setting loose her pet pot-bellied pig to roam the floor. Its dried feces remained stuck to the carpet under her desk, as the custodian had decided it wasn't his job to pick up pigshit.

Eventually, the custodian would report the health code violations to the Environmental Protection Agency. An inspector would come in to take readings of smoke and feces levels in the office, leading Ian Rae to issue an unprecedented memo banning smoking and animals—of both the household and barnyard variety—from the office.

For now, the gnats had free run in a once proud office that had become a bureaucratic Bosnia, with a staff that was double in size from the glory days, full of warring producers and reporters with their own armies and aims. All this chaos was reflected in the barnyard atmosphere of the physical surroundings.

The general belief among the workers was that their show was, indeed, trash. They could be forgiven the perception. Their leadership was a team of tabloid print reporters with no television experience or love of the form. *A Current Affair* had become a *News of the World* of the airwaves, living up to the credo of not letting facts get in the way of a story and living off stories that papered the British tabloids but were dismissed in America.

It was just like the wild ranting of Wayne at Nickel's bar way back in 1989—only now there was no one to stop it from becoming a reality. If a story was too good to be true, they'd *make* it true.

Here's how it worked: Say someone in the office heard—or decided to start—a rumor that Michael Jackson was caught en flagrante with his llama. The assignment editor in New York would call the L.A. office to check it out. If the story turned out to be unconfirmable—or untrue—it wasn't necessarily shot down or declared dead.

If the story was good enough, some tabloid vet in New York would then feed the deflated item to one of the many British tabloid newspaper journalists encamped in Los Angeles. The Brit would seize upon the rumor, pay someone as a supposed "unnamed source" to confirm it, then write the story as gospel for one of the outrageous London tabloids. The story would next be faxed from L.A. to London, published in England, then faxed back to the *A Current Affair* office in New York, where the staff would do a quick day-of-air story on what they knew never happened in L.A.

The story would include a shot of the British newspaper headline to show they were only reporting "what the world is talking about."

So a story that was generated in New York City, shot down in Los Angeles, concocted for England, published in London, and sent on its way back to New York City, would now air across America. The Fox lawyers would okay the story because it was attributed to the London papers.

No wonder wacko Jacko was gulping prescription pills by the bottle. No wonder no one took *A Current Affair* seriously anymore.

The show had committed the cardinal sin: it treated its viewers like fucking morons. No longer could the show be appreciated on any number of levels by any number of audiences, from college kids gathered around the dorm TV to other journalists chuckling at the in-jokes.

A Current Affair had become a cut-and-paste wastebasket of scandal, and the ones who had been there from the start, the ones who knew better, were merely feathering their own nests as the show slid headlong toward doom.

Wayne's Son of Sam segments were set to air on *Inside Edition* the first week of November sweeps. He'd given the *New York Post* serialization rights to photos and interview transcripts, but once Dunleavy's scheme was revealed, Wayne wrote a letter to Murdoch revoking permission, and handed everything to his pal Martin Dunn, the new editor of the New York *Daily News*. The week the interview ran on *Inside*, the *News* ran six consecutive front page stories.

With some quick typing and remembering from Dunleavy, so did the *Post*. They ran "spoiler" stories, the first under the banner:

HE'S LYING!

There was a fierce argument in the office. A man named Colin Ferguson had boarded a Long Island Rail Road commuter train and walked through the cars shooting and kiling people at random.

Dickie and Dunleavy were adamant about running a bite from a local black politician who held a press conference to call the gunman "an animal."

"We lower the show if we run that, mates," I argued, while Raf nodded in agreement. "He's not an animal. He's a man, a black man at that."

"That's bullshit," Dickie said. "He is an animal."

"Mate, when they were putting him into the police car, he looked at the reporters and whispered 'Help me.' If he was a white executive who snapped, you wouldn't be calling him an animal."

Dunleavy would hear none of it. "Of course he's a murderous animal! I've been in this business long enough to know that when some colomongo—"

Everyone, on both sides of the argument, stopped dead.

"What did you say?" I asked.

"Excuse me?" added Raf.

"What?" Dunleavy's air fizzed out.

"What did you call the guy? A 'colo' what?"

"A colomongo." Dunleavy hemmed and hawed a bit. "It means nutcase, mate," he said, weakly.

Laughter rippled around the room. "Doesn't sound like it means nutcase."

"Well, it does. It's not racial. It's a common term."

Dickie got back to the point. "Look, everyone wants to take out a gun and shoot people. But we keep it under control."

Uh-oh. The smiles faded. It was as if E.F. Hutton had spoken.

A few nights later, on the verge of November sweeps, it came to a head at Tommy McGrath's.

Raf and I were at the bar. He was excited that we were once again in command, and saw great promise in his Machiavellian role at the right hand of power.

Brennan was over by the payphone, spelling things out to Dunleavy. *A Current Affair* had been driven to its lowest point, quite possibly a depth from which they'd be unable to dig out, in part because of Dickie. Now Dickie was refusing to cooperate; his recaltricance was costing us valuable time. Now was our chance. The Wild Bunch was together again, ready to make one last ride into history.

Dunleavy shook his head. "Dickie's been through so much, mate," he said. "It's loyalty. I can't turn on him. I won't."

"Steve. This is the last chance."

Their voices got louder. Glasses knocked against the bar. Brennan was nose to nose with his mate of twenty-five years.

"Mate," Brennan said. "We're talking about your survival and the survival of the show. You've chosen the wrong horse, mate. Dickie is not the one. You've got to come on board."

There was silence for a moment, before Dunleavy's response reverberated through the bar and struck deep in Brennan's heart.

"No."

As far as Peter Brennan was concerned, it was over.

I sat with Dickie in the conference room and explained that I needed his cooperation. "I don't want to be executive producer, mate. I'm only here for the money and because Brennan needs me to be here. We can work together, you and me."

"No, no." Dickie screwed up his face and shook his head.

"You can be the boss. Everyone will answer to you while you and I come up with the show. All I want is to get the show happening and get some ratings. It'll be fun. Like old times."

"No, no, I've had it. I can't take it anymore. Too many bosses telling me what to do. I'm quitting. I'm getting Ian to find me another job in the company."

"That's not really quitting then, is it?"

He didn't quit. Dickie vaporized once again into ghost form. He announced his departure, yet he didn't leave. He stationed himself in a corner of the conference room with a word processor given him as a parting gift, and spent his days calling up onto his screen Internet pictures of women in bathing suits, often sighing in wordless criticism while I ran the show from the big table in the middle of the room.

"First off, all these file cards are coming off the wall."

"That's how we know what we're shooting."

"You might as well just fax a list to *Hard Copy* and *Inside*."

"Ian wants them there," Barry Levine offered.

"Too bad. From now on, we approach every show as a blank slate. We will go after day-of-air stories. We will go to the edge." I faced the leadership: Levine and Andrea Spiegel; Wendy Henry and Danny Meenan. "From now on, no more of these nighttime post mortems agonizing over stories. You see a story, Danny, you show me as soon as you get it. I'll give you an answer on the spot."

There were traces of smiles around the room. They faded when I told them there would instead be a seven a.m. meeting each day.

"We need to get an early start and we need to be first. I'll be here at seven. If you don't want to come, fine. But if you do, this will be your show. Things are going to be different. I can promise you one thing. This show will be fun again."

Peter Brennan knew only one way to reverse the fortunes of *A Current Affair* instantaneously: throw a whole lot of cash at something. As the most crucial month of November 1993 loomed, that something was Joey Buttafuoco.

Big Joey Buttafuoco had shot his mouth off so often in the past year and a half since his wife was shot that the District Attorney changed his mind and charged him with the statutory rape of Amy Fisher after all. Joey was headed to jail for six months.

"Don't worry. He'll be out in time for prom season," his new attorney said. Dominic Barbara was the Brandoesque lawyer who represented Jessica Hahn and appeared regularly on the Howard Stern show. Dominic went way back with Brennan and Dunleavy, funneling them great tabloid stories involving his clients on the Island, and representing Brennan in one of his divorces.

Now he was holding *A Current Affair*'s salvation. He had the words America was anxious to hear. Before he went to jail, Joey would come clean and admit for the first time that yes indeed, he'd fucked Amy Fisher. After a year and a half of infuriating women across the country by defending the big galoot, Mary Jo would announce she realized that her Joey was a cheating scumbag.

Sitting with Brennan and Dunleavy in the Asia restaurant, Dominic had the offer on the same table where John Terenzio had been feted at his farewell dinner.

I sat nearby and watched the negotiations. Not more than a couple of minutes passed before Dunleavy let out a scream and lunged over the table at his mate, Brennan.

Dunleavy calmed down and there were handshakes all round.

Later that night at the bar, Brennan told me what happened.

He'd asked Dominic: "What will it take to get the interview with Joey and Mary Jo?"

Dominic replied: "$500,000."

Brennan said: "It's a deal."

Dunleavy, ever out to save his boss a dollar, leaped.

"Wayne, I've been watching you, boy, and you are very unhappy. We've been in the middle of a fight between the forces of good and evil, and boy, the evil has overtaken you."

Wayne Darwen looked around the restaurant, embarrassed as the Reverend Donnie Dickerman clutched his hands and spoke a little too loudly. He laughed uneasily. "Mate, what the fuck is this?"

This was supposed to be a celebration. After all the headaches and heartache of the Son of Sam episode, he'd finally produced the segments for *Inside Edition*, had a one-hour special in the can to sell separately, and was sitting down to a good fucking steak at Kenny's on Lexington Avenue.

Now, with the plates cleared and coffee served, Rev. Dickerman was making his move. "Wayne, you must accept Jesus!"

The jailhouse preacher was getting louder and Maury Terry was looking on without a word.

"You must agree to give your life over to the Lord! You must be saved! You must be born again!"

"Maury—" People were looking up from their steaks at this Texas cracker and this wild-haired Aussie, holding hands, for fucksake! This wasn't funny anymore.

"Accept Jesus," the minister repeated.

"All right, mate! I accept! I accept Jesus!" Anything to get this guy to let go.

Out on the street, Wayne said goodbye to his friends and walked off alone toward his apartment. What a fucking joke! He cracked up, laughing into the night. He thought about the last six months, how his marriage had broken up, how he'd started drinking again, how his good mates betrayed him, how he'd been torn by the inner conflict caused by his contact with one of the century's most notorious serial killers. David Berkowitz could be saved, but he was beyond—

Wayne stopped on the corner and felt a warm glow inside his chest. He looked up, past the bright lights of the big city, toward something in the sky he could not see.

It was all he could do to keep from dropping to his knees. He realized, that yes, he did. He accepted Jesus.

Wayne was born again.

On the night before Halloween, River Phoenix died in convulsions on a sidewalk outside the Viper Room nightclub on the Sunset Strip. That following day, a Sunday, I set loose the forces of the L.A. office on the story, but by Monday morning it was clear my new team was getting its ass kicked. *Hard Copy*, we found, had interviews with people who were inside the Viper Room when he overdosed. They had video of the ambulance. Our team didn't even know about the 911 tape.

We were flying by the seat of our pants once again. I sent a producer to the makeshift shrine that had risen at the spot where the young actor died. I told him to shoot the nearby payphone and exteriors of the club.

On Monday's show, while *Hard Copy* used all its great material in a straight news report about the tragedy, we opened up *A Current Affair* to play the entire 911 call made by Phoenix's brother as River lay thrashing and dying only a few feet away. The tape played over pictures of the sidewalk, the payphone and the shrine. It was horrible and heartbreaking.

It rated.

Meanwhile, Barry Levine and I were writing all the reports for Mike Watkiss, who was on the road with Michael Jackson's troubled tour. Watkiss called in several times, asking to go back to L.A. so he could hire a secretary for the bureau. I reminded the bureau chief he was on the biggest story in show business history.

There was much work to do with the *A Current Affair* staff, and it was more than opening the windows to clear the smell of pigshit. We needed to open the windows and let some reality in.

A female reporter brought back a story of a murderous woman described in a tabloid newspaper as a "Marilyn Monroe lookalike." She repeated the description in her taped package, even though the videotape revealed the woman to more resemble Joe Torre.

David Lee Miller was covering the trial of Lorena Bobbitt, who'd chopped off her husband's penis. I told Miller and all other staff members that no one could use the word "penis" on the air.

"But why not? Dan Rather did!"

"David, David," I said, and related an old story about a guest who shows up your home at 7:30 each night and wants to be invited back again. Besides, working around the obvious stirred the imagination and got the old creative juices flowing.

The show was moving again.

After Maureen's writer Heidi ran out of the office in tears when Rafael and I edited the lead-ins she'd written, I relieved her of writing duties. Maureen stomped around and had a fit, but Faiman told her I was in charge and she settled down in a sulk.

It was typical. I was making her seem intelligent and helping her ratings, and she wouldn't speak to me. It didn't matter much; in fact, Maureen's sullen withdrawal made things easier.

To get the show on every day, I relied on a small portion of the staff—basically everyone I could see through the conference room door when I looked down the aisle into the newsroom.

"This is your show," I told them. "Anybody who wants to get a package on or be part of the show, has to get through you. Now where's the Julia Roberts tape?"

It was an important video we needed that morning. I'd asked one of the producers to get it.

"I'm not sure. I turned it over to an associate producer."

The associate producer had delegated the job to a production assistant, who turned it over to an intern. The tape was still missing. That's the way they worked: delegating and forgetting.

"No more delegating," I reminded everyone. "This is your show. You've got to take responsibility for it."

Quickly, they got the hang of it. Slowly, surely, *A Current Affair* was becoming a show again and I was becoming a producer again.

Days later, on the Friday before sweeps, Dunleavy called me in the late afternoon. We'd all be leaving at five a.m. the next morning, he said, to interview the Buttafuocos at Dominic Barbara's weekend house on Shelter Island.

CHAPTER TWENTY-FIVE:
BUTTAFUOCO SWEATS

"Don't worry," Dominic Barbara said, plopped like a great fat poobah on the black sectional couch. "You'll get your come shot."

"Our *what*?" Even the cameramen looked up when he said that.

"I know what you people want, I know what you call it in TV," he said. "The come shot. Don't worry. You'll get your come shot."

It didn't seem likely that afternoon as the $500,000 Buttafuoco spectacular got underway. Joey Buttafuoco, beefy and dressed in black, sat across from Dunleavy, leaning forward intently, foot tapping, fingers going like Tom Arnold, glancing nervously toward the bedroom door.

Dominic's wife Irma was supposed to take Mary Jo Buttafuoco shopping while we interviewed Joey in the living room of the house on the bay. Instead, she announced that she considered us cockroaches invading her home, added that she was menstruating, and left Mary Jo to her own devices in the guest bedroom.

Earlier, when we'd shot B-roll by the breakwater, Joey was acting like the star of his own music video, posing and brooding when he wasn't bouncing around like a teenager. That's how Dominic described him. "He stopped maturing at eleven, when his mother died. He dresses like a teenager, he acts like one."

Mary Jo, though, was all adult tragedy. After all, as they say, she had a fucking bullet in her head. A delicate woman with one eye wider than the other, her mouth drooping slightly from paralysis, she couldn't go out by the water with Joey because she was bleeding from the ear.

The $500,000 price tag weighed heavily on Dunleavy. He started out slowly, going over the details of Joey Buttafuoco's life. Joey was refreshingly insincere. When Steve got to the question about "the assignation," Joey stopped. He didn't know what the word meant. When Steve asked about the tryst, Joey thought he said "twist." Meanwhile, Dominic was interrupting every question and answer from the couch, telling Joey what to say—

Suddenly, there were moans and shouts from the bedroom.

"Uh, oh." Joey said, like a kid in trouble. It was Mary Jo. The interview was over. Joey got up to calm his wife.

"Are we doing this just for the money?" she screamed. "Why do this for the money?" Earlier, when Mary Jo voiced second thoughts, Dominic calmed her by scrawling a check for $100,000. The check had worn off. Mary Jo was going ballistic.

"She gets this way when the pain drugs kick in," Dominic said. It was obvious there was more to it. Either she was backing out of the deal, or Dominic never told her what she was in for.

At dinner, cameraman Kenny Fuhr was the first to get going after a couple of drinks, convincing Joey he should market those red and blue zebra-patterned workout pants he was known for wearing.

"Buttafuoco sweats!" Kenny said. "You'll make a fortune."

"Buttafuoco sweats. I like the sound," said Joey. He was considering the idea when Dominic barked down the table. "Mary Jo! you can do whatever the fuck you want, because you have a fucking bullet in your head! These guys here, they can't, because they don't have a fucking bullet in their heads. But you, you have a fucking bullet in your head, you can do whatever you want!"

Mary Jo was ill at ease until a couple of red wines helped her get it off her chest. "Let me tell you," she said, leaning close to me. "I was in my back yard, I was painting lawn furniture and I hear the doorbell ring. And there's this little girl on the steps. I opened the door. I didn't think she had a gun. If it was someone like Joey, a big guy, I would have automatically latched the screen door, but this girl..."

As the feast raged on around her, Mary Jo relived the fateful scene: the argument, the gunshot, lying on the porch, bleeding, the neighbors telling her later that she was clawing at the ground trying to get up without realizing it. It was awful, and worse, poor Mary Jo couldn't understand why people didn't see her as a victim; why anti-gun groups and victims' groups didn't call her up and ask her to speak; why she wasn't pitied...or even liked.

I was sure feeling sorry for her by then, this tiny woman with a side of her mouth dripping gravy from the effects of the bullet. Sitting next to her, Mr. Rock 'n' Roll was dreaming of selling his parachute pants. Buttafuoco sweats.

What could I say? I went into a speech about how feminists and the politically-correct crowd couldn't tolerate her for forgiving her husband and wanting to preserve her family, how she couldn't be forgiven because she survived. Mary Jo was supposed to die. This interview, I said, will turn the tide of opinion—I was laying it on thicker than the butter Dominic was laying on the hot rolls.

Back at the house, Dominic had ordered the Holyfield-Bowe fight on pay-per-view. Before we turned to the bout, Joey said he wanted us to watch a music video. The song was called "Snakeskin Voodoo Man" by a heavy metal band called Virgin Steele, a standard blues and a typical low-budget video production—except for the star.

It was Joey Buttafuoco—on his boat, on a motorcycle, in his Corvette—romping with an Amy Fisher lookalike. It was insane, and I knew it wasn't even the final outrage in this bizarre case. I couldn't stop laughing, tapping my feet and shaking my head. Joey lay back on the couch with his arm around his wife, crossing his legs and fondling a snakeskin boot. He was so proud. He was the Snakeskin Voodoo Man. After the video, he took his wife to bed.

As I wiped my eyes, Dominic had Steve in the kitchen, telling him how worried he was. Joey was set to go to jail in a week, on November fifteenth, but Dominic was afraid he'd get caught with another woman before he went in. That past Thursday night, Dominic said, Joey was at a whorehouse in Queens. He was going down on one, one was going down on him and a third had her tongue up his ass. Joey was a powderkeg.

The Holyfield fight was a good punch-up. A guy with a parachute dropped into the ring and got beat up himself. As we stood watching and rooting, Dominic was splayed out on the couch.

Then there was a smell; a sulfurous stench. Someone had let loose a silent, ungodly fart. The guests pretended not to notice. I mentioned that someone was sick. Apparently it was Dominic.

The next morning, the two camera crews set up out back for the Mary Jo interview while I sat in front of the bigscreen TV telling Joey some of my L.A. stories, like the time Raf saved me from that woman who showed up at the compound in Benedict Canyon with a knife.

"See! What if she killed Raf? You would've been in the same position as me," Joey said. "You didn't know she was like that."

"Well, uh, actually, I did have an inkling, Joey."

When I told him about the sisters who wanted Raf and me to find them a hitman, Joey Buttafuoco looked at me with awe. "And they want to put me in jail?" he said. "You are fucking crazy."

Joey gave me a high-five. It wasn't as good as having my mate David Berkowitz worrying about my soul, but it was a start.

"Look Joey," Mary Jo said, folding her hands over her chest, "I look like I'm dead."

When Mary Jo walked into the living room wearing pancake television makeup, she indeed looked like she belonged in the coffin. I could imagine her dying in her sleep in the next year, the bullet shifting in her head and her dying. This was the tragic element of the story that everyone seemed to miss. These were real people. This was real pain. This was real life that went out of control here, and what were we doing with it?

Mary Jo was articulate as she told the story of her life, leading to the day Amy Fisher came to her door. Then Dunleavy asked how she felt about Joey having an affair with the teenager.

"I choose to believe...he didn't do it," she said.

"Cut," I coughed. We stopped the interview.

"Steve, this is bullshit," she said, "and I'm not going to bullshit you. It isn't true. What do you want me to say? That he cheated and I forgive him? Fine. I said it. But it's not true." It was obvious she wasn't going to come clean. She and Joey had probably never even talked about what happened.

"How could you not believe this?" Dunleavy asked. "Joey told me himself. He admitted it."

"I said I *choose* not to believe," she replied. "Can't we just let the people use their imaginations and guess? Give them both sides and let them make up their minds?"

We stopped the interview and gave Dunleavy some time alone with Mary Jo while I accosted Dominic on the other side of the house. He acted very surprised Mary Jo didn't come through. Now it was clear that either he was holding back deliberately or she was not in on the bill of goods he sold us.

Mary Jo wouldn't budge. When the interview was over, she asked, "Is there anything else?"

"Not unless we want to start again from a different point of view," I said, disgusted.

"Don't I get any applause?"

We did Joey again in the living room where Mary Jo interrupted us the day before. Dominic promised he'd get her out of the house this time. Of course, he didn't. Irma stomped around, reminding us she was still on the rag and how low we all were.

Joey got into the same clothes as the previous day. We set him up in the middle of the room again and Dominic laid himself out on the big black couch. This time, he would make sure we got our "come shot," by putting the exact words into Joey's mouth.

"Ask him why he smiles all the time," he said to Dunleavy. Then to Joey, "The reason you smile is because it's a defense mechanism."

"Joey, as I ask you these questions, I notice, you keep smiling."

"It's a defense mechanism," Joey parroted.

Dunleavy asked about the shooting.

"Tell him you love your wife," Dominic said.

"I love my wife," Joey parroted. "I love my wife with all my heart." He gazed sincerely into the camera before reaching for his water cup. "How was that?" he asked with the smile of a pro.

When Dunleavy asked Joey if there was anything he had to say to Mary Jo, Dominic stopped the interview again. He brought Joey over, about two feet from where I was seated, and whispered, "When Steve asks you what you have to say to Mary Jo, I want you to think of your mother, when she died when you were eleven, and I think that way you might get some tears in your eyes."

"No, no, that's not my image," Joey said.

"Then look down so it looks like you're crying."

"No, no, I got somethin better," Joey said.

Dunleavy asked him: "Do you have any last words to say to Mary Jo?"

Joey shook his head. "I have no last words. This is a beginning."

The time had come for Dunleavy to ask if Joey did indeed have an affair with Amy Fisher.

"That's a hard one," Joey said. He looked to the bedroom door, behind which Mary Jo spoke on the phone. Irma wasn't watching her as she was supposed to. "I'm not gonna be married on Monday."

Dominic told Joey to admit fucking Amy Fisher once, and once only. When Joey said what he was told, Dominic grabbed my notepad. *"You got your money's worth,"* he wrote. *"You got your come shot."*

We left discouraged that Sunday, but after a lot of shouts on the phone to Dominic, we got another try at Mary Jo on Wednesday. This time we were at Dunleavy's house on Lido Beach, with three cameras for an interview with, and confrontation between, Joey and Mary Jo.

The couple realized they were going to lose the $500,000 if they didn't come through.

We got our come shot.

The first of the Buttafuoco shows aired on November twelfth. The Pizza Hut Corporation announced that the week garnered its highest volume of home pizza deliveries. They attributed the sales to the number of people staying in to watch the interview.

Once again, *A Current Affair* was on a roll. Dunleavy admitted to Peter that he'd indeed backed the wrong man. Dickie was a disappointment. Still, he wasn't happy I was using Rafael as my adviser and disregarding many of his more lurid ideas.

Peter Faiman took me for a drink at Asia.

"I'll be honest with you, mate. You're doing a great job. But you can't have Rafael as your second-in-command. He antagonizes too many people."

I'd come to divide the world between people who understood Raf and people who didn't. "Look," I said, "I'd trade twenty of the reporters in that place for one Raf. Raf is—"

Faiman looked at me deadpan. "Are you going to talk to me? Or are you going to yell a speech?"

"Oh, sorry, mate."

"That's all right. I understand. Now look. I spoke to Rupert," he said. "He wants to thank you for what you're doing. He thinks you're doing a great job. And he agreed with me when I told him I want you to be executive producer."

"Wow. I don't know."

"We'll help you. You won't be left on your own."

"I don't know, Peter. I enjoy the work. That's what I do best. I'd hate to be in a job where I have to spend the whole time going over budgets and being in corporate meetings."

"All care and no worries," he said. "I know about that. But you'll find you can never have creative control unless you have control over the budget and everything else."

"What's wrong with this world?" Raf stood at the bar at Tommy McGrath's and shook his head one too many times. I walked back from the jukebox where'd I'd played "Sweet Child O'Mine" one too many times myself. "Guns 'n' Roses, mate," I said. "This reminds me of L.A. Remember Slash?"

Raf laughed at his own stupidity. "What's wrong with this world?" He studied the bottom of his glass. "While you were playing your teenage songs, I began writing your book. I always thought I'd write *my* book. Now I know I'll wind up writing yours."

"Yeah, when I'm on the sidewalk in front of the Viper Room."

Raf couldn't believe I didn't want the executive producer job. He looked off toward the far wall and dictated the first few lines. "'I was approaching my fifty-third year. Burt Kearns was somewhere between thirty-seven and forty. He would change the date according to the situation. Steve Dunleavy was somewhere between fifty-seven and sixty...'"

"And the Afrikaaner says, ya, sergeant, ya, I was driving my car and hit two kaffirs in the road. One went through the windscreen and the other bounced off the fender and flew two hundred feet into the bush. I panicked, sir, I did, and buried them both."

It was the first week of December. I was approaching my thirty-ninth year, killing a Stoli and tonic while Dunleavy told a long joke at a big round table in Elaine's, the shabbily glamourous saloon on Second Avenue and

88th Street, legendary for its literary and celebrity clientele in the sixties and seventies.

Sitting to Dunleavy's right was young Shannah Goldner, step-daughter of "Ted" Williams, tabloid journo and Dunleavy's best friend until he died of alcoholism twenty years earlier, at thirty-nine. Shannah had been hired by *A Current Affair* as Dunleavy's minder, making sure he was pulled from the pubs in time for work. She also had a fine cinematic eye and was finally using it. She was with us for the Buttafuoco debacle and produced the series.

Shannah and Dunleavy had been dining at Elaine's a year earlier when they spied legendarily eccentric rock 'n' roll record producer Phil Spector, a colleague of Shannah's late father, fellow legendary producer George Goldner. Spector weaved to their table and accused Dunleavy of bedding the young woman. Ever chivalrous, Dunleavy responded by bloodying the little man's nose.

"'You say you hit these two blacks, sir, with your car? One went through the windscreen and the other bounced off and flew two hundred feet into the bush?'"

On this night, Dunleavy spoke in a spot-on South African accent as he drew out the joke about the Afrikaaner who showed up at a police station to confess his crime. It was typical Dunleavy, a joke whose setting could be transferred to any part of the world and the subjects to the victimized race peculiar to that location. In Australia, it's the two Aboriginals bonged into the Outback; in America, the redneck and the blacks.

In Elaine's, it was loud enough for the man seated alone at the next table to hear. Sam Shepard, the actor and playwright, couldn't hide his amazement.

"'Yes, Yes, I confess.' 'Hmm,'"—Dunleavy was in the voice of the sergeant now— "'I see no great problem here. The kaffir who went through the windscreen, we charge him with breaking and entering. And the one who was knocked two hundred feet into the bush, we charge with leaving the scene of an accident!'"

We all roared, though we'd heard it before. Dunleavy was deep into one of his drinking cycles. The pressures of the $500,000 Buttafuoco interview combined with the flux at *A Current Affair* had spun him into a two-week binge in which he'd been drunk pretty much constantly. In the thick of the bustling celebrity hangout, Dunleavy was in his own liquid, laugh-filled world. He paid no heed to Sam Shepard, and he didn't notice when actress Valerie Perrine took the table alongside. She and Shepard shared conversation while Dunleavy bellowed.

At one point, Kim Basinger swept into the room, luminous and beautiful in the most movie star of ways. She swept in another direction when she saw Dunleavy. He didn't notice.

By the time the food came, I was ready for Dunleavy to do something really embarrassing, possibly start a fight with the professorial Shepard.

Then he began to choke on his steak.

We all thought he was joking at first, until Dunleavy's gray pallor darkened to an actual blue. I was up and squeezing my way between chairs to attempt the Heimlich when Dunleavy coughed it up himself: a nice gooey gob of steak ejected into his red handkerchief, trailed by a long, thick rope of mucus and saliva. He wiped off his chin, put the handkerchief and meat in his pocket, and to Sam Shepard's obvious horror, resumed his drinking.

We settled up the bill and headed for the door, leaving with a nod and an amused look from Shepard, and recognizing a hint of the saloon's past glory days in the person of writer Gay Talese at one of the front tables. Someone said he was covering the Bobbitt penis trial for the *New Yorker*.

Outside, Dunleavy looked down the avenue, perhaps remembering his most embarrassing and life-threatening moment after leaving this restaurant on a snowy night not too many years ago. He and a female companion stopped to make love on a snowdrift when they were run over by a city snowplow. Dunleavy suffered a broken leg.

Tonight, legless, he accepted my help into a taxi and we headed downtown. "Did you notice Valerie Perrine behind you, mate?" I asked.

"Valerie Perrine the actress?"

"Yeah. The actress. She was sitting right behind you."

"Mate, I gang banged her years ago!"

Les Hinton looked at me with one eye.

"If you and Brennan have dreams about sitting on the deck of your house in Malibu and making millions in Hollywood, I can't help you. But if you want to be a good, hardworking newsman, I have an offer I believe is generous and fair."

Les was another former editor of the *Star* who'd been elevated all the way to the extraordinary position of chairman and chief executive officer of the Fox Television stations. He was based in Los Angeles and had flown to New York City on Rupert Murdoch's orders to sign me up as *A Current Affair*'s executive producer.

Les was a tall, youthful gent in his forties, with tousled, graying hair and an unhinged left eye that stared off behind his modish glasses toward a far wall no matter which way he was looking. The eye definitely had potential as a management tool. It certainly put the other person at a disadvantage. I, for one, wasn't sure where to look.

Les was offering me a deal. Two hundred thousand dollars a year, with a five or ten percent increase in the second year of a two-year contract. I could sign on for one year if I chose. I told Les he'd have to speak to my agent. I wanted a hundred thousand dollars more and written guarantees that I'd be able to turn certain *A Current Affair* stories into TV movies.

"Mate, we're talking about reputations and we're talking about the future and we're talking about your self-destructive tendencies." Raf lectured me at the Asia Bar. "You've got to take this job. This is the big chance for all of us."

I knew it was. I knew Rupert Murdoch was putting a lot of trust in me. Muriel Reis had written him a letter opposing my appointment as executive producer because I'd lied in a deposition during the Rob Lowe fiascos of 1989.

Murdoch tossed the letter and told Les Hinton to get me signed.

There was more to it, though. Aware of my hesitance, knowing I'd be involved in the day-to-day running of *A Current Affair* and wary of a potential loose cannon, Faiman and Hinton made it clear I'd be supported by a co-executive producer: Ian Rae.

"You and me are gonna be great friends, mate," Ian promised me. "We're gonna have lunch together, we're gonna drink together. We'll spend lots of time together. We'll be pals, me and you."

The next day, Ian fired ten freelance workers, including four on whom I'd relied to get the show on the air through sweeps. When I asked him to reconsider, he refused to budge. That's what I thought of when I thought about the future. After taxes, I'd be living on only a few grand more than I was making at *Hard Copy* with all care and no worries. It would be a struggle every day.

My kidneys were hurting. Every night in the bar, Dunleavy was punching me in the lower back and calling me a baby when I told him it hurt. It was his way of letting me know who was in charge, his way of getting me back for listening to Rafael. He was taking it out on my sides.

"Man, what does it matter?" I said to Raf. "I don't want to spend the next year with these people. It's gonna be a fight the whole time. It's not worth it."

"It *is* worth it," Raf said.

"Mate, you know what's worth it? That kid River Phoenix. What a way to fucking go. John Belushi dies in a hotel off the Sunset Strip? This kid dies on the fucking sidewalk in front of Johnny Depp's nightclub, puking on Christina Applegate on the fucking Sunset Strip. Mate, that's impressive."

For the past two months, I'd been living on chicken sandwiches and coffee, spending every night at that fucking Asia or Tommy McGrath's drinking beer and tequila and vodkas and tonics and feeling the twinges in my lower back like someone was squeezing the fucking lime juice out of my kidneys by hand.

I was killing myself all over again, bunking in a sublet apartment in the far West Village, stopping on the way home at a fake bikers' bar in the meat district called Hogs & Heifers, where sexy female bartenders danced on the bar whenever someone played "The Devil Went Down to Georgia" on a jukebox that was stuffed with George Jones, and was the only place where you could still get Pabst Blue Ribbon beer.

As Ian Rae spoke and Les spoke and Raf spoke, I thought of my Porsche, waiting covered in Peter Brennan's driveway in Beverly Hills. I envisioned driving with the roof folded in the back seat, the CD player blasting, heading east on the Sunset Strip, taking that curve past Tower Records and accelerating up the hill toward Sunset Plaza.

"You're stupid not to take this opportunity," Raf said.

I struck a match and held the palm of my hand over the flame. "I'm an outlaw," I responded. "On a steel horse I ride. And I'm wanted. Dead or alive."

"You're an asshole is what you are."

Raf and I continued our dialogue Saturday afternoon on a long walk through the city. We were approaching Washington Square Park in Greenwich Village when I noticed Dick Fisher pulling camera gear from the back of a truck.

Dick had been to Berlin with us. He was one of the cameramen on the Buttafuoco shoot. "Hey, look," I said. He's shooting *film*."

"Who cares."

We walked over and Dick introduced us to his assistant. "We're shooting that movie I was telling you about. I'm cinematographer."

Raf turned his head and looked into the distance.

"What are you shooting today?"

"Just a scene with two people walking through the park. If everybody shows up." Someone caught his eye. "Here he is." A handsome Irish kid in his twenties was under the arch. "Yo!"

We knew the kid, the writer, director, and star of the little project. He was the son of our pal the police spokesman and PR man. He jogged over and shook hands as he helped unload the gear. "I know your father," Raf said.

"Yeah, he's helping us with this little thing."

Raf and I walked on through the park. "See, mate," I said, "that's what we should be doing. We write all these scripts, we oughta shoot our own movie just like them."

"They're wasting their time."

"They're doing it."

"They're dreaming. You think Hollywood's gonna let them in? Dick Fisher? That kid? It's not gonna happen. He's wasting his father's money. You oughta be thinking about *A Current Affair*..."

Raf and I walked on toward Soho, leaving Edward Burns, Jr. to direct another scene for *The Brothers McMullen*.

---◆---

That week, *Variety* ran an item about *A Current Affair*.

> Although the newsmag has been far off its previous year's average in recent comparisons, it has risen more than a full rating point since it underwent a retooling just before the start of the sweeps and—at least through the previous week—leads *Copy* and *Edition* in the 18-34 and 18-49 demos.

It was funny to think that just a few months earlier, I was praying for another chance like Steven Tyler of Aerosmith, who made a wad of money, blew it all, and was allowed another go.

Now my chance was right in front of me.

I had a sitdown with Brennan at Tom McGrath's. From the time my name was first bandied about to take over the show, he'd stayed out of it. "Maybe Burt wants the chance to do it on his own," he said.

I told him I was considering turning down a job that people would kill for. I couldn't see myself spending the next year in the trenches, drinking myself to death while fighting all the different camps, doing it myself because so many of these people didn't get it when, in the end, they'd kill the show anyway.

"I only got into this because I needed the money. I did it for the money, mate, and it all went out of control. It happens every time you do something just for the money."

"You might want your own show, mate."

"It won't be my own show. It'll be Ian Rae's show. He's too erratic. One day we're best mates and the next morning he fires my key people."

"You're right."

"Fuck it. I'll take my chances in L.A."

"Ah, mate, we'll get some things happening in Los Angeles. Some ideas look good. *We'll have some fun.*"

I told them on a Friday I wasn't taking the job. Poor Ian Rae, home sick with the flu, phoned me in the office.

"Les Hinton just called to tell me that your agent told him you have decided you would rather remain in Los Angeles and don't want the job. Is this true?"

The steam was coming out of his ears, but he was being nice to me because he had to.

"Yeah, Ian. I'm sorry."

That afternoon, I told the staff that they'd have a new boss on Monday. No one believed me.

When I walked into the Racing Club, Dunleavy ran over. "Mate, mate, I've worked it out! I think I've worked out a deal!"

"It's too late, mate. I'm gone."

"No!" Dunleavy let out a wail and stood on the verge of violence, so Raf and I walked down the hill to the Sign of the Dove to have a drink away from everyone else.

Danny Meenan from the assignment desk stopped in and we sat at the bar for a final round.

Raf raised a rueful toast. "Always stick to your dreams. Never waver. Don't look back, look forward."

Danny added: "And remember, don't sit on vinyl with shorts on."

Raf was miserable. He felt he'd lost another chance to get back at the world. I felt bad because in the course of a month, so many people had become little kids to me, like poor Dunleavy, all alcohol-crazed, running around trying to patch up the deal on his own.

On Monday, Bill Ridley was flown in on the Concorde from London to take command of the show once again. Shannah told me it was a matter of days before things were back to the shambles of the past, with folks sitting around and Heidi writing the show again with her feet up on her desk doing crossword puzzles and Dunleavy running about doing screaming day-of-air pieces every morning and getting on the air as often as possible.

Poor Raf was out in the cold. With Peter and me gone, there was no reason for anyone to talk to him anymore.

Later that week, Peter Faiman called to say he was secretly glad I didn't take the job. He was negotiating with Howard Stern to take over Chevy Chase's late night spot on Fox. The show would take on the form of a news broadcast, he said, with someone reporting the news the way Robin Quivers did on the radio show, and Howard commenting on it.

"He speaks for the masses, the common man," Faiman said. "News is the one thing that's not exploited on television. It's all contrived comedy and comedy is tough to do."

He wanted me to be the producer.

I told Faiman that Stern's was the only show that could keep me in New York. I'd know something the second week of January when Stern decided if it was a go.

The triple black Mercedes 420 SEL slowed across from the Christmas tree lot at the wind-whipped corner of Charles and West Street. The tinted passenger side window rolled down automatically and the driver leaned toward the figure bracing himself against the frigid air skating across the river from New Jersey.

"Mate! Hop in!"

I got in and rolled the window up against the cold as Wayne took a right and made his way farther downtown. It was my last night in New York and we were having a final drink or ten.

We wound up, poetically, at Wayne's favorite strip bar, the Baby Doll Lounge, a corner dive on Sixth Avenue below Canal Street with signs in the window that actually said GO GO and TOPLESS.

There was a dingy bar and two low stages, separated from the aisle by a railing that gave the place a disturbing similarity to the cattle stall section at a state fair.

We bought light beers and watched the women dance. There were no My Bare Ladies among them.

We got back in the Mercedes and drove around lower Manhattan.

"You're lucky you're getting out, mate," Wayne said. "I'll tell ya, after all this Son of Sam bullshit, I'm going, too."

"Where to?"

"I don't know. I'm sitting on this Sam special. I'm fifteen grand in the hole right now and I gotta get something happening. Maybe Australia. Maybe I'll hide out in Sydney for a while, I don't know. But I'm gone."

We were on Sixth Avenue above 23rd Street. Wayne was pulling up in front of a classic old-style journo's hangout called Billy's Topless. There were no My Bare Ladies there, either.

The next day, I was on an American Airlines flight with Rafael, heading to San Diego, where he was mopping up the last of his *A Current Affair* stories and I would head off to Los Angeles to crank up my Porsche and see what Brennan and I could come up with next.

Wayne left town a few days later. When he resurfaced, he would be truly born again, living as a country squire on eight acres of good wooded land on a mountaintop outside Nashville, Tennessee, less than a mile from the home of George Jones.

Sometimes life just works out that way.

From Weekly *Variety*, December 27, 1993:

Affair exec take powder

HOLLYWOOD Three of the top executives running Twentieth TV's *A Current Affair* are out, replaced by a vet News Corp. exec with little TV experience.

Consultants Peter Brennan and Burt Kearns, whose bid to revamp the tabmag failed to pay off in ratings dividends in November sweeps, have exited the series along with senior producer Dick McWilliams.

Twentieth is bringing in longtime News Corp exec Bill Ridley, a Fleet Street vet who served stints as an editor of the *Boston Herald* and *Star* magazine, to oversee *Affair*...

Officially, Ridley will be the tabmag's second-in-command behind exec producer Ian Rae. But *Affair* staffers say Kearns—not Rae—was sitting in the exec producer chair during the sweeps and they expect Ridley to be there too...

Brennan, who was the show's creator and executive producer, had been expected to move on to other projects following sweeps...

Kearns, however, had been considered the odds-on-favorite to take over the show from Rae this month.

Fox Television chairman-CEO Les Hinton insisted that Brennan and Kearns "only intended to be there on a temporary basis." Other sources, however, suggested that Kearns wanted a great deal of money to take over the reins of the show. Rae, another News Corp vet, is said to have put up a fight, so Kearns left the New York-based program for a writing career in Hollywood...

In the same issue:

Crusaders: an affair to reckon with

HOLLYWOOD *The Crusaders*, a three-month-old weekly advocacy series dedicated to solving the problems of the little guy, has brought in a crusader of its own. Former *Current Affair* exec producer John Terenzio has jumped on board as a consultant...

CHAPTER TWENTY-SIX:
TO LIVE AND BE REBORN IN L.A.

We got a call from somebody who offered us pictures of
River Phoenix's body in the coffin—thank you, no thank
you, I don't even want to hear about it. And they faxed
them. It's like, 'Who's going to the fax and throw it away?'
—*Hard Copy's* Diane Dimond, *USA Today*

The Porsche was serviced, washed, waxed and rolling again. The roof was folded in the back seat and the CD player blasting as I headed east on the Sunset Strip, taking that curve past Tower Records and accelerating up the hill toward Sunset Plaza.

Raf was in the passenger seat, bitter in the second month of 1994. He'd been let go from *A Current Affair* and was altogether frustrated that Peter and I had wasted such a golden opportunity.

I lowered the music a moment. "So where you wanna go?"

"Let's go to the El Torito bar."

"Aw, mate, it's empty. You know that. It's always empty."

"The Nikko then." Raf was staying at the Japanese hotel on La Cienega. Brennan and I had rented a room there early one Easter Sunday morning a couple of years back. It was after closing time on the holiest day of the year; we spent the two hundred dollars just so we could raid the room's mini-bar. I regarded it as my most sinful act.

The Nikko bar was dead, though; a stark garden with a waterfall that made you have to visit the men's room every twenty minutes.

"C'mon, mate. That's always empty. It's boring. Let's have some fucking fun. Let's go to Sushi on Sunset."

"I'm not spending money! Fuck that!" We rolled past the popular sushi restaurant next to the Body Shop strip club and Raf sneered in the direction of the CD player. "What is this music?"

"Snoop Doggy Dogg, mate. It's my new theme song."

"Put on some George Jones."

"You got it." I fumbled for the music, approaching the palatial headquarters of the Directors' Guild and the corner of Fairfax.

"Genghis Cohen," Raf suggested.

"You hate that place." I made the right anyway. "You hate the music. You hate the bartender. And you complain about the food."

"Let's just go there." Raf gritted his teeth and shook his head. "I can't take it. I hate this boring town."

Boring? Los Angeles was literally still shaking from its most exciting event since the riots: a major 6.7 earthquake only weeks before. Freeway overpasses crashed to the streets; buildings crumbled; houses slid down mountainsides. The quake, in its own way, had brought the disparate Angelenos together in a way the riots were expected to but hadn't. People were suddenly alive, nervous, and aware; thinking twice before entering buildings, making sure not to stop their cars under highways or bridges when the light turned red; and when there was an aftershock—and there were hundreds, even thousands of varying degrees—eyes met and strangers exchanged jittery and embarrassed smiles when they realized the flash of fear they had betrayed.

There were cracks everywhere.

Rafael was angry, though; not because of what he'd missed out on, but because of what he might possibly attain. Earlier in the week, Peter and I had met up with Ron Ziskin and Shukri Ghalayini, a couple of guys who ran Four Point Entertainment, producing shows like *American Gladiators* and MTV's *Sandblast*. They'd wanted to do something with Peter Brennan, and off the top of his head at the restaurant downstairs from their offices, he suggested a show featuring Rafael. Raf would travel the country, finding stories and changing lives. "Sort of a reality *Hitchhiker*," was the pitch.

"Rafael Abramovitz?" Shukri was surprised.

"We're meeting with him this afternoon," said Ziskin.

We didn't know about Raf's plans. We did have a deal, though; just like that. Shukri and Ziskin liked it.

After lunch, Peter and I rushed off to page Raf, to fill him in before he showed up at Four Point, insulted someone, and blew the deal before he even knew he had one.

"What is this music?" Raf was still grumbling as we walked into Genghis Cohen, the strip mall kosher Chinese restaurant near the corner of Melrose that shared a parking lot with the Centerfold newsstand where Slash worked before he joined Guns 'n' Roses. The place was just as we'd left it. Behind the bar ahead of us was the miniature bottle-blonde bodybuilder who Raf had taken a dislike to in our last go-round in L.A. To the right was the Genghis

Cantina, the folk and lite jazz showroom and "industry" hangout.

We turned away from the music and took a booth in the dining room. Raf ordered the same garlic chicken and broccoli he ordered every time, a shot of Johnny Walker Black, and a pot of tea.

"That bartender has to be the most stupid woman in the world," Raf said unprompted, as the sound of acoustic guitar wafted in with the smells of mediocre Chinese food. "I hate that woman. And this music. What is this music? It's the worst music I've ever heard. They should put up a sign warning people that the sound of the music seeps into the dining area. Look at these people. In the turtleneck there. Is that a man or a woman? Look at these women in their stretched underwear with their big asses. This is the most boring town in the world. I hate this place."

"Can you pass the rice?" Raf's complaints had become as calming as a relaxation tape, but I wasn't buying them anymore. It took all this time for me to realize why this city had seemed such a dull place when Raf and I cruised around in the *Hard Copy* days.

I was with Raf.

I had a new attitude in my second coming to Los Angeles. This was a second chance to make it in a town that had spit me out.

Raf didn't want to stop in at the bar after dinner. "Let's go to the Bel Age," he ordered when we were back in the car.

"You hate that place."

"Fuck it. Fuck it."

Nabi was glad to see us at the Bel Age. Raf wasn't glad to see him. The drinks were too expensive. "This is boring," he said after one or two. "You're on your own; I'm out of here. You pay."

Raf went back to the Nikko. I only had to drive around the corner to my latest home: an apartment a few buildings away, on a hill in the middle of the area they called the West Hollywood Swish Alps. The building had its own gym, maid service and, on the roof, a pool that I looked forward to using until a xeroxed flyer was slipped under my door, reminding tenants not to swim if they were leaking infectious bodily fluids.

A Current Affair had kept an apartment in the same building back in the early years of the show. Their lease ended shortly after a crew used the flat to re-enact a murder scene. While everyone was off on a lunch break, a maid came in to change the towels, freaked when she saw fake blood splashed all over the walls, and before you knew it, half the West Hollywood Sheriff's Department was crawling through the building.

My apartment was on the fourth floor, with a balcony overlooking the L.A. basin. The studio where Dr. Dre recorded Snoop Doggy Dogg was at the end of the street. At the top of the hill, on the corner of Sunset just above the Bel Age, was the Viper Room. The notorious nightclub, from which bouncers set out River Phoenix to die, had become my latest local.

I wasn't returning to New York to produce Howard Stern after all. His late-night show on Fox didn't pan out. Everyone was blaming the pay-per-view television special he unleashed on New Year's Eve, a raunchy exercise that opened with Stern descending from the rafters on a commode and went deeper into the toilet from there. Word was Rupert Murdoch's beautiful wife Anna had seen or heard about Stern's onstage acts of perversity and degradation and forced her husband to cut off all negotiations.

Faiman told me that simply wasn't the case. Stern had notified Rupert and the Fox team of his intentions in advance. The deal's cancellation had more to do with Stern's fear of failing in a new medium, or, more likely, reports he earned about seven million dollars for his one-night stand on New Year's Eve. An entire season at Fox wouldn't bring him anything near that.

Stern suggested that Fox simply videotape his morning radio show and replay an hour of highlights at night. Fox didn't go for it, but the fledgling E! Entertainment cable channel did. The medium was obscure enough to pose no detriment to Stern's career if the show tanked, but indeed, the show quickly became E!'s biggest success and helped sell the channel in markets around the country.

Peter Brennan invited me to a lunch meeting at DelMonico's seafood restaurant on Pico Boulevard. A couple of guys from Fox were developing a tabloid TV sitcom starring Matt Freuer, the Canadian actor who played Max Headroom. They were looking for insights into the business and wanted to use Brennan for fodder.

He warned me not to give up too much to Dennis Klein and his partner, but once Klein mentioned he'd helped create not only *The Larry Sanders Show* but *Buffalo Bill*, which starred Dabney Coleman as an irascible TV host, Brennan said he'd give them whatever they wanted. *Buffalo Bill* was his favorite show ever.

The sitcom veterans sat rapt as Brennan wove tale after tale about the wild times and characters of tabloid TV. Then again, maybe they were amazed by Brennan's appearance. Rushing out of the house to make the meeting, he'd shaved on the run, and in the process sliced off a thick chip of his lip. He was spilling blood uncontrollably, all over his luncheon salad and onto the tablecloth, turning a white Kleenex red and starting on the napkin because he hadn't been able to find a styptic pencil.

The guys from Fox just laughed. Here was Mr. Blood and Guts Tabloid TV, bleeding all over the booth.

Brennan told them they could use the bit for their show.

"Mate, I can't believe it, that Dennis, he created *Buffalo Bill!*" Brennan had stopped bleeding, but he was still gushing about meeting the creator of his favorite TV show. We were back at the Formosa, where Tim Burton was holding court at the big corner table by the door.

"I was thinking," I said, "I should give them *The Fortune Garden*."

"Fuckin A. Why not?"

Raf put down his Johnny Walker Black. "That's stupid."

"Why? These guys actually get things made. Let's put it in their hands."

"Take my name off it."

"Mate," I said, "you're being negative."

"No, I'm not."

"You're getting bitter and twisted."

"That you're right about."

"Raf, I can't have that. I can't have somebody saying, 'No, I can't' all the time, when I know 'Yes, I can.'"

Later that night, I garaged the Porsche, hiked up the hill alone to the Viper Room, and set myself down at the tiny, neglected bar at the foot of the stairs, tended by a dirty angel of a beauty named Shannon, with a heart-shaped face and cascading ringlets of golden hair. I'd sit for hours watching her move, commenting on the ebb and flo of hip celebrity, and easing the conversation in another direction when she mentioned her boyfriend was a musician who played the upstairs room every Tuesday night.

The Viper Room should have spelled death to me, but instead it offered a sense of rejuvenation. This was the place where River Phoenix kicked into convulsions on a bad cocktail of heroin and cocaine, the place from which he was dragged foaming and twitching to die in an awful head-banging display out on the Strip. His death was the first major story I had tackled on my return to *A Current Affair*, and at times I was so fed up with the struggle and my lack of purpose that I envied the kid and the blaze of glory in which he went.

Now the Viper Room was my black-light coffin, my own angel of death was serving me double-strength vodkas and calling me "hon," and somehow I was feeling more alive than ever.

Shannon and I talked about F. Scott Fitzgerald, another drinker beaten by L.A., and his stories about Pat Hobby, the washed-up screenwriter doing whatever to make a few bucks in a town that considered him damaged goods. I knew she had a thing for F. Scott Fitzgerald. She had his name tattooed on her arm.

Peter Brennan brought me to Australia in February, to write and produce a pilot for an hour-long tabloid show with his partner, Peter Sutton.

It was high summer in Sydney. We worked long into the afternoons and drank deep into the mornings, impressed by the country's strides in making it easier and safer to stay pissed drunk twenty-four hours a day. Some local Mormons had started up a lucrative service called "We Drive You." A drunk could call from the pub and two abstaining missionaries would show up; one would drive the drinker home in his car, while the other followed to retrieve his partner.

Warwick Moss, the poet, actor, and host of the Sutton's Australian show *The Extraordinary*, came up with a twist on the game. He'd pay the Mormons extra to drive him and his car on a pub crawl from one end of the city to the other, then bribe them beyond their religious forbearance to allow him to drive the many miles up the coast to his home on Whale Beach.

When we were wrapped with the pilot, Brennan took me for a drive to his home, to visit his mother and brothers in the south Australian seaside village of Huskisson.

The three Brothers Brennan gathered on the outdoor patio of the Husky Pub. Their resemblance was uncanny. Yet even more striking was how Peter's two brothers represented the conflicting forces of his soul and the struggle that could have pulled him in either direction.

Lorrie was short and all solid muscle, with a chinstrap beard and tight, curly hair. He was the brother Peter had gone into business with so many years before on the *Sutherland Shire Seer*; the one who stayed behind and published his own newspaper, growing into the family man Peter might have remained had he sought rewards no farther than the shores of Oz.

Alan was what Peter Brennan may have become had his adventuresome side overshadowed his journalistic genius: a skinny, battered old salt with a droopy mustache and a long scar running down his chest, smoking on a single lung ever since a mistaken diagnosis of cancer had him cracked open like a lobster for unnecessary surgery.

Alan ran a small cleaning business in town. He'd recently moved to Huskisson and into a shack in Lorrie's backyard after years in Manila, where he ran one of the best whore bars on Mabini Street.

Alan had found a wife in Manila and brought her back to Australia with him. Only days earlier, she'd run away.

Mum sat at a picnic table with a bag of crisps and her shandy of lemonade and beer, looking serenely at her three surviving sons, together again. If only John could be here too, her beloved Johnny, the firstborn whose heart stopped at forty.

The brothers took positions in various sections of the open patio. Al sat close to his mother and sipped his beer gratefully. Lorrie stood with one foot on the low wall and peered out toward the peaceful dunes of the pristine Seven Mile Beach. Peter leaned against a pole, knocking off another cigarette and Touhey's Red.

The breeze was warm. The air was ocean pure. We were in a place so close to paradise. The brothers collected the silence that I at first took to be anger, friction, or at least resentment among them. I was mistaken. Peter Brennan was home. They were at peace.

They were Australians.

"So, Peter tells me you ran a nightclub in Manila." I sat across from Alan in the Huskisson recreation center, watching Peter and Lorrie play snooker.

He looked me in the eye and snarled. "I ran a whorehouse. Why don't you just come out and say it?"

"Okay, yeah, well, Peter didn't get so specific." I was anxious to hear more. "It sounds like quite a life. What did you do?"

"I ran the bar."

"Where did the girls come from? Were they like sex slaves?"

"They came from the country. Villages. They came on their own."

"Did they have pimps running them?"

"They had a mamasan."

"So are you glad you came to Huskisson?"

"Moving here was the worst mistake of my life."

"So—"

Alan's younger brother Peter sat himself next to us. "So, Allie, what do you think?"

"I think your friend asks too many facking questions." He narrowed his eyes threateningly. "He's like a facking cop."

I was convinced Alan Brennan was going to kill me. He was supposed to drive me to Lorrie's house, but he was off in another direction, staring ahead in determined silence, the cleaning equipment rattling in the back of his small car. I relaxed only when he pulled into the parking lot of the Husky Pub.

Inside over beers, he had something to get off his broken chest.

"I know you look down on me, and I'll tell ya, I don't give a fack," he growled. His face inched closer to mine. "I might not be educated and I might not be a fackin success but I'm facking proud of who I am and where I've been."

We were almost touching foreheads. I'd recognized his anger and was pissed enough to try some psychology.

"Who the *fuck* do you think you are?" I growled back. "Peter Brennan is a brother to me. And all the time I've worked with him, all we hear about is his fucking big brother Al who owns the fucking whorehouse bar in Manila. You're a fucking *legend*, mate."

"Peter's my brother," he said. "I love my brother."

"And he loves you. He's fucking proud of you."

"Yeah. Let's play some pool."

We played some pool and drank some more. When we made it to Lorrie's, Al stopped off in his shack and returned with something in his hands. "You're so fackin interested in my fackin life, maybe this'll give ya some help."

He tried to suppress a smile. He handed me a book.

Manila, copyright 1993, Alan Brennan, 344 pages.

> Of all the beautiful places in the Philippines, it's got me beat why I chose Manila. Then again, would I be any happier anywhere else? I doubt it. At least here, there's so much happening it leaves little or no time to dwell too much on the past...

Back in L.A., with the lights of downtown twinkling clear in the distance, Brennan, Rafael and I sat in my new apartment constructing Raf's pilot. We were calling it *Detour*. Raf stole the name from his daughter, who was working on a pilot with the publisher of the local *Detour* magazine. The script, we all wrote together:

> I made a detour once that changed me forever.
> And I did it at a time when I thought I'd seen it all.I was down in Mississippi, heading toward some story about a doctor who'd stepped over the line.
> I got delayed in a town called Belzona.
> And on the front page of the paper that day was a story about an execution that was gonna happen that very day.
> So I made a detour to the prison...

Each story would be told by Rafael in his inimitable style. Each would seem to be heading in a particular direction, then take a surprising detour at a crucial moment—a twist leading to a surprising conclusion.

We took a number of stories Raf shot for *A Current Affair* and *Hard Copy* and rewrote capsulized versions for the sell tape, constructing each around a pivotal moment other producers were bound to overlook. "There are stories all over the country," Raf's script concluded. "They happen every day. But the ones that stick with you are the ones that take an unexpected turn. The difference is recognizing the signs."

About an hour and a half east of Los Angeles, off the highway to Las Vegas near the high desert town of Lancaster, is a place called Lake Mirage, a wide expanse of flat cracked clay as far as the eye can see. Car commercials, music videos, and *Star Trek* episodes are filmed on the dry lakebed; the perfect stand-in for a distant, arid planet, it was even better for the shot of Raf's '67 Mustang driving in from nowhere through a cloud of white dust.

Raf and I had once driven a rented white Cadillac out there on another ride home from Las Vegas. We'd parked in the dead heart of the place and when Raf got out to look around, the wind picked up his hat and blew it toward the next county.

"*Fuck!*"

I'd laughed so hard I could barely point the camera as Raf chased the skipping Resistol until it vanished in the dusty horizon.

This time, we rode out with Brennan and a crew at dawn on a Saturday to shoot enough video to cover what we'd written for the pilot. The area held a variety of locations, from Joshua Tree desert to snow-topped mountains to lush farmland. We could make it seem as if Raf was driving across the country.

Raf wasn't happy that morning because Shukri and Ziskin had budgeted only a single day's shoot. Brennan and I accepted it; if we stuck with the plan, we'd be done by evening. Raf thought he deserved two days to make it right, and he was going to prove it by directing the crew to shoot every scene that caught his fancy, ignoring the shot list we needed to fill, including the entire script, which Raf would recite standing at a bar.

By late morning, with the sun moving across the sky, I spoke to him privately while he posed in his Mustang. "Mate, we've all got a lot of ideas, but we need to get some specific shots. Why don't we all try to agree before we have the crew break down the gear and reset each time. We won't be using a lot of this."

Raf snapped. "Who the fuck are you?" He stared me down from under his four-beaver hat as if he really were the leather-jacketed cowboy he was dressed up as. "You know, what the fuck did you even come along for, anyway? You're not adding anything to this shoot."

"Thanks, mate." I walked away off into the middle of the vast desert plain, knowing then that Raf's show would never get off the ground. He'd make sure of it. The indignities Raf felt he'd suffered at the hands of fools had boiled over. He'd gone out on a limb and pulled off the journalistic coup of the decade with his Amy Fisher ambush, yet he was vilified for it. He set the stage for our arrival at *A Current Affair* and found himself in reach of ultimate power—only to have me ignore his heartfelt counsel and turn down the chance. He couldn't believe that Peter Brennan and I gave it up to set up camp in this godforsaken phony city of Los Angeles.

Back in the real world, Olympic skater Tonya Harding was in hot water because her ex-husband had paid a thug to whack the knee of her competitor, Nancy Kerrigan. *Inside Edition* paid a great deal of money to accompany Tonya to the Olympics and tell her story with as much sympathy as a straight face could muster.

Bill Ridley and the gang at *A Current Affair* counterattacked by buying up her ex-husband, a weaselly bloke named Gillooly. Tens of thousands of dollars went to the man who would soon plead guilty to engineering the attack on the hapless young woman.

In TV terms, *A Current Affair* "owned" Gillooly, so one would assume they'd feel free to treat him as they wished, make points for their reporter by confronting him on the tough questions, and stand in for the rest of America who'd like to take a whack at the son of a bitch themselves.

Instead, it was a sympathetic Mike Watkiss looking on as Gillooly accused his ex-wife of being in on the attack and predicted she'd use her "charm" to get off.

"I'll always have great feelings for Tonya. Tonya is the finest skater that ever walked the earth, male or female," Gillooly said. Later, he'd sell videotapes of his and Tonya's wedding night lovemaking to *Penthouse* magazine.

Dunleavy's sober and judgmental treatment of Joey Buttafuoco had been an example of how a show could pay big money for an interview without compromising its tabloid sense of right and wrong. Yet, six months later, it would be business as usual. When Joey walked out of jail, Dunleavy was waiting in a white limo to cheer the fresh ex-con and squire him to a party.

Under the new regime, *A Current Affair* began a trend of taking the side of whatever lowlife they bought. From Joey to Gillooly to Rodney King assailant Stacey Koon, their payment of lucre for interviews, in effect, made them partners in the crimes.

Hard Copy, meanwhile, continued on its celebrity-centric route, to ratings success and some criticism for paying people to come out with sensational accusations against the likes of Michael Jackson.

In *USA Today*, one of the "Two Lindas" and Diane Dimond waxed disingenuous about their practice of paying for stories.

"I hate, hate, hate being lumped into this genre-bias tabloid TV," Ellman said. "I know what journalism is."

She admitted paying for interviews, but claimed agreements with sources didn't allow her to say how much. "Money changes hands for tape, for documents"—even on network news, she added, parroting the party line that tabloid shows don't pay people for their stories but for their goods.

"Yes, we pay (sources) for exclusivity for a limited period of time."

"It's an enormously incorrect perception that if you pay people they must be lying," Dimond told the newspaper. "I don't put stuff on the air that I don't think people are telling the truth about."

It was mid-March, 1994. Brennan and I were set up in a battered office on the second floor of a barracks-like building slapped up against LaBrea Boulevard in Hollywood, with an emergency door leading out to a landing overlooking a seedy discount store called the Bargain Circus.

We were in a far corner of KCOP-TV, a low-rated independent station owned by a conservative and cash-heavy corporation called Chris-Craft, whose owner was sitting on something like a billion dollars in cold, hard bills and was willing to spend a tiny portion on a new late-night television idea.

Brennan was executive producer. I'd be senior producer. The show would roll out in June on five Chris-Craft stations: New York, Los Angeles, Portland, Phoenix, and Minneapolis—in most cases right up against *Nightline, Leno* and *Letterman.*

While shows like *Hard Copy* and *A Current Affair* were spending somewhere close to half a million dollars every five days, we'd be on a shoestring budget of $125,000 a week. We didn't have a name for the show and we didn't have an anchor. What we did have was Brennan and me, and thirteen weeks to make it work.

That day, we toyed with a press release that might bring the show into better focus for the Chris-Craft people—and ourselves.

> United Entertainment Group, Inc., in association with Peter Brennan Productions will soon launch a national five-day strip program tentatively titled *Story of the Day.*
>
> The new show will examine or reveal one story each night in both package and interview form. Its endeavour will be to choose the story that is of the widest interest to the American audience on a particular night.
>
> Its format will be built around story content and host, flexible and popular in approach. It's a show that will accommodate humor and entertainment and probe the most talked about story of that day...

This would be the opportunity for Chris-Craft's first syndicated programming: Peter Brennan's latest brainstorm, an inexpensive late-night alternative to *Nightline*. This lowly show, not *Detour*, would be the one to take tabloid television to the next level. For years to come, it would also be the last.

We spent much of the next week editing Raf's pilot at Four Point. It was coming out better than we expected; a dusty, urgent, and emotional journey through the American soul set to a Ry Cooder soundtrack. This *Detour* thing might actually work, after all.

The final all-night edit session ended shortly before six a.m. on St. Patrick's Day. The sun was rising as we nosed Brennan's Jag out of the garage, heading off for food and, if there was a God in Los Angeles at that time of the morning, something to drink.

We lucked out, Brennan, Raf, and I, back on our side of the Hollywood Hills, when we arrived at Barney's Beanery. Through some harmonic alcoholic convergence, the venerable joint had begun a new serving policy that very moment, opening the bar at six a.m. with the debut of its "Heartstarter's Club."

The early opening was an experiment, and as the first to take part, we threw the test results off a bit by settling into a booth, ordering breakfast and the first of many rounds of vodka and orange juice. The waitress was amazed at our capacity for booze so early in the day and more than a little pleased when we told her we'd all just gotten out of bed and were on our way to the office.

That evening, Raf and I were at the Bel Age, where the alcohol soothed our psychic wounds and we wound up clinking glasses and exchanging hugs in this room of great triumph, each telling the other what a genius he was, vowing great things and promising to be friends forever.

"I love you, mate. I really do," Raf said. "You just have to know when to say you're sorry."

"I'm not sorry, Raf."

"You're not sorry about what happened in the desert?"

"That was you, mate."

"Here's how it works. I say I'm sorry, you say you're sorry, and we move on. Okay?"

"All right, I'm sorry then."

"See?" We clinked glasses again. "I had a friend," Raf continued. "I had one best friend. His name was Lenny and he died and I stood there as his coffin rolled into the crematorium. You see, I've been auditioning you for my new best friend."

Nabi edged over to point out two other bosom buddies on the couch in the corner. Warren Beatty and Sean Penn were buddies united at the bosom of Madonna. They were in animated conversation, Penn in his usual dark suit and white shirt with a slight potbelly pushing through, Beatty big and soft in his glasses, fat-ass corduroys, windbreaker, and white socks. It was a moment in time, watching two guys from two generations who'd both fucked and been fucked over by Madonna—a former beau and an ex-husband, both humiliated in one way or another and both new fathers—trading stories.

After a while, Beatty approached the bar to use the phone. The television was tuned to *Letterman*, and as Beatty began one of his fabled whispered conversations, Letterman was on screen introducing Carly Simon. Beatty whispered on, staring blankly at the screen a foot from his elbow as Carly Simon sang in pantomime.

Her most famous song, "You're So Vain," was written about Warren Beatty. He hung up, looked at the TV without reaction, and returned to his seat.

We were pretty drunk by then. "Hey," I told Raf, "if that was me, I would've put my hand over the phone and said, 'Hey Sean, I fucked her!'"

"Don't worry, that wouldn't have been you."

We went out to get the car, as usual parked by the valets right in front, shiny and deep blue under the bright night lighting. When Penn and Beatty came out for their cars, I pulled a still camera out of the glove box and, as a joke, handed it to Raf.

"Take their picture."

Raf got out and walked toward them. I couldn't believe it.

"Don't do it, dude," Sean Penn muttered, not threateningly.

Raf snapped. The front of the Bel Age lit up even brighter in the frozen flash.

We got the hell out of there.

CHAPTER TWENTY-SEVEN:
BUTTHOLE SURFERS & A MAD DOG
NIGHTLINE

I turned thirty-eight the day after they found Kurt Cobain with his brains blown out.

"If we were on the air today, we'd do that story, right?" Anita was right on target.

"We'd do a whole show on it. While Ted Koppel did something on Bosnia or Medicare, we'd be all over Seattle. We'd put together a package here, and do a two-way from the scene with a cop or a reporter who's covering the story."

It was April ninth. We had to be on the air on June sixth. Pete Schlesinger, an old television vet who was Chris-Craft's intermediary to the show, got us a good deal on a studio set from a friend who designed the sets for *Star Trek*. We'd broadcast from a dingy little studio no one was using with cameras that no one had used since the seventies.

Peter Brennan had decided this show would need to attract a female audience so he wanted a staff of women. There was Anita, the loyal assignment editor at *Hard Copy* who took a lot of knocks from Linda Bell for "switching allegiance" and was forced to leave shortly after we did. At Dunleavy's begging, Peter hired one of his former flames from the *New York Post* to work out of New York; to set up stories, Peter hired a woman he met on a plane. Dena was an intense blabbermouth with a law degree, no television experience, and an interest in witchcraft.

There were some runners, a couple of young kid production assistants, a segment producer to be hired later, and that was it, a ragtag bunch in the corner of a little shit station ready to take on the world with a half hour we needed to find a way to fill—just like *A Current Affair*.

Brennan didn't hire Raf for the show. He said he didn't fit into the concept.

April 11, 1994
To: Evan Thompson
From: Peter Brennan

Following are proposed titles for the new show.

STORY OF THE DAY	MAINSTREAM
THE DAILY AMERICAN	THE DAILY
SPOTLIGHT	THE AMERICAN
LEAD STORY	ON THE SCENE
SPOTLIGHT AMERICA	DEADLINE
AMERICAN SPOTLIGHT	DEADLINE U.S.A.
STORY ONE	DEADLINE STORY
THE STORY	REAL TIME
STORY U.S.A.	THE BIG STORY
ON THE SPOT	HEADLINE AMERICA

We still needed to fill two key positions. For the anchorman, Brennan wanted the news equivalent of Johnny Carson, a witty, avuncular charmer who was a Maury Povich with gravitas. For the reporter, well, we needed a good reporter. Brennan's ideal was a David Miller, the wild-eyed nervous nellie who'd rush to any scene and bark back the facts. My ideal was Raf, someone who'd cover the story as no one else would even consider.

We looked out into the great American news landscape. Aside from personal contacts and favorites, the only way to find these people was to call up the talent agents for tapes.

The tapes came in, each audition reel containing clips for as many as twenty anchormen or reporters, one after another, clone after clone. The anchormen were all old Ted Baxters with phony pontificating voices; the reporters stood in front of blazing row houses—unless they were the quirky ones, wearing bow ties, pedaling tiny bicycles or sitting in ice houses on the hottest day of summer.

The only anchorman who stood out was a tall Texan named Big John. I'd worked with Big John in New York City. He was a macho, goodhearted cowpoke with an ego the size of the Lone Star State. He liked an honest drink. He liked to make sure his female co-anchor didn't have more lines of copy to read than he did. Behind the bluster, Big John was a sensitive soul.

Big John was between gigs at his ranch in Texas when I offered him an audition for the host job. He was surprised and glad to hear from me; coincidentally, he'd be in town on Friday.

Big John was our only choice; we couldn't find anyone else in all

America. Still, we needed to make Chris-Craft president Evan Thompson think we were choosing from among a wide selection, so for audition day, we invited everyone who'd sent in a tape and résumé: the retired blowhard of an L.A. anchorman; the game show host; the oddball bulldog of a reporter who'd sent Brennan a fan letter saying Steve Dunleavy was his hero.

We sat each of them behind a makeshift anchor desk in the old studio and had them respond to questions thrown by Brennan. It was all for show, until Big John sat down and fielded embarrassing questions about his first sex experience, his mother, and other personal matters before he started to perspire and called off the session; he didn't like things being that far out of his control.

Afterward we stood out on the landing overlooking the Bargain Circus. Over cigarettes, Big John got teary and thanked us for considering him. He'd been having a crisis of confidence lately; after leaving an anchor gig in Miami, he was beginning to feel like a dinosaur, as if time and television were passing him by.

He said he'd recently gone to lunch with some young executives to talk about a new job; he ordered himself a drink along with his red meat, only one drink.

The next week he was hearing stories about it.

Brennan laughed. "You won't have that problem with us, mate."

"At our lunches, you can skip the food," I said.

Brennan invited Big John up to his house in Beverly Hills for a beer on Saturday afternoon. It was the same day we learned that Pat Harper, the anchorwoman who'd been hired to replace Big John in New York, died of a heart attack at her home in Spain.

Brennan was living in style on Summit Drive in Beverly Hills in a big white mansion that Fred Astaire built on the old Pickfair estate. When I arrived, Big John and Peter were seated at the bar overlooking the pool. Big John was reading something out loud. He paused to bring me up to date.

"This is a novella I've written. That's why I'm in L.A. A young gal I know is interested in turning this into a screenplay," he explained. "Now, the main character is a TV anchorman between jobs. And he's been dealt into a poker game in Louisiana."

Big John picked up the story from there, describing the minutia of each character's appearance and background, the cutting of the cards and the whisky on the table. He read the dialog in character, including the voice of the dusky Creole queen who'd bed down with our unemployed anchorman hero in a night of steamy bayou lovin'.

Big John read on...and on...and on. Twenty minutes later I realized he wasn't going to stop. Every time he flipped another page, I'd look over in hope of seeing a chapter's end. There was none. It was just one long story that wasn't ever going to finish and he was talking in that Creole lady's voice again...

He read on for forty minutes.

He took a breath.

Peter jumped in. "Burt! You need a beer!"

I made for the kitchen and came back with a couple of brews. Later, I'd learn that Big John had walked in the door a half hour before I did and began reading to Peter immediately. An hour later, he was still going strong.

Brennan and I realized Big John might be a problem.

When we were tossing around names for potential reporters, Alison Holloway's came up early on. She was the best we had at *Hard Copy* and we'd used her during our second stay at *A Current Affair*. She didn't seem likely to drop everything in London to come to Los Angeles, since she was anchoring the six p.m. newscast for the ITV network, and as far as we knew, was married, settled, and successful.

I gave her a call anyway. She was interested.

"We've got to go for some heavy topics to establish this new show," Brennan said.

"Real tabloid, right?"

"No. Real news, mate. We should call former presidents, do heavy issues like breast cancer."

"Breast cancer? I thought this was supposed to be an *alternative* to *Nightline*. Who's gonna watch that?"

"You don't understand. We need to establish ourselves as a serious show, lay down the groundwork, and then we can do what we want later."

"Yeah, but we've only got thirteen weeks."

"Don't worry about that." It was a theory as old and tested by time as Brennan's philosophy of writing a story by telling the story and telling it again. When reporters wrote articles about a show, they'd always go back to the clips of stories that appeared the week the show debuted. If we could get some chin-stroking subjects down in those opening days, our serious reputation would be written in stone.

"Yeah, but we don't want zero viewers, either."

"You've got to be patient. Look." Brennan leaned forward at the bar. "We go for a heavy issue like breast cancer. Can you imagine? As long as we take the high road, we can be showing bare tit! We can break barriers for television nudity and get away with it!"

"That's an idea."

"Can you imagine? Breast exams, take breast exams. We get Ann Jillian on and have her touching a tit!"

"Now you're talking."

"That's only the beginning. Yesterday, it was the caning in Singapore. Bare butts! We show bare butts..."

By the end of April, it appeared we'd be naming our show *Lead Story*, "lead" as in "leading the way" we hoped, and not "lead balloon." It also appeared this show would be understaffed, underbudgeted, underequipped, and underassisted by the KCOP staff whose facilities we were using. Not only was the show not drawing its staff from the KCOP roster, it wasn't working with the KCOP unions. We'd have to step carefully.

At the moment, we were more concerned with the show's content, filling up the first week's schedule with those serious topics Brennan wanted to go for, from ovarian cancer to censorship and living ex-Presidents. Brennan sent Dena, his airplane discovery, down to Georgia to follow Jimmy Carter around as he built houses for the poor. We set up shows on smoking, Scientology, the South African elections; sought names like Aaron Spelling, Steven Bochco, and Patti Davis. Most crucial, we went after Ann Jillian, Olivia Newton-John, Kate Jackson—any celebrity we could think of who might show us some bare tit.

Peter brought another of his misfits on board to help in the celebrity department. Gianni was a gangly, manicured Italian in canary yellows and powder blues who resembled a polished, openly gay Gomer Pyle. He'd used his unique experience as Sophia Loren's manservant in setting up his own publicity firm.

Gianni was the back door man. He'd arrange for celebrities to make quick, quiet money hosting TV pilots or cutting ribbons at European shopping malls, with payment in cash to avoid percentage cuts to their agents and managers.

His secret was a network of cooks, butlers, and houseboys who had personal access to the celebrities' lives, approaching them while cleaning their silver or serving breakfast in the kitchen. It worked especially well if the servant had seen his boss in bed with a thirteen-year-old the night before or was in charge of cleaning the blood off the sheets and walls.

Gianni had some success securing stars like Rod Steiger, Telly Savalas, and Jane Seymour for *The Extraordinary*—he even got the great actor James Woods to host the pilot for the American version.

For our new show, Gianni was assigned, or promised, a number of celebs of various luminosity: Shannen Doherty, Marlon & Christian Brando, Loni Anderson & Burt Reynolds, Mia Farrow, and Roseanne.

We'd see who he could come up with.

I was the only one at the Bel Age bar until a large, long-haired man flopped down a few stools away and ordered a beer. He looked familiar. I said the name out loud as I placed the face.

"Gibby Haines."

He looked up sharply with more than a trace of paranoia, shaken that he'd been recognized by someone nursing a vodka tonic and wearing a sports jacket. Gibby Haines was the singer for the Butthole Surfers. My old friend Nicky had turned me on to the group years ago in New York City.

I cursed myself silently for having the wasted mental capacity to know what Gibby Haines of the Butthole Surfers looked like, yet drank on in the acceptance that this very ability was what made me so effective in the tabloid TV business.

"Gibby Haines," I repeated with a knowing nod and a smile. I told Nabi I'd pay for his beer and told Gibby Haines I was a fan.

The singer hadn't come to the bar for conversation or recognition. "Uh, and what do you do, sir?" he asked politely.

"Aw, I work in television. Tabloid TV, you know."

He thanked me for the beer and slipped away. Later, I'd learn Gibby Haines was Kurt Cobain's roommate at the drug treatment center in Marina del Rey when Cobain went AWOL, made his way home to Washington State, and put that gun in his mouth.

Our bar scene was expanding. We'd begun meeting after work for early evening drinks at the Monkey Bar, the place on Beverly Boulevard that Jack Nicholson part-owned and where Madame Heidi Fleiss once ran her girls.

Recently opened to the general public, the Monkey Bar was a comfortable, dark bar constructed by a Hollywood set designer to look like it had been there for years. It was a relaxing place to drink and, as the evenings wore on, became stuffed with Heidi girl wannabees and the type of Valley B-girl willing to trade a blow job for a walk-on or, at the very least, a phone number and a promise for a drink that was blue.

The sun was still on its way down in the west and shining yellow through the open door and Peter was up using the phone when a middle-aged blond woman took a seat next to me. Her hair was like straw and her face as well-defined as a skull with skin stretched over it. She pulled out a sketch pad and began scratching away with a pencil. I froze when I noticed she was sketching me, so as not to ruin her picture and because I recognized the artist as Joni Mitchell.

Fuck, I thought, in twenty years they'll be selling her sketches or showing them in a museum and I'd be saying, "Look, that's me when I used to hang out in the Monkey Bar," and everyone'll say, "Yeah right, Burtie, have another."

Peter came back and didn't know who Joni Mitchell was even though

I kept nudging him and whispering her name. When he caught her drawing him, he called her on it and she slammed the sketch book shut.

"And what's your name?" he asked.

"I'm Joni."

"Hello, Joni. I'm Peter." We all got into a discussion about Richard Nixon, whose people were considering allowing to appear on the episode of our show dedicated to the living former presidents, but changed their minds because he had, only a few days earlier, died.

Word came the second week of May that Fox had taken some of the advice I'd given back in November and fired Maureen O'Boyle. The ratings of *A Current Affair* had slipped once again, to third place behind the imitators *Inside Edition* and *Hard Copy*, with ratings of 6.6, 6.7, and 7.3 respectively.

Her replacement would be Jim Ryan, the middle-aged, witty Irishman who'd found his niche hosting *Good Day New York* direct from the newsroom. His stint at *A Current Affair* was not to be so successful, thanks to the team that helped make O'Boyle such a rousing failure. The same week O'Boyle was fired, Bill Ridley was elevated to co-executive producer status with Ian Rae. There would be no slowing the show's inevitable slide to destruction.

Brennan had another brainstorm: forget the old man anchor idea and go for broke with Alison Holloway. He got her on the phone right away and asked if she'd come over within weeks for a job that could last three months or seven years. It would be her show.

She accepted.

Brennan left it to me to call Big John and tell him there'd been a change in plans, that the boys upstairs decided to go with a woman instead of a man.

"If it's any consolation, John, and I know it isn't, you were the best. Of all the anchormen in the country, you were the only one we would have gone for."

"And I do truly thank you for thinking of me."

"But they want a woman."

"You don't know what it meant just to know that I was still wanted," he said.

I hung up, imagining the sound of a double-barrel shotgun blast echoing across the vast Texas prairie.

It turned out Alison Holloway wasn't still married after all. Her union to the hip British TV producer who was friends with Faiman had ended in divorce, and Alison was now shacking up in the house she owned with a young ski bum she'd met in the French Alps.

She wasted no time quitting her job in London, packing her bags, and promising to send for the toy boy once she got settled in America so he could fulfill his dream of skiing off her millions on the slopes of Aspen.

As we neared the premiere date, Lisa, the very patient Chris-Craft liaison assigned to our show, could stay silent no longer. "Everything is so disorganized," she announced as the small staff gathered in Brennan's office. "No one knows what's going on!"

"Um, excuse me," I responded, quietly. "There are nine of us working here. Everyone knows his or her job. Our anchorwoman hasn't arrived yet. There's nothing to do before the show airs."

"Put your fears to rest," Brennan added. "We know our jobs and how to put on a show. This is only television."

That night, Brennan and I sat at the St. James Club next door to the new House of Blues. Drinking as usual, we noticed an ornate bottle, under lock and key in a glass case behind the bar.

"Don." We called the bartender over. "What's that?"

"Remy Martin. It's eighty dollars a shot."

We had one each. We decided it was worth the money, but left an afterglow of guilt.

"We have to go to the Bel Age, mate."

Brennan agreed to accompany me so I could confess to Nabi that we'd drank big expensive shots at someone else's bar.

"We sell the same thing," Nabi said. "We charge ninety-six dollars a shot."

Brennan headed home. I took a detour and stopped off for a nightcap at the Viper Room. Security guards wearing important-looking headsets like those goons from the House of Blues wandered in and out of the downstairs bar as my bartending angel Shannon poured my drink without me having to ask. Harry Dean Stanton wandered in looking lost. "Mr. Stanton is in the downstairs bar," someone's walkie talkie blattered, and a guard came to show the addled actor the way to the V.I.P. room upstairs.

In the main room, all black with green trim and gold Erte light fixtures, the actress Beverly D'Angelo was onstage with a cocktail trio, singing torch songs.

The crowd was full of Coppolaesque barroom celebrities like old man Stanton, Frederic Forrest, and Seymour Cassel, the type of celeb it wasn't worth telling anybody back home about because they wouldn't recognize the name.

I looked around for some action and thought I may have found it with the dark-haired woman swaying in front of me. She wore a long black punk dress and green sneakers. Her shoulders were exposed and she had a small clear mole on her back, dead center between the shoulder blades. She fit the profile of my L.A. women, except that a look at her face revealed her to be the actress Ellen Barkin, and I had no idea of the true color of her hair. I sidled alongside, smiled and she smiled back, that Ellen Barkin face all crinkles, her eyes and screwy mouth slits when she did. I said something in her ear. She asked me to repeat it. Her female handler looked concerned, and—

"Ellen. Please, join us at our table." It was the director Paul Schrader, overly formal, full of Viper smarm. She went.

I now had time to recognize that among the faces in the crowd were many tabloid reporters, including Brennan's daughter Yasmin, working undercover among the celebrities. Beverly D'Angelo did an acappella number called "Every Time I Fuck, I Fall in Love."

Tripping back downstairs, I tipped Shannon big and went home, staggered to the kitchen, took a jar of peanut butter and threw it off the balcony. I didn't consider I might have hit someone until I heard it crash and splat safely in the middle of the street.

I was sick of the fat I was pouring into my body, the vodka and beer and Remy and tequila and women in long black punk dresses who gave me nothing but a pain in my head.

There was no way I could know just how much my life was about to change.

With our June sixth debut approaching too quickly, I sat Brennan down and tried to be as realistic as possible. If we were going to get this show on the air, we needed people we could rely on.

"Well, who do we know?"

"You tell me. Who do we know who can do things the way we want them done? Raf and Wayne."

"Yeah, but Raf's going to be tied up with his own show."

"Let's bring him on freelance. Otherwise we're not going to get this thing on."

There was another small difficulty: the show's name, *Lead Story*. A friend back in New York wrote to tell me he noticed a weekly show by the same name on the Black Entertainment Television channel.

"What do we go with?" I asked. "*The Big Story. Story of the Day.* I like *The Big Story.*"

"No, mate, we need something classy, something that fits Alison. How about *Premier Story*?"

"Like *Premiere* magazine? Like a movie premiere?"

"No. Like this." He wrote it on a sheet of paper. "*Premier*. It means 'first,' or 'leading.' *Premier Story*, that's it."

This time the lawyers made sure no one owned the name. We gave the story to Steve Brennan at the *Hollywood Reporter*. It ran on May twentieth. All they got wrong was the spelling of the name.

Big *Story*:
Chris-Craft
slots newsmag

The British are coming—and headed straight into the late night TV wars via a new newsmagazine strip, *Premiere Story*, being pushed out for a summer launch by the Chris-Craft/United TV group.

Executive produced by TV magazine veteran Peter Brennan and helmed by leading U.K. anchor Alison Holloway... *Premiere Story* is being molded for a national launch in syndication as counterprogramming to the network talk shows and newcomer talk host Jon Stewart, who helms the upcoming late-night offering from Paramount to replace *The Arsenio Hall Show*...

The development of the new late-night challenger has already been creating a degree of interest from other stations around the country, particularly as it is hosted by a female anchor who could present a demographic alternative to the male-dominated talk show scene in the time slot.

"With the success that talk has had in late fringe, there is an appetite for reality programming in late fringe," said Lou Dennig, vp, director of programming at Blair Television, the New York station rep firm. "They are smart to start it off in June. If they can make it work during the summer there will certainly be room in the marketplace for it."

Alison Holloway came to town on the afternoon of Sunday, May twenty-second. She flew in from Florida where she'd been covering the Whitbread Round-the-World Yacht Race, her last assignment for ITV, and settled in at the Montrose Hotel, down the road and around the corner from the Bel Age.

When Peter and I arrived at her hotel late that afternoon, she was waiting in the lobby. She wore a white suit and carried a silver briefcase. I kissed her on the cheek and welcomed her to Los Angeles.

We met Peter's wife for dinner at DaVinci's, an old-guard joint in Beverly Hills where Dean Martin had a regular table. I wasn't concentrating on the food. I couldn't stop stealing glances at her. Alison was younger than I recalled, tan and blond, very cool and very beautiful.

After we dropped her at the hotel, I could only moan her name.

"Burt, she's our show," Peter said.

"Mate, she's the fucking franchise."

That week, I became Alison's guide to Los Angeles. I showed her the sights from the passenger seat of the Porsche, took her to restaurants and bars and dropped her at her hotel afterward, lingering longer each time as I watched her walk inside.

On a Thursday night, we had dinner at a sidewalk table on Sunset Plaza. We'd been drinking and I was braver than I might have been otherwise, asking and teasing her about her past.

"So you've been married three times?"

"And divorced. Do you think that's bad?"

"No. I think it's pretty cool. So let me get this straight. You're divorced from your first husband—"

"Whom I married when I was only twenty-one."

"—and you walk into this nightclub and there onstage is this comedian. And he notices you and makes a comment to your date—"

"It really wasn't like that."

"What was his name?"

"Jim. Jim Davidson. He's very popular back home."

"They call him 'Nick Nick,' I read that. What does that mean?"

"It was part of his act. He's very low class. He's a horrible man."

"Was he anything like Benny Hill?"

The chemistry was immediate, like nitro and glycerin. She was teaching me and I was teaching her. We began spending more and more time together, though I told her I didn't want to monopolize her time, and told myself nothing would come of it. Maybe that's why it came together so naturally.

One night after work, Brennan left us in the bar at the Mondrian. Alison wanted to carry on to the House of Blues, so we did. By evening's end, we wound up back at her hotel suite.

We wound up in her bed. We began to undress each other quickly, but stopped a moment before the final layer. Calvin Klein and the Gap faced Marks & Spencer.

"Look," I commented. "I'm all in black and you're all in white."

The satellite dish was late. It could transmit signals, but not receive them. The edit room was carved out of an equipment closet and the editor hadn't yet gotten the hang of the equipment. The 1970s studio cameras made the green set look gray and couldn't focus on Alison's fine features. The guy we hired as a segment producer turned out to be an idiot. The inexperienced producers had yet to line up a single guest for our debut show. A strike was looming among technicians at KCOP, and there was already sabotage because of resentment over a non-union show operating on the lot. We still didn't have a reporter.

We had Alison Holloway though, plus a very classy set and a campy Queen Anne desk for her to sit behind.

Premier Story was ready to roll.

PRESS RELEASE
Whitehead Associates
Public Relations
NIGHTLY NEWS PROGRAM DEBUT
Premier Story
PREMIER STORY, a nightly half-hour news
program that will explore the major stories of the
day, makes its debut with a special report on the
continuing assaults on the White House by the
religious right, the Republicans, President Clinton's
political enemies, and now the publication of Bob
Woodward's latest investigative book, *The Agenda:
Inside the Clinton White House...*

With our small staff, limited resources, and shaky technical equipment, we were forced to tape our first show a night in advance and cobble its segments together to feed out on Monday evening.

That Sunday night, we managed to assemble a panel of guests that was far-flung, potentially interesting, and by no means tabloidian. In the studio was Ben Stein, former Nixon speechwriter, actor, and, incidentally, KCOP commentator; Democratic party strategist Ann Lewis was glad to speak from Washington; and *Newsweek* political writer Jonathan Alter appeared from New York.

For good measure, just because he happened to be in town and was a recognizable name, we had California legislator Tom Hayden, former husband of Jane Fonda, in a separate final segment.

We finished the tape package on Monday. It included a Christian Broadcasting Network interview with sexual accuser Paula Jones, and another with an Arkansas State Trooper who claimed firsthand knowledge of Bill Clinton's sexual liaisons while governor.

"For Bill Clinton, the D-Day ceremonies in Europe appeared to some to provide a world stage on which he could hide in plain sight." Alison read the track. Brennan told her to speak slowly, so Americans would understand her British accent. "For while he met with the Pope and saluted the brave overseas, back home in Washington D.C., flames were licking at the front door of the White House.

"His accusers were coming from all sides, trying to torch the future of the forty-fourth president. And no one was sure where or how the next fire would ignite..."

We got the show done, four sections, ready to feed. The only problem was Ben Stein, whom we noticed after the fact was slumped in his chair and staring deliberately at Alison's breasts throughout the entire interview.

The Hollywood Reporter, June 8, 1994

TV review

The quest for truth takes many forms, the latest a daily hottest-topic report from the Chris-Craft/United TV group, *Premier Story*, which is sort of a mad-dog *Nightline*.

Monday night's premiere promised "the truth about Bob and Paula and Bill and Hillary"...

Although truth seems awfully variable these days, no real truths were forthcoming in this first half-hour, although a sense of panic was evoked by newly arrived English anchor Alison Holloway, who described "flames... licking at the front door of the White House" and "relentless accusers seem to be coming from all sides."

Tabloidian tone often is established by jolting, sometimes fatted language—i.e., (Paula) Jones may be "the ticking time bomb" for President Clinton. Fatuity also helps—as in the assertion the president was doing all these D-Day appearances in Europe "to hide from his pursuers."

The mood obviously was set by its exec producer, Aussie-born Peter Brennan....

Premier Story's first week carried on with the same sense of chaos we'd projected on the Clinton White House in our very first program. Each show had to be put together the night before and assembled the next day in painstaking, painful procedures on equipment that didn't work, and with editors who weren't familiar with the equipment.

On Tuesday, it was the story of two women who claimed to have been sexually harassed and abused at the Navy's Tailhook fliers' convention in Las Vegas. Wednesday was the breast cancer show, which didn't feature any celebrity "bare tit" after all; Raf, working freelance again, made his debut on Thursday, interviewing a father whose daughter accused him of sexual abuse after "repressed memories" were lured out by a therapist; Friday was Gianni's first "get," the long-awaited mystery guest.

It was a day to catch our collective breath, a full-show interview with *Premier Story*'s first celebrity guest. Gianni didn't get us Roseanne or Shannen Doherty. He didn't even get us Loni Anderson. No, this man with all the upstairs-downstairs connections made us hire a limousine to fetch Cliff Robertson.

Cliff Robertson, star of *PT 109* and *Charly*, two memorable movies made long, long ago, stepped into the office at about nine-thirty that morning. His wiry, thinning, combed-over hair and mustache were dyed motel furniture brown, his flight jacket and polo shirt specked with what seemed to be bits and stains of upchucked food. Something alcoholic sloshed in his coffee mug. His eyes floated, fighting for focus. He had yet to regain his land legs after the limo ride with Gianni. The man was stewed to the gills.

"We have to record this show day-of-air," Brennan insisted.

"We can't. It's not physically possible." We'd been on the air for a week and it was evident we were in serious trouble. "We don't have the facilities. The edit machines don't work. The editors don't know the rooms. The clearance people don't know how to get tape. You're letting the interview segments go long and we have to edit them down afterward. We can't do it."

"We have to."

Peter Brennan didn't like to confront problems and he especially didn't like to hear about them from me. This show was proving to be harder to get on the air than he'd anticipated. He and I were forced to split the two major jobs of getting the show on the air: he as line producer in the control room while I worked as segment producer cutting tape packages.

We had to work all that weekend preparing Monday's show. When our edit room went down, we had to commandeer one of KCOP's rooms and editors.

It was Sunday evening, June 12, 1994. I sat in the edit room with the KCOP editor, waiting through the grueling process of editing a segment on

Pearl Jam and their fight against the Ticketmaster agency.

The time was after ten p.m. Peter was in his office eating Chinese food with his wife and a couple of workers from *The Extraordinary*. Alison had just left to get some sleep before the next day's interviews.

As I worked, as Brennan ate Chinese, as Alison drove her blue Miata back to her new home in Laurel Canyon, we didn't know it, but our world was being transformed with the slash and thrust of a serrated knife. A few miles away, in a quiet neighborhood called Brentwood, in the courtyard of a condominium at number 875 Bundy Drive, a young mother named Nicole Brown Simpson and a young man named Ron Goldman were being butchered by person or persons unknown.

As they say in tabloid television, sometimes the Lord works in mysterious ways.

CHAPTER TWENTY-EIGHT:
"WHERE'S THE BAG, MR. KARDASHIAN?"

We got word from KCOP's newsroom wire in the late morning. "An ex-wife of football star O.J. Simpson and an unidentified man were found murdered outside her condominium in Brentwood."

Anita handed me the wire copy. "Hmmm," I said. "I wonder if he beat her to death."

Everyone in tabloid television knew that O.J. Simpson had been arrested for wife abuse some years back, but early word had it he was in Chicago at the time of the killings. We kept an eye on the story and carried on with our Pearl Jam show.

By late afternoon, things had changed considerably. After Simpson returned home from Chicago, a KCOP cameraman stood atop his truck and shot over the wall of Simpson's mansion, getting tremendous, exclusive video of the star in handcuffs. Either the cops had fucked up in a big way or O.J. Simpson was a suspect in a bigger way.

The studio crew was gone, so we tore apart the show in the edit room, brought Alison outside to tape a new open and intros and put together a package on the murder to lead the show. *Premier Story* was about to become a day-of-air broadcast whether we liked it or not, whether or not it was physically possible.

We were about to become the O.J. Simpson show.

Alison and I were on Rockingham Avenue outside Simpson's mansion the next morning, recording promos and shooting interviews and footage. The exclusive, secluded neighborhood off Sunset Boulevard had overnight become a media encampment. O.J. Simpson's home, rather than the scene of the crime, had become the center of the world's biggest story. Satellite trucks, microwave units, television crews, and reporters from around the world had taken over the neighborhood where Michelle Pfeiffer, the mayor, and many other celebrities lived in seclusion.

Most ironically, the family renting the mansion directly next door to the Simpson estate had moved out only days earlier. Fox TV chief Les Hinton had moved his family to a new assignment.

For Tuesday's show we ran extensive footage of the vivid videotaped moments that had flashed by in the past two days: Simpson arriving home and being restrained; detectives taking shoes from Simpson's house; a friend of Simpson's houseguest Kato Kaelin, showing up with the assumption that it was Kato who was killed with Nicole; and another little man taking a garment bag away from Simpson's gate the morning after the murders.

Our coverage looked different than anyone else's. We were devoting entire shows to one story and we weren't cutting up the tape into quick little soundbites. This wasn't the usual packaged reality; we were letting scenes roll. *Premier Story* had hit on a trademark style through necessity: the editing process was too slow to do a lot of cutting. We had to let tape run just to get the show on the air.

Soon, we'd be known for using a quick ten-frame burst of light called a "white flash" as a transition between scenes and interview segments. Other shows copied the innovation. We only came up with it because our editors took too long to do dissolves.

By Tuesday evening, Simpson hadn't been charged but it was apparent he was the prime suspect. The next morning, attorney Dominic Barbara, our Buttafuoco man, phoned in to Howard Stern's show. "Mr. Simpson—and I won't call him O.J. anymore because he's no longer a sports hero but an accused murderer—I think we have to get used to the idea that Mr. Simpson may face the death penalty."

We booked Dominic as one of the first of the attorneys who'd take up so much airtime as the Simpson case dragged over the next eighteen months.

Rafael Abramovitz, meanwhile, was momentarily energized by the story. He headed to the Mezzaluna Restaurant where Nicole had eaten her last meal, with an edge over the other journalists who took up just about every other seat. The manager was an actor he'd used in one of his *Hard Copy* re-enactments. He promised to give Raf an exclusive interview the following day.

Thursday's show was dedicated to the victims, beginning with Nicole's funeral, an endless procession of L.A. businessmen and their blond trophy wives. When O.J. Simpson arrived at the church doors to be escorted inside, our camera crew was in the middle of the media crush on the other side of the iron fence. The cameramen cursed one another as they jockeyed for space, called out to Simpson, and acted altogether unfunereal.

Premier Story was the only show to run the footage with full sound, to show what it was really like being there.

The second section was dedicated to Nicole's burial. The cemetery was closed to the media, so we paid a neighbor to let us shoot from his yard, using a long lens to capture the sad scene fifty yards away. The scene played out for six minutes with minimal sound.

The show ended with similar footage of Ron Goldman's funeral.

It was a risky style, but we found out the next morning that it paid off. Thursday's show outrated *Nightline, Leno,* and *Letterman* in New York. *Premier Story* was number one. *Premier Story* was on the map.

The next night, with O.J. Simpson avoiding surrender with his infamous low-speed Bronco chase, even Ted Koppel got on the Simpson bandwagon his highfalutin show had ignored all week. Of course, Ted apologized to his audience, explaining that occasionally his show had to diverge from the truly important stories to shine a light on the obsessions of the media in general.

I sat in a tape room watching the Simpson chase play out live on five different cameras on five separate monitors. This simple motorcade said so much about celebrity and race in America. That a black man could become one of America's greatest sports heroes and most beloved advertising pitch-men, that he could earn millions of dollars, marry a California beach blond, move into one of the richest, most conservative, and whitest neighborhoods in the country, that he could golf with presidents, believe he had "over-come" his blackness—yet wind up like Staggerlee racing down the road with the po-lice on his back—was both unimaginable and totally American.

As Simpson's alleged suicide note was read live on television by his friend Robert Kardashian, I was moved that he'd be enough of a man to take the blame and kill himself. As the Bronco rolled past cheering fans, I was touched. It was obvious these people were not applauding his crime, but in effect were saying goodbye to a fallen hero and encouraging him not to take his life. By the time Al Cowlings piloted the Bronco back to the Rockingham estate, I was certain O.J. Simpson would be shot dead by police on national television.

I held a thick yellow pad to take screening notes for a special live version of the show. As Simpson was apprehended peacefully, I pried the pad out of my mouth. I'd bitten straight through.

It was Saturday night. Brennan, Raf, and I were at the Bel Age, discussing the greatest story ever to drop into our laps.

"There's more to this, mate. There's drugs. There's Mafia, there's bad cops," I said. "We don't know who did this yet. Think about it. Who'd be easier to frame than O.J. Simpson if it were drugs? And who's this Goldman kid?"

"He did it," Raf said. Peter just listened.

"How can you say that? The cop who found the glove is a racist."

"He didn't plant the glove."

"Isn't it a little obvious, having Simpson drop both gloves, including one at his house, and have both of them found by a cop who'd been to his house before, supposedly knew Nicole, and has a paper trail of racism?"

"You're not doing anybody any favors with these bullshit theories about Simpson being innocent."

"You're a former civil rights attorney. You know how many black men have been framed in this country. How can you just go along with what the L.A. police say? What about Rodney King?"

"Shut him up." Raf looked over to Peter, who merely laughed.

"Simpson'll get off because of this cop!" I said.

"He's not getting off. That's all bullshit."

"How do we know? *You're standing in a bar.* You're supposed to be a reporter. You've spent every night at the bar with us while we plan the show. You can bet Dunleavy is on his hands and knees in somebody's bushes right now."

Raf put down his drink and looked at Peter. "I'm gonna kill him."

He walked out of the bar.

There's a popular Australian joke. An average bloke winds up on a desert island with Elle MacPherson and, after a few days, winds up having sex with her.

They've been doing it for weeks when the bloke says, "Elle, would you mind doing something a little, um, out of the ordinary? Would you mind dressing up in my clothes?"

"Sure." Elle puts on his pants and shirt.

"And would you be offended if I called you Bruce?"

"It's your fantasy."

"And would you mind walking down the beach there, away from me?"

"If that's what you want." Elle MacPherson starts walking.

"Go on, a little farther now." The guy waits until she's about fifty yards down the beach and he yells, "Hey Bruce!"

When Elle turns around, he shouts: *"Guess what? I just fucked Elle MacPherson!"*

My emotions were more complicated, but not too unlike those of the Australian bloke. I was having an affair with the host of our show, I was crazy about her, and yet, I felt I'd done something terribly wrong, upsetting the delicate balance of the show, the universe, and my relationship with Peter Brennan. It wasn't my place to do this.

Oh, but, shit, I wanted to tell my mates!

Alison Holloway was beautiful and worldy and more of a woman than I'd allowed myself to trifle with in the years since I left New York City. She'd been married three times, and because one of those marriages was to a popular, lowbrow comedian, she was a regular item in Britain's tabloid newspapers.

When Alison signed her deal to leave England for *Premier Story*, the tabs sent her off with headlines about how she'd become a "millionairess." She posed for the photogs in a long diaphanous skirt, holding an American flag behind her back like a bathtowel. One paper even ran a backlit shot, revealing the silhouette of her bare legs under her skirt, and they ran it side-by-side with a similar, legendary photo of Princess Diana. Alison was a princess!

I was a guy who'd promised himself to one day start on a five-year plan to normality: five years was how long I'd reckoned it would take me to ever feel anything for anyone again. In the years since I first walked into the office of *A Current Affair*, I'd stopped acting and actually become the character named Burt Kearns, the hard-drinking, hard-living boyo who bowed to the law of no man and especially no woman.

"You're getting on a roller coaster with me, darlin," I'd warn prospective girlfriends. "We're jet setters, a wild bunch who play by our own rules. If you climb on, you're going for a wild ride. You'll meet famous people, eat at the top restaurants, fly to exotic places; you'll go home with valuable prizes. But like any ride, it eventually comes to an ednd and you'll have to get off and let the next person on."

They'd buy it.

"Your heart is a fucking cemetery," Raf would say, and I'd tell him, "You're right, you look inside, you see it's Arlington, mate, green rolling hills with rows and rows of little white markers," and then we'd laugh, call each other geniuses, and drink some more.

This one, though, she lived that roller coaster life for real, and now I was the one hanging on. When one of Alison's friends from London visited for a weekend and I stayed away, I'd get in my car, blast Pearl Jam's "Rearview Mirror" at top volume and race down the winding Sunset Boulevard to the beach. I had the feeling in my stomach and didn't need a talk with myself or anybody to tell me what it was. I knew I was in trouble. I was fucking in love.

"No, you didn't. That poor woman." Raf shook his head. "You asshole. Now I can't touch her."

"She's unbelievable, mate. I'm in love."

"No you're not."

"I am. I finally met the woman who makes me feel the way these women felt about me. I could never understand what they were talking about. Now I do. She's incredible. We were in bed and she—"

"Please, stop! Stop! I don't want to hear." Raf feigned weeping. "This is very, very bad."

"No, it's a good thing. It's great, mate. We're like living together."

"Listen to me." Raf got serious. "You've got a show to worry about. And remember: She's an anchor. She thinks like an anchor. She's no different from any of the others. She's got only one goal and it ain't you."

I broke the news to Peter at the St. James Club. "I have to tell you, mate. I did something really bad. With Alison."

He nodded. "I know. It's not bad. It's fucking great. It was the night we were at the Mondrian, right?"

"How'd you know?"

"I could tell the way she was looking at you. She wanted to carry on. Good on ya."

"No, mate. I feel like I upset some kind of balance. It wasn't my place to do that."

"Bullshit; you look good together. Besides, it might make things easier if she's not bringing that skier, what's his name? Yam?"

"Yam, Yom. I think he's still coming."

"Don't count on it."

Raf went out and got a scoop. A sister of an investigating officer in the Simpson case told him what her brother revealed at a family dinner. Not only was a bloody glove found at the crime scene: there was also a ski mask.

"We have to go with it," Brennan said. We needed another exclusive to make some waves.

"We can't. Not yet," Raf said. "I only have it on one and a half sources. Let me work it. Let me be sure."

"Raf, we don't have time to let you work it. We need you to go on the air with it."

"You can go into makeup and everything," I said.

"Fuck you." Raf loved sitting on the set being interviewed by Alison as an expert witness. "Let me make another phone call."

Raf had misgivings but went on the air with the story because we pressured him. He could only hope his one-and-a-half sources were right.

They weren't.

The next day, Simpson prosecutor Marcia Clark said it was not a ski mask but some sort of knit cap found at the crime scene.

On Friday, Raf was called on his mistake by none other than Howard Rosenberg. The *Los Angeles Times* TV writer wrote a column criticizing television's obsession with the Simpson case, though his own paper was dedicating special sections to the investigation each day. "Call Them

Irresponsible, Throw in Unreliable Too" was ostensibly about the "loose tongues" of news shows reporting inaccurate tips from police sources.

> During Tuesday night's edition of TV's newest syndicated tabloid series, *Premier Story*, scrounging reporter Rafael Abramovitz repeated the ski mask story, confidently swearing by the "source" who fed it to him.
>
> On Wednesday, however, Deputy Dist. Atty. Marcia Clark, lead prosecutor in the case, said there was no bloody ski mask.
>
> Oh.
>
> ...What's a reporter to do if fed some hot scoop on the case from a source that he or she regards as reliable? Just ignore it? "No, seek confirmation from another source," (UCLA law professor Peter) Arenella said. Yes, yes, but that's Reporting 101, something that should be standard procedure on every sensitive story...

"Scrounging reporter? Scrounging reporter? That's it. I'm finished. I knew it."

"It's only Howard Rosenberg, mate."

"You guys have ruined my reputation. I told you we should have waited. I knew this would happen."

"You are a scrounging reporter, mate. Reporters scrounge, that's what they do. That makes you good."

"You guys, you guys think this is funny. It's not."

"Mate, if we did more scrounging, we'd get more ratings."

Wayne Darwen joined us at the beginning of July. We needed him. The Simpson case had changed everything. The show that had started out with a two-way and a tape package had become as complex as any prime access reality show—with less than a quarter of the budget.

We kept one, and sometimes two, camera crews on call at all times to chase down action at the courthouse and jail. Prosecutors, police, the defense, and family members were leaking information, pictures, and tapes faster than we could keep up, and with the pretrial hearings underway, events were moving even faster.

Peter Brennan studied the ratings of our show and *Nightline* and saw that they dropped precipitously when the taped segments gave way to interviews. We began to extend and add tape packages throughout the show, and as a result, hired on a couple of temporary field producers and convinced Wayne to fly up from Tennessee for a few weeks. He was the experienced segment producer we needed; what's more, the Wild Bunch was now four-fifths together again.

Wayne, though, had changed. He was a different person from the one we'd left in New York. If six months in Franklin, Tennessee had given him a new serenity, six days in Los Angeles brought back all the old fears he'd be sucked back into the life that almost killed him before he was born again.

Wayne knew we wanted him to stay on longer. He didn't know how to tell us he couldn't do it. He couldn't tell any of us he'd made his peace with the Lord. Instead, he began a friendship with a producer named Carla who had fundamentalist beliefs.

Raf, meanwhile, was disappointed and angry that Peter never asked him officially to take a role on the show. He felt betrayed that we made him go with the ski mask story and turned him into a scrounging reporter. He was certain he'd be screwed out of his new show in some way or another; and he couldn't get over the idea that I was with Alison.

Alison Holloway was the key to our success. She wasn't only beautiful, she was a brilliant, complete television journalist: authoritative, quick on her feet, and a terrific interviewer—a combination of Gordon Elliott and Chuck Scarborough behind a Queen Anne desk. Raf was wrong. Alison wasn't just another anchor. She was as good, and better than, any of us, spending hours in the edit room, even getting made up there before rushing off to the set.

America was taking well to Alison Holloway and she was taking well to America. She gave her ski bum the Spanish archer and never sent for him after all, though she let him remain in her London house for months.

It just worked out that I was spending most nights at her new home in Laurel Canyon, a four-story hillside custom adobe she was paying far too much to rent. We'd work together, drink together, eat together, sleep together, and get back to work the next morning.

I felt a real responsibility to Alison and to making this show work, constantly fighting to hire people who knew what they were doing; to get equipment that worked the way real TV worked. She was giving so much and Brennan was allowing so much to slip through the cracks.

I was caring a little too much. He didn't like hearing it.

Around the time Wayne arrived, Alison got a call from a casting director for Hollywood Pictures. The popular action director Tony Scott, a fellow Brit, had seen her on *Premier Story* and felt she'd be perfect for the role of a tough Australian TV reporter in his new film, *Crimson Tide*.

Alison went to Culver City for a screen test, reading pages and pages of dialog for the casting director. The next day's phone call made her literally jump for joy. She had the part. They sent over a contract for a day's shooting.

Then she got a call from *Hello!* magazine, a big splashy colorful kissyface version of *People* that was very big in Britain and Europe. The always-flattering glossy wanted to do a spread on Alison's new career in the colonies. Her old friend, journalist Simon Kinnersley, would write the story, asking Alison a few questions for the interview and making up the rest with her blessing; big, quiet photographer Alan Olley would take the photos.

The two Brits moved into the Laurel Canyon house for the weekend and the photo shoot got underway that Saturday morning. Lights were set up, clothing laid out, music played, and champagne uncorked. Alison's hair stylist Gary Lacy and a lighting assistant were on hand.

As things got underway, I went off to run some errands. When I returned an hour or so later, I saw that the bathroom tub was filled with water and bubbles. Alison was posing in the living room in a white pantsuit and sweater. I waited for a break before I broached the question.

"Umm, did someone take a bath?"

"Oh, no," she said, breezily. "They got some shots of me in there."

"Oh, you were standing by the tub, right? Sitting on the edge?"

"Oh no. Here." She grabbed a test Polaroid off the couch. It was a shot of Alison in the bubble-filled tub. She was apparently naked. You could see a good bit of her cleavage.

"Oh no, you can't do this."

"Oh, you can't see anything."

I thought of Diane Sawyer in her slit skirt in *Vanity Fair*, Deborah Norville breastfeeding in *People*—*Gunga Dan.*

"You don't understand," I told her. "If the tabloids here get a hold of this, you'd be finished. I mean, would Peter Jennings pose on his toilet?"

"Don't make me feel stupid."

"I'm not trying to—"

I called Brennan. "Tell them you'll cancel the shoot if they don't give up the film," he said. Then he laughed. "She doesn't understand. They do that sort of thing all the time in Britain."

"You saw her tits and everything, almost."

"Save the Polaroid."

Alison came back into the kitchen. "Alan promised not to use the bath shot. He says I can have the film if I want."

"Good. Get it from him."

We all headed off to Venice Beach for shots of Ally on rollerblades. She wouldn't do any swimsuit shots.

Premier Story had been on the air five weeks when the Simpson pretrial hearing ended on July eighth. Along with all the evidence revealed in the televised proceedings, many of the faces we couldn't put names to in the hours after the murders were identified and developed into important characters.

None was more intriguing than Robert Kardashian, O.J. Simpon's close friend and business partner. Kardashian read Simpson's supposed suicide note the day of the Bronco chase and later reactivated his law license to help in his friend's defense.

We had video from the morning after the murders showing Kardashian waiting at the mansion gate for Simpson to arrive home from Chicago. When Simpson was led in by police, Kardashian remained planted outside. A woman who'd accompanied Simpson from the airport walked over to Kardashian with a stuffed garment bag. She and Kardashian embraced. She put her head on his shoulder. It looked as if they were crying, but when I blew up the tape, it was obvious he was whispering something. His eyes scanned the scene.

When Simpson was led out to be driven to police headquarters for questioning, Kardashian took the garment bag and scooted away, unnoticed by anyone but another observant KCOP cameraman.

We noticed the man. We just didn't know who he was at the time.

We promoted a story on the Kardashian tape to run the following Monday, four weeks after the murders. It would be a look back at the mysterious doings outside the mansion and the people we didn't know then, but knew all too well now. It made for a good promo.

On Monday, July eleventh, editor Jack Foster and I squeezed into the tiny airless editing closet and began work on the piece. I had him slow the tape, stop and start it, even zoom in on faces in the crowd as I tried to find a story angle to fit the promo.

"Let it run in slow motion," I instructed him, sipping coffee as I watched little Kardashian, in his jeans and polo shirt, walk away with the suitcase.

"Can you make it slower?"

"Sure."

Slower. The police officers were concerned with keeping the cameras away from the car holding Simspon. Attorney Howard Weitzman seemed to make eye contact with Kardashian before calling over to the lead detective and placing an arm over his shoulder. Kardashian and the woman were on the move, walking past cops and detectives. Detective Bert Luper almost bumped into him walking out of the driveway.

The big Louis Vuitton garment bag—we could tell by the markings— was too heavy for the little man. He switched hands, and as he did, I noticed something. "Roll that back."

"You got it."

"Real slow." I leaned toward the screen. My eyes had to be fooling me.

Kardashian moved slowly in reverse. The bag changed hands. Three tags flew up from the handle.

"Freeze it!"

Jack did. "Back a little. Thanks."

Three tags: one said Hertz; the others were for American Airlines.

"Fuck me."

"What is it?"

"Fuck me."

Simpson, the Hertz spokesman, flew American Airlines to and from Chicago. It was O.J. Simpson's bag; the one he brought back from Chicago; the one police were searching for. They'd never found a murder weapon or bloody clothes—or the Louis Vuitton garment bag.

Robert Kardashian was getting away with O.J. Simpson's bag—and who knows what else.

Holy shit.

Jack, veteran of many a story, realized what we had. He whistled and smiled. "Wow."

I got on the phone to Brennan's office. Raf picked up.

"Is Peter there?"

"He's on the other line."

"You guys better come over to the edit room, like now. I think we solved the case."

"Is this more of your bullshit—"

"I'm not kidding. Put Peter on the phone."

"Hall-lo."

"Mate, you've got to get down here now. I've got something really big. A major heavy. A major fucking heavy."

The picture was frozen on the screen: Hertz and American Airlines Premium Class.

"Well, fuck, you've solved the case, Burtie." Brennan lit a cigarette and took a deep drag.

Raf shook his head. "Holy shit. You did it. This is fucking big. I don't believe this."

The only question was the identity of the woman; the one who handed Kardashian the garment bag in the first place. She looked like Cathy Randa, Simpson's faithful assistant of twenty years; yet she seemed a bit heavier than in the other pictures we'd seen of her.

Stephen Green, a budding filmmaker who was creating our tape library singlehandedly, pulled out a tape of Randa at the pretrial hearing. We still couldn't tell.

"Push in on the side of her head."

Jack blew up the courtroom video. She was wearing the same earrings in court that she wore the morning after the murders.

Everything was falling into place. Cathy Randa had come from the airport with Simpson. When Officer Thompson grabbed Simpson and took his shoulderbag, she was able to carry out the garment bag, unmolested.

It looked like we had ourselves a conspiracy.

"Let's get hold of the cops." Raf was pumped up. He called the LAPD detectives and Bert Luper was in our office within the hour. Our camera crew videotaped as he and his fellow detectives watched the tape and shook their heads. "That's the bag we're looking for, all right."

It had been four weeks since O.J. Simpson arrived home from Chicago, four long weeks since the day Robert Kardashian took the bag, and five weeks since our show had made its debut.

I wrote a piece for Raf to read. He added the section about the detectives and tracked the story before he went off to makeup so he could talk about the discovery on the set.

> Watching the tape in slow motion rang the bell for
> our senior producer Burt Kearns.
> He called me up to the editing room.
> He showed me what he had spotted.
> It all looked strange—too strange to be just
> anyone's bag.
> Strange enough to find out if the cops investigating
> the case were interested in this piece of video.
> Bert Luper and his partner were at the OJ mansion
> the morning that Kardashian walked off with the
> bag.
> Bert Luper was in Chicago looking for the murder
> weapon.
> What we didn't know was that he was after this very
> garment bag.
> They screened the tape, and it was all too clear what
> this bag meant to them.
> That it was the "V" bag they had been looking for.
> The designer garment bag that left with OJ for
> Chicago.
> A bag they believed contained evidence in the case.
> A bag that was on the scene in plain view; which
> turned out to be the perfect place to have it go
> unnoticed.

⸺◆⸺

"You've done it, mate. You've made your bones," Raf said in all seriousness. "I had the Chambers tape and the Amy Fisher tape; now you have this. You're up there with us now. This was your baptism."

"It's bigger than that!" Wayne enthused. "This is a movie!"

"He's right," Brennan agreed. "We should write the treatment now."

"Think of the story!" Wayne was truly excited. "You have this producer who's a fuckin congenital liar, he can't ever tell the truth, he's the one who finds a piece of tape of Elvis in a fuckin hardhat and he says Elvis designed the Las Vegas Hilton—"

"He had the blueprints. He did help design the Hilton."

"—and then he gets the fuckin scoop of the year and we don't believe him because we're used to him exaggerating all the time! It's the greatest! *The Boy Who Cried Bag!*"

"You've got something there, mate," Brennan said.

"So, what do we do next?" I asked. "With the bag story, I mean."

"We wait."

"We should have Raf go after Kardashian."

"No," Brennan said. "This is going to blow the case wide open. Let's let it settle and see what everyone does with it first."

Wayne was still thinking up angles. "This is gonna send Simpson to fuckin prison for life. You oughta be careful, mate. That Al Cowlings is gonna come after you."

"We don't even know if Simpson did it," I said.

"He did it," Raf said.

"Hey, I admire Kardashian," I said. "He's the best friend a man could ever hope to have. Without question, he went over the line for his friend."

"Now we know why he renewed his legal license," Raf said. "So he can't be forced to testify."

"I feel bad ratting him out."

Wayne chuckled and lit a cigarette. "The Boy Who Cried Bag, that's it, yeah."

"I can't believe it," Raf shook his head.

Brennan lit up as well. "Let's just see what happens next."

What happened next was even more astounding. Everyone else in town tried to take credit for the discovery.

I couldn't believe it. This wasn't a story that people were fighting for; it wasn't in the air—nobody was poring over old videotape looking for clues. This Kardashian bag story came out of *Premier Story*'s edit room, and if we hadn't run out of stories to promote, Kardashian would have gotten away with it.

Even worse, this cowardly theft of historical credit actually began in our own building. The KCOP news team was upset we didn't notify them of our scoop in advance or mention it was their cameraman who shot Kardashian with the bag. The next morning, they sent a reporter to interview us about the discovery, but ran a segment that night that didn't mention *Premier Story* at all.

It was small-town, small-time bullshit, but nothing compared to the gall of KCBS. The newsroom where Linda Bell's husband landed not only ran the bag story without mentioning *Premier Story*, but they had Associated Press run a story around the country that gave a KCBS reporter credit for nailing Kardashian with the bag.

One of the more blatant credit-takers was Harvey Levin, a chunky attorney-turned-reporter who played a nasty-tempered Geraldo with an adenoidal voice. Levin went on the air a couple of days later with a scoop of his own. "Sometimes it pays to go back and study the old footage to see what we missed the first time around," he said, as if it were his idea. "That's what we did..."

Levin's scoop was tape of Marcia Clark leading a search of Simpson's mansion. According to the "time code," the hour and minutes displayed on the video, she was snooping around the property an hour before a search warrant was issued. If true, the result could be devastating to the prosecution, barring important evidence and removing Marcia Clark from the Simpson case.

The next day, KCBS made Harvey Levin apologize over and over again. He said he was wrong, claiming the time code on the tape referred not to 9:45 a.m., but 9:45 p.m., the time the tape was fed from a remote truck outside Simpson's mansion. Being that the time code for 9:45 p.m. would have read 21:45, it's more likely that KCBS or Levin reached some agreement with prosecutors not to blow their case so early in the game.

Levin looked like a buffoon. He deserved everything he got.

"The bag" became *Premier Story*'s hook. It gave us an identity and it gave Alison a memorable tagline. For weeks after the discovery, she ended each show with the line, "Where's the bag, Mr. Kardashian?"

We hired a plane to fly over Los Angeles, from Brentwood to Hollywood to downtown L.A., trailing a banner that read "Where's the bag, Mr. Kardashian?" Producers and reporters, even spectators, began to hound O.J.'s friend by shouting the question whenever he appeared in public.

He'd eventually have to face the music in court.

We wanted to take the story to the next step and find the bag. Brennan got one of his private eye connections to start calling every marina along the local coast to see who rented small boats in the days following the murders.

Brennan was convinced the bag was dumped in the Pacific, and when a porn star told some reporter that her boyfriend Al Cowlings told her the murder weapon "sleeps with the fishes," his hunch seemed to be borne out.

In the meantime, he had another idea.

"Let's buy a Louis Vuitton bag that's exactly like Simpson's, let's attach Hertz and American Airlines tags, and let's dump it in the ocean so it washes up on shore at Malibu."

"Should we make it bloody?"

"No, just a bag. Let's see what happens."

"You can't do that," Raf said.

"Yeah, I guess you're right."

Nick Loiacono was on the phone. Nicky, who'd taught me the TV ropes back on the assignment desk at Channel Five, had become something like a brother, through ups and downs and his restless time in Los Angeles at *Hard Copy*. Nicky was back in New York now, working across the river in New Jersey for NBC's America's Talking cable outfit, producing a show called *Bugged*, on which people came in or called in to talk about whatever happened to be bugging them.

Nicky had given us the phone number to the control room, offering us the chance to vent our spleens about anything that bugged us. This time it was Nicky who was bugged, and very upset.

"Look, man, I'm really sorry. I had no idea this was going to happen, but you guys gotta know about it, it's really bad."

"Whoa, whoa, Nicky, man, it's all right. What happened?"

"See, I've been getting any celebrity types I know to call in and talk about what's bugging 'em. I found Joe Pepitone and Martin Abend—you know, the usual. Anyway, I called Barry Nolan, he's been a good guy, people know him. Barry says great, he'll say he's bugged they don't spend enough money on curing childhood diseases."

What Nolan actually said, live on *America's Talking*, deviated slightly from the plan.

Wayne, Raf, Brennan, and I sat in Brennan's office while Nicky played the tape over the speaker phone.

"You know what bugs me? I work for two very hardworking women. They call them the Two Lindas, and they've worked very hard to make this show a success," was Nolan's gist. "Last season, this place was run by a bunch of Australians. They were a boy's club, and if you wanted to be in it you had to drink with them. All they did was get drunk, and that bugs me…"

Brennan smiled slightly and sadly as the man whose career he created damned him on the speakerphone.

Raf shook his head. "This is very bad."

"Why? Why would he say that?" was all Wayne could say.

How could this pontificating pipsqueak pipe on about the man who made him a star and possibly a millionaire on the basis of his Irish good looks and prematurely gray hair? I could picture Linda Bell next to Nolan, rubbing her fleshy shoulder against his as the phonebook-sitting ventriloquist's dummy followed her script.

Nicky got back on. "That's it, man. I'm sorry. I didn't know."

Brennan laughed. "It's all right, Nicky. No harm done." He hung up and stood for a cigarette.

"You oughta sue," Raf said.

"I think I'll call my lawyer. Give him a scare."

CHAPTER TWENTY-NINE:
GUD'BY T'WAYNE & HELLO, HI-8 JOE

Wayne and I sat at the end of the Monkey Bar. "You're looking good, though, mate. A lot better than you did in New York."

"I've dropped eighteen pounds in four weeks. It's entirely due to stress. It's amazing."

"Yeah, and Alison. She's good, ain't she."

"She is. I'm like Kato with her. I haven't been like this before." I pulled out my Vietnam Zippo and held my palm over the skipping flame. "I can still do this."

Wayne looked on in shock and grabbed the lighter. "Stop that! Don't be an asshole, mate."

It was early July. *Premier Story* was days away from moving its offices and studio off the KCOP lot to the campus of the Hollywood Center studios a mile or so east. It was a good time to move. Technicians were about to launch their strike against the cheapskate KCOP management, and we'd been smoked out of our dinky old studio. The board in the control room had blown up during a pretape session, with sparks, flames and everything, and we'd been forced to broadcast from the KCOP newsroom. Every time our stage manager called for quiet and counted down to an interview or an intro, people in the newsroom would drop tapes on the floor or do "Blow me!" coughs. They were jealous.

Peter had made Wayne an offer that would keep him in L.A. for the next three months. The money was generous and he felt loyalty to his mates, but Wayne didn't want to be in Los Angeles.

"Mate, I miss my dogs."

"Yeah, but isn't this great? We have a show. It's what the first days of *A Current Affair* must have been like. We're gonna change the fucking business."

"I was thinkin', mate, I could work with you guys from Nashville. I could get you all kinds of stories from there."

"Wayne, we need you here. At least til we get it under control."

Wayne looked into his beer. "I don't know. I hate this town. L.A.'s a bad place."

"Mate, stick with us."

Two days before the move, Wayne made his.

I entered the office that morning as I usually did, on the run, passing Wayne and one of the producers sitting together at a word processor.

"Hey," I said to her. "Why aren't you at the courthouse?"

She was assigned to cover a news conference that was set to begin in a matter of minutes.

"It's all right," Wayne said, looking straight at the screen. "She's writing a script with me."

"No, it's not all right. I've got to put on a show. We need the news conference. Go."

"Mate! I need her to help me with the script."

"I'll help you with the script. We've got all day." To the producer: "Get the crew and get down there."

"Fuck you!" Wayne yelled. "Fuck this Mickey Mouse fucking operation!"

E.F. Hutton had spoken again. Everyone in the place turned their heads and froze.

"Come into Peter's office," I said.

Wayne ran in after me and I slammed the door.

"Don't ever pull that shit in front of the staff."

"Fuck that, mate! I can't get any help in this fucking place. If I want to use her, I can use her!"

"I'm the senior producer here. I have to run a show. I assigned her to the courthouse for a reason. You'll get your help."

"Fuck this power tripping bullshit!"

"Wayne, it's not power tripping. It's management and it's getting the show on the air."

"Well, fuck this, fuck this!"

I tried to look into Wayne's eyes. They were looking everywhere but into mine. I knew what he was doing. It was the same explosion when he walked out of *A Current Affair*. Wayne couldn't find a graceful way to refuse Peter's three-month contract offer so he was choosing a path of blazing glory.

"I'm not gonna take it." He was still going. *Adios, mi amigo.* "I'm not listening to you." Thanks for your help. "I'll fuckin walk, mate." See you in Nashville. "If I don't get that fuckin woman to help with my fuckin script, I'll fuckin walk out!"

I gave him the out. "Go ahead and walk!"

Wayne turned on his heel, flung open the door, rounded the corner, and kicked open the bar of the emergency door to the Bargain Circus overlook. He ran down the steps.

It was eight a.m.

I took a breath, picked up my coffee, and walked to the doorway. Everyone in the office pretended they hadn't been listening to every whisper-shouted word behind the door.

I opened the door to the landing as calmly as possible.

Wayne was running down LaBrea Boulevard.

They gathered behind me slowly, Anita and Carla and Julie and Stephen, watching Wayne's figure get smaller as he headed toward Melrose.

"Is he okay?" Anita asked.

"I don't know."

"Aw, Wayne's a good guy, he'll be back." Carla lit a cigarette.

"I don't think so," I said. "I don't think he will."

"He just went like that?"

"Yeah, he flipped out. Just like he flipped out when he quit *A Current Affair*. I think he must be on drugs or something."

Peter was angry. He'd scheduled a quick vacation that weekend. Wayne had done the unthinkable, pulling out on deadline.

"I think he wanted to go back to Nashville," I said.

"Doesn't do us any good. Shut the door."

I did and sat down.

"I think we have our savior."

"Who's that?"

"Dunleavy."

"He'd never leave Murdoch."

"Believe me, mate, he's coming. He thinks it's his last chance."

"Well, it is, isn't it."

"Can you imagine, Alison and Dunleavy?" Brennan smiled wider than I'd seen him smile in months.

We were set up in a two-story bungalow with a palm-shaded yard at the back of the Hollywood Center Studios, the bustling hive that served as the studio in the film *The Player*. Don Adams was taping a revived version of *Get Smart* in the nearby soundstage. Donald O'Connor and Mitzi Gaynor had written their names in the cement walkway to *Premier Story*'s new front door.

Our new digs, with refrigerators and cable-ready TV monitors, gave us the aura of chic California success, yet the problems remained. The editing equipment, now stuffed into small rooms off the kitchen and hallway, remained inferior. The editors and technical staff were working around shifts at other shows; they were often wearied and unprepared.

We whipped them like horses and somehow crossed the finish line each evening. There was no break from the work. Brennan and Alison and

I did the brunt of it: the writing, the editing, the producing. Relief came when we hired a couple of more segment producers, including Dunleavy's minder-turned-producer, Shannah Goldner. We needed it. *Premier Story* was getting bigger and more expensive than originally anticipated. The miserly $125,000 weekly budget began creeping toward $150,000, but still nowhere near what the other tabloid and reality shows cost—and they were looking to us for direction.

Raf moved in and out of the orbit. His anger flared again when he learned how much Brennan offered Wayne to come on board.

"Mate, I had to offer him more because we wanted him full-time," Brennan explained. "I can't go to Chris-Craft and tell them I want to give you the same, because you're only part-time. You have your own show to worry about and you could be leaving at any time."

Oh, yeah. Raf had his own show. *Detour* was taking shape.

There were at least a dozen people crammed into Alison's spacious corner office for a meeting about *Detour*. Aaron Spelling's new Worldvision syndication arm had bought into the project with Four Point. Chief Karen Miller loved the concept, loved the tape, and loved Raf. She loved it all so much she wanted to add a smidgen of her own ideas to make it that much better and give it her imprint.

Compromise had begun as everyone in the big circle spoke about turning the twelve-minute pitch tape into a Hollywood extravaganza, with film and everything.

Everyone had ideas. A dresser and her assistant sat balancing on their laps swatches of various-hued denims and catalogs from Ralph Lauren and Calvin Klein so Raf could be suited in a phony designer version of the genuine articles he wore in everyday life and on the tape. An Asian man wearing a long purple dress held up cards of different colors for the graphics. A pair of art designers explained their ideas for the opening.

"I see oil derricks, pumping up and down!"

"Men with jackhammers!"

"Raf's car rides through a construction site!"

"Silos!"

I could see where this was going.

"Now, we'll reshoot the car scenes on film," Karen Miller said. "We'll need a cinematographer."

"I've got some candidates," Brennan said.

"And Raf will do one more story. It should be a woman's story. A woman who makes a choice in her life."

We'd already done some research. "We have that story down near the Everglades," I said. "A woman was accused by the local paper of having

AIDS." There were glances and visible shivers around the room. "It was a phony rumor. She fought back."

"That's great."

"Now, the logo—"

The designers had an idea worth every penny and plexiglas award they ever got: a "Detour" road sign.

"Oh yes, we can put it on the side of the road at the construction site..."

There were more detours ahead. Brennan was suddenly vague about whether Raf would definitely be hosting the show. In any case, he said, Raf would have a piece of it and he signed to Four Point, not Worldvision, as either producer or host.

Raf was certain he'd get screwed out of the deal one way or another. For safety's sake, he called in a chit from an old friend in Beverly Hills and got himself a meeting with an agent at CAA.

Raf wanted to be protected. Boy, did he get a wrong number.

On August tenth, *Hard Copy's* era of "The Two Lindas" ended when co-executive producer Linda Ellman resigned unexpectedly with the comment that "tabloid television is not my life."

"While some industry sources referred to the obvious tensions that would have arisen between two executive producers working together under tense conditions, this was dismissed as a reason for Ellman's resignation," Steve Brennan wrote in the *Hollywood Reporter*. "One source suggested she is in talks about the possibility of running her own show."

Paramount Television issued a statement giving her equal credit for guiding the show "to its highest ratings in its five-year history." The statement said there were no immediate plans to replace her.

There was no comment from the other co-executive producer, Linda Bell. It had taken her five years and there were many bodies in her wake, but she had done it.

Linda Bell had won.

"Listen to me. We've got to concentrate on *Detour*, mate," Raf said. "*Premier Story* is a done deal. Forget this. Come with me."

"I can't, mate, it's day by day with *Premier Story*."

"Yeah, you're riding high now. But remember, you're gonna fall."

Raf was angry that I was spending time with the anchor of the show. I knew it, but as successful as we thought the show might be, *Premier Story* remained an uphill climb.

Under ordinary circumstances, the O.J. Simpson case would have been a godsend to a show like ours; a tabloid story we could make our own.

Indeed, in the early weeks, as *Nightline* turned up its nose, *Premier Story* ran away with the coverage and ratings.

By now, though, O.J. Simpson was everywhere, always, from local to network news, morning shows to talk shows. Each had its own angle, and by the time 11:30 came around, people were ready to hear Jay Leno crack some tasteless jokes about the whole mess.

Premier Story was one of the bunch—making as much noise as we could while broadcast on a mere five stations. We kept breaking news, and expanded our horizons to embrace other big tabloid stories of the day: Prince Charles admitting adultery; the suicide of porn star Savannah; interviews with the likes of Jane Seymour, Tonya Harding, and John Wayne Bobbitt (exhibiting his mended member through skintight bicycle shorts); the Roswell UFO incident; the bizarre wedding of Michael Jackson and Lisa Marie Presley; the mysterious drowning of Jackson's former sister-in-law, DeDe.

Then there was the other black sports hero caught in a tragic murder case. Chicago Bulls basketball icon Michael Jordan saw his world destroyed when his father and confidante James Jordan disappeared in July 1993 while driving through North Carolina.

Two weeks after James Jordan went missing, his red Lexus 400 turned up smashed and stripped; a few days later, a John Doe body that had been dragged from a swamp weeks earlier was identified as the famous father.

The coroner had to use dental records to make the I.D.; the morgue had no refrigeration unit, so the body had been cremated. All that was saved were a .38 calibre slug pried from the victim's chest, $10,000 in dental work, and his fingertips.

By the summer of 1994, there were two young men accused of the murder and speculation they may have been railroaded. The questions reached a bizarre crescendo when one of their attorneys claimed the senior Jordan wasn't dead at all—that he'd faked his death because he was on the run from gamblers.

"Imagine that," I said, "You're sitting in some bar in the Caribbean, watching the story on satellite TV, and you look over and there's an old guy next to you with no teeth, holding his beer with both hands because he has no fingertips."

Michael Jordan, meanwhile, had quit basketball and was burying his grief not by chasing the killers but by chasing a baseball dream in the muggy Deep South where his father had disappeared. Michael Jordan, superstar, was now Michael Jordan, outfielder for the AA Birmingham Barons of Alabama, a team down a rung or two in the Chicago White Sox farm system.

It was a poignant and wonderful summer for Jordan. While Raf went down to Robeson County to check out the murder investigation, I came up with a way to capture the baseball story.

It was time to create another character.

Joe Guidry was a twenty-one-year-old kid from Louisiana we'd hired as a tape transcriber and who was now working as a production assistant, runner, and helper in the tape library. He was conscientious, good-natured, and, many days, came to work wearing a Michael Jordan basketball jersey. Joe's head was shaved. He was a dead ringer for Michael Jordan.

I called Joe into my bright new California office and asked him about his goals in the television business. Joe wanted to be a producer. He was taking television and radio classes at a community college and volunteering as a cameraman at a public access cable station when he wasn't using his motor scooter to do errands for *Premier Story*.

"You ever use a Hi-8 camera?"

"Like a home video? Yes, I have."

"You ever been out on the road before?"

"No, I have not."

"Wanna go?"

We got Joe credentialed and sent him down to Alabama to cover the Birmingham Barons and get as close to Michael Jordan as he could. I told Joe to wear his Michael Jordan jersey and act like a fan, figuring they looked so much alike, the star would feel sorry for him and give him an interview.

Hi-8 Joe was born.

Joe spent a week in Birmingham, joining the Barons for their homestand against the Memphis Chicks. He had many memorable meetings with his hero: during batting practice, in the dugout, and on the field. Most all of them consisted of Joe calling out Michael Jordan's name and Michael Jordan ignoring him.

A couple of days in, an attractive ballpark worker named Cheryl took pity on the plight of the young lookalike. Perhaps she could be of some help. Her cousin was Jordan's maid.

Joe called the cousin that afternoon and she promised to ask Jordan to give Joe an interview.

She soon called back. "Michael says no."

Joe proved his journalistic savvy that night, when he and Cheryl drove up to the guardhouse at Michael Jordan's gated community.

"We're here to pick up Michael Jordan's maid. We're the maid's ride," Joe said, and after Cheryl gave a few identifying details, they were waved through; Joe driving with the Hi-8 on his lap.

They were in front of Jordan's two-story brick mansion. A basketball hoop was set up in the driveway. Joe shot surreptitiously and got out with the maid.

The next morning, Joe was with the press pack in the club house.

"Hey! You! C'mere." It was Michael Jordan, sitting on a bench in front of his locker.

"Me?"

"Yeah, you. C'mere."

Joe stood before his idol.

"I hear you came by my house and were shooting and stuff."

"Well, yeah—"

"Don't you be doin that. That's not cool."

"I'm just doing my job." Joe could barely get through the journalist's standard reply before bursting into laughter.

Jordan waved him off in disgust, but back on the field, Joe was unrelenting.

"Yo, Michael! Mike! Mike, talk to me!"

Jordan finally gave Joe a few words on-camera as he walked to the showers after a practice. It had something to do with not agreeing that Joe looked anything like him at all.

We dedicated the entire Labor Day show to Joe's pursuit of his hero, Michael Jordan. Alison and Joe sat on the edge of the set to introduce and talk about the segments. We called it "Michael & Me," in a nod to Michael Moore's hunt for a meeting with General Motors boss Roger Smith in *Roger & Me*.

The show ended with a similar twist: hours after Joe had gotten on a plane to return to Los Angeles, Michael Jordan held his first free-for-all news conference.

Two days after Labor Day, we only had to look in the *L.A. Times* to see the new problem the uncooperative KCOP had foisted upon us. It was bad enough their half-hour newscast was running ads saying that only idiots watched the news after eleven. Now Ricky Feldman, the station's general manager, had bought up and was crowing about a block of late night programming that had little chance of succeeding but every chance of burying *Premier Story*.

"They fit the profile of my station," he told the paper, "which is few older people and lots of young adults."

It was unclear what audience would tune into this batch. The block began at 10:30 with a show called *Last Call*, a Brandon Tartikoff vehicle described as a "younger, humorous *McLaughlin Group*." It was hosted by Brianne Leary, a co-star in the TV series *CHiPs* back in the seventies, and featured a bunch of hiply-dressed young folk making light of the news.

This was followed by a show called *The Newz*, spelled with that wacky "z" to telegraph to the viewer that it was bound to be a laugh riot— "laugh" spelled "l-a-f-f!"—a nightly sketch comedy show in the spotty tradition of *Saturday Night Live*. The zany press photo showed the kooky cast wearing straitjackets.

"Featuring an ensemble cast of stand-up comics and improvisational actors and a team of writers grounded in the *Harvard Lampoon*," the *L.A. Times* hyped, "the show will spoof the day's news and events and include recurring characters such as Andy and Abby, a couple of combative columnists dispensing advice on relationships."

Yeeee-hah! They would have done better dredging up the old gang from *FUNY*.

Premier Story was sandwiched in at 11:30, followed by Paramount's desperate replacement for Arsenio Hall, Jon Stewart, an MTV wisenheimer in Doc Maartens and black t, obsessed with homoerotic, backside-oriented humor.

"We're going to baby it a little," Ricky Feldman told the *L.A. Times* about *Premier Story*, frustrated he couldn't move the show because it was owned by his parent company, Chris-Craft. He was actually more concerned with saving money. "You can spend millions for, let's say, *Who's the Boss?*, and you have hundreds of episodes, and what if people don't want to see them anymore? If first-run doesn't work, you drop it and go on to something else. But if it does work, then you have a franchise, a huge hit like Ricki Lake turned out to be."

Meanwhile, he was cutting the throat of Chris-Craft's own chance at a franchise.

Back in New York, Dunleavy was feeling the effects of a knife in the back.

The assailant was the self-righteous, leftist filmmaker Oliver Stone, whose new movie was a blood, gore, and drugfest called *Natural Born Killers*. The film was intended as an over-the-top, rock 'n' rolling indictment of the media's glorification of violence and murderers, but was damned as a celebration of the same.

Key to Stone's broadside was a character named Wayne Gale, an Australian tabloid TV reporter played by Robert Downey, Jr. Wayne Gale was a slimy, soulless, grandstanding, and, ultimately, demonic scumbag. Downey Jr. and Stone helped publicize the movie by telling the media that Wayne Gale was based on Steve Dunleavy.

Indeed, a year or so earlier, Downey, Jr. did follow Dunleavy on his daily rounds, sat in on production meetings, watched him interview heavyweight champion Riddick Bowe, and joined him at bars.

"He's a rather tiny, obsequious man who spent three days with me drinking my beer," Dunleavy recalled when asked to comment on the actor. "Never asked me one question. Anyone who doesn't ask a question of a supposed subject is either arrogant or stupid. You pick which one."

Dunleavy told the New York *Daily News* he phoned Downey, Jr. after the movie's release, "fully prepared to do an interview about his alleged sendup of me, and got a wall of silence. Four thousand secretaries later, he wouldn't talk to me."

He could only feel disappointment over the young chameleon Downey, Jr. Dunleavy's wrath was reserved for the *auteur*, Stone. "Please don't think that I feel outraged and/or angry," he told the paper. "I'm kind of detachedly amused by the whole stupidity of it. This from a man who has made millions upon millions of dollars out of blood, guts and scar tissue. He has happily made millions out of exploiting every blood cell spurted out of the human body."

"I don't begrudge him making a buck—he's got two alimonies to pay. But leave the moralizing to the priests and rabbis."

The irony in Dunleavy's situation was that he may have been Stone's public target, but he wasn't the true model for Wayne Gale.

Wayne Darwen was. Around the time Downey, Jr. followed Dunleavy, he also hung around Tribune, where Darwen and Geraldo were in full swing. Downey, Jr.'s creation dressed and walked like Darwen, made references to ex-wives and secret girlfriends—the Gale character even sucked up to the serial killers for a big exclusive interview just as the real Wayne had befriended Berkowitz.

Dunleavy was a more promotable target.

Raf returned that week to Lake Mirage to reshoot the desert *Detour* scenes on film. The shoot didn't go well. Raf was stiff in his designer cowboy duds, and when he was revving up his '67 Mustang to record engine sounds, he accidentally threw it into gear and smashed the front end of his beloved ponycar to bits.

The sound of the car, the crash, and Raf's curses were priceless.

It was Raf's idea the first time around to record his track in a pub, telling the stories to Brennan. For the new pilot, we'd redo his dialog in a diner on the corner of Santa Monica and LaBrea.

Alison was leaving town that night; she was returning to London to fulfill some commitments she'd left behind. Her substitute host was to be David Lewis, a bear of a bearded attorney we'd used on a regular basis in two-ways about the Simpson case.

Lewis had a big reputation. He'd represented Manuel Noriega and had managed to get a hung jury in the first trial of Carolyn Warmus, the crazy

Westchester schoolteacher who shot her boyfriend's wife dead before going off to give the unwary widower a blowjob in the parking lot of a Holiday Inn.

Though David Lewis wasn't exactly an electric screen presence, it was one of Brennan's hit-or-miss inspirations to use him. We moved Alison's Queen Anne desk off the set and lugged out a scuffed old office number. We could only hope the ratings would hold.

Lewis arrived in town as I was driving Alison to the airport, me a bundle of hyper turmoil because I knew she'd be seeing the ski bum for the first time since she'd left him three months earlier and was worried she wouldn't come back.

I kissed her goodbye at the metal detector and walked through the big International terminal with a heavy heart that could only be lightened by something Russian and distilled. I slipped into a terminal bar, took a seat next to one of those weenie rotisseries, and settled in with a double Stoli and tonic.

What an experience it was, being the only one who wasn't knocking back a quick one with an eye on the clock before rushing off to fly away. Everyone had somewhere to go; everyone but me.

I had five Stoli and tonics on my pub crawl of the hideaway lounges of LAX; a lone presence of drinking calm in a place where everyone was on the move. Alison was in the sky by the time I had a skycap point me back to the parking garage. I was as drunk as I'd been since we'd first gotten together and she began luring me from Brennan and my barposts to her bed in Laurel Canyon.

I wondered for the first time what it meant, if I was missing something, and whether this was why Peter and I were having so many disagreements about the direction of the show and the way things weren't working—whether our connection was weakened because we were no longer meeting at the point of clarity so many hours down the drinking line.

I put my old driving skills to use, pointed the Porsche down Century Boulevard, and called Wayne on the cell phone. Wayne had committed a journalistic sin running off on deadline, but when I'd spoken to him a couple of days later, he was back in Nashville and seemed to have forgotten what happened. We hadn't spoken much since that day.

"How are ya, mate?" he asked. "How's Ally?"

"She's good, she's good. She went back to England for the week, so I'm on my own."

"Watch out, mate, don't go gettin yourself arrested on Hollywood Boulevard."

"Yeah, right. How are you?"

"Fine. I could use a little mazuma if you know what I mean, so if you guys have any work down here, I'm up for it. You know, I needed to get away from L.A. Everything was movin too fast."

"I understand."

"Yeah, I'm on my back porch right now, I got the hot tub goin, my dogs at my feet..."

We spoke all the way up LaBrea to the diner.

Raf and Peter were replaying the barroom scene, only in this new Aaron Spelling version, it was over coffee instead of beers. Peter sat at the counter with his back to the camera; Raf flubbed the lines again and again.

I poured myself into a leatherette booth and watched.

"You know, that mother had a choice. And it was her choice," Raf recited, before stopping the take and trying again.

"Can I say something?" I slurred.

Peter and Raf looked at each other and rolled their eyes.

"What?"

"It's very off-putting, all this talk about 'choice,' it's like a feminist buzzword, mate."

"It's in the script now."

"Yeah, well, I think you're gonna have problems in the South, cause this word choice means abortion, a woman's right to choose and all that."

"Karen Miller wants the word in." Brennan said it quickly.

"Karen Miller?"

"It's her money, mate."

"You let Karen Miller write the script?"

Raf sighed. "Can we get on with this? I don't have all night."

Jim Ryan, the witty anchorman for *A Current Affair*, once told one of the funniest jokes I'd ever heard. He was sitting over a drink at the old Racing Club as the sun was going down, when he said, "What's the difference between this place and an elephant's fart?"

I couldn't tell him.

"Well," he said in all seriousness. "This place is a barroom. An elephant's fart... is a *BAR-OOOM!*"

Now, Ryan was dealing with an elephantine decision forced upon him by Ian Rae and other Fox executives: whether to share the anchor desk the way it was done at *Hard Copy*. Lisa Gregorisch, a close friend to Rupert's daughter Elizabeth and the latest news director at Fox's Channel Five, had the perfect co-host: a newswoman and pal named Penny Daniels.

Jim Ryan didn't have to think long. He was daily at the mercy of people who didn't know how to produce television, who'd stuck him behind Maureen O'Boyle's New Age desk, covered him in Frank E. Campbell makeup, shot him in harsh lighting, and had him looking more like a purse-lipped Mr. Blackwell than the smart New Yorker everyone knew he was.

Enough was enough. Ryan said no, and went back to his day job anchoring *Good Day New York*, beating the networks morning after morning with his sleeves rolled up and sharp wit aglint.

Penny Daniels suddenly had *A Current Affair* to herself, and no one was sure why. She was a horsefaced young woman who acted out her lines with hand movements that approached the elaborateness of signing for the deaf. She had no connection to the show or, as far as anyone knew, tabloid television. No one could figure why the suits didn't go for the obvious choice.

Life away from Murdoch? Life without security? Dunleavy was back at Tommy McGrath's bar, drinking and thinking seriously about options he'd never considered.

He was double-fucked. Still huffing and puffing in pursuit of every exclusive he could get his hands on, he hoped secretly that his excellence and loyalty might be rewarded and he'd be tapped for the anchor job. After all, he was the spiritual leader of the show, the father confessor and hod carrier all in one.

There was no way. In light of the *Natural Born Killers* fiasco, Dunleavy's was the last face Fox wanted fronting its failing tabloid show.

On the other side of the country, Brennan saw the cracks opening in his mate's fragile ego. He went for it in a quick phone call to Max Robins at *Variety*. One small item was all it took.

Is Dunleavy A "Premier Story"?

A Current Affair chief correspondent Steve Dunleavy is being ardently courted by the folks at the upstart syndicated newsmag *Premier Story*. "It's an open secret that I'd love to steal him away. There's nobody better than Steve," says *Premier Story* executive producer Peter Brennan, who worked with Dunleavy when he ran *Affair* a few years back. "I've talked to him a bunch of times about coming over and I know that where he's working now is not a happy place, so maybe I'll be able to tempt him to leave and start having some fun again." Rumors have been coming out of *Affair* that since the departure of fiftysomething anchor Jim Ryan that Dunleavy, who is in the same age group, may be vulnerable as well...

For the first time, Dunleavy was considering a move, seriously.

"*Woof!*"

Bill Beltran hit the buttons on the console and barked the old film editor's affirmation of a completed edit. Fuckin Woof. The pictures on the monitors reversed, sped up, slowed down, and ended in a perfect segue. *Detour* Part Two was actually taking shape.

Brennan and I were trying hard on this one. We'd be starting a show for our mate, giving Rafael the glory he deserved and, we hoped, getting him over the insecurity that had him seeing defeat at every turn.

We'd been editing for days, though, and the going was slow. Raf spent most of his time down at the bar, obsessing over his Johnny Walker Black, stopping into the edit room to say he didn't like a shot I chose or the length of a dissolve. I'd grumble, do it again, and Bill would say "Woof."

There was one underlying problem with this second version of the *Detour* pilot. Nothing could replicate the natural rhythms of the first. That one came together instinctively. We spent hours whittling away words that didn't fit and finding shots that did. This one had fingerprints all over it. Karen Miller had her additional dialog; the film footage was inferior to the Lake Mirage video shot by cameraman Russell Lorette; and that extra story about the woman fighting the AIDS rumor didn't fit stylistically.

When Raf asked to bring his future son-in-law, a music video director, along to the Everglades, Brennan and I assumed he wanted only to show off his know-how and put the successful whippersnapper in his place. One look at the tapes though, and it was obvious Raf put much of the directing into the young man's hands. There was even a reversal shot, in which the reporter re-asks a question so his face can be shown. Raf was a crusader against such fakery. This reversal showed him with a sympathetic glisten in his eyes.

Raf had to deal with his own conscience on that one. He'd screened the AIDS rumor story. Around nine, he made his way up from the bar to tell me which shots and soundbites to use.

"Okay, mate," I said. "We're ready for the Everglades shot."

Raf stood there. "What's the rush? I know where it is."

"What tape's it on? We're on a roll here."

"Calm yourself down."

"C'mon, man, Bill's waiting. We're on a deadline here. Let's slap it in."

I don't know if it was the Johnny Walker Black or Alison or *Premier Story*, whether Raf was angry that I'd dropped the booze weight, or that he simply couldn't take the pressure.

"Don't talk to me that way."

"What?"

"Nobody talks to me that way." Raf was staring at me, angry.

"Scuse us, Bill," I said. "Let's take five."

I walked out of the edit room and Raf followed. "Mate, what's going on here? I've been editing for hours. We need to start on your section so we're not here all night."

"What are you, on speed? Calm down."

"If you don't know where the shots are, just tell me."

"Nobody talks to me like that."

Ron Ziskin walked by, noticing the two weirdos having it out in the middle of his office.

"Mate, what is your fucking problem?" I said. "Please, let's get this done. We're supposed to be working together."

"Fuck you."

That did it. The coffee, the hours working both shows, the unappreciation— "No. Fuck you. Do it yourself."

We were out by the elevators now. I pounded the down button with the heel of my hand. We faced each other like a couple of drama queens in an Edward Albee play.

"You're fucking high," Rafael said.

"You know, man, we're doing this for you. Me and Peter, we're going out of our way so you can have a fucking show."

"I don't want you doing anything for me."

"Maybe that's your fucking problem. But you know what, you're a fucking asshole."

"Watch how you speak to me."

"Fuck you. Fuck you."

Raf stood there, his face full of rage. It was a like a breakup of lovers, and there was no turning back.

"There's a reason you don't have any friends, mate," I said. "Do it your fucking self. I'm off this."

The elevator doors opened. I got on.

Raf volleyed. "Fuck you."

I returned. "Fuck you."

The doors closed.

When Brennan returned, I was waiting outside on Cahuenga Boulevard to tell him I'd joined that club of people who refused to work with Rafael Abramovitz. Peter could choose which of us he wanted to edit the *Detour* tape.

The choice was obvious. Raf flew back to New York the next day. I never saw him again.

CHAPTER THIRTY:
JEFF GREENFIELD IS A BIG FAT
HUMORLESS PUTZ

Premier Story hit its stride the final week of September.

The trial of O.J. Simpson began with jury selection in downtown Los Angeles on a Friday, September 23, 1994. Tall scaffolding was erected and trailers set up in a huge media encampment in the parking lot of the Hall of Records across the street. Vendors were in place with their "Don't Squeeze the Juice" buttons and "Free O.J." baseball caps. Protesters had their placards. Tourists had their cameras. Police had their hands full.

Premier Story had a new idea. We were going to do the show from outside the courthouse. Alison would get to prove just how good she was on her feet, on the run.

We spent some money on this one, including three camera crews. One we placed on a tenth-floor balcony across the way. Two roved around to catch attorneys, key players, and other activity on the short, tree-lined street.

Most of the network reporters and anchormen divided their time between a media room upstairs, where no cameras were allowed, and the scaffolded encampment around the corner and across the street that was dubbed "Camp O.J."

This was typical hands-off network television, another Brandenburg Gate where the Brokaws and Gumbels and Rathers could stand in front of their cameras with a nice tableau of the action behind them, while actually being far and safe from it.

The grunts, the cameramen, lowly general assignment reporters, and producers, stationed themselves in "The Pit," at the foot of the stairs that led from the sidewalk to the metal detectors at the courthouse door. The Pit was where we set up a director's chair and microphone for Alison to open the show and provide commentary as the melee raged behind her.

We were in place. Julie and Rio and Beth and the other *Premier Story* kids had our coffees and pads and tapes. Hi-8 Joe roamed the parking lot looking for faces he'd become familiar with in transcribing all the Simpson footage.

There was a commotion up around the corner. Born-again attorney Robert Kardashian was arriving, performing his real function—bringing a fresh suit for his pal O.J. to wear in court. Alison jumped up and told one of the crews to follow.

I turned to Brennan. "Uh, should we get her to come back?"

He smiled and shook his head. "I don't think we'd be able to stop her."

Alison dived into the roiling crowd toward Kardashian, the only woman amid the beefy cameramen and mike-holders. A couple of people on the edge of the crowd were already shouting, "Where's the bag?"

She pushed her way through. "Mr. Kardashian, hello. I'm Alison Holloway, good morning, Mr. Kardashian. I've been asking you for some time—" The cameraman moving at her right had had enough of her pushing him out of the way. He responded by swinging his heavy Beta camera and clocking her in the head with the fifteen-pound battery. There was an audible knock, like a hammer against wood, but Alison didn't skip a beat. "—where the bag is? Will you tell me now, Mr. Kardashian?"

They were at the bottom of the pit. Kardashian mumbled a few words but walked inside without giving up anything.

Alison sidestepped the crowd and beckoned the cameraman closer. "Well, you know, I was saying earlier how dangerous it can be to be in the middle of that sort of frenzy, when these people arrive and you try to get some sort of quote, you try to talk to them and you try to get in there—I hadn't done that before," she confided to the camera. "And I've come off, I think, worse for wear. Let me just—oww!"

Alison leaned into the lens and pulled back her bangs to reveal a lump the size of a Grade A jumbo egg directly over her right brow. She smiled and kept on talking. "One of the cameramen hit me with the back of his camera. I actually think he knew he was doing it, cause he said to me, 'Get out the way,' and I wasn't going to get out the way and this is the result."

She looked into the camera as if it were a mirror and mussed her bangs to cover the wound. "Oh, well, I'll just pull my hair over it. I hope it's okay."

She shrugged and walked off camera. Cut.

Brennan and I stood stunned and amazed. She was sensational. We had our promo. We had our show. We had our new direction.

"Somebody get her some ice."

With *Premier Story*'s new persona, tabloid TV had taken over the news. Nobody was doing television like this and word about Holloway's performance spread over the weekend. With a camera crew and a microphone and a small troupe of producers with Hi-8 cameras and notepads, *Premier Story* managed to bring the viewer into the middle of the chaos and make some sense of it.

Ironically, it was Geraldo Rivera who summed it up best the next week when he invited Alison to be a special guest on his afternoon talk show. He called her work "a remarkable look at the insanity surrounding this case; a different look than what you've been seeing on your evening news programs at what its like outside that courtroom."

Macho man Geraldo, of course, he of the broken nose in the neo-Nazi talk show brawl of Nov. 3, 1988, was most impressed with Alison's beaning by the camera. "Alison did a great job," he said. "A fantastic job. She got that big knot on her head so she's got her Purple Heart now."

We were back on the scene Monday, with the same successful mix: Alison would run the media gauntlet and get in her questions as she walked with Simpson attorneys Robert Shapiro and Johnny Cochran; Joe would recognize some obscure cop from one of the tapes he'd transcribed and get in a few intelligent questions while others looked on in ignorance; we'd mix in important happenings in the courtroom, briefings from the pool reporters who had seats inside, and reports from producer Tom Marshall covering the pressroom.

Alison and I would leave in the early afternoon, stock up at McDonald's, and map out the show's structure on the way to the office. Then we'd divide up the work in the edit rooms.

The shows became a commentary on the media as well as the justice system; unlike the ponderous pundits who look down from a place safely removed from the scene, we were reveling in the thick of it, getting people and places the "big boys" wouldn't even notice.

There was John Roberts, Dan Rather's heir apparent at CBS, sitting with his little laptop outside a trailer in Camp O.J., complaining, "The problem with this story is there's a dearth of pictures"—while four-story scaffolding loomed over his head and a circus performed around him. There was the now-deceased rapper, Tupac Shakur, at court to face another weapons charge, recognizing Alison and expressing concern about her head wound.

There was the reporter from a city in the Midwest, so excited to be covering such a big story. "We're in a trailer with about seven ABC affiliates from around the country and we're all great friends now. None of us knew each other before," he said, as if Camp O.J. were actually some sort of Camp Runamuck. "We're all cooperating, swapping tapes: 'Did you get this? Who got Shapiro today? Did anybody get O.J. at the jail?' All switching and swapping and you don't usually see that in the media."

"No, of course not," Alison said, smart enough to just let him talk.

"That's very unusual."

"So where's the sense of rivalry now? Has it gone completely?"

"I think we put it aside for now, because I think we've all realized that very few of us are ever gonna get an exclusive with this and the best thing to do is be cooperative and please the bosses back home."

Perhaps we were revealing *too much* about the media.

By Tuesday, Alison was a celebrity herself outside the courthouse, a beautiful blond dynamo in a smart pantsuit getting in everyone's faces and business as the day's session got underway. A morning radio show doing a live remote from the sidewalk called Alison over for an interview. The reporter had one question: "Were there this many people at Benny Hill's funeral?"

We were making our way back from shooting at Camp O.J. when we noticed someone had taken over our spot in the pit.

I nudged Brennan. "Holy mack'rel, will you look who it is."

"Oh, yes, oh, yes," he said, and took Alison by the arm and pointed out the person we were talking about. Alison laughed and told Jay Kay the cameraman what she'd do next. He rolled, she gave a wink, and talked to her friend the camera.

"Something interesting has happened this morning. I came to the courthouse steps to take up my usual position down there at the base of the steps—and someone was standing in our spot. Jeff Greenfield, reporter for *Nightline*. They've finally decided to come down. They must have thought it's a good idea."

It was beyond great. *Nightline* was chasing us again, deigning to cover a story that *Premier Story* had run away with the past two nights. What was even better: Greenfield was in our space, and he looked like a boob, standing on a small stepladder looking down at the mass of media and clucking his tongue in disapproval, while a man in sports jacket and dark glasses held Greenfield's luggage—and the ladder, so his star wouldn't tumble.

We couldn't ask for a broader target; now Alison was on her way with a big smile on her face to shake Jeff Greenfield's hand and ask him a few questions. This was Gordon Elliott shouting through a bullhorn at Bryant Gumbel's boat; *Hard Copy* pouncing on Maury Povich down the street from the Fox building.

If anyone would see the humor, it would be the wiseacre "new journalism" pioneer Jeff Greenfield, who came all the way from New York to do a critical commentary on the media's O.J. obsession.

Alison was making her way through the crowd as Greenfield stepped gingerly off the ladder. "There he is now," she informed the camera. "Blue shirt; having a chat to his producer. Let's go in. Let's go have a word." Greenfield noticed the woman and camera heading his way. "Jeff. I'm Alison Holloway from *Premier Story*."

He backed off as if confronted by a bad smell. "I know, but—"

"Can I shake you by the hand? I very much enjoy your program and I saw you down here for the first time today. What made you come down today?"

Greenfield hemmed. "No, no." Then he hawed. "I don't want to talk about that; it's not appropriate for me—"

"Really?"

"Yeah, it really isn't."

Around them, producers from other networks and stations were nudging cameramen. Cameramen were hoisting their gear and shooting the confrontation between the upstart late night show and the mighty *Nightline*—which had apparently pulled rank and muscled into *Premier Story*'s battle-won spot by the door.

Alison carried on with a smile; taking the piss, as they'd say. "I just thought it would be fun to have a very brief chat—"

Greenfield looked embarrassed, yet patronizing. "No, the last thing—"

"No, I understand you're tied up. We're all very busy down here. I just think—"

"I know. No, but I appreciate it and thanks for the kind words. But I'd just as soon—"

"Okay. Well, nice to see you. And see you around for the duration of the trial—"

"Oh, no." Greenfield laughed at her. Was she kidding? Lower himself like that? "No."

"We're here for the long haul," Alison said. "I'm sure we will."

Other journalists laughed at the confrontation. As Greenfield muttered something to his producer-bag holder, the thought of him laughing at us like that really rankled.

I whispered to Joe: "Go over and ask him what he thinks of *Premier Story*. Ask him why he wouldn't talk to Alison. Ask him what he's scared of."

Joe ambled over with his Hi-8. "Excuse me. Why wouldn't you speak to Alison Holloway?"

Greenfield gulped and turned away from the camera. "No."

"Who are you with?" Joe had been asking many journalists which organizations they represented. Edited together, it would make an impressive end-of-show montage. Greenfield felt himself to be a man who needed no introduction.

"Why wouldn't you speak to Alison?"

There were more hearty laughs from comrades waiting for the next burst of activity. Jeff Greenfield, the man who for years pontificated about the media, who in 1988 said news had been taken over by "electronic barbarians; the carriers of the basest impulses unrestrained by shame, or for that matter, pride," was seeing the camera turned back on him.

"What do you think of *Premier Story*?"

"Shall we just walk over there?" Greenfield suggested to his producer-ladder holder. They snatched the bags and set off toward the safety of Camp O.J. across the street.

Joe followed a few steps behind. "Why wouldn't you speak with Alison Holloway? Why are you running away?"

Greenfield skittered away to derisive laughter from the grunts in the pit. Our cameraman, Jay Kay, kept his distance as Joe followed the pair across the street. Spectators, vendors, cops and journalists alike looked on with a smile. Yeah, who's he to drop in from the airport to stand on a ladder, survey the scene, have a glass of Perrier at Camp O.J., and then fly back first class to file a report saying that all us people who care about this case are idiots?

Jeff Greenfield, to paraphrase Tom Wolfe, his buddy from Elaine's, was being mau-maued.

"What do you think of *Premier Story*?"

Greenfield and his manservant were safely across the road, entering the guarded Camp O.J., seconds from shaking young Joe, when they were assaulted from the front. A tall man in a permapress suit accompanied by a cameraman stepped forward to welcome the star to the isle of civility. "You know, usually you're the guy looking at the media," he crowed in a Southern-fried anchorman's voice. "Today, the media looks at you too, right?"

Jeff Greenfield gave him a pained, "Are you an asshole?" look.

"Richard Belcher with your ABC affiliate in Atlanta," the man said, extending a hand and sucking up to the big network boy at exactly the wrong time.

"Hi," Greenfield mumbled, giving an ix-nay on the alk-tay jerk of the head toward Joe that Belcher didn't notice. "How you doin."

"Fine. You got time for six hundred questions we're gonna ask you?"

This man from his Atlanta affiliate was worse than the kid with the camera standing nearby. Greenfield muttered. "Yeah, um, but I think we oughta just wait until this rather unpleasant young man is finished."

Joe laughed in good-natured surprise.

Belcher pressed on with forced joviality, trying to make an impression on his bigtime colleague. "He's one of about twelve with *Premier Story*. Have you met him?"

"No, but I, you know—"

"My name is Joe Guidry," Joe said, extending his free hand. "How you doing?"

"No," said Greenfield. "I have no interest in shaking your hand. This is the kind of lack of civility that I really think is unfortunate." He turned to Belcher. "So we're not going to do anything until he is...weary."

Belcher looked at Joe. "Can I have a second with him?"

"No problem," Joe replied.

"Can I?"

Greenfield sighed. "No, I'm—"

"I'm just asking *him*," Belcher said a little too sharply to Greenfield. He had no idea what the bigshot from New York had been through. "See, I've cut my separate deal with him."

Joe realized he was being treated like some kind of gang member. "I just wanted to ask him who he was with," he said.

Greenfield shook his head. "Well, we're not gonna get into—" Belcher stepped in it again. "Jeff Greenfield, with ABC News," he said confidentially.

"ABC News? Okay."

Greenfield rolled his eyes. "See, that's just what—" He sighed, defeated.

Belcher pressed on with his interview. "But look, you've made, for years—"

Greenfield turned his back to Joe's camera and shook his head. He wasn't going to answer any questions.

"I'm not interviewing you," Belcher said. He was getting fed up. It was clear that Greenfield had gone from journalistic hero to pompous poop before his very eyes. "But this is part of what you do expertly, is to observe this kind of stuff. Is this the first time you've seen one like this?"

Greenfield shook his head again, and for the first time his bag handler spoke.

"*He's still shooting!*" Snitch. Rat fink!

The good old boy was getting fed up. "I'm not. I'm not."

"He is." Greenfield winced as if he was having a particularly unpleasant attack of intestinal gas. There was an uncomfortable silence.

Joe broke it. "Who was that guy who was holding your ladder? Is it like, do you just hire him as a ladder holder?"

That did it. Greenfield turned to the camera and stuck his damp face close to Joe's lens. "You don't get it, do you?"

"I'm just asking a question."

"No. This is *in*-civil," Greenfield lectured, using the old and scholarly form of the word "uncivil" to describe what he deemed to be a young man's impoliteness and lack of courtesy. "It's rude. It's invasive. And it's part of the problem. And you are part of the problem, not the solution." Greenfield was winding up into his best journalism schoolmarm lecture. "This is not the way to do journalism. And I feel very sorry for you if you have any hope for a career in it."

"This is unpleasant business." He picked up his bags. "Okay?"

Joe stayed put as the *Nightline* commentator, valet in tow, harrumphed off behind the Camp O.J. scaffolding.

"Thank you," Joe said and, after a moment, added, "Are you hiring?"

The Greenfield segment was the talk of the courthouse the next morning. We'd gotten an item into *Page Six* of the *New York Post* that made it seem old Jeff was a spoilsport putting the whammy on Joe Guidry's chance at a career. The phones and fax lines at *Premier Story* were ringing with calls from newsrooms back in New York—ABC included—congratulating us for taking the piss out of a holier-than-thou media commentator and showing him to be too prickly and ungracious to share a word or two with the woman whose show was beating the pants off *Nightline* on the Simpson story.

Not everyone was laughing. Alison was having a coffee in The Pit when someone came over and warned her. *Nightline* was striking back. They were going to be looking at the media, all right. They were focusing on *Premier Story*.

We went about our business. Alison was interviewing a sidewalk musician who'd been detained by police after following Johnny Cochran into the courthouse, when I got a nudge from someone else—an ABC cameraman was a few feet away, shooting Alison.

I went up behind her and whispered in her ear. Alison turned around and told Jay Kay to follow. "Hi," she said to the ABC cameraman. "Why are you shooting me?"

The ABC veteran laughed, then sidestepped the question and Alison as he did a humorous dance around his camera and tripod. It was all good fun on the sidewalk—until a sharp voice cut through all the others.

"You're interviewing my cameraman?"

It was another of those bizarre, fortuitous television moments. Until then, Alison had been the only woman on a sidewalk crowded with sweaty male journalists, photographers, and street people. Suddenly there was another female. She was blond, too, and her haircut was quite similar to Alison's. Only she was about twenty years older and tough as a leftover Thanksgiving turkey.

"Hello, I'm Alison Holloway from *Premier Story*," Alison said.

"Judy Muller." She was another reporter from *Nightline*, taking over from Jeff Greenfield, who was probably in bed with an icebag on his head. She looked at Alison as if she were performing some unnatural act, talking to the cameraman—the cameraman Judy Muller told to shoot Alison. "Why are you interviewing my cameraman?

"Everybody is interviewing everybody else. Why are you interviewing me?"

The crowd pushed closer, eager for a fight. Our second cameraman, Chris Telford, moved in as well. Hi-8 Joe crouched and shot up from the sidewalk. Judy Muller's cameraman zoomed in as well. The exchange that followed was something out of Beckett.

"I'm trying to find out why you're interviewing us."

"Because it's sort of the media show, isn't it? Everybody's interviewing everybody else. Do you think it's a good idea?"

"Lemme ask you a question, Alison," Judy Muller said, her eyes in a mean squint and the lines on her face growing taut, "when you yell questions at Kardashian like, 'What's in the bag' and 'Where is the bag,' clearly you don't expect an answer like, 'My God, you've broken the case, let me tell you right now, here on the sidewalk.' That's part of your shtick, correct?"

Alison seemed taken aback. "Gosh, that's a very abrupt, upfront and very direct question. Um, I wouldn't ask a question unless I expected an answer. But you wouldn't ask me that question unless you expected an answer. You know, we go round in circles."

"But you don't expect an answer when you, when you ask that on the sidewalk?"

"Oh, I might, but I might not. I might, but I might not. You know, it's a very important issue. Let's not get away from what we're dealing with here. That's a very important issue. Let's not make light of it, okay?"

"I don't make light of it. But don't we make light of it when we conduct that sort of thing on the sidewalk?"

"Are you saying you wouldn't conduct that sort of thing on the sidewalk?"

"That's what I'm saying, yeah." Judy Muller's face was stretched back in a rictus grin. She looked like she wanted to kill.

"Are you?" Alison said. A print reporter scribbled notes. Everyone else waited to see who would throw the first punch. "Oh."

"No?"

"Oh, you're holier than thou," Alison said. "No, I don't think so."

"Okay, thanks."

With that, they backed off. Judy Muller turned and slipped into the crowd.

I turned and smiled. "Hey, Joe!"

Judy Muller corraled her cameraman and producer and was rushing toward the safety of Camp O.J. Waiting for the traffic to pass, she noticed the young man with the Hi-8 camera behind her.

Joe tried to get a question out. "Do you think—"

"Do me a favor," Judy Muller growled.

"Yes, ma'am," said Joe, following. "I just want to ask you a question, just a couple of questions."

"I don't want to answer any. Bye!"

They were across the street. "No questions? None at all?"

"Nope!" Judy Muller pretended to be hard at work. She had the cameraman set up his tripod and shoot the CNN correspondent doing a standup on a plywood stage.

"Don't you want to know what's inside of that bag?" Joe asked. "Don't you want to know what's inside of that bag, ma'am?"

"Go away, fella." She pointed out something to her producer.

"Please?" Joe was unfailingly polite. "Wouldn't you like to know what's inside of the bag?"

Judy Muller put a hand to her lips and put her face into the camera like Jeff Greenfield did. "Shhhhh! We are recording," she whispered.

"Excuse me." Joe stood silent, the camera fixed on the woman's hawklike profile. After a long pause came an almost inaudible whisper from Joe. "Don't you want to know what's inside of the bag? Don't you want to know what's inside of the bag?"

Judy Muller turned her head slightly to the camera and said from the corner of her mouth, "Fuck off, fella."

Joe was stunned. He giggled like a little kid who'd just heard a bad word. "Oh, you don't have to use profanity, now."

Judy Muller and her crew moved on. "Thank you very much, ma'am," Joe said, meaning it. "Thank you. Tell Jeff I said hi!"

Fuck off fella! We had our promo for that night's show. Sure, we put a bleep over most of the "fuck," but you sure got the message.

It was the highlight of our story about how the folks at *Nightline* focused their cameras on us because of the Jeff Greenfield incident. We re-ran highlights from that segment, followed by Alison's encounter with the cameraman and the entire Judy Muller showdown, unedited, bouncing among three cameras and climaxing with Hi-8 Joe and the immortal, "Fuh-*bleep*-cough, fella."

I had to feel sorry for Judy Muller. She couldn't report what it was really like in front of the courthouse. Her segment was rush-released to Peter Jennings' *World News Tonight* broadcast, a two-minute, well-balanced report on the "media circus" that described Alison as "one reporter who uses the shtick of asking Robert Kardashian what he did with O.J. Simpson's garment bag," followed by Alison's soundbite: "It's sort of the media show, isn't it? Everybody's interviewing everybody else."

Fuck off, fella.

The mainstream media was not about to let us off the hook so easily. Just as Peter Brennan waited for the other news shows to go after Robert Kardashian once we exposed the bag story, so ABC News gave us our comeuppance through other channels.

Both were in the print media.

The first was from Jeff Greenfield himself in his nationally syndicated newspaper column.

Victim of the Press

> I have just gone through an experience I heartily commend to anyone who practices journalism for a living: I have been mauled by the media.
>
> I was at the site of the O.J. Simpson trial, where I felt as if I were witnessing the Chernobyl of American journalism—a wholesale abandonment of any sense of proportion. A team from a third-tier tabloid show approached, camera rolling, microphone outstretched, asking for comments.
>
> I declined; politely, I believe.

From there, Jeff Greenfield relived the horror: the video camera pointed at his face, the questions yelled toward him, asking why he was afraid...

Yet, the commentator admitted the ordeal served him right; that even those not in the journalism trade should experience stalking by camera, if only to understand how the invasive lens can make anyone seem to be hiding something or "on the edge of a temper tamtrum."

The blame, Greenfield concluded, could be laid on the "real" journalists, like the ones at *60 Minutes*, who've "repeatedly bent the conventions of news-gathering...for the sake of drama and ratings."

> Now, pretend journalists use the techniques of dramatic news shows, while putting aside any pretense of values...

You might guess who fired the next shot across our bow: Howard Rosenberg, using his column in the *L.A. Times*:

Premier Rises to
Top of Sleaze Beat

> ...Who wouldn't be for yanking TV from the O.J. Simpson courtroom if that would result in the erasure of such pernicious skulkers as *Premier Story* and its obnoxiously smug British host, Alison Holloway?

But of course, it wouldn't. They and their
commando colleagues do their damage outside the
courtroom...

Premier Story plays it like a game. During one
recent week, the show recruited a young schnook
named Joe—a sort of tabloider in training—to roam
the exterior of the Los Angeles Criminal Courts
Building with a camera person and generally harass
and bait anyone he could find in hopes of
provoking a TV-worthy response.

Presumably, that would include someone giving
him the finger...

Rosenberg wrote that the apparent goal of *Premier Story* and "the
smarmy Holloway" was to create mischief—as well as "to wittily do unto the
media what the media has been doing unto others." Indeed he criticized the
"frenzied pack journalism" outside the Criminal Courts Building, and stated
that by dispatching a "correspondent as high-ranking" as Greenfield, *ABC
News* "had sucked down into the same cesspool."

Thus, it wasn't that Joe's targets were so high
that gave this entire exercise a kind of sad futility
but that he and *Premier Story* had found a way to
descend even lower...

We didn't need to seek revenge. A few weeks later, Ted Koppel and
Nightline provided it for us.

When I heard about the *Nightline* segment, I had the tape brought into
the office and watched it with Brennan. We couldn't believe our eyes. What
a fool!

We set aside a minute or so at the end of that night's show for a package
making use of the clip. Alison set it up in the intro by mentioning that our
Hi-8 Joe discovered there were imitators out there. We dissolve to Jeff
Greenfield's infamous invocation: "This is not the way to do journalism."

Freeze on his face. Joe begins the track: "Boy, was I disappointed. I
finally got to meet one of my journalistic heroes, Jeff Greenfield, at the O.J.
Simpson trial, and he tells me that."

"This is unpleasant business," Greenfield adds.

"I know it's unpleasant, but I still wanted to get into TV," Joe continues.
"So, in order to facilitate our special access to parts of America normally not
open to a television news crew, I proposed that I would go into these areas
alone with a Hi-8 camera.

"And I got exclusives with people like Prince Charles—and Kato! But I couldn't forget the hurtful words from Jeff Greenfield of *Nightline*."

Greenfield: "This is not the way to do journalism."

Joe: "So get this. This week, I accidentally turned on *Nightline*—sorry, Alison—and there was Ted Koppel himself, doing a story in prison. And guess how he shot it?"

Here we see Ted Koppel from the previous night's *Nightline*. Ted is wearing a neat denim shirt, and he holds a Hi-8 camera as he is led by guards into a cage with another man.

"In order to facilitate our special access to parts of the prison normally not open to a television news crew," Ted intones in voiceover, "we proposed that I would go into these areas alone with a Hi-8 camera..."

There's Ted, looking like Charlie Brown in his safari outfit, holding the biggest goddamn Hi-8 camera you could think of, with a huge shotgun mike sticking off the front and all of it attached to headphones sitting like earmuffs on his Alfred E. Neumann coiff.

They cut to Ted's POV of a prisoner. Ted asks, with squeaky insouciance: "So, you're in maximum lockup, right?"

Dissolve from the con to Hi-8 Joe. "This is not the way to do journalism," he just manages to get out, cracking up.

"But it works," Alison adds with a smile and wink. "Doesn't it, Ted?"

CHAPTER THIRTY-ONE:
MAKIN' WICKY-WACKY ON THE TITANIC

Alison Holloway, Premier Story anchorwoman:
O.J. is to the Brit host what the Iranian hostages were
to Ted Koppel and Nightline.
—*Newsweek*, October 17, 1994

Peter Brennan had a big smile as he hung up the phone in the control room. He wrote two words on a sheet of paper and pushed it in front of me: *Done deal.*

"Come outside."

We stood in the Hollywood Center lot. He lit a cigarette and clapped his hands. "It's a done deal, mate. We did it."

"We're being syndicated?"

"No. But this'll ensure it. Dunleavy, mate. He's going to do it."

"No."

"Yes. He says it's ninety-nine point nine percent done. He's gonna sign with us. He's coming."

"Dunleavy's gonna leave Murdoch?"

Brennan could hardly control his enthusiasm. Of all his inventions, scams, and feats of brilliance, this would be the most satisfying. He'd fuck over the Pig, he'd stand equal to Murdoch, he'd show Dunleavy his true worth. "He will. They owe him some money from all his years at the *Post*, so he's talking to Ken Chandler about that. But that's it."

"How'd you do it?"

"I had to convince Chris-Craft that if we wanted someone with Dunleavy's experience and prominence, we'd have to give him more than a thirteen-week contract. He needs some guarantees, just cause of who he is."

"He agreed?"

"He agreed."

"Fuckin A."

For the first time in weeks, Brennan seemed light on his feet. The Wild

Bunch was back for one more ride, and we had Annie Oakley leading the pack. "This is gonna be great, mate," he said. "Steve and Alison."

"It'll be over the top."

"Oh, it'll be great."

Steve Dunleavy was serious. After years serving his boss as a company man grateful for his paychecks, he realized he had but one last chance to make his stand. It was bad enough running around for Bill Ridley, but Penny Daniels? He got no respect, no respect at all. Who pulled them through William Kennedy Smith? Who got them Buttafuoco? Who wrestled a bear? He wasn't going to be alive forever. It was time for some recognition.

Ian Rae had handled it pretty well. He was shocked, he stuttered; he'd be alone now. He was the last loyal soldier, but he said he understood. He respected Brennan and he knew his mate Dunleavy would be in good hands.

Dunleavy was even getting a meal out of it. Ian was treating him to a celebratory dinner at Elaine's. No hard feelings.

The two old tabloid mates lorded over a prime table at Elaine's, but Ian Rae seemed preoccupied, looking at his watch and barely touching his light beer and thick pasta.

"'Scuse me, mate, Oy've gotta make a quick phone call."

Dunleavy smiled at an attractive female tourist a few tables away. In the old days, he'd have had her in the back of a cab. He had other things to think about now.

The waiter was at the table. "Mr. Dunleavy, there's a phone call for you at the bar."

Dunleavy took a sip of vodka and walked over, a bit light-headed.

Ian held the phone, whispering and literally bowing as he spoke. When he saw Dunleavy, his eyes shifted and he thrust the receiver forward. "It's the boss," he blurted.

Indeed, it was Rupert Murdoch, speaking ship-to-shore from his yacht, moored off the Italian coast. Dunleavy found himself standing at attention and fixing his tie without even realizing he was doing it.

"Steve, old mate?" Murdoch sounded like he was next door. "What's this I hear about you being unhappy? Leaving the fold? What can we do to make things right..."

Heading into November, *Premier Story*'s thirteen-week commitment from Chris-Craft had been extended to twenty-six, but there was still no word whether they'd put us into syndication. Our latest hire, producer Simon Bohrsmann, flew in from London the very day we were heading off to Las Vegas to shoot a segment on the Rolling Stones' appearance at the MGM Grand.

He came along and watched in jet-lagged disbelief as we gathered crew and producers at the Flying Monkey Bar in the casino and power-drank before heading out to do standups on the overpass above Tropicana Boulevard.

We were back in that hyped-up, oxygenated, air-conditioned world and couldn't wait to get done with the shoot so we could decompress over the gaming tables—but things didn't work out as smoothly as Vegas usually ensures.

Despite its transition from finger-snapping night world to Bermuda-shorted family vacationland, most of Vegas still maintained its swinging palm-greasing persona. Not so at the brand-new MGM Grand, whose casinos stretched for football fields and whose hotel sprawl dwarfed the Kremlin. This was Hollywood all the way.

We were greeted by a slick and shifty Hollywood PR man in a spangly MGM Grand baseball jacket who treated us as if we were trying to get pictures of plutonium rods at a secret nuclear reactor rather than a bunch of wrinkly old rockers going through the motions on a well-promoted world tour.

He guided us to the velvet rope that led to the arena where the Stones were performing and wouldn't let us go a step farther.

Fuck this. I'd been getting by on four or five hours of sleep a night since the summer. We'd been working through seven time zones and four countries, including Switzerland, where Alison and I had jetted off to cover the mass suicide of the Solar Temple cult—fifty dead bodies and the story didn't make a ripple here because not a one was American—and Mexico, to which Alison and I sneaked off for a dirty weekend in Cabo and wound up in the emergency room at Cedars-Sinai shaking like junkies with shygilla from eating ceviche. We'd been from courthouse to edit room to studio to bar to airplane and back again. We were stretched to the limit and with each passing day it seemed it was all for nothing, that Chris-Craft was going to pull the plug no matter what we did because they didn't have the balls to go for greatness.

I left Alison with the camera crew and went with Hi-8 Joe out behind the arena and around the security zone where Rolling Stones equipment trucks and getaway cars were stationed. When the big old South London roadie hassled us by shining a penlight into the camera lens, I hassled back, egging him on for a fight.

When the Stones were heading into the encores and the cops told us to scram, Joe and I scrambled into a Portosan and hunched over the squat hole peeking through the air vents at the stage door twenty yards away. When the door opened and the big roadie led the tiny, spindly old musos toward their van, Joe and I burst out of the portable toilet like

Butch and Sundance, only Joe was shooting a Hi-8 and I was laying cover in the form of a decoy, being swarmed by the burly old security guys the way the Forest Lawn forces got me at Sammy's funeral.

I was fed up, over-tired, and happy for a fight. "Don't touch the camera," I warned. "Don't touch the press. It's not gonna look good on TV in L.A. and New York."

Charlie Watts looked on with curiosity, Mick Jagger with disdain as the doors to their getaway vans slammed shut amid the riot.

"Be careful, we don't want you to get run over by the van, mate," said the road manager, giving me a nicely-placed elbow to the gut.

We got our pictures and reconvened at the Flying Monkey Bar.

Almost simultaneously, my old buddy Jim Sheehan was on his first assignment for us in New York City. Princess Diana was in town, possibly looking to move to America; his only mission was to get the story and get something no one else had.

It came together outside the Carlyle Hotel. The New York media waited in the rain for Diana's car to roll out of the parking garage toward her next engagement. Only Sheehan had plans for an encore after everyone got the flash-popping, five-second shot for that night's news. He knew that Diana's motorcade would get stuck at the red light around the corner at Park Avenue and 75th Street.

He made plans in advance with his camerawoman and after Diana's car rolled by, the two of them took chase.

The camera was rolling the entire time as the pair huffed and puffed in the middle of the street to the side of the towncar. Diana was in back. The camera light reflected off the tinted glass of the passenger window, but the outline of Diana was clear.

The princess gave one of her patented demure smiles to the camera, but what stood out was her eyes, that strange combination of lens seduction and the terror of what might happen next. She was clearly surprised that her driver hadn't made a clean getaway from the gangbang, and she was trapped, literally in a corner of the backseat, perched as far away from the camera as possible.

Jim Sheehan knew what he had. If only they could get closer—and then traffic started to move and there was a bump and suddenly the camera picture went out of control, coming to rest on the street, catching the screeching tires of the getaway cars.

Our camerawoman had been run over, her leg clipped, deliberately it seemed, by Diana's tail car, a U.S. State Department escort. She was all right, but Sheehan had the presence of mind to call Eddie Burns, who told him to file a report at the 19th Precinct, and then convince the camera-shy camerawoman to sit down for an interview.

We pumped up the story over the next few days, demanding a formal apology from Buckingham Palace and doing what we could to turn the altercation into an international incident. We even hinted that we might seek criminal charges against the Princess herself.

After police viewed the videotape, they declined to file charges. "It was a minor thing," Det. Jerry Nichols said later. "But because of the people involved, it was blown out of all proportion."

Dunleavy remained at Fox. In the aftermath of his failure of nerve, the opening for a *Premier Story* reporter became more urgent.

Peter Brennan fell back on the old standbys. David Lee Miller from *A Current Affair* expressed interest in the job, and threw around his weight, demanding he be flown out to Los Angeles "to inspect our facility" before making any decisions about working for the genius who invented him.

Brennan was still a fan of Miller because of the way he'd run after stories back in 1986. I told him he was living in the past, but that it was his call.

We were booking Miller a plane ticket when he called and said he'd signed an extension of his contract at Fox. He had no qualms telling Peter he never had any intention of joining our little show after all. He was only using his former mentor's good faith offer so he could bring it to Fox as a bargaining chip.

Brennan shrugged and said it wasn't personal. I told him it was very personal and that we should file the asshole under "Herdrich."

"We're fighting for our lives here, and he took advantage of us," I said. "It's lower than low."

"Oh, calm down, mate," Brennan said. "It's only television."

Alison Holloway would be shooting her movie scene any day now and there was excitement on both sides of the Atlantic. We at *Premier Story* saw it as another great promotional tool; back in London, Alison had the town painted green when the latest issue of *Hello!* magazine came out with a five-page photo spread and interview.

**WITH HER TURBULENT PRIVATE
LIFE LOST IN THE PAST AND AN
EXCITING CAREER IN AMERICA
TELEVISION PRESENTER
ALISON HOLLOWAY
INVITES US TO HER NEW
HOME IN LOS ANGELES**
'Back home, I'm famous for having been
married to Jim Davidson. The marriage

actually lasted for less than a year
and I've been working for 17 years.
But that mistake stuck to me like glue'

The photos showed Alison in various poses in her rented home and on the beach. There was a bathtub shot after all, but the tub was dry and empty and Alison wasn't in it. The pommies (the Aussie word for British people, probably from "pomegranate," rhyming slang for "immigrant"), it was later explained to me, have a thing for bathtubs.

The article was in question-and-answer form, though most of it was made up by Alison's friend Simon Kinnersley after a brief chat. It focused, as did most of the coverage in Great Britain, on Alison's marriage in 1987 to the music hall comedian Jim Davidson. The wedding had taken place amid great fanfare; the divorce, within the year, amid lurid tabloid headlines that were more embarrassing to Alison in her career as a serious journalist than the bruises and black eyes she had to hide with makeup when she went on the air during their marriage.

When the marriage ended, Davidson was all over the British tabloids with his "poor little me" stories. Alison never said a word publicly and instructed her friends to keep quiet, too.

The *Hello!* article touched on poignancy when it had Alison saying she came to America partly to escape the spectre of that union. "I came to realize that it was never going to go away," she said. "I was always going to be one of Jim Davidson's exes. I'm not looking for excuses; I can understand why some TV bosses had reservations about taking me on...I realize that it has absolutely nothing to do with my ability to do the job. The question is, can this woman be seen as a serious newsperson or will she be regarded as the ex-Mrs. Jim Davidson whose face was all over the tabloids?"

The next questions touched on why she'd been married and divorced three times by age thirty-three. *Is there a man in your life at present?* "No. I know it sounds an awful cliche, but I really haven't had time..."

The article ended with Alison speaking about her future, allegedly saying "I've just made my first movie. Well, it was one day's filming! I play a TV anchorwoman in a film called *Crimson Tide*..."

In reality, filming was still days off, and despite repeated calls, Hollywood Pictures wouldn't send her a copy of the script or even the portion containing her lines.

Alison couldn't go down and film the part unless she knew the context. This was a macho, boyo Simpson-Bruckheimer production and you never knew what those guys might be up to.

The script arrived the day before Alison was scheduled to show up at the studio. She tore open the package and flipped through the pages to find her part.

As written, the movie opened like a documentary, with purported voiceover from Tom Brokaw: "Six days ago, in response to continued Serbian attacks on Macedonia...the President of the United States ordered massive bombing runs..." The lines seemed to be written specifically for the NBC anchorman. They contained no "I's."

Ted Koppel turned up on TV on page five. "That was footage taken yesterday," our competitor would say. "But a half hour ago, surrounded by hostile forces, rebel leader Vladimir Radchenko threatened to use his nuclear arms on the United States..."

Alison's character appeared on page nine. She was the only real-life journalist playing someone else: an Australian reporter based on Janna Wendt, an overtly sexy star of the Australian *60 Minutes* and, at the time, a candidate to add some sex appeal and youth to the aged American show.

> CLOSEUP: ON A TV: WE SEE: VLADIMIR
> RADCHENCKO, the Russian rebel leader and
> fanatic, in a pre-recorded interview with SARA
> TURKCANNON, a pretty Aussie reporter. She
> repeats a question, shocked.
> > TURKCANNON
> > ...so what you're saying is; if Russian
> > nationals were harmed...
> They cut to "office on an explosive handling
> wharf": Watching Radchencko on TV are all the key
> officers of the USS Alabama...
> ON TV: The young Aussie reporter shifts... and as
> she does the boys can't help but notice her chest.
> > LT. LINKLETTER (TSO)
> > Oh my God...play that back.
> > She's got huge tits buried beneath
> > that shirt.
> Tape rewinds, but their laughter fades as the
> interview plays on...

That was it. After all the flattery and all the pages she'd read in the audition, Alison was being set up as the target of a tit joke.

Alison stared in disbelief. "I can't do this."

I read the script again. "You can't do this."

"I know. This is outrageous."

"No, Ally, it's better," I said. "You can get more publicity turning it down. You'll be standing up for women everywhere."

"I'm just a pair of tits to them."

"Welcome to Hollywood."

Brennan's agent Barry had taken on Alison as a client. When he called Hollywood Pictures, the casting director was firm. "Alison Holloway will honor her contract and show up for filming tomorrow." He told the woman to read Alison's scene. She phoned back immediately and apologized.

I planned a news conference at the *Premier Story* office and began sending out feelers to some of the entertainment shows. Greg Agnew sought out Alison often while covering the Simpson case for E! Entertainment News. He demurred, saying E! couldn't run the story because they relied on the kindness of movie studios. The assignment editor at *Extra*, the new syndicated competitor to *Entertainment Tonight*, said basically the same thing.

A few more calls elicited the same answers. There was a reason the city's only gossip column was the *Los Angeles Times*' postcard-size summary of Liz Smith. We were in a closed company town.

The only man with enough power to rise above the fear was ancient Army Archerd. His column on page two in *Variety* was the first thing industry people read over their orange juice in the morning.

He made Alison the lead.

> Good morning: *Premier Story* anchor Alison
> Holloway's face turned crimson when the
> seventeen-year veteran British newscaster received
> her script of *Crimson Tide*, for which she auditioned
> and says she was to play an Aussie TV reporter.
>
> In her scene for the Simpson/Bruckheimer
> atomic sub thriller for Hollywood Pictures, a
> submariner, after watching Holloway's taped report,
> says, "Play that back. She's got huge tits buried
> beneath that shirt."
>
> Holloway said, "I will be turning it down—flat.
> Now I want to know if, in my test, they were
> focusing on my face or my breasts!" (She was
> wearing "a

Neal Travis ran an item in the *New York Post* in which Alison expressed hope that Ted Koppel and Tom Brokaw would be gentlemen enough to turn down the picture. In the end, both their roles went to former newsman Richard Valeriani. The tit scene was deleted.

Hollywood Reporter
Market briefs Nov. 3

Premier Story, the new nightly news strip executive produced by Peter Brennan (*Hard Copy, A Current Affair*) is picking up considerably on Secaucus, N.J.'s WWOR-TV. It averaged a 3.5 rating/9 share for the week of Oct. 17-21, up 50% in the time period from last year. The show airs on the United Chris-Craft stations with a national syndication rollout envisaged. Award-winning British TV reporter Alison Holloway hosts.

"Pack up your troubles, come on along, where lights are dreamy and life's a song! In Honolulu, across the sea, makin' wicky-wacky down in Waikiki!"

Wearing a tuxedo and crooning into a microphone by the piano at the bar in the St. James's Club Hotel, Richard Halpern could have been a ghost from the heyday of the art deco restaurant, where at a table outside by the pool, Tim Robbins once heard the pitch to end all in *The Player*.

Richard, the man of a thousand voices, was now working mornings as *Premier Story*'s promo announcer. This singing was his night gig, and he'd dedicated the 1930 Sophie Tucker tune to Alison, who was at the bar consoling Shannah, still weepy after Dunleavy did an about-face and decided to remain with Murdoch.

"I feel like he's a dead man," Shannah said through her tears. "Like he decided it's time to die. I'm so sad for him."

Alison whispered some soothing words, then turned to smile and raise a glass to Richard, who was singing only for her.

"The hula dancers are sure good news! Those joy dispensers are a cure for the blues! It's absolutely the place to be—makin' wicky wacky down in Waikiki!"

Jim Sheehan and Simon Bohrsmann sipped light beers and discussed potential neighborhoods for bringing up their kids when they moved to L.A. permanently.

I was in a corner by the phone with Brennan, arguing strategy. In the past week, we'd been packing the show with short, shoddy packages and clips, throwing on phone call interviews and multiple guests when fewer would have worked better.

"Alison, out on the street, one story, on the move—that's our claim to fame, mate." I was frustrated. "That's how we're making our mark and pushing this whole thing onto the next level."

"Yeah, but it ain't rating."

"We have to give it time. A few days in a row, at least. Right now, nobody knows what we are."

"Look," Brennan said wearily. "We need to get the ratings up in sweeps. This is the only way I know how to do it, the same way we did it back at *A Current Affair*, mate. Give 'em enough stories to keep 'em hanging on, so if they don't like a story, there's always the next one."

"We're losing our identity; it's turning into a mess. And with Lisa running that desk, I never know what's going on."

"Aw, mate, this is too fucking hard, this isn't fun."

Richard was on to Fannie Brice, circa 1916. "This is a song for Jewish Indians," he said by way of introduction to the jaunty tune. "*Me and the Chief talk, but ve don't known vut we speak. I keep his wigwam way up in Cripple Creek. And he calls me 'Eagle' cause I got a beak! It's a beak! It's a beak! But I'm an Indian!*"

"I don't mind Lisa. I don't mind being out of the loop. I just don't like being lied to."

"Welcome to journalism, mate."

"*I'm an Indian!*" The formally-dressed pianist knocked out a jaunty pow-wow beat. Richard held two fingers in a V-sign behind his head for feathers, while smacking his lips in a "woo woo!" chant as he did a rain dance around the microphone stand.

December began with whores. Prostitutes camped out in Alison's office, selling what had come to be, in their young lives, their most valuable asset: information.

It was time to sell out Heidi Fleiss. The Hollywood Madame was finally going on trial for running a call girl ring, so her call girls were running to *Premier Story* to tell the world her secrets.

There was Suzy Sterling, a stunning and stunningly dim blond Heidi nicknamed "The Sex Toy." Suzy told a Hollywood whore-with-a-heart-of-gold story straight out of a modern-day Busby Berkeley musical: a high school cheerleader from New Jersey leaves her fiance at the altar, runs off to Tinseltown with dreams of becoming an actress, winds up splitting time between turning over bodies in a tanning salon and tending bar, meets a streetwise, snappy broad named Heidi, moves into Heidi's place in Benedict Canyon, and learns to use her rah-rah skills to become something of a star, getting paid to dress up like a pom pom girl and perform "sis-boom-bah" cheers saluting the penises of biggies like Charlie Sheen.

Victoria Sellers was next. The daughter of Peter Sellers and Britt Ecklund had fake orange hair, slot machine eyes, and weepy stories about a daddy who neglected her, and a friend, Heidi, who was once her partner running hookers out of exclusive Hollywood nightspots but now wouldn't speak to her because Victoria was telling Heidi tales for money.

Victoria had a lot to cry about. She was facing weapons charges, having recently been arrested along with her latest boyfriend, an L.A. gang member.

For days, Victoria and Suzy and colleagues with names like "Brandi" lolled around Alison's office in Laura Ashley dresses, looking for all the world like country club daughters with too much makeup and too much time on their hands.

Even Heidi's mother got into the act. Ellyn Fleiss was a frizzy-haired hippie mom from the Los Feliz hills who was eager to, and did, demonstrate how she could still get her leg up on a ballet barre in the downstairs rec room. She portrayed her Heidi as a damaged, troubled child taken advantage of by older men. Then she added that most people probably wished secretly that they too could make a bundle the same way Heidi did.

It was time to get back to O.J. With his *Extraordinary* show out of production, Brennan put the laid-off staff to work with a series of dramatized events leading up to, and following, the murders. Constructed around courtroom testimony and records, it was classy and controversial material.

The show's budget was climbing. We were pouring everything we could into each ratings point during sweeps and the weekly cost was now somewhere on the far side of $150,000—once or twice hitting $170,000— but it was paying off. Ricky Feldman's late-night line-up had long since cancelled, and our late-night ratings in New York were better than *A Current Affair*'s, the show that cost $500,000 a week and ran in the peak viewing hour.

Each day, though, was a fight to get on the air followed by quick decompression at the St. James's Club or the Monkey Bar where Brennan and I would fight more over the direction of the show.

In the past six months, I'd proven, and become confident in, my ability to know how to get ratings and run things. Brennan had reason to want to keep me under his wing.

"I'm really not stupid about this," I said. "I've been doing this a while. I know what works."

"Look, this is an experimental show," Brennan said. "Chris-Craft is experimenting, so whatever happens, happens. It's too much work, anyway."

Experimental. I poured out the foamy backwash of my Bud Light and watched Alison talking to Simon down the bar. When Brennan used the word "experimental" regarding the show, I knew we were done for. He knew something we didn't. *Premier Story* was dead.

To get *Premier Story* operating at a functioning level for an extended period of time would have entailed the hiring of tested professionals who could replace the anchorwoman and management staff in the field and edit rooms. It would have required an increase of about another $50,000 to each week's budget.

A $220,000 weekly budget would allow us to hire more producers and a top-notch field reporter and still run at less than half the cost of other tabloid-reality shows.

To roll out the show into syndication would take a slightly bigger outlay. Chris-Craft would have to commit to a year's worth of programming, while allocating eight to ten million dollars in advertising and promotions; all in all, it would cost them twenty to twenty-five million dollars to get a successful syndicated show off the ground.

Chris-Craft didn't have the confidence, or the stomach, for it. The last week of November, Brennan called me into the office.

"We're on hiatus as of December second," he said.

"What does that mean?"

"It means we're cancelled."

Celebrity Service is a daily daybook of entertainment events, press availability and contact numbers for actors, musicians, and public figures out promoting their latest product. Subscribers receive a multi-paged listing on their fax machines each morning.

Every fax package features a separate page dedicated to the "Celebrity of the Day," highlighting the career and recent project of the most prominent or publicity-needy famous person.

On November twenty-second, the Celebrity of the Day was Linda Bell. "Under her helm, (*Hard Copy*) has garnered its highest ratings ever in 1993-94 and the strongest launch in its six-year history this season."

Premier Story was featured in the *New York Post* a few days later:

Premier Story nears end

TV's lowest-rated tabloid news show, *Premier Story*, will air its final show Friday night, the program's producers announced.

But the series may be revived in syndication, Chris-Craft/United Television said. The show was launched last summer and a spokesman described its brief run as a test to gauge audience reaction. "The Chris-Craft stations were utilized as a laboratory to determine the show's appeal," he said.

The company is pulling the show off the air while it looks for a national syndicator. Chris-Craft says it hopes to have *Premier Story* back on the air in syndication by next fall...

It was funny and, I suppose, fitting. *Premier Story*'s obit was written by Alex Monsky, the son of my first TV news director and founder of *Hard Copy*, Mark BvS Monsky.

CHAPTER THIRTY-TWO:
BEAT THE MEATLES

It was the second month of 1995. Alison, Brennan, and I were having lunch under the warm winter sun at the Petit Fours sidewalk cafe on Sunset Plaza. Out on Sunset Boulevard, a specially rigged truck towed a beat-up BMW convertible with a camera mounted on the driver's side door. Gene Hackman, almost unrecognizable with a goatee and cap, drove. John Travolta was plumped up in the passenger seat, fat and pink, every ounce the movie star with a white shadow of scalp peeking from the top of his head. The car was pulled up the Strip again and again, and every time someone yelled "Hey, John!" from the sidewalk or passing car, Travolta would turn his head, turn on a big white smile and wave, and they'd have to drag the BMW by one more time.

We weren't working. Since the demise of *Premier Story* in December, I'd taken Alison to Aspen and she'd brought me along to England when she returned home to shoot a season of a quiz show called *All in the Mind*.

London was cold and rainy and everything I expected, only smaller. The rooms in the houses were cramped and people huddled around television sets watching their four channels the way they once tuned in the radio during the blitzkreig or to hear the Queen's Christmas message. The country still labored in the echo of the air raid sounds of World War Two. Signs of the bombing were visible everywhere, from the lines of row houses broken by prefab concrete structures or vacant lots, to the hunched determination on the faces of the old folks, pressing on, always with a glance toward the gloomy skies. The later campaign of IRA terror kept the new generation head-down against the wind.

There weren't any Mary Quant, Twiggy, Marianne Faithful swinging London birds in plasticene miniskirts with legs up to there. There were fake punks in green hair, deisel fumes, and rental signs on every other building reading "TO LET" that caused me every single time I saw one to think of "toilet."

I wondered how someone as fearless and vibrant as Alison had come from such a tiny land.

Then again, it was January.

We weren't long in London. Alison was taping a season's worth of episodes in the BBC North studios in Manchester, the rainy industrial city whose newspaper's front page that week proclaimed that its center boasted the worst air pollution in all the land.

A local rock band called Oasis was making waves. Alison's ex-husband Jim Davidson was on many billboards, pitching a tabloid newspaper's lottery game. I got a look at one of his comedy albums in a record store. The cover showed him at a urinal flanked by two large black guys who pointed at his dick and laughed.

When Davidson turned up on the telly hosting a snooker show, smarmy in a tux and doing his "nick nick" jokes, Alison told me to turn it off. "He's not funny," she said. "He's a horrible, violent man and it makes me sick to see him."

I was fascinated. The guy looked like a young Dunleavy, though shorter, rougher around the edges, and not as smart.

We got up early one morning so Alison could appear on a morning talk show called *Richard & Judy* to promote *All in the Mind* and talk about her new career in the states. The show was taped in studios built into a renovated dockside complex on the Mersey River in Liverpool. Richard asked about the O.J. Simpson trial. Judy was most interested in how much money Alison made.

After her segment, Ally was driven back to Manchester to rehearse and I stayed behind to wander Liverpool. This was Mecca to me, birthplace of the Beatles, the cultural influence that most shaped my life. When I was a boy, their music showed me that the future could—and should—be whatever I wanted it to be. The dream they portrayed led me to my tabloid mates. Brennan was Lennon, the cynical genius; Dunleavy, the showman McCartney; Wayne was George Harrison, younger, with an overshadowed talent; and Raf—well, I guess Raf would have to be Stu Sutcliffe, Lennon's friend who quit the group before it became a success because he was an artist, not a musician—only to go home and have his brain explode.

I guess that made me Ringo.

It didn't take me long to find my way. A re-creation of the Cavern Club was a short walk downtown on Mathew Street at the entrance to a cheesy and lightly-traveled Beatles tourist district that included memorabilia shops and pubs with names like McCartney's and Lennon's. There was the sad "Eleanor Rigby Statue" on Stanley Street, which the tour map described as "a touching monument" sculpted by song and dance man Tommy Steele out of "love for Beatles music and concern at the lack of tangible tributes to them in their home city," though in a singular act of self-promotion, Steele charged the city "half a sixpence" for the work in honor of his signature movie from the sixties.

The city fathers had been farsighted enough to allow the Royal Life Insurance Company to construct the Cavern Walks Shopping Centre on the hallowed site of the original Cavern Club, a pitiable two-story complex with stores that sold beads and ceramics, described as "a permament monument to the Beatles" with Cynthia Lennon-designed doves and roses above the entrance and a statue of the Beatles in the atrium.

Disappointed, I headed back to the Merseyside Tourist Welcome Center and boarded a Beatles *Magical Mystery* tour bus. There was a surprising number of tourists for this midweek January morning, though the only other American was a young man in an Army jacket who looked like the guy who killed John Lennon. He said he was a soldier on leave from his post in Germany, though his hair was too long and he seemed too pudgy for active duty. The other fifteen riders were Japanese tourists. None spoke English and each held a home video camera.

I sat in the front seat of the school bus behind the driver. The tour guide was an actress in a local theatre company who apologized that the usual gaudy bus was out of service and became more discouraged when the crackly cassette player went dead during the opening of the song "Magical Mystery Tour," embarrassed we'd have to settle for her commentary as she pointed out the sights.

"There's the registry office where John Lennon married Cynthia Powell in 1962. Brian Epstein was best man. Paul and George also attended...to your right you will see the Liverpool Institute on Mount Street where Paul and George both attended school...there's the Anglican Cathedral. Paul auditioned for the church choir in 1953—unsuccessfully...we now enter the neighborhood once known as the Dingle...to our right halfway down Madryn Street is number nine, the house where Ringo Starr was born...to the left you'll recognize the Empress Pub. It was pictured on the cover of his first solo LP, 'Sentimental Journey'..."

The tour continued in what to our guide and driver was monotony unaccompanied by music. We rolled out of the more harsh neighborhoods toward lush parkland and rolling green hills under blue suburban skies. "We're heading into the neighborhood where John Lennon grew up. They called him a working-class hero. That's a load of boll— rubbish, as you'll see."

It was amid the greenery that the bus paused on a hill and the guide pointed out a church partially hidden by trees. "Now we arrive at St. Peter's Church. On sixth July 1957, in the church hall, John and Paul were introduced for the first time...251 Menlove Avenue. John Lennon lived here as a teenager with his Aunt Mimi and Uncle George, in the room above the garage. You'll notice the sign warning tourists to keep off the property. If you look out the windows to the right, you'll see the spot where John's beloved mother Julia was hit by a car and killed while crossing the road. John wrote the song 'Julia' in her memory and if the blinkin' tape recorder worked, I could have played it for you..."

The bus stopped for pictures on Beaconsfield Road at the gates to the old Strawberry Fields children's home, and we stood outside the tidy brick building at 20 Forthlin Road where McCartney grew up. "This was the last McCartney family home. They were here only a matter of months when Paul's mother Mary died. Paul's father lived here until 1964, when he had to move out in the middle of the night because of all the fans who'd come round."

There was the football field through which young Paul would run with his guitar to jam with his new mate John...I was like a Jew in the Holy Land. My heart was full of the modern myths and legend that informed my life. My camera broke on the corner of Penny Lane while I focused on the shelter in the middle of the roundabout.

I took it as a sign.

That evening, at a small wrap party for the quiz show, the BBC people were fascinated that I'd managed to spend an entire day in Liverpool.

"That must have been a singularly excruciating experience, old bean. I say, how did you manage to fill the hours of boredom?" the director asked.

"No. It was incredible. I saw the church where John Lennon and Paul McCartney first met. I stood at Strawberry Fields. I—"

Lips pursed. Glances were exchanged. Could the Yank be taking the piss?

"You all have to understand," I explained. "I'm from America. When I was growing up, the Beatles were the most important influence on my life. To people my age, they were everything. And to us, Liverpool only existed in black and white. Just like the picutres. But today, after all these years, it was in color! I had no idea it was full of parks and trees—"

The BBC people exchanged more looks of sarcastic amazement.

"No, I understand." One particularly artistic chap, dressed out in black, nodded in appreciation. "I understand how you as a Yank would be fascinated. But then again," he chuckled. "There must be other cultural sites you're anxious to see—the National Gallery, say, or Stratford-Upon-Avon."

"Well, yeah, sure, there's one I'm really looking forward to."

Ally winced as everyone leaned forward expectantly. "Ah, right. Now what would that be, then?"

"Well, I really want to visit Benny Hill's grave."

We arrived back in the States in time to dump off our bags and fly off to Las Vegas for the NATPE convention. The annual shindig of the National Association of Television Program Executives was the big showcase for syndicated shows being sold or promoted for the next season, and the convention hall was crawling with the new crop of afternoon talk show hosts anxious to grab a piece of what Ricki Lake had fallen into. There was Lake's former producer Charles Perez, who'd borrowed her studio one weekend to tape a pilot for a show of his own, casting himself as a wholesome "Geraldo Next Door" while hoping no one recognized him as Charlie Dabney, the tongue-kissing gay-next-door who popped up on an episode of MTV's *Real World*; Gabrielle Carteris, who got her own show because she *played* the smart girl on *Beverly Hills, 90210*; Tempest Bledsoe, because she was the overweight smartypants daughter from *The Cosby Show*; and Carnie Wilson, simply the fat girl from Wilson-Phillips some channel surfers might mistake for Ricki Lake.

The star of the bunch of tubby freshman misfits was Gordon Elliott, fresh from his hiatus and rarin' to go, yet already being tamed and molded from barrier-breaking behemoth to cuddly wallabie, currently advertised in the trades in a large-as-life fold-out ad that kept folding out until it reached Gordon's full six feet, seven inches.

Detour had its own foldout ad in the trades as well, though it couldn't have been what Raf anticipated.

Worldvision was pushing the show in its clubby showcase next to the massive set-up for Paramount Television, where Frank Kelly and Linda Bell stretched their smiles and pressed the flesh.

Like the other major distributors, Worldvision's "booth" was an actual prefabricated office, with climate control, comfortable couches, a bar, and private rooms in which deals could be made. *Detour* was among the shows displayed in huge ads on the walls, but Rafael Abramovitz was nowhere to be seen—in person or photo. In an amazing fulfillment of self-fulfilling prophecy, he'd helped screw himself out of his own show.

Detour was meant to be a show unlike any other, hinging on Rafael's unique talents and storytelling abilities. Things changed as more people got their hands on the project, adding their ideas and taking them farther from the source.

In the end, Raf was left with no guarantee the show would be built around him. His deal with Four Point gave him a piece of the show and a role as host or producer. He didn't know that the CAA agent he'd enlisted for security represented not only Four Point, but the actor Keith Carradine, who was, as they say in Hollywood, "available." The agent, who was supposedly trying to get the best deal for Raf, was working both sides of the fence while at the same time whispering to the guys at Four Point that maybe they didn't need Raf to host the show after all. Maybe they'd prefer a "Raf type," the more telegenic and well-known Carradine.

Somewhere along the way, Raf and the concept of *Detour* were derailed altogether.

By the time *Detour* went to NATPE, Raf was out of the picture. The second pilot tape we'd produced was scuttled and replaced by a slick, garden-variety sales tape voiced by a stock announcer. The thick cardboard insert that appeared in the trades the week prior to the convention showed a picture not of Raf and not of Keith Carradine, but of Peter Brennan.

"He came from Down Under and smote the competition..." the copy began in a crude imitation of what the ad people thought to be the *Detour* style. Brennan hung around the Worldvision booth as the living embodiment of the show, but when station group managers asked what the show was about, he really couldn't say.

No one knew anymore.

Prospective buyers thought Brennan was being cagy and planned for *Detour* to be another sex and scandal show like *A Current Affair*.

Detour was dead.

Alison and I moved together into a house in the Hollywood Hills, with a view of the city and bedroom doors that opened onto a pool. This was the L.A. life we'd heard about, the one I envied when I'd visit Neal and Tolley high above Sunset Plaza, sipping tequilas and watching the traffic helicopters hover below.

I'd felt guilty when *Premier Story* ended, as if I, finding Alison, was the only one leaving richer. Our relationship to that point had been passionate yet polite, always on our best behavior, both of us wanting to get it right. Living together for real, we put aside the politesse and got into the ugly muck of what real love was all about.

We had to work at it. We had a big house, big dreams, and for the first time in either of our careers, were both out of work as we held out in hope of another show of our own.

Peter Herdrich and Dennis O'Brien were working at Young & Tomlin's *Inside Edition* clone, *American Journal*. Their boss, Charlie Lachman, another former *New York Post* editor, brought Alison to New York to offer her a job as a reporter. The show, he promised, was moving into brave new territory, packed with two-minute stories covered top to bottom with music by avant-garde composer Philip Glass.

Alison turned him down.

We continued meeting up with Brennan every evening at the St. James's Club—sold and renamed The Argyle—strategizing and trying to find a way to get syndicated. I wanted to sell the *Premier Story* concept lock stock and barrel. If that wouldn't sell, I had many more—proposals and pitch tapes for shows with names like *Hidden America, Team Holloway,* and *The Big Story.* Each made use of the best elements of *Premier Story*: Hi-8 cameras to get places the big cameras couldn't, writing and style that would bring reality television to a more sophisticated level, and the special talents of Alison Holloway.

I'd even produced a pilot for Chris DeRose, the animal activist from the *Hard Copy* days. His "Last Chance for Animals" group was based in an office on the Sunset Strip; his volunteers were B-movie actresses, *Playboy* models and heavy metal musicians who'd be happy to kill people who mistreated animals. The show would follow them on rescue mission raids and poke around their private lives—sort of a reality combination of *77 Sunset Strip* and MTV's *Real World.*

I called it *Wild Life*: "Sex and Dogs and Rock 'n' Roll."

Peter Brennan wasn't much interested in any of it. "What we should do is take over a TV station in the middle of nowhere, mate," he said. "In Kansas somewhere. Cover one town for an entire year."

Peter Brennan was sick and tired. He would have preferred to live on a beach or spend a year playing tennis, but responsibility, with his wife and kids, now spread among two homes in Bel Air and the Marina Peninsula, left him with an acute need for money.

He had little interest in reviving *Premier Story.* In his eyes, the show was damaged goods. Any potential buyer would wonder why Chris-Craft didn't run with it. Peter held Alison in high regard as a producer and on-air talent, but held it against her that she wasn't American. As someone who shaped American values and ideas with his invention of tabloid television, he didn't like the subjects discovering that the wizard behind the curtain was a man from Oz. He was convinced that Americans didn't want foreigners telling them what to think.

Peter Brennan lusted for the ultimate American host. "If I could only get Roseanne to do a talk show, that would be it," he dreamed at the Argyle. "She'd be the one person who could beat Oprah."

Roseanne was otherwise engaged.

Brennan found the next closest thing: her bulldyke sister.

Geraldine Barr helped invent the "domestic goddess" persona that evolved into Roseanne's hit television series, but along with other members of Roseanne's support team, was cut off by her sister after Tom Arnold came along. Geraldine went off to lick her wounds in San Francisco, where she wrote a tell-all book that included belittling comments about the size of Tom Arnold's penis.

If Alison Holloway was Brennan's most classy, telegenic and accomplished frontperson, Geraldine would be his most hideous and untrained. She was Brennan's id, unfettered by beauty or depilatory, overweight and mannish, with crooked teeth and a braying voice.

Ah, but that braying voice sounded like Roseanne's, and that fat package could be a Bizarro world, TV-movie version of America's number one sitcom star. Brennan poured all his egalitarian impulses into this one, imagining an all-American show that stripped television to its Aussie roots: *A Current Affair* and *Premier Story* and a night in a pub all boiled down to the flannel-shirted lesbian little sister of the angriest and straightest-talking sitcom star of our time.

It was a little bit Howard Stern, a little bit Ross Perot and a skidmark off *Beavis & Butt-Head*. Brennan called it *News To Me*:

> *News To Me* is a daily magazine-like format that presents and strips bare the formal language and presentation of news as we know it.
>
> It is a blue-collar, no-bull dissection of the day's hottest stories with an eye to demolish sacred cows, expose the double standard, ridicule the pompous, revile unfairness, pummel false celebrity and honor plain truth and the common man.
>
> The subject matter is the story that all America is talking about today. Geraldine will...carve up new movies and television shows...honor a local hero...phone a legislator's office about a stupid rule...and get viewer phone polls to let the power brokers know when people are fed up and are not going to take it anymore...
>
> She is straight-up, common sense, simple, perceptive, critical; yet optimistic. She has, through it all, great faith in the common wisdom of the people. She is the average viewer.

Unfortunately, Geraldine wasn't a television performer. The show didn't fly.

Born-again Wayne Darwen surfaced shouting "hallelujah" in March. From his retreat in Franklin, Tennessee, with his two dogs and new woman, he'd formed a one-man production company called Mountaintop Television and turned to grass roots Americana for inspiration.

"I've got the ultimate, mate, a show where we ride down the backroads of America into all those little out-of-the way places and talk to the common man, people we never see on television."

"Sounds like your neighbors."

"Mate, no shit! You won't believe, I've got Hatfields & McCoys right down the road—and there's a guy, Old Man Osborne, he lives next door to a millionaire, and he craps in a fackin outhouse! You oughta come down here, mate, living's cheap; we can have fun."

"Ah, I'm kind of committed to L.A.—"

"L.A.'s bad air and bad people, mate. Come down to Nashville, clear your mind, cleanse your soul. Get yerself a piece of land—"

I changed the subject. "So who's your host?"

"Ready for this? I know his son. Merle Haggard."

"Merle Haggard."

"Fackin' A! He rides his tour bus across the country, and we talk to people on the way. We call it *Merle's 'Merica*."

Maureen O'Boyle's career was born again. After being dumped from *A Current Affair*, she won the attention of Roger Ailes, the rotund former Republican strategist who was now a television consultant for Warner Brothers. Warner's signed up Maureen as weekend anchor for *Extra*, their version of *Entertainment Tonight*, and her big expressive head proved to be far better suited to spouting TelePrompTer copy and inane hypey-talk than the down-home realism required by *A Current Affair*.

Television, though, works with a strange logic. Maureen was so good being dumb on *Extra* that Warner's was preparing to launch her into the smart person's arena, with a pilot for her own talk show.

If Maureen was "hot," *A Current Affair* was turning a dangerous icy blue and being wheeled into intensive care one last time. If ratings were a heartbeat, the doctors would have the clappers pressed to the show's chest and be shouting "clear!"

The granddaddy of tabloid television was now in third place behind *Inside Edition* and *Hard Copy*. The dreadful *American Journal* was less than a tenth of a ratings point behind, and while reality shows in general were taking a beating because of the ubiquitous O.J. Simpson trial, the very survival of *A Current Affair* was on the line. Fox needed to import the finest surgeons in a last-ditch effort at revival. They came up with Bob Young and John Tomlin.

The producers from the original *A Current Affair* were returning to the Fox fold, years after jumping ship and making a bundle with *Inside Edition* and *American Journal*. Word spread that both men resented the assignment. They'd signed a deal to create new shows, but the small print on their contracts allowed Fox to press them into this action first.

The problem was time. Young and Tomlin wouldn't start at Fox until the end of May. With three crucial months and one vital sweeps period in the interim, Fox honchos Peter Faiman and "J.B." Blunck needed to take stopgap measures.

Once again, they turned to Peter Brennan.

"It's rent money, mate," Brennan said when I argued that the job would be a step back for our successful team. He signed a short-term deal that had him working out of the L.A. office, coordinating coverage of the Simpson trial and gently taking control of the show, which was being manhandled by Bill Ridley and Barry Levine, the newspaper hacks who still didn't get it: that papers can be hot, but televison is cool.

Peter Brennan walked into *A Current Affair* with a pack of Marlboro Lights, a deliberately foggy demeanor, and a pocketful of twinkling charm. He was there to get in and out, richer and unscathed, but when he suggested Alison and I come on board to help out, I decided it should be all or nothing. Youngie and Tomlin didn't want the show; fifteen months after I'd refused to take it over, I had reason to. This would be the perfect place to pick up where we'd been dropped off at *Premier Story*, a half-hour a night to move the genre to a higher ground.

I drew up a plan to revive our careers and make *A Current Affair* relevant once again.

> March 9, 1995
> Long Term Proposal for *A Current Affair*
> Cut to the chase. This is the only future for a dying show:
>
> *A CURRENT AFFAIR*
> THE NEW NATIONAL TABLOID NEWSMAGAZINE
> WITH ALISON HOLLOWAY IN LOS ANGELES
> AND STEVE DUNLEAVY IN NEW YORK CITY

The memo ran for a half dozen pages, detailing plans for turning the show around. Everything boiled down to a few proposals: Move the main office to Los Angeles; fire the staff and hire people back on an invitation-only basis; replace the hackneyed style with maturity and wit; bring back the guts, the confidence to determine the most important story and angle of the day; and, most crucial, team up Dunleavy and Holloway as hosts.

"Two foreign accents that scream all that's great about America... Dunleavy is the tabloid legend, the mad dog reporter who's a combination Errol Flynn and Crocodile Dundee; Holloway the intrepid young correspondent and producer, the smart mysterious blond whose Queen's English and regal bearing barely hide a sexy, saucy wit. The new *A Current*

Affair would be truly national, international, upbeat and once again over-the-top..."

This was my version of Brennan's rallying speech in Tarrytown five years earlier. It was the type of thesis I should have nailed to the door of Rupert Murdoch's mansion above Benedict Canyon. Instead, I showed it to Brennan before handing it to Faiman.

Brennan was adamant. He told me not to send it, but to settle down and take whatever money I could get out of them.

The proposal went unseen.

CHAPTER THIRTY-THREE:
KATO SUCKS & NICKY DIES

The Los Angeles bureau of *A Current Affair* had been moved several times within the Fox Television Center since the show's glory days, its location reflecting its status within the Fox organization. At the height of Barry Diller's pique, the office was shifted from a high floor with a panoramic view to a low building at the back of the lot. As years passed, the view kept getting closer to the ground.

When we arrived at the Fox Television Center in April 1995, the office was so close to the ground, you had to look up to see dirt. We followed the guard's directions through a parking garage and down a dimly-lit hall lined with utility lockers. The ceiling panels were shattered, rusted, and muddy, with multicolored wires and asbestos silver tubing hanging down like guts through the ruptures. Plastic pots on the floor caught water dripping in a steady stream from the earth above. We were no longer in a building, but in an underground tunnel beneath the parking lot. This was the new home of *A Current Affair*'s L.A. bureau, windowless, airless, with everything but a canary in a corner cage to warn when the toxic gases seeped in. One literally could not get any lower.

Things could get stranger, as they did once we turned the corner to the office. *A Current Affair* was sharing its space with a Fox news magazine show called *Full Disclosure*.

This was the latest project from Van Gordon Sauter, the former executive producer of Dan Rather's *CBS Evening News,* hired on by Murdoch, in part because Sauter was married to California state treasurer Kathleen Brown, who was making a run for governor.

Sauter's wife would lose to a Johnny Carson lookalike named Pete Wilson, while Sauter and his erstwhile *CBS Morning News* producer David Corvo failed with their first Fox enterprise, a "hip" knockoff of CBS's yuppie newsmagazine *West 57th*. The show was *Front Page*, the one whose star correspondent was Ron Reagan, Jr.

Full Disclosure was to be Fox Television's first investigative newsmagazine since Gerald Stone sank *The Reporters*, with a pair of hosts also brought on because of their Murdochian connections.

Judith Regan was News Corps' backroom star, a beautiful, savvy New York City book editor who'd guided both Howard Stern and Rush Limbaugh to best-seller status.

Andrew Neil was a former editor of the *Sunday Times* of London and early executive at Murdoch's Sky Television. He was an even more confounding choice than Regan, who had no television experience at all.

Bulky, bumpy, and brimming with overconfidence, Neil was a Scotsman who spoke with a thick burr and whose noggin was capped by a thicket of wiry hair that led the British tabloids to dub him "Brillo."

It would be up to the Sauter gang to polish this raw gem for American television. They permed, colored, untangled, and brushed back his troublesome coif, yanked off his dickie, stripped him of his British bon vivant regalia and dressed him up in Edward R. Murrow drag, with colorful tie, rolled-up sleeves, and bright suspenders.

In the end, he looked like a *Saturday Night Live* parody of Larry King who rolled his r's to boot.

Great money was poured into *Full Disclosure*. Teams were dispatched to bring back stories from around the world. Neil himself ventured with a producer to seek out the Moscow Mafia. Yet it didn't take long for Fox executives to realize that the show had as much chance of surviving as Ron Reagan Jr.'s.

Full Disclosure was cancelled before it ever aired. Judith Regan went back to her books. Andrew Neil was given a million dollar golden handshake, allowed to keep his new clothes, and offloaded back to England with a grand announcement on arrival that he was retiring to France to write his *Sunday Times* memoirs.

For the rest of the staff, holders of healthy contracts, business went on as usual, as it proceeded the day we returned to *A Current Affair*. Phones rang. Stories were investigated and lined up for shooting. Producers, reporters, and assistants turned up their noses at the lesser types from *A Current Affair*.

There was one minor problem.

They had no show.

These people were working for a show that did not exist. This wasn't the Fox catacombs. This was the frigging *Twilight Zone*. Yet it seemed perfectly normal compared to what was going on at *A Current Affair*.

The L.A. bureau was now the fiefdom of Mike Watkiss, that bantam bodybuilding reporter with the Dunleavy pompadour. As bureau chief and

West Coast correspondent, Watkiss strutted around the office in a constant state of partial undress, preening shirtless while giving commands, his pants undone as he changed among his everyday Western attire to jacket and tie for on-camera standups to be inserted into the show, to the skin-tight spandex he paraded in on the way to athletic workouts.

Watkiss was a strange duck. In my last tenure at *A Current Affair*, Ian Rae considered firing him, saying his on-air attire of suspenders, shirtsleeves, and conk made him look like a South London bookie. When word got back to Watkiss that Ian Rae didn't like his look, he changed it.

Watkiss dyed his hair blond.

By the time I returned to *A Current Affair*, Watkiss had washed out the lighter tresses in favor of a jet-black dye job, his pompadour accented by pencil-thin Bret Maverick sideburns; but in case viewers forgot about his tonsorial confusion, several of Watkiss's stories included footage from past interviews, showing him with black hair, then blond, sometimes brown and back to black. Not once did anyone tell Watkiss he was out of his fucking mind. No one was going to tell him, now. He was riding high with his greatest success yet: appearing as an *A Current Affair* reporter in the hit movie *Dumb and Dumber*.

Watkiss took it personally that Brennan and I were treading on his turf. "He doesn't get it mate," Brennan warned before I arrived. "He's angry because we've taken over his office. He doesn't get it: we've taken over the show."

"Get in here quick, mate." I passed Watkiss buttoning his shirt in the hall and followed Brennan into his office cubicle off the *Full Disclosure* room. "Do you have a jacket and tie?"

"At home," I said. "Why? I don't think I have a tie anymore."

"You might be called as a witness in the Simpson trial."

"What?"

The prosecution had gotten around to Robert Kardashian and the garment bag. They were ready to argue that Kardashian should be forced to testify about what he did that morning after the murders, because he'd reactivated his legal license afterward and was therefore not protected by client confidentiality laws.

Two detectives were on their way to pick up a copy of the tape.

"Didn't you tell them they'd have to get a subpoena?"

"Fuck, no! Let em have it."

Visions of me on the witness stand perspiring and stuttering like the second coming of Kato churned my gut. "Yeah, but Peter, in America, journalists don't give up their notes or tapes unless they're forced to. It's part of the Constitution and the first amendment and freedom of the press and all that."

"Fuck that! Mate, think of the publicity here." Where was Raf when we needed him? "This is exactly what we need. Give 'em anything they want as long as they mention the show!"

I sighed and waited for the detectives.

Judge Lance Ito put the bag issue on hold. Ultimately, the tape wasn't used in court and Kardashian would claim he never looked inside the bag, dropped off the bag in O.J. Simpson's business office and never saw it again. The hopes of ever getting to the bottom of what really went down will probably have to wait until everyone is dead.

"You guys are running the show. Do what you have to do," Faiman told me on the phone. "Bill Ridley answers to you and Peter."

All of a sudden, *A Current Affair* had a new agenda, dedicated entirely to the O.J. Simpson trial. Penny Daniels would anchor the show from location in Los Angeles, though she required a portable TelePrompTer to get through the two-line intros. Dunleavy would be set loose to do what street dogs do best. Alison was a special correspondent and, Brennan promised, would present the biggest sweeps special of them all—just as soon as he nailed it down.

"We should take advantage of this, mate," I said. "We have free rein. Let's do what we do best."

"We can't. Let's just help them along, help them with their scripts, and when the time's up, let's get out."

Peter Brennan and I had arrived at an impasse that was fraying our working relationship beneath the Simpson trial on the overhead television set. I was anxious to take power and use *A Current Affair* for our own ends, but Peter didn't want to put anything in place that would help Young and Tomlin succeed, or take measures that would have him blamed for the show's ultimate failure.

"We have a chance to take over. We shouldn't waste our time," I insisted. "We should take it."

"Mate." Brennan sighed and held up his glass for another Stoli, splash of soda and twist of lemon. "It's just rent money for now."

We were in a new pub. The movable binge had settled into a satellite office "over the road" from the Fox Television Center.

With its glittering Arabian Nights sign and two-story building, the Dunes Motel might have been a passable resting place for travellers and tourists, had it not been located across Sunset, around the corner from the homeless encampment on the freeway overpass, on a strip of hotsheet hotels in one of the dicier sections of Hollywood.

The Dunes had a bar, though, tucked off in a corner of the parking lot, that was a tiny oasis of civility, similar in spirit to the warm pubs found in every village of the United Kingdom. It was a cocoon of conviviality and good cheer, with above average food, payphones, and only a swinging door to let in the afternoon sun.

This hidden room in the dead zone of Sunset was among the most welcoming we'd found in all Los Angeles.

"It works both ways." I tried a different approach. "If you want the ratings to go up, we've got to give them a reason to tune in. We can write whatever we want for Watkiss or Miller or McGowan—but people won't believe them because they're identified with a show that lies."

"That doesn't matter."

"Let's use this show, mate. Use it for ourselves. It can be anything we want it to be. It's a half-hour of airtime to fill."

Like Dunleavy in Tom McGrath's bar back in 1993, challenged by Brennan to ride with the Wild Bunch once more, Brennan himself shook his head again. "No."

Alison's debut on *A Current Affair* was a drastic change from the usual menu. The show, which had passed off as many as six bite-sized news reports a night, would be dedicated to a single subject: a mondo verite visit with potential Simpson defense witness Dr. Kerry Mullis, a Nobel Prize-winning DNA expert whose excessive tastes for women and LSD threatened to overshadow his expertise.

The story would be told as we best knew how: with Hi-8 camera cutaways, tight, plain-spoken narration, and smarts. It was as big a jolt as the Michael Jackson special Brennan and I had cooked up two years earlier.

This time, Brennan preferred to err on the side of familiarity. "You can't have it go so long without narration," he said, viewing the first segment. "This isn't *Premier Story*, mate."

"All I'm doing is television the best way I know how."

"Mate, this is too drastic a change for this show."

"A change is what the show needs."

"We can't come in and bomb the fucking place."

"I'm trying to treat viewers like they're intelligent."

"You can't do that."

"What?"

Brennan sighed. "Look, any intelligent viewer this show had is gone now. They don't watch anymore. The people who do watch it, expect shit. They won't understand this."

"You're telling me to dumb it down."

"If you put it that way, yeah."

"Mate, I never thought I'd hear you say that."

There were several young assistants in the L.A. office, but the only one I could rely on was a kid named David Rothenberg. David was eighteen. He usually wore a baseball cap and jeans. When people first looked at him, they were often repulsed, as his face and body had been scarred horribly in a notorious fire.

When David was six, his father brought him to a motel near Disneyland, and rather than lose custody of the boy to his estranged wife, set the room and David on fire.

The child survived, but only barely. His fingers were burned down to stubs. Layers of skin were melted away. Thirteen years and close to a hundred operations later, David remained trapped in a life of unimaginable pain and incredible courage.

Steve Dunleavy had met David five years earlier when he did a story on the case for *The Reporters*. "The Comeback Kid" segment became legendary for Dunleavy's over-the-top prison confrontation with David's father. When Dunleavy taunted, "Truth is, people out there right now think you're the biggest son of a bitch on two legs," he caused the man to convulse in sobs.

Dunleavy also interviewed David's mother. When she began to cry, he took out his pocket handkerchief, said, ""Reporters aren't supposed to show emotions," and cried along.

A couple of years later, *GQ* magazine accused Dunleavy of "faking" the crying shot the way William Hurt did in *Broadcast News*, turning the camera around after the interview and turning on the waterworks, while claiming he'd used two cameras to capture the scene as it occurred.

Anyone who knew Dunleavy could tell you the question was beside the point, that whether he turned the camera around or not, he cried for real. Dunleavy was successful because he had a real heart, and he was truly moved by David's bravery. He stayed close to the boy, visited him when he was in Los Angeles, and got him that job in the L.A. office.

David was a good kid. His mouth curled easily into a smile and he still had the most expressive, bright, and soulful eyes. There were few in the office as helpful as he was.

I identified with the kid. People were put off by my appearance, too. I was angry, the former Prince of Darkness stomping around in a new uniform of jeans, Timberland boots, and shoulder-length hair, caught in a news bureau where no one read newspapers, where simple requests went unheeded, where people were being allowed to destroy the show that gave me the opportunity to tell the truth. The anger filled me every time I walked into the underground office, the same way frustration took over in my days at *Hard Copy*.

I felt an obligation to Alison and a determination to change television the way we did, against all odds, with *Premier Story*, but now, Peter Brennan, the man who taught me never to underestimate the audience, was telling me to dumb things down.

Sweeps was approaching, and Peter Brennan knew only one way to reverse the fortunes of *A Current Affair* instantaneously: throw a whole lot of cash at something. As the most crucial month of May 1995 loomed, that something was the wedding of Nicole Brown and O.J. Simpson.

Back in 1983, Simpson had hired a small company to videotape the festivities on the Rockingham estate. There were hours of raw footage, beginning in the early morning when the bride was dressed by her sisters, through the ceremony itself—during which O.J. Simpson was baptized—and ending with the wild reception.

Somewhere along the way, the tapes got into the hands of a couple of guys from San Diego. Their dream was to sell first-run footage to a tabloid show, then market a wedding videotape through mail order. Word of their intentions had circulated in Hollywood and New York for months; several shows got a look at the highlights, but there were no takers.

It wasn't the quality. That was undeniable. It wasn't the price; at this stage in the Simpson game, a half million dollars was confetti. The problem was ownership. Despite the fine-print releases the newlyweds may have signed over to the videographers, there was no doubt O.J. Simpson owned the copyright, both to the ceremony at his home and to his own image.

Sitting in the L.A. jailhouse, writing books, autographing photos and footballs, and communing with his expensive team of lawyers, O.J. Simpson was bound to sue the pants off anyone who tried to sell what could turn out to be valuable property in the future.

Dunleavy was among those who'd made desperate efforts to damn the law and go full speed ahead broadcasting the tapes. To his frustration, nothing could be done. If his competition at King World and Paramount couldn't find a way around the law, there was no way the supercautious Muriel Reis would okay spending half a million dollars on the prize.

It took Brennan less than a week to come up with the solution: a foolproof plan to spend the money, beat O.J. Simpson at his own game, and return to Muriel Reis' eyes the infatuated sparkle of a schoolgirl in love.

In the meantime, I was staking out stories relating to other characters in the Simpson case. The next opportunity presented itself with the premiere of a Pauly Shore movie called *Jury Duty*, which after its completion had scenes added and dialogue re-looped with "O.J. jokes" to cash in on the murder case.

The premiere in Westwood would continue the theme, promising lookalikes for prosecutor Marcia Clark and Judge Lance Ito, a white Bronco parked at the curb, and Shore's "date" for the evening, prosecution witness Kato Kaelin.

With his shaggy hair and dimbulb persona, Kaelin had won some affection as the village idiot of the Simpson trial, yet his eagerness to use his friend's murder to jumpstart his Hollywood career, combined with his lack of candor about Simpson's actions the night of the murders, had made him one of the more despicable figures in the case.

We arrived to tell the story between the lines, pointing out some of the ironies most of the media didn't notice while they fawned over the B-grade guestlist. There was the billboard atop the cinema advertising the film *Murder in the First*, and the small cemetery adjoining the parking lot, where Marilyn Monroe was entombed and Dominique Dunne, daughter of Simpson trial watcher Dominick Dunne, strangled by her jealous boyfriend, was buried.

Kaelin himself was protected by a publicist from the high-powered Lee Solters firm as he waltzed past the receiving line of cameras and reporters with his new friend Pauly, then ran straight for the open door of a limousine waiting to speed him away.

Later, Hi-8 Joe videotaped Alison as she drove from the theatre on Wilshire Boulevard, turned right on San Vicente, and rolled into Brentwood, past the Mezzaluna restaurant and left onto Bundy Drive. It was a take-off on Detective Philip Vanatter's videotape, recently played in court to demonstrate the short distance between the murder scene and Simpson's mansion.

We showed that Kaelin joined in the exploitation of his friend's death only six minutes from the place she was slaughtered.

I was happy with how the segment turned out, though it wouldn't be the lead of the show; Dunleavy had the spot with a story on the police criminologist who'd fumbled much of the evidence.

Yes, Steve Dunleavy was back in town, carrying the banner for the failing regime back in New York, and accompanied by a small team of female producers who cheered the scripts he wrote, brushed the dandruff off his pinstripe suits, and accompanied him on his drinking jags.

They couldn't, however, help him stretch the lead story his status commanded to longer than two minutes and thirty seconds. Once he got past his "From the farming fields to the killing fields" line, Dunleavy realized he was coming up more than two minutes short.

Brennan stopped in my edit room minutes before it was time to feed tape to New York. "Mate, can you stretch this Kato piece?"

"I thought you wanted it shorter."

"Dunleavy can only go two fifteen," he said. "I need two more minutes or we're gonna have a hole."

"No problem." I added an interview with Anna Nicole Smith.

"Were you responsible for the piece on Kato Kaelin?" Barry Levine was calling from the New York office.

"Yeah. Alison and I did it." I knew they'd call. I waited for the congratulations.

"That was the worst piece of shit I've ever seen on this show. It was an embarrassment. That section on Dominick Dunne was over the top. It was disgraceful."

I waited for him to laugh. "Are you serious?"

"Yes, I'm serious." Levine was obviously talking for a crowd on the other end. "You should be ashamed."

I spoke calmly and without inflection. "Who the fuck are you?" I asked. "You have the balls to talk to me like that? To me?"

"That's what I think. You know, our ratings may not be very good, but we're proud of everything we put on the air," said the notorious supermarket tabloid hack. "Eight minutes for that was a disgrace."

I thought of Dunleavy's producers pulling yellow highlighting markers over transcriptions of an interview they'd watched in person the night before, and how they didn't know enough about television to fill five short minutes.

"Who the fuck are you?" I demanded. "You got a problem, talk to Brennan."

He slammed down the phone. I slammed into Brennan's office and told him what happened.

Brennan chuckled. "It's that whole crew back in New York, mate. They're upset because we've taken over. He was just putting on a show for Ridley and the rest."

"Yeah, well, we're not taking over the show, and if I have to take this shit and be insulted by ungrateful bastards like that Bartleby-the-Scrivener check-writing son of a bitch, let's really take over."

Brennan sat calmly. "Call Levine back," he said. "And tell him there was a meeting last week, and you and I were the only ones to vote that he shouldn't be fired."

Later that day, I found the reason behind Levine's outburst. We'd criticized and mocked Kato Kaelin, who a few months earlier had been paid $50,000 by A Current Affair to walk along a beach with Dunleavy and say nothing relevant about the case. Kaelin was considered a "friend" to the show, just as Joey Buttafuoco and Jeff Gillooly were friends, and therefore beyond criticism.

What Levine didn't know was that Lee Solters' people found a new way for Kato to cash in on his notoriety: an autograph-signing tour of midwestern shopping malls. Next stop was Denver, Colorado, and we were going to be on his weasel ass like suntan oil.

It was the old *Premier Story* team, Alison and Hi-8 Joe and Jay Kay and me, that arrived in Denver, where the Kato Kaelin battleplan was in action: he'd make a couple of paid appearances for a local rock 'n' roll radio station, then, to offset any negative publicity, spend an hour signing autographs for charity.

It was with weariness, not the exhilaration of the chase, that we set up in front of a designer jeans shop in the Villa Italia shopping mall in the suburb of Lakewood. By the time Kato Kaelin came running through the store, waving to the crowd amid heavy metal fanfare, there were more than a thousand people jammed against the barricades, spilling over into the press area, leaning over the second-floor balcony, holding up children to be kissed, handing over gifts, chanting his name, and straining to touch the hem of his tight-fitting garments.

I realized then that all the bad tabloid TV had done had been funneled into this depressed shopping mall. This was the cult of celebrity at its most perverse, the natural extension of Joey Buttafuoco's snakeskin voodoo boots, with souvenir t-shirts and everything.

The deejay lowered the triumphal music and handed Kato a microphone.

"How's everybody up there in the bleachers?" he asked cheerfully. There was a distracted rumble and Kato worked harder to fill the void. "They can't hear you on the radio! Louder!"

The reminder that their hysteria was being broadcast to all Colorado seemed to inject a sense of shame throughout the mall. The locals went quiet for a moment, as if suddenly asking themselves what they were doing there.

It was in that momentary silence that a voice rang out, loud enough for everyone at home to hear:

"Y o u   s u c k !"

Later that night, I was having second thoughts about everything, most especially about the validity of tabloid television. After all we'd worked for, it had come down to this, sitting in a rental car half an hour before midnight, staking out the back door of an ice-skating rink in Denver, Colorado, waiting to ambush Kato fucking scumbag leech Kaelin when he left the stage of the heavy metal concert thrashing away inside.

It belonged in a journalism textbook: When you find yourself staking out Kato Kaelin outside an ice-skating rink in Denver, Colorado, you will have reached the nadir of your career.

Worse, I was dragging Alison through it.

I pulled out my cell phone and called home to check for messages. Beep. "Burt. This is Dave Peterkin. Nicky Loiacono's been involved in a serious traffic accident."

Nicky, my first boss in television, the purest newsman and most loyal friend I'd know; if he knew where I was now, he'd be ashamed for me. An accident? My first thought was: who did he kill? "He was hit by a car in Fort Lee, New Jersey. He's got severe head injuries. He's on life support. I thought you'd want to know."

Oh, Nicky.

I paged my friend, Bob O'Brien, a reporter for the *10 O'Clock News*, and he called back from Elaine's. "He was out drinking after work with his friends from *America's Talking*. Walking to his car when a drunk driver came through a light and hit him. It's bad, bro. He was dragged about fifty yards. Turns out there were two cops behind the car. One of them got out to take care of Nicky. The other one caught up with the woman at the tunnel."

"It was a woman."

"Yeah. She was so drunk she didn't know where she was."

"Ironic, huh?"

"You tell me."

"Fucking Nicky. Is he gonna make it?"

O'Brien exhaled. I could hear the restaurant clatter before he spoke again. "The doctors say it doesn't look good. But you know what I say? Nicky's a fighter. And I know him, man. I know he's gonna fight and in a few months, we're all gonna have a drink with him right here."

"I'll come back for that."

"You'd better."

"So let me know what I can do. I'll be home tomorrow."

"Love you, man."

"Fuck! You're so fucking angry all the time." Peter Brennan had been waiting at the bar at the Hollywood Athletic Club, the swank modern pool hall in the building where Errol Flynn and the Barrymores once ran around in towels. It was midway between the Dunes and civilization on the Sunset Strip in more ways than one.

"I've had enough of this, mate." He turned with his Stoli and soda. His face was flushed. "You gotta stop this."

"Yeah, I'm angry. I'm trying to help run the show, I got people sabotaging me left and right. I ask to have papers in the morning, I don't get the papers. I can't ask why things don't get done—"

"Yeah, but throwing pens around edit rooms?"

That morning, I'd tossed a Bic pen in the air when Brennan told me fifteen minutes before deadline to take two minutes out of the Kato piece. "I was sticking up for the story."

"That doesn't do me any good. I'm trying to get a show on."

"You're right, mate." I sighed and we both relaxed. "I know I'm not helping you. I'm really not. I shouldn't be there if I'm not. I'm turning into Raf."

"No you're not. Raf would say everything was broken and not have any suggestions on how to fix them."

"I say everything's broken and no one listens to my suggestions."

"Look, this is only television. Just have some fun with it."

"I can't. I'm Raf. I've become Raf."

Peter Brennan needed a way out. On April nineteenth, he got one when a bomb destroyed the Federal Building in Oklahoma City. As far as Brennan was concerned, *A Current Affair* was no longer the O.J. Simpson show. He put Bill Ridley in charge of Oklahoma City coverage and sent half the staff to do standups in front of the rubble like all the local and network newspeople.

For now, the heat was off.

Nick Loiacono, meanwhile, was as good as dead. He'd remained in a coma the week after the accident and surgery to relieve pressure on his brain had little effect. He was officially pronounced brain dead, and it was only a matter of time before they pulled the plug.

After I got word, I left the office and went over to the Dunes with Dunleavy. It was amazing how despite the egos and clashes back at the office, everything was all right once we got to the bar. To Dunleavy, there truly was a difference between business and friendship. We had a laugh or two, at least one about Rafael.

Like a kid too prideful to come out and apologize or ask to play ball, Raf had lurked along the sidelines since he'd walked out on *Detour*, speaking periodically to Peter Brennan, sussing out job opportunities. Brennan assigned him to go after fallen evangelist Jim Bakker, who'd soon be released from prison, but when J.B. found out about it, Raf's job was cancelled. We had to laugh.

That night, Alison and I walked down the hill to the Sunset Strip to the Bel Age to tell Nabi and Dmitri the news about Nicky. They were very sad. In the past year, Nicky had kept in touch with them and they always said the place was never the same since he left.

We were all very quiet. Once in a while, Nabi would come over and look at us, teary-eyed. We ordered dinner from the restaurant and sat and ate and told Nicky stories while MTV videos ran on the television behind the bar.

"There's a band," I said to Alison, nodding at the screen. "Hootie and the Blowfish. How's that for a name, huh? Hootie and the Blowfish."

I alternated between a beer and single malt Scotch.

Suddenly someone was standing next to Alison. It was the heavyset guy in the expensive track suit who'd been drinking alone at the other end of the bar. He was thumbing through a wad of bills.

"What will it cost for her to give me a blowjob?"

I put my drink on the bar. "What did you say?"

"I said how much for her to give me a blowjob."

There wasn't half a second that passed before my fist landed with a crunch, flat in the middle of his nose. The guy staggered back, and as I went to my right, trying to get around Alison sitting between us, he charged back at me. Bang. I punched around Alison and hit him again as he tagged me on the chin.

The two of us rolled toward the couch in the middle of the room. Alison was on the guy's back, grabbing hanks of his hair and screaming, "How dare you!" while I shouted for her to get out of the way and fought like one of the Bowery Boys, trying to avoid hitting the wrong person. He was on top of me on the couch and then a hard left had me atop him, pounding him in the face. Nicky was my best friend. He taught me how to listen to a police scanner. I punched again. He taught me about boxing. He even took me to a Butthole Surfers show. I kept punching. Someone was telling me to stop. Nicky was the first person to teach me what it was to be a friend. Insult my beautiful Ally? I kept punching until the security guards pulled me off, and when they did I charged the guy again.

It took the police and their plastic handcuffs to get me sitting down by the door as they sorted out the stories.

"Mister Burt, please, be quiet," Dmitri implored. "This man, he is a lawyer. He is very bad man. Very bad. Just be quiet."

I wasn't quiet. I had righteousness on my side. I wanted to press charges, but the cops said if I did, my opponent would press countercharges and we'd both be hauled down to the station. He was a lawyer and he had a case: someone told the cops I threw the first punch.

They removed the handcuffs. I called Brennan and asked what I should do. He said to get the hell out.

The adrenaline was surging as Ally and I walked up the Strip on the way home.

"Those bastards," I said, "Why didn't Nabi and Dmitri stick up for me?"

"Because the other guy was a guest at the hotel."

I'd never hit somebody like that. That was something Nicky would do. I thought about people's spirits passing through and I realized I did it for Nicky.

"Poor Nicky. Nicky's dead," I said. I stopped on the sidewalk across from the Roxy, on the Strip where Nicky and Raf and Brennan and Dunleavy and Wayne and I had too many drinks and drove too many times when we shouldn't have and I thought of all the years that brought us here, back to *A Current Affair*, like we'd never been anywhere at all.

The tears were dropping from my eyes as I thought about Nicky being hit by that car, Nicky being dragged, Nicky being dead. I sat down on a wall and had myself a good cry for Nicky. It was the first time I cried since December 8, 1980, the night John Lennon died. Ally got me home.

Nicky died on April 25th.

CHAPTER THIRTY-FOUR:
DUNLEAVY'S REWARD

The highest-paid minds in television's legal departments pondered for months how to get away with running O.J. Simpson's wedding video.

Peter Brennan came up with the answer in a matter of days: get Nicole's parents on board. Lou and Juditha Brown had no legal rights to the video, but once they gave their blessing to the deal, there was no way O.J. Simpson could argue. Simpson fighting his in-laws over the picture of his bride would be like killing her all over again.

Our old friend Muriel Reis came out to Los Angeles from New York to handle the final contracts. As it now stood, *A Current Affair* would only have to pay the holders of the video about $200,000 for rights to a half-hour of footage. An additional $50,000 would convince the Browns to be happy about the release of the tapes and the sale of the video called *Memories of Nicole*.

These wedding tapes would present the first sympathetic view of their daughter. Until this point, Nicole was pitied, but regarded as a hard-bodied California wife with artificial breasts and a wild lifestyle; a voice on a 911 call that was by turns hysterical and manipulative. The wedding video showed Nicole in her maiden glory, when her love for O.J. Simpson crossed all boundaries and taboo. We'd hear her voice on what was supposed to be the happiest day of her life.

For O.J. Simpson, the fallout could be ruinous.

The wedding video was the payback Peter Brennan had promised Alison. The woman who'd received national attention for her coverage of the Simpson case would be *A Current Affair's* special correspondent, taking viewers through a weeklong examination of the tapes.

As the day approached, however, Dunleavy moved in. Brennan brought up the subject matter-of-factly at the Dunes. When he was challenged, he reacted with annoyance. "Mate, it's what Faiman wants. We have to give a piece to Dunleavy. He worked to get the tapes. They'll split the story. That's that."

Brennan was watching out for his mate. I knew there was no fighting it and told Alison the same. I insisted only that Dunleavy's New York contingent have nothing to do with the editing. They were already anxious to take dialog out of context, add dramatic music and get straight to the scene where O.J. whips out a knife—to slice the wedding cake.

The fallout from my terms was not a long time coming.

The tapes would begin airing on Monday, the first of May. On Friday, April 28th, a mid-morning decision was made to have Steve and Alison scramble to the beachside community of Dana Point to interview Nicole's parents about their support of the project.

Alison and Steve climbed into a limo with a collection of producers and sped off to the scene, an hour and a half away. They were cutting it close. The show had to be fed out by noon. There was no time to do anything but whip off the interviews and feed them back from a microwave truck on the scene.

Brennan was back in the Fox control room with two of Dunleavy's New York assistants as the interviews were fed back from Dana Point. The young women flirted with the control room engineers while Brennan worked two phones, trying to speak to a producer on the scene. None was in the truck as the tapes were fed.

Ultimately, Brennan asked me to turn the interviews around: Alison with Nicole's mother Juditha; Dunleavy handling Lou, the father. We made the deadline, but not without consequence. It seemed Dunleavy had shot his interview with two cameras—perhaps he'd learned from the Rothenberg scandal—but the second camera tape never made it to the edit room or the finished piece.

That afternoon, Dunleavy was led to believe that I left his face out of the segment deliberately. Dunleavy's producers, who'd traveled with him to Los Angeles, worked him into a frenzy over it. This was *my* payback for cutting them out of the wedding project.

O.J. Simpson struck back as expected in another courtroom on Monday, seeking an injunction to prevent the airing of the video, claiming it breached his copyright and invaded his privacy. Beverly Hills attorney Anthony Glassman called the sale of the tape "morally repugnant," claiming the video was made solely for little Sydney and Justin Simpson, and that profits could just as easily go to one of Nicole's sisters as it could her children.

The judge turned down his motion to supress the show, though he reserved decision on whether the *Memories of Nicole* videotape would be allowed to go on sale.

The show went on, with Penny Daniels doing a brief throw to Steve and Alison hosting from a phony newsroom set. Everything was in place for the week, five full shows taking us through the wedding day, culminating on Friday when the groom cuts the cake and the couple head off on their new life together.

Dunleavy was once again being produced by those with his best interests in mind. He spoke off the cuff and without alliteration. His narration of the video was sparing and low-key. He and Alison looked good together.

All plans changed after Monday's show, when Muriel stepped in once again.

If we were to run the rest of the video, she said, we'd have to present it like an old-fashioned *A Current Affair* package, with lots of narration. Otherwise, she said, it would seem we were simply playing O.J. Simpson's property rather than reporting on it.

Brennan and I had another disagreement on that one. He was happy to go along with whatever Muriel wanted.

I stood at the urinal in a men's room on a different floor from the *A Current Affair* office. Jim Sheehan walked in. We looked at each other and laughed. We knew why we were avoiding the usual men's room: Mike Watkiss.

Watkiss wanted to punch me out. I got the first inkling a couple of weeks before, when I passed him in the office and asked how he was doing.

"Fine, mate." His voice dripped theatrical sarcasm as he stared me down. What's eating him? I shrugged and carried on, only to be told later about the rumor that I wanted him taken off the air. Dunleavy said he was there when Watkiss went crazy in his office, punching a hole in the wall, pretending it was me.

Events escalated. Alison told me Watkiss had stared her down at the coffee machine. Jimmy Sheehan reported being bumped by the mighty mite in the hall. I knew what was next. I'd be standing at the men's room sink, he'd sucker punch me and everyone would say I was asking for it.

"He wants to kill you, mate," Dunleavy said. He thought it was a good laugh. "Ah, go outside and settle it with your hands like a couple of men."

I went into Brennan's office and demanded, "I want it on the record, mate. This guy is out to get me and he's gonna sucker punch me one day and everyone's going to say I deserved it. I want it on the record that I'm under physical threat because I don't have medical insurance and I'm not going to fight the guy in the office."

Brennan laughed.

"No. Fuck this," I said. I called Jimmy Sheehan over.

"It's true," Sheehan said, embarrassed. "He's been acting threatening. Staring at me when I walk by. Bumping me. I don't even use the men's room because I'm worried I'm going to get punched."

Brennan apologized and we made the complaint official.

They had a memorial service for Nick Loiacono on May thirteenth in New York. I wrote a eulogy for Bob O'Brien to read in my absence. Before sending it off, I handed it to Dunleavy to read in Brennan's small office. Dunleavy was a friend of Nicky's, too.

When I looked in a few minutes later, he was on the couch, alone, reading, holding his handkerchief and bawling like a baby.

The month went downhill from there. Bill Ridley was relieved of his duties and prepared to fly back to England. When Brennan berated me because someone told him I'd insulted David Miller's work, I quit, but returned the following week when he apologized, admitting it was a set-up from the ones who didn't like all us *Premier Story* people being there, taking over their show.

With Ridley gone, Brennan decided to spend the last two weeks in New York. He brought Watkiss with him. The little guy pranced proudly. "I'm in the witness protection program," he bragged.

The ultimate indignity came on May 18th, when general managers around the country began hearing about *A Current Affair's* "imminent cancellation." The rumor spread so quickly that Greg Meidel, the president and chief operating officer of Fox TV, was forced to issue a memo to the show's staff, insisting that the "nasty and inaccurate rumor...could not be further from the truth, as all of us at Twentieth have high expectations for the long and successful future of *A Current Affair*."

The rumors were started by salesmen from the rival King World, who were anxious to move in on the failing *A Current Affair* time slots. The memo took everyone at the show unawares, and seemed to be one of those self-fulfilling death knells, especially in light of the article in the next day's issue of *Daily Variety*:

> The program, which has reached record low ratings in the mid 4's over the past few weeks, saw more than a quarter of its audience disappear in the first full week of the May sweeps, compared to the same period a year ago...
>
> Magazine shows have suffered because of increased cable viewership and an overdose of (Simpson) trial coverage earlier in the day. *Affair* has been hurt even more because of trial-related access preemptions in Los Angeles, the nation's second-largest TV market...

It was all over for us by the last week of May. Young and Tomlin were arriving any day. We packed up our tapes and left the underground fortress for the last time. The infighting, the egos and the jealousies had gotten us nowhere. Brennan had done what he could to keep the show on an even keel and get out clean with a wad of money. Dunleavy had done all he could to protect the weak and remain loyal to the ones who were thrown in over their heads and were sinking the show. I'd done my best to use the show by bringing it to a higher level and giving Alison as distinct a role as possible.

In the end, everything was washed away in too much alcohol.

On Thursday, May 25th, Steve Dunleavy ran another story about Joey Buttafuoco. Joey was arrested on Sunset Boulevard in Hollywood for allegedly propositioning a policewoman masquerading as a hooker. He was in town to appear on a show called *Liars*.

The following night, Alison and I had everyone over to the house. Dunleavy's New York contingent, the ones from *Premier Story*, all of us sat around and drank to the end of a very bad time. The women danced and Dunleavy acted out most of the songs from *Guys & Dolls*. It was around three a.m. when the CD changer landed on Frank Sinatra's *Come Dance with Me* album. Dunleavy got up and and did a soft shoe singalong as everyone applauded and laughed. Then he grabbed Alison, took her in his arms and the two of them waltzed and tangoed to "Dancing in the Dark."

He led. She spun. Their bodies moved as one, dipping and stepping around the couch and across the living room. I sat at the dining room table and held my hands in front of me, palms out, creating a camera frame and following them as they danced.

"That's the show," I said. "That's the promo. *Steve Dunleavy and Alison Holloway: Dancing in the Dark.*"

Steve Dunleavy was back in New York on the last day of May. Bob Young and John Tomlin were set to take over *A Current Affair* the very next day, starting with a general staff meeting at 10 a.m., where they'd be introduced and the new agenda would be put into motion. The entire staff of the L.A. bureau had been flown in for the occasion. It would be a new day, and perhaps, finally, a good day for *A Current Affair*.

Dunleavy had planned to call his mate Youngie for a drink at O'Flanagan's on First Avenue that last night of May, but someone from the assignment desk called about a hot story that needed chasing down. Of course, there was no one else on the inflated staff who'd give up his or her evening to do it. Dunleavy put off the drink.

Dunleavy would never forget the date or the time. It was Thursday, June 1st, 1995. He was sleeping in his apartment on East 34th Street when the phone woke him at 7:20 a.m.

It was Youngie. "Mate, you've got to meet us for breakfast at the Royalton at eight."

Dunleavy looked at the clock. He wasn't mistaken. Eight a.m. was but forty minutes away. "Uh, mate, I can't make it by eight. I've got to shower and—and I thought we were all gonna meet at the office at ten. I'll see you then."

Youngie's voice was solemn. "Steve, it's very important. You have to come. Peter Faiman wants to have a word."

"All right, mate."

Dunleavy had gotten up and out of countries on shorter notice than that. He could tell from his former photo editor's voice that something was up. One of two things was going to happen in thirty-nine minutes: He was going to be offered the anchorman's job at *A Current Affair*, or he was going to take a long walk off a short pier.

It didn't matter which. He was ready for either choice. The options alone made him feel very important.

What would a man wear on his wedding day? What would he wear in his casket? Dunleavy chose his dark blue Armani suit, a light blue shirt, blue tie, cufflinks and his tassel casual shoes.

Bob Young, John Tomlin and Peter Faiman were waiting in the eatery at the trendy hotel on 45th Street. Dunleavy made a quick check of the faces. Youngie, in his pants and jacket, was very cordial. Tomlin, the big lug, was downright glum. Faiman was strictly business.

"Mate, have something to eat?"

"Great breakfast here."

The two new executive producers were falling all over themselves.

"No, no," Dunleavy said. "Just coffee for me."

There were a few more words of cordiality before Faiman went into a preamble. "As you know, Steve, we have a meeting today, and Bob and John will be introduced to the staff. And things as you well know are going to be heading in a new direction. John and Bob are well aware of the tremendous contribution you've made—"

Dunleavy knew what was coming next, and despite all that had come to pass, he felt it his obligation to spare them the discomfort and dishonor of having to give him the news.

"Whoa, whoa, whoa!" Dunleavy pushed back in his chair and held his hands up to end the charade. "Mates, I can see where this is going. I'll save you the words!"

Youngie broke in. "Steve. We want to make it very clear that we want you to stay in the organization."

Stay in the organization? Where the hell else could he go?

Dunleavy left them in the Royalton lobby. They had a meeting to preside over and a show to take over. He walked down 45th Street and loosened his tie as he headed toward his apartment.

On the corner of 35th and Second, he stopped in at his local diner, the Gemini. He took a seat at the counter and ordered what he ordered every time he stopped into a diner for breakfast: bacon and eggs—sunnyside up, of course—with white toast, black coffee with sugar—and no potatoes.

He felt, strangely, at ease as he dug into the food, and wasn't annoyed at all when he was recognized by people stopping in to pick up coffee or waiting at the counter to pay their checks.

"Steve Dunleavy! Oh, man, can I have an autograph, guy?"

"Steve! Sorry to bother you, but I love your show!"

"Whatcha doing tonight? Something on that fuckin O.J., I hope."

"Go get em, Steve!"

"Sorry 'bout the napkin, it's all I got."

"Steve Dunleavy, I can't believe I'm meeting Steve Dunleavy."

Dunleavy signed the autographs. He looked at the family pictures of strangers. He insisted he pay for his breakfast.

Back at the apartment, Dunleavy popped off the cufflinks and left them on the dresser. He kicked off the casual tassels, hung up the Armani suit and light blue shirt and put on jeans and sneakers.

The meeting at *A Current Affair* would be starting any minute now. It was the first day of June. He didn't even think of having a drink. "I drink for fun," he'd tell anyone who asked, "not to ease pain or mask emotions."

Dunleavy went for a walk along the East River. There was nothing like New York. God, he loved this town.

Dunleavy got a call from one of his producers on Friday.

"Are you all right?"

"Of course I'm all right," Dunleavy said with a laugh.

"Those motherfucking bastards," she said before breaking into tears.

She wanted to meet Dunleavy for a drink. He didn't want to go to Tommy McGrath's; it would be a bit too humiliating. He suggested someplace quiet, away from the crowd. Here's a laugh. He suggested O'Flanagan's over on First, the place he was going to meet Youngie for a drink the night before the big ten a.m. meeting.

The drink that had to be cancelled when work got in the way.

Word of his demise hadn't yet reached the papers, so it was a happy greeting he got from the bartender as he started on his first vodka tonic.

He watched as the door opened and his producer entered the bar. Another producer followed her in, and then another. Dunleavy's eyes, as he'd put it, were as wide as dollar bills. They'd all come, the entire office it seemed, crowded around him at the bar and trying to grab a piece of him.

Even Youngie was there, and he had tears in his eyes like all the rest. Dunleavy held his emotions in check until he caught another face beaming wistfully from the crowd. Tommy McGrath himself had come to say goodbye.

After a weekend at home on the Island with his wife Gloria screening as many phone calls as possible, Dunleavy was back to business on Monday, back in that blue Armani suit walking to the News Corp building at 1211 Sixth Avenue in midtown.

The secretary didn't keep him waiting long at all. She ushered him right into the Boss's office, where Rupert Murdoch was seated behind his big desk.

"Steve!" Murdoch rose and greeted his hard-working alter ego with great affection. He was very friendly, even fatherly.

"So," Murdoch said. The two Australians looked each other in the eye. There wasn't much that had to be said. They both knew what had happened, and why. "So, what do you wanna do?"

Dunleavy was more relaxed than he'd ever felt in the presence of the great man. "Well, I guess I've been effectively fired from television—"

Murdoch nodded. "Ummmm. Well, what do you wanna do? Do you want to go to the *Post*? You wanna write? What do you want to do?"

"I reckon I'll go to the *Post*."

CHAPTER THIRTY-FIVE:
THE LAST LAUGH

*Hard Copy executive producer Linda Bell Blue will replace
Jim Van Messel as executive producer of top-rated syndication
magazine* Entertainment Tonight *on July 5.*
—*Hollywood Reporter*, June 12, 1995

Tomlin and Young announced their four million dollar plans for *A Current Affair* the day after Linda Bell got the second wish from her TV genie. *A Current Affair*, the rebel, devil-may-care maverick of television that inspired so many imitators, would now officially seek to become an imitator of *Inside Edition*.

The new leaders cast themselves as the originators of *A Current Affair*, come back to set things right with a list of ironclad rules to "restore credibility": there'd be no more paying for stories—unless necessary, and in that case the terms of the deal would be disclosed on the air; no more "ambush" interviews—unless the subject had turned down three official requests for conventional interviews; and no more re-enactments.

There would be a new emphasis on investigative reporting, with a twenty-person investigative unit, gutsy show business pieces, and a new Washington bureau to watch out for governmental misdeeds.

There would be new graphics, a new set—even new music. The old "ka-chung" would remain, if only for old times' sake.

The question was why they'd bother. The answer it seemed, was time slots. *Variety* reported that Fox TV boss Greg Meidel "said Twentieth decided 'it would be a much better investment for us to work on the existing show rather than shelling out thirty million dollars or so to come up with an idea for a new show' that would have to build an audience from scratch in an increasingly crowded syndication marketplace."

Most important, *A Current Affair* needed a new anchorman to represent all the upstanding journalistic values this clean team held in high regard. Behind the scenes, Tomlin and Young worked frantically to get Geraldo Rivera.

8MM
A new concept in reality television

Did you hear the one about the American, the Aussie and the Brit who took a car ride across America in search of the World's Second Largest Ball of Twine?

It's no joke. What they found when they got there, and the people they met along the way, have inspired a new reality television program that delivers the antidote to trashy tabloid and talk television.

Welcome to *EIGHT MILLIMETER 'MERICA—8MM* to you. Think Charles Kuralt meeting Dennis Miller— *48 Hours* crossed with *National Lampoon's Vacation.* Three top producers venture into the American heartland, armed only with a map, Hi-8 cameras and their own unique perspectives. Their mission: find that elusive species...the forgotten

The casino was an impressive sight from the river or the road; two giant candy-colored Stratocaster guitars crossed like swords against a kind of supersize Hard Rock Cafe. Inside, it was a no-frills barn, loud and sloshing with jumbo plastic cups of keg beer, and crowded with field and factory workers and other working Joes with their wives who'd stopped on the way to Memphis or drove in from towns like Clarksdale, Hushpuckena, Indianola, and Yazoo City. The Lady Luck Rhythm & Blues Casino on the banks of the Mississippi River outside the town of Lula was our last stop before crossing the big muddy into Arkansas.

Wayne and Alison and I were taping our pilot for *8MM*, the show that grew from Wayne's Merle Haggard idea. The three of us were using our own money, Hi-8 cameras, and wits every time we pulled off the road; Wayne and I cowering behind Alison as she greeted people with a big smile and a right royal British accent.

We made the trip in a Jeep Cherokee, followed by two more SUVs packed with country rock musicians who composed a soundtrack along the way from the Hank Williams, Jr. Museum on Nashville's Music Row, down Route 412 to the Perry County Jail, through a town full of black people called Whiteville, to Memphis and Graceland, before hooking south down Dylan's Highway 61. From here it would be on to Little Rock, the Rose Law Firm and the McDonald's restaurant where Gov. Bill Clinton once stopped on his morning jogs to grab a bite and use the payphone to call his girlfriends.

This was the first time I'd seen Wayne since he ran away from *Premier Story*. He was surviving on freelance work from Young and Tomlin at *A Current Affair*. Here at the roulette table in the big casino on the Mississippi, I tried to convince him it was time we took over television again.

"Naw, mate," he said. "All's I need is enough to make the mortgage each month. Bob and John, they treat me okay."

"Of course they do! You're worth so much more. You're taking orders from idiots who inherited what you invented."

"Mate, I'm not interested in running it any more. I'm happy to be working. People hear of me, they think I'm some sleazy alcoholic nutcase, cause of what I did in the past. Well, all I can do is show 'em what I do now."

"Mate, everybody's made money off this genre except you, me, Raf, Peter, and Dunleavy! McGowan made millions. The cameramen got rich investing in Starbucks. Young and Tomlin have their own industry. And us, we're hardly even in television! We gotta cash in."

Wayne smiled and shook his head. "I look at it this way," he said. "These young guys made the money off my back and I'm at peace with that. I used to wanna be Keith Richards. I don't wanna be Keith Richards anymore. I wanna be John Lee Hooker. Keith Richards has the money. John Lee Hooker doesn't have anything. But he has the respect. People sit at his feet for wisdom, mate."

"I used to be Keith Richards. Now I'm John Lee Hooker." Wayne lit a cigarette and smiled beatifically.

I followed his gaze to the wheel, spinning one way while a little white ball raced in the opposite direction. Where it stopped nobody knew. I kept my chips at a corner of the table: five on 31, three on 34, two on 35. The wheel slowed. If the ball dropped and one of my numbers hit, I moved the chips around. By the time we left, I was up $500. This was easy; it sure was a lot easier than trying to sell television shows.

A twenty-ton garbage truck rolls through a neat suburban neighborhood, racing by a man in his bathrobe holding two Hefty bags. The truck barrels on, past a garbage dump and over a cliff.

An announcer intones with great weight: "We took out the trash."

The TV commercial and print ad for *The New A Current Affair* represented only one volley in Young and Tomlin's attempt to lift the show out of the ratings doldrums and into a newsy, respectable direction. The offices in New York were converted into a clean, streamlined network-style newsroom. Local and network news producers were brought on to staff the investigative units and Washington bureau. The Elvis shrine was removed from the wall.

There was nary an ounce of flash nor flair to be seen. Negotiations to hire Geraldo Rivera as host had broken off around the time he leaked to the media he was holding out for a Fox late-night show in addition to the *A Current Affair* job. Fox changed horses quickly, announcing the hiring of a man named Jon Scott.

Scott was one of the original reporters on NBC *Nightline*. He was thick-browed, colorless and humorless; in a way, the "anti-Maury." Yet on September eleventh, he would be the anchor of *The* New *A Current Affair*.

In August, *GQ* magazine was on the stands with an issue saluting "The Cheesing of America" and placing special blame on Rupert Murdoch's Australian tabloid scoundrels for cheapening American culture beyond redemption. The article gave special credit to Steve Dunleavy and Peter Brennan and added, "there are even honorary Aussies, such as Rafael Abramovitz, an attorney-turned-reporter who has worked for Brennan at *A Current Affair* and *Hard Copy*, and Burt Kearns, Brennan's trusted lieutenant, who has been known to address colleagues unironically as 'mate.'"

While basking in the honor that was meant to be an insult, I returned to Great Britain with Alison to gather a crop of stories for *The Extraordinary*, Brennan and Sutton's syndicated paranormal show. We'd taken jobs as producers; Brennan said it was an easy way to make "rent money" until we got another show off the ground, though as time passed, he seemed less interested in doing it again.

Peter Brennan was working double duty, producing the pilot of a new courtroom show conceived by Doug Llewelyn, the *People's Court* reporter who was left in the cold when Judge Wapner hung up his robe. This one starred a New York judge named Judy Scheindlin.

Brennan got the gig in a roundabout way. Audrey Lavin had resurfaced as a divorcee, and recommended him to her new boyfriend, a TV executive whose company was underwriting the show. Larry Lyttle's company was backed by Aaron Spelling's syndication arm, Worldvision. The woman he answered to was Karen Miller, the one who added "choice" to *Detour*.

It was a small world, after all.

We were in a bookstore off the Edinburgh's Royal Mile, buying up research material after shooting a segment on a pub haunted by the ghost of the real-life Dr. Jeckyl and before heading to the annual arts festival to interview a modern dancer who had no legs.

I left Alison in the local history section and wandered over to the show business books, scanning the covers and spines in hope of finding another tome on the life and work of Benny Hill.

My eyes stopped at a paperback featuring a photo of a man in a tuxedo.

The Full Monty was the title. It was the autobiography of Alison's second husband, the comedian Jim Davidson.

I went straight for the index, and finding there wasn't one, flipped through the text and the guy's life until it came to the part about Alison. I knew some of what went on during their short and unhappy marriage but never pressed Alison for the details. Now curiosity had the better of me.

Davidson started at the beginning. By his account, they hadn't met in a comedy club after all. Alison was anchoring the news at the HTV station in Bristol; she interviewed Davidson when he appeared at the Bristol Hippodrome, in a Christmas "pantomime" show of *Cinderella*.

He decided she was his Cinderella. He wrote her a note, asking for a date. She wrote back that her "Prince Charming" boyfriend wouldn't understand.

He got the date. They were married. Then came the horrors that made their way into the tabloids, like the times he blackened her eye or bruised her body. In his book, the comedian played the abashed little boy, saying that Alison was too obsessed with her career and keeping up appearances. He became depressed and fat in their Bristol estate, he wrote, and they would fight.

Davidson explained away each assault on his lovely princess bride as accidental bumps or defensive moves. He portrayed himself as the innocent bystander when recalling the day Alison's brother responded to his abuse by punching him in the nose.

The comedian even went after Alison's mother. Everybody knows you don't go after a person's mother.

As I stared at the page, I realized my hands were shaking and my mouth was dry. Davidson didn't tell the story of kicking Alison down the stairs the day they returned from their honeymoon or her shame when she appeared on the air with pancake makeup covering the bruises. This was no *mea culpa*; he was blaming the victim. It was the most cowardly treatise since O.J. Simpson's book.

I was going to kill him.

I didn't say anything as we walked across the river bridge to meet up with the crew at the Deacon Brodie pub. At Heathrow for the flight home, I stopped in at a newsstand, where copies of the book were displayed across an entire wall. I thought of buying up every one to throw in the trash, but figured the big sales would only make them stock more.

Jim Davidson, with his ugly, racist jokes, smarmy tuxedo, and music hall quiff; he beat her in person, he beat her in hardcover, and he beat her in paperback. He was going to get his.

"What I've spilled in vodka, I could have gotten China drunk. What I've puked, I could fertilize the Sahara!" Dunleavy held his glass high and followed up with a frightening graveyard cough. He had a terrible cold and the air conditioning here in the back room of Denny's was turned up way too high. "Ah, I'm crook, I'm ratshit, mate. My eyes have bags for a trip to Moscow."

"Why don't you have a sleep?"

"Nah, nah. We'll have that later. For now, there's work to do."

It was the first week of September 1995 and how far we'd fallen. A few years ago, it was the Columbia Bar & Grill a short walk west on the corner of Gower; a few months ago, the hospitable Dunes. Now we were in the chilly backroom bar of a Denny's fast food diner across Sunset from the Hollywood Center Studios where Brennan had set up shop for *The Extraordinary*.

It was another bar few knew existed, with a clientele of waylaid tourists in liederhosen or Bermuda shorts, speaking other languages and wondering where all the stars were. I was never entirely at ease drinking there—always expecting the masked gunmen with the sawed-off shotguns, ordering everyone to lie face-down on the floor—but at least the Bud Lights came in wide-mouth bottles and were the coldest in town.

Dunleavy blew his nose again. He did his best to keep up a brave face since he was booted so unceremoniously from *A Current Affair*, but the strain was showing.

On Monday, *The New A Current Affair* would debut with its new host and new direction. Every article written about the show in the past few months pointed to Dunleavy as the symbol of its sleazy and disgusting past: paying Joey Buttafuoco, fighting with Michele Cassone, confronting David Rothenberg's father. Ever the company man, Dunleavy took the abuse and demotion without question. He slid into a job as columnist for the *Post* and drank away his rage when the kids there didn't treat him with the respect due the man who led the paper in its gory glory days. Dunleavy even shared drinks with Bob Young.

"Sorry, mate, you know I couldn't make any of these changes if you were around," his mate Youngie told him. "You'd fight me tooth and nail, and you'd stick up for all the weak ones we'd have to get rid of. It was the only way I could do it."

"Ah, it's only business, mate," Dunleavy said with resignation. He was on the giving end so often he knew he had to be gracious in receipt. Now he was in Los Angeles awaiting the end of the O.J. Simpson trial, living frugally at the Sunset Hyatt, where he was careful to not spend too much of his boss's money on expenses.

Dunleavy checked into the Hyatt for luck ever since he'd gotten his first L.A. scoop while staying there in 1967. Little Richard lived at the hotel. To see the two of them, trading autographs, pompadours touching at the sports bar downstairs, was nothing short of historic.

I was living in comparative splendor at the Bel Age. Alison and I were in the midst of a "row," as they say in England; I'd moved out for a few days until things cooled down.

Our relationship had certainly been through its share of crises, the two of us having spent the past nine months in a constant state of career flux, not working, working together, being together twenty-four hours a day, worrying about money for the first time in years, and living the strain of not knowing what was happening next. So here we were, Dunleavy and I, killing time until Brennan made it over from *The Extraordinary* office, and here I was, holding the idea that would bring both him and Alison the glory they deserved.

"I saw it in my head when you and Alison were dancing in the living room. The new show."

"Oh, mate. We were pissed," Dunleavy said.

"Yeah, but that was it. You're a team. You're Nick, she's Nora. No— you're Simon Templar, the Saint."

"Ah, yes, St. Steve, bless you, my son." Dunleavy made the sign of the cross over my head.

"No, not Simon Templar, who'm I thinking of? The guy from *The Avengers*, what's his name? John Steed. You're John Steed. And Ally is Emma Peel."

"How could she throw me out of my own fucking house? I've lived on every hotel on the fucking Strip this summer and I never even did anything wrong!"

"Ah, it's women, mate." It was late into the night and we were drinking in my room at the Bel Age. Dunleavy nursed a Heineken. "And remember, she's a good one."

"Fuck it." I threw back another shot from the tiny tequila bottle I'd pulled from the minibar. "You know, I put a fucking hit on her ex-husband and this is the thanks I get? I oughta cancel it, goddamn it."

"You did what? You're crazy."

"That fucking baggy pants comic who beat her, mate, I hired some guys to break his fuckin knees."

The tabloid life had come full circle. After weeks mulling over how to punish Jim Davidson for abusing Alison, I'd decided an old-fashioned Irish kneecapping, by bullet or sledgehammer, seemed most appropriate. Me, the onetime tabloid prince, who'd produced so many stories about contract hits, who'd been solicited along with Rafael because of our alleged expertise, was now on the same dead end street.

"Mate, you're talking crazy," Dunleavy said. "Don't even talk like that."

"You and Brennan did it." I was an honorary Australian. I was too far away to pop the guy in the kisser on my own, so the next best thing was what they'd do. "You tried to take out the Pig!"

"That's bullshit, it's just a fucking story."

It may have been legend, but it was the most famous Dunleavy and Brennan legend of all: that in the early years of *A Current Affair*, the two of them decided in a late night drinking bout that Ian Rae had brought them such misery that he deserved to die. The two of them were pissed as a couple of wine cellar rats, full as a state school, but Dunleavy managed to find the bar phone and dial up an old buddy, a union man known to take care of such requests.

He slurred his instructions, went back to the vodka and didn't realize what he'd done until a few hours later, when he awoke, draped across a desk in the *A Current Affair* newsroom, to see Brennan passed out in the chair, head back and snoring.

"Pete, Pete, mate, wake up!"

Brennan responded with mumbles.

"The Pig! The Pig!"

"Fuck the Pig. The Pig must die," Brennan mumbled.

"Oh no, tell me I didn't, mate. Did I call in a hit on Ian Rae?"

"Fuck the Pig." Brennan resumed his snoring.

Dunleavy grabbed the nearest phone and dialed in haste. He cleared his throat when a woman answered. "Good morning, I'm so sorry to wake you, but this is a bit of an emergency. Would Tom be home?" Dunleavy tried to sound as awake and matter-of-fact as possible at six a.m. "He what?" Dunleavy felt his stomach drop. Tommy had left for work already. He'd left for work. He was off to execute the Pig.

Dunleavy began to cry.

Two hours later, the pair were in Brennan's office, working on coffee and alibis. "All right, mate," Brennan said, "if we did, it's too late. There's nothing we can do. It was a tragic mistake."

"Mistake? Mistake? I called in a hit on Ian Rae! It's not free, you know. What was I thinking? What were we drinking—"

"Good mornin, mates!" The words preceded the arrival of stumpy Ian Rae, scratching his ass and greeting the men with whom he shared matehood.

Brennan looked like he'd seen a ghost. He fumbled his coffee and it splashed across the morning papers.

"Ian!" Dunleavy's face brightened. It was a miracle. He jumped up, embraced the vice president of news, and ushered him in as if to shield him from any gunman's sight. "Ian! It's so good to see you!" Dunleavy kissed him as Brennan glanced nervously at the rooftops across 67th Street and lowered the window shades.

Ian Rae fought to break free of Dunleavy's slobbering kisses. "Get off me, ya facking crazy bloody poofter!"

Ironically, it was Peter Brennan who'd disabused me of the knee-capping earlier in the week.

"Forget about it," he counseled. "Let it be."

"I can't, mate. He lied. He lied about Ally in the papers, he attacked her in his book. He even said things about her mother!"

"It's different over there. Why do you think Ally's lawyers told her not to bother suing? The people who matter don't read that crap, and the ones who do, don't believe it. They say all kinds of things in the tabloids. Nobody takes them seriously. They use it to wrap the fish and chips. And besides, you break his knees, everyone will feel sorry for him."

"He's got to pay—"

"Listen to me. I've found that these things have a way of working themselves out. People like that meet their own fates."

I thought of telling Dunleavy the truth as I pulled the covers over my head and waited for him to leave the hotel room. He'd passed out only a few hours earlier, sitting up at the bar in my Bel Age mini-suite, denying the Ian Rae incident and mumbling incoherently in a gutteral drawl until he was a burble of snores. Now, somehow, in superhuman fashion, he was up, eating breakfast, blowing his nose, drinking the last Molson from the minibar and on the phone to the *New York Post* city desk looking for another story.

"Get up. Get up!" he demanded. "If you don't get up, I'll bugger you!" Dunleavy yanked a big stiff handkerchief from his pocket and blew his nose lustily. He was sick as a dog.

"Go away," I managed to moan.

"This will not do!" Dunleavy went for the bottom of the bed and pulled up the covers, exposing my bare feet. "This is how the Philippino police get answers out of suspects. The old bottle torture." With that, he began whacking the soles of my feet with the Molson bottle. The pain sent me into a jig on top of the mattress. I was up.

"Goddamn it."

"C'mon. Let's go into the office."

"Let me eat first." I called room service and looked out over L.A. I could see my old apartment building down the road, and to the west, the hotel where Alison stayed when she first came to L.A. I just wanted to go home.

"This flu is turning into pneumonia," Dunleavy said.

"You got anything to take for it?"

"I have these prescription pills, but I'm loathe to take them."

Dunleavy was afraid to put medicine into his body. Something so healthy could kill him.

"Just take one, at least. You don't wanna be in the hospital when the verdict comes."

"You're right." Dunleavy pulled the container from his pocket and popped a colorful capsule. Within a minute, he bolted for the bathroom.

I sat by the window eating Dunleavy's leftover toast, listening to him vomit violently. What sounded like gallons of liquid splashed into the commode and across the bathroom walls. The man who never ate, whose entire intake seemed to be poisonous alcoholic liquid, was expelling every last drop in full-throttle spews; all of it triggered by a tiny health-restoring pill.

The groaning and gushing continued. I realized that Dunleavy was going to die in my hotel room off the Sunset Strip not a hundred yards from where young River Phoenix breathed his last. He would die in the bathroom like Elvis. There would be police and camera crews and the silver pompadour would be poking out from under the coroner's sheet, and I'd be trapped as part of the Dunleavy myth, a short listing in some future edition of *Hollywood Babylon*.

Dunleavy emerged from the bathroom drenched in sweat, looking like a vampire who'd glimpsed the dawning sun; which, I guess, he was. "It was that damn pill," he complained.

I parked the Porsche in the Hollywood Center Studios visitors lot, over the road from the Denny's where the troubles began twenty-four hours earlier. A long queue of tourists stretched along the edge of the parking lot, all waiting to be the studio audience for that day's taping of *America's Funniest Home Videos*. There was an audible buzz as they watched Dunleavy unfold himself from the passenger seat, smooth down the wrinkles of his charcoal gray pinstripe Hong Kong suit, and comb back his silver hair.

"Look, it's that guy from *A Current Affair*," one of the tourists said as the line began to move.

"It's Steve Dunleavy!"

Dunleavy preened in the attention. He walked proudly across the parking lot, with all eyes on him. Then, suddenly, he gulped and leaned forward, and as the fans watched in horror, projectile-vomited another gusher of yellow water onto the hot blacktop.

The jurors in the O.J. Simpson case began deliberations on Monday, October second. About four hours later, they sent word to Judge Lance Ito that they'd reached a verdict.

That evening, we sat at the bar at the Argyle amid the excitement and tumult accompanying the impending announcment. Alison and I had been with the case from the beginning. Now we were reduced to sitting with Brennan watching everyone else confer with authority.

"It's guilty, mate, it's guilty," said Dunleavy. "When the jury walked into the courtroom, no one looked at Simpson."

"They're saving it for a surprise."

David Miller was in town representing *The New A Current Affair*. He agreed with Dunleavy. "It's definitely going to be guilty. They asked for a re-read of Alan Park's timeline testimony. That means they think he had enough time for the killings."

"Time line, time line." Dunleavy nodded.

"You guys are way off," I said. "They'd never convict O.J. Simpson this quick."

"I'm afraid so, mate."

I may not have been working for a tabloid show, but I never stopped following the trial. When the jury came back so soon, I was certain it would be "not guilty." Johnny Cochran was masterful in his summation; the pedestrian Marcia Clark and Christopher Darden had blown an open and shut case.

"Guys, have you been watching the trial? There's no way they can convict him based on what went down."

"Oh, Burt's a contrarian," Miller sniffed.

What did I know? I was killing time on *The Extraordinary* and cutting pilot tapes whenever I could get some free editing time. He was the big reporter for *The New A Current Affair*, a faux news magazine with a batallion of faceless reporters.

The verdict was announced at ten the next morning.

Three days later, we were standing in a massive empty soundstage next to the one where we once taped *Premier Story* at the main Hollywood Center Studios. Linn Taylor, *The Extraordinary's* office manager, used her Australian charm to pull a few strings and got me three free hours. A few more tugs and she'd gotten me a spotlight on a pole and a smoke machine.

Now we had to wait for the stars. Alison and Steve were in a booth at the Hollywood Canteen on the next block, having a necessary wine or two before shooting the framework for the pilot I was creating for them.

They returned a little more relaxed. Alison wore a spangly short cocktail dress that made her look like a million bucks though it cost her only $29.95 at Ross. Dunleavy was suave in a rented tux.

We killed the lights. We hit the smoke machine. The empty soundstage was pitch black. We trained the spotlight on the couple and somebody hit the CD player. The horns began to pump. Frank Sinatra began to sing: *"Dancing in the dark, til the tune ends, we're dancing in the dark and it soon ends..."* Steve and Alison began to dance, sweeping around the same soundstage in which Astaire and Rogers once danced, looking as otherworldly and magical in the portable monitor as I'd envisioned all those months before in our living room. This would symbolize their partnership in this new tabloid magazine show I had in mind.

This was what television was all about.

CHAPTER THIRTY-SIX: PITCHING & BITCHING

Barry the agent didn't know what to make of *Dancing in the Dark*. "I think it could use someone like Jimmy Breslin."

"*Jimmy Breslin*? I know he's your client, Barry, but what's he gonna do? Cut in on them dancing?"

"Ah...I think it needs the American element. You've got two foreigners there. It won't fly. But Breslin—"

"But Breslin is like pushing seventy."

"I don't know. I just don't think there's enough of a show there."

I felt I owed Barry. When I was offered the executive producer role at *A Current Affair* back in 1993, he never pressed me to take the job and he didn't charge me a commission. "It's more important to be happy," he said. "Fuck the money. Life is too short."

Well, life was getting even shorter now, and we couldn't wait around any longer. Peter Brennan was tied up producing yet another TV pilot, a cutesy animal show called *Amazing Tails*. His boss was Audrey Lavin; she'd finally found her nice niche. Peter didn't have much choice; it was payback for her getting him the *People's Court* show. He didn't tell me he took the job, probably because I was trying to pitch *Wild Life*, that animal-themed show of my own.

I realized I had to watch out for myself. Barry hadn't set up a single meeting for me or Alison, on any of our projects. Alison's recent high-profile appearance, hosting an ABC-TV special, was arranged through her hairstylist.

So that's why we had Barry up at the house, to sit him by the pool and lay out everything in no uncertain terms.

Barry lit a Monte Cristo cigar and nodded. It seemed he finally was getting it. "You know what you two should do?" Barry was a dead ringer for the comedian Gilbert Gottfried. "A movie. Not even anything big. You do a little movie that will play a long time in one theatre. Like that *Rocky Horror Picture Show*."

"A movie."

"You do a movie the gays will love. That's a big enough audience right there. It'll play for years in that theatre on Santa Monica Boulevard. It'll play in the Village. That's the key."

"Let me make sure I have this right," I said. "You're telling us we should make a gay movie."

"Right. Or write a book. A book you could turn into a movie. That way you get it from both sides."

"You're telling me I should write a book I can turn into a movie that can play on Santa Monica Boulevard. For gays."

Barry puffed his cigar and nodded. Problem solved.

I looked at Alison. I looked at the house and the pool and the prospect of being evicted for non-payment of rent.

"Barry." I tried to be calm. "We're television producers. We have shows we need to push. Alison is a very talented correspondent and anchorwoman. We have to work in television."

This was the price of independence. Every day, we'd stop at a bar on Sunset to meet with Peter Brennan to throw around ideas or simply get an idea of what was in the air. After a while, we weren't even making plans; we were simply drinking. It was one thing to repair to the pub after working our asses off all day and making great television by the seats of our pants; quite another to putter around *The Extraordinary* office for a few hours, then wander over to fucking Denny's at one in the afternoon. We were on the outside looking in and we drank like we were kings of all we could see.

I thought of that Merle Haggard song Wayne had played for me, about the young man who lived it up on the brink of success, always certain his friends would pull him back if he fell too far.

"Now I'm paying for the days of wine and roses," Hag sang, "a victim of the drunken life I chose. Now all my social friends look down their noses, cause I kept the wine and threw away the rose."

I looked at Alison being as polite as possible. I looked at Brennan, all red in the face and vaguely depressed, and I wished Rafael was still around to prod him, to say, "This is very bad, we are wasting time and money, you guys gotta get on the ball," to act as some sort of moral compass and get us back on track.

Raf was long gone. He was somewhere in New York City, where he'd haunt the *A Current Affair* pubs, looking for work, palling up to reporters and producers he'd resented in the past. When Raf wanted to write a column for the *Post*, Dunleavy set him up to meet with editor Ken Chandler, but Raf got insulted by some imagined slight and the deal went up in smoke before any spark was even lit.

Who knew what Raf was doing now? He never called.

I put down my wide-mouth Bud Light and piped up from out of nowhere. "You know what the problem is? We kept the wine and we threw away the rose."

Everyone ignored me.

Alison and I found a different way on our own. Despite, and more likely because of, the rocky times we'd survived, we realized we were in love. We decided we were going to stay together and we were going to push our projects, Barry or Brennan or not.

We decided we would have a baby.

On the evening of December sixth, Alison handed me a present. I sat at the dining room table and studied the small box, tied off with a ribbon and a sticker showing it was from the Fred Segal store on Melrose. I figured it was a wallet or something similar. I opened it with great drama.

Inside was a pair of baby booties.

On the other side of the table, Alison was holding her breath.

I hugged her. "It's great."

"Are you happy?" she asked.

"Of course I am. We planned this, didn't we?"

Alison brought out a pregnancy picture book showing that at this stage, our child was like a tadpole.

"It's funny," she said. "The doctor asked if I planned the pregnancy."

We both knew the next question had she said no.

A few days later, Barry the agent came through. He said he showed the *Wild Life* pilot to his friend Henry, who loved it and had the connections to pitch it. Henry Schleiff had been chairman and CEO of Viacom for six years until he lost out in a power struggle with his friend Frank Biondi. Since then, he'd been set up with a comfy production deal, pushing through specials like the sexual marionette show, *Twisted Puppet Theatre.*

Brennan and I met Henry at the Four Seasons Hotel on the edge of Beverly Hills. He was a living Dave Berg cartoon, a gangling forty-eight, with cropped silver hair, wire-rims, and a colorful sweater. He veritably hopped in his seat with enthusiasm, talking on his cell phone and taking notes as we prepared the pitch over lunch.

"'*Baywatch* with animals.' That's great," Henry said. "And what I like about this is that the volunteers, the people who work for this guy DeRose, they're as lost as the animals."

The Four Seasons restaurant was filled with industry people. Brennan was the only one in jeans, a workshirt, and windbreaker. He said he'd worn

438

suits to too many unsuccessful pitch meetings and refused to get dressed up for any more.

Copies of the *Hollywood Reporter* were scattered on tables and about the floor. Henry picked one up and laughed at the cover photos of sixteen women included in the issue's list of the most powerful women in Hollywood. "This is one cover where you can't say, 'Had her, did her, fucked her,'" he said.

"Yeah," Brennan said, as we all laughed with him. "But you could say, 'She fucked me. She fucked me, she...'"

Lucie Salhany's picture was on the cover, the number four most powerful woman in Hollywood. The woman who'd taken control of *A Current Affair* during the Terenzio era was now back at Paramount, starting up their mini TV network, UPN.

We were headed to her office to pitch *Wild Life*.

"I don't like it. This is not *Baywatch*," Lucie said. Her office was on a stretch of Wilshire Boulevard in Brentwood, not far from the Bundy Drive murder scene. There was a poster for a Rita Hayworth movie called *Femme Fatale* behind her desk and thirty-five framed photos of her son, husband, and self on the TV cabinet. "If I put this against *Friends* or *Party of Five*, I'd be killed."

Lucie Salhany's fledgling weblet was full of failures except for the *Star Trek* franchise; now she was trying to clone *The X-Files* with a show called *Nowhere Man*. In the wings, she said, was *Phone Calls from the Dead*.

Henry countered with an idea for *Paladin Meets Ghostbusters*.

We found it was one thing to come up with an idea for a hit show, quite another to get those in power to understand what we were talking about.

The woman in charge of late-night alternative programming at Fox didn't understand. She was in her thirties and exhausted. Days earlier, she'd given birth to her second child in fifteen months.

"This is the first pitch I've ever gotten with the tagline, 'Sex and dogs and rock 'n' roll,'" said the middle-aged woman calling the shots at the USA Network. She didn't get it either, though her young assistant was excited that one of the *Wild Life* volunteers was the drummer for the heavy metal band Poison.

It was the same wherever we went. Back at UPN, we pitched an idea that was red hot and out of the headlines: putting Princess Diana on trial for treason. Salhany's number two man Mike Sullivan expressed great interest, saying it looked like a solid "go" and a good way for him to get a free trip to London. I could tell by the look in his eyes it wasn't going to happen. He was afraid, but couldn't admit the idea was just too far out there for him.

Still, we pitched on.

Faye Resnick was flirting with the waiters. She was dark-haired, dark-skinned, and striking among the beautiful crowd at Drai's restaurant on La Cienega. She supposedly was scared for her life after writing the best-selling tell-all about her friend Nicole Brown Simpson, yet here she was, the life of the party.

We watched her slip into the ladies room as we continued drinking in the lounge of low couches and chairs at the front of the restaurant. Drinking at Drai's was like being at an Irish wake without a body.

"So I hear you have a problem with me working for Audrey's pilot," Brennan said. We were both pretty pissed, having just finished dinner with Neal and Tolley Travis, who were in from New York. They looked great. Brennan looked very tired.

"I don't have a problem with you. I have a problem with her. She betrayed us at *Hard Copy*. She wasn't there when we needed her most—"

"Ah, I've known Audrey for years. It's just rent money."

Our conversation escalated. Alison asked us to keep our voices down. We all stopped talking when Faye Resnick emerged from the toilet. She was wearing a different outfit. Maybe she believed she was being followed, after all.

There was a tension between Peter Brennan and me that wasn't there a year ago, and it was only heightened by Henry Schleiff's enthusiasm for my projects. I wasn't a lieutenant any more. Peter didn't want or need a partner. We didn't agree on how things should be done. Or maybe we just weren't drinking together enough.

It wasn't Peter's fault. He was doing things the way he—the way we—had done for years. It was me who couldn't afford to wait any longer; I had responsibilities now, a reason to stand on my own—

That baby inside Ally's belly confirmed the choice I'd made. I'd chosen the woman. John Lennon's choice led to the final step that broke up the Beatles. I was breaking up the Wild Bunch.

Dean Martin died on Christmas morning. We'd taken Alison to his favorite restaurant the night she arrived in America. Before his health got too bad, he'd hold court on Monday nights at the Hamburger Hamlet down the hill from our house. I'd seen Dino sing at Bally's in Las Vegas a couple of years ago, and a couple of Christmases ago was the last time I'd seen Nick Loiacono. As I wrote in the eulogy read at his memorial, "It was Christmas night, 1993. Nicky got off work and we wound up at the old Folk City bar in the Village. We drank tequila by the window. Every shot the bartender poured was a triple. And then a new bartender took over. She only poured regular-sized shots. When Nicky told her we preferred the first bartender, she explained he wasn't a bartender at all—but a customer filling in while she was in the ladies room. Nicky convinced her to let the customer be our personal bartender the rest of the night. When it got too late, Nicky walked off into the subway on Sixth Avenue and that was it...

Alison and I drove to Las Vegas on December twenty-ninth, and rolled into the driveway of the Sands Hotel just before 7 p.m., the exact time the Las Vegas Strip was remembering an old star.

Dean Martin 1917-1995.
We dim our lights in tribute

read the Sands' electronic marquee, the new sign of Vegas. Local TV camera crews were set up on the grass beneath the old marquee, the one with the black plastic lettering advertising Bob Newhart and Mary Wilson of the Supremes like it was 1964 all over again. It looked like the marquee Dean and the Rat Pack posed under in that famous photo, all these old swingers in their forties who should have known better, squinting in the five o'clock sun.

They dimmed the lights on the Strip when Sammy died in 1990. It didn't work out so smoothly in the new Vegas. The little old marquee in front of the Sands went dark, but all around, lights flashed and music played and you really had to concentrate to notice anything different. The TV crews shot their assignments obediently, pretending the Strip was going dark while a pirate ship battle raged on with smoke pots, flashes, cannons, and tourist roars in the lagoon at the Treasure Island casino across the boulevard. They'd run the footage silent and no one would be the wiser.

By the time we left Las Vegas, Alison and I agreed we'd be getting married. "I just thought you might have a problem with being married, cause you've been married three times," I mentioned while strolling through the Forum shopping mall at Caesars Palace. "Maybe you don't like being married."

"I don't have a problem being married," she said, taking my hand. "I just have a problem with some of the assholes I married."

I was also carrying fifteen hundred dollars in winnings and the nagging suspicion that my roulette system worked—as if I'd discovered the scam to beat three-card monte or something. It seemed so easy: start with a hundred in dollar chips. Find a corner. Put seven chips on one number, three on the number next to it, three on the number above. Stick to it until one hits, and invariably, it would, often in a big payoff, 280 dollars or so. Pocket the two hundred—the initial stake, doubled—move off the number that hit and start playing the one next to it; keep playing until the chip pile grows or everything but the profit is gone.

We arrived home on New Year's Eve. There was a message from Steve Dunleavy on the answering machine. For the past six weeks, he'd been in Bosnia, filing a report a day for the *New York Post*.

He'd arrived in Tuzla in the freezing cold waiting for the C-130s to arrive with the first contingent of U.S. Army peace enforcement troops, and had traveled all over the scarred country with a Moslem driver, interpreter, and fixer named Aleya Dedijic.

For some reason, this particular experience had a profound effect on the old journo. After years of infighting in tabloid TV, being so certain of where he stood, Dunleavy's prejudices were skewed each day in the aftermath of true civil war, in the real Bosnia.

Dunleavy would later speak highly of the alcohol he was able to seek out, the white lightning called loza, Slivovitz plum vodka, and the surprisingly tasty Slovinian beer. It was the people he couldn't get out of his mind, though; the Moslems with blue eyes and blond hair, the grandmother running through a mine field to a garbage dump to dig up food for her granchildren.

He shared Christmas dinner with the American soldiers at the Tuzla airbase: Army turkey and no booze. "Burt and Ally. Have a Happy New Year," his message said. "God bless you all. Pass it on to Pete. I'm back from Bosnia, safe and sound. I'll never take a hot shower for granted again." Then he cleared his throat. He'd choked himself up again. "Bye for now."

CHAPTER THIRTY-SEVEN:
THE BUTT-SKETCH ARTIST
& THE END OF AN ERROR

Wayne Darwen called on the seventh day of 1996, the day before Elvis's birthday. He was in New York, editing packages for *The New A Current Affair* and pitching *8MM*.

"Mate, I was talking to Youngie," he said. "He wants *8MM*."

"What do you mean 'wants it'?"

"Well, not like we expected. He wants to give us a five-minute segment once a week on *A Current Affair*."

"Tell him thanks, but no thanks."

"Good, good, that's fine. I'm playin' good cop, bad cop, mate. He's interested. And if things don't work out, we have something to fall back on."

"Hold out for a show. Anyway, I might have something happening on this end. Peter and I are pitching with one of Barry the agent's friends, a guy who used to run Viacom."

There was a pause. "What's his name?"

"Henry Schleiff."

Wayne let out a yell. "What? Henry Schlieff?" He pronounced the name like "thief."

"You know him?"

"Mate, he ripped me off when I was selling my Madonna special. No way am I working with him. Sorry. I'd rather go hungry."

Wayne called again three days later. "Mate. *A Current Affair*'s just been cancelled. It's fucking bizarre, I was standing here when it happened.

"But look," he was whispering now. "Youngie wants you to come here with the *8MM* tapes. He's pitching new shows to Murdoch over the weekend and he wants to use *8MM* as a segment in one of them."

"Have him pitch *8MM* as a show on its own."

"I don't think they'll do that, mate."

"Fuck it. Those assholes just killed *A Current Affair* and they want to turn our show into a fucking segment? No way. Hold out."

The cancellation announcement to the staff spread around the country within minutes. Anchorman Jon Scott was taken off the show immediately, with the claim that he was on assignment. Penny Daniels and Bill McGowan would alternate in the months the show remained on the air. Panic among the *A Current Affair* staff was quelled somewhat with the vague promise that many would be kept on to work on new Fox projects. The leaders among them took the next step. They began planning a party.

Daily Variety, Jan. 11, 1996:

AFFAIR TO DISMEMBER
Venerable tabmag out after losing clearances

Marking the end of an era in syndication, Twentieth TV will pull the plug on the venerable tabloid magazine *A Current Affair* at the finish of the season.

A massive creative overhaul this season came too late to save the nine-year-old mag, which was cancelled after it lost clearances in New York, Los Angeles and Chicago.

The program's demise, less than two weeks before the National Association of Television Program Executives conference, has set off a wild race to grab its primary early- and late-fringe time periods...

The straw that ultimately broke *Affair*'s back was NBC-owned WMAQ Chicago picking up the new Warner Bros. talk show with Rosie O'Donnell. The talker would have bounced the tabmag out of its 4 p.m. slot when the O'Donnell show premieres in June...

"I'm sad in two ways," Maury Povich told the papers. "Professionally and personally, it gave me back my name. If it weren't for *A Current Affair*, I'd still be known as Mr. Chung."

There were few other tears shed among the media as word spread that the era of tabloid television was over. The decision to have Young and Tomlin declare they were "taking out the trash," allowed everyone to remember the fallen show as "trash television."

"Fox TV producers took the trash out of *A Current Affair*, and now the whole show is in the Dumpster," read the New York *Daily News* lead, under a headline that read, "For TV's ex-trash champ, *Affair* is Over."

"I have some notes here on the new improved, trashless *A Current Affair*," Marvin Kitman wrote in *Newsday*. "On Nov. 2...*ACA* became the first program to proudly air pictures of Hillary Clinton's crotch...Nov. 6 was the day *ACA* had the honor of being the top bidder for the *National Enquirer's* Paula Barbieri sex video...Nov. 7...a report on something called the 'date rape drug,' which they got all hysterical about...then they proceeded to show the pictures of a gangland shooting four times in slo-mo...next came a story on the country's biggest child sex ring...This was the new cleaned-up *ACA*. So you can imagine how trashy it was before the cleanup."

"The truth is, it has been years since *A Current Affair* has competed very well in the compete-or-die arena that defines the genre," wrote Eric Mink in the *Daily News*. "In fact, *A Current Affair* has been getting its clock cleaned by Paramount's *Hard Copy* ever since the pedophilia accusations against Michael Jackson broke and continuing through the frenzy of the O.J. Simpson case."

The only appreciation came from Rupert Murdoch's *New York Post*. TV critic Michele Greppi wrote, "*Affair* really did change TV, and not just by hanging tawdry tinsel and raucous recreations on the ivory towers of journalism. Or by giving us Maury Povich's raised eyebrow...

> *Affair* trafficked in reality— or recreations of it— and trickled up, from the local station level instead of down, from the studio level. It set off an unprecedented gold rush that would lead not just to imitators but to a seachange in TV itself. The medium got flashier and grittier, from network news to talk shows to prime-time comedies.

Dunleavy was on the phone from New York. "I spoke to the Boss," he said. "'They didn't do too much of a job spending my thirty million dollars.' That's what he said about Youngie and Tomlin. 'They didn't do too much of a job spending my thirty million dollars.'"

Murdoch didn't think too much of Young and Tomlin's hour-long pilot either—a collection of re-voiced *20/20* packages hosted by Jon Scott. Veteran newswoman Jane Wallace was hired and fired from the project the same day when she refused to put her voice on someone else's segment on Elvis Presley.

Dunleavy was excited. He saw an opportunity. He wanted Murdoch to see *Dancing in the Dark*. "Get a pen," he said. "Copy down this letter:

Dear Boss, we came up with this in two hours.

Anyone who asks why we're dancing doesn't get it.

Steve D.

"Just that, that's it; send that and the tape to Murdoch's office in Century City Monday morning."

Brennan said I shouldn't do anything rash; that Dunleavy was probably pissed and I should speak to him Monday morning before I did anything.

By Monday, Dunleavy had changed his mind.

"The body lies dead on the table." Wayne was on the phone from Nashville. His field-producing gig was cancelled along with *The New A Current Affair*. John Lee Hooker was back on the mountain.

"Tabloid television, *A Current Affair*, it was all really about humanity, but it got lost in the shuffle," he said. "An *A Current Affair* story was really about people. It really got fucked up because these assholes mutilated it. Tabloid does not exist. It doesn't exist on *Hard Copy*, *Inside Edition*—it hasn't existed on *A Current Affair* in a long time. It died because they took the soul out of it and everyone lost sight of what it was.

"So if you're going to write anything about it, mate, the first line is 'The body lies dead on the table.' I was there when they pulled the plug. I was there when the bean counters came in and it died officially. 'The body lies'— no— 'the body lies cold on the table,' and this is your title: 'Tabloid—colon— The Autopsy Report.' Mate, come down to Tennessee, we'll write it. We lift it out of the gutter by analyzing it. You give it a sort of scholarly academic level; you excuse all the bad stories by adding the analysis. Anecdotes and analysis and interviews. 'Now It Can Be Told.' Once tabloid was assimilated into the news, once the network assholes got into it...it died. Killed by amateurs."

I told Wayne the autopsy idea was perfect. "It's true, when you think about it. The body had severe liver damage, a bad case of cirrhosis, bruising about the ribs where it was beaten, stab wounds in the back, dead brain cells..."

It sounded like a dog breathing, or like Bill Beltran making lots of quick edits. Quick woofs, one after the other.

"That's the baby's heartbeat," the doctor said.

Woof woof woof. Woof.

Doctor Karen Kornreich smeared a bit of KY jelly right above Ally's pubic line. Allie lay flat out, her pants off, her waist and legs covered by a giant paper towel. I sat by her feet, next to the biohazardous waste container, and put aside the baby magazine article about sex during pregnancy.

The doctor held a small doppler microphone attached by phone cord to a radio speaker. "It's like a needle in a haystack, but we can probably find the baby's heartbeat," she said.

"I thought I felt it right below my navel a few weeks ago."

"No," the doctor said with a heard-it-before smile. "That might have been gas. It's only this big." She pointed to her fingernail, then moved the doppler around some more. "Ah. There it is. Hear it?"

The doctor had a finger entwined in Ally's pubic hair as she held the mike to her belly and twisted the speaker around.

Woof woof woof.

"It's really fast," Ally said.

"It's perfect. It's at 160. As it grows, it will be somewhere between 120 and 150."

"It's a baby, all right."

This was definitely a Beverly Hills medical office. I walked toward the room where Ally was waiting with her pants off and stopped in my tracks when I bumped into the nurse with the bright orange hair from the TV show *ER*. Connie Brazelton wasn't working; she was a pregnant patient.

Down the hall was the office of Dr. Wayne Huizenga, the young sports doctor who testified for the defense at the O.J. Simpson trial. Robert Shapiro had hired him to give O.J. Simpson the once-over after the murders.

I wondered if O.J. had brought Nicole to Dr. Kornreich. Among the family Christmas cards on one of the bulletin boards was a family photo of a young mother and two kids in winter clothes, dad in pajamas and a bathrobe: Hugh Hefner. Same crowd.

Don Simpson's drug-sodden body gave out on January nineteenth, as the notoriously excessive Hollywood producer keeled over in the toilet with a book in his hands, just like Elvis. Don Simpson was the bad boy of Paramount when I arrived in town, producer of that *Crimson Tide* movie Alison read for. He lived on Stone Canyon Road in Bel Air, a few houses down from Peter Brennan's. He was fifty-two. His obit in the *L.A. Times* included a glowing tribute from Heidi Fleiss, who remembered him as "not just a customer, but a close friend."

> PEP TALK: Greg Meidel, who recently took the reins of the MCA TV Group, is quickly making a reputation as a guy who'll do whatever is necessary to win. At a meeting to rally his staffers recently, Meidel talked about the need to hustle, knock back shots of tequila, and, if necessary, kiss ass. When one of the execs present asked for the boss' exact definition of the latter, Meidel demonstrated, literally, on the exec..." —*Variety*, Jan 23.

Rosie O'Donnell's big round face shined down like the woman in the moon. At the latest convention of the National Association of Television Programming Executives, she was everywhere in ads promoting this year's model in syndicated television: nicey-nice talk shows, a reaction to the detritus that television's geniuses unleashed the previous year. As we rode the escalator to the convention floor, Rosie's big round face smiled down from a humongous poster, framed by big photo faces of Maureen O'Boyle and Jenny Jones. Maureen O'Boyle plus Rosie O'Donnell equals Jenny Jones. Or maybe Rosie O'Donnell minus Jenny Jones equaled Maureen O'Boyle. In any case, this year's NATPE did not bode well for our type of television.

Las Vegas, the city of bad odds, was the perfect place for the big convention. Most of the shows being hawked were sure to be cancelled by midyear if they were picked up at all. The prime time television stars who roamed around were most likely to succeed by selling off old episodes to be rerun until eternity. Everything else was hit or miss.

Gordon Elliott was the only star equal in physical stature to the pro wrestling superstars who outnumbered and outweighed the latest talk show hopefuls two to one. Gordon's show was rating for shit, but he'd survived the freshman season with a new look—bearded and somewhat gaunt, like a hostage just released by Islamic extremists. He was just as jumpy as a guy who'd been chained to a radiator, and with good reason. Gordon's wife was back in New York, ready to give birth at any time, and he was poised to hop a jet at the first sign of contractions. Angus Alexander Elliott was on the way.

We moved through the type of depressing circus where you know the animals are abused to make them do their tricks, past a booth that was among the most popular and well-suited to an ass-kissing business. The "Butt Sketch Artist" was a gentleman who drew amusing caricature sketches of people's rear ends. There was a line of suits waiting to be immortalized.

Peter Brennan's business was once again at the Worldvision booth. His *People's Court* show was being sold under the name *Hot Bench*, apparently a legal term that had something to do with quick decisions, but was applied to give a little vavoom and sexy pizazz to the tiny dynamo Judge Judy, who courted the station managers like a TV veteran.

Worldvision's other attraction was a talk show that replaced scandal and voyeurism with a thick slathering of Velveeta. *The Jim J. & Tammy Fae Show* paired mascara-oozing evangelist Tammy Fae Bakker with forgotten camp comedian Jim J. Bullock, Paul Lynde's successor on the old *New Hollywood Squares*. The idea for the new talk show, believe it or not, was Dunleavy's, an epiphany that struck him when he covered, choreographed, and participated in Tammy Fae's most recent wedding for *A Current Affair* and watched the idea fly from his hands.

Dunleavy seemed to be the only *A Current Affair* alum missing from the convention floor. Audrey Lavin was there as dutiful companion to Larry Lyttle while flogging her *Amazing Tails* at a tiny booth around the corner. Reporters from *A Current Affair*, cut loose and drifting like Major Tom outside the capsule of television, wandered about gladhanding anyone who might deem them still employable.

Even Mike Watkiss was there, leading a lollipop guild of former *A Current Affair* tape editors, tromping booth-to-booth trying to stir interest in a nice show called *Heroes*. When Watkiss saw me, he hung back, with his head down. He should have been ashamed of himself. The previous spring, he wanted to punch me out because he thought I didn't want him on the air. He couldn't have known that if I'd taken over *A Current Affair*, he and Dunleavy would have been the only reporters I'd have kept. Watkiss was distinct enough to make effective—though I might have had him dye his hair.

Of course we found a bar that we made the center of our tabloid universe. It was at Caesars, near the check-in, overlooking the casino and baccarat room where, shooting an *A Current Affair* "Vegas Week" six years earlier, Rafael stood in awe of the dealer and his dance of the seven decks, where Wayne wrote Maureen O'Boyle's scripts after we arranged for her to be a showgirl at the Aladdin. We laughed so hard at what we'd done, and when Maureen became anchor she had tapes of the show and all related footage destroyed secretly, like porny pictures from her past.

We wound up at the roulette table, Brennan and Gordon Elliott and Peter Sutton and the boys, all of us crowded around in a frenzy of noise and chips, drink orders and cheers for the little white ball bouncing around the spinning wheel. Most everyone spread their chips all around the table. I stuck to my three numbers and hit for $300 on the first spin.

Peter Brennan kept winning, not knowing how or even when he won because he's color blind. I kept my eight chips on number 32 every time, spreading a few more chips nearby in my usual fashion.

The stubbornness was making Gordon's beard itch. "C'mon, spread 'em around, mate!"

"He has a system," Brennan said.

"But is he having fun?" Gordon demanded.

"It's not about fun," Sutton and I said in unison.

Gordon's friends made it a joke. On every spin, they each added a chip to my pile on number 32. I played until I ran out of cash, and had to borrow a hundred from Brennan.

The group was so loud and hands were moving so many which ways, the pit boss replaced the friendly dealer with an unsmiling vet. Everyone was stacking their chips on number 32 now. The pile was nearing twelve inches high, climbing and teetering.

"You bastards," I said as the wheel spun and the ball zipped around the perimeter. This time I moved my chips to the 35.

"Are you nuts?" Brennan grabbed my chips and balanced them on the 32. The pile was more precarious now.

"No more bets."

The ball bounced across the wheel and came to rest at number 32.

Everyone won hundreds of dollars each. The pit boss and dealer exchanged scowls. I gave Brennan his hundred and in a chorus of hoops and hollers, we walked. I was vindicated. My system worked.

Hours later, it was down to me and Peter Brennan at the bar.

"I think we may have complicated things with the Australian show," I told him. We'd been shooting a pilot show for a network in Sydney. Alison would be the star.

"How do you mean?"

"We're having a kid."

"What?" Brennan's face brightened like it hadn't in a long time. "Oh, that's fucking great!" He hugged me and kissed my face. "You and Ally are validating the relationship. It's such good news!"

We ordered a couple of more. Alison had gone up to the room, feeling unwell in the early months of pregnancy. "You've done it. Great. I love you two, it's so good that after all this bullshit, moving into hotels, everything's on track. It's a good thing."

"I thought it might complicate things, with her hosting the Australian show and all."

"Bullshit. It'll make it better."

We watched the diehard gamblers carry on into the night.

"How do you feel?" Brennan asked.

"I don't know. I don't think it's really hit yet."

"You're scared to death. Aren't you?"

"Nah."

"You're scared to death," Brennan insisted. "That's all right. It's a great thing. The best. And Ally. I really like her. I trust her. She's a good fucking woman. You're lucky. I love you guys. We're always gonna be family, remember that." Whether it was the vodka talking or not, it didn't matter. We hadn't drunk this late together in years, really. "I'm proud of you. You're a lucky man. Alison is an honest, straight-up woman. It's hard to find that. In men, or women. She's a good fucking woman—"

"Burt Kearns?" The bartender held up the phone. It was Ally, calling me home.

"A kid? As in Ally's pregnant? Ally's pregnant. When you said you're having a kid, I thought you meant a goat. That's great. Great. What am I saying? That's terrific!" Steve Dunleavy was on the phone. Ally picked up the extension and he carried on. "I remember Ray Kerrison's wife, she was a devout Catholic, but she got pregnant and she had an incredible craving for canned beer. It had to be canned beer. Here she was, a devout woman, she spent the first six months of her pregnancy pissed all the time. No, love, I couldn't be happier for you..."

"What if it's the Anti-Christ?" Wayne threw in a little old tabloid TV Prince of Darkness humor when I told him the news. "Naw, heh heh. You got a name?"

"Not yet."

"Name it Anna Nicole," he suggested. "Nah, call it Brennan. Give it a good strong Irish name. You want a boy or a girl?"

"I think it'll be a girl," I said.

"Yeah. That's better," he said. "Girls are easier to intimidate. Is Ally happy? I'm sure she'd be happier if it were a different father. Heh heh. When's it due?"

"August. Beginning of August."

"Ah, a Leo, like me. I'll be Elvis' death age this year. I was born three days after his death day. Strange."

Back at the Argyle, Brennan had an idea. He said Alison and I shouldn't get married, or if we did, we should keep the news very quiet. That way, when the story made the British tabloids, we'd get a headline to cherish:

ALLY'S
LOVE
CHILD!

I didn't know if Rafael heard the news. I hadn't seen or heard from him in more than a year, since I walked out of the *Detour* editing session and he walked out of the Wild Bunch and our lives. Word was that he'd given up on television and gone back to the law, taking a job as an attorney in Barry Slotnick's office. Slotnick was a flamboyant tabloid TV regular who'd defended subway gunman Bernhard Goetz, members of the Gotti and Colombo crews, and engineered a "rough sex" excuse for a young man accused of strangling his girlfriend with his high school graduation tassle.

One would think that Slotnick represented everything Raf found cheap and demeaning in what he saw as a noble profession. "I only handled death penalty cases," Raf used to say. Now, people were laughing about his new work, calling him an ambulance chaser.

CHAPTER THIRTY-EIGHT:
DON SIMPSON MEETS BUTTERBEAN

I stood on Stone Canyon Road in Bel Air on a brick driveway at the open gate of Don Simpson's estate. It was a proper shingled mansion surprisingly close to the road, with a wall low enough to get a good view of the windows and a gentle tinkling stream running under the path to his front door. A couple of issues of the *Beverly Hills 213* gossip rag lay in plastic bags on the bricks.

This was how our lives worked. Peter Brennan, Alison, and I standing in Don Simpson's driveway, the best at what we did, but having to do it for a TV pilot for a show to run in Australia.

As Ally did her standups, I watched her image on the portable monitor, fixed her hair, helped her with line readings, and held the reflector stand in the breeze. Looking at the small picture, I thought how good Alison was at this. I wondered what this past year and a half had done to her; whether she was the same woman before I met her. Was she the same self-producer from London, the same confident journalist, or had I dragged her down? I didn't know. I looked at her, thinking this is the woman who's having my child, and wondered why she chose me.

The phone rang at 8:30 a.m. Jim Sheehan was on the line.

"Quick," he said. He sounded in a panic. "Put on 95.5 FM. You've got to pitch one of your shows."

"What are you talking about?"

"Brandon Tartikoff. He's on the radio and he's giving listeners thirty seconds to pitch a show."

Jim was serious. It had come to this.

There was HBO. There was even CBS. There were more before Barry's friend Henry set us up to pitch *Hidden America* to Jerry Offsay at Showtime in the big building on Lankershim, over the hill in Universal City. Henry had big connections there, since he ran the entire operation as chairman of

Viacom a few years back.

This time, we brought Alison along.

Offsay liked the idea and he liked Alison. He suggested we tailor the concept to Showtime's existing lineup: tying it to the Mike Tyson-Frank Bruno fight in March.

We had a special.

Peter Brennan stopped by in the morning, freshly showered and wide awake. I'd called him and said we needed to talk, and he knew what to expect as I laid it out at the table in the dining room.

"On this Showtime special, mate, I need to get equal credit. You're going off on your own projects and you can't be responsible for us. I need to establish this production company of ours and establish myself as an executive producer."

"You're right. I don't see any problem with that."

It was simple as that. Peter Brennan and I were now on equal footing.

Now we were at the bar at the Argyle for a purpose. This was where Brennan set up shop. Our boxing special would focus on four up-and-coming fighters whose stories we'd contrast with the big Tyson fight in Las Vegas. We had a teenage Olympic hopeful at the L.A. Boxing Gym; Butterbean, the 300-pound novelty heavyweight everyone called "The Great White Nope;" a beautiful female boxer; and a contender in one of the anyone-can-enter, anything-goes, Tough Man competitions.

Earlier in the week, we almost ran off to Tenerife in the Canary Islands to shoot at Frank Bruno's training camp, but Showtime's sports chief Jay Larkin put a stop to it. He didn't want us anywhere near his fight—and he didn't like Henry Schleiff.

"Good," Brennan said, glad to save the Tenerife money. "Maybe now we can do a special people really want to watch. I was thinking. We should make it like *Red Shoe Diaries*. Put that female boxer in a fake locker room and hire actresses. Use lots of steam. We can have nudity."

I'd been out of work too long. "Mate. We have an hour on Showtime. We have the opportunity to do something really great here, to get out of this tabloid rut we're all stuck in. We should do a really heavy documentary. We can win a CableAce Award!"

There was silence and a smirk. I realized we were caught in a whirlpool of lowered standards. "It's only television" was taking on an entirely different context.

"I met a man here in a snow-covered town called Bay City, on the shore of a Great Lake at the northernmost edge of the American heartland. Here, in the the state of the Michigan militia, there is a man who a factory complex, and in back, next to an actual crematorium, runs a little boxing gym where he trains angry young men in an effort to build the next Great White Hope..."

I was imagining how Rafael would lead this story if he were still in television. Alison and I were in Bay City, Michigan, all right, a frozen little town near Lake Huron. If Wayne were doing the story, he'd mention it was the hometown of Madonna.

We were here to find Butterbean, the comic oddity with the shaved head and red, white, and blue trunks.

That weekend, it snowed in Las Vegas. "I've seen this before." The valet parker at Caesars held open the car door in the middle of an actual blizzard. "In the movies. *Miracle on 34th Street* or something."

The sight was almost frightening. Caesar's and the Mirage were barely visible behind post-it size snowflakes, like it was the end of the world or the aftermath of a nuclear bomb. I wished we had a film crew to shoot the big casinos in the snow. Later, we could use it for a movie about the apocalypse. The blizzard would be gone in an hour and forgotten and everyone would wonder how we pulled off the special effects.

The night before, Butterbean boxed a man whose record was one win and three losses and who hadn't fought in three years. He managed to squeak through with a TKO. When we weren't following him, we trailed a beautiful young female boxing champion who was in the game to make money for her daughter's future. It was her manager's idea to put his fighter in a bikini and shoot her posing in the fountain of the Caesars Forum mall.

The papers would say it last snowed in Las Vegas in 1990. Wayne and I were in town for that last storm. We'd just arrived to shoot "Vegas Week" material for *A Current Affair*. That was when Wayne got Maureen to dress up as a showgirl and I shot a piece on the Liberace Museum that we promoted as the discovery of the little-known "Mrs. Liberace." The story was true. She was his sister-in-law.

There was more snow the very next day. We were in downtown Anchorage, Alaska, shooting the Alaskan Tough Man competition, where oil field workers, Eskimos, street people, and big men on campus bashed each other's skulls for the title of Toughest Man in Alaska. It turned out the top contender was a twenty-two-year-old bookworm with no confidence and size seventeen feet.

Anchorage was where we found what tabloid had truly wrought. Crystal was a round-card girl, flouncing about in her high heels and

Budweiser bathing suit between rounds, with a smile as bright as the Northern Lights and a body as unstoppable as the Iditerod dogsled race beginning the morning after the fights on the street behind our hotel.

Crystal was anxious to be interviewed about how she got into the round card game. She invited us to the home she shared with her husband and son, a little white house in a neighborhood of little white houses, tucked behind a towering pile of plowed snow on the end of a deadend street. She wore a pink angora sweater and kept a copy of William Bennett's *Book of Virtues* on a table beside her as she spoke of how her life had changed for the better in the years since she was addicted to crystal methedrine.

Crystal now worked as an all-nude stripper and lap dancer at a Klondike bawdyhouse called the Great Alaskan Bush Company. She brought out her scrapbooks and pointed with pride to spread-eagle shaved-crotch shots from men's magazines and family nudes of herself and her husband.

She was so excited about getting on television that she invited us to tape her show that night at the Bush Company. She strutted in a star-spangled costume, sequinned from top hat to heels, to the tune of James Brown's "Living in America," stripped off, skimmed a few faces, and bent over so her chin touched the floor and the spotlights touched places that should have been reserved for her husband, who sat at a table near the bar and watched impassively.

Crystal then painted fluorescent white stars on her nipples, a blue field on her chest and red and white stripes down her belly, pressed a white t-shirt to her torso and draped the body flag over our cameraman's head. It was then I realized I'd seen Crystal before. A few years back, we'd had her on *Hard Copy*, when she competed in the Stripper of the Year competition in Las Vegas. Living in America, indeed.

On March third, Anthea Disney was named president and chief executive of HarperCollins publishing, an arm of Rupert Murdoch's News Corporation that wasn't living up to financial expectations despite blockbusters like Howard Stern's *Miss America*.

After her success as editor-in-chief of *TV Guide* and a time bringing News Corp's Internet service on line, Anthea arrived at HarperCollins as she did at *A Current Affair*, with no experience in the business but the full support and confidence of Rupert Murdoch.

"I guess I have delivered for him so far," she told *The New York Times*. "When I cease to deliver for him, he will undoubtedly cease having confidence in me."

Henry Schleiff warned us that the Showtime executives would want to view some of the edited footage before we were done. "It's important," he said, "whatever you do, don't show them everything. Show them a couple of minutes. If you show too much, they'll feel obligated to make changes. Just give them a taste."

The only other thing he asked was that his production company get an onscreen credit: "Cheesy Puppet Theatre, Inc." Brennan ran to look at the contract specifications to make sure the credit didn't have to go at the beginning of the special.

Peter Brennan worked out a cut-rate editing deal with a house in the Valley that put together his *Hot Bench* pilot—which was now, in the prevailing nicey-nice television spirit, renamed *Judge Judy*.

The place was run by an old-timer named Bill who worked on a modified AVID system in which all tapes were transferred to video discs for editing. It was supposed to be quicker, but by the end of day one, it was obviously not. Bill was an old sailor with a big smile and a swollen neck who was used to editing three-camera sitcom shoots, not fast-paced reality.

Brennan was unyielding about us staying put. Then he went home and left Alison and me to do the job. From the start, it had been impossible to get him to commit time or attention to this project; ever since I demanded equal credit and urged us all to aim high.

Alison and I were stuck in the Valley editing day and night for two long weeks. When we weren't writing the rest of the special or shooting pickup footage, we took our meals in the facility's cafeteria while in the edit room across the hall, an editor doctored a sitcom, cutting the three-camera shoot down to a half-hour show, and pumping up the canned laughter along the way. Loud rolling waves of guffaws and gales of hilarity echoed after every stupid one-liner. The editor added the laughs, made them louder, faking it like Tony Roberts did in that scene from *Annie Hall*.

On March twelfth, I surrendered, giving up officially on my dream of getting a CableAce Award or even creating a quality show. That was the day Peter Brennan went off to New York for meetings on other projects, leaving a script on our young Olympian unfinished.

It was a message, I knew. Peter Brennan was showing me by example how to be an executive producer. Lieutenants do the work. When he returned a couple of days later, Peter took all our completed segments and, despite Henry's warning, showed everything to the executives at Showtime. The suits felt obligated to make suggestions: move segments, remove others, rewrite, add track, make part one, part three...

Peter called me in the edit room from his car phone to tell me he'd agreed to all their requests.

"You did what?" I lost it. "Didn't you explain to them, part three can't be part one? That there's a structure?"

"What structure? It doesn't matter!" he said from the car.

"It fucking-A does matter. You haven't been sitting in these edit rooms for two weeks. This is bullshit. It won't get done!"

I was feeling like Rafael being told we were switching around his Chappaquiddick segments. Peter made me feel even more Raf-like.

"You know, this isn't worth it," he said. "Every little change, you freak out. You're the biggest problem here."

"I'm the biggest problem."

The special didn't matter to him. It was only television.

Alison flew to Las Vegas the weekend of the Tyson-Bruno fight to shoot the opening for the special and scenes from the fight.

We had three days left to finish editing, and it would mean working around the clock to get it done. Peter Brennan and Henry Schleiff went along to Vegas, too.

By Tuesday, I was getting through the final section of the show when Alison came into the edit room. She'd just gotten results from her amneocentesis. The fetus was fine.

I gave her a squeeze and she slipped a napkin into my hand. She'd scrawled across it: "You're having a son."

We took a break and went into the parking lot. "I thought you didn't want to know."

"I wanted to get emotionally attached," Alison said. "I haven't been getting attached to it in case something was wrong. And now that I knew it was all right, I didn't like the idea of someone else knowing when we didn't. Are you disappointed? You wanted a girl, didn't you?"

I didn't know. I was going to have a son. Wayne was right. With a girl, it would probably be easier. Now, knowing it was a son, I could only think of my father and me and how difficult it could be. You have to be a man to be a father to a son.

Peter, Alison and I showed the finished special to the Showtime executives that night. They told us to remove everything we'd shot over the weekend at the Tyson fight. That was Jay Larkin's doing. Henry had taunted him in Vegas and lost the pissing match.

We went back to the edit house to make those and other changes. As I got down to work, I realized Peter Brennan had disappeared.

He called an hour or so later from the bar at the Argyle and told me not to be concerned with the footage we had to cut out or didn't have time to edit in.

"Let me tell you about Steve McPartlin's first story for *A Current Affair*," he said. The former sportscaster came back realizing he hadn't asked the right questions, and, in fact, had missed the essence of the story. "John Tomlin told McPartlin not to worry. The audience only knows what's on the screen. And there's an unspoken understanding with the audience that what you put on the air is the best there is and that you didn't have anything better. So they don't know what didn't get on..."

He lectured while I worked, explaining why, when we needed to shorten the special, I shouldn't excise the duller sections he'd slapped together about the young Olympic hopeful. "We need it so people will forgive us for running the tawdry shit about the female fighters. It's the same as putting 'save the dog' stories in the Aussie tabloids. Those guys at Showtime don't understand. John and Bob didn't understand..."

I didn't think Brennan understood that the old formula might not apply to a one-off cable special that needed to be as intense as possible. We had no time or room to beg forgiveness. Just as we had no time to be sitting at a bar talking on the phone, looking back on the good old days.

I handed the phone to Jimmy Sheehan and asked myself when it was that I stopped understanding.

In the early morning hours, Jim and I drank beer in the edit house parking lot, waiting for the Midnite Express courier to take the tape overnight to New York. We got back to the house around three a.m. and we watched the special, playing the ending over and over. A fighter skipped rope under the credits:

Written and Produced
by Peter Brennan and Burt Kearns
Reported and Directed
by Alison Holloway

Ending with:

In memory of Nick Loiacono

Ally went to Florida to tape segments for a second ABC special. This time, I was glad she was working with professionals. She deserved better than us.

Henry called a meeting for eight a.m. Friday at the Four Seasons before our next pitch meeting. Henry and Barry the agent were there when I arrived; Brennan wasn't. Henry sat across from me in his green sweater and yellow golf shirt. Barry was at my right, nose in the *Hollywood Reporter* as Henry explained why I'd be getting less money than him or Brennan. Peter Brennan, you see, had the name Henry could sell. Henry, you see, was the bigwig who did the selling. "You have to admit," he said, "as a producer, you know the industry is full of producers. I love the way you write, you have an ability to see things, but you're the fungible one."

Henry was angry that Brennan and I listed ourselves as his fellow executive producers in the credits. He said he and Brennan discussed the situation at the bar the night before. I was Brennan's number two, he said. Brennan and he decided I'd be line producer. Six specials or so down the line, I might be promoted while he and Brennan moved on to other projects. I was "fungible."

I looked at Brennan's empty place setting. He was an hour late. That was highly unusual. I was pissed—American style. "I worked out this executive producer credit with Peter a long time ago," I said. "The only thing you asked was that your Cheesy Puppet company get a mention. This entire project was my idea. If I wanted to be a line producer, I could've stayed at Fox. I didn't give up jobs, lose money, spend my own money, and spend a year and a half creating shows to be anybody's number two. I was Peter's number two seven years ago. I was a fucking line producer in 1983. I'm doing this to get a name for myself. I came up with this show—"

"I must say, eighty percent of this show is Burt's," Barry mumbled. "I gotta say, he did turn down the executive producer job at *A Current Affair*..."

Peter Brennan showed a little while later, my Teflon brother, acting like he didn't know anything was up.

When I got home, I looked up "fungible" in the dictionary. Then I knocked off a letter, firing Barry as my agent and telling him to replace me. I didn't want Henry anywhere near any of my projects.

"I'm sorry, mate, but I warned you," Wayne said when he called. "The same fuckin thing happened to me..."

I turned forty on April ninth.

CHAPTER THIRTY-NINE:
THE GAMBLER

Alison and I were married in the Little White Chapel in Las Vegas at three o'clock in the afternoon on Saturday, April 13th. The bride was painfully beautiful in an electric powder-blue pantsuit from Rodeo Drive. I wore a double-breasted navy Armani jacket over a blue cotton t-shirt, black jeans and cowboy boots. John Hallenborg, an old friend from my newspaper days, was along as witness and photographer.

The chapel was on Charleston Boulevard on the downtown side of Stupak's tower near the beginning of the Strip, with a big sign advertising it as the place Joan Collins and Michael Jordan were married—though not to each other. It was the only wedding chapel in town with a drive-thru window.

Inside were a couple of counters for registration and souvenirs like bride and groom flute glasses and pink leg garters; the walls were covered with mirrors and photos of young black athletes and old stars like Judy Garland, Mickey Rooney, Mel Torme and Wayne Newton; there was a framed tabloid article about Nick Kane of the Mavericks, who got hitched at the drive-thru window.

The two small chapels off the lobby resembled mini-mortuaries. One had folding chairs and a relief of a waterfall; the other was a proper shadowy chapel with white pews and a makeshift altar.

An young Latino in an Army dress uniform ushered in his chubby senorita. She wore a faded wedding dress and when she shook her hair, revealed an ornate gang tattoo on her exposed back. A pair of *Natural Born Killer* types mumbled a request for details: she was a dusty *Grapes of Wrath* gal in t-shirt and jeans, hand-pulling her skinny Starkweather man; a cherry whitebread couple brought their tux and gown in carrybags. An entourage of black people from Compton moved into the main chapel. The bride told Ally she'd been chasing her man to the altar for twenty-two years.

The minister looked like George Grizzard and spoke like Liberace. When it was our turn, he shut the doors, started up a tape of creepy background music, and adjusted the video camera. The room was semi-dark and very hot. I felt the heat prickling my forehead, back, and legs. He told Alison to stand at the side of my heart and the ceremony began.

We walked up the short aisle. "Ah, you've done this before," I joked to Ally.

The minister spoke about streams and rivers and waters of love as I perspired and we both tried not to laugh. He asked if I took Alison as my lawful wedded wife.

"I do!" I replied, and Ally was crying. We exchanged rings. I couldn't see because my glasses were in my pocket. The folks from Compton made joyful noise outside. The minister stopped once or twice to adjust the video camera and then made us form a stack with our hands. "Burt, your hand is on the bottom because you're the foundation. Alison on top, because in marriage the woman will always have the upper hand."

My hands were soaking wet. I didn't realize til then. "I now pronounce you man and wife," he said. "Now kiss your wife!" I did, first a gentle kiss, then another—and then we gave each other the tongue.

We flew back that evening for a night at the Peninsula Hotel in Beverly Hills, but first celebrated at our favorite roulette table in Caesars. We went home with $2,700 between us. It was the omen we needed. God and luck had blessed our marriage.

Peter Brennan called on Monday.

"Is what I hear true?"

"Haaaa!"

"That you got married?"

"Yeah."

"Congratulations!" Ring. "Fuck these phones. Are you home? I'll call you back!"

Brennan called back. He'd been in New York when we ran off to get hitched. He said it was a "lost week." When he wasn't out all night with his mates, he and Henry pitched more ideas to HBO. The cable network, he said, wanted very graphic, rough-edged violence: dead bodies and autopsy footage.

Brennan had also visited the control room of Gordon Elliott's show, "as a friend visiting a friend," and when the producer saw him, she exploded, called a staff meeting, and announced she was leaving at the end of the season.

Afternoon talk was changing. Now that Rosie O'Donnell was a hit, Gordon would finally be allowed to do what he did best, doorknocks and live remotes and chaos. He only hoped it wasn't too late. All the other talk shows were going "nice," too.

Brennan mumbled that Barry was working out a deal for him to be paid as Gordon's consultant.

We all had a celebratory drink at the Argyle that night. "I'm proud of you for doing the right thing," Peter said in my ear and laughed. I wasn't sure if he was joking. Shannah didn't waste time handing me the invitation:

! WORLD EXCLUSIVE !
ACA Alumni pay your last
respects at the gala
"A Current Affair"
good-bye party!

<u>Black Tie Invited</u>
Saturday Night, May 4th 1996
8 pm to Midnight

New York Armory,
67th Street & Park Avenue

Featuring:
* Open Bar!
* Open ACA Casket!
* Gourmet Buffet Dinner!
* Music & Dancing!
* Celebrity Guests!
* ACA Funeral Service!
* ACA Gag Reel!
* Other Shocking Surprises!

THERE IS NO COST TO ATTEND
Mandatory R.S.V.P. By April 25th
We must know if you are bringing a guest.
Seating is limited. No R.S.V.P., No party!

B.Y.O.S.A.
Bring your own shocking allegations.
<u>And bring a memento to place in the coffin!</u>

The invite was printed in color on tabloid newspaper-sized paper with an *A Current Affair* headline, logo, contract, and collage of newsclip items like "*A Current Affair* is both the lowest form of journalism and the lowest form of television, a lethal combination." It gave a pretty accurate picture of how the survivors felt about the deceased.

I could only think one thing: first they killed the show and now they were dancing on the grave.

Peter seemed a bit upset he wasn't invited to the wedding. When he mentioned seeing Raf at a hotel in Manhattan, I went out of my way to steer the conversation somewhere else. "Did you see the *Enquirer* had a picture of O.J. wearing the Bruno Magli shoes?"

When John Hallenborg stopped in at the Argyle a night later, Peter Brennan was at the bar, drinking alone. Brennan was very downhearted, he reported, and spoke about how sad he was at losing me, that I'd be unavailable for his projects and that he hadn't been invited to the wedding.

"I've always been available for Peter," I said. "He's got a nice cushion with the *Judge Judy* show, he's working out other deals with Gordon and in Australia. He's even doing more specials with Henry. I'm the one who's fucking broke."

"I don't know. He's a very depressed man," John said.

Funeral *Affair*

Good thing those guys from *A Current Affair* have retained their senses of humor, even as the EKG machine attached to their long-running show has just a few beeps left.

Look for *ACA* alumni like Burt Kearns, Maury Povich, Peter Brennan, Rafael Abramovitz, Bill Ridley, Maureen O'Boyle, Diane Dimond, Steve Dunleavy and Wayne Darwen to show up at the show's official wrap party at the Armory May 4. To keep the mood light, we hear the folks are preparing to stage a mock funeral, complete with a coffin filled with tapes of classic segments and bloopers.

Rupert Murdoch is footing the bill, though at this point he might be wishing he opted for cremation.

It hit me while I was walking the dog. It really was over with Peter Brennan. He didn't want to tell me, but he'd signed a one-year contract as executive producer of this new *Judge Judy* show, he was moonlighting on Gordon's show, he was still pitching shows with Henry Schleiff, and I had nothing to do with any of it.

He was telling me it was time to be my own man and go off on my own.

A year earlier, I felt I was paying the price for my relationship with

Alison; two months ago, it was the price of ownership.

I'd made a decision to sail with the pirates, but in the end it was every man for himself. Wayne was hiding from temptation and keeping his demons at bay; Dunleavy was a prisoner of his low horizons; Rafael was exiled by his anger; Peter had been caught in the dreams and promise of a decade earlier; and I was the one kidding himself all this time, believing that somehow we were all going to ride off together like some kind of Wild Bunch.

They recorded the final episode of *A Current Affair* on May first. Maury Povich made a surprise appearance opening the show, before turning it over to Bill McGowan, who anchored a low-key retrospective that was a bit condescending and better suited to *Inside Edition* than to the iconoclastic, tradition-mooning thunderbolt that *A Current Affair* had seared across the television landscape.

It was all so polite.

> When Maury bid you welcome more than ten years ago,
> little did any of us know that we'd enjoy a dizzying
> decade together before we bid you farewell.
> Hello everyone. I'm Bill McGowan and it's with a
> great sense of pride and, I'll admit, a bit of sadness
> that we welcome you to this last edition of *A Current Affair*.
> For years, the critics have said that for better or worse,
> we created a new television genre...
> but the fact of the matter is...you did.
> Every night, we asked you to come and sit around our
> modern-day campfire...and luckily for us,
> you seemed to enjoy the kind of stories we told.
> Of course, not all ten thousand some odd stories we told
> were works of art...but many of them were memorable...
> probably because they were about people just like you.
> The popularity you, the viewer, gave to this show helped transform
> the extraordinary events of average people into headline news...

Twenty-seven minutes later, it was over. McGowan had a wistful smile and a glisten in his eye.

> And believe it or not, that's all we have to say.
> Normally at this point, we show you what's coming up tomorrow.
> But as you know by now, there is no tomorrow for *A Current Affair*.
> All of us will be moving on to new challenges, but we will always

have a special place in our hearts for this time we spent with you.
It's been rewarding and fun, and on behalf of the entire staff,
I'd like to thank all of you for making it possible.
We've been thinking of what would provide the proper closure and
really there's only one thing left to say
and only one man who can say it—

This was the point when Gordon Elliott would chop his way through the wall of the set with the ax he used on the Berlin Wall, hacking a hole wide enough to let in Dunleavy, Rafael, and a team of producers and hangers-on from Tommy McGrath's over the road. The gang would run amok, tear down the flats, throw pies, pop champagne bottles, and set the anchor desk ablaze. Fistfights would break out; blouses would be urged open; the studio would fill with smoke. Firemen from up the street would run in and blast everyone with their hoses; a fat lady would be singing in the corner; Brennan would toss a dwarf toward her—

No, in the end, McGowan tossed to Maury Povich, who cocked an eyebrow and said, "Until next time America" with his most lecherous leer, and that was it.

No Gordon, no Dunleavy, no Raf, no nothing.

A Current Affair would go out with a whimper and an unctuous smile.

In the end, it was only television.

It would be a fitting and fine conclusion to say we all reunited at the *A Current Affair* party, 'then joined in a mass embrace and sang a chorus of "Auld Lang Sine."

It didn't happen that way.

Peter Brennan was the only one of us five to show up at the crowded bash at the 67th Street Armory. He said he got very pissed and didn't recognize most of the people who attended.

Steve Dunleavy was in Tel Aviv covering the Israeli elections for the *New York Post*. He wouldn't have made an appearance at all had not Maury Povich put up five thousand dollars for a satellite hookup so Steve could joke around on a big screen.

He did imitations of Peter Faiman, Ian Rae, J.B., and Brennan, drank from a bottle of Heineken and removed his false front tooth.

Tomlin and Young, blamed for killing the show, stayed away from the party. Anthea Disney sent a taped message. Maureen O'Boyle was there, walking around proud and tall with an "I told you so" grin, letting everyone in on the status of her new talk show. She'd be Rosie O'Donnell's lead-in in New York.

Bill McGowan read a funny poem he'd written and there was an actual funeral procession as some black-clad female producers emitted loud fake wails as they accompanied a prop coffin toward a mock funeral ceremony.

"Shut the fuck up! Show some fucking respect!" Steve McPartlin yelled at the top of his lungs, trying to quell the talking, drinking, and carrying on that continued while the former tabloid team members acted out the death rites and placed humorous gag gifts, including the tapestry of Elvis, into the prop casket.

Barry Levine handed out a hundred-page commemorative pack of articles and clippings that put special emphasis on the final days.

Wayne Darwen arrived in New York that night to edit a segment for *American Journal*. He checked into his hotel, changed into evening wear, and was about to leave for the party when he was overcome with a foreboding that stopped him from moving.

He knew that if he went to the Armory and allowed himself to be dragged back all those years, something very bad would happen. So he remained in his hotel room, watching television and praying until the hours passed.

Rafael Abramovitz planned to attend the farewell bash. He called one of the organizers to RSVP.

"I'd like to bring my wife," said the man who helped create the genre and brought the show its highest ratings.

"There's not enough room," he was told. "You can bring a guest, but it has to be someone who worked on the show."

"Fuck it."

Raf stayed home.

I didn't attend either, and a conversation with a friend in New York got me quoted in the *Daily News'* *Hot Copy* column, saying: "I couldn't bring myself to travel to celebrate with the people who killed the show and watch them dance on the grave."

That weekend, I was in Las Vegas with Alison, kicking the roulette system up a notch, starting with five hundred dollars broken into five dollar chips and sticking with the numbers 4, 13, 6 and 7. I'd hit now and then, with the takes big enough to make up for the stake and then some.

In the evening, I won three thousand dollars at the Mirage alone but lost nine hundred when Ally wouldn't get off her table and I kept playing to kill time.

The loss kept me up that night. I made it all back the next morning.

"What better story is there than this? A guy turns forty, gets married, he's having a baby, he has no money, and he goes to Las Vegas to make it." Jim Sheehan was half laughing, half disgusted.

"Jim, I'm telling you. When I fill out a form and they ask my occupation, I'm not putting writer or TV producer any more. It's professional gambler. From this day on, I'm a professional gambler."

"Calm down. Take a glycerine tablet."

"I need a nickname. 'Three-Number Burt.'"

"I have to work. I'm on the clock."

I walked alone from the Omnisphere entrance of Caesars Palace toward Las Vegas Boulevard on my way to the moving sidewalk that would dump me off at the white tiger entrance to the Mirage casino. People passed on a moving sidewalk above me under a spinning Planet Hollywood sign. Barry Manilow smiled from the Mirage billboard where Siegfried & Roy usually posed.

It was eleven a.m., I was down nineteen hundred dollars and knew I was bound to be down much more. The sky was deep blue and the heat was palpable on my neck and forehead. The spice of the second Bloody Mary tingled in my dry mouth.

I was forty years old, married for one day less than a month with a child on the way, and after twenty years making a living as a journalist, I'd left my pregnant bride and faithful dog at the Los Angeles Airport and gotten on an America West shuttle to Las Vegas to try and make the rent by gambling away credit card cash advances on a Friday morning.

At six p.m., my pregnant bride and faithful dog would be waiting in the car outside the terminal at LAX to pick up daddy from his workday.

The worst had occurred.

I had become a character out of an Elmore Leonard book.

Funny thing was, it wasn't necessarily a bad feeling.

On June fifth, Connie Chung had a news conference in Beverly Hills to announce her return to television in a daily syndicated show produced by DreamWorks, the new studio headed by Steven Spielberg, Jeffrey Katzenberg, and David Geffen.

Katzenberg began. "I am very pleased and excited to be be able to introduce you to one of the genuine great news icons."

Connie came out with an introduction of her own. "I do have an announcement about my show, but I'm only half the story. The other half is right back there. Maury."

Maury Povich joined his wife, announcing he was giving up his talk show in two years to co-host a half-hour show dealing with "the story of the day." Neither Maury nor Connie could define the show so early on. They said only that it will "evolve," focusing on the story folks are talking about around the water cooler or dinner table, and "really tackle it in-depth with some real analysis of it."

The show didn't yet have a production team or any stations signed on, but it all sounded so fucking familiar—Maury Povich and Connie Chung, dancing in the dark.

It was the morning after a Vegas trip that paid off the Blue Cross bills. I awoke to see Alison's smiling face. "Oh, I had the funniest phone call," she said. "Audrey Lavin was on the phone."

"How'd she get our number?"

"She said she had forty animal stories that need to be written for her show and wanted to know if you'd write them."

"What did you tell her?"

"I said you were out. We talked about babies, because she's pregnant, too."

The phone rang. It was Audrey.

"Sorry," I said. "I'm really too busy."

"Do you know anyone who might be interested?"

"No, I'm sorry. I'm out of the loop."

"Okay."

"Thanks."

"Thank you. Bye."

I was leaving it up to the wheel to tell me what to do, where to go, whether I was doing right or wrong; to tell me where it was all heading. I'd put my fate in control of the wheel, the one named JOHN HUXLEY LONDON with two red diamonds at the hub. It was mid-June at the MGM Grand; one last stop at the tables after dinner before driving home through the desert night.

The decor was *Wizard of Oz*; the tables were crowded; there was another fight that weekend at Caesars. Ally encouraged me to take the lone empty seat at the ten-dollar-minimum table. Whoever had been there before me had not done well. There was a fresh wet splash on the felt where a drink had toppled. I took my chips and proceeded to lose. I was going down and fast. All my brand-new hundreds with the big Ben Franklin heads were leaving. The wheel was telling me something and I wasn't sure what it was.

Earlier, I was thrown for a loop when Hallenborg explained the odds were more against me than I thought. "The casino pays out 35 to one, but the odds are one in 38," he said. "Think about it. Thirty six numbers plus the zero and double zero." It wasn't luck, I said. It was more than karma. It was the system. I should have kept my winnings and gone home. In a half hour, I was physically beaten, exhausted, another three hundred dollars in the hole.

I got up and stood at the table where Ally placed a small stack of dollar chips and ordered another two hundred in fives. Fuck it, I'd go home five hundred in the hole. I hit the four on the first spin and I hit again. I put fifteen dollars on the thirteen, watched the wheel and bang, five and a quarter. I was back where I started before I began to lose.

"I'm cashing out." The dealer seemed shocked. The female pit boss came over and said I could be rated if I kept playing.

"No. Thank you. I'm out."

For the first time, I felt it in my chest. Stunned, I had to sit at a slot machine. The wheel had taken it all away and then, with minutes to go before I slumped away defeated, *gave all the money back*. I could hear what the wheel was telling me. It was saying, "Look, you amateur. You mean well. You want to be romantic. Well, look around. There's your romance. Look around at real despair and wasted lives. Look at the fat, lonely, tumor-ridden losers who have to work every day just to survive. Look at the people who don't have the options. Look at the woman you're with. I remember when you were here at that Rolling Stones concert for *Premier Story*. You got drunk at the Flying Monkey Bar. You fought. She was going to go back to England but she stayed. She stayed with you; she's your wife now and she's having your son.

"Amateur. Here's your money back. Take it and go. It's time to grow up, kid."

CHAPTER FORTY:
TABLOID BABY

Before I had kids, I was waiting for my life to begin.
It was always: when this happens, when that happens...
and all of a sudden one morning, I woke up and that feeling
was just gone. It felt to me like the beginning of some life that
I had worked really hard and waited very long to get to.
—Bruce Springsteen

Ally's water broke a few minutes after midnight. By one-thirty Wednesday morning, August seventh, we were in a birthing room in Cedars-Sinai Hospital. She was propped up in bed, attached to a machine to monitor her contractions; I was sprawled on a chair.

The room on the corner of the third floor had a wide window overlooking the hospital's helicopter pad, Beverly Boulevard, and a vista of the Hollywood hills. There was nothing we could do but wait. Our child would be born before the calendar changed.

Dawn broke over the hills at five thirty in the morning. On the television over the door, the broadcaster on the CBS early morning news told of a British woman who'd aborted one of her healthy twins because she couldn't afford to keep them both. The story was followed by video of a two-headed baby born in Mexico. The child, which the newscaster explained was actually a set of Siamese twins sharing a single body, was not expected to survive the day.

Outside on the corner of San Vicente, the numbers on the Hard Rock Cafe's world population sign continued to click upward while the total rain forest acreage fell.

As the morning progressed, Ally's pain intensified. She developed a mild fever and her legs began to shake uncontrollably. An anesthesiologist administered a numbing epidural before afternoon. Ally relaxed and was aware of her contractions only through the monitor printout that measured her changes like a seismograph.

471

Doctor Kornreich stopped in several times throughout the afternoon. She promised we'd have our son by evening.

"They're being called 'drive-by deliveries,' women giving birth and being sent home the same day," read the KNBC anchorwoman at 5:20. "But that could change in this state. We'll have that story..."

In the next room, a woman let out a yowl of pain. The nurse watching Ally smiled. "Don't worry," she said. "She didn't have an epidural."

Dr. Kornreich returned just after six p.m., and at 6:15 Alison had her legs in the stirrups and was starting to push. The epidural dulled the pain and she pushed with all the strength in her overtaxed body each time the nurse called out another contraction on the monitor.

I held her leg and pressed one knee toward her chest, whispering in her ear while the nurse held the other leg and Dr. Kornreich coached. Alison's face turned blue with the strain.

The ordeal was repeated every few minutes. It was past seven p.m. The TV monitor was silent, but stuck on CBS. As Alison pushed as hard as she could, images from the show *Hard Copy* flashed by on the screen. There was Michael Jackson, Madonna, and Howard Stern. O.J. Simpson was somewhere in the crowd. These were the faces and personalities that in the past decade drove my career, whose actions became our obsessions, whose handlers we taunted, now diced and chopped into bite-sized bits in a cheapened version of what we started. There was Loni Anderson. All these useless people who guided the pirate ship that led me to Alison and led us here. None of them mattered any more. All that mattered was in this room.

Alison kept pushing as *Hard Copy* segued into *Entertainment Tonight* with more celebrities and more meaningless images. There was Max Robins, who chronicled the tabloid years in *Variety*, now a big shot at *TV Guide* being interviewed in New York. Max's wife had twins. Eddie Burns, Jr. pushed the movie that would follow his tremendous success with *The Brothers McMullen*...

"Push!" Doctor Kornreich coached. Have this baby! C'mon Alison, have this baby!"

As the credits rolled, the doctor told me to lean over and look. There was his head. The tabloid shows were over. If the baby didn't come out on the next set of contractions, she'd be forced to go for a Caesarian.

It was eleven p.m. in Manhattan. Steve Dunleavy stood in Langan's Bar on West 47th Street between Sixth and Seventh Avenues, under the watchful eye of the actor Michael Caine, whose head appeared in a large photo on the wall.

Caine owned Langan's in London. The Irishman who ran this joint had put up Caine's picture so people would think this place was connected to the classy British restaurant.

Though Dunleavy had heard the story before, he sipped his vodka and tonic and laughed as owner Des O'Brien told it again.

In the morning, Dunleavy would be off to San Diego to cover the Republican National Convention for the *New York Post*.

Farther uptown, in an apartment nine floors above Columbus Avenue, Rafael Abramovitz was in for the night. He put aside his paperwork from the law office and sat back in front of the television.

He had another idea for a show that could get him back on the air. He'd call Brennan about it in the morning. For now, it was WPIX and the beginning of another *Seinfeld* rerun. *Seinfeld* made him laugh.

It was 10 p.m in Nashville, Tennessee. Wayne Darwen was in the audience at the Ryman Auditorium, home of the original Grand Ole Opry. Onstage, Elvis Costello performed to promote his new album, *All This Useless Beauty*.

"What song was he playing at exactly ten?" Wayne thought about it when I asked him later on the phone. "Hmmm. What's appropriate? 'Pump It Up.' Yeah, that was it, 'Pump It' — no wait, I know, 'Alison.' Yeah, 'Alison.' He was playing the song 'Alison.' Now that I think of it, at exactly ten p.m., Elvis Costello was performing the song 'Alison'..."

The clock struck exactly eight o'clock p.m. in Los Angeles. Peter Brennan sat in an editing room in Hollywood, overseeing production of a cable television special he'd sold with Henry Schleiff. He was doing this one on his own.

"Have this baby!" Dr. Kornreich yelled one more time. "This is it, push!" At exactly eight p.m. in this birthing room on the third floor of Cedars-Sinai Hospital, Alison Holloway pushed once more and a child emerged in a gush of fluids, wrapped in his umbilical cord, covered in blood, guts, green powder, and his own black shit.

It had taken fourteen hours of labor but our son had fought his way out and made it into a world of all this useless beauty.

"Don't worry if you don't hear him cry right away," the doctor said as she handed the newborn to be placed under a warmer. "You will."

"It's our baby," I told Alison, snapping a photo and kissing her as we heard the healthy scream. "I love you."

I stumbled around the bed, pulled the Hi-8 video camera off its tripod and joined the intern at the warmer. He handed me scissors and after I cut what remained of the umbilical cord, the child clutched my finger with his perfect little hand.

I picked up my son and I held him to the window overlooking Beverly Boulevard and the Hollywood Hills. I pointed out the Sunset Strip and the side of the building covered by a poster for a movie called *Jack*, in which Robin Williams plays a child who ages with extraordinary speed.

"This is it, kid. This is your town and this is your world. I'm your father, and that's your mother and we're both real glad you're here. Welcome, Sam."

We named him Sam; Sam Peter Holloway Kearns. Sam, because after reading all the books full of 20,001 names for babies, it seemed a good solid name.

We named him Peter after Peter Brennan, to whom we all owed so much, the man who taught me about life and friendship and made all of this possible.

I insisted we add Holloway to his name. I wanted Sam to always be aware of the accomplishments of his mother, who was better than all of us combined.

Peter Brennan visited the next day, held Sam and stared at his face. "Look at that face. That's innocence. He'll never be so innocent as this moment ever again."

"It's official. His name is Sam Peter Holloway Kearns," I said.

Brennan looked up with an embarrassed, suspicious smile. "What's this 'Peter'?"

"Ah, just because there was a question about the paternity."

We laughed and he spoke to the baby. "I'm your old Uncle Peter, the old drunk you'll get to know." He looked up. "How old will I be when he's eighteen? Is there any chance I'll be alive?"

Wayne called with congratulations. "Mate. When you have your first grandson, he'll be the Son of Sam. Heh heh."

There was a message on the answering machine at home. "This is Dunleavy. Remember, you must christen the little bugger!"

We never heard from Raf. When he was told about the birth, he said it was good. When he was told the child's name, he sounded startled. "Sam Peter?" he asked. "Is it Peter for Peter?"

I sat by Alison's hospital bed with Sam sleeping in my arms and I wondered what he'd learn from his old man and what it was I had to teach him. I knew I'd tell him about old Pat Doyle and all about Nicky—I'd have a lot to tell him about Nicky—and let him know how dangerously close he'd come to having Nicky's name. I'd tell Sam about the Beatles, and about my four friends and how they helped make his life a reality. The five of us changed the world, and funny enough, our partnership lasted just about as long as the Beatles' did. One of us went back to the law, one of us went back to newspapers, one of us went back to the country. One of us went back to Las Vegas, again and again.

The only one of us still working in television was the man who started it all, and he'd always be searching, too.

"Peter Brennan," I'd tell Sam. "You were named after him, you know." I'd tell him how Peter Brennan founded a whole new genre of television, how he taught me what was important in life, how we lied to tell the truth and how we robbed so we could give it away, how we were a team; I'd explain to Sam that business is business but a friend is a friend and that no matter how bad things seemed, he must always remember:

It's only television.

I looked at Sam asleep in my arms and realized he and his mother were the ones who had taught me the most. Then I thought of his birthdate, August 7, 1996: 8-7-9-6. Hmmm. 6-7-8-9. I couldn't wait to play the combination at roulette.

In the days to follow, the world would change again.

Peter Brennan separated from his wife and ran off to New York to produce Gordon Elliott's return to the type of television he'd made back in the glory days of *A Current Affair*.

Sam Peter Holloway Kearns was two weeks and one day old on the evening Brennan was expected in the bar of a Chinese restaurant on West 47th Street called the Dish of Salt. Waiting for him were Steve Dunleavy, Ian Rae, and Rafael Abramovitz, all gathered to celebrate a bittersweet anniversary: the first episode of *A Current Affair*, broadcast exactly ten summers before.

These ten years and thousands of drinks later, Dunleavy balanced another vodka and tonic and did a graceful dance to the payphone, speaking for a few minutes in a mock slur.

"I have a man who wishes to have a word with you," he told the person on the other end as he beckoned Rafael from the bar.

Abramovitz the attorney sipped a concoction of his own invention, a combination of Jack Daniels, soda and a splash of Rose's lime he called a Westsider. He still wore the cowboy boots though the Resistol hat stayed in the closet at home. When Dunleavy waved, he smiled and strutted over.

Dunleavy handed him the phone and slipped back to his mates.

"Hello," Rafael said, unable to keep the smile from his voice. "You named the kid for Peter?"

I sat at home and listened intently to hear his voice over the barroom noise. It was the first time I'd spoken to Raf in almost two years. "Of course. Who else?"

"That's very good. Congratulations. Now—" He took a deep breath and laughed on the exhale. "Don't you think you owe me an apology?"

"For what?"

"For having behaved badly in an edit room." All this time had passed and somehow Raf had turned it all around. He'd never change. "You know you gotta do it," he said, "because I'm fifty-five years old. Life's too fucking short. You gotta learn to apologize. You gotta grow up; you're a father now. You gotta say, 'Rafael, I'm sorry.' You say I'm sorry and then I say I'm sorry and then we move on."

"But Raf, I'm not sorry."

"Picture it. You're in a confession booth. Say it..."

It was good to hear his voice and so familiar to hear him wasting the special moment demanding I apologize for the choices I made. "Don't you miss any of this at all?"

I realized I didn't. Ally fed Sam in the next room. It was past dark on West 47th Street; the sun still shone in Los Angeles. I was looking to the future while my friends drank to the past. "You can't have that attitude because friends are more dear than anything in the world, more important than honor, more important than wealth, more important than anything in the universe because you only connect with very few people and we're all sinners and we have to say we're sorry. I'm not even Christian and I'm offering you this opportunity..."

Raf droned on, and as he did I knew I wasn't sorry for anything. I didn't have to look beyond the next room to know what was most important. Before he gave up on getting an apology and offered congratulations on my having a son, my friend Rafael had helped me once again.

He made me realize I'd grown up, after all. I didn't know what was going to happen next, or where we'd all meet or work again, but I was sure of one thing.

I wasn't a tabloid baby anymore.

EPILOGUE:
1999
Summer of Sam (& John-John)

For all the ponderous, agonized media navel-gazing over
the rampant tabloidization of America, the consumer
would be well-advised to consider his own interests.
To put it in a nutshell, if he wants to know what really
happened, he should check out the sleazebags.
—"In Defense of Tabloid Sleaze,"
Mark Steven, *The Wall Street Journal*

Three years later, it was mid-July and turning out to be the Summer of
Sam in more ways than one. Somehow I'd found myself working in a dingy
ground-floor office on the corner of Sunset and Gower in the seedy heart of
Hollywood, cranking out segments for a new breed of reality show that
strings together clip after clip of sensational video footage, undated,
suspended in time, with thrill stacked upon thrill and every picture telling
a story all its own.

The future had arrived but the past kept shouting over my shoulder.
Somehow, I'd found myself sharing the office with Wayne Darwen. Wayne
was standing behind me, wearing a HEADLESS BODY IN TOPLESS BAR t-
shirt under his black demin jacket, looking at the world through tinted
glasses while screaming on the telephone to Maury Terry, his partner in the
1993 Son of Sam interviews.

"You tell him to *fuck himself!*" Wayne shouted, gesturing with an unlit
cigarette he wasn't allowed to smoke indoors. "Tell that serial-killing son of
a bitch to put down his Bible and pick up his gun. He was a lot more
effective!"

With the release of a new Spike Lee movie, Son of Sam was a celebrity
again. Maury Terry was trying to cash in by flogging the old interview tapes.
Wayne was caught in the middle. Born-again killer David Berkowitz had

been writing him letters, begging Wayne not to help promote the film, while at the same time giving new interviews and hawking a line of "Christian" videos, including one called Son of Sam/Son of Hope.

"Tell that prick if he asks for loyalty he has to give it back," Wayne rasped. "I held out in deference to him wanting silence and all I see is him talking! And how dare he call Spike Lee evil when the movie's based on his *ultimate evil*! Tell him I'm disgusted..."

I sighed and peered through dusty blinds to see Mike Myers as Austin Powers, mocking us from the world's tallest billboard on the side of a building a few blocks west. A few blocks in the opposite direction, Peter Brennan was running *Judge Judy*, heading into its fourth season as one of the most successful and lucrative shows in syndication. Dunleavy was back in New York tapping out furious Son of Sam recollections for the *Post*. Rafael was making ends meet with his law firm on lower Fifth Avenue. It was the perfect, predictable end to the decade and the century. As Austin Powers might say, "It's *tabloid*, baby..."

Then, that evening, two days before the thirtieth anniversary of Chappaquiddick, John-John Kennedy's plane went missing.

Three years is several lifetimes in television, but they pass all too swiftly in the life of a child. Sam—our Sam—is a little boy now, and three years spent raising him, and sharing a glimpse of the world through his eyes, are enough to wash away at least a few layers of tabloid cynicism.

The old excitement of dancing behind the messenger of misery just ain't the same when you've got a kid. The realization dawned in the weeks after Christmas Day of the year *A Current Affair* was cancelled, Sam's first Christmas, the morning a woman named Patsy Ramsey dialed 911 to report that her little girl JonBenet had been kidnapped.

Dunleavy made the story a subject of outrage in his *New York Post*. Though he was exiled to print, he was a logical television guest on January 17, 1997, when the *Leeza* show marked close to a month without an arrest in the case. Talk about the Prince of Darkness: Dunleavy arrived at the studio in Los Angeles just as word came that Bill Cosby's son Ennis had been murdered near Mulholland Drive and the 405 Freeway.

Dunleavy stayed in town for a week, holed up in a Holiday Inn in Santa Monica, making and waiting for phone calls to advance the Cosby mystery. At home, I kept him up-to-speed on developments by channel-surfing the local newscasts and adding my own spin. "I've got this theory, mate, from reading between the lines," I told him a few days after the crime. "It doesn't add up that this was random. Nobody's saying it, but from all the clues, I think Ennis Cosby had to know his killer."

Dunleavy seemed to shrug off the suggestion. After all, it was bullshit, and forgotten until two mornings later, when I pulled up at the Centerfold Newsstand and was sucker-punched by the front page of the *Post* blaring from the rack:

Steve Dunleavy reports
from Los Angeles:
COSBY
HAD TO KNOW
KILLER

"Ennis Cosby had to know his killer," Dunleavy wrote. "For the Los Angeles Police Department to even suggest it was an 'opportunistic robbery' is to give scant respect to his memory..."

A graph or two down, he referred to a "source" that I recognized to be me. I stared at the paper in shock, and later, driving home along the Sunset Strip, in shame. Two shattered parents had just buried their son on the family property. It wasn't right to play around like this any more. Things were different now that I had a son of my own.

A lot of us in the old crowd shared that queasy feeling in May, when the tabloid climate we'd created came back to bite us on the ass with Marv Albert's arrest for allegedly biting a female acquaintance on the back. Marv's fiancee was Heather Faulkiner, who'd produced segments for us at *Hard Copy*. Heather and I worked together back at WNBC, on the old *News 4 at 11*. Marv was our sportscaster. Of all the colleagues who could have been stung in a sex scandal, Marv and Heather were among the least deserving. There was a real story between the lines here, only no one seemed interested in covering it.

Then again, just when you thought you were out, they pull you back in. Just like that, Princess Diana, the tabloid princess, was dead. It was as if the tabloid decade smashed head-on into centuries of history and for a while there, the media was pegged as the drunks behind the wheel. That very morning, August 31, 1997, a *Hard Copy* crew was setting up on my patio. Alison was being interviewed as a Royal expert. The role continued through the sad week and led to a regular gig as a *Hard Copy* special correspondent. It also led to my last tabloid television adventure.

January, 1998: Sonny Bono was dead, and Alison was headed to England to gather up sweeps stories for *Hard Copy*. Few people knew that I'd wangled a quiet deal to come along as producer.

It was like old times, finding someone who'd tell us that Princess Grace had been involved in a sex cult, getting tape of a new British TV show that broadcast full frontal male nudity—and coming up with an ultimate Diana conspiracy, claiming her body wasn't buried on an island at her family estate, after all.

"The Spencers bury the family pets on the island. It's known as the Isle of Dogs," Alison's journo mate Simon Kinnersley told our camera. "And we have to remember the water table on the island. Once you start digging down more than a couple of feet, you're going to be in water."

Local whispers had it that Diana was actually entombed in the family crypt at St. Mary's Church just up the road from the Althorp estate. The island ruse was said to be an excuse to keep tourists from trampling the quaint village, and to charge admission to mourners.

While Alison interviewed a local news reporter in the graveyard, I slipped inside the tiny church with a Hi-8 home video camera. The little old ladies posted near the "No Cameras" sign were many pews behind as I made my way to the iron gates of the Spencer family chapel. Nineteen generations of Diana's family were buried beneath the stone floor. Amazingly, on that very floor was the outline of fresh cement. It was obvious the crypt had been opened.

The story was exclusive. Combined with that secret church video, it was explosive. The new executive producer at *Hard Copy* said it was, yet she handled the dynamite in the only way format would allow, cutting the segment to under three minutes and giving the story what Diana's family neglected to give her: a proper burial.

The only time most of America would even notice the phony grave claims was months later, when Diana's brother denied them on the premiere of *Fox Files*.

Frank Sinatra died in May, the same night they ran the final episode of *Seinfeld*. The tabloid shows were feeling a death rattle of their own as *Seinfeld* reruns began snatching up the prized timeslots that lead into primetime. The tabloids were once masters of that domain, but with the Fall 1998 season approaching, the surviving shows were pulling in less than half the viewers reached in the heyday.

In August 1998, *Hard Copy* replaced its anchor team with a smiley young man named Kyle. There were secret plans afoot to change the show's name to *First Person*, but when Steve Brennan broke the name-change story in *The Hollywood Reporter*, station managers who'd received the news on golf courses threw their clubs into the air and stopped the name change from taking place. News media of all stripes ran stories on the final death knell for tabloid television.

Hard Copy's cancellation wasn't announced until the following April, but everyone knew it was over by year's end. The "tabloid shows" no longer offered an alternative take on anything. Geraldo and Diane Dimond were an evening news team on CNBC. Bill Clinton and Monica Lewinsky might as well have been a news anchor team themselves. *Dateline NBC* was on five nights a week. CBS's *60 Minutes* had broadcast a man being put to death. There was a stable of former *A Current Affair* producers entrenched at ABC's newly-expanded *20/20*.

A new generation of journalist had infiltrated and taken over the network ranks, the first generation trained entirely on the tabloid shows and indoctrinated on the Murdoch mantra of exclusivity and exploitation. They call them the "Tabloid Babies" and they're crawling all over the place.

The last television news revolution of the Twentieth Century may have fizzled out before anyone admitted it ever even occurred, but three years later, tabloid television and network news are unrecognizeable compared to what they were when it all began. Former network newsreader Deborah Norville may be hosting *Inside Edition*, but it was her successor at NBC's *Today* show, Katie Couric, who was on the scene in Littleton, Colorado, a couple of mornings after the massacre at Columbine High in April 1999. Katie sat with a fair-haired teen and a large black man. Methodically, surgically, Katie prompted the boy to recount in excruciating detail how he'd witnessed the man's son be selected and executed because of this race. All the while, the director dissolved smoothly from cutaways of the father hearing it for the first time, to meaningful closeups of his big hand clutching the boy's. It was a heartbreaking, powerful television, too much for this father to watch. That's how good it was.

In fact, it was *too* good. After the commercial, co-host Matt Lauer congratulated Katie for one of the most emotional interviews ever. Later that week, NBC News issued a press release celebrating increased viewership thanks to the massacre.

Yes, the twain have met, they've mated, and Murrow's legacy of idealism has exchanged fluids with Murdoch's rules of cynicism. The mingling of the two in a more acceptable arena has led to the creation of something bigger, yet something less. In short, tabloid television gained the world but lost its soul.

Just look back on the week of John-John, seven days to deification for the poster boy of American celebrity culture, with the networks devoting more coverage to his death than they did to Princess Diana's.

Over at CBS, Dan Rather, who made his network bones by jumping the gun reporting the death of JFK, gets all teary-eyed on air over memories of glimpsing the son at posh eateries; Connie Chung gets to host ABC's *Good Morning, America* when Diane Sawyer calls in sick with grief for two days running; NBC's Maria Shriver is home with the family—her family, *the*

Kennedy family—just as she's hyping her new children's book about death; and Fox is lining up the legal guns against *Entertainment Tonight* for stealing-—*off a satellite feed*-—footage of John-John that the network may or may not have acquired from a Kennedy family member on its payroll as a correspondent.

Now that's tabloid, baby!

Three summers later and the only places to get the stories between the lines seem to be Howard Stern's radio show or the likes of Matt Drudge on the Internet. We're still waiting for justice in the case of JonBenet, who would have been nine yesterday. The satellite trucks have pulled out of Atlanta following another mass murder and headed back to Columbine in time for the new school year, and Sam Peter Holloway Kearns has spent the day chasing Goofy and Tigger around the Happiest Place on Earth.

Today is Sam's birthday. Our boy is tall and he's healthy and he's three years old. John-John Kennedy turned three the day he saluted his father's casket in that picture the networks kept showing. John-John was a member of the media when he died, and the last issue of *George* magazine that he edited featured Rob Lowe on its cover. See? The fucking story never ends. The journey of the *21st Century Tabloid Boy* is already under way.

August 7, 1999
Disneyland

WHERE ARE THEY NOW ?

MAURY POVICH, original host of *A Current Affair*, stars in his own daily talk show produced by Universal Television. The DreamWorks newsmagazine he was to anchor with his wife, Connie Chung, went up in smoke when DreamWorks couldn't secure time slots. In the grand tradition of Geraldo Rivera, Maury recently hosted a Fox special on the opening of an ancient Egyptian pyramid.

CONNIE CHUNG has returned to television as a correspondent for ABC News and cohost of *20/20*, competing for exclusives with Diane Sawyer and Barbara Walters.

GORDON ELLIOT, jolly giant, suffered the cancellation of his afternoon talk show in 1997. Buena Vista Television paid him to remain off television for two years, in anticipation of his return as host of the new *Let's Make A Deal*. After plans for the show were scrapped in May 1999, he returned, at least temporarily, to his familiar role as "doorknocker" for *Good Day New York*.

MAUREEN O'BOYLE, who replaced Maury Povich as host of *A Current Affair*, lost her Warner Brothers talk show, *In Person with Maureen O'Boyle*, in 1997. Her fat contract, however, led Warners to make her host of its syndicated magazine show, *Extra*. In April 1999, Maureen played herself on *The Larry Sanders Show*. In May 1999, Maureen used her show to announce her pregnancy.

DIANE DIMOND, correspondent for *A Current Affair* and *Hard Copy*, signed a million-dollar deal with Warner Brothers in April 1997, also with the promise of her own talk show. Instead, Warners made her a reporter for *Extra*. In 1998, she quit to become Geraldo Rivera's cohost on a nightly news show on CNBC.

ANTHEA DISNEY, former *A Current Affair* executive producer and

Maureen O'Boyle's confidante, remains an important player in the Rupert Murdoch organization. She was promoted in September 1997 from chief of HarperCollins publishing to chairman and CEO of its parent company, the News America Publishing Group. In February 1999, Rupert Murdoch inserted another key player above her in the coporate hierarchy: his son, Lachlan.

BOB YOUNG and **JOHN TOMLIN**, creators of *Inside Edition* and Dr. Kevorkians of *A Current Affair*, have again followed the trail blazed by Peter Brennan, this time with Rysher's *Judge Judy* competitor, *Judge Mills Lane*, a court show starring the referee in the infamous Mike Tyson "ear biting fight."

PETER FAIMAN, *'Crocodile' Dundee* director, *A Current Affair* guru, and Fox programming chief, is an independent producer and director based in Hollywood. In 1999, he created and executive produced Miramax Television's first reality pilot, *The Best Money Can Buy*, and the Travel Channel series, *Adventure Crazy*. He is also directing television coverage of opening ceremonies for the 2000 Olympics in Sydney, Australia.

JOACHIM BLUNCK ("J.B."), *A Current Affair* co-creator and Fox exec, was the original executive producer of *The Howie Mandel Show*. He's moved on to other projects.

GERALDO RIVERA, tabloid godfather and host of *Now It Can Be Told*, was the subject of an intense bidding war between Fox and NBC News. Fox wanted him to anchor their new news network. NBC won. In addition to his two daily talk shows on the CNBC cable network, Geraldo was promised prime time network specials, appearances on the *Today* show, and $4 million.

BILL McGOWAN, *A Current Affair* reporter, became a field producer for the failed CBS News magazine *Public Eye with Bryant Gumbel* (though Gumbel was applauded by his superior, Andrew Hayward, for his promise to "resist the tabloid instincts that have crept into nonfiction television.") He is now a producer for ABC's *20/20*.

DAVID LEE MILLER, *A Current Affair* reporter, was hired as London correspondent for the Fox News network in 1997. He was subsequently transferred to Jerusalem and later reported from Kosovo.

DICKIE McWILLIAMS, *A Current Affair* senior producer, returned to print, working for the *New York Daily News*. He was fired when Pete Hamill took over. He is now a field producer for *Extra*.

PETER HERDRICH, tabloid TV double agent, is senior producer of *Inside Edition*, which in 1996 became the first syndicated newsmagazine to win journalism's prestigious George Polk Award for its hidden camera report, "Door to Door Insurance."

JOHN TERENZIO, *A Current Affair* executive producer, is senior vice president and exective producer of Fox Sports News.

BARRY LEVINE, *A Current Affair* deskman, left his job as managing editor of *Extra* amid a scandal in May 1999. According to reports, he promised to pay a daredevil known as "The Human Fly" to parachute off the World Trade Center, but instead tipped off police and arranged to videotape the man's arrest. When the stuntman asked for his money, Levine allegedly replied, "We don't pay criminals." He was hired immediately by the *National Enquirer*. "The Human Fly" sued *Extra* for $2.3 million. Then, in July 1999, he miscalculated a leap from a cliff in Norway, and plunged to his death.

IAN RAE, vice president of Fox News and co-executive producer of *A Current Affair*, was transferred to a post somewhere within the new Fox News network.

MURIEL REIS, *A Current Affair* attorney and censor, is chief counsel for the Fox Television stations. Near the end of the O.J. Simpson trial, she sent Peter Brennan an audition tape, in hopes of pursuing a sideline as an on-air legal expert.

RUPERT MURDOCH controls 30.1 percent of News Corp, the media conglomerate that includes the Twentieth Century Fox movie studio, Fox TV, the Los Angeles Dodgers, major newspapers in the United States, England, and Australia, and satellite TV networks on several continents. In June 1999, he was divorced from his wife of 32 years. That same month, at age 68, he married Wendi Deng, a 32-year-old former executive with his Hong Kong-based Star Television service. *Forbes* estimates his net worth at $7.2 billion.

BARRY DILLER continues to change the face of world media as he continues his quest for world media domination. He's extended the Home Shopping Network and Ticketmaster onto the World Wide Web, while expanding his empire through USA Networks, Inc.

BRANDON TARTIKOFF died of Hodgkin's Disease in September 1997. In June 1999, he got another show on the air when Showtime revived his pet project, *Beggars and Choosers,* a satirical series about network television programming.

JEFF GREENFIELD, the "big fat humorless putz" from the O.J. Simpson trial, left ABC's *Nightline* for CNN.

JOHN PARSONS PEDITTO runs an award-winning production company, Parco International, which over five years has produced a hundred hours of documentary and "non-fiction thriller" programming seen on 38 international networks. Among his productions were the award-winning HBO specials, *Talked to Death, Dead Blue,* and *Panic.* He also co-produced a feature film, *Jane Doe*, starring Calista Flockhart and directed by his son, Paul.

LINDA BELL BLUE is executive producer of *Entertainment Tonight*. In July 1999, her show was threatened by Fox News with a $500,000 lawsuit for allegedly pirating footage of John-John Kennedy. The matter was settled without comment in August.

RON VANDOR and **CHERI BROWNLEE**, Linda Bell's subordinates at *Hard Copy*, eventually became co-executive producers of the show. When ratings plummeted, they were "dumped" into a new show called *Real TV* (based on an idea by Peter Brennan). Under their leadership as executive producers, the show became a surprise hit. After ratings dipped, they were fired in June 1999.

ALAN FRIO, former *Hard Copy* anchor, has returned to Los Angeles as anchorman at KCOP-TV (*Premier Story's* former home).

TERRY MURPHY and **BARRY NOLAN**, *Hard Copy's* anchor team, were fired in 1998.

FRANK KELLY now shares the title of President of Paramount Domestic Televison. The co-president was embarrassed in 1997 when actor George Clooney announced a boycott of *Entertainment Tonight*, revealing that Kelly had reneged on a signed agreement not to run stories about Clooney on *Hard Copy* if the actor cooperated with *Entertainment Tonight*. In 1998, Kelly led a massive overhaul and "softening" of *Hard Copy*. In April 1999, he announced the show's cancellation.

EAMES HAMILTON YATES, legendary *Hard Copy* reporter, is an acclaimed director and writer of documentaries, specials and features. He won a CableAce award for the HBO documentary special, *Talked to Death,* which exposed the story behind the "Jenny Jones Murder." Eames' documentary *Dead Blue* was a groundbreaking study of depression. His most recent project was *Panic*, featuring Kim Basinger.

AUDREY LAVIN, tabloid television's secret weapon, is married to Larry Lyttle, chief of Big Ticket Productions, which runs, among other successful series, *Judge Judy* and *Judge Joe Brown*. They have two children.

JOE GUIDRY ("Hi-8 Joe" from *Premier Story*) is an acclaimed field director and digital cameraman, and has shot his first television public service spot—on film. He runs his own company, Video Joe Productions.

EDWARD BURNS, JR. had a starring role in Steven Spielberg's picture, *Saving Private Ryan*. He continues to write and direct his own films, and recently co-starred with Robert DeNiro in a movie directed by John Herzfeld, director of the first Amy Fisher TV movie.

BARRY THE AGENT was thrown out of his house by his wife.

HENRY SCHLEIFF, Barry the agent's friend and founder of "Cheesy Puppet Theatre, Inc.," is CEO of Court TV.

JIM DAVIDSON, comedian, has tried to rehabilitate his image on British television as a game show host and aspires to become a Tory Member of Parliament. Each holiday season, he stars in a smutty "blue" pantomime show entitled *Sinderella*. In February 1998, he placed forty-first in a newspaper poll of the Britain's fifty most unpopular people.

NEAL TRAVIS, formerly of *Hard Copy*, thrives with his daily column, *Neal Travis' New York*, in the *New York Post*. He is a full-time resident of The Hamptons.

ALISON HOLLOWAY, host of *Premier Story*, returned to a regular role on American television the day after Princess Diana was killed. She has been a special correspondent, host, and producer for syndicated series, network specials, and documentaries in America, Great Britain, and Australia. In 1998, she hosted the pilot for a British version of *Entertainment Tonight*.

And what of the Wild Bunch?

STEVE DUNLEAVY, mad dog reporter for *A Current Affair*, is a star columnist for the *New York Post*. A typical, memorable column was filed the day the body of Gianni Versace's killer Andrew Cunanan was found on a houseboat in Miami. Entitled "If that's Andy, let's hope he died painfully," the piece concluded with the lines, "Oh, I wish I could have been in a small room with Andrew Phillip Cunanan. He was younger, he was fitter than I am. But I will tell you one thing. Whoever won, it would not have been as painless as that .40-caliber bullet going through his diseased brain."

RAFAEL ABRAMOVITZ is an attorney with a private practice in Manhattan. In May 1999, he represented Barry Levine in his unsuccessful fight to keep his job at *Extra*.

WAYNE DARWEN interrupted his twilight career as a journeyman field producer to return to television management in August 1997 as managing editor of the nightly syndicated show *Strange Universe*. After a brief return to the beaches of Australia, he has settled into a spiritual, sober, and successful life as a television producer in Los Angeles.

PETER BRENNAN married Lisa Lew in April 1999. The happy couple makes their home in the Hollywood Hills .Brennan is executive producer of daytime television's runaway hit show, *Judge Judy*, and its companion, *Judge Joe Brown*. He also helped produce a public access talk show hosted by Joey Buttafuoco.

BURT KEARNS returned to television in February 1997 as a special consultant to the syndicated series *Strange Universe*. He was named executive producer that summer. Restyled as "the reality show of the millennium," *Strange Universe* was cancelled in December, two years and one month before the millennium's arrival. Kearns lives in Malibu with Alison and Sam,producing and pitching shows and specials, and learning the rules of craps.

ACKNOWLEDGEMENTS

This book would never have seen the light of day if not for the support, assistance and belief of some very important people. Topping the list are Paul Sherman, attorney, adviser, and friend, who read the manuscript, demanded to know why it hadn't been published, and made sure it was; and Van Hill, who took the chance to publish this.

The ones who gave great encouragement, assistance and advice from the earliest stages include John Hallenborg, Steve Powers, Neal Travis, Norah Lawlor, Ed Breslin, Richard Price, Jeff Madrick, Elli Wohlgelernter and Eames Yates.

My sounding board, conscience, and best friend through the living and the writing has been Jim Sheehan.

There are the ones who were more than generous with their time, memories and help in getting the story right, though they should bear no responsibility for the story that's told: Shannah Goldner, J.B. Blunck, Peter Faiman, Ken Fuhr, Barry Levine, Linn Taylor, Maury Terry, Cheridah Walters and Brett Hudson.

There are many other talented people who were there through the years. Among them: Cindy Adams, Ginger Akers, Andrew Backwell, Simon Bohrsmann, Doug Bruckner, Jerry Burke, Ed Burns, Sr., Bob Campbell, Bill Cassera, Chris DeRose, Diane Dimond, Riva Dryan, Gordon Elliott, Heather Faulkiner, Penny Goodleaf, Frank Grimes, Bob Guccione, Jr., Video Joe Guidry, John Johnston, Carla Kaufman, Ross King, Nancy Kramer, Gary Lacy, Santina Leuci, Lisa Lew, Audrey Lavin Lyttle, Bill McGowan, Legs McNeil, Dick McWilliams, Danny Meenan, David Lee Miller, Warwick Moss, Maureen O'Boyle, Bob O'Brien, Devin O'Connell, Kim O'Mahony, John Parsons Peditto, David Peterkin, Ian Rae, Muriel Reis, Howard Stern, Peter Sutton, Debra Weeks, Barry Weiner, Barbara Wellner, and of course the men without whom there would be no tabloid genre to write about in the first place, Geraldo Rivera and Maury Povich.

The journalists and columnists who chronicled the tabloid years through its ups and downs were invaluable in their insight, impartiality, and accuracy. I salute and thank Steve Brennan, J. Max Robins, Jim Benson, A.J. Benza, Jefferson Graham, Jeff Greenfield, Michele Greppi, Gerri Hirshey, Richard Johnson, David Kamp, Simon Kinnersley, Marvin Kitman, Irv Letofsky, Howard Rosenberg, George Rush, and Linda Staasi.

At Celebrity Books, Sandra Laughlin read the mansucript, saw its potential, and put in many hours to make it happen; Cary Johnson believed in the book and my gambling system; and my editor, Bethany Snyder, has undergone a crash course in tabloid from which I can only hope she one day recovers. She made everything sharper and helped cut to the chase.

None of this would have been possible without the friendship of four men of great talent. Their trust in allowing me to chronicle this lost part of television history was crucial.

The likes of Steve Dunleavy will never be seen again. He managed to turn "My Favorite Year" into my favorite decade. Rafael Abramovitz taught me secrets about writing and life that will always be with me. I hope to keep winding up in offices with Wayne Darwen for as long as I work (though I hope the surroundings improve). He's the most loyal of friends and a rock star on the stage of life. Peter Brennan gave me a life and opportunities I could otherwise only imagine. His generosity, compassion and heart more than equal the genius he's brought to television.

Thanks, mates—and I ain't pissing in your pockets, either!

Finally, thanks to some very understanding people on the home front. My parents, Burtsell J. and Anne Kearns, offered untold encouragement and support; Geoff and Sylvia Holloway were always there with a helping hand, a sense of humor, and a cup of tea; Samantha Fox helped keep everything together; and we'd be lost without the inestimable help and patience of Yolanda Cruz.

Then there's Alison, about whom not enough good things can be said. She is the love of my life, Sam's mama, and my better. This could not have been written without her by my side.